ABHINAVAGUPTA
PARĀ-TRĪŚIKĀ-VIVARAṆA

The Secret of Tantric Mysticism

English translation with notes and running exposition by

JAIDEVA SINGH

Sanskrit text corrected, notes on technical points and charts dictated by

SWAMI LAKSHMANJEE

Edited by

BETTINA BAUMER

MOTILAL BANARSIDASS INTERNATIONAL
• DELHI •

Abhinavagupta
Parā-triśikā-Vivaraṇa

The Secret of Tantric Mysticism

JAIDEVA SINGH

MOTILAL BANARSIDASS
INTERNATIONAL
DELHI

Reprint Edition: Delhi, 2024
First Edition: Delhi 1998

ISBN : 978-93-90696-03-1 (Cloth)
ISBN : 978-81-19394-58-6 (Paper)

Also available at
MOTILAL BANARSIDASS INTERNATIONAL
41 U.A. Bungalow Road, (Back Lane)Jawahar Nagar, Delhi - 110 007
4261 (basement) Lane #3,Ansari Road, Darya Ganj, New Delhi - 110 002
203 Royapettah High Road, Mylapore, Chennai - 600 004
12/1A, 2nd Floor, Bankim Chatterjee Street, Kolkata - 700 073
Stockist : Motilal Books, Ashok Rajpath, Near Kali Mandir, Patna - 800 004

Printed in India
MOTILAL BANARSIDASS INTERNATIONAL

CONTENTS

List of Charts

PREFACE

The last six years of Thakur Jaideva Singh's life were devoted to the study of the Parātrīśikā Vivaraṇa of Abhinavagupta with that full concentration of which he was still capable at the ripe age of 93. He did not have the satisfaction of seeing the fruit of his labours in published form. After a short but severe illness he passed away on 27th May 1986.

Jaideva Singh spent two summers in Kashmir (1980-81) to study this difficult text at the feet of his Guru Swami Lakshmanjee, the only living representative of the full Kashmir Śaiva tradition both in its theory and practice, *śāstra* and *yoga*. Without his understanding of the tradition and illuminating exposition, this text would have remained obscure. Swamiji has corrected the Sanskrit text published by the Kashmir Series (KSTS), which contained many mistakes, basing his emendations both on the available manuscript material and on the tradition. He has also devised the charts illustrating the text. After completing the translation, Jaideva Singh spent two years preparing a lengthy introduction. He read many Sanskrit texts and other works of philosophy and mysticism, but unfortunately he did not leave behind any notes for the planned introduction, which he had not committed to paper before his illness. The day before he was admitted to hospital, he said to me, as if it were his final testament: "Kashmir Śaivism is the culmination of Indian thought and spirituality." In a sense, this text led him to his own fulfilment, which may be expressed in the words of the Parātrīśikā: *anuttara*, Ultimate Reality, or *khecarī-samatā*, identification with the universal Consciousness.

After his death the task of editing the book was entrusted to me. Pandit H.N. Chakravarty helped in revising the text and translation, for which we would like to express our gratitude. The author's translation, which was partly handwritten and evidenced many corrections, had to be edited and retyped. With the exception of a very few corrections, his translation has been left unchanged. It should perhaps be mentioned that sometimes his own "exposition", without which the text would not be understandable, has been inserted in the translation. Except at a few places where brackets have been added to indicate the additions, no attempt has been made to change the style of the translator. In this his last work Jaideva Singh has shown his full mastery of the art of translation, which means more than a literal correspondence to the original. In spite of the great difficulties of both language and content, he has succeeded in bringing out the originality of Abhinavagupta's thought and the beauty of his language.

While Jaideva Singh was working on the text, two other translations of it were published: One in Hindi by Nilkanth Gurtoo[1] which he saw before completing his work, the other in Italian by R. Gnoli[2] which he had no time to compare with his own since he received it when he was already ill.

The present Preface can in no way be a substitute for the author's introduction that he was prevented by illness from writing. It is only intended as a help towards situating the book in its proper context, without claiming to be a study of its contents, tempting though such a study would be.[3] This is one of the deepest and most difficult texts of Kashmir Śaivism or Trika in general and of Abhinavagupta in particular, and the present translation can become the starting point for further research, not only in the field of Kashmir Śaivism, but of comparative mysticism as well.

The Text

Abhinavagupta[4] wrote two commentaries on this short and condensed Tantric text: one called *Laghuvṛtti* (Short Commentary) and also called *Anuttaratattvavimarśinī* ("Reflection on the Ultimate Reality"),[5] and this present *Parātriśikā Vivaraṇa*, which he also calls *Tattvaviveka* or *Tattvavivaraṇa* and *Anuttaraprakriyā* in his *Tantrāloka* (IX, 313 with Jayaratha's Comm.: *anuttaraprakriyāyām iti śrīparātriśikāvivaraṇādau ityarthaḥ*, Vol. VI, p. 249).[6] Since this text is quoted in the Tantrāloka, Abhinavagupta must have written it before his *magnum opus*. The two commentaries differ not only in length but also in interpretation. The commentated text, which consists of only 36 verses and which is supposed to be a part, or indeed the essence of *Rudrayāmala* (*Tantra*)[7] is generally known as *Parātriṃśikā*, "The Thirty Verses on the Supreme". Abhinavagupta however rejects this title because there are actually more than thirty verses, and because he prefers the title which indicates the meaning of the text: *Parātriśikā*. This title, accepted by him, is explained as "The Supreme Goddess of the Three", or more explicitly: "The Supreme Goddess who transcends and is identical with the Trinity (Trika)."[8] The "three" refers to the three Śaktis: *icchā* (will), *jñāna* (knowledge) and *kriyā* (activity), or *parā*, *parāparā* and *aparā*, or else the three states of *sṛṣṭi*, *sthiti* and *saṃhāra*, and *a fortiori* to the content of the Trika, i.e. Śiva, Śakti and *nara*. Another possible title, one given by Abhinavagupta's predecessors, was *Parātriṃśakā*, which is explained by them as: "That which speaks out (*kāyati*) the three (*tri*) Śaktis (*śa*) of the Supreme (*parā*)."

The *Parātriśikā* has also been called *Anuttarasūtra* by the earlier teachers, "The Sūtra or essence of the Unsurpassable, the Ultimate Reality" (p. 276, KSTS), and elsewhere *Trikasūtra*, which Jayaratha explains as: *śrītrikasūtra iti, trikaprameyasūcikāyāmśrīparātriśikāyām ityarthaḥ* (Tantrāloka XII, 15, vol. VII, p. 101). This shows the great importance given by Kashmir Śaivism to this revealed text as the "index to the entire subject-matter of Trika system."[9] In fact it is one of the most authoritative and venerated texts, along with *Mālinīvijaya Tantra* (mostly called *Pūrvaśāstra* by Abhinava). This importance is also proved by the fact that Somānanda wrote a commentary on the *Parātriśikā* called *Vivṛti*, which is unfortunately lost and to which Abhinavagupta frequently refers. Maybe some obscure passages of his Vivaraṇa would become clear if we were in possession of Somānanda's Vivṛti. Other commentaries quoted by Abhinavagupta are also not available at present, namely those of Kalyāṇa and Bhavabhūti.[10] There is a later commentary by Lakṣmīrāma (alias Lasakāka, 18th-19th cent.)", and others about which we have little knowledge.

The Tantra is in the usual form of question and answer—a fact which itself becomes the subject of metaphysical reflection for Abhinavagupta: Bhairava answers the questions of Devī, which are related to the "great secret" (*etad guhyam mahāguhyam*..., v. 2—this also justifies the English subtitle). Abhinavagupta also calls it *trikaśāstra-rahasya-upadeśa*[11] ("The teaching of the secret of Trika doctrine," p. 52, KSTS), and he makes it clear that this is not a text for beginners but for advanced disciples or even for enlightened ones: *nijaśiṣya-vibodhāya prabuddha-smaraṇāya ca* (V. 5 of his introductory verses). He thus presupposes in his readers both knowledge of the Trika doctrines as well as spiritual experience. This expression of his shows precisely the function of such a text: to enlighten those who are still on the way and to remind the enlightened ones of their own experience. Any mystical text addresses itself to both types of readers simultaneously.

The language of both text and commentary is very often a secret language, used on purpose to hide the real meaning from the uninitiated. Not only that, but most words, verses or passages have a double meaning and can be interpreted on several levels, e.g. on the levels of *parā*, *parāparā* and *aparā*, or in the context of *śāmbhava* or *śākta upāya*, etc. The translation contains these different possibilities of interpretation. It should also be mentioned here that the verses in Apabhraṃśa have not been given in the translation because their language is no longer understood even by Kashmiri Pandits.

Abhinavagupta's interpretation of the verses is variable in the sense that he dwells at great length on the first nine verses but gives a much shorter commentary on the latter part of the Tantra. The interpretation of the very first verse alone covers 50 pages of the printed text in the Kashmir Series edition. In order to understand Abhinavagupta's approach we must be aware of the importance of sacred language and of a revealed text. Since the Tantra is also called a Sūtra, he says that a Sūtra contains manifold meanings and can be interpreted in a variety of ways—which does not however mean in an arbitrary fashion. He thus shows his full mastery of exegesis, taking every word of the Tantra to its extreme possibilities of interpretation. The best example of his hermeneutical genius is to be found in the sixteen interpretations of the term *anuttara*—even the number 16 is significant because it indicates completeness or fullness.[12] Abhinavagupta's exegetic approach consists in combining fidelity to the text with an incredible freshness and originality. In the Indian tradition there are certain commentators who distort the original text in order to superimpose their own view on it and others who blindly follow to the letter the text in question. Abhinavagupta's genius is to infuse life into each syllable of the text.

The Background

The Divine Consciousness is identical with the Supreme Word (*parā vāk*), and hence every letter or word is derived from and ultimately inseparable from this Consciousness. "She (the supreme *vāk*) is, in the most initial stage, stationed in the Divine I-consciousness which is the highest *mantra* and which is not limited by space and time." (p. 3-4 KSTS). Therefore the analysis of language is inseparable from that of consciousness. *Mantra* and the whole metaphysics of the Word is at the centre of this text. Modern philosophy of language could learn a lot from Abhinavagupta's subtle speculation on the Word, *vāk* (*logos*), which extends from its mystical dimension to the intricacies of Sanskrit grammar and linguistic speculation, from psychological subtleties to philosophical reasoning. Abhinavagupta is a master in all these fields and he has not left any aspect of the word. Because of the multiple dimensions of meaning contained in letters and words etc., language as a whole has been understood as a complete symbolical system. The Word *is* the symbol. The four stages of *vāk* as *parā*, *paśyanti*, *madhyamā* and *vaikhari* represent a gradual descent (or ascent) from the undifferentiated, transcendental level to the differentiated, gross level.

The Sanskrit language, of course, lends itself with particular clarity to the type of mystical-philosophical speculation on letters, words and sentences of which Abhinavagupta is so fond. For example, the very word *aham*, 'I', as the centre of consciousness, has been analysed as: *a* standing for Śiva and *ha* for Śakti. *Aham* is "the natural, innate *mantra* known as the Supreme Word (*parā vāk*) of the Light of Consciousness (*prakāśasya*, i.e. Śiva)." (p. 55, KSTS). In a kind of pun it is turned around into *ma-ha-a* to show the return movement from external manifestation, represented by *ma* (standing for *nara*, the individual), through *ha* (standing for Śakti) to *a* (standing for Śiva or *anuttara*). Thus the two movements of expansion and retraction of consciousness are contained in the two *mantras aham* and *ma-ha-a*. The very first letter of the alphabet, *a*, indeed stands for Śiva or *anuttara* as the source of the whole manifestation: the external creation, the development of language (the alphabet) and the revelation of consciousness. Then follows the symbolical identification of the vowels with qualities or Śaktis, e.g. *ā* stands for *ānanda* (bliss), *i* for *icchā* (will), *ī* for *īśanā* (lordship), *u* for *unmeṣa* (unfolding), etc. Another important symbolical understanding of the letters is that the vowels are called *bīja* (seed) and are identified with Śiva, while the consonants are *yoni* (womb) and are identified with Śakti. This implies the inseparability of Śiva and Śakti, of vowels and consonants in language.

A great part of the reflection on the meaning of letters is centred around the two ways of arranging the letters of the Sanskrit alphabet, *Mātṛkā* and *Mālinī*. In the words of Jaideva Singh: "Trika philosophy maintains that the entire manifestation is an expression of *parā śakti* or *parā vāk* or transcendental logos. This *parā vāk* is creative energy. Every letter of the alphabet represents energy in some form. The letters of the alphabet are arranged in two schemes in Trika, viz. *Mātṛkā* and *Mālinī*. *Mātṛkā* means the little mother or phonematic creative energy. *Mālinī* literally means the Devī who wears a *mālā* or garland of fifty letters of the Sanskrit alphabet......The main difference between *Mātṛkā* and *Mālinī* consists in the arrangement of letters. In *Mātṛkā*, they are arranged in a regular order, i.e. the vowels come first and the consonants come next in a serial order. In *Mālinī*, they are arranged in an irregular way, i.e. the vowels and consonants are mixed and no serial order is observed."

Another aspect of the mystical-philosophical meaning of language can be seen in the following example. The simple fact that Bhairava in the first person addresses Devī in the second person becomes for Abhinavagupta the starting-point for a deep philosophical reflection on the nature of the three grammatical persons and their pronouns: I, you, he (she, it) (*aham, tvam, saḥ*). These three are a part of the triadic structure of reality (*sarvaṃ trikarūpam eva*, p. 73, KSTS), and they are related to the trinity of *nara* (he or it), Śakti (you) and Śiva (I), and thus to the three levels of *apara, parāpara* and *para* (the lowest or objective, the intermediate and the transcendent levels). But since the trinity does not consist of closed entities but of a relationship where one can be transformed into the other, and the lower can be assumed in the higher, all kinds of interactions between the three persons are possible. For example the third person, which may even be a lifeless object, if it is addressed personally becomes a 'you' for the one who addresses it and thus shares in the Śakti-nature of the second person. The example given is the vocative: "You, O mountains!" But the same object in the third person can even be transformed into the first person, into an 'I', as in the words of Kṛṣṇa in the Bhagavad Gītā: "Of mountains, I am Meru." On the other hand, a person or 'I' addressing another person or 'you' experiences a kind of fusion of his 'I' with the 'I' of the person addressed, that (common) I-feeling being of the nature of delight (*camatkāra*) and freedom (*svātantrya*). Communication is communion in the same *ahaṃbhāva*. The pure, unlimited, absolute 'I' is only Śiva who is self-luminous consciousness. "The notion of 'you' i.e. the second person, though indicative of separateness, is actually similar to that of 'I'. Therefore both you and I are described as genderless." Abhinavagupta gives several examples from common speech of how the three grammatical persons are interrelated and merge in each other, in order to show that everything, even insentient objects, is ultimately related to the absolute I-consciousness of Śiva. Even the three numbers of singular, dual and plural are related to the three principles of Trika: the singular being Śiva, the dual Śakti and the plural *nara*, i.e. the level of multiplicity. The restoration of plurality into unity or of the objective world into Śiva, is indeed the characteristic par excellence of release from bondage: *anekam ekadhā kṛtvā ko na mucyeta bandhanāt* (p. 79, KSTS).

This may suffice as an example of how Abhinavagupta is able, by analysing grammatical structures, to throw light on reality in toto, because, as he himself says, language and the rules of grammar reflect consciousness. This is not limited to Sanskrit but applies to all languages, for "there is no speech which does not reach the heart directly." (p. 80, KSTS).

Metaphysically speaking, the Parātrīśikā Vivaraṇa explains and illustrates the Tantric principle or dictum: *sarvaṃ sarvātmakam*, "everything is related to everything else." This awareness of the interrelatedness and oneness of all things as an expression of the freedom of the Divine, is extended to the ultimate degree. What it implies is not a chaotic confusion of dimensions of reality, but an inner relationship which follows the principle of the reality and its reflection: *bimba—pratibimba.* Just as in a mirror right becomes left and left right, in the order of creation the Ultimate Reality is inversed, and in order to return to the Source this inversion has to be rectified. Hence the highest principle is related to the lowest (Śiva to the earth) and so forth (see the charts), in other words: transcendence is in immanence and immanence in transcendence. This is the key to the speculative (in the literal sense) play with the letters of the Sanskrit alphabet and the *tattvas* or principles of reality. Therefore Abhinavagupta comments at length on the famous verse of the Mahābhārata: (XII, 54, also Yoga Vāsiṣṭha):

YASMIN SARVAṂ YATAḤ SARVAṂ
YAḤ SARVAṂ SARVATAŚCA YAḤ /
YAŚCA SARVAMAYO NITYAṂ
TASMAI SARVĀTMANE NAMAḤ //

"In whom everything is, from whom everything comes,
who is everything and everywhere,
who is immanent in all things, eternal,
him, the Self of all, do I adore."
(my translation, different from Jaideva Singh)

In the spiritual realm—which is of course inseparable from all else—the ideal is enunciated by the Tantra in the first verse as *khecarī-samatā*: sameness with the power of consciousness. *Khecarī* is the Śakti moving in the free space (*kha*) which is an image of consciousness. The soul or individual knows in reality only two states: *khecarī-vaiṣamya,* dissimilarity, estrangement from the Divine Consciousness-power or the essential nature, or *khecarī-samatā* (or *-sāmya*) which is a state of harmony and identity with the divine I-consciousness. The first is the state of ***paśu,*** the bound individual, the second is the state of a *jīvanmukta* or of *pati,* the Lord himself, for: "*Khecarī-sāmya* is the highest state of Śiva both in life and liberation."

These are only a few hints at the content of this profound work from which the reader can draw direct inspiration. Even Abhinavagupta himself, after completing his commentary, says in all humility: "I have briefly concluded it according to (the teaching of) my *guru* and the Āgama. As to what happens by resorting to this I-consciousness, ask your personal experience. I have only shown a little bit of the path. One should not rest contented with this much..."

* * *

It has not been possible to print the Sanskrit text and translation alternately, because most of the translated passages were too long to make such a division useful for the reader. However, the page numbers of the Sanskrit text printed at the end have been indicated before every passage of the translation, so that the reader can follow the text alongwith the translation.

Since both in the translation and in the notes every technical term has been explained, it was not found necessary to add a Glossary. The Index will be useful in tracing the explanations of the specific terms of Trika and of Parātrīśikā.

Finally, I would like to thank Swami Lakshmanjee for all his guidance and inspiration, and especially for blessing this book by giving it a dedication praising both Abhinavagupta's genius and Śiva, the unsurpassable: *abhinavacamatkārātmane śivāya namaḥ*!

Varanasi
27th May 1987
and
Vasant Navarātra 1988

Bettina Bäumer

Notes

1. Nilkantha Gurtoo, Śrī Parātriṃśikā. Delhi (Motilal Banarsidass), 1985.
2. Raniero Gnoli, Parātriṃśikā tattvavivaraṇam. Il commento di Abhinavagupta alla Parātriṃśikā, Roma (Seric Orientale Roma), 1985.
3. The reader may consult the introduction by R. Gnoli, or in Hindi by N. Gurtoo.
4. We need not go here into the life and works of Abhinavagupta. Apart from the well-known study by K.C. Pandey, we may refer to two recent publications: V. Raghavan,

Abhinavagupta and His Works, Varanasi (Chaukhambha Orientalia), 1980, and N. Rastogi, Introduction to the Tantrāloka, Delhi (Motilal Banarsidass), 1987.

5. This commentary has been translated into Italian by R. Gnoli (Commento Breve alla Trentina della Suprema, Torino, Boringhieri, 1965), and into French by A. Padoux (La Parātrīśikālaghuvṛtti de Abhinavagupta, Paris, Publ. de l'Institut de Civilisation Indienne, De Boccard, 1975).
6. Cf. N. Rastogi, op.cit., pp. 55 ff.
7. Cf. T. Goudriaan and S. Gupta, Hindu Tantric and Śākta Literature, Wiesbaden (O. Harrassowitz), 1981, pp. 40 and 47. The Vijñāna Bhairava, among other texts, is also attached to the Rudrayāmala.
8. The form Parātrīśikā is also used by Kṣemarāja and Jayaratha whenever they quote this text.
9. N. Rastogi, op.cit., p. 56.
10. Even their identity is not certain. Cf. Tantrāloka XIII, 149.
11. Published in the KSTS, vol. 69 (1947).
12. Cf. in another context the *ṣoḍaśakalātmaka soma*, p. 274, KSTS, etc.

ABBREVIATIONS

A.G.	Abhinavagupta
A.P.S.	Ajaḍapramātṛsiddhi (Utpala)
Bh.G.	Bhagavad Gītā
I.P.K.	Īśvarapratyabhijñā Kārikā (Utpala)
KSTS	Kashmir Series of Texts and Studies
L.V.	Laghu Vṛtti (on Parātrīśikā)
M.V.T.	Mālinīvijaya Tantra (also Mālinīvijayottara)
P.K.	Pratyabhijñā Kārikā (same as I.P.K.)
P.T.	Parātrīśikā
P.T.V.	Parātrīsikā Vivaraṇa
Ś.D.	Śivadṛṣṭi
Sp.K.	Spanda Kārika
Sv.T.	Svacchanda Tantra
U.	Upaniṣad
V.Bh.	Vijñāna Bhairava
Y.S.	Yoga Sūtra (also P.Y.S. for Patañjali Yoga Sūtra)

अ. प्र.सि.	अजड प्रमातृसिद्धि
ई. प्र.	ईश्वर प्रत्याभिज्ञाकारिका
कठ	कठोपनिषद
प. त्री.	परात्रीशिका
प्र. का.	प्रत्यभिज्ञा कारिका
भ. गी.	भगवद्गीता
म. भा.	महाभारत
म. भाष्य	महाभाष्य
म. वि.	मालिनी विजय
यो. सू.	योगसूत्र
व. प.	वाक्यपदीय
व. म.	वामकेश्वरीमत
वि. भै.	विज्ञानभैरव
शि. दृ.	शिवदृष्टि
सा. का.	सांख्यकारिका
स्त. चि.	स्तव चिन्तामणि
स्प. का.	स्पन्द कारिका
स्व. तं.	स्वच्छन्द तन्त्र

PRELIMINARIES

(Parentage of Abhinavagupta and a desire for spiritual well-being.)

Vimalakalāśrayābhinavasṛṣṭimahā jananī
Bharitatanuśca pañcamukhaguptarucirjanakaḥ.
Tadubhayayāmalasphuritabhāvavisargamayaṃ
Hṛdayam anuttarāmṛtakulaṃ mama saṃsphuratāt. (1)

Translation

(There is *double entendre* in this verse)

First Interpretation

May my heart[1] (i.e., the reality which is designated as *jagad-ānanda*, the divine beatitude made visible in the form of the universe), whose very nature is manifestation[2] bursting into view by the union[3] of both, viz., Śiva and Śakti (*tadubhayayāmala-sphurita-bhāva-visargamayaṃ*), which is the very emblem of supreme immortality be fully flourished (*saṃsphuratāt*).

Ubhayam or 'both' refers to *jananī* or mother and *janaka* or father. The *jananī* or mother is the *Śakti*, the universal Divine Energy which expresses its stamina in ever fresh creativity that is inspired by pure, absolute autonomy[4] (*vimalakalāśrayābhinava-sṛṣṭimahā*)—the father is Śiva who is perfect and complete in Himself not lacking anything whatsoever (*bharitatanuḥ*) and whose zest in creativity is brought to realization by five powers[5] (*pañca-mukhaguptaruciḥ*).

Notes

1. *Hṛdaya* or heart here refers to *jagadānanda*, the divine beatitude which is immutable, which never declines, which is visible in the form of the universe, which is the very core of manifestation. Cf. Tantrāloka I, 1 with Jayaratha's Commentary.

2. Jayaratha explains *visarga* as *bahirullilasiṣāsvabhāvaḥ*, i.e. it is the very nature of the Divine to manifest Himself externally.

3. Union or *yāmala* denotes the *sāmarasya* or perfectly unified or undifferentiated state of Śiva and Śakti which is the pair and origin of all differentiation.

4. The word *kalā* in this context means, as Jayaratha puts it, *Svātantrya-śakti* i.e. absolute autonomy.

5. 'Five powers' refers to the main powers of the Divine, viz. *cit* (consciousness), *ānanda* (bliss, beatitude), *icchā* (will), *jñāna* (knowledge) and *kriyā* (activity).

Vimala or pure in the text means 'not having any of the *āṇava*, *māyīya* and *kārma malas*'.

Second Interpretation of the Verse

May my heart[1] which is full of the supreme quintessence of reality (*anuttarāmṛtakulaṃ*), and which is the product of the exuberance of emotion due to the mating of both (i.e. my father and mother) (*tadubhayayāmalasphurita-bhāvavisargamayaṃ*) expand in supreme consciousness.

The mother (*janani*) is one whose name is constituted by the letters (*kalā*), *vi, ma, la* (literally whose name rests on the letters *vi, ma, la*,[2] *vimalakalāśrayā*) and whose delight consisted in giving birth to Abhinavagupta (*abhinavasṛṣṭimahā*). The father is one whose glory is known by the appellation Siṃhagupta (*pañcamukhaguptaruciḥ*)[3] and who is complete in himself (*bharitatanuḥ*[4]).

Notes

1. *Hṛdaya* or heart in Śaivāgama refers to that centre or *madhyadhāma* from which all the five sensory activities or *jñānendriyas* proceed and to which they return. In yogic parlance, it is known as *suṣumnā*.

2. The name of Abhinavagupta's mother was Vimalā.

3. '*Pañca*' in *pañcamukha* is derived from the root '*pañc*' (I.P.A. *pañcati, pañcate*) which means 'to spread out'. *Pañcamukha*, therefore, means 'one whose mouth is wide open' i.e. '*siṃha*' (lion). Siṃhagupta is a short form of Narasiṃhagupta which was the name of Abhinavagupta's father.

4. He is said to be '*bharitatanu*' or complete in himself, because he had *samāveśa* or compenetration in Śiva-Śakti.

Jayaratha in his commentary on Tantrāloka, vol. I, 1st verse says that Abhinavagupta was '*yoginībhūḥ*' (one born of Yoginī) for himself. *Yoginībhūḥ* is one whose father is a '*siddha*' (a perfect one in *yoga*) and whose mother is *yoginī*. One born of the union of *siddha* and *yoginī* is known as *yoginībhūḥ*.

Second and third verses are expressive of homage to the Devī (goddess).

Second Verse

Yasyāṃ antarviśvam etad vibhāti
Bāhyābhāsaṃ bhāsamānaṃ visṛṣṭau
Kṣobhe kṣīṇe' nuttarāyāṃ sthitau tāṃ
Vande devīṃ svātmasaṃvittim ekām. (2)

Translation

I bow to that one goddess in the form of Self-consciousness[1] in whom this universe which appears as an external objective existence in the state of manifestation, shines (*vibhāti*), on the extinction of that delusive understanding[2] which makes one identify oneself with one's vehicles, inwardly (*antar*) in the state of Supreme Reality[3] (*anuttarāyāṃ sthitau*).

Notes

1. '*Svātmasaṃvitti*' means the consciousness of the Real Self, not of that psycho-somatic state which masquerades as the Self.

2. *Kṣobha*, literally 'agitation' means here that disturbing delusive understanding which uproots us from our real mooring and makes us identify ourselves with our vehicles, and thus shows the universe as external to the Divine Consciousness.

3. *Anuttara* or Supreme Reality is that state in which the external objective existence is felt as only an expression of the Self or Divine Consciousness. External has a meaning only with reference to the empirical consciousness identified with its vehicles, not to the Divine Consciousness. The external world is like a reflection in the mirror of consciousness which, though not different from the mirror, appears as different from it.

Third Verse

Naraśaktiśivātmakaṃ trikaṃ
Hṛdaye yā vinidhāya bhāsayet
Praṇamāmi parām anuttarām
Nijabhāsāṃ pratibhācamatkṛtim. (3)

Translation

I offer my homage to the wondrous delight of that consciousness which is supreme (*parām*) and unsurpassable, which is effulgent by its own light, which while having within itself the group of the three, viz. phenomenal reality (*nara*), the Universal Spiritual Energy (*śakti*), and Śiva makes them appear externally.

Fourth Verse

(Homage to the Guru or spiritual guide)

Jayatyanarghamahimā vipāśitapaśuvrajaḥ
Śrīmānādyaguruḥ Śaṃbhuḥ Śrīkaṇṭhaḥ parameśvaraḥ. (4)

Translation

Hail to the primordial Guru Śambhu,[1] Śrīkaṇṭha[2] the great lord who is full of radiance (spiritual light), whose greatness is beyond all evaluation, and who cuts asunder the bondage of the group of bound souls.

Notes

1. Śambhu-Śiva who as Śrīkaṇṭha was moved with pity for suffering humanity and inspired Durvāsas to spread the message of Śaivāgama. Therefore, he is the primordial Guru of this Śāstra. Śambhunātha was the name of Abhinavagupta's *guru* in Trika and Kaula Śastra. Therefore there appears to be a *double entendre* in the word Śambhu. In that case, *ādya guru* would mean initial *guru*.

2. *Śrikaṇṭha*: This is one of the names of Śiva. It is said that he was touched by pity for suffering humanity. He, therefore, commissioned the sage Durvāsas to revive the teaching of Śaivāgama. The sage divided the teaching of Śaivāgama into three classes: *advaita* (non-dualistic), *dvaita* (dualistic) and *dvaitādvaita* (non-dualistic cum dualistic) and taught them to Tryambaka, Āmardaka, and Śrīnātha, respectively. Tryambaka was the founder of the Advaita School to which Abhinavagupta belongs.

Fifth Verse

(The purpose of Abhinavagupta's Commentary)

Nijaśiṣyavibodhāya prabuddhasmaraṇāya ca
Mayābhinavaguptena śramo'yaṃ kriyate manāk. (5)

Translation

For the clear understanding of my pupils and for refreshing the memory of those who are already proficient in this Śāstra (this philosophical discipline) I, Abhinavagupta, am making a little exertion (in writing this commentary).

THE TEXT WITH THE COMMENTARY

Śrī Devī uvāca

ANUTTARAṂ KATHAṂ DEVA
SADYAḤ KAULIKASIDDHIDAM
YENA VIJÑĀTAMĀTREṆA
KHECARĪ-SAMATĀṂ VRAJET (1)

Meaning of Important Words

Anuttaram: the Supreme, the unsurpassable, the Absolute Consciousness; *sadyaḥ*: immediately, spontaneously, *kaulika*: pertaining to *kula* or the supreme energy of Śiva appearing in the entire cosmos. Consisting of the body, senses, worlds etc. *kula* also means *ghanatā*, i.e. solidification, concretization (of consciousness); *siddhi*: accomplishment, perfection of achievement; fulfilment of aim; spiritual power. *Kauliki siddhi* therefore means the achievement of identity of the individual consciousness, of the empirical I with the perfect I-consciousness of Śiva which has become concretized in the form of the cosmos, an achievement which comes about in this very physical body.

Khecarī-'bodhabhūmisañcāriṇī satī iyaṃ saṃvit śaktiḥ (L.V., p. 11), the Consciousness-power moving about in the sphere of universal knowledge. *Khecarī*: '*khe carati iti khecarī*, means literally that which moves about in *kha* or sky. *Kha* or sky is the symbol of the unobstructed expanse of Consciousness. Here according to Abhinavagupta, it means *Saṃvid-śakti* or consciousness-power.

Translation

The exalted goddess said (to Bhairava): "O God, how[1] does the unsurpassable divine Consciousness[2] bring about immediately[3] the achievement of the identity of the empirical I with the perfect I-consciousness of Śiva which comes about in this very physical body[4] and by the mere knowledge of which one acquires sameness with the Universal Consciousness-power (*khecarī*)?"[5]

NOTES

The Devī is the *parāśakti* who on the plane of *paśyanti* and *madhyamā* puts a question as the Devī in order to bestow grace on human beings, and on the other hand being poised in *anuttara* answers as Bhairava.

1. *Katham*: How i.e. '*kena prakāreṇa*'—in what way, by what means.

2. *Anuttaram*: the unsurpassable Divine Consciousness is so called, because, as Abhinavagupta puts it, it is the Experient of all, and there is none other that can make it his object of experience. It is the universal subject *par excellence.* "*Tasya tu cidātmanaḥ svaprakāśasya na grāhakāntaram asti iti anuttaratvam*" (L. V. p. 1). "*Anuttara* is so called, because there is none other who can act as subject of that Self-luminous Universal Consciousness." It is the Eternal Universal Subject of all experience.

3. *Sadyaḥ*: Immediately i.e. at the very moment when it is known. In Laghvī Vṛtti, Abhinavagupta adopts the reading '*svataḥ*' in place of *sadyaḥ*. *Svataḥ* has been explained in Laghvī Vṛtti as '*svatantrataḥ*' i.e., by its absolute autonomy.

4. *Kaulika-siddhiḥ*: means '*kule dehe bhavā kaulikī siddhiḥ*', i.e. an achievement that occurs, that is experienced in this very physical body. There are two important words in this phrase, viz. *kaulika* and *siddhi*. *Kaulika* is the adjective from *kula*, happening or occurring in *kula*; *siddhi* means achievement, the desired fulfilment. What is this achievement, what is this fulfilment? The achievement is '*cidaikātmya*' i.e. identity with, unification with *cit* or universal Consciousness. *Kula* includes *deha* or physical body. So, '*kaulika-siddhi*' means the achievement of the unification of the empirical consciousness with the Divine Universal Consciousness in this very body. The limitation of the individual consciousness disappears, it is transformed into unity-consciousness, and the individual views the world and life in a different light. *Kula* on the macrocosmic plane, is the divine creative energy, the *parā vāk* which brings about the phonematic emana-

tion up to '*ha*', the manifestation of the universe. On the microcosmic plane, it refers to that energy which works in the human body. *Kaulika siddhi* thus brings about the perfect harmony of the microcosmic with the macrocosmic.

There are, however, many shades of meaning of *kaulika siddhi* which will be clear from the translation of the Vivaraṇa commentary of Abhinavagupta.

5. *Khecarī-samatā.*

Khecarī: A.G. in L.V. says, '*khecarī bodhabhūmisañcāriṇī sati iyaṃ saṃvic-chaktiḥ.*' (p. 2). '*Khecarī*' is the Consciousness-power that moves about on the plane of *bodha* or the universal Divine Consciousness. What are the characteristics of this *bodha*? A.G. says, 'They are *avikalpatvaṃ, pūrṇatvaṃ. Bodha* or the Universal Divine Consciousness is (1) thought-free (*avikalpa*) and (2) it is *pūrṇa* i.e., whole, complete, undivided, unconditioned, integral. In one word, it is not limited or determined by any external condition. *Khecarī*, therefore, is the *śakti* that pertains to this plane of consciousness.

Samatā means 'sameness'. So '*khecarī-samatāṃ vrajet*' means he acquires the same integral, unconditioned, undetermined consciousness as that of Śiva or the Divine.

One who does not rise to that level does not have the experience of *khecarī*. As A.G. puts it in L.V., "*Tatprakārāparijñāne tu na khecarī abodharūpe vedyāṃśe sañcaraṇāt*" (L.V., p. 2), "one who does not have the experience of that level does not have the experience of *khecarī*, because his consciousness moves about in *abodha* which is only objective-external like blue colour or jar or cloth or internal like pleasure, pain, etc." *Abodha* in this context is a technical term meaning empirical consciousness. A.G. clarifies this idea further by saying: "*Tata eva vedyaiḥ nīlādibhirniyantriteti na pūrṇaśaktiḥ*" (L.V.2). Since the empirical consciousness is determined, conditioned by 'blue', etc., therefore it is not *pūrṇa*, not integral, not unconditioned. The consciousness of the *khecarī* level alone is unconditioned and hence *pūrṇa* or whole in itself.

Commentary

Text

From *parameśvaraḥ* on p. 2 upto *devī ityucyate* on p. 3, l. 5

Translation

The Highest Lord ever brings about the five-fold act.[1] He is in fact the very Grace itself, being always equipped with His Supreme Divine Energy (Śakti) whose very nature is Grace (it should be borne in mind that Śakti never considers herself as different from Śiva.[2]) (The Supreme Divine Energy or *parā* Śakti expresses itself in *parā vāk*). This Śakti which is full of the thought of Grace for the entire world is, to begin with, non-different (in the undifferentiated or *nirvikalpa* state) from *paśyanti* who is *parāmarśamayī* i.e. who is always cognizant of the essential nature of the Divine and who has a hundred powers which are boundless in operation which however will be described later. She (the Supreme *vāk*) is, in the most initial stage, stationed in the Divine I-consciousness which is the highest *mantra* and which is not limited by space or time. In that stage she (*parā-vāk*) abides without any distinction of question and answer which will start in *paśyanti*.

The *parāvāk* which is non-dual i.e. identical with the (supreme) consciousness is present in all experients[3] always in her integral nature (of knowership and doership) uniformly in all states i.e., even at the level of *paśyanti*, *madhyamā* and *vaikhari*. Therefore, *paśyanti* comprehends in a general indeterminate (*nirvikalpa*) way whatever is desired to be known if it is awakened by due causal conditions just as one who has experienced variegated colour like dark, blue etc., as in a peacock's tail and whose experience is determined by many impressions, positive and negative, recalls only that particular colour which is awakened by the proper causal condition of the memory. At the time of initial indeterminate knowledge in *paśyanti* in which there is no distinction in the word and its referent, there was obviously not any sense of difference between the word and its referent.

Madhyamā, however, which shows the difference between the word and its referent is concerned with its comprehension only in the same location (*sāmānādhikaraṇya*) i.e. in the *antaḥkaraṇa* or the inner psychic apparatus.[4] In *vaikhari*, on the other hand, there is a clear difference between the two i.e. between the word and its referent.[5]

When this regular, fixed relation of the word and its referent (*vyavasthāyāṃ*) is proved in one's own experience, it will be found that what is the stage of *parā vāk* is the power of non-*māyīya* word and is of the nature of the highest truth. It is unconventional (*asāṃketika*), natural (*akṛtaka*), having as its essence the stamp of the highest truth, and is inspired by the truth of the energy of the *mantra* of I-consciousness, the principle of which will be described in the sequels.

She abides in the subsequent conditions of *paśyantī* etc., also, for without her there would accrue the condition of non-manifestation, in *paśyantī* etc., and thus would arise the contingency of absolute insensateness (*jaḍatā*).

In that stage (i.e. in the *parāvāk* stage), there is absolutely no thought of difference such as 'this' (a particular entity or individual), 'thus' (a particular form), 'here' (particular space), 'now' (particular time). Therefore, beginning with *paśyantī* which is the initial creative state of the energy of the highest *mantra*, up to *vaikharī* in which manifestation of difference of all the existents has proceeded fully, this *parāvāk* full of the wondrous delight of her own self, resting within her own self which is all Light, continues pulsating (*sphurati*). That pulsation is I-consciousness whose highest truth is uninterrupted continuity.[6] This matter will be clarified further on. In that (*parāvāk*) alone, in the *paśyantī* stage in which there is just an incipience of difference, in the *madhyamā* state in which there is an appearance of difference (inwardly in the psychic apparatus), which consist specifically of *jñāna* (knowledge) and *kriyā* (activity) respectively—*jñāna* which is the predominant attribute of Sadāśiva and *kriyā* which is the predominant attribute of Īśvara, the wondrous delight of I-consciousness which encloses within itself the joy of objective existence of innumerable universes is fully operative. Therefore, Supreme Consciousness even while appearing as *paśyantī* and *madhyamā* actually experiences Herself as the Supreme Consciousness. It is this Supreme Consciousness (*parā saṃvid*) that is said to be 'Devī' (goddess).

NOTES

1. The five-fold act refers to (1) *sṛṣṭi* or manifestation, (2) *sthiti* or maintenance, (3) *saṃhāra* or withdrawal or absorption, (4) *vilaya* or veiling the essential nature, (5) *anugraha* or revealing the essential nature i.e. grace.

2. As the Śakti (the Divine Energy) is never different from Śiva (the Supreme Lord), it is all the same whether one calls Śakti as *anugrahātmikā* i.e. Grace incarnate or Śiva as *anugrahātma* or Grace incarnate.

3. She is present in all experients and in all conditions as the innermost Supreme or Divine Consciousness. The experients can be divided under seven broad heads, viz., *sakala*, *pralayākala*, *vijñānākala*, *mantra*, *mantreśvara*, *mantramaheśvara* and *Śivapramātā*. She is present in all of them.

4. The difference between the word and its referent is, in the stage of *madhyamā*, only in a subtle mental state; it has not yet been externalized. *Samānādhikaraṇa* means in the same location, i.e. *antaḥkaraṇa* or the psychic apparatus.

5. In *vaikharī*, there is *vyadhikaraṇa vimarśa* i.e. the location of the word is in the mouth, but the location of the referent is in external space.

6. The highest truth of the Divine I-consciousness is that its continuity is uninterrupted (*avicchinnatāparamārtham*). It is always present in everything. It never takes a holiday. It cannot be escaped from. Nothing can elude it, or give a slip to it. That is why Śiva is said to be immanent in the universe.

Text

Different implications of the word Devī:

From *iyatāpaśyantyādisṛṣṭikrameṇa* on p. 3, l. 5 upto *devatāvyavahāraḥ* on p. 3, l. 14

Translation

(She is called Devī because of the following reasons:)

1. Because in the succeeding order of creation from *paśyantī* down to external manifestation like blue etc., she sports with the creative delight of her consciousness, for the root '*div*' from which the noun *Devī* is derived means 'to sport'.

2. The Divine Bhairava transcends everything and abides in an all-exceeding eminence. Because of His desire to remain in that state i.e. because of His desire to overcome and surpass everything; and abiding in transcendental eminence who is none other than that Divine desire is called Devī, for the root

'*div*', from which the word 'Devī' is derived also means *vijigiṣā* i.e. 'the desire to overcome and surpass' (there being no difference between Bhairava and His divine energy, Bhairavī).

3. Because of her carrying on the activities of life in so many innumerable ways of knowledge, memory, doubt, ascertainment etc., she is called *devi* for the root '*div*' also means 'to carry on the activities of life'.

4. Because of shining in the forms of 'blue' etc. which appear everywhere, (she is called Devī) for the root '*div*' also means to shine or irradiate.

5. Because of being adored by all who are (inevitably) possessed by Her (Devī's) light and are devoted to Her (she is called Devī) for the root '*div*' also means 'to adore'.

6. Because of Her access to all things according to Her will, separated though they may be by space and time, (she is called Devī), for the root '*div*' also means 'to go, to have access to'.

7. Hence 'divinity' (*devatā*) applies especially to Bhagavān Bhairava. Devī is (reasonably) applied to Bhagavatī also, for she is His very Śakti. This interpretation of *Devi* is supported by the Science of Grammar which declares that the root '*div*' is used in the sense of 'sport, the desire to overcome or surpass all, behaviour, irradiation, adoration, and movement'.

Thus the epithet *devatā* is applied also to Viṣṇu, Brahmā etc. inasmuch as they partially partake of the divinity which is particularly applicable in its wholeness only to the Highest Lord and, which is the same thing, his Śakti.

Text

The rationale of the past tense in 'said' (*uvāca*):

From *evam bhagavati paśyanti madhyamā ca* on p. 3, l. 14 upto *sphuṭayiṣyate ca etat* on p. 4, l. 15

Translation

When the glorious *parāvāk* becoming *paśyanti* and *madhyamā* (i.e. in the stage of *paśyanti* and *madhyamā*) thus recollects Herself, "I myself as Parāvāk Devī said thus", then (i.e. in that state of recollection), shining forth (*ullasat*) in that form (i.e. as *parāvāk*), she regards Her own *parā* stage as past in accordance with the fact of difference brought about by *māyā*, because in comparison to Herself that stage (of *paśyanti*) is the commencement of *māyā*, and because of her travelling through the passage of inner senses (in the case of *madhyamā*) and outer senses (in the case of *vaikhari*), whose life consists in manifesting difference, she regards the *parā* stage as past (*parokṣatayā*).

The today of Brahmā is not limited by the (human) day whose division of day depends on the (apparent) motion of the sun. The measure of his today is determined by many *kalpas*.[1] The day of Viṣṇu and others is even longer than that, and in the case of Yogīs the term day is used even for one-thousandth part of the human day on account of his inward motion of *prāṇa* (breath).[2] Thus how can the concept of today or the present which is unsettled and fictitious apply to unfictitious Consciousness (which is beyond time)?

According to this principle, *parāvāk* who fulfils the sense of the past in all its aspects, viz. *sāmānya bhūta* (*luṅ* i.e. aorist), *anadyatana* (*laṅ* i.e., imperfect) and *parokṣa* (lit. i.e. past perfect) reflects thus in the first person of the *parokṣa* (past): "I the same Parāvāk Devī unseparated from Śiva (*vācya*) and the Śāstra (*vācaka*) or from the word and its referent thus said.' This is the sense of the use of the past tense.

(An example of such reflection about the past in the present may be cited from common experience:)

"While asleep, I, indeed, bewailed". In this experience, there is the proof of reflection about the past in the present. In the above example, the person does not remember the past experience, for he did not have that experience in the past (and remembrance is only of a past experience). Now after awaking, he experiences that state in astonishment either by the great reliability of the statement of another person or by perturbation due to affections in his body through sobbing etc., caused by excessive bewailment, exuberant singing etc. This is not unbelievable. "In an insane condition or in the condition of being asleep, I, so they say, uttered moaning sound"—in this statement, there is a reference to the past even without any objective experience in insanity, dream, swoon etc. In the *parā* (supreme) stage, there is, indeed, total absence of any object whatsoever.

Only because this is the experience of the fourth state, the experience in this is identical with the experient whereas in insanity etc., the experience is due mainly to the excess of bewilderment. This is the main difference between the two. The pastness is, however, common.

Thus every experient whether situated in the position of a teacher or disciple, etc. or in any other capacity, is able to carry out all his dealings always by entering her (*parāvāk*); therefore he apprehends her only (in every state). When it is stated, "The goddess said", it means "I (Parāvāk) only always know everything in an undifferentiated way in the highest stage (*parābhūmau*), otherwise this (question-answer matter) would not acquire clear expression in the stage of *paśyantī* and *madhyamā*." This is the sense of the statement: "The goddess said." It is in this way that the later statement, "Bhairava said," should be considered. There also, the sense of the statement is, "I, only as Bhairava i.e., without the division of Śiva and Śakti (*guru* and *śiṣya* in this context) said," "Only being predominantly the divine Energy, it is in her aspect of her creative nature that She (*parā*) uses the term '*aham*' (I). Thus being predominantly the possessor of that Energy, the delightful experience of Bhairava in His aspect of withdrawal or absorption assumes the form of '*ma-ha-a*.'"[3] This will be clarified later.

NOTES

1. *Kalpa* is a fabulous period of time, according to which a day of Brahmā is one thousand *yugas* or a period of four thousand, three hundred and twenty millions of years of mortals.

2. The time occupied by a *yogī* in *samādhi* in one circuit of respiration covers centuries of external years.

3. *Aham* and *Ma-ha-a*: '*Aham*' consists of three letters, viz. '*a*', '*ha*' and '*m*'. In this '*a*' denotes Śiva, '*ha*' denotes Śakti, '*m*' denotes '*nara*' i.e., all objective existents. Thus '*aham*' denotes the state of manifestation or expansion (*prasara*) of the Divine in objective existence. *Aham* is known as *sṛṣṭibīja*. *Ma-ha-a*: This is the reverse process of *aham*, i.e., the process of the withdrawal or absorption (*praveśa*). In this '*ma*' denotes '*nara*' or objective existents, '*ha*' denotes Śakti, and '*a*' denotes 'Śiva'. This is known as *saṃhāra-bīja* or the process of withdrawal. In both cases, Śakti is the medium. In '*ahaṃ*', Śakti is the medium

through which Śiva passes into phenomena. In *ma+ha+a*, again, Śakti is the medium through which manifestation is absorbed into Śiva. That is why Śakti is said to be the entrance door in Śaiva philosophy "*Śaivī mukhaṃ ihocyate*".

The Final Resting Place of all questions and answers

Text

From *etacca paśyantī madhyamābhuvi* on p. 4. l. 15 upto *tacchāsana pavitritānām yatnaḥ* on p. 6, l. 12

Translation

This is the experience of the highest consciousness characterized by will power (i.e. of *parāvāk*) in the stage of *paśyantī* and *madhyamā*, characterized by *jñāna śakti* (power of knowledge). This is the aim of all the Śāstras (the texts indicating the spiritual discipline) from beginning to end; therefore, there is the actual experience of the energy of the highest *mantra* of the I-consciousness of the Divine in *jñānaśakti* (power of knowledge) only which is the characteristic of Sadāśiva because of the appearance of the former, i.e. the question of the Devī and the latter, i.e. the answer of Bhairava therein in the form of the construction of the words "*Devī uvāca*' and '*Bhairava uvāca*' by means of the letters, *D, e, v, ī, u, v, ā, ca* and *Bh, ai, r, a, va, u, v, ā, ca*.

It has been rightly said in Svacchanda Tantra: "The God Sadāśiva Himself assuming the position of both teacher and pupil revealed the Tantra by means of former and latter sentences i.e. by means of question and answer." (Vol. IV, KSTS, p. 20).

Thus the power of grace of the Divine is always and in all experients uninterrupted. Therefore, she (the power of Grace) alone, the life and soul of Trika Śāstra, constitutes the highest relationship (between the experients and the Divine Consciousness).

In the matter of *anuttara*, i.e. in order to attain to *anuttara* (the unsurpassable, the Supreme), all other kinds of relationship,[1] e.g. *mahat, antarāla, divya, adivya*, etc. are in accordance with the said teaching, aimed at the Supreme only. The same thing has been said in Trikahṛdaya:

"The highest Lord is always intent on creativity (*visargapara-*

maḥ) through His Śakti. He showers grace, manifests and withdraws without any restraint (for grace only)."

Thus there is always the active presence of *anuttara*. So the inner content i.e., question-answer which appears in the consciousness of the highest Lord in an undifferentiated way because of its being the highest truth, is thought of in the *paśyantī* stage in an indeterminate form (in *nirvikalpa* form) with a desire to put it in apportionment of letter, word, and sentence; it is posited with a sense of separateness in the *madhyamā* stage in a determinate form (i.e. in *savikalpa* form); it is finally expressed in the form of question and answer in the *vaikharī* stage i.e. in gross speech consisting of *māyīya* letter, word and sentence, such as 'how the unsurpassable etc.'

This is that unobservable face (i.e. Śakti) of Bhairava full of the feel of manifestation, of which the essence is the unsurpassable I-consciousness, full of the stirring joy (*kṣobha*)[2] brought about by the union (*saṃghaṭṭa*) of Śiva who is symbolized by '*a*' and Śakti who is symbolized by '*ā*' which is the source of the appearance and extension of manifestation according to the Trika system of philosophy and Yoga, which is the original (*maulikaṃ*), enduring state (*dhruvapadam*) and the life of all living beings. Therefore, it is not right to associate the Divine with a particular station[3] etc., for in the absence of any limitation in His case, designation of a particular place for Him is thoroughly unjustifiable.

The fact of question and answer (*vastu*) is an ever present reality which is in the first instance, i.e. at the level of *parāvāk* without division (i.e. without the division of a question and its answer). Therefore, this is all what is meant to be said here. The Self who is the natural state of all existents, who is Self-luminous, amusing Himself with question-answer which is not different from Himself, and in which both the questioner (as Devī) and the answerer (as Bhairava) are only Himself, reflects thus as I, "I myself, being thus desirous of wonderful delight knowing the truth as it is, appear as question and answer (*tathaiva bhavāmi*)." So the book begins with, "The Devī said—how the unsurpassable etc.", says in the middle, "Bhairava said, Listen, O goddess," and ends with "This constitutes Rudrayāmala (the pair of Śiva and Śakti)."

Moreover, from all the Śāstras which have come out from five sources[4] up to worldly dealings—all this is said to be the highest relationship (*paraḥ sambandhaḥ*)

"In my explanation I, Abhinavagupta, have revealed the entire hidden wealth of question-answer mode which has to be kept secret, which is the quintessence of the teaching that makes one identify oneself with Śiva and which always leads oneself in experience to the state of Bhairava."

However with a desire for the good of my pupils, I am summing up the whole teaching in the following verses: "In all dealings, whatever happens whether it is a matter of knowledge or action—all that arises in the fourth stage (*turyabhuvi*) i.e. in the *parāvāk* in an undifferentiated (*gatabhedaṃ*) way. In *paśyanti* which is the initial field of the order of succession (*kramabhūjiṣu*), there is only the germ of difference. In *madhyamā*, the distinction of *jñeya* (object of knowledge) and *kārya* (action) appears inwardly, for a clearcut succession is not possible at this stage (*sphuṭakramāyoge*).

Moreover, *madhyamā* or *paśyanti* fully relying on *parā* which is ever present and from which there is no real distinction of these (*bhṛśam parām abhedato adhyāsya*) (later) regards that state as if past like a mad man or one who has got up from sleep.

This state of the unsurpassable will be explained in this way (i.e. the subject-matter, nomenclature, connexion, and purpose).

The same thing has been said by revered Somānanda in his commentary[5] (on Parātrīśikā) in the following words:

"After the initial pulsation of Energy in the form of *Devī uvāca* of revered Bhairava who is (always) intent upon the fivefold act...".

I who have been purified by his (Somānanda's) commentary am attempting only to clarify the difficulties (lit., to cut asunder the knots) that have remained in that commentary.

NOTES

1. There are six kinds of *sambandha* or relationship between the teachers and the taught:

(1) *Para-sambandha*: in which the questioner and the answerer, the teacher and the taught are both Śiva. It is the highest relationship. It only means the resolution of all doubts by entering *anuttara*, i.e. the highest divine consciousness.

(2) *Mahān sambandha*: in which the questioner is Sadāśiva and the answerer is Śiva.

(3) *Antarāla sambandha*: in which the questioner is Anantabhaṭṭāraka and the answerer is Sadāśiva.

(4) *Divya sambandha*: in which the questioner is the sage, Nandakumāra and the answerer is Anantabhaṭṭāraka.

(5) *Divyādivya sambandha*: in which the questioner is the sage, Sanatkumāra and the answerer is Nāndī.

(6) *Adivya sambandha*: in which both the questioner and answerer are human beings.

2. *Kṣobha* in this philosophy indicates the urge of manifestation.

3. For instance the association of Śiva with the Kailāsa mountain, etc.

4. The five sources from which all the śāstras have come out are the five aspects of Śiva, viz. Īśāna, Tatpuruṣa, Sadyojāta, Vāmadeva, Aghora. Īśāna predominantly represents *cit śakti*; Tatpuruṣa predominantly represents *ānanda śakti*; Sadyojāta represents *icchā śakti*; Vāmadeva represents *jñāna śakti*, and Aghora represents *kriyā śakti*.

5. This commentary is not available now.

TEXT

From *uktaḥ sambandhaḥ* on p. 6, l. 12 upto *sambandhābhidheyaprayojanāni* on p. 7, l. 11

TRANSLATION

The relationship has already been described. Now, we are going to describe the *abhidheya* or subject-matter. *Triśikā* is a compound word. This is its analysis 'the *iśikā* of the three' (*tisṛṇām iśikā*). 'Of the three' means 'of *icchā* (will), *jñāna* (knowledge), *kriyā* (*activity*).' The three are also designated by such other words as *sṛṣṭi*[1], *sthiti*, *saṃhāra* (with reference to the physical plane) or '*udyoga*', '*avabhāsa*' and '*carvaṇā*' (with reference to the spiritual plane). '*Īśikā*' means '*Īśvarī*', the goddess who governs and controls the three i.e. *icchā*, *jñāna* and *kriyā* or *sṛṣṭi*, *sthiti* and *saṃhāra*, or *udyoga*, *avabhāsa*, and *carvaṇā*. It should be borne in mind that '*iśanā*' or governance or control in this context means "being non-different or identical with that which is to be governed or controlled." Therefore, the revered goddess '*parā śakti*' (i.e. the supreme divine Consciousness) who at once transcends this division of three (viz. *sṛṣṭi*, *sthiti*, *saṃhāra* etc.) and is identical with it is the *abhidheya* or subject-matter of the book, and because of its connexion with *parā*, the title (lit., name) of this Śāstra is *parātriśikā*.' Another reading of *triśikā* given by venerable teachers is '*triṃśakā*', and owing to the similarity of words, they give the following etymology:

"That which speaks out (*kāyati*) the three *śaktis* or powers" is *triṃśakā*. The word *triṃśikā* derived from its connexion with thirty (*triṃṣat*) verses is not correct. Even thus, it is not the number of verses but only the sense of *triṃśakā*, that should be adopted. For instance, it has been said in Tantrasāra[2]:

"The sense of Triṃśakā has been declared by you in a range of a crore and half verses."

The relationship of the title of the book and the subject-matter is that of the supreme, for both refer to the same Reality. This has been practically pointed out already.

The aim or purpose of the Śāstra is liberation of all experients in life-time, experients who have become entitled for this knowledge of the unsurpassable (*anuttara*) derived from grace in the form of excellent descent of divine Śakti (power). This liberation connotes penetration with complete identity in the essential nature of Bhairava and unification with perfect I-consciousness which is the delightful flash of one's own essential Self and is the achievement of one who by the realization of his essential nature regards the entire multitude of the categories of existence supposed to be bondage as mere different aspects of his sportfulness which is the expression of the abundance of his delight.[3]

It is averred that liberation is deliverance from those things (the categories of existence) which are conventionally considered to be bondage, deliverance of the individual who lives and grows in the body, *prāṇa* etc.[4] whose field of activity is the inner and outer senses (*jñānendriyas* and *karmendriyas*), and which (i.e. the body, *prāṇa* etc.) are as drives[5] and whose life consists in strenuous endeavour.

If all the impressions (*saṃskāra mātra*) caused by *māyā* (i.e. the impressions of difference) vanish, what does the announcement of such liberation signify and with reference to what is this liberation?

The same idea has been expressed in Spandakārikā (in the following lines):

"He, who has this understanding (viz., that the universe is identical with the Self), regards the whole world as a play (of the Divine), and thus being ever united (with the universal Consciousness) is, without doubt, liberated while alive" (Sp. K. II, 5).

This will be clarified shortly. Thus this realization (i.e., identity of oneself with the perfect I-consciousness of Bhairava) constitutes the purpose of the Śāstras and so this purpose is the culmination of the object of human existence. An inquiry about the purpose of purpose is uncalled for. So the connexion, the subject-matter, and the purpose have been described.[6]

NOTES

1. In the classification according to *sṛṣṭi* etc., there are five aspects, viz. *sṛṣṭi*, *sthiti*, *saṃhāra*, *pidhāna* or *vilaya* and *anugraha* and according to *udyoga* etc., there are also five aspects, viz. *udyoga*, *avabhāsa*, *carvaṇā*, *bījāvasthāpana*, and *vilāpana*. Here according to three-fold classification, *pidhāna* and *anugraha* have been included in *saṃhāra*, and *bījāvasthāpana* and *vilāpana* are included in *carvaṇā* for the sake of uniformity

2. This book is not available now.

3. *Mukti* or liberation does not mean deliverance from the categories of existence but rather identity with the essential nature of Bhairava or in other words with the perfect I-consciousness which is the essential nature of one's own Self.

4. Etc. refers to *puryaṣṭaka*.

5. By 'drives', Abhinava does not mean that they drive one to misery, but that they drive or push the individual to higher life; their very short-coming acts as a stimulus for rising to a higher life.

6. This refers to what is known as *anubandhacatuṣṭaya*, or four indispensable elements of any *śāstra*. They are (1) the *prayojana* or purpose or aim, (2) the *adhikārī*, i.e. one who is competent for the study of the particular *śāstra*, (3) *abhidheya*, the subject-matter of the *śāstra*, (4) *sambandha* or relationship or connexion between the title of the *śāstra* (*abhidhāna*) and the subject-matter (*abhidheya*).

(1) Abhinavagupta says that the *prayojana* or purpose of the

śāstra is *mukti* or liberation, but he scouts the popular idea of *mukti* as deliverance from the vehicles of the Self or from the categories (*tattvāni*) of existence. He valiantly maintains that *mukti* only means identification of the self with the Supreme I-consciousness of the Divine.

(2) Abhinava has not directly used the word *adhikāri*, but has suggested it in '*vibhoḥ paraśaktipātānugrahavaśotpannaitāvadanuttarajñānabhājanabhāvānāṃ*' (P.T., p. 6, l. 22) i.e. they alone are fit to study this *śāstra* in order to attain *mukti* who are oriented towards the Lord through grace.

(3) With regard to *abhidheya* or subject-matter, Abhinava says that it is *saṃvidbhagavatibhaṭṭārikā parā* (P.T., p. 6, l. 15) i.e., the Supreme Divine Consciousness, the Supreme Divine Śakti that ever flashes as I and expresses itself in *parāvāk* or Supreme Sound.

(4) So far as *sambandha* is concerned, Abhinava says, "*abhidhānābhidheyayośca para eva sambandhaḥ tādātmyāt*" (P.T. p. 6, l. 21), the relationship of the subject-matter and the book is that of the Supreme, for both refer to the same Supreme Reality.

Text

From *atha granthārtho vyākhyāyate* on p. 7, l. 12 upto *ityādi* on p. 11, l. 11.

Translation

Now the meaning of the text is being explained. (Abhinava takes up the first word of the first stanza, viz., *anuttaram* for explanation. He has explained it in sixteen ways).

1. *Uttara* may be interpreted as 'more, additional', '*an*' means 'not'. '*Anuttaram*', therefore, means '*na vidyate uttaram adhikaṃ yataḥ*', i.e. 'Than which there is nothing more, or additional'. The other thirty-six *tattvas* (categories of existence) upto Anāśrita Śiva[1] whose very existence is proved by their entrance into the consciousness of highest Bhairava (i.e. which owe their very existence to Para Bhairava) point to the Consciousness of Bhairava as something more than or superior to themselves. Not like this is the highest, most perfect Consciousness of Bhairava (i.e., the Bhairava-Consciousness does not point to anything more or higher than itself), because of its essence being unrestrained, nonrelative, delightful flash of knowership.

2. *Anuttara* is that state in which there is neither question, nor answer (i.e. in which a question formulated in '*Devi uvāca*' or an answer formulated in '*Bhairava uvāca*' does not arise). It is that ocean of supreme Consciousness, from which arises infinite knowledge upto that of Anāśrita Śiva, and by which the pupil becomes competent for the clarity of the question to be raised. It is, in fact, that Reality which is ever awake. In that state how can there ever be an occasion for another answer (than the perfect Bhairava Consciousness) which comes from a preceptor or Guru?

3. '*Uttara*' means crossing i.e. liberation. This is the liberation accepted by the dualists. This does not go beyond the fixed order of things.

According to this, one has, first of all, to enter from the stage of body to the stage of *prāṇa,* then the stage of *buddhi,* i.e. one at first considers the body to be the Self, then the *prāṇa,* and then the *buddhi* to be the Self, then the stage of *prāṇa* (the universal *prāṇaśakti spandanākhyāṃ jivanarūpatāṃ*), then the state of the void which connotes the dissolution of all objectivity, and then on attaining the highest pitch (*atiśayadhārāprāptau*) of the successive diminution of all the *malas* (limitations), the emprical individual is freed on the manifestation of the state of Śiva. All this stupendous ascension is, indeed, futile (for were not the previous stages also the expression of Śiva?).

4. Similarly, rising of the *śakti* from the navel to the heart, then to the throat, then to the palate, then to the top of the head (*brahma* i.e., *sahasrāra*), then to the Bhairava *bila* (the point above the *sahasrāra*) in an upward succession is ascension. *Anuttara* signifies that in this Śaiva Āgama, mounting to Bhairava by an upward succession through the six *cakras* is not indispensable (*na vidyate uttaraḥ* i.e. *ūrdhvataraṇakramaḥ yatra*).

5. *Uttara* also means 'that from which one has to go beyond' i.e., bondage or the world. It also means 'crossing over' i.e. *mokṣa* or deliverance.

Therefore, *anuttara* is that in which there are no such crossings (i.e. according to *anuttara,* the world is not really bondage, and when the world is not bondage, the question of deliverance does not arise).

6. *Uttara* also means speaking in a limited way (about Reality) e.g. 'It is like this, it is like that', i.e. limiting Reality in these

ways. Therefore, *anuttara* is that which has not got limitations. It is unlimited, infinite Reality.

7. Even pointing to Highest Reality[2] by the mere word 'this' is also limiting it, for such indication is also limitation. Thus because of its sense of exclusion (*vyavacchedakatvāt*), even a simple denotation as 'this' is only a *vikalpa* i.e. a mere thought-construct, because of its essence being 'limitation' (*vyaccheda-prāṇameva*). Therefore, so long as an empirical experient (*māyīyaḥ pramātā*) is desirous of entering *anuttara* (the Supreme Reality) so long he remains in *vikalpa* (thought-construct) of a particular form (i.e. in *samādhi*). In this context, (it must be borne in mind) that that which is indeterminate (*avikalpitaṃ*) and necessarily inherent in everything (*avinābhāvi*),[3] that is really *anuttara* (Supreme Consciousness), for without it even a determinate concept cannot appear (*tadvinā kalpitarūpāsphuraṇāt*). In fact, in *anuttara* (*tatra*), contemplation, concentration etc. (*bhāvanādeḥ*) are wholly inapplicable. Therefore, it (*anuttara*) has been declared (by Somānanda) to be beyond contemplation, *karaṇa*, etc. Not that *bhāvanā* is wholly useless, (i.e. it can only bring about the purification of mind, but not the realization of *anuttara*). Such *anuttara* (i.e. the *nirvikalpa*, thought-free *anuttara*) abides even in the life of the work-a-day world (for those who have its awareness). It has been (thus) said by myself in one of my hymns:

"Slender (*pratanu*) rain falling continuously (*avicchidaiva patan*) is not visible in the far-spreading sky (*vitata iva nabhasi*) but it is clearly visible in juxtaposition with the tree of the forest or the eaves of the roof of a house. Even so, the Supreme Bhairava, being too subtle, never appears in the range of experience. Under the circumstances, it is only by its connexion with means which depend on space, form, time, pattern, and state that that consciousness is generated instantaneously in them in whom the awareness of Bhairava is subdued—the consciousness that is indicative of thy presence, O Lord !"

So it will be said further that what is posited as an answer is really no answer. Now we proceed further with the explanation of *anuttara*.

8. Thus the *śākta upāya* is said to be higher than the *nara* i.e. *āṇava upāya*. *Śāṃbhava upāya* is higher even than that (i.e. *śākta upāya*). Even in *Śāṃbhava upāyas* there is a hierarchy among them-

selves in the forms of *bhūta, tattva, mantra, mantreśvara,* (*śakti* etc.). Again even among physical elements, there is a hierarchy in the form of the earth, water etc. The dreaming is higher than the waking, sleep is higher than that (dream); the fourth state (*turya*) is higher than that (sleep); the state beyond the fourth (*turyātita*) is higher than that (i.e. the *turya*). Even in the waking condition there is a hierarchy of these states among themselves through four[4] varieties. I have conclusively discussed this matter in detail in Śrīpūrvapañcikā.[5] I have not described it here in detail, because that will serve no useful purpose, and will unnecessarily increase the volume of the book. This kind of *uttaratva* (hierarchy) only shows higher and lower and contains the delusion of dualism.

9. *Uttara* (in *anuttara*) is used in an abstract sense in which there is no indication of superiority or inferiority as in the division of *brāhmaṇa, kṣattriya, vaiśya, śūdra,* the lowest caste (the caste last in order).

10. *Uttara* (is used) in the sense of *śaktis* like *paśyanti*[6] etc.

11. *Uttara* may mean *śaktis* like Aghorā and others.[7]

12. *Uttara* may mean '*para*' etc.[8] *Anuttara* is that where these don't exist.

13. *Anuttara* may be analysed into *a+nut+tara*. The noun '*nut*' is derived from the root '*nud*' which means to impel, to push, and *tara* means crossing, going beyond the worldly existence. *Nuttara* would, therefore, mean 'going beyond the worldly existence through impulsion' by the process of initiation.

The *guru* (spiritual guide) sets in motion his own consciousness in the consciousness of the disciple. Thus he (the *guru*) applies an initiation which is intended to bring about liberation (*mokṣadā*) by means of the process (*paripāṭyā*) of the central point (*viṣuvat*)[9] etc. which is devoid of the movement of *prāṇa* (exhalation) and *apāna* (inhalation) breaths which assume the utterance of *haṃsa*, and is the junction of both and by the difference of *sthāna*[10] on the *sakala niṣkala*[11] initiation and through the practice of *yojanikā*[12] initiation on the occasion of the last function of the complete oblation.

Now in all these, how is this kind of mockery made of the unsurpassable consciousness (*anuttara caitanya*) that is self-luminous, omnipresent, unmodified, i.e. unrestricted by the limitation of space, time and form?[13]

Therefore *anuttara* is that in which a crossing over does not occur by such impulsion as will be said in: "Thus initiation that leads one to liberation is achieved only in the case of one who knows the Truth in reality" (P. T. v. 26).

14. '*An*' from the root '*an*' 'to breathe' with the suffix '*kvip*' means one who breathes. Thus '*An*' means *aṇu* or the empirical individual whose life consists in breath and who considers his gross body (*deha*) or the subtle body (*puryaṣṭaka*) etc., i.e. *prāṇa* as the Self. Similarly *ananam* may mean life (*prāṇanā*), existing in the body etc., consisting of different powers devoid of I-consciousness, as in the case of one who is known as *śūnya-pramātā.*[14] So *anuttara* would mean superiority over the empirical individual and the *śūnya-pramātā*, having preponderance over everything, because of its being the highest truth, i.e. because of its being Bhairava Himself.

In this world full of sentient and insentient existents, the non-sentient ones exist because of their dependence on the sentient ones. The life of all living beings consists indeed in the afore-mentioned divine powers of knowledge and action in the case of other experients also (*paratra*) as in one's own. Only the bodies etc. appear as different.

And that which is life appears in every one without any distinction i.e. life appears in every one whether he is *deha-pramātā*, *puryaṣṭaka-pramātā* or *śūnya-pramātā*. This indeed is the highes truth. As has been said by revered Utpaladeva:

"Knowledge (*jñāna*) and activity (*kriyā*) are the very life of living beings." (P.K. I, 4)

Thus life consists only in knowledge and activity, i.e. knowledge and activity alone are symbolic of life.

15. *Anuttara* may be analysed as *a*+*nut*+*tara* meaning the *tara* or flotation of the *nut* or impulsion of '*a*'. 'A' is the Śakti (*kalā*) who is above the range of *māyā* (*amāyiya*), who is not found in Śruti-śāstra (i.e. in the Vedic tradition), who is the bliss (*camatkāra*) of the very waveless ocean of consciousness abiding in the natural, supreme Light, who covers both the initial and the final stage of the perfect I-consciousness (i.e. both '*a*' and '*haṃ*' the Sanskrit word for 'I'), which comprehends the entire cosmos

which is the expression of the creative delight of Śakti. *Nut* i.e. impulsion is the culmination of the expansion (*visargāntatā*)[15] of that (i.e. *kalā*). *Taraḥ* means the flotation or swimming of that *nut* i.e. the continuance of that state over everything else. (The sense is that though *anuttara* in its expansion is denoted by Śakti and *nara*, yet it is never separated by these. It pervades up to the very end).

16. *Anuttara* is now analysed as *anut+tara*. 'A' in *anut* means *avidyamāna* (not existing), '*nut*' in '*anut*' means impulsion i.e. successive action (*kramātmakā-kriyā*) depending on the duality of going and coming i.e. movement in space and time. So '*anut*' means that in which there is no impulsion of the successive movement (*kriyāmayī preraṇā*).

This '*anut*' is well-known among people as *ākāśa* (ether) etc. i.e. *śūnya* or void (for in *ākāśa* or void, there is no possibility of coming and going etc.).

'*Tara*' is a sign of comparison, meaning better, higher. So '*anuttara*' means higher even than *ākāśa* or ether.

In '*ākāśa*' (ether) etc. also there may be said to be successive action on account of incidental contact with a jar or various other incidental contacts and on account of constant and intimate connexion as that of sound. In the supreme Consciousness, however, which has as its essence, the sovereign power of thoroughly uninterrupted, absolute Freedom, which has I-consciousness full of the entire multitudinous objectivity characterized by thisness, the condition of which is accepted (*svīkṛta*) by Śiva but is viewed with hesitancy (*śaṅkyamāna*), by Anāśrita Śiva, with a feeling of ease characterized by delight in differentiated objectivity (*vicchinna-camatkāramaya-viśrāntyā*), which is ever beyond all appearance (*nirābhāse*), but which is always shining in manifestation, in which what was non-appearance for Anāśrita Śiva has been accepted as appearance by Śiva (*svīkārābhāsīkṛtānābhāse*), the activity of I-consciousness is successionless, because of the absence of the relativity of space and time which are characterized by objectivity (in manifestation) and absence of objectivity (in withdrawal), which is full of the delight of its own consciousness, well known in the *matsyodarī*[16] and *mata śāstra*. This successionless I-consciousness is the *anuttara* (supreme, unsurpassable).

(Now Abhinavagupta takes up the question as to why the word *anuttara* has been used instead of *anuttama.*)

According to the rule of grammar, the suffix *tamap* (i.e. *tama*) is used (in the superlative degree of adjective), denoting that which surpasses everything (*atiśayamātra*), but the suffix *tarap* (i.e. *tara*, denoting comparative degree) has been used here which shows only a comparison of two things. For instance when we say, 'This is whiter', what we mean is that of two things both of which are white, one has more whiteness (*atiśayena śuklaḥ*) than the other. But in the sentence 'of these white things, this has more whiteness'—what is the additional sense in this? For instance in: 'This palace is white, this cloth is white, this swan is also white', that which has the greatest whiteness is said to be whitest (*śuklatama*). The palace is also white, the cloth is also white—what additional information has been given in 'the whitest'? Therefore in the *tamap* suffix, the formation of the sentence in the above way is inappropriate. The *tamap* suffix does not describe anything more than the *tarap* suffix.

This is what is meant to be said: "The *tamap* suffix is used when a particular correlative is not intended to be spoken about (i.e. when there is no comparison between two), the *tarap* suffix is used with reference to a correlative (i.e. when there is comparison between two). The secondary word (*upapada*) is used when there is a distinction made by a dual number with reference to a correlative." One only is a correlative. 'Of the two, this is more white'—in this, a third is not acknowledged. For expressing specific ascertainment, the first is considered to have a correlative. There is no expectancy of more than two in comparison. There is comparison of only one simultaneously with reference to the other. In using the *tamap* affix by way of gradation, one does not get any additional information. The use of '*tarap*' and '*tamap*' suffix in the sense of graded or comparative value is only conventional; it has no regular or proper derivation. It is not in accordance with the sense of '*tarap*' and '*tamap*' suffix. If *tarap* and *tamap* indicate graded excellence, so may *tārya* and *tāmya* also. Enough of displaying ability unnecessarily regarding a matter a bit of which we have heard from scholars.

Here it is in order to indicate graded correlatives along with '*uttara*' that the *tarap* suffix has been used. Even if there were no occasion to express correlatives, the usage of '*anuttamam*' would also have borne the same sense.

So in another Āgama, it has been said:

"There is no one to whom that unspecified Highest Reality (*anuttamam*) is unknown which, however, is not known even now to the wise who have become perfect in *sādhanā* (spiritual praxis)."[17] (Even now means even when so-called *jñāna* has been acquired.)

Thus the unsurpassable (*anuttara*) is that whose essence is absolute Freedom, which is not determined by time, i.e. which transcends all temporal concepts, which is an embodiment of activity (*kriyāśakti*)[18].

The same thing has been said by revered Utpaladeva in the following lines:

"It is only in worldly activity that there is succession, due to the Lord's power of time (*kālaśakti*) but there can be no succession in the eternal activity (*kriyāśakti*) of the highest Lord (which is of the nature of *vimarśa*) just as there is no succession in the Lord Himself" (I.P.K. V. II, 1, 2).[19]

Thus this unsurpassable Reality (*anuttara*) has been explained in sixteen ways. In the Trikasāra[20] also, it has been said:

"*Anuttara* is the heart (centre) of all. There is a knot in that heart. Knowing that knot to be sixteen-fold, one should perform one's actions at ease."[21]

Similarly, "The knot abiding in the heart can be untied only by *Anuttara* Himself."

NOTES

1. The following form the thirty-six *tattvas* or categories of existence according to this commentary:

Mahābhūtas (gross physical elements)	—5	(earth, water, air, fire, ether)
Tanmātras	5	(*rūpa, rasa, gandha, śabda, sparśa*)
Jñānendriyas	5	
Karmendriyas	5	
Buddhi, Manas, Ahaṃkāra	3	
Prakṛti	1	
Puruṣa	1	

Māyā together with her five *kañcukas*	6
Śuddha vidyā	1
Īśvara	1
Sadāśiva	1
Anāśrita Śiva and his Śakti	2
	36

2. The Highest Reality cannot be designated as 'this' for that would only objectify it, whereas the Highest Reality can *never* be objectified. It is the Eternal Subject.

3. *Avinābhāvi* is that which is necessarily inherent in everything. The *akalpita* or indeterminate is the *avinābhāvi*, for without the indeterminate, the determinate (*kalpita*) cannot exist.

4. Details of these *upāyas* are given on page 215 of Tantrāloka, vol. I. (KSTS ed.)

5. These four varieties are (1) *jāgrat-jāgrat*, (2) *jāgrat-svapna*, (3) *jāgrat-suṣupti*, (4) *jāgrat-turiya*.

6. This book is not available now.

6. These *paśyanti*, *madhyamā*, etc. are *śaktis*, and not gradations of speech.

7. The Śaktis (powers) referred to are:

(1) Aghorā Śaktis that lead the conditioned experients to the realization of Śiva.

(2) Ghorā Śaktis that lead the *jivas* towards worldly pleasures and are a hindrance in the way of liberation.

(3) Ghoratarī Śaktis that push the *jivas* towards a downward path in *saṃsāra*.

8. These are:

(1) Parā which brings about a sense of identity with Śiva.

(2) Parāparā Śaktis which belong to the intermediate stage, they give a sense of unity in diversity.

(3) Aparā which brings about only a sense of difference.

These Śaktis carry out their function through Aghorā, Ghorā and Ghoratarī Śaktis.

9. *Viṣuvat prabhṛti* = *viṣuvat* etc. *Viṣuvat* in a general sense means middlemost, central. In a specialized or technical sense, it means equinox—a point where day and night become equal. The idea common in both cases is a central point where two forces become equal. *Haṃsa prāṇa* means *haṃsa-rūpi prāṇa*. '*Ham*' is a

symbolic word for the utterance indicated by *prāṇa* (exhalation) and '*saḥ*' is a symbolic word for the utterance indicated by *apāna* (inhalation) breath. So '*haṃsaprāṇa-śūnya-viṣuvat*' means that central point where both *prāṇa* and *apāna* are equally balanced, the middle-most point where there is neither *prāṇa* nor *apāna* (*haṃsaprāṇādiśūnyaviṣuvat*), the zero point intermediate between *prāṇa* and *apāna*. It is at such a point that the *guru* impels the consciousness of the disciple in the universal consciousness. *Prabhṛti*, i.e. *et cetera* refers to *abhijit*. It is also symbolic of the meeting point of the *prāṇa* and *apāna*. The difference between the two is that in *viṣuvat*, the neutral or zero point comes at the end of *prāṇa* and commencement of *apāna*, whereas in *abhijit*, it comes at the end of *apāna* and commencement of *prāṇa*.

10. *Sthāna-bheda* refers to the difference of *bāhyadvādaśānta* and *āntaradvādaśānta*.

11. *Sakala* and *niṣkala* initiation:

Sakala initiation is for one who after realization of the Supreme wants to remain in the world and help others in their realization of liberty. By initiation, the future and past *karmas* of such a disciple are destroyed, but his *prārabdha karma* (i.e. *karma* which has commenced to bear fruit) is untouched so that he may remain in the physical body in order to liberate other souls. A parallel may be noticed in the Bodhisattva of Buddhism.

Niṣkala initiation is for one who only wants his liberation and is not concerned with the liberation of others. A parallel may be noticed in the Pratyeka Buddha of Buddhism.

For details, see Tantrāloka, 15th Āhnika, verse 30 ff.

12. *Yojanikā dīkṣā*: In this, the *guru* unites the consciousness of the disciple to a particular *tattva* according to his desire. Cf. "*tato yadi bhogecchuḥ syāt tato yatraiva tattve bhogecchā asya bhavati tatraiva samastavyastatayā yojayet*", Tantrasāra, p. 159.

13. It is not modified by *deśa* (space) i.e. it is *vyāpaka* or all-pervading, not modified by *kāla* (time) i.e. it is *nitya* or eternal, not modified by any particular *ākāra* or form, i.e. it is *viśvākāra* i.e. all-containing.

14. *Śūnya pramātā*: having the experience of only void. He is devoid of I-feeling in respect of the various powers of the senses; he is also devoid of the sense of objectivity. He has simply life without even the breath.

15. The culmination of the Śakti in her *visarga* or expansion consists in *ahaṃ*, of this '*a*' is symbolic of *abheda* i.e., unity '*ha*' is symbolic of *bheda* or diversity, the *anusvāra* or dot on '*ha*' is symbolic of *bhedābheda* i.e. unity in diversity. These three are known as *para visarga*, *apara visarga* and *parāpara visarga*.

16. *Matsyodari*: The belly of the fish keeps throbbing inwardly without any external movement. So the I-consciousness keeps throbbing without movement.

17. The wise want to know it by reason, and fail miserably. The common people know it instinctively as the ground of all existence.

18. Here *kriyāśakti* includes *jñānaśakti* also.

19. There is no succession in I-consciousness. It is uninterrupted. So it is beyond time. The *anuttara* is the Lord's I-consciousness, and so successionless i.e. beyond temporal concept.

20. Trikasāraśāstra is not available now.

21. The sixteen knots are the following:

Reality is expressed in (1) *prameya* or object, (2) *pramāṇa* or knowledge, (3) *pramātā* or subject of knowledge, (4) *pramiti* or non-relational knowledge, i.e. knowledge without subject-object relation. Each of these four has four states viz. *sṛṣṭi*, *sthiti*, *saṃhāra* and *anākhya*. Thus altogether, they make up sixteen.

TEXT

From *tata idṛk* on p. 11, l. 11 upto *vyākhyātam* on the same page, l. 16.

TRANSLATION

(Now Abhinavagupta gives three interpretations on *kathaṃ* (how) of the verse.)

('*Kathaṃ*' may be taken in the sense of an Instrumental Case—*tritīyārtha*. Then its meaning will be like the following:)

1. In what way (*kena prakāreṇa*) is such *anuttara* to be realized: by abandoning the *uttara* or the world or otherwise?

(It may be taken in the sense of Nominative Case, *prathamārtha*. Then its meaning will be like the following:)

2. What is this way? Since *anuttara* is all this multitude of knowledge (*jñāna*), object of knowledge (*jñeya*) (and knower i.e. *jñātā*) which meets on all sides mutual opposition consisting of

difference, therefore, there are bound to be superiority and inferiority. What is this kind of *anuttara* with higher and lower grade?

(It may be taken in the sense of Locative Case, *saptamyartha*. Then its meaning will be like the following:)

3. In which way is there *anuttara* in liberation or even in what is supposed to be bondage? Since there is no definite rule regarding taking the '*thaṃ*' suffix in the sense of any particular case, and since it can be taken in a general sense of kind or sort, this question beginning with '*kathaṃ*' concerns only kind or sort. The word '*deva*' has already been explained.

(Now Abhinavagupta explains *sadyaḥ kaulika-siddhidaṃ* of the verse.)

Text

From *kulaṃ sthūla sūkṣma* etc. on p. 11, l. 17 upto *kimapareṇa vāgjālena* on p. 13, l. 10.

Translation

(First interpretation of *kaulika-siddhidaṃ*)

'*Kula*' is gross (*sthūla*), subtle (*sūkṣma*), and ulterior (*para*), *prāṇa* (life-breath), *indriya* (senses), *bhūtādi* (the five gross physical elements) both in a collective sense (i.e. in the sense of totality of manifestation),[1] and in the sense of cause-effect. As has been said: "By reason of action (only) in collaboration with another" (Y.S. IV, 24).[2]

So *kula* or totality is so called, because Consciousness itself abides in the various forms of objectivity[2] (*yathāvasthānāt*)[3] by means of coagulation[4] and Consciousness itself (voluntarily)[5] assumes bondage by its own Freedom. It is said: "The word '*kula*' is used in the sense of coagulation and kindred." (*saṃstyāne bandhuṣu ca*).[6]

Without Consciousness which is Light itself, no entity which is devoid of the light of manifestation (*aprakāśamānaṃ vapuḥ*) can acquire existence.

Now '*kauliki*' is that which is related to the whole universe including the body; *siddhi* or achievement is the acquisition of bliss (*ānanda*) by turning round (*parivṛtya*)[7] to have a firm hold on that very principle i.e. the light of the universal consciousness (*tathātva-dārḍhyaṃ*), in other words, identity with the perfect I-feeling of Śiva, who is the highest Consciousness and whose nature is *spanda* or the eternal throb of delight in manifestation (*hṛdaya-svabhāva-parasaṃvidātmaka-Śiva-vimarśa-tādātmyam*). So '*kaulika-siddhidaṃ*' is that which enables one to have such achievement. In other words, by achieving identity with *anuttara*, the .otality of manifestation becomes like that *anuttara* itself.

As has been said in the following lines:

"By means of negative and positive proof[8] (*vyatireketarābhyāṃ*) there is settled conviction concerning the Self (*nijātman*) and objectivity (*anya*, lit., the other). Such conviction is known as fixity (*vyavasthiti*), firm standing (*pratiṣṭhā*), complete attainment (*siddhi*), and final beatitude (*nirvṛtti*)."

(Interpretation of the word *sadyaḥ*)

The word '*sadyaḥ*' is used in the sense of 'on the same day' (*sa* = same, *adya* = day). As has been said previously, there is no fixity of the day or the present (i.e. it is only conventional). So, '*sadyaḥ*' in this context means at the same instant. Sameness here does not connote sameness of the moment, but rather 'terminating in Reality' (*tattvaparyavasāyi*), for it is in this way that the word *sadyaḥ* is to be understood. Therefore if *sadyaḥ* is to be taken in the sense of 'at that very moment', then on account of the limitation of the present moment, the past and future moments would be rejected, and thus the present whose life consists in its being reckoned relatively with reference to the past and the future will also have to be rejected.

For the *kula* (total objectivity) that has been described (so far) is the collective whole (*cakra*) of the rays[9] of the divine Sun, viz. Bhairava and is of the essence of Light (in its external aspect). When, however, that (*kula*) acquires *nirodha* (rest, stoppage) by identification with the inner supreme Bhairava Consciousness, then it is full of the relish of the ambrosia of supreme bliss, is *anuttara* (transcendent to all aspects and phases), beyond space and time, eternal of the form of *visarga*,[10] and ever-risen. The same thing has been said in Vādyatantra[11] in the following lines:

"Having retained (within one's essential nature) one's entire group of *śaktis* (that are extroverted) and having (thus) drunk incomparably the most exquisite nectar (of Self-realization), one should abide happily in that state[12] (of self-realization), unrestricted by the past and the future."

At another place, I have described in detail the non-restrictive characteristic of both these times (i.e. the past and the future).

(Second interpretation of *kaulika-siddhidaṃ*)

Kaulika-siddhi means *siddhi* or achievement of definite experience of objects derived through *kula* i.e. by means of the body, *prāṇa*, and *puryaṣṭaka*. The *siddhi* (achievement) consists in the definite grasp of blue, pleasure etc. (i.e. objective and subjective experience) which are completely diverse (lit., whose life consists of diversity). *Kaulika-siddhidaṃ*, therefore, means that which gives i.e. brings about the definite grasp of objective and subjective phenomena by means of *kula* i.e. by means of the body, *prāṇa*, and *puryaṣṭaka*. Indeed it is the body, mind, etc., which, through the penetration in them of the energy of the eternal '*a*' i.e. 'Śiva', and His externalizing Śakti symbolizing '*ha*', the energy that is beyond the sphere of time and that mounts the intermediate stair of *prāṇa* etc., which bring about the success in the form of the definite perception of the existing entities.[13] As has been said,

"It is rather by coming in contact with the power of the Self that the empirical individual is equal to that (i.e. the divine Being)" (Sp. K. I, 8).

Similarly,

"Resorting to that power (of *spanda tattva*), the divinities, Mantra etc., being endowed with the power of omniscience proceed to carry out their assigned functions towards the embodied ones just as the senses of the embodied ones by resorting to the power of *spanda* proceed to carry out their (specific) functions" (Sp. K. II, 1).

(Third interpretation of *kaulika-siddhidaṃ*)

Kula means—though *kula* of the form of Śiva-Śakti is close at hand, i.e. though it is present in every one, it is not realized by all. *Siddhi* means, according to the principle already described, liberation in life itself (in the form of identity with the divine consciousness) generating the much sought-after supernormal powers, *aṇimā*[13] etc. *Sadyaḥ* means spontaneously without any effort or anticipation (*anākalitam eva*) i.e. without contemplation (*bhāvanā*)[14], *karaṇa*[15] etc. So '*kaulika-siddhidam*' means that which brings about liberation in life (in the form of unification with the divine consciousness) generating spontaneously without the effort of contemplation etc., the much sought-after powers of *aṇimā* etc.

As has been said by revered Somānanda:[16]

"Because of Śiva's being present always, what is the use of contemplation, *karaṇa* etc.?" (Ś.D. VII, 101)

Similarly, (it is said in the following lines):

"Having once acquired the knowledge of omnipresent Śiva with firm conviction through experience (*pramāṇa*), the scripture, and the statement of the *guru*, there is nothing to be done any more by means of *karaṇa* or *bhāvanā*." (Ś.D. 5b-6).

(Fourth interpretation of *kaulika siddhidaṃ*)

"*Kaulika* means *kule-jātā* i.e., born or sprung in *kula*. *Siddhi* means the achievement of the appearance of diversity, beginning with the expansion of '*ha*', the expression of Śakti's delight and ending with the evolution of the multitude of external existents. That which brings about such achievement is *kaulikasiddhidaṃ*.

It is *anuttara* itself of the nature of eminent Light, which has implicitly within itself the expansion of the universe as identical with consciousness,[17] that explicitly evolves diversity through the abundance of the delight of power issuing from its own unsurpassed Freedom. *Māyā* or *prakṛti* which is not Light of Consciousness (*aprakāśarūpaṃ*) cannot be the cause of the manifestation of existents. If that is supposed to be of the nature of Light, then it certainly is the exalted Lord Bhairava Himself. Then what is the use of another snare of words?

NOTES

1. *Kula* or the totality of manifestation appears in three forms, viz., gross (*sthūla*), subtle (*sūkṣma*) and the ulterior (*para*) either as material object or as the body. In the case of the body it is known as *sthūla śarīra*, *sūkṣma-śarīra*, and *para* or *karaṇa śarīra*. In the sense of cause-effect[3] it means that *bhūtādi* or *pañca mahābhūtas*, the five gross physical elements, viz., earth, water, fire, air, and ether are the effect of *sthūla* or gross matter, the *indriyas* or

senses are the effects of subtle or *sūkṣma* matter, and *prāṇa* is the effect of the *para* or ulterior matter.

2. This is a quotation from Patañjali's Yoga-Sūtras (IV, 24). The full Sūtra is as follows:

tadasaṃkhyeyavāsanābhiścitramapi parārthaṃ saṃhatyakāritvāt.

i.e. "That, viz. the *citta* or mind though variegated by innumerable sub-conscious impressions exists for another (i.e. the *puruṣa* or Self) by reason of its acting in collaboration with another i.e. because of interdependently joint causation."

3. *Yathāvasthānāt* means that every material object appears in its own space, time and form.

4. *Āśyānarūpatayā* or 'by means of coagulation' means that subtle energy of consciousness assumes the solid form of matter, but even in that thickened mass of matter, consciousness does not lose its nature, even as water in becoming ice does not lose its nature.

5. The *kula* or totality of matter assumes bondage or limitation not by any compulsion, but *bodhasvātantryādeva*, by the inherent Freedom of the divine Consciousness, i.e. the divine Consciousness voluntarily descends into the limitation of matter.

6. The double entendre in '*bandhuṣu*' cannot be brought out in translation. The word '*bandhu*' is derived from the root '*bandh*' which means to bind. '*badhnāti manaḥ snehādinā iti bandhuḥ*'. A kindred or friend is called '*bandhu*' because he binds the mind by affection etc. In *bandhābhimānāt*, A.G. suggests that '*kula*' binds or limits not only in the sense of matter, but also in the sense of kindred or friend.

7. *Parivṛtya* is a very significant expression in this context. *Parivṛtya* means 'turning round, going back' to its origin. '*Parivṛtti*' the noun form of the verb '*parivṛt*' is a technical word of this system. It is defined as '*idantātmakaṃ viśvābhāsam ahantātmani pūrṇābhāse saṃsthānaṃ*'—the entire objective manifestation appearing as 'this' abiding in the full blaze of perfect I-consciousness of the divine'. The *kaulikī siddhi* comes when the fragment returns to the whole, the perfect I-consciousness. The objective phenomena then appear as a ray of the noumenal Light.

8. '*Vyatireka-itarābhyāṃ*'—'*Vyatireka*' means exclusion, a *negative proof*, '*itara*' means other than *vyatireka*, i.e. *anvaya* or positive proof. *Vyatireka* is defined as '*yadabhāve yadabhāvaḥ*' i.e. it is that

where in the absence of one, the absence of the other also occurs. '*Anvaya*' is defined as '*yatsattve yatsattvam*' i.e. it is that where in the presence of the one, the presence of the other also occurs.

9. Rays or '*raśmicakra*' means *śakti-cakra* or the collective whole of the *śaktis* of the Divine.

10. '*Anuttara dhruva*' is the '*a*' or the supreme Śiva, the first letter of '*aham*'. *Visarga* is the expansion of '*aham*' upto the *anusvāra* i.e. the nasal sound which is marked by a dot on '*ha*' in *ahaṃ*. Thus '*a*' in *ahaṃ* represents Śiva, '*ha*' represents 'Śakti', the *anusvāra* represents the fact that though Śiva is manifested right upto earth through Śakti, he is not divided thereby; he remains undivided (*avibhāgavedanātmaka-bindu-rūpatayā*).

Visarga: The very nature of *anuttara* or Śiva-Śakti is *visarga* or expansion which has two aspects, viz., *sṛṣṭi* or expansion in manifestation upto *nara* or phenomena and *saṃhāra* or return movement from phenomena to Śiva. The whole cosmic play of *sṛṣṭi-saṃhāra* is of the nature of *visarga*. The *visarga* is indicated in *sṛṣṭi* with two dots above one another (:) and also by the dot on *ahaṃ* which is only half *visarga*. Half of '*ha*' is known as full *visarga* and half of this *visarga* is *anusvāra* or *bindu* (.).

11. Vādya Tantra is not available now.

12. '*Vartamāne*' here means *svarūpalābhadaśāyāṃ* i.e. in the state of one's realization of his essential nature.

13. *Anuttara* symbolizes '*a*' and *visarga* or Śiva's externalizing Śakti symbolizes '*ha*'. The body, *prāṇa*, etc. cannot bring about the definite perception of objects by themselves. It is the energy of the inner Divine 'I' which by enliving them enables them to have objective and subjective experience.

14. In the non-dualistic Śaivāgama all these powers are interpreted in the light of identity with Śiva or Bhairava who is our own essential Self. Thus

(1) *Aṇimā* is the power of assimilating the entire manifestation to the *cit* or the Divine Consciousness which is our essential Self.

(2) *Laghimā* is the power of discarding all sense of diversity.

(3) *Mahimā* is the acquisition of the sense of all-pervasiveness of the Divine.

(4) *Prāpti* is the power of abiding in one's own essential Self.

(5) *Prākāmya* is the power of viewing the variety of the world as the delightful play of the Divine.

(6) *Vaśitva* is unity-consciousness with all.

(7) *Īśitṛtva* or *Īśitva* is the power of abiding as the Divine Consciousness without interruption.

(8) *Yatrakāmāvasāyitva* is the power of developing *icchā-śakti* characteristic of Śiva.

14. *Bhāvanā* in a general sense includes *dhāraṇā* (concentration), *dhyāna* (meditation), *samādhi* (absorption); in a specific sense, it means creative contemplation.

15. *Karaṇa* is one of the *āṇava upāyas* in which the aspirant contemplates over the body and the nervous system as an epitome of the cosmos.

16. Somānanda lived in Kashmir in the ninth century A.D. He wrote Śivadṛṣṭi, and a commentary on Parātrīśikā which is not available now. He was the great-grand-teacher of Abhinavagupta.

17. The entire objective manifestation exists in *anuttara* as a form of Consciousness or *vimarśa*.

Text

From *tathā yena anuttareṇa* on p. 13, l. 10 upto *vijñātamātreṇa* on p. 13, l. 17

Translation

(Now Abhinavagupta explains '*yena vijñātamātreṇa*' of the first verse in different ways.)

(First interpretation of '*yena-vijñātamātreṇa*')

'*Yena*' means *anuttareṇa* i.e. by which *anuttara*.

Vijñāta means *viśeṣeṇa jñātā* i.e. distinctively known, very well known.

Mātreṇa—This consists of two words *mā*+*tra*. *Mā* means *mātrā* i.e. *mānena* or *pramātmanā*, meaning 'by means of the knowledge (of the Self),' *tra* means *trāṇam* i.e. *pālanaṃ* or protecting, nourishing, maintaining or *patitva* i.e. rulership, guardianship.

So, *trāṇam* means protection of the *pramātā* (knower), *pramāṇa* (knowledge and means of knowledge), *prameya* (knowable object) and *pramiti* (right conception). So, *mātrā* is one that protects or maintains by the knowledge of the essential Self *pramātā*, *pramāṇa* etc. Therefore, *vijñātamātraṃ* means 'that *anuttara* by which the above *mātrā* is very well known'.

(Second interpretation of *vijñātamātreṇa*)

That which is very well known i.e. known with firm conviction, is already known. Being once already fully known (*sakṛd-vibhātātmatvāt*) it is not to be known again. *Jñātamātram* means already known as on object (*jñeyaikarūpatvāt*), for instance a jar, never a subject (*na tu kadācit jñātṛ-rūpam*). So, *vijñātamātra* means that which is already known as an object. Similarly, it also means *māyā* which is known as an object bringing about diversity.

Now, *vi-jñātamātram* is that in which both the known (*jñātamātra*) i.e. objects such as jar etc. and *māyā* have ceased ('*vi*' in this context meaning '*vigata*', i.e. ceased). Therefore, *vi-jñātamātreṇa* is that in which objects such as jar etc., are no longer objects but being identified with the subject appear as one's own light, and where *māyā* no longer prevails.

Three ideas have been brought about in the above explanation: (1) It is *anuttara* by means of which is maintained that Self through which alone exist the pleasures of *pramātā*, *pramāṇa*, *prameya* and *pramiti*. (2) The Self once recognized one requires no further support through *bhāvanā* etc. (3) The object cannot replace the subject. That in which the object and *māyā* do not prevail is *vijñātamātra*.

Text

From *khe brahmaṇi* on p. 13, l. 17 upto *uktanayena* on p. 18, l.3.

Translation

(Now Abhinavagupta offers an explanation of *khecarīsamatā*)

The meaning of *khecarī* is as follows. That Śakti is *khecarī*, who abiding in *kha*, i.e. *brahma* (i.e. *cit*) which is identical with herself roams about i.e. functions in various ways (*carati*). This *khecarī* in her universal aspect functions (*carati*) in three ways. She (as *gocarī*) brings about a knowledge of objects, (as *dikcarī*) effects movements, such as grasping, relinquishing, etc., (as *bhūcarī*) exists in the form of objective existents. Thus this *khecarī* exists as *gocarī* in the form of *antaḥkaraṇa* (the inner psychic apparatus), as *dikcarī* in the form of *bahiṣkaraṇa* (i.e. outer senses), as *bhūcarī* in the form of objective existents, as blue etc., or subjective existents as pleasure etc.

Similarly, in the individual aspects, the *śaktis* that are known successively as *vyomacarī* in the void (of consciousness) in which the distinction between subject and object has not yet appeared, as *gocarī* in the form of *antaḥkaraṇa* in which there is just appearance of knowledge, as *dikcarī* in the form of the outer senses suggesting the appearance of diversity in which state there is diversity of the knower from the knowable object, as *bhūcarī* in the form of *bhāvas* or existents in which there is preponderance of clear diversity in the objects, are in reality, according to the principle enunciated, non-distinct from *khecarī* which abides in the essential nature i.e. *anuttara*. Thus that Śakti of the Supreme Lord is only one. As has been said,

"His *śaktis* constitute the entire universe, and the great Lord is the possessor of all the *śaktis*." Or according to another interpretation: "There is only one possessor of Śakti, viz., Maheśvara and the entire phenomenal manifestation is the varied form of His *svātantrya śakti* (sovereign autonomy)." Consequently she (*khecarī*) is indicated in feminine gender.

It would not be proper to have a fixed, regular order or separateness between *khecarī śakti* whose sphere is the self, *gocarī* whose sphere is the *antaḥkaraṇa* or mind, *dikcarī* whose sphere is the senses and *bhūcarī* whose sphere is external objects, because in that case an intimate connexion between them would not be possible, and also because as completely separate from *khecarī*, they would not appear at all (merely through the activity of the senses).

That very *khecarī* is perceived separately (from the Divine) in the form of desire, anger, etc. However, the *samatā* or sameness of *khecarī* means the perception of her full divine nature everywhere (in *śabda* or sound, *rūpa* or form and colour, *rasa* or taste, *gandha* or smell, *sparśa* or contact) because of her being of the nature of perfect Bhairava. Even an iota of the ignorance of the nature of the integral *anuttara* amounts to a contrary state of the mind. It is this contrary state that constitutes transmigratory existence (*saṃsāra*).

In this state, there is active display of *āṇava mala* bringing about as it does the sense of extreme smallness in oneself because of his considering himself as thoroughly imperfect, of *māyīya mala* which is due to perception of diversity which comes about because of the longing for making up (lit. filling) for the limitation caused by *āṇava mala*, of *kārma mala* which arises because of laying hold of the residual traces of good and evil actions done under the influence of *māyā*.

When owing to the absence of limitation, the aberration (*vaiṣamya*) of the modes of the mind caused by the non-recognition of the essential nature ceases, the very states of anger, delusion, etc., appear as only an expression of the consciousness of the perfect, revered Lord Bhairava Himself. As revered Somānanda has said: "Śiva is that whose very nature consists in the expansion of His Śaktis" (Śivadṛṣṭi, III, 94). Similarly, "Whether it is the state of pleasure (the expression of *sattva*) or of pain (the expression of *rajas*), or of delusion (the expression of *tamas*), I abide in all of them as the Supreme Śiva" (Ś.D. VII, 105).

"In pain also, the purpose is steadiness through the efflorescence of the essential nature by means of endurance" etc. (Ś.D., V. 9).

Even the states of anger etc., exist because of their identity with the wondrous play of the (divine) consciousness, otherwise their very existence would be impossible (lit., otherwise the very acquisition of their nature would be impossible). The divine sense-goddesses themselves carrying out the various play (of life) are like the rays of Śiva-sun. The sense-divinities[1] by combining among themselves become of innumerable sorts. They are either of terrible or beneficent kinds arrayed for various appropriate purposes (*parikalpita-tattatsamucita-saumya-rudraprakārāḥ*) and employed for terrible (*raudra*) actions of *uccāṭana*[2] and *māraṇa* or for gentle, beneficent actions (*śāntyādirūpeṣu karmeṣu*) and in the *mata śāstra*[3] etc., are said to be worthy of worship as deities according to their division as *kṛtyā*[4] etc. They constitute the family of revered Bhairava. As has been said, beginning with: "One should assume the crow-faced pose for *uccāṭana*" and in: "they are the rays of the God of gods and hold the power of '*ka*' and other groups of letters."

If the real nature of these rays i.e. *śaktis* is not realized, then concealing (*tirodadhatyaḥ*) the wondrous play of the divine Consciousness which remains without any differentiation even in the midst of differentiations (*vikalpe'pi nirvikalpaikasāraṃ*), they bring about the state of *paśus* (limited experients) by worldly snare, by means of the multitude of various kinds of letters, by means of the *ghoratari śaktis* who carry on their sports (i.e. *devatātmanā*) in the form of various kinds of concepts (*vikalparūpeṇa*) by entering them (i.e. the limited experients) in the form of fear arising from doubt.

As has been said in the following lines:

"*Mahāghoras* are the deities of the *pīṭhas* who delude people constantly", and in: "They push those limited experients down and down who are engrossed in objects of pleasure." And also in:

"Being deprived of his glory by *kalā*,[5] he (the individual) becomes a victim of the group of powers arising from the multitude of words and thus he is known as the bound one." (Sp. K. III, 13).

When their real nature is known, then these very mental states (such as anger, delusion, etc.) bring about, by the means referred to (viz. *khecarī-samatā*) liberation in life itself. As has been said:

"When, however, he is firmly rooted in that supreme *spanda* principle, then bringing the emergence and dissolution of the *puryaṣṭaka* entirely under his control, he becomes the real enjoyer and thenceforth the lord of the collective whole of the *śaktis*." (Sp. K. III, 15).

This is what is meant by the knowledge of their (i.e. the states of desire, anger etc.) real nature. These states of anger, etc., at the time of their arising are of the form of *nirvikalpa* i.e. they are sheer energy of the divine.

So even when an aberrant thought-construct (*vikalpa*) (such as *kāma* or *krodha*) arises (which at the time of arising is non-aberrant) and is influenced by the varied words which are the outcome of the multitude of letters, it is not united with the group of the *śaktis* associated with the multitude of the letters so that it cannot annul the yogī's nature determined by his earlier state of *nirvikalpa*. The thought-constructs are not entirely detached from the indeterminate state of consciousness (*nirvikalpa*) which is only another kind of *vikalpa* or thought. It is only the indeterminate consciousness (*nirvikalpa*) which by the power of its autonomy (*svātantrya*) differentiates from itself the various entities (*bhāvas*) from which are derived the differences of the gross elements (*labdhabhheda-bhūtādi*) known as *vijñāna-*

cakra and is thus the master or regulator of it (i.e. the *vijñāna-cakra*).

Therefore, homogeneousness (*sāmya* or *samatā*) of the *khecarī-śakti* constitutes liberation. This homogeneousness (sameness) of the *khecarī śakti* is due to the awareness of the essential nature of the *anuttara* (i.e. the unsurpassable Absolute Reality) which is constantly present and which arises from the bliss of the recognition of the completion of the union of the divine Śakti with Śiva, and acquires stability by the realization of the consciousness of bliss of both (*ubhayavimarśānandarūḍhi*).

Śiva intent on creativity in the form of expansion by means of the energy of the great *mantra* of the Supreme primal word, viz. the perfect I, in union with Śakti, in whom the urge for expansion is implicit, and in whom abounds the bloom of the compactness of their energy, becomes engaged in the act of creative expansion.[6]

Now whatever enters the inner psychic apparatus or the outer senses of all beings, that abides as sentient life-energy (*cetanarūpeṇa prāṇātmanā*) in the middle channel i.e., *suṣumnā* whose main characteristic is to enliven all the parts of the body. That life-energy is said to be '*ojas*' (vital lustre), that is then diffused as an enlivening factor in the form of common seminal energy (*vīrya*) in all parts of the body.[7] Then when an exciting visual or auditory perception enters the percepient, then on account of its exciting power, it fans the flame of passion in the form of the agitation of the seminal energy.

As has been said:

"By conversation or contact with the body etc."

Of the form, sound etc., even a single one, because of its being made powerful by the augmented vigour referred to previously, can bring about the excitement of the senses pertaining to all other objects also. Since every thing is an epitome of all things for all people, even memory or idea of a thing can surely bring about agitation because of the excitement of innumerable kinds of experiences like sound etc. lying subconsciously in the omnifarious mind. Only well-developed seminal energy (*vīrya*) containing the quintessence of all experiences (*paripuṣṭa-sarvamaya-mahāvīryameva*) can bring about full development and endow one with the power of procreation (*puṣṭi-sṛṣṭikārī*), not its immature state (*apūrṇam*) as in the case of a child, or its diminished state (*kṣīṇam*) as in the case of an old man. When the seminal energy that has been lying within and identical with one's Self in a placid state (*svamayatvena abhinnasyāpi*) is agitated (*vikṣobha*) i.e. when it is in an active state, then the source of its pleasure is the Supreme I-consciousness full of creative pulsation, beyond the range of space and time (*adeśakālakalitaspandamayamahāvimarśa-rūpameva*), of the nature of perfect Bhairava-consciousness, the absolute sovereignty, full of the power of bliss.

Even a (beautiful) figure brought into prominence by the meeting of two eyes affords delight only by the device of its union[8] with the mighty seminal energy (*mahāvisarga-viśleṣaṇa*-yuktyā*) which stirs up the energy of the eyes (*tadviryakṣobhātmaka*); such is also the case when the ears hear a sweet song.

In the case of other sense-organs also, the perception by itself (i.e. without its union with the seminal energy) cannot acquire full expansion because of the springing up of energy only in the sense-organ itself (*svātmani eva ucchalanāt*).

So in the case of those in whom the seminal energy has not developed (*tadvirya-anupabṛṃhitānāṃ*), in whom the pleasure of love that excites the seminal energy as in other cases, is absent, who are like stone, to whom the beautiful figure of a charming young woman with large and handsome hips, with face moving to and fro and with sweet, soft and melodious song cannot give full delight. To the extent to which an object cannot bring about full excitement to that extent it can provide only limited delight. If there is complete absence of delight, it only spells insentiency. Engrossment in a profuse delight alone excites the seminal energy and that alone signifies a taste for beautiful things (*sahṛdayatā*). Excessive delight is possible only to those whose heart is expanded by seminal energy which has the boundless capacity to strengthen sensibility and which is established in them by repeated association with objects of enjoyment.

In grief also, there is the same wondrous experience of delight (to those who have *khecari-sāmya*). Whatever pleasure is derived from one's wife and son, the pleasure which is animated by seminal energy, and which abides in the heart (*antarvyavasthitam*),

---

* *Viśleṣaṇa* in this context means not separation but union: *viśeṣeṇa śleṣaṇaṃ* i.e. uniting in a definite characteristic way.

when contrary to all anticipation (*bhāvanā-asadṛśa*) there is an apprehension of the loss of the loved one aroused by tears and shrieks, that very pleasure becomes the cause of grief (*kṣobhātmakaṃ*) and when that grief reaches its climax (*vikāsaṃ āpannaṃ*) and one thinks that that pleasure will not be experienced any longer, then owing to despair (*nairapekṣya-vaśa*) the nature of that grief is suddenly turned into distinct joy (*camatkriyātma*) (owing to the expansion of the essential nature or *khecarī-sāmya*), so it has been said:

"Even in grief, by the expansion of the essential nature etc." (Ś.D. V, 9).

When there is the dissolution of *prāṇa* and *apāna* (*marudādi*), in *suṣumnā* which, as the central channel, is full of the storage of the energy of all the senses, then one's consciousness gets entry into that stage of the great central *suṣumnā* channel where it acquires union with the pulsation of one's Śakti (*nijaśakti-kṣobha-tādātmyaṃ*), then all sense of duality dissolves, and there is the perfect I-consciousness generated by the abundance of the perfection of one's own inherent Śakti. Then by one's entry into the union of Śiva and Śakti (*rudrayāmalayogānupraveśena*) which consists in the bliss of their essential nature of manifestation and by one's complete integration (*viśleṣaṇa*) with the expansive flow of the energy of the great *mantra* of perfect I-consciousness, there is the manifestation of the *akula* or *anuttara* (absolute) Bhairava-nature which is beyond all differentiation (*nistaraṅga*), unalterable and eternal (*dhruvapadātmaka*).

In the case of both sexes sustained by the buoyancy of their seminal energy, the inwardly felt joy of orgasm (*antaḥsparśa sukhaṃ*) in the central channel induced by the excitement of the seminal energy intent on oozing out at the moment of thrill (*kampakāle sakalavīrya-kṣobhojjigamiṣātmakaṃ*) is a matter of personal experience to every one. This joy is not simply dependent on the body which is merely a fabricated thing. If at such a moment it serves as a token of remembrance of the inherent delight of the Divine Self (*tadabhijñānopadeśadvāreṇa*) (i.e. if at such a moment one realizes *khecarī-sāmya*), one's consciousness gets entry in the eternal, unalterable state (*dhruvapade*) that it realized by means of the harmonious union (*viśleṣaṇa*) with the expansive energy of the perfect I-consciousness which constitutes the venerable

Supreme Divine Śakti (*parābhaṭṭārikārūpe*) who is an expression of the absolutely free manifestation of the bliss of the union of Śiva and Śakti denoting the Supreme Brahman. It will be said later that 'one should worship the creative aspect of the perfect I-consciousness' (P.T., Verse 29b).

It is rightly said, "As the great banyan tree lies only in the form of potency in the seed, even so the entire universe with all the mobile and immobile beings lies as a potency in the heart of the Supreme" (P.T. Verse 24).

Similarly, "This is the achievement of the reward of *mantra*. This is the union of Śiva and Śakti. By the practice of this, one achieves the power of omniscience." (P.T. Verse 35).

At another place also, it has been said:

"O goddess, even in the absence of a woman, there is a flood of delight, simply by the intensive recollection of sexual pleasure in the form of kissing (lit. licking), embracing, pressing etc." (V. Bh. Verse 70).

The above has been said in the following sense:

Even when the contact with a woman is intensely remembered, that is reflected in the sexual organ (*tatsparśa-kṣetre*) and in the central channel which is the channel pertaining to the natural, supreme Śakti (*madhyama-akṛtrima-parātmaka-śaktinālikāpratibimbitaḥ*). Then even in the absence of contact with an actual woman (*tanmukhyaśāktasparśābhāve'pi*) the intensive memory of the contact excites the seminal energy pertaining to contact with women which lies in it (in the central channel). In this connection, it has been said, "At the time of sexual intercourse with a woman, complete union with her is brought about by the excitement which terminates in the delight of orgasm. This only betokens the delight of Brahman which in other words is that of one's own self." (V.Bh. Verse 69).

Further, "By love, one should understand the achievement pertaining to Kula."

The eminent, venerable Vyāsa has also said:

"Every womb is my great Śakti (*mahat-brahma*). I deposit the semen in it. From that occurs the birth of all beings, O son of Bharata." (Bh. G. XIV, 3).

The venerable Somānanda also says in his commentary (on Parātrīśikā):

"The question of the Devī in amorous union with Bhairava though pertaining to *para-sambandha*[9] was put to Bhairava from the standpoint of *mahat*[10] and *antarāla*[11] *sambandha* in complete harmony with *parasambandha.*"

Enough of this long introduction to the esoteric teachings of Trika-scripture. So, according to the principle set forth above, this is what is meant by the first verse, that it is *anuttara* which gives *kaulikasiddhi* and which if understood brings about *khecarī-sāmya*.

NOTES

1. The activities of the senses as they occur are known as *indriya vṛtti* and lead only to worldly activities, but if they are given a turn towards higher consciousness, they are transformed into *indriya-śakti* and are known as *karaṇeśvari*, *marīci-cakra*, etc.

2. *Uccāṭana* and *māraṇa*: Employment of a *mantra* by which a person is completely distracted is known as *uccāṭana* and a *mantra* for killing a person is known as *māraṇa mantra*.

3. This is a system of Tantra teaching *dvaitādvaita*.

4. *Kṛtyā* is a goddess with whose help tāntrikas destroy the enemies.

5. *Kalā* here means the *śakti* of letters.

6. This cryptic sentence of Abhinavagupta defies translation. The following ideas are involved in this sentence.

(1) Śiva is of the nature of '*sāmānya-prakāśa-spandana* i.e. is full of the pulsation of general creativity.

(2) Śakti is of the nature of stimulating the general potential creativity of Śiva into *viśeṣa-vimarśa-maya spandana* i.e. into specific manifestation of *śabda* or sound, *rūpa* or form and colour, *rasa* or flavour, *sparśa* or touch, *gandha* or smell.

Therefore the union of both is a *sine qua non* of the rich variety of manifestation.

(3) This union bespeaks the expansion of '*a*' *kalā* of *anuttara*. The first stage is the *śānta-vīrya* or only *prakāśa* of Śiva. Second is the stage of *vimarśa* or rich variety of manifestation.

(4) The Absolute is androgynous in nature. The male principle is represented by Śiva and the female principle is represented by Śakti. It is out of the union of the two that there is manifestation.

7. This means that it contains the *ojas* or vital lustre of *śabda* (sound), *rūpa* (form), *rasa* (savour), *gandha* (smell), *sparśa* (touch).

8. *Viśleṣaṇa* here means *viśeṣeṇa śleṣaḥ*, definite junction or union. *Mahāvisarga-viśleṣaṇa* is a technical word of the system which means that all joy arises by union with the perfect I-consciousness.

9. *Para sambandha* or the relation between the teacher and the taught is that in which the teacher and the taught are both Śiva.

10. *Mahat* or *mahān sambandha* is that in which the questioner is Sadāśiva and the answerer is Śiva.

11. *Antarāla sambandha* is that in which the questioner is Anantabhaṭṭāraka and the answerer is Sadāśiva.

Exposition

There are four important points in the long commentary of A.G. on this verse, viz. (1) What does the dialogue between the Devī and Bhairava actually mean? (2) The connotation of *Anuttara*, (3) What is *kaulika-siddhi*?, (4) The concept of *khecarī-samatā*.

We may take up these points one by one.

1. What does the dialogue between the Devī and Bhairava mean? '*Devī uvāca*' means, 'The Devī said' i.e. put a question, and *Bhairava uvāca* means 'Bhairava answered'. Does this refer to some remote past in which there was a dialogue between the Devī and Bhairava? What does the past tense connote? Who is the Devī? Who is Bhairava?

A.G. says, "*Paraiva ca saṃvit 'Devī' ityucyate*". The Devī is none other than the Supreme Divine Consciousness which is not an abstract idea but living, throbbing Conscious Power, or Energy (Parāśakti), the Supreme Verbum (Parāvāk), constantly pulsating as 'I' (*ahaṃ vimarśa*). And the question is nothing but Self-reflection. As A.G. puts it, "*Tat paśyanti-madhyamātmikā svātmānam eva vastutaḥ parasaṃvidātmakaṃ vimṛśati.*" The Devī while appearing as *paśyantī* and *madhyamā* knows Herself to be the Supreme Consciousness.

Who is the questioner? A.G. reveals the following answer: "*Aham eva sā parāvāgdevī-rūpaiva sarva-vācyavācakāvibhaktatayā evam uvāca.*" "I myself as the same Supreme Divine Speech-power undifferentiated from all words (*vācaka*) and their referents (*vācya*) spoke thus."

A.G. says: *Evaṃ paramārthamayatvāt parameśvarasya cittattvasya, yadeva avibhāgena antarvastu sphuritaṃ, tadeva paśyantibhuvi varṇa-pada-vākya-vibhajayiṣayā parāmṛṣṭaṃ, madhyamāpade ca bhedena sthitaṃ vastupūrvakaṃ sampannaṃ yāvat vaikharyantaṃ 'anuttaraṃ kathaṃ' ityādi bhinna-māyiya-varṇa-pada-vākya-racanāntaṃ.*

"So, the inner content i.e. question-answer which appears in the consciousness of the highest Lord in an undifferentiated way because of its being the highest truth, is thought of, in the *paśyanti* stage, with a desire to put it in the apportionment of letter, word and sentence, is posited, with a sense of separateness in the *madhyamā* stage, and is finally expressed, in *vaikharī* stage, in *māyiya* form i.e. in gross speech consisting of letter, word and sentence."

At the *parā* or highest stage, there is neither question nor answer. There is simply Truth. It is only when it is to be revealed that it assumes the form of question and answer and is expressed in words.

Finally, A.G. sums up the issue in the following words: *Etāvadeva atra tātparyam—svātmā sarvabhāvasvabhāvaḥ svayaṃ prakāśamānaḥ svātmānam eva svātmāvibhinnena praśnaprativacanena praṣṭṛ-prativaktṛ-svātmamayena ahantayā camatkurvan vimṛśati.*

"This is all what is meant to be said here. Self who is the natural state of all existents, who is self-luminous, amusing Himself with question-answer which is not different from Himself, and in which both the questioner (as Devī) and the answerer (as Bhairava) are only Himself, enjoys self-reflection."

So the divine dialogue is, in the ultimate analysis, a spiritual monologue, a sort of self-reflection, self-recollection.

This also solves the enigma of the past tense. At the *parā* or supreme level, there is the eternal Truth which is timeless. So there is neither question nor answer, neither past nor present, nor future. It is only Reality shining in its own light. Reality, not static, but dynamic, pouring itself out (*prasara, visarga*) in manifestation, throbbing with self-expression. It is only when the Truth of the *parā* level is to be described or revealed that it descends to the *paśyanti* level, embodies itself in the form of the Devī, and the divine dialogue starts. So '*uvāca*' or reference to the past is *logical*, not *chronological*.

2. The connotation of *anuttara*.

A.G. has explained the concept of *anuttara* in sixteen ways from different points of view. In his Laghuvṛtti, A.G. gives the gist of the connotation of *anuttara* which covers all points of view. "*Uttaram utkṛṣṭam uparivarti, tacca jaḍāpekṣayā grāhakarūpam. Tasya tu cidātmanaḥ svaprakāśasya na grāhakāntaram astīti anuttaratvam. Tena anuttaraṃ saṃvidrūpam sadā sarvatrāvabhāsitaṃ pūrvāparadeśa-kālavihīnam anapahnavanīyam*" (L.V., pp. 1-2).

"*Uttaram* means higher, superior. In comparison to the insentient, it is the subject or experient. Hence *uttaram* means higher, superior. Since, of the self-luminous Consciousness, there is no other experient, since it is the universal Experient, therefore, is it *anuttara*. Therefore, *anuttara* is the supreme Consciousness, eternal, omnipresent, beyond time and space, undeniable Reality."

3. *Kaulika-siddhi*:

A.G. interprets *kaulika-siddhi* from two points of view, the extroversive and the introversive.

From the extroversive point of view, *kaulika-siddhi* means '*kulāt āgatā siddhiḥ*', i.e. achievement of definite experience of objects like jar, a piece of cloth, etc., derived from *kula*. '*Kula*' means '*prāṇadehādiḥ*' *prāṇa*, body etc. So '*kaulikasiddhidaṃ*' means *prāṇadehādeḥ āgatā siddhiḥ bhedaprāṇānāṃ nīlasukhādīnāṃ niścayarūpā tāṃ dadāti iti*, i.e. that which brings about definite and certain objective experience like blue and subjective experience like pleasure, through *prāṇa*, *manas*, body etc. (to the empirical experient). Does the mind-body complex bring about this experience by itself? No, the mind-body complex is only the medium. It is *anuttara*, the unsurpassable Reality that brings it about through the medium of mind-body. "*Śarīrādayo hi jhagiti anuttara-dhruva-visarga-vīryāveśena akālakalitena prāṇādimadhyama-sopānārohenaiva bhāvānāṃ tathātvaniścaya-rūpāṃ siddhiṃ vidadhate.*" Indeed it is the body, mind, etc. which through the penetration in them of the energy of Śiva and Śakti, the energy that is beyond the sphere of time, that mounts the intermediate stair of *prāṇa* etc., that brings about the success in the form of the definite perception of the existing entities."

So *kaulika-siddhi* is definite perception through the medium of *kula* or mind-body complex, brought about by *anuttara*.

From the introversive point of view i.e. from the point of view of the return movement, *kaulika-siddhi* means the following: '*kula*' means the totality of gross, subtle, and subtlest manifestation. This is only congealment of the Supreme Consciousness. '*Kule bhavā kaulikī siddhiḥ*' i.e. it is the *siddhi* pertaining to the total complex of gross, subtle manifestation. *Siddhi* here means "*tathātva-dārḍhyaṃ parivṛtya ānandarūpaṃ-hṛdayasvabhāva-parasaṃvidātmaka-śivavimarśatādātmyaṃ tāṃ siddhiṃ dadāti.*"

"*Siddhi* or achievement is the acquisition of bliss by turning round to have a firm hold on that very principle, i.e., the Light of Universal Consciousness; in other words, identity with the perfect I-feeling of Śiva who is the highest Consciousness and whose nature is *spanda* or the eternal expression of His delight in manifestation." It is *anuttara* which brings about such achievement.

4. The concept of *khecarī-samatā*:

The main objective of Devī's question is *khecarī-samatā*. This is the focal point round which the entire dialogue between the Devī and Bhairava revolves.

This is a compound word, the components of which are (1) *khecarī* and (2) *samatā*. We have, therefore, to understand the connotation of these two words. Let us, first of all, take up the word *khecarī*. '*Khe*'' is the locative case of *kha* which means sky, void, or *brahman*. In this context, it means '*brahman*' (the Absolute) and *carī* means that which moves about. As A.G. puts it, "*Khe brahmaṇi abhedarūpe sthitvā carati iti khecarī*," "*khecarī* is that which, while stationed in *brahman* or the Absolute in indistinguishable unity, moves about." In other words, *khecarī* is the dynamic divine consciousness. It is this divine Consciousness-Power that in manifestation appears in the form of the empirical experient, when she is known as *vyomacarī*, in the form of the psychic apparatus, when she is known as *gocarī*, in the form of the outer senses, when she is known as *dikcarī*, in the form of the objective existents, when she is known as *bhūcarī*.

At the empirical level, every experience, whether it is a matter of perception such as sound, form, savour, etc., or a subjective state of mind, such as *kāma* (passionate longing) or *krodha* (wrath) appears as distinct in its own right, having nothing to do with the Universal Consciousness. When it is viewed in this light, i.e., as something in its own right, clamouring imperiously for its gratification then it is *khecarī-vaiṣamya* i.e. contrary to the actual nature of *khecarī*.

When, however, all perceptions and subjective states of mind like *kāma* and *krodha* are regarded only as an expression of *khecarī* or the Divine Consciousness, when they are viewed *subspecie aeternitatis*, then even these states throw back the mind of the aspirant in the sweet embrace of the Divine; then they serve only as liaison between the human and divine consciousness.

As A.G. puts it, "*Saiva khecarī kāma-krodhādirūpatayā vaiṣamyena lakṣyate; tasyāḥ samatāsarvatraiva paripūrṇa-bhairavasvabhāvāt.*"

"When *kāma* and *krodha* are viewed only as aberration of the mind, then they constitute *khecarī-vaiṣamya* or heterogeneity of *khecarī*. The *samatā* or homogeneousness of *khecarī* consists in viewing every object and state as the nature of integral Bhairava.

Again "*svarūpāparijñānamayatadvaiṣamya-nivṛttau malābhāvāt krodha-mohādivṛttayo hi paripūrṇa-bhagavadbhairavabhaṭṭārakasaṃvidātmikā eva.*"

"The *vaiṣamya* or disparateness of *khecarī* is due to the ignorance of the essential nature of *anuttara* or the Absolute. When this ignorance is removed, then all limitations of the empirical consciousness disappear and with the disappearance of these limitations, even *krodha*, *moha* etc., appear as of the nature of the perfect divine Bhairava-consciousness."

By *khecarī-samatā*, the aspirant feels divine Presence everywhere, in every object, in every state, even in passion and wrath. It is an attitude which has to be constantly maintained. His whole outlook on life is changed.

In this context, A.G. examines the question of sex. Sex is usually considered to be only a biological phenomenon, only an animal instinct having nothing to do with the Divine, and is looked down upon with monkish disdain. A.G. turns his *tāntric* microscope upon the problem and examines it with shattering candidness. According to him, sex is only a microcosmic aspect of a macrocosmic divine creative energy. The thrill of sex is only a pale reproduction of the thrill of this divine creative energy. The divine creative energy radiates from the union of Śiva and Śakti. It has to be borne in mind that Śiva and Śakti are not two separate realities, but only aspects, the *prakāśa* and *vimarśa* aspect of one Reality, and their union is a sort of hermaphroditic or androgynous union.

In the mammalian kingdom, energy is stored in the central channel of the spinal column which is the generating, storing as well as the distributing centre. According to A.G. whatever is taken in, whether in the form of food or perception (e.g. sound, visual awareness of form, savour, contact, etc.) is converted first in the central channel in the form of *ojas* (vital energy); then this *ojas* is converted into seminal energy (*vīrya*) which permeates the whole body. All reproductive and creative functions are performed by this energy, Whether it is the enjoyment of good food, beautiful scenery, sweet music, entrancing poem, the embrace of a dear one, everywhere it is this energy that is at play. It is the representative of the divine energy (*khecarī*) on the physical plane. Even passion, anger, grief, owe their life to that divine energy. When that energy is used as a distinct form of mere physical, chemical, biological or psychic energy, then it is *khecarī-vaiṣamya*, the heterogeneity, the disparateness of *khecarī*. When everything is viewed and used as a form of divine energy, as

A motion and spirit that impels
All thinking things, all objects of all thoughts
And rolls through all things

then it is *khecarī-sāmya*; then it is the homogeneousness of *khecarī*. This *khecarī-sāmya* leads to liberation, liberation from the octopus-like hold of the sensuous life.

"*Khecarī-sāmyameva mokṣaḥ. Tat ca anuttara-svarūpaparijñānameva satatoditaṃ parameśvaryāḥ śivātmani saṃghaṭṭasamāpattyā ubhayavimarśaānandarūḍhi.*"

"Homogeneousness of the *khecarī-śakti* constitutes liberation. This homogeneousness of the *khecarī-śakti* is due to the awareness of the essential nature of the *anuttara* which is constantly present and which arises from the bliss of the recognition of the completion of the union of the divine Śakti with Śiva." It is not simply the knowledge of energy qua energy that brings about liberation, but the constant awareness of the energy in close embrace with the Divine that brings about the miracle.

"*Aṇumātramapi avikalānuttara-svarūpāparijñānameva cittavṛttīnāṃ vaiṣamyaṃ. Sa eva ca saṃsāraḥ.*"

"Even an iota of the ignorance of the nature of the integral *anuttara* amounts to a contrary state of the mind. It is this contrary state that constitutes transmigratory existence."

How does *khecarī-sāmya* bring about liberation? The answer is "by transformation of the mind." *Khecarī-sāmya* does not mean locking oneself up in a room and meditating for a few minutes. It means awareness of the Divine every minute in the hum-drum routine of life. When the divine Presence is felt constantly whether one is eating, drinking, sleeping or looking into office files, when the whole life becomes *yoga*, then is it *khecarī-sāmya*. Then the mind of the aspirant is completely transformed. *Khecarī-sāmya* is that wonderful alchemy which transmutes the gross psychic element of the aspirant into the solid gold of divine consciousness. There ensues the miracle of the dissolution of the human consciousness into the divine consciousness. Thenceforth, it is not he that lives, but it is his Lord that lives in him. In his L.V., A.G. interprets *khecarī-samatā* as *avikalpatvaṃ*, *pūrṇatvaṃ* and *devīrūpatvam*, as consciousness free of thought-construct, integral and divine.

Text

ETAD GUHYAṂ MAHĀGUHYAṂ KATHAYASVA MAMA PRABHO

Translation

"Tell me this secret, this greatest secret, O Lord who are my very Self (*mama sva*)" or: "Tell me (*kathayasva*), O my Lord (*mama prabho*) this truth which, though largely unhidden (*mahā aguhyaṃ*), yet remains a secret."

Commentary

Text

From *guhyaṃ aprakaṭatvāt* on p. 18, l. 5 upto *tasya āmantraṇamātmana eva* on page 20, l. 19.

Translation

This is a secret mystery, because of its not being evident for though it abides in *guhā* (cavern) or *māyā* in which the essential nature remains unknown, it is not evident.[1] Moreover, it is largely unhidden, for it is known to everyone as the source of delight. (In its ultimate analysis), it is the goddess *śuddhavidyā*[2] herself who abides undivided in the different states of knower (subject), knowledge, and knowable (object). The three-cornered one,[3] however, becomes in the state of *māyā*, percipient of differentiation which is excessively reflected therein. *Māyā* also, being the source of the emanation of the universe, is actually divine knowledge (*śuddhavidyā* or *śivavidyā*) itself. Therefore, according to the principle enunciated, this *śuddhavidyā* or divine knowledge, when not known in this aspect, is called *mahāguhā*[4] (the great cavern), because of her being three-cornered in the form of knower etc. (that appear as different) on account of her exalted state of nondifferentiation being concealed from view. In the Trika Śāstra,[5] she alone (viz. *śuddhavidyā māyā*) is, actually the object of worship as the three-cornered divinity.

It has been (rightly) said:

"She is the three-cornered great spiritual truth (*mahā-vidyā*) of the three aspects (Śiva, Śakti and *nara*), the abode of all joy (whether external or *cidānanda*), the substratum of universal expansion i.e. both subjective and objective (*visargapadaṃ*). Therefore, she should be worshipped in all the aspects of *pramātā* (knower), *pramāṇa* (knowledge and means of knowledge) and *prameya* (objects of knowledge). Similarly, "The one divine Light who permeates in *pramāṇa*, *prameya* (*artha*) and *pramātā* never sets i.e. is ever present."

Now in this great cavern of *Māyā* whose heart is full of pure divine wisdom (*śuddhavidyā*) which is the vast creative movement, the origin of the emergence of the entire universe, the return movement in the form of *ma-ha-a* that occurs by its own inherent dynamism of delight is, indeed, a great secret. By means of this secret it is intended to indicate that there is a return movement from objective manifestation indicated by '*ma*' (*nara*) and '*ha*' (*śakti*) towards the essential nature (of the Self) which ends in the repose of Self-consciousness which signifies divine Freedom or in other words uninterrupted Bhairava-Consciousness indicated by '*a*'. Of manifestation, the delightful form of the energy of the natural, innate *mantra* known as *parā vāk* (the Supreme divine utterance) is I (*ahaṃ*). As has been said:

"The repose of all manifested phenomena in the Self is said

to be I-consciousness." (APS 22) i.e. the real I-feeling is that in which in the process of withdrawal, all external objects like jar, cloths etc., being withdrawn from their manifoldness come to rest or final repose in their essential, uninterrupted *anuttara* aspect. This *anuttara* aspect is the real I-feeling (*ahaṃ-bhāva*).

This is a secret, a great mystery.

In the process of expansion, the changeless, unsurpassable, eternal, reposeful venerable Bhairava, is of the form '*a*' which is the natural, primal sound, the life of the entire range of letter-energies (*sakalakalājāla-jīvanabhūtaḥ*). He in the process of expansion assumes the '*ha*' form (the symbol of Śakti), for expansion (*visarga*) is of the form of '*ha*' i.e. Kuṇḍalinī[6] Śakti, and then he expands into a dot symbolizing objective phenomena (*nara rūpeṇa*) and indicative of the identity of the entire expansion of Śakti[7] (i.e. the entire manifestation) with Bhairava. (Thus the expansion is in the form of *ahaṃ* or I. After this A.G. describes the return movement of manifestation in the form of *ma-ha-a*): Similarly, the lowest part or the last phase of objective manifestation (*ṃ* or *nara*) with its three powers[8] whose life consists of the trident of the *parā*, *parāparā* and *aparā śakti*, in its return movement through its union (*viśleṣaṇa*) with that *visarga*, viz. '*ha*' *śakti*, gets its entree into *anuttara*, i.e. '*a*' which is the fundamental unalterable stage. This will be clarified proximately.

Thus there is *a-ha-ṃ* in expansion and *ma-ha-a* in withdrawal or return movement.

(A.G. now sums up the mystery of *mahāguhya*:)

In the *ma-ha* (*mahe* i.e. in the great Reality) which is the highest bliss as described earlier, that which is '*a*' according to the previously described principle, that '*a*' is the mysterious secret. This is the great secret, this is the source of the emergence of the universe. Also by the delight emanating from the union of the two (viz. Śiva and Śakti), it is clearly manifest (*aguhya*) inasmuch as it is the delight of all.[9]

(Now A.G. interprets *sva mama prabho*:)

'*Sva mama*' means 'my very self'. '*Prabho*' is a form of address and means, by bringing about such wonderful manifoldness, you are indeed capable of appearing in any form. A form of address connotes the face-to-face presence of the addressed one towards the addressor or his identity with him. So, it has a greater connotation than an ordinary noun. As has been said,

"An address has a greater connotation than a mere noun." I have conclusively proved it in my 'Śrī Pūrvapañcikā'.[10]

'*Etat kathaya*' or 'tell me this' means that though this truth is undifferentiated in the form of the Primal Creative Sound (*parāvāk*), yet kindly put it in a series of well-knit sentences in the stage of *paśyanti*, etc. As has been said earlier,

"The Lord Himself assuming the role of teacher as Śiva and disciple as Sadāśiva etc."

It has been decisively shown earlier that there is identity between venerable *parā* and *paśyanti* etc.

The word 'mine' indicates an object (*idaṃbhāva*) related to an individual subject (*pratyagātma-sambandhitvasya*). The secret that is implicit in this relation is that '*m-ha-a*' is really speaking '*a-ha-m*'. In 'this appears to me', the quintessence of the idea of appearing is I-consciousness[11] (*yat bhāsanaṃ tasya vimarśaḥ ahaṃbhāvaikasāraḥ*). The I-consciousness (*a*+*ha*+*m*) from the point of view of the return-movement of the subject (*bhāva-pratyupa-saṃharaṇamukhena*) to the subject is *m*+*ha*+*a* as has been said earlier. As has been said,

"The ascertainment of a definite object as 'this' amounts to its relational reference to (lit. resting in) the essential nature of the Self. This reference constitutes I-consciousness (*ahaṃ-vimarśa*)."

At another place also (it has been said):

"The determinate knowledge (*adhyavasāya*) in the form 'this is a jar' transcends the limitation of name and form of the jar and is (really speaking) a form of the *jñānaśakti* of the highest Sovereign, and shines as the Self (i.e. as one with the self), and not apart as an object denoted by the word 'this' (I.P.K., I, 5, 20).

It has been rightly said by revered Somānanda in his commentary (on Parātrīśikā):

"The vowel '*a*' is pure Śiva".

The same idea has been described by me in detail.

(Now A.G. gives another interpretation of '*sva-mama*' taking it as one word, and by analysing it into (*su*+*a*+*mama*).)

'*Su*' means *suṣṭhu* i.e. duly, aptly, '*a*' means *avidyamānam* i.e. not present i.e. absent; '*mama*' means *viśvaṃ* i.e. the universe. So '*sva-mama*' means to whom full of I-consciousness the universe (as something apart) is simply nothing. The life of the possessive case consists in denoting the possessed as something different. '*Viśva*' or the universe which is qualified by the possessive case '*mama*' i.e. 'mine' is not (denoted by '*a*' in *su+a+mama*) any thing apart from 'I'.[12]

Though the yogīs initiated according to other systems (i.e. Sāṅkhya-Yoga and Buddhism) or the *vijñānākala* and the *pralaya-kevali* (according to our own system) do not have the idea of '*mama*' in a certain state (e.g. in the state of *samādhi* or absorption), yet there is the residual impression in them which has the tendency for difference; on awaking into their previous state, owing to the residual impression becoming active, it grows into I-consciousness identified with the body. In order to remove even the residual trace, the prefix '*su*' has been used in the sense of '*suṣṭhu*' (duly, aptly).

As has been said by myself in a hymn:

"That thought, viz. 'Nothing is mine' by which the senseless creatures are reduced to wretchedness incessantly, that very thought viz. 'Nothing is mine' means to me 'I am everything'. Thus I have attained a lofty position".

(Another interpretation of '*sva mama*' by means of a *bahuvrihi* compound from the point of view of Śiva:)

"*Sva mama*' may be analysed into *su+ama+ma*. '*Su*' stands for '*śobhana*' i.e. excellent; '*ama*' means knowledge, '*ma*' means *mānam* or realization. Now a *bahuvrihi* compound is thus formed out of these three words, '*su—śobhanena amena mānam yasya sa svamama*'. Thus '*svamama*' is one who, being His own Light itself, through excellent knowledge (*śobhanena amena*) has realization (*mānam* i.e. *avabodha*) by means of the knowledge of non-dualism derived from the communication of the highest truth (*amena* i.e. *paramārthopadeśādvayātmanā jñānena*), knowledge which is free from the slightest trace of the foul stain of dualism (*śobhanena dvaitakalaṅkāṅkanākālusyaleśa-śūnyena*).

(From the point of view of Śakti:)

Now, '*amā*' is one who knows (*amatīti*). This is taken as one word and means the goddess Parāśakti who moves freely in all fields of knowledge. This '*amā*' is *a+mā*, '*a*' has a negative force, meaning *avidyamāna* i.e. not present, and '*ma*' means '*māna*' i.e. both knowledge or *jñāna* and its absence i.e. *ajñāna*, i.e. who is the ever-present substratum of both[13] (*nityoditatvāt*). That goddess is known as *amā*.

(From the point of view of *jīva* or the empirical individual based on *bahuvrīhi* compound within another *bahuvrīhi* compound, e.g., 1. *suśobhanā amā yatra* 2. *tasyām sā yasya*:)

She is '*su*' i.e. excellent being ever present. (This gives the explanation of '*sva*'+'*ma*'. Now remains '*ma*' of the phrase '*svamama*'). The remaining '*ma*' implies *māyā*'. Now, '*sva mama*' means: "He in whom even in *māyā*, i.e. even in the ordinary life of *pramāṇa* (knowledge) and *prameya* (i.e. object of knowledge) *su amā* i.e. the excellent *amā* as described is always present." Thus there is a *bahuvrīhi* compound within another *bahuvrīhi*. What it means is that the Highest Lord even in the ordinary life consisting of *pramāṇa* etc., is always endowed with His highest Śakti, being nondual. (Since there is no difference between the Devī and the Lord,) addressing the Lord means addressing Herself.

NOTES

1. In his L.V., A.G. says, "*nanu grāhakarūpaṃ sarvasya hṛdaye sphurati tatra kim praśnena. Satyaṃ sphuritamapi na tattvato hṛdayaṅgamibhūtam. hṛdayaṅgamibhāvena vinā bhāvamapyabhāvena rathyāgame tṛṇaparṇādivat.*"

"Well, does not Reality shine as the perceiving Experient in the heart of all? Then what is the relevance of a question about it?" "True", says A.G. "though it shines in everyone's heart, it is not intimately assimilated by the heart as existent. So though present, it is as if non-present, just as the grass and leaves on the path of someone who passes on in a chariot (though present are not noticed by him)."

2. '*Śuddhavidyā*' in this context does not mean the *śuddhavidyā tattva*, the fifth category in manifestation. It means the pure, divine knowledge or Śivavidyā.

3. *Śuddhavidyā* becomes '*trikoṇā*' or three-cornered in manifestation. The three corners are *pramātā*, *pramāṇa* and *prameya*, i.e. the experient, experience and means of experience, and object of experience. Vide the illustration of *trikoṇa* or *triśūla*:

Trikoṇa or the triangular form of manifestation

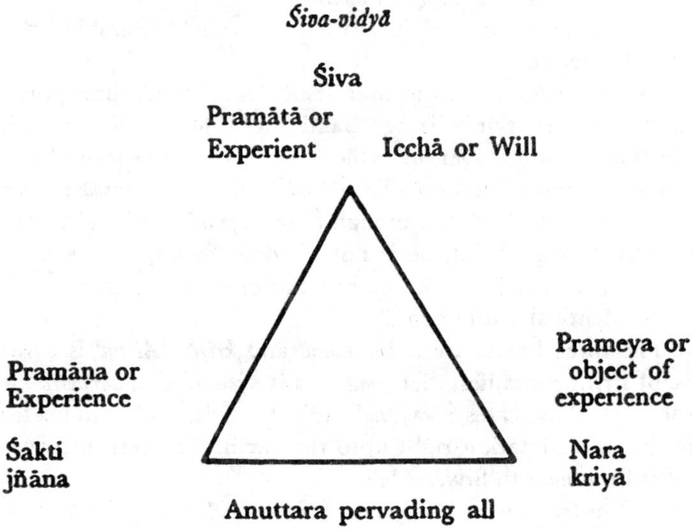

Triśūla or three-pronged Reality

4. The triangular form of *māyā* is symbolic of cavern in which the secret of manifestation is hidden. It is also symbolic of the female or generative organ. Therefore, *māyā* has been called '*jagat-janana-bhūḥ*', "the source of the emanation of the universe."

5. The Śāstra is called *trika*, because it deals with three aspects of Reality, viz. *pramātā-pramāṇa-prameya* or *icchā-jñāna-kriyā* or Śiva-Śakti-*nara* or *para-parāpara-apara.*

6. In Śāradā script '*ha*' is written as *s* which resembles the form of Kuṇḍalinī.

7. In the process of *sṛṣṭi* or manifestation, '*a*' symbolizing Śiva expands into '*h*' symbolizing 'Śakti', and terminates into *ṃ* or the *anusvāra* or dot over '*ha*' which completes the process of the expansion or manifestation. The '*bindu*' (dot) or *anusvāra* over '*ha*' represents the fact that though Śiva is manifested right upto the earth through Śakti, he is not divided thereby, he remains undivided; his expansion or manifestation in the form of Śakti remains identical with Him.

8. The three Śaktis are *icchā*, *jñāna* and *kriyā*. '*Ahaṃ*' is symbolic of *sṛṣṭi* or manifestation, *ma-ha-a* is symbolic of *saṃhāra* or retraction; '*a*' indicates Śiva, '*ha*' indicates *Śakti* and *ṃ* indicates '*nara*' i.e. manifestation right upto the earth. The return movement is from *nara* to Śiva or '*a*'.

9. A.G. interprets *mahāguhya* in three ways here: (1) *Maha*+*a* +*guhyam*. In the great blissful manifestation, the presence of '*a*' of *anuttara* in all its phases is a great mystery (*guhya*). (2) *Mahā*+*guhyam*: Śiva-vidyā in the form of Māyā—the great cavern is the source of all manifestation. This is another great mystery. (3) *Mahā*+*aguhyam*: Though a great mystery, it is not entirely beyond experience, for the identity experienced in the union of male and female and in the union of the experient and the experienced object is well known to everybody.

10. This book is not available now.

11. Any experience without its relation to an experient would be meaningless.

12. *Ṣaṣṭhi*—the possessive case denotes the possessed as something different from the possessor as in the word '*rāja-prāsāda*', the king's palace, palace is something different from the king, but the universe is not anything different from Śiva or I.

13. This hints to that plane of Śakti where *jñāna*, *ajñāna* and their cessation—all abide in *saṃvid* or divine consciousness.

Introduction to the second verse (p. 20-21)

The next verse by gathering up the substance of the many

questions raised in one and a half verses above is meant to clench the issue.

Text

HṚDAYASTHĀ TU YĀ ŚAKTIḤ
KAULIKĪ KULANĀYIKĀ /
TĀṂ ME KATHAYA DEVEŚA
YENA TṚPTIṂ LABHĀMYAHAM // 2 //

Translation

O Lord of all the gods, tell me about that *kauliki śakti* who resides in the heart (i.e. in consciousness), the Śakti who is the chief source of the entire manifestation and who is the presiding deity of all manifestation so that I may have full satisfaction.

Commentary

From *sarvasya* on p. 21, l. 1 upto *uttaru ehu aṇutula* on p. 23, l. 4.

Translation

(Interpretation of *hṛdayasthā*)

Hṛdayasthā = *hṛt*+*aya*+*sthā*. *Hṛt* is the supreme conscious base of all objective experiences like blue etc., and subjective experiences like pleasure etc., and also of the empirical experients conditioned by the body, *prāṇa* and *buddhi*. *Ayā* (plural of *aya*) means knowledge of manifold, varied objects like jar, cloth etc., brought about by its own freedom. *Sthā* means this scintillating *śakti* abiding in them. So '*hṛdayasthā*' means the scintillating Energy abiding in the knowledge of varied objects brought about by the supreme conscious base of all objective and subjective experience and experients by its own freedom.

(Interpretation of *Kulanāyika*)
(On the plane of *anuttara*)

Kulanāyikā means who is the presiding deity (*nāyikā*) of *kula* i.e. body, *prāṇa*, pleasure etc., in other words of objects, experience and experients. She is called *nāyikā*, because it is she who brings into manifestation all objects of experience, experience and experients (*śarīra-prāṇa-sukhādeḥ sphurattādāyini*), the vital energy of the collective whole of Brāhmī and other goddesses (*brāhmyādi-devatācakrasya vīryabhūtā*). On the plane of Śakti, she is the innermost core of the entire sensory and nervous system (*nikhilā-kṣanādicakrasya madhya-madhyama-rūpā*), and on the plane of *nara*, she is the female and male generative organ, the source of all production (*jananasthāna-karṇikā-liṅgātmā*).

(The following is the interpretation of *Kaulikī*:)

1. *Kaulikī* is one who though immanent in all manifestation (subjects and objects) is herself *akula* i.e. transcends it (*kule-bhavā akularūpā kaulikī*).

2. Or one who abides in '*kula*' but is '*akula*' (i.e., sheer consciousness (*cinmātra*) distinct from *kula* or manifestation) is '*kaula*' (i.e. Śiva). She in whom this *kaula* or Śiva abides in identical form is *kaulikī*. The entire range of manifestation (*kula*) abides as such because of its being rooted in the light of *akula* (i.e. Śiva).

As has been said,

"But by coming in contact with the power of the Self, an individual becomes equal to that" (Sp. K. I. 8).

Similarly:

"Resorting to that power (of *spandatattva*), the divinities '*mantra*' etc. together with the sacred formulae which serve as their indicators, being endowed with the power of omniscience proceed to carry out their assigned functions towards the embodied ones just as the senses of the embodied ones by resorting to the power of *spanda* proceed to carry out their (specific) functions" (Sp. K. II, 1).

Deveśa is a form of address, meaning, the Lord of the gods, Brahmā, Viṣṇu, Rudra, etc.

Instead of '*tāṃ me kathaya*', the reading in revered Somānanda's commentary is '*tan me kathaya*', and he explains '*tat*' as 'therefore' (*tasmāt*) or it may mean 'Tell me that by which I may attain the satisfaction of the highest bliss i.e. I may enjoy the freedom derived from the bliss of the highest non-dualism." There is also another reading '*brajāmi*' instead of '*labhāmi*'. (The meaning in both readings is the same.)

By the word '*aham*' or I in '*labhāmyahaṃ*' is always to be understood 'the life and soul of all experients'. Having understood by the teaching the nature of I as described, one obtains the satisfaction of knowing oneself as the Divine, the satisfaction of complete I-consciousness. This has already been made clear before. The revered Somānanda has also interpreted '*hṛdaya*' in his commentary as :

"*Aya* or advancing (of the mind) i.e. *jñāna* or knowledge in the *hṛt* or the Supreme centre of consciousness."

"Abhinava has composed this commentary on the question (of the Devī) which elucidates the essence of Trika for cutting asunder inevitably (*haṭhāt*) the knot of *māyā* existing in the ether of the heart, for the mind which is engrossed (*saktaṃ*) in destroying for ever the māyic ignorance which is the root of all ill (*aśiva*), the mind in which Śiva has penetrated (*Śivena niveśitaṃ*) and which is a thirst for drinking the nectar of the bliss of Śiva."

In order to open the entire treasure pertaining to the question, Bhairava said. The sense of the past tense in 'said', has already been explained. What is the use of repeating it again? Bhairava is one who sustains and maintains the universe (indicated by '*bha*', from the root '*bhṛ*', meaning to sustain, to maintain) and who sounds the great *mantra* of Self-consciousness, i.e. who has constantly the awareness of Self (indicated by '*rava*' or sound in Bhairava). Only here the predominance is that of Śaktimān (i.e. Śiva) from the point of view of the return movement (of His expansion) in the form of *ma+ha+a* which has already been described earlier.[1] This will be made clearer further on. So, the following is the purport of the introductory part of the dialogue.

The initial *spanda* of *Saṃvit* or divine Consciousness

"The divine Supreme Consciousness-Power not different from Bhairava on the point of expansion according to Her essential nature, is said to be supreme *icchāśakti* (Voluntary Power). Her actual expansion as *jñānaśakti* (cognitive power) assumes the *parāparā* or *paśyantī*[2] form and as *kriyāśakti* (conative power) the *aparā* or *madhyamā*[3] form etc.[4]

The nature of the question

Now, the inquiry about the nature of *parāśakti* who expands in the form of the universe is said to be *praśna* or question. The Devī who is that very Śakti is the initiator of the question about Her (i.e. *parāśakti*).

The consideration of the nature of this expansion is said to be the most excellent organ of speech (*para-vaktra*) and that consists of both question and answer.

That very organ of speech constitutes the return movement pertaining to absorption beginning with '*m*' i.e. the *jīva* (empirical individual) who has limited consciousness (*aparasaṃvitterārabhya*) reaching the inner *śakti* i.e. (*parāpara-saṃvitti*) '*ha*' (*antastarām*) and finally getting absorbed in the compact mass of bliss of the highest consciousness—*anuttara* or '*a*' at once (*parasaṃvid-ghanānanda-saṃhārakaraṇam muhuḥ*).

Bhairava in whom the entire expansion of the universe is involved inwardly abides as the perpetual responder. As the dual process of expansion and retraction is beyond time, therefore, this question-answer is the truth that is of uniform nature.[5] This is *para saṃbandha*[6] associated with *anuttara*. My revered guru Śambhunātha has already expounded it as the pith and core of Trika Śāstra.

NOTES

1. In *sṛṣṭi* or expansion, it is Śakti who has the predominance, in *saṃhāra*, or the return movement, it is Śaktimān or Śiva who has the predominance.

2. *Paśyantī* retains the truth of unity of the *parā śakti* and contains the germ of diversity of the *aparā śakti*. Hence she is called *parāparā* i.e. *parā*+*aparā* (the supreme cum non-supreme).

3. *Madhyamā* is that stage of expression in which diversity has commenced in a subtle form. Hence she is called *aparā* or non-supreme.

4. 'etc.' includes *vaikharī* in which there is complete diversity.

5. There is no difference between the question and answer at this stage. The question itself is the answer. In the empirical level of reality, the questioner is one, the responder is another; the question occupies one moment of time, the answer occupies another. At the empirical level, there is succession in expansion and retraction. At the met-empirical level, it is *akrama*, successionless, beyond time. That level is the domain of eternity—timelessness. Hence there is no dualism of a questioner and a responder, a question and an answer. It is the heartbeat of Reality sounding the eternal aye of creative activity.

6. *Parasambandha* is the highest relationship between the ques-

tioner and the responder. In this, Śiva Himself is both the questioner and the responder.

There are other five kinds of relationship between the questioner and the responder. They are given below:

1. *Mahān saṃbandha.* In this, the questioner is Sadāśiva and the responder is Śiva.
2. *Antarāla saṃbandha.* In this, the questioner is Anantabhaṭṭāraka, and the responder is Sadāśiva.
3. *Divya saṃbandha.* In this, the questioner is Nandakumāra Ṛṣi and the responder is Anantabhaṭṭāraka.
4. *Divyādivya saṃbandha.* In this, the questioner is Sanatkumāra Ṛṣi and the responder is Nandī.
5. *Adivya saṃbandha.* In this, both the questioner and the responder are human beings.

Text

ŚṚṆU DEVI MAHĀBHĀGE
UTTARASYĀPYANUTTARAM /3/
KAULIKO'YAṂ VIDHIRDEVI
MAMA HṚDVYOMNYAVASTHITAḤ /
KATHAYĀMI SUREŚĀNI
SADYAḤ KAULIKASIDDHIDAM /4/

Translation

Listen, O most illustrious one, 'the *anuttara* or the unsurpassable one is the unsurpassable even of the proximate one' or '*anuttara* means even the answer amounts to no answer'. The plan of creation in accordance with *kula* abides in the ether of my heart. I am revealing unto you, O goddess, that which brings about spontaneous fulfilment pertaining to *kula*.[4]

Commentary

From *devi iti*...on p. 23, l. 11 upto *ucyate* on p. 24, l. 12.

Translation

The word '*Devi*' has to be interpreted as has been done previously.

(First interpretation of *mahābhāgā*)

She who has the supreme one i.e. Śiva as her aspect.

(Second interpretation of *mahābhāgā*)

The word *bhāga* has to be derived in this context from the root '*bhaj*' which means to partake of, to adore. Here, it is taken in the latter sense. So *mahābhāgā* means 'she who being adored according to the instruction described and about to be described gives the great divine power'.

(Third interpretation of *mahābhāgā*, the word '*bhāga*' being used in the sense of portion)

Mahat – the great one i.e. Anāśrita Śiva who is known as the great one; *bhāga* = a portion, a fraction. So *mahābhāgā* means she of whom the celebrated great one, i.e. Anāśrita Śiva is just a portion, for she enfolds within herself the initial one also of the entire thirty-six categories.

(Fourth interpretation of *mahābhāgā*)

She whose portion is *mahān* i.e., *buddhi* category. *Mahān* has been called a portion from the distributive or analytic point of view ('*vibhāgakalāpekṣi*'). It is the divine Śakti herself who is a compact mass of consciousness that is called *buddhi* in the matter of settling in their proper forms of different objects and actions brought about by her own freedom. As has been said by revered Somānanda:

"In the sphere of differentiation (*aparasthitau*) i.e., at the level of man where differentiation prevails, she (*parāśakti*) is known as *buddhi* which in its subtle all-pervasive condition is always the innate (*sahajam*) universal consciousness of Śiva." (Ś.D.I, 26-27).

(Fifth interpretation of *mahābhāgā*)

'*Bhāga*' may mean difference or separation. By the '*matup*' suffix, the word '*bhāga*' means that which has difference or separation i.e. a separate entity. In separate entities, ascertainment is made by differentiating one thing from another. Though pure ascertainment of objects (*prāsādātmaka-viṣaya-niścayo*) i.e. the indeterminate aspect (*nirvikalpa*) of *buddhi* does not touch i.e. does not concern itself with the pleasant and unpleasant aspects of the different objects present in the world, yet that *buddhi* (in its determinate or *savikalpaka* aspect) brings about the perception of objects as separate from one another. It is universally admitted that there is a flow of the attribute of *sattva* in the case of the pleasant states of *buddhi*, for the pleasant states of *buddhi* are of the form of *dharma* (righteousness), *aiśvarya* (power or sovereignty), *jñāna* (knowledge), and *vairāgya* (freedom from worldly desires). If one gets entrance into the deepest layer i.e. in the *prathamābhāsa* or the initial, indeterminate state even in the pleasant aspect of *buddhi*, then through that he will find himself perpetually in the domain of supreme bliss underlying that aspect.

(Sixth interpretation of *mahābhāgā*)

Mahābhāgā may be analyzed into *maha+ā+bhāga*. '*Maha*' means *jagadānanda* i.e. that bliss which is entirely uninterrupted, perfect, integral, independent, expression of divine Freedom; '*ā*' means '*iṣat*' or slight; '*bhāga*' means fraction. So *mahābhāgā* means the Devī of whose *jagadānanda*, bliss, only a slight fraction is available (to people). Whatever happiness there is in life, that is possible only by entering the Universal Creative Energy (*visargaśaktau*) who is the highest abode of the Supreme bliss. It appears in small limited measure (in life) only because of the *visargaśakti* not being realized in her internal essential aspect.

Bhaṭṭanārāyaṇa has given expression to the same idea (in his Stavacintāmaṇi):

"All the delight that is noticed in all the three worlds (viz. *bhava*, *abhava* and *atibhava*) is only a drop of whose delight, to that God, the ocean of delight do I bow." (St. C. Verse 61).

(Seventh interpretation of *mahābhāgā*)

Mahābhāga may be interpreted as '*ma-ha-a bhāgaḥ yasyāḥ sā mahābhāgā*' i.e. she who betakes herself to that form which has been declared by the previous principle as *ma-ha-a* is *mahābhagā*. What is meant to be said is that the delight of the highest Lord which expands in the form of '*aham*' is the essential form of Śakti, and that is the nature of revered *parā*.

Commentary

From *ata eva* on p. 24, 1.12 upto *prasaktānuprasaktyā* on p. 25, 1.21.

Translation

Therefore that highest goddess hears everything. Abiding as she does in the form of the power of hearing, she has that sovereign power (*svātantrya*) which consists in effecting congruous and suitable connexion by blending all sound in a meaningful whole—the sound which is clear to the ear but is only a succession of a mass of confused vibrating syllables. Without this power of effecting congruous connexion, an experient though hearing particular words lost in confused buzzing sound says, in common usage 'I am not hearing them'.

An object of sense-perception which is merely confused buzzing sound without its being blended in a sensible whole is also said to be 'heard'. This is the common usage. But in reality, the confused sound only enters the ear; it does not enable the listener to grasp the words denoted by the sound and therefore it remains only a confused mass of sound (*tathā bhavet*), for being different from the words, it is merely buzzing sound. When it is intended to enunciate the words, then there cannot be the production of confused sound, for there is no ground for it. When there is the desire to speak sensibly, then there is the enunciation of clear words, and with the enunciation of clear words, there is no occasion for indistinct, confused sound of the same kind. Those very words when they are not clearly enunciated and so cannot be knit into a meaningful whole are said to be mere confused sound. For one attentively intent on knitting the words in a sensible whole, there may be clear comprehension to some extent. Therefore in such a case, it is the congruous connexion of the words which can be of use. It is the goddess *parāśakti* (the supreme creative power) who brings about the congruous connexion. It has been rightly said,

"Mantra, Mantramaheśvara etc. resorting to that power etc." (Sp. K. II, 10). In fact "hears, sees, speaks, seizes" etc. are only aspects of the goddess alone. As has been said by the Divine in Vedānta:

"That by which one (i.e. the experient) knows colour and form (*rūpa*), taste, smell, contact, sound, the pleasure of sexual intercourse is this Self alone. What remains in this world (which is not known by the Self)?" (Kaṭha U. II, 3).

Hearing does not mean simply lending the ear to some confused, loud utterance of words. Śiva Himself thus laid down in Svacchanda Śāstra on the occasion of the division of *japa* (repeating a *mantra* in a murmuring tone):

"That which is heard only within oneself is known as *upāṃśu japa*." In this the Self alone hears in *madhyamā* stage, not anybody else.'[3] This is what is said.

When the organ of utterance (*sthāna*) and the mode of articulation (*prayatna*) are distinctly marked, then with the junction and separation of the teeth and the lips, even words uttered in very low tone may be audible to a person sitting very close and there would arise the contingency of the *japa* becoming *saśabda* i.e. *japa* with audible words. It has been said:

"That which is audible to others is known as *saśabda japa*". In *upāṃśu japa* (*atra*), there is no particular advantage even to a man who is sitting close by, for it will be inaudible to him. Another person may notice the movement of the tongue and the junction of the lips (of the performer of the *japa*), yet he cannot hear him, for the words are not audible externally (*varṇasya bahirātmalābhābhāvāt*), for the *japa* is being performed only in the *madhyamā* stage. Only the performer can hear it (*ātmanā eva śravaṇaṃ syāt*).

By the impact of air, clear words are effected, but the impact is not so strong as to make it audible externally. Even the movement of lips in this *japa* does not enter the stage of marked utterance of words, but is confined to itself till that *japa* lasts. If the movement of lips, hands, etc., occurring at that time (i.e. at the time of *japa*) is stopped and in its place there is distinct articulation by means of the organs of utterance, and in the effectuation of words, if there is soft or loud production of sound in succession so as to be audible near or far, then it is, in every way, heard by others. Then it will be sound of the level of *vaikharī*. Enough of elaboration of this incidental reference.

Notes

1. *Parābhaṭṭārikā* is the very power of learning. She hears everything that is ever uttered in the universe.

2. Her sovereign power (*svātantrya*) consists in *saṅkalanānusandhāna. Saṅkalana* means effecting congruous and suitable connexion of distinct sounds and *anusandhāna* means blending them in a definite, meaningful whole.

3. What is meant to be said is that in *upāṃśu japa,* even the aspirant carrying on the *japa* cannot hear the *mantra* with his physical ears. 'He hears it within himself' only means that he experiences the mantra as a *spanda* or throb of his self-experience.

Exposition

The Devī is none other but the Śakti of Bhairava Himself. A.G. gives seven reasons why the Devī is called *mahābhāgā.* Now A.G. says that there is an esoteric meaning in asking her to hear. She is the power of hearing itself. While others cannot make out anything from confused, buzzing sound even though it is heard by the ear, she can always make out the sense of all sound whether it is clearly pronounced or is only indistinct, confused sound.

Text

From *saiva parameśvari* on p. 25, l. 22 upto *sṛṇu devi iti* on p. 28, l. 11.

Translation

That very supreme goddess who hears everything has by the form of address (viz.,' O goddess, listen'), clearly been indicated as Śakti. Everything in the universe is of the form of *nara,* Śakti and Śiva.[1] Therefore everything in the universe consists of the triad. That, which is only confined to itself (as an object), is insentient and comes chiefly under the category of *nara,* as for instance, 'the jar is lying (on the ground).' The above has reference only to the third person (*prathama puruṣa*) which is left to be supplied after the first and second person (*śeṣaḥ*).

That which appears even as 'this', when addressed, becomes completely enveloped with the I-feeling of the addressor. The 'this' which is different from the addressor, when addressed as 'you', becomes a form of '*Śakti*'. In 'you are standing' this is the meaning of the second person, and the principle of addressing viz. as I am standing, even so this is standing. Ordinarily, the I (*ahaṃbhāva*) of the other person is different from the 'I' of the person who is to address, but in the process of addressing, the addressor assimilates the delightful autonomy of the addressed characterized by I-feeling to his own, and considering it as identical with the uninterrupted delight of his own I-feeling starts addressing him. In this light, he is addressing him in the true sense of the second person. This sense in which the addressor and the addressed, though different, become one in the addressing is indicative of the *parāparā* goddess (whose characteristic is identity in diversity).

(On the other hand) in the freedom of the uninterrupted delight of I-consciousness completely independent of any reference to anything else, expressed in the form 'I am standing', it is in every respect (*sarvathā*) the revered *parā* (highest) *śakti*[2] that is at work. In that lies the pre-eminence of the first person. As has been said, "Since I transcend the perishable and also the imperishable, therefore, am I known as the highest *puruṣa* i.e. as the first person." (Bh. G. XV, 18).

Here the verb '*asmi*' (am) has been used with reference to 'I', the first person, to indicate its pre-eminence over both the perishing and the imperishable.

Here in every case, it is not the limited I identified with the body that is referred to. The limited I (identified with the body) being an object of the senses is obviously incompatible with that (the real, unlimited I). Thus this (i.e. unlimited) I is of the nature of the self-luminous Śiva. Therefore of the (universal, unlimited) Consciousness (*bodha*) which is self-luminous, there is neither any diminution nor augmentation. Both diminution and augmentation being of the nature of *aprakāśa* cannot be an aspect of the Light of Consciousness (lit., cannot enter consciousness). The middle state which is only relative to the state of diminution and augmentation is also nothing. Therefore the notion of I which is inseparable from the universal consciousness of Śiva (*tadbodhāvicchedarūpa*) and free from all relativity is not applicable to situations of augmentation, diminution, and the middle state between these indicated by thisness, i.e. objectivity and absence of objectivity (i.e. the state of *śūnya* or void). The notion of you i.e. the second person which, though indicative of separateness, is actually similar to that of I. "Therefore both you and I are described as genderless" (i.e. they are used for both genders). The application of number etc., i.e. dual and plural of these words according to the usage depending on the enumeration or difference of the body is appropriate from the point of view of *parā-parā śakti* in the dual and *aparā-śakti* in the plural. The difference determined by the Śakti of the Divine Freedom is considered as one in the case of several bodies which can be traced in such usages as 'we two, you two, we all, you all."

Augmentation etc., being associated with the body cannot be even figuratively employed in the case of consciousness, for diminution and augmentation cannot be reasonably applied to consciousness.

"Everything is an epitome of all". According to this universal principle, even the insentient third persons (*narātmano jaḍā api*) shedding their insentiency can become entitled to the use of second and first person (*śakti-śaivarūpabhājo bhavanti*), for instance, in 'listen, O mountains', the third person has been treated as second person, in 'of mountains, I am Meru', the third person has been treated as the first person, in 'I, Caitra am speaking' the first person has been treated as the third person. The second person which pertains to *śakti*, can by shedding its *śakti* character, acquire the aspect of the third person, for instance, in 'you whose fear has vanished, are fortitude (lit. the power of fortitude) itself', 'you' not being used as a form of address has appropriately acquired the aspect of the third person. Usage like '*bhavān*' (you) with particular, subsequent use of words like '*pādāḥ, guravaḥ*' (revered one) which are used only in the case of another person, being used as third person which is characteristic of *nara* is fairly recognized. The second person also which is characteristic of *śakti*, shedding its particular use acquires the aspect of first person which is characteristic of Śiva, for instance, "O dear friend (female friend), O loved one, thou art I" is an accepted usage. The first person also characteristic of Śiva, shedding its aspect of first person which is *cit*, betakes to the aspect of the third person characteristic of *nara* or second person characteristic of *śakti*. In the following expressions, "Who am I?" "This one am I," "O I", "Fie to me," "Oh to me" etc., the uninterrupted autonomy of I is subdued, and it is chiefly the separate 'this one' that becomes predominant. In such a case, it is as if separateness characteristic of *aparā śakti*, in other words, *nara rūpa* or third person that becomes prominent. In 'O I' etc., Śiva contacts the throb of *parāparā śakti* (i.e. enters the sphere of second person). But in such cases, the preceding state acquires the succeeding state without transgressing its previous nature.[3] Thus the third person characteristic of *nara* can clearly mount to the stage of the second (the Śakti stage) and even to the first person (i.e. Śiva stage) but the contrary course of mounting cannot be admissible.[4]

Each of this triad without giving up its nature, becomes of three forms, viz. singular (Śiva-*bhāva*), dual (Śakti-*bhāva*) and plural (*nara-bhāva*). It has been said,

"One thing becomes dual, and after becoming dual, it becomes plural." Of one and the same thing, when it is only one, then it connotes the nature of Śiva, since there is no other as counterpart. When there is a counterpart, then it is the nature of Śakti. In the case of many denoting difference, there is the nature of *nara*. Thus we have '*ghaṭaḥ*', one jar denoting oneness, and thus Śiva-*bhāva*, '*ghaṭau*', two jars, denoting Śakti-*bhāva*, '*ghaṭāḥ*', many jars, denoting the aspect of *nara*. In a copulative compound (*dvandva samāsa*) in which the members, if uncompounded, would be in the same case and connected by the conjunction 'and', we have an example of many things forming a sort of unity, thus denoting Śiva, e.g. '*ghaṭapaṭapāṣāṇāḥ*' (jar, cloth, stones). In a verb also, e.g. '*tiṣṭhati*' (one is standing or sitting) denotes Śiva: '*tiṣṭhataḥ*' (two are standing or sitting) denotes *śakti*, '*tiṣṭhanti*' (many are standing or sitting) denotes *nara*. In fact, the entire manifestation is the expansion of *kriyāśakti* brought about by one alone (i.e. by Śiva). As has been said:

"By reducing the many (i.e. the *nara-rūpa* and *śakti-rūpa* to one (i.e. Śiva-*rūpa*) who is there who will not be liberated from bondage?"

Therefore, when the third person (*nara*), the second person (Śakti) and the first person (Śiva) are used together, simultaneously there is the absorption of the lower in the higher and higher, because it is the higher that contains the truth of the lower, e.g. in '*sa ca tvaṃ ca tiṣṭhathaḥ* (he and you are standing), the number of the verb '*sthā*' (to stand) is used in the second person which indicates that the third person (*nara*) has been absorbed in the second (*śakti*). In '*sa ca tvaṃ ca ahaṃ ca tiṣṭhāmaḥ*' (he, you and

I are standing), the verb '*tiṣṭhāmaḥ*' which is the plural number of the verb in the first person has been used even for the third and the second person which is indicative of the fact that the third and second person are absorbed in the first. It is only this state of complete understanding, the essence of the residual traces of the innate, perfect I-consciousness which is followed by the grammarians in their descriptive rules. Similarly, even in local dialects, e.g., the language (e.g. Pāli) used by the Buddhists or used in Āndhra or Dravidian region, this manner alone of speech and meaning (lit. expressed by words) which originally follows the instinctive feeling of the heart, conveys by its delightful impression this form (viz., the form of *nara*, Śakti and Śiva) of understanding.

As has been said by myself:

"That is no speech which does not reach the heart directly." So in every way, this kind of comprehension is innate. As has been said: "Without the form of *nara*, Śakti and Śiva (*tair*), there is neither word, nor meaning, nor mental movement." In Mālinīvijayatantra also, it has been said:

"As the one Śakti of Śiva (*śambhoḥ śaktirekaiva śāṅkarī*) abides, presiding over the entire class (of words, in first, second and third person), even so has she been related unto you." (M.V. III, 34).

In Tantrasamuccaya also, it is said:

"This universe is established always and is in every way involved in third person (*nara*), second person (Śakti) and first person (Śiva) both in the dealings of worms and the all-knowing."

Thus this universe consisting of the third, second and first person (*nara-śakti-śivātmakaṃ*) has been explained according to the teaching of the traditional clear comprehension. This all-inclusive order of experience (*sarvaṃsahaḥ pratipattikramaḥ*) consisting of the third, second and first person has been manifested by the free will of the highest Lord. So enough of elaboration of a topic which can appeal to the hearts of only a few people who have received the teaching from a *guru*, who are of refined taste, who are well-read (lit., who have heard from the learned people a great deal), and who have been purified by the descent of the Supreme grace. So, 'listen, O goddess' has been explained.

NOTES

1. In the context of *trika* or triad, viz., Śiva, Śakti and *nara*, '*nara*' represents all objective phenomena from the earth upto *māyā*; 'Śakti' represents Śuddhavidyā, Īśvara, and Sadāśiva, and 'Śiva' represents Śiva and Śakti.

2. In the first person, it is the *parāśakti* that is at work. From the point of view of the triad, first person is the state of Śiva. In the second person, it is the *parāparā śakti* that is at work. So, the second person, from the stand-point of the triad is the state of śakti. In the third person, it is the *aparā śakti* that is at work. So the third person from the standpoint of the triad is the state of *nara*.

3. The meaning is that the Śiva-aspect abides in the Śakti-aspect, and the Śakti-aspect abides in the *nara*-aspect. Thus the Śiva-aspect pervades all of them.

4. The *nara-rūpa* first rises to the Śakti-*rūpa* and then to Śiva-*rūpa*. It cannot rise to Śiva-*rūpa*, leaving aside the intervening Śakti-*rūpa*.

EXPOSITION

A.G. has tried to show that when Bhairava in the first person addresses the Devī in the second person, it should be understood that the Devī is not different from Bhairava. In order to prove this point, he has given a number of examples of the usage of speech in which the second person is assimilated to the first, and the third to the second. A.G. has been at pains to prove that these kinds of usages in speech in all languages are not a matter of mere accident or convention, but serve as a pointer to the metaphysical truth, viz. that Śiva and His Śakti are one, that just as in grammar there is first the singular number, then the dual and finally the plural, that just as in speech, there is firstly the first person, then the second and finally the third, even so in manifestation, the singular number and the first person are symbolic of Śiva, the dual number and the second person are symbolic of Śakti and the plural number and third person are symbolic of *nara* or objective phenomena. Further, just as the third person has to surrender itself to the second, and the second to the first in order that they may be used together, so also the *prameya* (object) or *nara* has to surrender itself to *pramāṇa* (knowledge) or Śakti, to be known, and *pramāṇa* has to surrender itself to *pramātā* (knower) for its final fulfilment.

Commentary

From *uttarasyāpi* on p. 28, l. 11 upto *ityuktam* on p. 33, l. 21.

Translation

That which is said, viz. how it is the *anuttara* of *uttara* is the answer of Bhairava.

(Different senses of *uttarasyāpyanuttaraṃ*)

1. As has been said before (viz., everything is the epitome of all), the proximate one (*uttaramapi*) is also identical with the non-proximate (*anuttara*). It cannot exist otherwise. Therefore, the proximate also setting aside its character as proximate becomes non-proximate. The text reads, '*uttarasyāpi anuttaraṃ*'. '*Uttarasya*' is the 6th or the genitive case, and the genitive case is (also) used in the sense of '*anādara*' i.e. ignoring or setting aside i.e. absence of consideration or dis-regard. So '*uttarasyāpi anuttaraṃ*' may mean the proximate setting aside its character as proximate becomes non-proximate. Even this difference (of the proximate one i.e. from the earth upto *anāśrita* Śiva' acquires this character (of difference) by resting wholly on the undifferentiated (i.e. *anuttara*).[1] As has been said in the following:

(This is a difficult verse. The following is its prose order:) "*Paravyavasthāpi pare tāvat kartuṃ na śakyate yāvat paraḥ na ātmīkṛtaḥ : yataḥ paraḥ pare buddhaḥ.*")." "Even the ascertainment of difference (*paravyavasthā*) cannot be made in the different objects (*pare tāvat na kartuṃ śakyate*) so long as the Supreme is not assimilated to oneself (*yāvat paraḥ na ātmikṛtaḥ*), since the different object (*paraḥ*) is known (*buddhaḥ*) only in the Supreme (*pare*) i.e. the different object has its *raison d'être* only in the Supreme."

2. *Uttara* may mean the posterior. So '*uttarasyāpi anuttaram*' may mean, "even the posterior part of the book cannot offer its answer."[2]

3. Even of my answer given in the *paśyanti* stage which is the first expansion of *parā*, this *anuttara* is the highest truth i.e. this non-answer (*anuttara*) or silence is the highest truth.

4. *Uttara* may also mean the phenomena—desirables, knowables, and actions—prompted by the trident, viz. *icchā-śakti*, *jñāna-śakti* and *kriyā-śakti*. *Anuttara* is that stage where all the above and *uttara* cease.

What after all is that *anuttara*? The answer is 'that is *anuttara* from which proceeds *kaulika vidhi*'. *Kaulika* has been previously explained as 'that which is of the nature of *kula* and *akula*'[3]; *vidhi* means 'the great manifestation' (*mahāsṛṣṭi*)[4] or the *tattvas* from *anāśrita* Śiva upto *śuddhavidyā* (*śuddhādhvā*). '*Vidhi*' is socalled because of its being executed. Now *anuttara* is that from which proceeds this 'great manifestation' i.e. *mahāsṛṣṭi*[4] which enfolds within itself hundreds of crores of unlimited *māyīya* (phenomenal) creations. As has been said, "That from which proceeds everything." So, this universe consisting of *cit-pramātā* i.e. *śūnya pramātā*, *citta* i.e. *puryaṣṭaka pramātā*, *prāṇa* i.e. *prāṇapramātā*, *deha* i.e. *deha-pramātā* (i.e. four kinds of experients), pleasure and pain i.e. subjective experiences, senses i.e. means of experience, the five elements and jar etc., i.e. subtle and gross objects of experience abide without difference in one, supreme, divine Consciousness as simply form of consciousness (*bodhātmakena rūpeṇa*). Though the divine universal consciousness never ceases to exist, for it ceasing, there will be the contingency of universal darkness, yet there does not exist difference consisting of reciprocal absence (of objects), for all objects are omnifarious in that state (*viśvātmāna eva bhāvāḥ*). If all things were not situated in that universal Bhairava Consciousness, then even the initial indeterminate perception which is of use in urging the senses towards their objects would not be there. Therefore, the entire multitude of existents exists there, without the appearance of appropriate objectivity (lit., thisness), identically with I-consciousness only, void of all differentiation. There is absolutely no difference there whatsoever. In that universal Bhairava consciousness, the entire manifestation (*kaulika vidhi*) lies clearly (*spaṣṭaḥ san*) at rest.

All this (universe) consisting of thirty-six categories, though created by Śiva who being of supreme Śakti, is of the nature of universal creative pulsation (*sāmānya spanda*) rests in that consciousness itself in its own form which is predominantly Śakti i.e. characterized by particular creative pulsation (*viśeṣa spanda*).[5] This is what is meant by the inherence of objects in their own nature which is consciousness. As has been said "In which all things exist."

This multitude of objects (*tadetat*) of the nature of Śiva and Śakti, Śiva whose characteristic is universal creative pulsation (*sāmānya spanda*[5]) and Śakti whose characteristic is particular creative pulsation (*viśeṣarūpam*) though only of one form (*ekātmamapi*) has been determined separately by the Lord only as an aid for teaching, but really speaking it is only one, viz. *anuttara* who is the essence of the creative energy viz., the autonomous I-consciousness.

What is the nature of that in which this process of creation (*kaulika vidhi*) is inherent? Bhairava says, "It inheres in the ether of my heart" (*mama hṛdaya-vyomni*). Now heart (*hṛdaya*) in this context means the receptacle of all the existents.

Existents from blue etc. upto worms are, in their final analysis, simply nothing unless they rest in consciousness (*cidaṃśa-aniviṣṭānāṃ*). 'Blue' etc. belong really to the experient. The essence of blue etc. consists in its being incorporated in uninterrupted I-consciousness, as in 'Blue appears to me".

('*Mama hṛdayavyomni*' may be interpreted in many ways)

First interpretation: In '*mamahṛdayavyoma*', '*hṛdaya*' means the receptacle of innumerable objects like blue etc.; '*vyoma*' means that where the universe of particular objects (*mamakārātmakaṃ viśvam*) is '*vita*' i.e. is held wholly in an implicit manner in that ether which is devoid of all difference (*śūnyarūpaṃ*).

Second interpretation: '*Mama*' means 'of the consciousness which expresses itself both in difference (*apara-saṃvitti*) and non-difference (*para-saṃvitti*); '*hṛdayam*' means the final resting place i.e. I—'*ahaṃ*'. The *vyoma* of that also means, by the form of the return movement of *ahaṃ* i.e. *ma+ha+a*, the *nara* form i.e. the objective phenomena represented by '*ma*' being dissolved in the dot i.e. the *anusvāra* over '*ha*', enters the *kuṇḍalini śakti* represented by the letter '*ha*' and finally entering the '*a*' letter which represents the integral, unimpeded delight of *anuttara*, which is identified with all, it becomes that (i.e. *anuttara*). This is the ether of my heart. Therefore, that from which this universe proceeds, that in which it rests that one alone, the eternal, the one whose nature cannot be veiled which is self-luminous (*prathamānaṃ*), which can never be denied (*anapahnavānīyam*) is the *anuttara*, the unsurpassable Absolute. As has been said:

"Inasmuch as nothing can veil His nature, there cannot be the obstruction anywhere of his in whom all this world rests and from whom it has come forth." (Sp. K. I, 2).

Even if He (Śiva) is supposed to be obstructed by a cover (e.g., *māyā*), He still shines by His freedom in the form of that cover itself,[6] and thus the Lord is always of the nature of knowledge and activity. The particle '*yat*' (of which *yasmin sarvaṃ* or *yatra* and *yataḥ sarvaṃ* or *yasmāt* are different forms) conveys the sense of all the cases; on account of its fitness of relation with another sentence (e.g. *idaṃ sarvaṃ sthitaṃ*), it stands here in a special position i.e. it is used in the sense of the locative case (*yasmin paramaśiva*) i.e. the Supreme Śiva in whom it rests, and on account of its fitness with another sentence (e.g. *idaṃ sarvaṃ nirgataṃ*), it is also used in the sense of the ablative case (*yasmāt paramaśivāt*) i.e. the Supreme Śiva from whom it emanates. This is the clear, direct sense. That which is the source of the expansion of universal manifestation (*kaulikaḥ sṛṣṭi-prasaraḥ*), in the sense of the ablative case (*yasmāt ca nirgatam* or *yataḥ sarvam*), that which abides in the ether of my heart, in the sense of the locative case (*yatra sthitaṃ* or *yasmin sarvaṃ*), that indeed is *anuttara.*

Thus having established that the *anuttara* is the centre of both the expansion and the absorption of the universe, Bhairava now establishes the expansion, which is technically called *kriyāśakti-visarga* which means *visarga* or external expansion of the *spanda* of *kriyāśakti* which is of the nature of *vimarśa.* He begins with '*kathayāmi*' (i.e., I am telling you).

That very aspect of expansion is *a-ha-m* (I), *para* (supreme), *anuttara* (unsurpassable). Even in its regular succession of external expansion consisting of *paśyantī* and *madhyamā* denoting *parāparā śakti*, and *vaikharī* denoting *aparā śakti* its unbroken continuity is the highest truth. '*Kathayāmi*' means: 'I am expressing it by the use of appropriate names the series of utterances upto *vaikharī* that arise from the venerable *parā śakti* and are expressed in varied scriptural and worldly forms. It has been said, "Who is everywhere".

Whether in the initial stage of *parā* or the final stage of *aparā* i.e. *vaikharī*, both of which are the expression of revered *parāśakti* and also in its stage of expansion in the form of *parāparā* i.e. in *paśyanti* and *madhyamā* forms, it is throughout the display of the immutable *anuttara*. Venerable Somānanda has also said the same thing in his commentary on Parātrīśikā. "*Kathayāmi*" means "I (Bhairava) say owing to the eagerness of the enquiry; that it is I who being present as Consciousness in all, declare this." It is this explanation which my heart, purified by the reasoning of the guru, teaching of the scripture, and personal experience, (*yuktyupadeśasaṃskāraiḥ*) has fully accepted.

(Now A.G. gives different interpretations of *sadyaḥ*)

First interpretation: The nature of the highest Lord is said to be '*sadyaḥ*'. '*Sadyaḥ*' may be analyzed into *sat*+*yaḥ* meaning '*yaḥ parameśvaraḥ tat sat*' i.e. what the greatest Lord described as Bhairava, *akula*, *anuttara*, *dhruva* is, that is all this *sat* or existence, in other words *kaulikavidhi* or the plan of creation. (So *sadyaḥ* means—He who is this whole universe). No object whatsoever can exist apart from the veritable Bhairava who is both *prakāśa* or Light and *vimarśa* or the consciousness of that Light as I.

In all matters, there are three terms, *sattā* (existence), *sambandha* (relation), and *arthakriyā* (purpose). Even though they are considered to be different (*parābhimatānāmapi*) by others, the *raison d'être* of all of them is *sattā* i.e. being (*sattāhetutā*). Without *sattā* (being), there cannot be the possibility of even *saṃbandha* or *arthakriyā* (*sattā-ayoge tathāiva-anupapattiḥ*). If one requires to find out another being of being or another purpose of purpose, then there would be the contingency of *regressus ad infinitum*. *Sattva* or *eternal* being is that by which alone do other things derive their life and the apparent form (*prakāśamayatā*) of which is brought into being by its *vimarśa*. That being is Bhairava Himself full of the I-feeling which is the quintessence of the consciousness of His Freedom.[7]

2. Or *sadya* may be interpreted as '*sati-sadrūpe yasyati yatnaṃ karoti* i.e. he in his nature as *sat* i.e. as Śiva exerts, i.e. is active, for Śiva is the very life of the power of activity. This *sadya* may be treated as neuter gender by adding the suffix *kvip*. Some elderly teachers have adopted the reading *sadyat* (*sat*+*yat*) instead of *sadyaḥ*. It has been said in Siddhasantāna:[8]

"The power that shines in appearances (such as jar, cloth etc.) is *sat* itself i.e. Śiva."

In Spandakārikā also it has been said:

"That (Reality) is *sat* in the highest sense." (Sp. K. I, 5)

Venerable Somānanda has also said:

"That which is *sat* or Śiva is the highest reality (*paramārthaḥ*). Since the universe is pervaded by that highest Reality, therefore the universe is also Śiva. Thus His nature has been declared. It has been rightly said, "He who is all"."

(A.G. now comments on *kaulikasiddhidaṃ*)

The expansion of the power of activity of this very *anuttara* is being explained by the statement *kaulikasiddhidaṃ*:

The word '*kaulika*' has already been explained. Its *siddhi* or perfect fulfilment is now being explained. That by which the being so i.e. the true nature (*tathātva*) of *kaulika* is fixed and corroborated, is its perfect fulfilment i.e. *anuttara* is the true fulfilment of *kaulika vidhi*, the creative process. In that highest experient, viz. the unsurpassable divine Consciousness, everything—*kula* and *akula* i.e. Śiva and Śakti—becomes that very Consciousness where all that is perceived and known acquires the firmness of that very nature itself (*pratīyamānaṃ sarvaṃ tathātvadārḍhyaṃ bhajate*).

It has been said:

"Trika is higher than the highest."[8]

At another place also, it has been said:

"The Śaiva system is higher than the Vedic, the left-hand doctrine is higher than Śaiva, the right hand doctrine is higher than the left; the Kula system is higher than the right-hand doctrine; the Matam is higher than the Kula, the Trika is higher even than that; in fact, it is the highest of all."[9]

In Niśācāra[10] Śāstra also, we find the following:

"The teacher who has been initiated as *ācārya* in the left-hand path and is considered to be knowing the supreme truth (according to left-hand path) has to undergo the ceremony of consecration in Bhairava *mārga*, he also has to receive fresh initiation in the Kula *mārga*, he who has received initiation in Kula has to receive initiation in Kaula *mārga* and even he who has received initiation in Kaula *mārga* has to receive fresh initiation in the Trika *mārga*."[11]

In Sarvācāra[12] also, it has been said:

"The teacher who has received initiation in the left hand path and is considered to be knowing the Supreme truth has still to undertake the purificatory ceremony successively in the various Bhairava systems, viz. Kula, Kaula and Trika."

This alone is the mode of Śiva that in all the stages whether of the common man, the Veda, the Śaiva Siddhānta, the left hand path, the right hand path, the Śākta system (Kula) and the Mata system, it is He that abides as the highest experient. As has been said:

"He who is eternally all, to Him, the Omnifarious one do I bow."

So, "all this is verily the *anuttara*"—proclaiming this as the central point of his thesis, venerable Somānanda has said in his commentary on Parātrīśika: "What occasion is there for much talk, everything is *anuttara*, because of being *anuttara*."

Pointing out how others have expounded this, leaving aside such (lucid) exposition would amount to a fault. Though a dialogue carried on with those who are without any knowledge of grammar, logic, traditional teaching and have no personal experience would be shameful, yet in order to bring to the knowledge of sensible people the sample of their exposition, I am putting down here their explanation of *anuttara*. This is how it begins:

"By the use of the words *anuttara* etc. in one and a half verses, the question pertaining to Śiva has been put. In *hṛdayasthā tu yā śaktiḥ*' the question pertains to Śakti. In that part of the book which contains the answer, viz., "*Śṛṇu devi...uttarasyāpyanuttaraṃ*," the explanation offered is: "Listen about *uttara*, i.e. the expansion of Śakti, and also about *anuttara*, i.e. the expansion of Śiva." In this case, if the explanation is from the point of view of Trika, there arises the contingency of a third question regarding *nara*. If the explanation is from the point of view of *yāmala*, even there, it is not two separate beings—Śiva and Śakti whose connexion is known as *yāmala* so that a separate question about each could be justified.

The meaning of '*atha*' also (occurring in the subsequent verse) would not fit in. Of two homogeneous realities, the word *atha* indicates the definite priority of one and the definite immediate sequence of the other. Without the ascertainment of the nature of *uttara* (i.e. Śakti), a question about *anuttara* (i.e. Śiva) is unreasonable.

In some old books, another such verse is also noticed: "O Lord, I have heard the description of the spiritual knowledge pertaining to *trika* and so through your favour I have also acquired knowledge pertaining to *uttara*."

Therefore that which the teachers have taught in accordance with the commentary of venerable Somānanda will alone do good to all.

"Abhinavagupta has made the blazing Sun of commentary manifest that is bent on extirpating the darkness (*tāmasa*) due to misleading, wretched commentaries lacking the refinement of good teaching and tradition, that makes the heart-lotus, purified by the discipline of *trika* bloom, that, by its flashing lustre, melts the coagulated stream of innumerable bonds."

So that is said to be *anuttara* from which this *kaulika* creation emerges, in which it stays, and of which it is constituted.

(Here ends the *bimba* portion of Parātrīśikā)

(Now begins the *pratibimba* portion of Parātrīśikā)

So, what is the *kaulika* mode of manifestation? How does it proceed from *anuttara*? How does it stay in it (i.e. *anuttara*) alone? How is it (i.e. *kaulika vidhi*) the form of *anuttara* itself?

It has been said that it is the *anuttara* even of the posterior part of the book. It is for the explanation of all this that the Lord Bhairava proposes to devote the posterior part of the book with a desire for decisive ascertainment in detail for the sake of those pupils who have become adroit by acquiring the understanding of the knowledge of reality which is the essence (*niṣkarṣaṇa*) of the well-reasoned explanation of the *guru* (*yukti*), teaching of the traditional scripture (*āgama*) and personal experience (*svasaṃvedana*).

There is the complete satisfaction of realization for those whose manifold impression of the ideas of difference has been utterly destroyed by so much of solid teaching in the form of the question beginning with '*anuttaraṃ katham*' and concluded with two and a half verses and in the form of the answer beginning with '*śṛṇu devi*', and ending with a decisive statement in one and a half verses and who have attained to the state of *jīvanmukti* (liberation in life) by entering the stage of *anuttara*.

Therefore, I proclaim with upraised arm that those who have been purified by firm conviction may rest contented with so much only. Now the other part of the book is begun for a thorough deliberation of the *kaulika* state inherent in the spotless mirror of *anuttara* who is the supreme Bhairava.[13]

NOTES

1. The '*uttara*' or proximate one i.e. the entire manifestation from the earth upto *anāśrita* Śiva which is full of difference cannot exist without resting on *anuttara* which is *abhedabhūḥ*, the stage of non-difference i.e. pure undifferentiated Consciousness.

2. It has already been said that the Devī asks questions from the stage of *madhyamā* and Bhairava answers from the stage of *paśyanti*. But *paśyanti* itself is the first external expansion of *parā*. How can it describe the state of *parā*? So in spite of all the explanation offered by Bhairava in the *paśyanti* stage, the nature of *parā* really remains unanswered (*anuttara*).

3. '*Kula*' means Śakti and '*akula*' means Śiva. '*Kulākulātma*' means that in which Śiva and Śakti are fused into one.

4. *Mahāsṛṣṭi* means creation from *anāśrita tattva* upto *Śuddhavidyā* (*śuddhādhvā*), creation from *māyā* upto earth is known as *avāntara sṛṣṭi* (*aśuddhādhvā*).

5. '*Sāmānya spanda*' or universal creative pulsation is the nature of Śiva; *viśeṣa spanda* or the creative pulsation of particulars is the nature of Śakti.

6. The cover, *māyā*, *mala*, etc., are not anything outside the Lord. They owe their existence to Him and are dissolved in Him.

7. The first interpretation of '*sadyaḥ*' says '*yaḥ sat*'—He i.e. *Parameśvara*, the Highest Lord is *sat* i.e. this universe itself. The second interpretation of '*sadyaḥ*' says that the *sat* or the universe is He i.e. Bhairava Himself. What is meant to be said is that Śiva is the universe and the universe is Śiva.

8. *Trika* is designated as the highest, because it teaches that whether it is the initial manifestation of (1) Śiva, or (2) Śakti—

i.e. Energy in all her multifarious aspects, or (3) *nara* i.e. objective phenomena, it is throughout *anuttara.*

9. Śaiva is a technical term in this context. It connotes the system of dualistic philosophy or Śaiva Siddhānta prevalent in South India. The word *vāma* means beautiful, appealing. In this system, the five *m*'s were allowed under certain conditions. They were *māṃsa* (meat), *matsya* (fish), *madirā* (wine), *mudrā* (food of parched grain) and *maithuna* (sexual intercourse). *Dakṣa* or *Dakṣiṇa ācāra* (right hand path) is said to be superior to the *Vāma* or the left-hand path. It is full of *vidhi* and *niṣedha* i.e. do's and don'ts. A.G. says in Tantrāloka, "*Dakṣiṇaṃ raudrakarmāḍhyam,*' i.e., the '*Dakṣiṇa* path is full of terrible practices.' In *Kula*, a great emphasis was laid on *caryā* which means due observance of certain prescribed practices. *Mata* is said to be higher than Kula. Not much is known about Mata. Jayaratha has mentioned eight Āgamas pertaining to Mata, but they are not available now.

10. This is not available now.

11. The Bhairava Śāstra mentioned in this verse is the Rudra Bhairava Śāstra, not the non-dualistic Bhairava Śāstra advocated by Parātrīśikā. There was a good deal of similarity between Kula and Kaula, but as mentioned in note No. 9, in Kula, the greatest emphasis was laid on *caryā*. In Kaula *mārga*, the greatest emphasis was laid on universal unity consciousness. Both Kaula and Trika are non-dualistic, but in Kaula *mārga*, emphasis is laid on all the methods, viz. *jñāna, caryā, kriyā,* and *yoga*, whereas in Trika emphasis is laid mostly on *jñāna* and *yoga.*

12. This book is not available now.

13. The previous portion of Parātrīśikā is known as *bimba grantha*, and from now onwards it is known as *pratibiṃba grantha,* for in the previous portion, it is the nature (*svarūpa*) of *anuttara* that has been described. From now it is its external manifestation or expansion that is going to be described. On the analogy of a mirror, the divine source of light is known as *bimba* (in its process of *saṃhāra* or withdrawal) and its reflection in its own mirror is known as *sṛṣṭi* or manifestation or expansion.

Exposition

In this portion of his commentary, A.G. has shown that the *raison d'être* of the entire manifestation (*kaulika vidhi*) is *anuttara,* the Absolute Divine Universal Consciousness. He has adopted the following ancient verse of Mahābhārata (Śāntiparvan XII, 47,58) as the core of his thesis and enlivened it with his own penetrating insight (also Yoga Vāsiṣṭha VI, 36, 18):

"YASMINSARVAṂ YATAḤ SARVAṂ
YAḤ SARVAṂ SARVATAŚCA YAḤ /
YAŚCA SARVAMAYO NITYAṂ
TASMAI SARVĀTMANE NAMAḤ" //

"To that omnifarious one do I bow, in whom lies all, from whom all starts, who is all, who is all round, and who is always constitutive of all."

First of all, he takes up '*yataḥ sarvam*' i.e. from whom proceeds all, and after elaborating the expansion of manifestation from the Divine, concludes with the following remark:

"*Kauliko vidhiḥ kulākulātmā vidhiḥ mahāsṛṣṭirūpo yasmāt prasṛta etat eva anuttaram*";

"That from which proceeds Śiva-Śakti, the divine insight of creativity itself is this *anuttara*."

Next, he takes up *yasmin sarvam*—i.e. in whom resides all this, and sums up his arguments by saying,

"*yasminsarvaṃ—atra spaṣṭaḥ sannayaṃ vidhiḥ kaulikaḥ sthito viśrāntiṃ prāptaḥ*";

"In whom clearly rests all this universal manifestation"—that is *anuttara*.

After this, he takes up '*sarvataśca yaḥ*,' who is all round, and concludes with the following remark:

"*Prathamaparyantabhuvi parabhaṭṭārikātmani tatprasarātmani ca parāparādevatavapuṣi anuttaradhruvapadavijṛmbhaiva.*"

"From the first stage of *para*, the highest, then its expansion in *parāpara*, and finally up to the last stage of *apara* or manifestation of the gross material world, it is all round the expansion of the immutable *anuttara*."

Now he takes up *sarvaṃ yaḥ*, and aptly quotes in this connexion a line from Śrī Somānanda:

"*Yatsattatparamārthohi paramārthastataḥ Śivaḥ*";

"That which is Existence is the highest Reality, the universe is of the nature of that Reality, therefore everything is Śiva."

Finally, he says that it is *anuttara* who is constitutive of all and to whom we bow as the all—'*yaśca sarvamayo nityaṃ tasmai sarvātmane namaḥ.*' This is the highest philosophy and at the same time the highest religion.

Text

ATHĀDYĀSTITHAYAḤ SARVE SVARĀ VINDV-
AVASĀNAGĀḤ /
TADANTAḤ KĀLAYOGENA SOMASŪRYAU
PRAKĪRTITAU // 5 /
PṚTHIVYĀDĪNI TATTVĀNI PURUṢĀNTĀNI
PAÑCASU /
KRAMĀTKĀDIṢU VARGEṢU MAKĀRĀNTEṢU
SUVRATE // 6 /
VĀYVAGNI-SALILENDRĀṆĀM DHĀRAṆĀNĀṂ
CATUṢṬAYAM /
TADŪRDHVAṂ ŚĀDI-VIKHYĀTAṂ PURASTĀT
BRAHMAPAÑCAKAM // 7 /
AMŪLĀ TATKRAMĀJ JNEYĀ KṢĀNTĀ SṚṢṬIR-
UDĀHṚTĀ /
SARVEṢĀM EVA MANTRĀṆĀM VIDYĀNĀṂ CA
YAŚASVINI // 8 /
IYAṂ YONIḤ SAMĀKHYĀTĀ SARVATANTREṢU
SARVADĀ /

Translation

The *kaulika vidhi* or the manifestation of the Universe is as follows (*tadyathā*):

5. The fifteen (*tithayaḥ*)[1] viz. '*a*' etc. (*ādyaḥ*)[2] are all the vowels ending in a dot, i.e. *anusvāra*. At their end, through the connexion of *kriyā śakti* (*kālayogena*)[3] occur what are known as *soma* (moon) and *sūrya* (sun).[4]

6. In the five classes of consonants beginning successively[5] with '*ka*' and ending with '*ma*' (*kādiṣu makārānteṣu pañcasu vargeṣu*), there are the categories of existence (*tattvāni*) beginning with the earth and ending with *puruṣa* (*pṛthivyādini puruṣāntāni*)[6], O Goddess with excellent pious observation (*suvrate*).

7. There are the four *dhāraṇās* pertaining to *vāyu* (air), *agni* (fire), *salila* (water) and Indra. After that, there are the well-known '*śa*' etc.[7], which further on, are known as five *brahma* (*brahmapañcaka*).

8. Therefore, beginning with '*a*' and successively ending with '*kṣa*' it is known as *sṛṣṭi* or manifestation. O glorious one, this manifestation consisting of '*a*' to '*kṣa*' is always known in all the Tantras as the source of all the *mantras* and the incantations (*vidyānām*).

NOTES

1. '*Tithayaḥ*' is the plural of '*tithi*' which means a lunar day. As there are fifteen '*tithis*' in each fortnight of the lunar month, the word '*tithi*' is used symbolically for fifteen. So '*tithayaḥ*' means fifteen

2. *Ādyāḥ* = *a* + *ādyāḥ* which means '*a*' etc.

3. *Kālayogena* = "*kālaḥ kalanā sūkṣma-kriyāśaktiḥ tasyāḥ yogena sambandhena.*" The word '*kāla*' here means subtle *kriyāśakti* and *yoga* means connexion. So, '*kālayogena*' means through the connexion of *kriyāśakti*.

4. *Visarga* means expansion. This is a two-way track: (1) the *saṃhārātmaka* or the centripetal track or the track of withdrawal towards the centre, and (2) *sṛṣṭyātmaka* or the centrifugal track, the track of projection or manifestation.

Visarga is expressed with two dots—one above the other viz. *Soma* or moon represents the upper dot; the dot representing the centripetal track, the track representing the return movement towards the centre, the *saṃhārātmaka* track; *Sūrya* or Sun represents the lower dot, the dot representing the centrifugal track, the track representing the external expansion from the centre, the projection or manifestation of Śiva in the cosmos.

The sixteen vowels from '*a*' up to *visarga* represent the nature of Śiva, and the consonants from '*ka*' to '*ha*' represent Śakti. '*Soma*' represents '*praveśa-rūpa kriyāśakti*' (the return movement of *kriyāśakti*); and *Sūrya* represents the *prasara-rūpa kriyāśakti* (the expansion of *kriyāśakti*). There are two modes of *kriyāśakti*, viz. (1) *Śiva-vartinī*, and (2) *paśu-vartinī*. *Vimarśa* or Divine Self-consciousness is *Śiva-vartinī kriyāśakti*.

5. Successively : The Sanskrit word *kramāt* means two things : (i) *kramāt--krama* + *ad* (= *kramāt*) as swallowing all succession i.e. without any real succession, and (ii) successively. This points to the truth that in Śiva, there is really no succession and that succession is spoken of in relation to the empirical individual.

6. Classes of letters together with the *tattvas*, organs, etc., are given below:

(1). Letters:	*ka*	*kha*	*ga*	*gha*	*ṅa*
Tattvas or the gross elements	*pṛthivī*	*jala*	*agni*	*vāyu*	*ākāśa*
(2). Letters:	*ca*	*cha*	*ja*	*jha*	*ña*
Tanmātras	*gandha*	*rasa*	*rūpa*	*sparśa*	*śabda*
(3). Letters:	*ṭa*	*ṭha*	*ḍa*	*ḍha*	*ṇa*
Organs of actions	*upastha*	*pāyu*	*pāda*	*pāṇi*	*vāk*
(4). Letters:	*ta*	*tha*	*da*	*dha*	*na*
Organs of sense	*prāṇa*	*rasanā*	*cakṣus*	*tvak*	*śrotra*
(5). Letters:	*pa*	*pha*	*ba*	*bha*	*ma*
The psychic apparatus, the primal matter (*prakṛti*) and limited experient (*puruṣa*)	*manas*	*buddhi*	*ahaṃkāra*	*prakṛti*	*puruṣa*

(6). The *dhāraṇās* or *antaḥstha* letters are the following four: *ya, ra, la, va*. '*Ya*' symbolizes *vāyu-bīja*, '*ra*' symbolizes *agni-bīja*, '*la*' symbolizes *salila-bīja*, '*va*' symbolizes *Indra-bīja*. The word *bīja* indicates that these letters are to be used as *mantras* for *vāyu* etc. These are connected with *māyā* together with her *kañcukas* (coverings). '*Ya*' is connected with *rāga* and *niyati*; '*ra*' is connected with '*vidyā*', '*la*' is connected with '*kāla*' and '*kalā*', and '*va*' is connected with '*māyā*'.

7. '*Śa*' etc., means *śa, ṣa, sa, ha, kṣa*. Of these, *śa* represents *mahāmāyā*, *ṣa* represents *Śuddha vidyā*, '*sa*' represents Īśvara, '*ha*' represents Sadāśiva, and '*kṣa*' represents Śakti. This group is known as *brahmapañcaka*.

Commentary

From *tatrākulam* on p. 34, l. 17 upto *iti sthitam* on p. 38, l. 22.

Translation

That *anuttara* itself whose nature is '*a*' is all this universal manifestation (*kaulikasṛṣṭirūpam*). This is what is being ascertained here.

'*Atha*' (the first word of the above verses) is connected with that manifestation (*tatsṛṣṭi*). The meaning is that it is *anuttara* that constitutes the universal manifestation. Though according to the principle laid down earlier, in manifestation also, there is no succession (of earlier and later) which is entirely related to time, yet so long as there appears the difference between the taught and the teaching brought about by the Lord Himself through His Free Will, so long the fact of succession (of earlier and later) has to be admitted. So, it is with reference to this appearance of succession, that the word '*atha*' has been used in the sense of immediate sequence (*ānantarya*) i.e. subsequently it is '*akula*' itself that appears in the form of the manifested universe. The word '*atha*' (now) has not been used to indicate immediate succession of answer after the question of Devī. The word '*atha*' has been used here for clear apprehension of the meaning of a point arising in the sequential order of a homogeneous object of inquiry pertaining to the same doctrine[1] (*ekapraghaṭṭakagata*). Otherwise there can be in every case an occasion for the use of '*atha*' even in the sense of immediately after silence. If it is said 'Well, it may be so. What is your trouble in such use?', the reply is, 'None whatsoever, except that such use is not found in experience.'

Venerable Somānanda gives the following interpretation of '*atha*':

"'A' of '*atha*' indicates Śiva and '*tha*' Śakti" and refers to Āgama in support of it. He explains '*atha*' as *anuttara*. Both '*tha*' and '*ha*' are used equally in the sense of mutual perpetual pervasion. Thus '*ha*' denotes Śakti, '*tha*' also denotes Śakti. Therefore, '*atha*' has been used in the sense of '*aha*' because of its being non-different from Śakti that manifests endless objects at the very initial expansion of bliss and because of its depending on the highest *nāda* of *parāhantā* (the Supreme I-consciousness) which is the very life of all beings. I have not examined this point in detail, for I am not directly aware of such an Āgama. He was directly acquainted with such Āgamas and thus interpreted this book of pithy teaching (*sūtra granthasya*) which is capable of bearing hundreds of reasonings and usages. He expanded in detail the subtle differentiation of meaning of powder (*dhūli* used in the sacrificial rites at initiation) or symbolic scripts of *mantras* (i.e. '*atha*' meaning Śiva and Śakti) in that sense on the basis of this book and other Āgamas. I who am purified by his teaching, who have a desire to purify myself by removing the difficulties occurring in his book, am indifferent to such interpretations as he has arrived at. Subtle difference of meaning of the *mantra* depending on imaginary and symbolic interpretation of the letters of a word may be of use to some, but cannot be of use to pupils of all countries and all times. Therefore I have not described it in detail. Such an interpretation is of no use to those who have the benefit of personal experience and the rational explanation of the teacher; it is only easy to be managed by those who simply depend on their own imagination. For others who are not acquainted with that teaching, the impartation of that teaching will be of no use. Enough of this which creates an interruption in the subject under discussion.

Now I follow the proposed topic. *Ādya* in the verse means *a*+*ādya* i.e. '*a*' which is the first of the vowels. Or '*athādya*' may be taken together and analyzed as '*atha*+*ādya*'. In this case, the '*tha*' of '*atha*' is used only for the sake of ease in pronunciation.

The meaning again would be '*a*' which is the first of the vowels. In this context the word '*ādya*' has not been used merely in the sense of the 'foremost of an order', nor in the sense of 'proximity' etc., but rather that whose existence continues in '*a*' etc., i. e. in '*a*' and all other letters (*a ādau bhavaḥ iti ādyaḥ*). So it is being decisively propounded here that '*a*' is the stage of the highest sound (*parāvāgbhūmiḥ*) in which alone of these letters there is the non-conventional, eternal, natural form consisting only of consciousness. In the nature of consciousness, the omnifariousness of everything (*sarvasarvātmakatā*) is always present. That highest Divinity, viz. *parā* (who is only the dynamic form of *anuttara*), though consisting of the highest stage of non-differentiation is teeming with endless variety, containing within Herself as she does the *parāparā* expansion of *paśyanti* etc.[2] The maxim 'that which is not there may be elsewhere' will not hold good in her case. Seize (mentally) that goddess, viz. consciousness, known as the initial ever-creative activity of I-feeling (*prathamām pratibhābhidhām*), void of even a trace of the foul stain of limitation.

Whatever mobile and immobile objects there are—all these abide in the venerable, divine, supreme consciousness of Bhairava (*saṃvidi bhagavad-bhairava-bhaṭṭārakātmani*) in their truest, invariable form (*pāramārthikena anapāyinā rūpeṇa*), in the form of the perfect, supreme I-consciousness (lit., in the form of the quintessence of sheer divine energy, *vīryamātrasārātmanā*), in their true nature which is brought out by the unfoldment of endless variety that is perceived at the time of the emergence of hundreds of things that are about to appear in a slightly most indistinct, a slightly more indistinct, or a slightly indistinct form (*tadudbhaviṣyat-īṣadasphuṭatama-īṣadasphuṭatara-īṣadasphuṭādi-vastuśatasṛṣṭikālopalakṣyamāṇa-tattadananta-vaicitryaprathonnīyamānatathābhāvena*).

Parābhaṭṭārikā who is the stage of omniscience (*sarvajñatābhūmiḥ*), the highest truth without any limitation (*asaṅkucitaparamārthā*) and natural is suddenly resorted to by those who are established in intensive awareness of that state (*tathāvadhānātiśaya rūḍhaiḥ*), who are purified by utmost grace (*parānugraha-pavitritaiḥ*) and those whose impurities in the form of uncertainty, doubt or other synonymous terms owing to non-belief in that have been completely ground down by grinding on the grindstone of continuous spiritual discipline (*abhyāsakramaśāṇanigharṣaniṣpeṣitattadapratyayarūpakampādyanantāparaparyāyavicikitsāmalaiḥ*). Even in the case of those who are assailed by doubt, the omniscient stage of consciousness appears, on certain occasions[3] when they are able to view Reality, in a slightly limited form, though not in its full, natural form.

Venerable Kallaṭa has rightly said:

"By the gradual elimination of *tuṭi* from the movement of exhalation and inhalation, there is the acquisition of omniscience and ominipotence."

Now this matter (the omniscience of Parābhaṭṭārikā) which is to be known only by one's own experience is being explained by reasoning.

(A.G. uses at first *anvaya tarka*, i.e. reasoning by positive means.)

Indeterminate consciousness (*nirvikalpa saṃvid*) is that which by its efficacy (*sāmarthya*) brings something within comprehension which by its subsequent suitability for a particular purpose (*arthakriyāyogyatādivaśa*) finally acquires confirmation as a state of the Self and thus receives firm concurrence which precedes all successive determinate perceptions like blue etc., which are considered to be mutually incompatible (*virodhāvabhāsisaṃmatakramikavikalpyamānanīlādiniṣṭha-vikalpa-pūrva-bhāvi*) and pervades undivided all those blue, yellow perceptions etc. which are admittedly incompatible (*tattadvikalpaniyaviruddhābhimata-nilapitādyābhāsavibhāgi bhavati*), as for example in the integral perception of a picture (in which the difference of the various parts is not marked), or the integral perception of one standing on the top of a hill (*śikharastha*) or the integral perception of a peacock's tail (in which the different colours like blue etc., are not separately noticed).

(Now A.G. uses *vyatireka tarka*, i.e. reasoning by negative means.)

That indeterminate consciousness (*nirvikalpa saṃvid*), however, which does not pervade undivided the various incompatible percepts like blue, yellow, etc., cannot be (considered to be) prior also to the endless determinate percepts such as blue, yellow, etc., brought about by its own efficacy, as for instance, a perception pinned totally to the blue. But it, known by different names such as *unmeṣa*, *pratibhā* etc., does occur in the interval between two different determinate ideas or percepts, one that has just terminated and the other that is about to arise (*astamitodeṣyat*). This is what is extolled as the indeterminate consciousness in the Tantras (*śabdāgama-gitaṃ nirvikalpakaṃ*), precedent to what in conversation are considered to be mutually incompatible determinate percepts or ideas, such as blue, yellow, etc.

Therefore it (the *nirvikalpa saṃvit* or indeterminate consciousness) abides undivided among the endless determinate percepts. The interval between the two determinate ideas can by no means be denied because of the difference between the two ideas. That interval consists of consciousness only, otherwise (i.e., if consciousness is not present in the interval), on account of the extirpation of the residual traces of consciousness caused by that interval or gap (devoid of consciousness), memory, congruous link, etc. between the consciousness preceding the gap and the consciousness succeeding it would become impossible.

Since there is no disagreement among all the teachers regarding *pratibhā* or indeterminate consciousness having the above characteristic, therefore it is free from the fallacy of *asiddhi* or the non-probative reason. Since it does not depend on the understanding of any conventional sign, it is sheer indeterminate consciousness (*avikalpatva*).

In the matter of natural, non-conventional indeterminate consciousness which is identical with pure consciousness which is quite different from the insentient, there cannot be any similarity with determinate consciousness, for in it differentiation has not appeared. Objects are known only when their characteristic difference is marked. Determinate perceptions do not arise without the indeterminate consciousness because they lack the freedom for emerging by themselves. This freedom belongs only to indeterminate consciousness, for it is only indeterminate consciousness that serves as means for the recollection of the conventional signs etc. How can the recollection of conventional signs etc. be possible without the experience of indeterminate consciousness? In such consciousness, according to the previous principle, there is the absence of the limitation of time, etc. Thus the one divine indeterminate consciousness (*pratibhā*) defined by my weighty statement is of this kind i.e. of unlimited nature, the very Self of all. Not only in the beginning and the end but in the intervening state also, she is the origin of the emergence of the other present, past and future determinate apprehensions. Those who are adept in discrimination have experienced *ālaya-vijñāna* i.e. unified or integral knowledge in this very way (i.e. in the way of indeterminate consciousness).

Agreement of the determinate apprehensions occurring immediately after the indeterminate one has already been shown. Therefore, there is no non-probative reason (*asiddha hetu*) for the *probandum* (i.e. that which is to be proved viz., the determinative perceptions), nor can it be said that the *prātibha jñāna* is confined to only indeterminate consciousness which remains uniformally the same, which allots separate positions to the various determinate perceptions (*vikalpas*) and which is not opposed to *prātibha jñāna* or which is usually concerned with bringing about determinate perceptions and only appears in pure indeterminate form now and then (*kadācit*), nor is there complete exclusion or separation of the determinate consciousness (*asya*) from the indeterminate consciousness (*tataḥ*). Therefore, there is no contradiction (*na viruddho*) between the indeterminate consciousness and any other apprehension, nor is indeterminate consciousness simply an occasional and not uniform ground (of the determinate consciousness) (*nānaikāntiko*), nor is there an exclusion from it of even any dubious, opposite thing (i.e. even opposite things have their *raison d'être* in the indeterminate consciousness). In similar examples also, e.g., the integral perception of a picture etc., faults like the non-provability etc., of the reason (viz. the indeterminate consciousness) stand rejected. When the faults concerning the main reason are rejected, there remains no occasion for finding faults in examples similar to the main reason. By others also it (i.e. the indeterminate consciousness being the ground or reason of the determinate one) has been practically settled. Therefore, why take the trouble of repeating it ! This matter has been finally settled:

"That which moves in the prior, intervening, and posterior state of the apprehension of all the objects of sense (*nikhilavaiṣayikāvabodha-pūrvāparāntaracaraṃ*), which is universal (*nikhilātmakaṃ*), which is endowed with the splendour of the highest Śakti (*paraśaktibhāsi*), that indeed is the divine creative consciousness (*prātibhaṃ*). To one who is absorbed in that consciousness (*tasyāṃ pralīnavapuṣaḥ*), how can depression (*glāniḥ*) brought about by the lack of this divine consciousness (*abhāvavaśopaklṛptyā*) ever occur?"

"The ignorant man does not observe the magnitude of the delightful enjoyment of the most precious wealth (*paradhanasukhāsvāda*) lying in the body, *prāṇa* etc.[4] and feels overwhelming depression[5] in his heart. If the Supreme goddess who feels particular relish in bringing into being the entire universe (*nikhilajagatisūtisarasā*) enters his heart, then oh ! she sportively functions as the full and final oblation (in reducing to ashes the depression that had been plagueing him)."

A similar idea has been expressed in Spandakārikā: "Just as a plunderer carries away the valuables of the house, even so depression saps away the vitality of the body. This depression proceeds from ignorance. If that ignorance disappears by *unmeṣa* how can that depression last in the absence of its cause?"[6] (Sp. K. III, 8).

Also in the following verse:

"That should be known as *unmeṣa* whence the rise of another thought takes place in the mind of a man who is already engaged in one thought. One should experience it introspectively for oneself." (Sp. K. III, 9),

Further:

"The wise ones describe ignorance or in other words the primal limiting condition (*āṇava mala*) as the root cause of the *māyīya* and *kārma mala*. That very seed (viz., *āṇava mala*) even of the worn-out tree[6] of transmigratory existence is consumed instantly in the supreme blazing fire of supreme consciousness (*parāsaṃvit*)."

As has been (rightly) said:

"*Mala*, they say, is nothing but *ajñāna* or ignorance of one's real nature. This ignorance is the cause of *saṃsāra* or *māyīya mala* which again serves as the cause of *kārmamala*". (M.V. I, 23)

So also, (it has been said):

"If that ignorance disappears by *unmeṣa*, how can depression last in the absence of its cause?"

Thus has been described the nature of indeterminate consciousness (which also pervades the determinate consciousness). If it were otherwise than this i.e. if the indeterminate consciousness did not pervade the determinate consciousness also in all its phases, then which and by what could the following be so closely linked, viz. the destruction of depression, the emergence of depression from ignorance (of one's essential nature), and the destruction of ignorance by means of *unmeṣa*. In that case, all this would be like an investigation into '*nṛ*' and '*pa*'[7] i.e. would be merely futile.

So, the goddess, the highest power of creative word (*parāvāk*) is of the form of all the letters, beginning with '*a*' and ending with '*kṣa*', expands by enfolding within herself the venerable *parāparā* form etc., inherent in *paśyantī* etc., that are about to arise by her free will, has the essence of the creative delight which is identical with the consciousness of diverse manifestation consisting of all the elements, worlds and objects that have been undisputedly brought about by being included in her progressive expansion (*tadgarbhikāravaśāvivādaghaṭita-sakalabhūta-bhuvanabhāvādiprapañcaprabodhaikyacamatkārasārā*), is of the nature of the highest Reality consisting of astonishing facts brought to light by the presence of Lord Bhairava (*parameśvarabhairavabhaṭṭārakāvirbhāvaprathitatathāvidhādbhutabhūtaparamārthasvarūpā*), is the Supreme Creative Power that reveals within her pure mirror of Self endless manifestation, maintenance and absorption (*svātmavimaladar-*

paṇanirbhāsitānantasṛṣṭisthitisaṃhāraikyamayamahāsṛṣṭiśaktir). It is established that this is what has been decisively proved completely by Lord Bhairava by means of the verse '*athādya*' etc.

Notes

1. The question of the Devī and the answer of Bhairava refer to the state of Reality i.e. *svarūpa-vimarśa*. Therefore, both are homogeneous objects of the same doctrine.
2. See the charts for clarity.
3. Vide verse 75 of Vijñāna-Bhairava.
4. 'Et cetera' refers to *puryaṣṭaka* and *śūnya pramātā*.
5. The depression is due to the lack of recognition of the essential nature of the Self.
6. The 'worn out' (*jīrṇa*) tree suggests that the *māyīya* and *kārma mala* have been eliminated, but since the *āṇava mala* is still lingering, it supplies sustenance to the tree and so, although it is worn out, it does not fall.
7. If '*nṛ*' and '*pa*' are pronounced together, then it means a king, but if '*nṛ*' and '*pa*' are disjoined and are uttered after an interval, they would mean nothing. Even so if *glāni* is connected with *ajñāna*, and *ajñāna* is removed immediately by *unmeṣa*, then the sequence is understandable, otherwise not.

Exposition

This long commentary of A.G. serves only as an introduction to the eight verses by means of which Bhairava answers the question of the Devī, viz. "How does *anuttara* bestow *kaulika siddhi*?"

The actual interpretation of the verses will follow later. In this introductory portion A.G. has stressed the following two points:

1. *Kaulika sṛṣṭi* or the universal manifestation is not something different from *anuttara*. It is *anuttara* itself that appears as *kaulika sṛṣṭi*. As he puts it '*tadeva anuttarapadaṃ, sṛṣṭirityarthaḥ*—it is *anuttara* itself that is this vast manifestation.

2. The entire manifestation abides in the creative energy of the Divine. This creative energy is *parāvāk*, the energy that sounds forth the universe. The *parāvāk* is the *paranāda*, the creative throb of the Divine Mind which at a lower level takes the form of sound. The energy of the *parāvāk* flows into various letters from

'*a*' to '*kṣa*' which as conscious forms of energy bring about the manifestation of the universe. The letters in their original form are not merely conventional as they are at the human level.

The *parāvāk* is dynamic, creative consciousness. The nature of this consciousness is *nirvikalpa*, indeterminate, undifferentiated. According to A.G., *parāvāk*, *pratibhā*, *unmeṣa*, *nirvikalpa saṃvid* are almost synonymous; they refer to the same creative energy of the I-consciousness of *anuttara*. All determinate objects, perceptions, ideas covered by the blanket term *savikalpaka* inhere in the *nirvikalpa saṃvid* and emanate from it. The entire *kaulikī sṛṣṭi* or universal manifestation is simply an expression of *nirvikalpa saṃvid*. A.G. has used *nirvikalpa saṃvid* in a very wide sense, in the sense of the divine creative consciousness, the very life of all manifestation.

Commentary

From *tadevaṃ sthite* on p. 38, l. 22 upto *iti* on p. 51, l. 22.

Translation

It being so, the meaning of the verse is now being decisively fixed. The letters from '*a*' to *visarga* denote *Śiva tattva*; those from *ka* to *ṅa* denote the five elements from the earth up to the ether; those from *ca* upto to *ña* denote the five *tanmātras* from smell up to sound; those from *ṭa* to *ṇa* denote the five *karmendriyas* (organs of action) from the feet upto the tongue; those from *ta* to *na* denote five *jñānendriyas* from the nose up to the ears; those from *pa* to *ma* denote the group of five i.e., *manas*, *ahaṃkāra*, *buddhi*, *prakṛti*, and *puruṣa*; those from *ya* to *va* denote through *vāyu bīja*, *agni bīja*, *jala bīja* and *indrabīja*, *rāga*, *vidyā*, *kalā* and *māyā tattvas*. These are also known as *dhāraṇās*, because they make the *aṇu* or the empirical individual think of the universal powers of Bhairava differently (*pṛthagbhūtatayā*). There are two causatives involved here, owing to the causer and the caused being of two forms.[1] So, in one's own self which is light, highest and perfect state, identical with Bhairava, and universal are held the states of *kalā*, *vidyā*, etc., as has been said in Śivadṛṣṭi: "Self alone who shines as bliss (*ānanda*), and consciousness (*cit*), whose advance of will-power (*icchā*) is un-impeded, moves forward in all the objects as Śiva whose knowledge (*jñāna*) and activity (*kriyā*) are ever prevalent" (Ś.D.I. 2).

In Spandakārikā also, the same idea has been expressed: "In whom resides all this".

So also, the Lord assumes these states (of *rāga, vidyā, kalā, niyati*) which are held in His shining Self by His own light by veiling Himself, that is to say, He manifests by adopting the state of thisness (i.e. objectivity) whose nature is insentiency. Then again He encompasses all this objectivity with I-feeling. So this state of the Lord as Sadāśiva and Īśvara which is pure Śiva-consciousness (*śuddhavidyāmayi*) has been hinted at by one causative form of the verb '*dhṛ*'. In this case also the encompassing of thisness with I-ness can happen only when that which is to be encompassed (viz., thisness) has already been effected. And from the point of view of the pure Lord who is all consciousness, thisness denoting difference cannot remain in that state (i.e., as something different or separate from consciousness), and so in the event of the non-occurrence of that which is to be encompassed, the encompassing of this with I-ness cannot properly be upheld. In that case, there cannot be any propriety in considering Śiva in the capacity of an encompasser. And without his encompassing activity, nothing whatsoever can appear, because of the absence of a proper cause. This has been declared by me many a time. The 'this' or external appearance, however, does occur. This only means that the 'this' or external appearance, though now different from the (divine) light does appear externally through the power of the Lord Himself, for any other cause (than the Lord) is impossible. In one's consciousness also, one can bear witness to the fact that it is the (divine) consciousness that appears in all forms. Thus it is clear that while the universe is the Self itself, i.e. identical with the Self (in its transcendental aspect), it appears differently as 'this' (in its immanent aspect). The 'this' appears only appositionally in the I which is all light (as in the case of Sadāśiva or Īśvara).

So from the above, this is what is most certainly indicated, viz., it is the Lord Himself who knows all the different knowables (e.g., *kāla, rāga,* etc.) of any knower whatsoever in the manner of 'I', i.e. in the manner of *śaktis* identical with Himself. Whoever may be the knower (i.e. the limited, empirical experient), he too, because of his appearing as a knower, is the Self itself. So he relies on such limited *śaktis* (i.e. *kāla, rāga*, etc.) and through these (i.e. limited *kāla, rāga*, etc.) he experiences the state of the knower (*vedaka*) and knowables (objects) as (totally) different. Through *rāga* (passionate desire) etc., only He (Śiva) has been reduced to the status of a *paśu* (an empirical individual) etc. So *rāga* etc. assume, according to the principle stated previously, the position of the inciter (lit., the causer) of Śiva to regard in a limited way those states which otherwise He regards as His *śaktis*.

Therefore, the second causative verb (*ṇic*) having come into operation, those (i.e. *rāga, kāla*, etc.) becoming the sole cause of Śiva being designated as *jīva* (empirical individual) are spoken of as *dhāraṇā*. Even if a causative form of a verb is in operation, the connexion with the meaning of the root of the verb is never lost (*prakṛtyarthānvayānapāyo*), so in this case also, the causative force of the root *dhṛ* can be applied only to that which has *prakāśa* (i.e. is conscious) i.e., it can be applied to *rāga, vidyā, kalā* because they are *śaktis* as they, being conscious are *dhriyamāṇa* i.e. can be caused to operate and they in their own turn become operators.

As has been said by myself in Śivadṛṣṭyālocana[1] (a commentary on Śiva Dṛṣṭi):

"He alone can be impelled who has the competence for being impelled." Bhartṛhari has also said (in Vākyapadīya):

"In the case of one who has not yet commenced to act (but has the capacity to act), verbs with reference to question (*pṛcchā*) etc. are used in the imperative form (*loṭ*) when a direction or command is to be given (*praiṣe*). But when a direction or command is to be given to one who has commenced to act, then it is a matter of the use of the causative form (*ṇic*)."

What is known as *kañcuka* (covering) in other Śāstras has been designated as '*dhāraṇā*'. As has been said in Tantrasāra:

"*Vidyā, māyā, niyati* etc., use their own states as bonds for the *paśu* (the limited, empirical individual). Therefore, they have to be purified with effort." ('To be purified' means 'to unite with *anuttara* by *anusandhāna* and to dissolve in it.') Somānanda has explained the word '*dhāraṇā*' in the sense of limbs or constituents from another point of view (viz. the *advaita* or nondualistic point of view). In his commentary, he means to say that in the case of limited empirical individual (*parapakṣa*), all states like *rāga*, *kalā, vidyā* should be taken as objective (*dṛśyatva*) with reference to the Self.

Such is his particular manner of interpretation: "He who does not know fully the standpoint of the supreme experient (*svapakṣa*)[3] and that of the limited, empirical individual (*parapakṣa*) himself sinks in the ocean of doubts. How can he enable others to cross it?"

The letters from '*śa*' to '*kṣa*' denote the group of five categories viz. Mahāmāyā, Śuddhavidyā, Īśvara, Sadāśiva and Śakti. Above the category of *māyā*, and below the category of Śuddhavidyā, there must be another category as the abode of the Vijñānākalas. As has been said "Above *māyā* and below Śuddhavidyā are the Vijñānakevalas." If Mahāmāyā is not accepted as a category (lit. in the absence of the category of Mahāmāyā), then the abode of *pralayakevalis* being in *māyā* category, and that of the Vidyeśvaras in Śuddhavidyā, which would be the abode of the Vijñānākalas? Therefore, it has been declared in Pūrvaśāstra (i.e. Mālinīvijayottara) that the Vijñānākalas have only one *mala* (limitation), for though they are below the stage of Śuddhavidyā, there does not appear in them the limitation (*mala*) known as *māyīya*, because in their case, the display of different objects caused by differentiation does not occur. So they have only *āṇava mala* which is ignorance (of one's essential nature). They alone being enlightened through the grace of Śuddhavidyā become entitled to the status of Mantra, Mantreśvara and Mantramaheśvara. In Mālinīvijaya itself (*tatraiva*) it is said, Anantabhaṭṭāraka enlightened (lit. awakened) the limited experients, viz., the eight Rudras (*jīvān*) who have attained the status of Vijñānākala (p. 3. v. 19),
and also :

"Having united them to Śuddhavidyā, Īśvara and Sadāśiva, he (Anantabhaṭṭāraka) similarly manifested seven crores of Mantras together with their regions of administration."

In some Śāstras (other than Trika) Mahāmāyā, on the assumption of the absence of *mala* (limitation) pertaining to difference i.e., absence of *māyīya* and *kārma mala*, is accepted as the last part of Śuddhavidyā category. At some places, because of its being an impediment in the form of *āṇava-mala* which is ignorance of the essential Self, the state is considered to be the last or extreme end of *māyā*, just as in some Śāstras, the *rāga* category is supposed to be adhering to the empirical individual, therefore, it is not considered separately, just as here itself, *niyati* and *kāla* are not described separately (from *rāga* and *kalā*) in the Trika Āgama. According to this view, the five *brahmas* as denoted by *śa, ṣa, sa, ha* and *kṣa* are Śuddhavidyā, Īśvara, Sadāśiva, Śakti and Anāśrita Śiva, respectively. This will be clarified later. They are known as '*brahma*' because the root '*bṛh*' from which the word '*brahma*' is derived means 'to grow great' and 'to make grow'. These categories are called '*brahma*' firstly because they transcend difference (*bhedasamuttīrṇatvāt*) (from the point of view of *bṛhatva* 'growing great') and secondly because they bring about the production of the universe of differentiation (*saṃsāra-sūtikartṛtvāt*) from the point of view of *bṛṃhakatva*—'making grow'). These thirty-four categories having been settled according to the procedure of the Śāstra resort to '*a*' only, as that is the initial and primal letter.

In this connection, this is what is to be examined. Firstly there is the Śiva *tattva* assigned to the '*a*' class (i.e. '*a*' to *visarga*), then there are the five elements (in *kavarga*) etc., and finally there is '*śakti*' (assigned to '*kṣa*'). What is this particular order in the descent of the mantras pertaining to *sṛṣṭi, saṃhāra* and *sthiti*?[3] In all the Śāstras e.g. in Mālinīvijayottara, Siddhātantra, Svacchanda Tantra, the arrangement of letters denoting the various *tattvas* or categories of existence from '*kṣa*' upto '*a*', from the *tattvas*—the earth (*pṛthivī*) upto Śiva is given in the same manner.

It is said in Mālinī-Vijayottara:

"The initial one i.e. *pṛthivī aṇḍa* is pervaded by *dhārikā*;[4] in that, only one *tattva* i.e. *pṛthivī* (earth) is acknowledged. While considering the succession of *varṇa** (letters), *pada* (word), and *mantra*, it is only *kṣa varṇa, kṣa pada*, and *kṣa mantra* that should be regarded separately in succession." (M.V. II, 50).

In the same book (i.e. in the same Mālinīvijayottara Tantra) according to Mālinī in which there is a mixed arrangement of the vowels and the consonants consisting of the letters '*pha*' etc., the arrangement of the categories earth (*pṛthivī*) etc. begins with the

(*Continued on page* 104)

*In this system, any *varṇa* or letter is called *arṇa* or mantra, for soteriologically, it protects one who reflects on it (*mananāttrāyate*).

CHART 1

THE VARIOUS AṆḌA OR ELLIPSES CONTAINED IN ANUTTARA

Anuttara is all-pervasive. The name of the *kalā* is Avakāśadā *kalā* according to Trika. In other Saivāgamas it is called Śāntyatīta-*kalā*. Its presiding deity is Anuttara itself. It is beyond all the *tattvas*, but contains all the *tattvas* in itself. It is beyond all the *mala* or limitations, but comprehends all the *malas*. Its state is one of *abheda* or non-difference, and it is beyond all the *adhvas*.

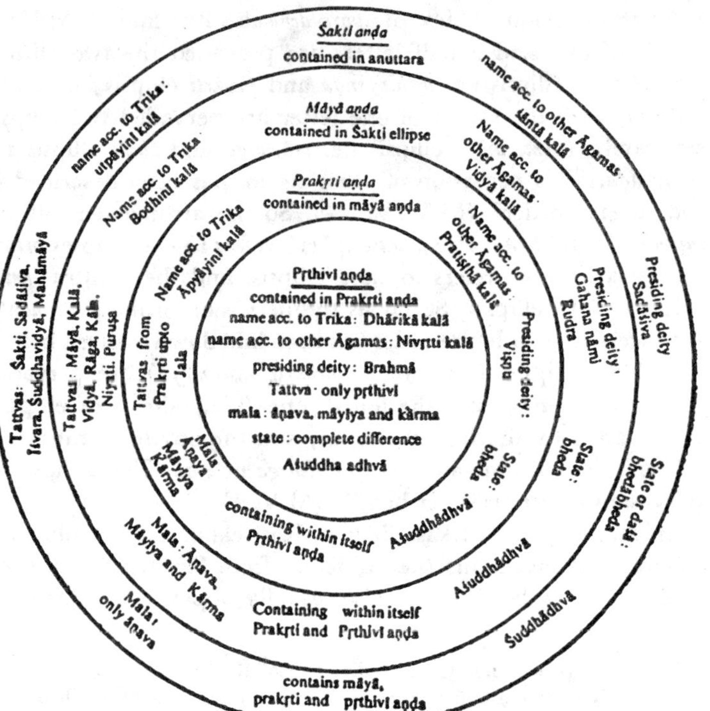

last letter '*pha*'. In *Mātṛkā*, in which there is no mixed arrangement of the vowels and the consonants and though in it the assignment of the *tattvas* to various letters is different, there is the same assignment of the category earth (*pṛthivī*) to the last letter in both. The relevant verse regarding Mālinī* is as follows:

"The earth category has been mentioned in '*pha*' and from '*da*' up to '*jha*' i.e., from water up to *pradhāna* or *prakṛti*, one should mark twenty-three categories successively" (M.V. IV, 15).

Again in the same book, it is said according to the three *vidyās*.[5] There is the *mantra* of one letter (i.e. *auṃ*) in Śiva *tattva* (*niṣkale*) and the other two, viz., one of three letters i.e. *aghore* and the other of one letter i.e. *hrīṃ* (*tryarṇaikārṇadvayam*) are in the other two (*dvaye*) i.e., in Śakti and Sadāśiva" (M.V. IV, 19).

According to *parāparā devī*, '*auṃ*' refers to Śiva *tattva*, and '*aghore*' refers to Śakti *tattva*. It is in this way that the order of the successive *tattvas* has been fixed.[6]

From the point of view of *aparā devī* also it is said: "With the *mantra* of one and a half letters are pervaded the two ellipses (viz. *pṛthivī* ellipsis i.e. *pṛthivyaṇḍa* and *prakṛti* ellipsis i.e., *prakṛtyaṇḍa*), with the *mantra* of one letter are pervaded two ellipses separately (viz., *māyā* ellipsis i.e. *māyāṇḍa* and *śakti* ellipsis i.e. *śaktyaṇḍa*. This pervasion of *apara mantra* has been described in the reverse order[7] (M.V.IV, 24), So the arrangement of the *tattvas* is as follows. The *mantra* '*phaṭ*' refers to two ellipses *pṛthivī* and *prakṛti*, '*huṃ*' refers to *māyā* ellipsis, and the mantra '*hrīṃ*' refers to *śakti* ellipsis. So far as the pervasion of the *para mantra* is concerned, a different order has been laid down as given below:

"Three ellipses (viz. *pṛthivī*, *prakṛti* and *māyā*) are pervaded by the phoneme, '*sa*', the fourth one (viz., the *śakti* ellipsis) is pervaded by the trident i.e., *au*, and the one that transcends all, viz., Śiva is indicated by the *visarga* i.e., *aḥ*. This is how the pervasion of *para* is described.[8]" (M.V. IV, 25).

In the *mantras* Mātṛkāsadbhāva, Ratiśekhara, and Kuleśvara, different arrangements (i.e., different from Parātrīśikā) also are noticed.[9] In other Tantras also, usually opposite arrangements

*The arrangement of letters according to Mālinī is the following:
n ṛ ṝ ḷ ḹ th c dh i ṇ u ū b k kh g gh ṅ ī a v bh y ḍ ḍh ṭh jh ñ j r ṭ p ch l ā s aḥ h ṣ kṣ m ś aṃ t e ai o au d ph.

are given in many ways. But in this i.e. Parātrīśikā, an altogether different arrangement is noticed. So to one proficient in Āgama, this appears as destructive of one's own principles, as sometimes a bangle of glass or shells gets shattered by the clash of its own components. Nor can it be merely conventional so that it could be considered to be opposite even if determined in varied ways according to the fabrications of a man's fancy, as for instance, the southerners designate 'boiled rice' with the word '*caura*' and the inhabitants of Sindha designate 'thief' with the same word, and 'boiled rice', they designate with the word '*krūra*'. The Kāshmīris, however, indicate with that word (i.e. *krūra*) husked barley, wheat and rice. If it is to be treated as conventional, it cannot be definitely determined because of its being unsettled, because of its being unconcerned with the highest truth and because of its uselessness concerning the relation between that which is to be purified and the purifier (*śodhya-śodhaka-bhāva*). If it is said that even a conventional word derives its existence from the Will of God, that it cannot be anything whatsoever without the Will of the Highest Lord, and that it is well known that convention comes forth by the will of God, for peace is gained by the *āpyāyana*[10] ceremony that is performed for the welfare and prosperity (of a particular individual) and that ceremony depends entirely on the name, word, script etc., which are entirely conventional, then my reply is that everything can be acquired only by one conventional word (for all countries, all times and all men), why should there be the necessity to resort to other conventions (for different countries, times etc.)? If one has to depend on convention only, then will arise the problem of endless conventions coming down from one's own Śāstra, from another Śāstra, popular conventions, conventions of particular assemblies, conventions coming down from a host of teachers, convention particular for each different person and so on. This problem will also have to be examined. It may be said that there is no use going into these details. 'The relation between the purifier and that which is to be purified will be the same in any case and this is enough to achieve our object'; this also uttered by and heard from illiterate people is indeed becoming to themselves.

If it is said that God's will is perfect, it is not open to dis-

(*Continued on page* 108)

CHART 2A

THE IDENTITY OF THE ORIGINAL SOURCE (BIMBA) AND ITS REFLECTION (PRATIBIMBA)

ka	Pṛthivī
kha	Jala
ga	Agni
gha	Vāyu
ṅa	Ākāśa
ca	Gandha
cha	Rasa
ja	Rūpa
jha	Sparśa
ña	Śabda
ṭa	Upastha
ṭha	Pāyu
ḍa	Pāda
ḍha	Pāṇi
ṇa	Vāk
ta	Ghrāṇa
tha	Rasanā
da	Cakṣu
dha	Tvacā
na	Śrotra
pa	Manas
pha	Ahaṃkāra
ba	Buddhi
bha	Prakṛti
ma	Puruṣa
ya	Rāga
ra	Vidyā
la	Kalā
va	Māyā
śa	Mahāmāyā
ṣa	Śuddhavidyā
sa	Īśvara
ha	Sadāśiva
kṣa	Śakti

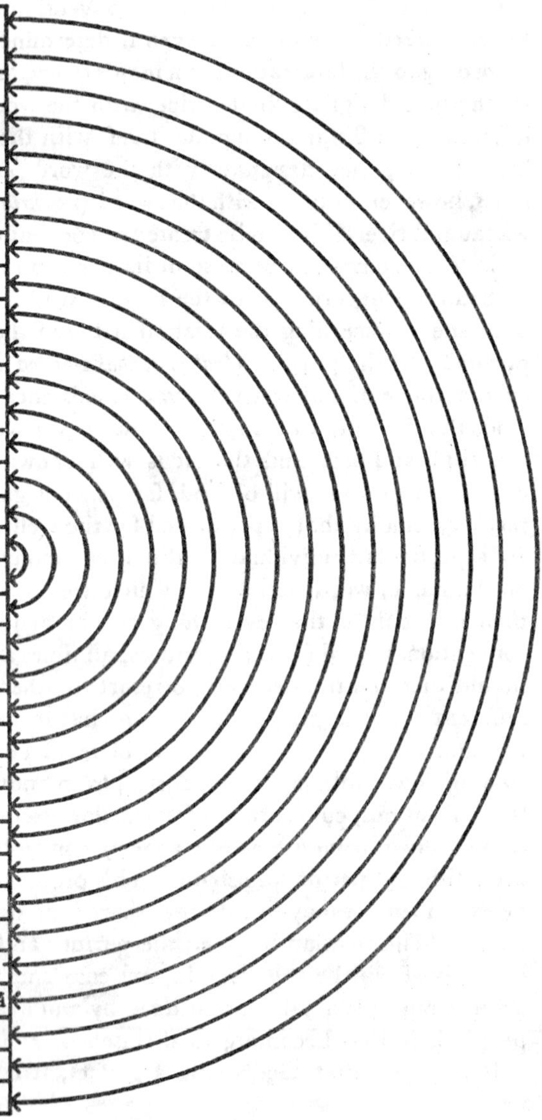

CHART 2B

THE TRANSPOSITION OF THE TATTVAS (CATEGORIES OF EXISTENCE) IN REFLECTION (PRATIBIMBA)

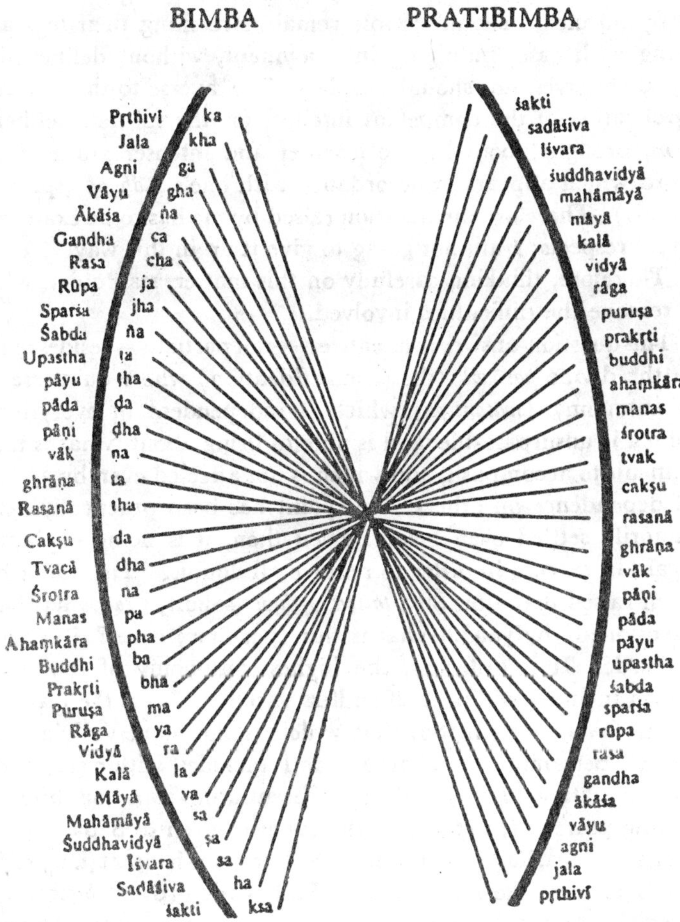

cussion, then enough of useless efforts like reading and concentrating on books, exposition, discussion etc. This heavy burden should certainly be abandoned. One should then sit quietly. God's will alone would save one who is to be saved. It is His merciful will that makes one depend on such thought.

By no means should people remain stretching their legs and lying with ease, indulging in enjoyment, without deliberating for themselves, nor should people sit idle, averse to the constant application of the competent intellect for the subtlest deliberation, brought about by the intenser and intenser grace of the Lord which appears in accordance with one's *sādhanā* (spiritual praxis). Therefore the question raised by me has to be examined in all respects; I am not going to give it up in this way.

Therefore, thinking carefully on this matter, stay quiet, while I remove the difficulties involved.

This question-answer in its entirety—not partially—resides really in the divine *parāvāk* (the cosmic Ideation) whose quintessence is autonomy (*svātantrya*) which is independent of everything, which is unsurpassable and is able to bring about what is most difficult to accomplish, and which is not affected even by an iota of dependence on others. This point has been practically satisfactorily settled even before. Even then, it is being explained again in extenso in order to remove all doubts. The doubt has been raised that after Śiva *tattva*, *pṛthivī* (solidity) *tattva* has been mentioned (by you). What is this (peculiar) order? I say it is no order. It is orderless, the highest autonomy of the Lord which includes within itself endless variety. This is the teaching of the Trika system. So, that which is the highest divine Ens (*para*) pertaining to Bhairava and includes within itself the differentiating (*apara*) and the differentiating-cum-non-differentiating powers, (*parāpara*) abides superior even to Sadāśiva and Anāśrita Śiva, having made even the latter one her seat (i.e. presiding over even the latter one). (*Parā* is the orb or *bimba*, and everything else is the *pratibimba* i.e. reflected or represented form.)

For instance Pūrvaśāstra i.e. Mālinīvijaya at first refers to Sadāśiva in the following words: "Sadāśiva who is the gigantic departed one, smiling and both conscious and unconscious should be meditated upon as the seat of *parā* or the Supreme divine Śakti" (M.V. VIII, 68), and concludes by saying that Sadāśiva who has entered the *nādānta*[12] state is her seat, and then having said that "all this is her seat," declares: "From his (i.e. Sadāśiva's) navel rises the trident of Śakti (divine Energy) with three prongs which should be meditated upon" (M.V. VIII 69). The three prongs referred to are "Śakti, Vyāpinī, and Samanā". There also (i.e. higher above the Śaktis), the Supreme abode of *unmanā* i.e. the state of *ūrdhvakuṇḍalinī*, in the form of three white lotuses has been described, in the words "this is the most distinct seat" (M.V., p. 48, v. 70). So far as the three lotuses on the prongs of the trident are concerned, they form the seats of the goddesses (*parā-paśyantī*, *parā-madhyamā*, and *parā vaikharī*).* Though this is known as supreme *paśyantī* and is the ultimate limit of *jñānaśakti* known as *nāda* (i.e. as the state of Sadāśiva), yet this has only to be passed over, for the state of Parā is higher than this (see the picture introducing the Parātriśika Vivaraṇa). As has been said in Śivadṛṣṭi: "What according to us is *jñānaśakti* and is really the level of *parā-paśyantī* as expressive of Sadāśiva state is to the duffers, the grammarian's the highest state."[13]

The *buddhi* that is introverted towards the inner spiritual Self is the level of *parā-paśyantī*. Its presiding deity is Rudra i.e. Para-(supreme) Sadāśiva. The *parā-paśyantī* comes to an end in *jñāna-śakti* which is a state of Para-Sadāśiva, and this state of Para-Sadāśiva is the Śakti of Anāśrita-Śiva.

The presiding deities of *manas* and *ahaṃkāra* introverted towards the Self are respectively Para-Brahmā and Para-Viṣṇu. Their field of activity is limited respectively to *parā-vaikharī* and *parā madhyamā*. Therefore, their final resting abode (*pratiṣṭhā-bhūḥ*) is the *kriyāśakti* of Para-Īśvara and Para-Sadāśiva.[14] This is proved by Āgama and supported by personal experience.

Therefore, over *parā-paśyantī* is the stage of goddess *parā* where everything appears and is also apprehended as identical with Herself.

---

*In Śaiva philosophy, there is the *bimba-pratibimbavāda* i.e. the principle that the main factors that exist in the lower sphere have their original source in the higher sphere. The *paśyantī*, *madhyamā*, *vaikharī* that exist in manifestation have their original forms at the higher level of *parā*. Therefore, the original forms of these at the higher level are called *parā paśyantī*, *parā madhyamā* and *parā vaikharī*.

They are seated in the following order: The Parā is seated on the middle lotus, the Parāparā on the right and the Aparā on the left.

Though in the stage of Śuddhavidyā and also of Māyā or the state of *pralayākala*, *bhāsanā* (i.e., the existence of *prakāśa* and *vimarśa*) abides in identity, yet in that stage, the apprehension of 'this' (i.e. objectivity) is different. In Śuddhavidyā, the entire multitude of subjects and objects is reflected in the sole 'I'. It is apprehended only as fully dominated by the I-consciousness, such as "*I am this*".

Thus both of these (*etat ubhayam* i.e. both *I* and *this*) being reflected in the common substratum of the supreme consciousness appear as identical and so are said to have a common substratum (*sāmānādhikaraṇyam*).

Therefore all existents share the *parāparā* state (i.e. the state of identity in diversity) in the stage of Īśvara, and in the stage of Māyā (and also of *pralayākala*) they share the state of *aparā* (i.e. the state of differentiation).

One should not understand from this that the Īśvara state and Māyā state are themselves *parāparā* and *aparā*. (It is only their *prameyas* or objects at their stage that are the *parāparā* and *aparā* states.) Therefore, there is no room for doubting that what the Āgama (viz. Rudrayāmala) has affirmed is contrary to what the venerable Utpaladeva has said about *parāparā* with reference to Īśvara.

In the case of Mantramaheśvara, the I-feeling though having knowledge as its highest truth, is however, different from the I-feeling of Īśvara and Śuddhavidyā which is *aparā* i.e. of a lower order. My experience (*saṃvit*) tells me that 'this' i.e. the I-feeling of Īśvara and Śuddhavidyā is only *this* i.e. of a lower order than the I-feeling of Sadāśiva, Śakti and Śiva.

The *vijñānākalas*, however, have only an awareness of 'I' which though of the order of knowledge (*bodhaikaparamārthe api rūpeṇa*) is devoid of the experience of 'this' i.e. objectivity. Because of their non-awareness of objective reality, they have only an awareness of 'I' and, therefore, they are in the category of *aprabuddha* i.e. unawakened. The *pralayakevalis* are non-aware of both 'I' and 'this'. Therefore they are decidedly unawakened.

In the stage of *pralayakevali* and *śūnyapramātā* (*māyāpade*—which is the abode of *śūnyapramātā*) though by means of the light of indeterminate consciousness (*nirvikalpakatābhāsena*), there is an underlying sensibility of that sort (i.e. indeterminate consciousness), which is the very life (of determinate consciousness), though they owe their very existence to the grace of the indeterminate consciousness only and cannot be in any way separate from it,[15] yet the later dealing and judgement of such experients (i.e. when they have risen from the state of the experience of the void) are determined by consciousness of difference and are only of the nature of determinate consciousness (*vikalpātmaiva*), as for example, "This is body etc., I am only I, i.e. the one who is the knower, this is a jar, what is 'this' is only an object of knowledge etc.".

In the case of the condition of such an experient (i.e. *pralayākala* or *śūnyapramātā*), it is only the indeterminate consciousness that has the capacity of bringing about a consciousness of that sort (*tasyaiva avikalpasaṃvidātmanaḥ tathā sāmarthyaṃ*). For though none other than the *nirvikalpa* one is known to be the cause of that kind of consciousness (i.e. the determinate consciousness), even if any other cause is supposed to be its origin, it will ultimately end only in that kind of undivided universal consciousness (i.e. *nirvikalpaka* or indeterminate I-consciousness). It is because of this capacity of the indeterminate I-consciousness that its power of bringing about endless variety (in manifestation) is proved to be invariable.

In the being of this indeterminate I-consciousness, its sovereignty of the creativity never ceases. In *vaikhari* stage or in *madhyamā* stage in which there is subtle *māyiya* objectivity (i.e. where there is a subtle difference through the force of *māyā*), this kind of apprehension of difference (*bheda-vimarśa*) is not possible if it is completely excluded from the indeterminate I-consciousness (*bhāsanātireki*).

In the supreme consciousness, however, as is the *prakāśa* so is the *vimarśa* for carrying it out in practice. Therefore in that, all things appear completely identical with consciousness, just as water is in water, or flame is in flame, not simply like a reflected image. Whenever this supreme goddess (*parā*) is described for the purpose of teaching, she is brought within the sphere of cognizance only by being considered from an inferior point of view.

Similarly Bhairava who is of the nature of light (i.e. spiritual light of consciousness) is self-proved, beginningless, primal, the ultimate in all respects, and present in everything. What else is to be said regarding Him?* He displays His Light identically (*svaprakāśam prakāśayati*) in the expansion of all the categories of existence (e.g. the 36 *tattvas*), all the objective phenomena (*bhāvas*), and views them all as Himself (*tathaiva ca vimarśati*) in His self-delight (*camatkāratve*) which never vanishes (*anapeta*). That which is this perception in that way (i.e. as identical with Himself), makes His self-revelation (*bhāsana*) evident in lakhs, crores, ten crores (*arbuda*), ten *arbudas*[16] of endless future (*bhāvi*) manifestations and absorptions to be brought about by *māyā* and thus he appears in those very forms (*tathārūpaṃ eva bhavati*).

Even while appearing in various forms, if he had not considered the initial and intervening, i.e. the rise and expansion of objectivity as being based only on *prakāśa,* then the possibility of the doubt regarding the deviation of the initial (i.e. the Bhairava consciousness) and the succeeding state (i.e. the expansion or dissolution of objectivity) could not have been removed, and consequently the entities of the world would have been unknown, owing to which there would have been the disruption of full identity and non-establishment of the real state of Supreme Bhairava. This would have led to the breach of the close adherence of the lower *paśyantī vāṇī* etc. which depend on Bhairava. So the venerable *parā,* owing to the continuation of such states would remain *parā* only in name. If Bhairava consciousness or *prakāśa* had by its very nature not taken to such consideration, then the would-be objective universe would neither have appeared, nor would have expanded. "Let the multitude of objects not be based on a solid foundation; let it remain imperfect; down with this talk of non-difference; let Bhairava as the foundational support of everything remain unproved; let the so-called supremacy of *parā* bear the stain of difference", all such talk is not proper.

So this alone is possible and appears appropriate also that the light of Bhairava, at the very first stage of external manifestation, having its objective the earth category, through *vimarśa-śakti* continues to move towards earth only in its march of descent.

*Bhairava is primal, because He is the Source of everything. He is the ultimate, because everything finally rests in Him. He is present in everything, because it is His energy that is manifest in everything.

Completeness of every *tattva according to* the theory that every *tattva* is an epitome:

Thus that very last *tattva*, viz *pṛthivī* (earth) while maintaining its character as earth (*sa hi caramo bhāgaḥ tathātāvat svātmarūpaṃ bibhrat*) and holding within itself all the innumerable earlier *tattvas* (e.g., water—*jala*, fire—*agni*, etc.) as inseparable from itself, appearing in that form (*bhāsamāno*) and viewed in that aspect (*vimṛśyamānaḥ*) is complete in itself. Its precedent *tattva* also (i.e. *jala* or water) having the posterior *tattva* (i.e. *pṛthivī* or earth) as its background, being identical with the appearance and perceptibility present in the earth category (*vṛtta-pūrvaparipūrṇābhāsā-sāravimarśa-tādātmyāt*) and not renouncing the completeness of its posterior *tattva* (i.e. the *pṛthivī tattva*) inevitably brings within its compass the fulness of all the preceding *tattvas* also (*svayaṃ ca svarūpanāntariya katāhaṭhakṛṣṭasvapūrva-pūrvatarādi bhāgantarā-bhogo*) and appearing and being carefully considered in that way is integral in the same way (as the *pṛthivītattva*). Thus one by one, all the preceding *tattvas* (*agni*—fire, etc.) not being separated from their posterior two or three ones, including within themselves the delightful existence of their antecedent *tattvas* in accordance with the non-divergence from the nature of Bhairava which has accrued to them, are perfectly integral. Thus that category becomes a form very proximate to its chosen self-luminous Bhairava and that form becoming a self-chosen abode of rest is designated Bhairava. You, who are proficient in thinking of Bhairava, become engrossed in meditating on Him. An undivided sight from a distance of a wilderness without limitation of associated objects like pond, mountain, tree etc. or even with these limitations (*tadvatyapi*) providing a wholeness of vision offers a well-known means of entree into Bhairava-consciousness. As Vijñānabhairava puts it: "One should cast one's gaze on a region in which there are no trees, or mountain, or even wall. His mental state being without any support will then dissolve and the fluctuations of his mind will cease." (V. Bhairava, verse 60). Otherwise if there is partial perception, then if the perception beginning with the first part of the same is only of parts (i.e., is not an integral perception), then what is the difference of Bhairava-consciousness from the other lower states of consciousness which are full of difference and are avowedly fragmentary? The difference lies in the fact that Bhairava-consciousness expressing as it does the delight of the unity of endless variety of existence is considered to be integral as compared with other states of consciousness which are fragmentary. Those who have received proper training and have penetrated into the divine consciousness know this difference themselves. If the heart-lotus of some animal-like men has not blown under the ray of grace falling from the highest Lord, then hundreds of words of mine, even though their hearts be pierced with sharp needle-like words can neither make the heart-lotus blow nor make it accomplish (the objective). On a (thing like) jar also, one similarly casts an integral look. In this case also, the indeterminate consciousness instantly (*jhagiti*) takes in a view of the jar as a whole (not of its constituent parts), and then forms all kinds of determinate ideas about it and they starting from the bearest ultimate part enter into the interior and the interiormost aspect and finally dissolve again in the indeterminate state. Therefore, there is no use in referring to other similar cases. Similarly in this matter also, the Śiva principle is inherent in all cases (i.e. even in the earth category) as an indeterminate reality, and having the elegant autonomy of generating determinate states is, though itself beginningless, decidedly the prius of all reality. There is no difference of opinion in this matter. This Śiva principle can be considered complete only if it abides also in the ultimate earth category. So also, the consciousness of earth (*dharā-saṃvit*) can display it as identical with central Reality in spite of its appearance as an object only when it is able to display the awareness of all the categories as inherent in the earth category.

[The completeness of *pṛthivī tattva* according to *vamana-yukti* i.e. the principle of projection.]

It is the essential nature of Śiva which is the real state of the earth category (*svarūpa-satattvaṃ ca asyāḥ avasthānaṃ dharāyāḥ*). How? By the process of projecting downwards (*adhara-vṛttitayā*) i.e. by the process of Śiva's projecting His manifestation down to the earth (*vamanayuktyā*). [The process of downward projection i.e. *vamanayukti* is described in the following words.]

Śiva *tattva* expands into Śakti *tattva* (*paripūrṇa prasara*). By His autonomy is effected a state (i.e. the state of Sadāśiva) in which the sense of non-difference (with manifestation) is not so fully established (as in Śiva *tattva*) (*tatsvātantrya klṛpta aprarūḍha-abheda*); with this as the preceding *tattva* comes into being a *tattva* in which the appearance of difference (i.e., the appearance of manifestation) is homogeneous with the *tattva* (i.e. the state of Īśvara) (*tatpūrvaka-eka-rasabheda*) and there is the *tattva śuddha-vidyā* in which there is the appearance of difference (*bhedāvabhāsa*) (which, however, is dominated by I-consciousness); again through His power, there comes into being a state in which the autonomy of consciousness is gradually contracting, i.e. Māyā (*tattva, vaśodita saṅkucāt-citsvātantrya-sattāmaya*); then appears the experient dominated by *māyā* (*māyā-grāhaka* or *māyā-pramātā*) of which the group of five i.e., the group of the five *kañcukas* or coverings is his sphere of experience (*tadgrāhyacakra*), then comes into being undifferentiated *pradhāna* or *prakṛti* (*avibhedātmaka pradhāna* i.e. *prakṛti* in the state of equipoise of the three constituents), then its evolute *buddhi tattva* (*dhitattva*) and the evolute of *buddhi tattva*, viz. *ahaṃkāra* (the I-making principle) which is the origin of *manas*, the organs of sense (*jñānendriyas*) and the organs of action (*karmendriyas*) and the *tanmātras* or the primary elements of perception (*tanmūlakaraṇa-pūrvaka tanmātra*) which expand into the gross elements, viz. ether, water, etc., and finally into *dharā* or earth. (Thus the real state of the earth category is the essential nature of Śiva.)

[The *paripūrṇatā* or completeness of *pṛthivī* (earth category according to *grasana-yukti* or the process of dissolution.]

As long as the earth-category remains by *ākṣepa* i.e. (*ākṣepeṇaiva*) by the process of *grasana* or gradual dissolution in the previous categories, it indicates the own-being (*svarūpa*) of Śiva. As it points to the (five) *tanmātras* by means of the five objects of sense, so they being suggested by it, in order to substantiate their own form (*nijasvarūpopaklṛptaye*) point to their earlier well-established origins (*samākṣiptaprāktanaprātiṣṭhika-mūla*) which again have a series of uninterrupted preceding origins of their own (*antaraparamparānubandhisvakapūrvaka-mūlāni*). It is not at all right to say that what is accepted as a *material cause* does not continue in its effect. It may be said in certain cases that the instrumental causes etc. are somehow not connected with the effect (but this cannot be said with regard to the material cause). This has been discussed by me threadbare elsewhere in another treatise dealing with causation. A discussion of it here will only disturb the smooth progress of the present topic (*prakṛta-vighātakam*). Therefore, it is not being discussed in detail here.

[The following describes the series of the categories of existence by *grasana-yukti* i.e. by means of the order of absorption into Śiva.]

Thus (according to the reverse order), it is at first the earth which has completeness. Then it is water which also having absorbed within itself the characteristics of all the *tattvas* appears and is apprehended in completeness. It having absorbed within itself the wondrous, *prakāśa-vimarśa* present in the earth category (*tadbhāsāvimarśa-camatkāraṃ antaḥkṛtya*) becomes complete by the transmission of the *saṃskāra* (residual traces) of the completeness of the earth category. Finally, the earth itself is but the integral divine consciousness i.e. the very Self of Śiva. Thus even a limited space (*pradeśamātram api*) contains the entire form of Brahman. The Śāstras (scriptural texts) have declared it as their finding that, "Each *tattva* (category of existence) has the characteristics of all the thirty-six *tattvas*." Such is also the teaching of Spanda Śāstra (as in the following verse): "When the *yogī* wishing to see all objects by pervading them all i.e., infusing them all with the light of his consciousness, then what is the use of saying much, he will experience for himself (the splendour of that vision)". (Sp.K. III. 11). One should lay this to one's heart. By the last quarter of this verse, the same fact has been indicated. So what else is to be said?

(Establishment of the dependence of all the *tattvas* on Śiva-tattva by logical argument.)

When a thing cannot exist without a particular characteristic, then that particular characteristic is its very nature (*svarūpa*), just as being a *śiśama* (*śiṃśipā*) means having the nature of tree (i.e. there cannot be a *śiṃśipā* without its being a tree). When the expansion of the fixed order of things is set aside through the autonomy of the supreme Lord, then a thing may happen even without that which is its nature. The succeeding *tattvas*, earth, etc. cannot come into existence without the preceding *tattvas*, viz. water etc. Therefore, they i.e. the preceding *tattvas* are the characteristics of the succeeding. The category of earth cannot exist without the category of water, for it is in the medium of firm support (*dhṛti*) only that solidity is found (and there is solidity in earth because of the presence of water).[18] In this way, in a regular order, the (five) gross elements (*bhūtāni*) cannot exist without the five *tanmātras*. These senses also cannot exist without the inner psychic apparatus consisting of *buddhi*, the ascertaining intellect, *ahaṃkāra*, the I-consciousness and *manas* (the idea and image making faculty). All these cannot exist without the primal, undifferentiated, compact subtle root-cause i.e. *prakṛti*. How can *prakṛti* exist without the limited experient i.e. Puruṣa (*saṃvidātmakaṃ ca antareṇa*) who is fettered by the snare of time (*kāla*), limited efficacy etc. (*kalādi*) which are the characteristics of experience (*saṃvidātmakaṃ*) which he has imposed upon himself only by his own limitation (*saṅkocavaśādeva ca svātmārohita*). How can there be limitation of the unlimited consciousness (i.e. how can there be a limited *puruṣa*) without the autonomy (of the Divine) which is the cause of that limitation and of which *māyā* is another name (i.e. this limitation comes about by *māyāśakti* which is only another name for the *svātantrya* or autonomy of the Divine)? This state of limitation by the divine autonomy in the form of *māyā* does not come about without the slightly unlimited reality (*iṣat-asaṅkucita* i.e. *śuddha-vidyā*), unlimited reality (*asaṅkucita* i.e. Īśvara), slightly expanding (*iṣad-vikāsi* i.e. Sadāśiva) and fully expanded reality (*vikasvara-rūpam* i.e. Śakti), standing as it does in opposition to the gradually proportionate shrinkage of that whose very essence is limitlessness (*asaṅkucitatā-sāratāratamyāpekṣi*). All these realities are simply nothing without Bhairava who is absolutely autonomous and the very quintessence of perfect Light. This regular order of the categories is admitted to be true according to one's own experience. Śruti (scriptural text) also says, where can the earth category which is inclusive of water be found without its solidity? (i.e. the solidity of the earth is due to adhesiveness and adhesiveness is not possible without liquid). So if we say that the earth has in it also its preceding category, the water, how does it perturb us? On the contrary, it will only be in support of the supreme consciousness (*parā saṃvit*) which is the perfect, omnifarious, revered Bhairava Himself.

The Form of Time in the Bimba area of Parā

On the occasion of coming into existence of *parāparā* (supreme-cum-non supreme) *vāṇi* which is *paśyanti* and *aparā* (non-supreme) which is *vaikharī*, in other words, on the occasion of future and past times, the entire corpus of Time appearing in the three forms (present, past and future) in accordance with the difference of the categories of existence (*tattvas*) which are slightly distinct (*iṣat-sphuṭa* in *paśyanti*), more distinct (*sphuṭatara* in *madhyamā*) and fully distinct (*sphuṭatama* in *vaikharī*) abides in the splendour of revered *parā* (the supreme transcendental consciousness) in the form appropriate to *parā*.[19] That which is to arise (i.e. the future *parāparā* state) and also that which is the last (*aparā* state) decidedly sparkles in the initial light (i.e. in the ever-present *parā*-state). Futurity is posited only with reference to *clear difference* that is to arise in what is undifferentiated. For instance 'The *kalki* (incarnation) will appear and will destroy those who are intent on vice'—if this statement referring to the future had not been experienced in an earlier present, then how could this statement be made in the Purāṇas? If it is said that in some previous creation, there was *kalki* who destroyed the wicked as described, then the question arises, 'Is the *kalki* referred to the same or another one? If it is said that he is another one, then how is one to know that he is really another one (lit. how will it be evident to consciousness?).' If it is the same *kalki*, why is there a difference in the time of his appearance? If it is said 'that he is not bound by time', how is it to be proved? If it is said that he is not bound by time because he, being the very nature of consciousness, is omnifarious (*citvād-viśvarūpatvāt*) then why is not the statement made by me, viz., that there is every thing in the venerable Bhairava who is invariably present on the tip of my tongue and in my heart, who is consciousness transcending the sphere of time, who is perpetually inseparable from the universal Energy, who is identical with the universally acknowledged hundreds of manifestations and absorptions which appear through the contraction and expansion of Energy exercised by His absolute autonomy and who is the supreme Lord, honourably accepted with open eyes, or why does not one describe it in an open-throated way after having ascertained the truth for oneself?

Therefore, this fact is perfectly established that so long as Śiva who is beginningless and endless, who is self-luminous, whose essence is autonomy which is integral and inherently independent, who enfolds within Himself the entire multitude of categories, whose highest truth is His own Self, who, because of His being eternally present, who, because of His being in harmony with everything, because of His conferring grace on all, abides as Bhairava beyond the sphere of time, in *parā* or supreme consciousness which would not tolerate even the very word of 'a particular state' (*avasthāśabda vyapadeśa-asahiṣṇau*), so long according to the doctrine of this Śāstra He abides in the form of total manifestation (*mahāsṛṣṭi*), not in a succession of particular limited manifestations. This is perfectly in harmony with the view of this Śāstra. Because of His enclosing all the categories one by one and the entire multitude of categories collectively in one hemispherical whole (*sampuṭikaraṇāt*), He abides in the manner of a hemispherical bowl (*saṃpuṭayoga*)—this is the tradition of our revered teachers. It will be said that 'beginning with the stage of *paśyanti*, there is the play of partial bondage (*pāśāṃśollāsaḥ*) on account of the commencement of difference. Therefore up to *paśyanti* the principle of the relationship of that which is to be purified and the purifier (*śodhya-śodhaka-bhāva*) is undeniable. As has been said:

"O virtuous one, beginning with the earth up to Sadāśiva, all the categories are to be known as usual being connected with production and destruction." (Sv.T. V, 548).

The Principle of Bimba-pratibimba

Paśyanti who has the nature of *parāparā śakti* (i.e. the nature of supreme cum non-supreme Energy) is like a mirror, constituting the energy of *parāśakti* herself, in which *parā* shines as a reflection. That form, which is always the same both in its original condition and reflection, is not called reflection, as the mere reference to the face (*mukhaparāmarśa-mātramiva*) is not reflection, because of its nature being merely the original face. That, however, which, though being the same, appears in another way, as for instance, the image of the face, in a reverse order, the front as the rear, the left as the right, this also and that also (i.e. as similar)—that alone is called reflection. That (i.e. the reflection) is only similar (to the original) not dissimilar. Therefore, *parā-bhaṭṭārikā* (the supreme consciousness) while casting in the transparent mirror of *parāparā* who has as her essence *paśyanti*, her reflection full of the categories, earth etc., in their separate forms (*apūrṇa-pṛthivyādi tattva-sāmagrī nirbharam*) and thus having a succession of separate categories (*tattattathāvidhoktakramaṃ*) is present even in the separate categories because of her enclosing inwardly within herself the natural, integral, absolutely true and invariable apprehension of '*ka*' and other letters (*antastathāvidha-sahajākṛtrima-pāramārthikānapāyikādi-parāmarśa-kroḍikāreṇaiva*) and displays those letters '*ka*' etc. in an integral way different from their nature.

Therefore, when *parā* casts, in the homogeneous, transparent mirror (of *parāparā* whose essential nature is *paśyanti*), the reflection of the categories which are apprehended as earth, water, etc. and are identical with herself, by bringing about differentiation by means of her autonomy (*tathollasadbhedasūtraṇayā*), then a reverse order of the categories—earth etc., is produced. That which in the supreme consciousness (i.e. *parā*) is *śakti tattva* becomes (by reflection) in *parāparā pṛthivitattva*, that which is *pṛthivi tattva* becomes *śakti-tattva*. This is the position of *pṛthivi* etc. in *parāparā* from '*kṣa*' upwards.

It has been declared by me many a time that there cannot be any change in Bhairava who is always integral, infinite, and autonomous, for there can never be any excess (or diminution) in consciousness (which is Bhairava).[20]

In the apprehension of the highest consciousness (*paramātmani parāmarśe*), all the categories of existence are only of the nature of consciousness (i.e. they are all Śiva). The supreme truth of that apprehension is the expansion of *śakti* from *ka* to *kṣa*. Therefore, in the highest consciousness (*parā*) there is complete absence of difference. In *parāparā*, there is non-difference in difference according to the principle of reflection. When the *parāparā* state which has the form of a garland of letters from *ka* to *kṣa* holds as reflection the categories existing in *parā* which is situated at a level higher than itself, then of the non-*māyiya*, inaudible (to the gross sense), supreme *k* to *kṣa* letters, the categories (*tattvāni*) acquire a reversal of order i.e., the upper becomes lower and the lower upper. The sense is that this happens through the power of the nature of the original (*bimba*) which is in the upper level, acquiring a lower level in reflection. So in the statement that 'there is *pṛthivī tattva* in *kṣa*,' there is no contradiction, from the point of view of that which is to be purified and the purifier. Because of the invariable continuity of the *parā* state, even in that i.e. even in *parāparā* state there is the continuous succession of *ka* and other letters (*kādivarṇasantānaḥ*).

Because of the appearance of *paśyantī* in the bosom of *parā*, because of the emergence of *madhyamā* state within *paśyantī*, and because of the propensity of *vaikharī* present in her (i.e. *madhyamā*) nature, *varṇa* (letter), *mantra* (word) and *pada* (sentence) successively arise, but these (not being purifier) remain at the level of *śodhya* (that which is to be purified).[21] However, let this matter alone. This is not germane to my thesis. I have conclusively discussed this point in Śrīpūrva (Mālinīvijaya) and Pañcikā.

Clarification of the State of Mālinī etc.

Though it has been declared that according to venerable Mālinī, there is a different arrangement of the letters etc., still let those who are devoted to the Lord (*parameśvaraḥ*) and whose knots of ignorance have been shorn asunder by the teaching of Trika, understand the subject under discussion after complete ascertainment. That which has been said viz., that there are divinities, in the highest consciousness or *parā śakti* surpassing the highest point[22] of *paśyantī* viz., the *śakti* of Anāśrita-Śiva, should not be forgotten by the noble selves.

Thus the state of *madhyamā śakti* (i.e. *parāmadhyamā*) is being described which abides in the area of *parāsaṃvit*, but has descended to the level of *parāparā*. *Madhyamā* (*parā madhyamā*) within Her own sphere of authority which is the sphere of *kriyā-śakti* of Īśvara being of the nature of containing clear objectivity (like jar, cloth, etc.) in a veiled form at every step superimposes the word in the object or referent, or object in the word.

If the referent is universal, its denotative word has to be universal. It is in such a state that the superimposition of each other which are of a swinging or oscillating nature (*lolibhāva*)* is pos-

---

**Lolibhāva* in this system is a technical word. This means that both word (*vācaka*) and its referent (*vācya*) are so intimately associated that the one signi-

sible, not otherwise. A piece of cloth even if it is shorter by three or four fingers than another piece of cloth cannot cover it completely. Word and its referent can become universal if they are associated together by nature. Vowels which are of the nature of germ (*bīja*) and consonants which are of the nature of their receptacle (*yoni*) denote Śiva and Śakti respectively and, therefore, the former is denotative and the latter is the denotated.

As has been said: "In this realm of letter, Śiva i.e. the group of vowels is said to be *bīja* i.e. germ or semen, and Śakti or the group of consonants is said to be the womb or receptacle". (M.V. III, 12). "The realm of letters has two aspects—(1) *bīja* and (2) *yoni*. Of these, the vowels are considered to be *bīja* (germ) and the consonants beginning with '*k*' are considered to be *yoni* (their receptacles)" (M.V. III, 10). Being thus described in Pūrva Śāstra (i.e. Mālinīvijaya), Śiva, not abandoning His nature of the experient, is the *vācaka* or the designator, and Śakti who abides in objectivity is the *vācya* or designated. In the (common) world of difference also, every *vācaka* or significant word is successful only when it is identified with the state of the subject in its two aspects of vowel (*pratipādaka*) and consonant (*pratipādya*). We shall explain presently that the coagulation of the germ (*bīja*) in the form of the vowel denotative of Śiva is the *yoni* or womb denotative of the consonant in the form of Śakti, for it is because of the *bīja*-letter or vowel that there is an expansion of the *yoni*-letter or consonant.

Therefore, if there is union of *bīja* (germ) in the form of vowels with the womb in the form of consonants, in other words, if there is the homogeneous union of Śiva and Śakti, then what a pleasant surprise; without any effort, without tilling and sowing will be generated both *bhoga* (enjoyment) and *mokṣa* (liberation).

The *bīja-varṇa* or vowel is adequate in itself and the *yoni-varṇa* or the consonant is equally so. Therefore, which is the cause and which the effect? Such argument does not disturb us who are making a statement about consciousness which is teeming with infinite variety. Even in worldly dealings dominated by *māyā*, speech which imparts clarity to the successive letters and words

---

fies the other. At the level of *madhyamā*, they are so identified with each other that one can denote the other. This is what is meant by *adhyāsa* in the Trika system.

and being of the nature of light, brings about thinking and has the nature of bringing about a unified sense (*ekaparāmarśasvabhāvaiva*). By others (the followers of other doctrines and the grammarians) this i.e., the supreme consciousness (*parāsaṃvid*) has been proved by laboured deliberation. In this system, it is established effortlessly to those who earnestly take to its teaching. Therefore, we do not insist on one's going to the house of a teacher of grammar, the only gain of which will be a little refinement of speech (body of words). So, (by following this Trika system) questions or doubts pertaining to succession or non-succession or priority and posteriority (of letters) or words in respect of *piṇḍamantra*[23] consisting of nine letters and *mahā-mantras*[24] are solved by themselves.

Description of the Pattern of Mālinī

So, revered Mālinī *mantra* alone is of the chief, supreme state of Śakti at the level of the intermediate state i.e. at the level of *paśyantī* situated at *parāparā* level. Therefore, it has been said in Pūrvaśāstra (Mālinīvijaya):

"The knowers of *mantra*, in order to achieve the desired object of the followers of *mantra* and tantra should practise in matters of *nyāsa*, the *nyāsa*[25] of Mālinī which is free of particular prescription (of rites) and has a mixed arrangement of vowels and consonants, for the sake of *śākta* body." By this statement, it has also been declared that Mālinī has a mixed arrangement of vowels and consonants. At another place also, it has been said: "One should direct the *mantra* neither towards *nara* (i.e. limited beings and objective phenomena) nor to Śiva, the supreme *tattva*, but to Śakti. They i.e. *nara* and Śiva cannot bestow enjoyment and liberation, for *nara* is insentient, and Śiva is powerless (for power resides only in Śakti)."

Notes

1. This book is not available now.
2. *Svapakṣa* means '*parapramātṛ-pakṣa*', the supreme experient; *parapakṣa* means *mitapramātṛ-pakṣa*, i.e. the limited empirical individual.
3. *Sṛṣṭi* pertains to *kriyā*, *sthiti* to *jñāna*, *saṃhāra* to *icchā*. *Sṛṣṭi* is the *avatāra* of *aparā śakti* which is predominantly governed

by *jñāna-śakti* and *saṃhāra* of *parā śakti* which is predominantly governed by *icchā-śakti*.

4. *Dhārikā* pervades *pṛthivī tattva*, *āpyāyinī* pervades *jala tattva*, *bodhinī* pervades *agnitattva*, *pavitri* pervades *vāyutattva* and *avakāśadā* pervades *ākāśa tattva*.

5. The three *vidyās* refer to *parā*, *parāparā* and *aparā*. *Parā* is that which rests in the Absolute only as Will to manifest. It is only *icchā śakti*. When with *jñāna śakti*, the form of manifestation is determined, then this mixed state of *icchā* and *jñāna śakti* is *parā-parā vidyā*. When by means of *kriyā śakti* manifestation is finally brought about, then the *vidyā* is known as *aparā*. This is the empirical condition consisting of *pramātṛ* (the experient, the subject), *pramāṇa* (experience and means of experience) and *prameya* (object of experience).

6. In Śiva *tattva*, there is the *mantra* of one letter, viz. *auṃ* in Śakti *tattva*, there is the *mantra* of three letters, viz. *aghore*; in Sadāśiva *tattva* there is the *mantra* of one letter, viz. *hrīṃ*. The full *mantra* referred to is: *oṃ aghore hrīḥ paramaghore huṃ ghorarūpe haḥ ghoramukhi bhīme bhīṣaṇe vama piba he ru ru ra ra phaṭ huṃ haḥ phaṭ*.

7. The *mantra* of *aparā devī* is *hrīṃ huṃ phaṭ*. The *mantra* *phaṭ* is of one and a half letters. This covers the *pṛthivī aṇḍa* and *prakṛti aṇḍa*. The *mantra hrīṃ* is also of one letter. It covers *Śakti aṇḍa*. The entire cosmos consists of the evolution of Śakti *aṇḍa* in *anuttara*, *māyīya aṇḍa* in Śakti, *prakṛti aṇḍa* in *māyā*, and *pṛthivī aṇḍa* in *prakṛti*. See diagram (Chart 1).

8. This refers to the *mantra Sauḥ*. '*Sa*' represents the three cosmic spheres (*pṛthivī*, *prakṛti* and *māyā*) i.e. the 31 *tattvas* of Śaiva philosophy from *pṛthivī* upto *māyā*. '*Au*' represents *śuddhavidyā*, Īśvara and Śadāśiva together with *icchā*, *jñāna* and *kriyā*. The *visarga* (the two dots—one above the other) represents Śiva and Śakti. This is the pervasion of *parā*.

9. Mātṛsadbhāva or Mātṛkāsadbhāva *mantra* is *h*, *s*, *h*, *phreṃ* (Tantra 30, 47-49), Ratiśekhara *mantra*: *r*, *l*, *y*, *u* (Tantra 30, 10), Kuleśvara *mantra*: *jh*, *kṣ*, *hūṃ* (Tantra 30, 16).

10. In Āgama, various ceremonies are performed for mental peace, physical health etc. These are known as '*āpyāyana*' ceremonies.

11. By '*preta*' or 'departed' is meant one who is not a being of

the terrestrial world. Sadāśiva has been called '*mahāpreta*'—the gigantic one who is not a being of the terrestrial world, because other *pretas* i.e. other souls who have departed from this world (after death) still retain their sense of difference, but Sadāśiva has absolutely no sense of difference. He is, therefore, *mahāpreta*. The use of *mahāpreta* for Sadāśiva is figurative, the word '*prahasantam*' (smiling) has been used for Sadāśiva in order to show his joy in serving as a seat for *parā* (the transcendental Śakti). The word 'Īśvara' in the quotation refers to Sadāśiva, not to Īśvara-*tattva*.

Sadāśiva has been designated as simultaneously both '*sacetana*' (conscious) and '*acetana*' (unconscious). He is '*sacetana*' (conscious) with reference to his identity with the transcendental Śakti, and *acetana* (unconscious) with reference to the sense of difference that prevails in the world.

12. All the categories of existence have two aspects, viz. (i) the original orb and (ii) its reflection. Their original orb is in the *parāśakti*. No reflection has any existence unless its original orb (*bimba*) is present in *parā*. The supreme original orb is decidedly *parā*; the *bimbas* or original orbs of the remaining *vāṇīs*, viz., *paśyantī*, *madhyamā* and *vaikharī* are also present in *parā*. In the quotation borrowed from Mālinīvijaya, it has been indicated that even the three goddesses, in the form of energy, viz. *parā paśyantī*, *parā madhyamā*, and *parā vaikharī* abide on the three lotuses that blossom on the three prongs which emerge from the navel of Sadāśiva. The venerable *parāśakti*, however, presides over even the above three.

There are the following *mātrās* (morae) of *praṇava*, viz. *a*, *u*, *m*, *bindu*, *ardhacandra*, *nirodhī*, *nāda*, *nādānta*, *śakti*, *vyāpinī*, and *samanā*. The eighth one, viz. *nādānta* is a state of Sadāśiva. There is also the twelvth *mātrā*, viz. *unmanā* which constitutes the seat of the venerable *parā* that transcends all these. The three white lotuses with reference to *parā* indicate *sṛṣṭi*, *sthiti* and *saṃhāra*. Venerable *parā* is above even the *ūrdhvakuṇḍalinī*. She is there in the form of divine Energy. Therefore, her sea` is described as *parama āsana* i.e. as the most distinct seat, for this seat stretches as far as *parā* Herself (*parāparyantatvāt*).

Nādānta is indication of the 8th *mātrā* (e.g. *a*, *u*, *m*, *bindu*, *ardhacandra*, *nirodhī*, *nāda*, *nādānta*, *śakti*, *vyāpinī*, and *samanā*). *Nādānta* points to the state of Sadāśiva. The yogī experiences the 12th *mātrā* i.e. *unmanā* of *praṇava* when he has succeeded at first in dissolving the first eleven *mātrās* in *cidākāśa*. *Unmanā* is also called *ūrdhvakuṇḍali pada* which is the special seat of *parā*.

13. The grammarians believe that there are only three stages of *vāk*, viz. *paśyanti*, *madhyamā* and *vaikhari* and consider *paśyanti* to be the highest stage. The Trika philosophers, on the other hand, maintain that there are four stages of *vāk*, viz., *parā*, *paśyanti* *madhyamā* and *vaikhari* and consider *parā* to be the highest stage.

14. The statement made in this paragraph will be clear from the following table:

Levels of the Three Bimba Vāṇis

No.	*Antaḥkaraṇa* introverted towards the inner self	The *bimba vāṇis*	Presiding deity	State of creative categories according to Trika
1.	Buddhi or Prajñā	Parā-paśyantī	Para-Sadāśiva	Jñāna-śakti aspect of Para-Sadāśiva.
2.	Ahaṃkāra	Parā-madhyamā	Para-Viṣṇu	Kriyā-śakti aspect of Para-Sadāśiva.
3.	Manas	Parā-vaikharī	Para-Brahmā	Kriyā-śakti aspect of Para-Īśvara.

15. *Pralayākala* and *śūnya-pramātā* are states in which the soul lies unconscious in sleep due to *moha* for a long time. There is, however, one difference between them. The movement of *prāṇa* and *apāna* goes on in a subtle way in the *śūnya-pramāta* till they lie unconscious in *pralaya* i.e. the dissolution of the world. The *sañcita karmas* of both are, however, present as *saṃskāras* in this state.

16. A *lakṣa* = 100,000; a *koṭi* = ten *lakṣas*, an *arbuda* = ten *koṭis*, a *parārdha* = two *arbudas*.

17. The category of earth (*pṛthivi tattva*) is the ultimate aspect of manifestation. It contains all the preceding *tattvas* from *jala* (water) upto Śiva-*tattva* according to the principle 'everything is an epitome of everything else.'

18. By *kāṭhinya* or solidity is meant 'compactness of being firmly or densely united'. There cannot be solidity in the earth, unless the earth elements are densely united with the water atoms-element.

19. The *parā* state is ever present, the Eternal Now; *parāparā* state is future; the *aparā* state is past. The sense of 'abiding in parā in the form appropriate to *parā*' is the following:

In the *bimba* of *parā*, the future and past are present in this form of *bimba* i.e. as ever-present which is the appropriate characteristic of *parā*, because in *parā* Time is not based on the sense of relativity which is the characteristic of the empirical consciousness.

Summary of the completeness of the earth category according to the principle of Śiva's projection upto the earth i.e. Vamana-yukti (Involution):

1. Complete equipoise of *Ahaṃ* (I) and *Idam* (this i.e. objectivity) – Śiva tattva
2. Expansion of Śiva into *A-ha-m* – Śakti tattva
3. By means of Svātantrya Śakti (autonomy of Śiva), loss of *abheda* or non-difference, the emergence of *idam* (this) in *aham* (I) – Sadāśiva tattva
4. The incipience of subtle difference by a breach in non-difference – Īśvara tattva
5. *Bheda* (difference) and *abheda* (non-difference) equally balanced – Śuddhavidyā tattva
6. Shrinkage of *abheda* (non-difference) and appearance of *bheda* (difference) – Mahāmāyā tattva
7. Complete *bheda* or difference – Māyā tattva
8. The empirical individual abiding in *māyā* – Puruṣa tattva
9. The progeny of Māyā by which the empirical individual is completely affected – Kāla, Vidyā, Rāga, Kalā and Niyati tattva
10. The homogeneous state of *sattva, rajas*, and *tamas* – Prakṛti tattva
11. The first aspect or modifications of *prakṛti* – Buddhi tattva

12. Two aspects or modifications of *buddhi*	=	*manas tattva and ahaṃkāra tattva*
13. Modification of *ahaṃkāra* tattva	=	The five *jñānendriyas*, and the five *karmendriyas*
14. The primary general object of perception	=	*Śabda, sparśa, rūpa, rasa* and *gandha tanmātrās*
15. Modifications of the subtle tanmātras into concrete elements	=	*ākāśa, vāyu, tejas* and *jala tattva*
16. The ultimate limit of the entire manifestation	=	*Pṛthivī tattva* (earth category)

20. Bhairava Consciousness which is *anuttara* transcends both *bimba* and *pratibimba.* That consciousness is represented by the vowels which are not amenable to the doctrine of *bimba-pratibimba.* The vowels always represent Śiva on every level whether primordial-*parā* or the ultimate *vaikharī.*

21. *Varṇa* or letter starts in *parā* and *paśyantī*; *mantra* or word starts in *madhyamā* or *parāparā* and *pada* or sentence starts in *vaikharī*, or *aparā*. Purification means that in *sādhanā* or spiritual discipline, *pada* which is in *vaikharī* has to be raised to the level of *varṇa* in *paśyantī* and *parā*.

22. The *paramakoṭi* or the highest point refers to the *antakoṭi* of *paśyanti*. The *ādi* or initial *koṭi* of *paśyantī* is *Īśvara tattva*; the *madhya* or middle *koṭi* of *paśyantī* is *Sadāśiva tattva*; its *antakoṭi* is *anāśrita Śiva*.

23. *Piṇḍamantra* of nine letters is the following: *h, s, r, kṣ, m, l, v, y, ṇūṃ*. This is a *mantra* without the interruption of vowels in between.

24. *Mālā mantras* are those like "*Oṃ namaḥ Śivāya*" in which the words are syntactically connected.

25. *Nyāsa* is a technical term. It means mental assignment of the various parts of the body to different deities accompanied with *mantra* or prayer with particular gesticulations.

26. *Śākta-śarira*: body charged with *śakti* or divine energy.

Parāparā-saṃvitti

The pervasion of *tattvas* in Mālinī on the basis of Mālinīvijayottara Tantra.

na, ṛ, ṝ, ḷ, tha, ca, dha, ī, ṇa, u, ū, ba, ka, kha, ga—the first sixteen letters are pervaded by Śiva-Śakti tattva.

Serial No.	*Varṇa or arṇa i.e. letter*	*Tattva*
1.	gha	Sadāśiva
2.	ṅa	Īśvara
3.	i	Śuddhavidyā
4.	a	Māyā
5.	va	Niyati
6.	bha	Kāla
7.	ya	Rāga
8.	da	Vidyā
9.	ḍha	Kalā
10.	ṭha	Puruṣa
11.	jha	Prakṛti
12.	ña	Buddhi
13.	ja	Ahaṃkāra
14.	ra	Manas
15.	ṭa	Śrotra
16.	pa	Tvak
17.	cha	Cakṣu
18.	la	Rasanā
19.	ā	Ghrāṇa
20.	sa	Vāk
21.	aḥ	Pāṇi
22.	ha	Pāda
23.	ṣa	Upastha
24.	kṣa	Pāyu
25.	ma	Śabda
26.	śa	Sparśa
27.	aṃ	Rūpa
28.	ta	Rasa

29.	e	Gandha
30.	ai	Ākāśa
31.	o	Vāyu
32.	au	Tejas
33.	da	Jala
34.	pha	Pṛthivī

Parāparā Saṃvitti

The pervasion of *tattvas* in Mātṛkā (from *a* to *kṣa*)

a, ā, i, ī, u, ū, ṛ, ṝ, ḷ, ḹ, e, ai, o, au, aṃ, aḥ

i.e. all the vowels are pervaded by Śiva *tattva*. The pervasion of the *tattvas* by other letters of Mātṛkā is given below:

Serial No.	*Letters*	*Tattvas*
1.	ka	Śakti
2.	kha	Sadāśiva
3.	ga	Īśvara
4.	gha	Śuddhavidyā
5.	na	Mahāmāyā
6.	ca	Māyā
7.	cha	Kalā
8.	ja	Vidyā
9.	jha	Rāga
10.	ña	Puruṣa
11.	ṭa	Prakṛti
12.	ṭha	Buddhi
13.	ḍa	Ahaṃkāra
14.	ḍha	Manas
15.	ṇa	Śrotra
16.	ta	Tvak
17.	tha	Cakṣu
18.	da	Rasanā
19.	dha	Ghrāṇa
20.	na	Vāk
21.	pa	Upastha
22.	pha	Pāyu

23.	ba	Pāṇi
24.	bha	Pāda
25.	ma	Śabda
26.	ya	Sparśa
27.	ra	Rūpa
28.	la	Rasa
29.	va	Gandha
30.	śa	Ākāśa
31.	ṣa	Vāyu
32.	sa	Agni
33.	ha	Jala
34.	kṣa	Pṛthivī

Exposition

In this section, four important points deserve attention, via. 1. Phonematic manifestation, 2. The principle of evolution in Śaivāgama, 3. The principle of everything being an epitome of everything else, 4. The state of *bimba-pratibimba* or the original orb and its manifestation.

1. *Phonematic manifestation*

According to Śaivāgama, *vimarśa--śakti* or the self-verbalising and the self-revelatory aspect of the *anuttara* or the Supreme consists of the eternal awareness of 'I' or *Aham* (in Sanskrit). The Supreme is not simply *prakāśa* or light of consciousness, but *prakāśa-vimarśamaya* or light and energy of awareness simultaneously which is potentially the germ and source of all manifestation. Thus the Supreme is a biune principle.

This *Aham* of the Supreme contains all the letters of the Sanskrit alphabet which consists of 50 letters. The 16 vowels from '*a*' to '*aḥ*' are forms of Energy representing the Supreme that is transcendent to manifestation. The remaining 34 phonemes which are consonants are also forms of Energy manifesting the various *tattvas* or categories of existence. So the phonemes are not merely inert letters, they are creative powers of the universe. The universe is not simply visible phenomenon of the Divine; it is the utterance of *Parāvāk*, the verbal Power of the Divine. Manifestation is known as *varṇa-sṛṣṭi*, phonematic creation in Śaivāgama.

The phonemes are known as *Mātṛkā*, the little mothers who are

(*Continued on page* 134)

Chart 3

THE ARRANGEMENT OF LETTERS ACCORDING TO MĀTṚKĀ IN PARA-SAṂVITTI IN SARVĀGRA-RŪPATĀ

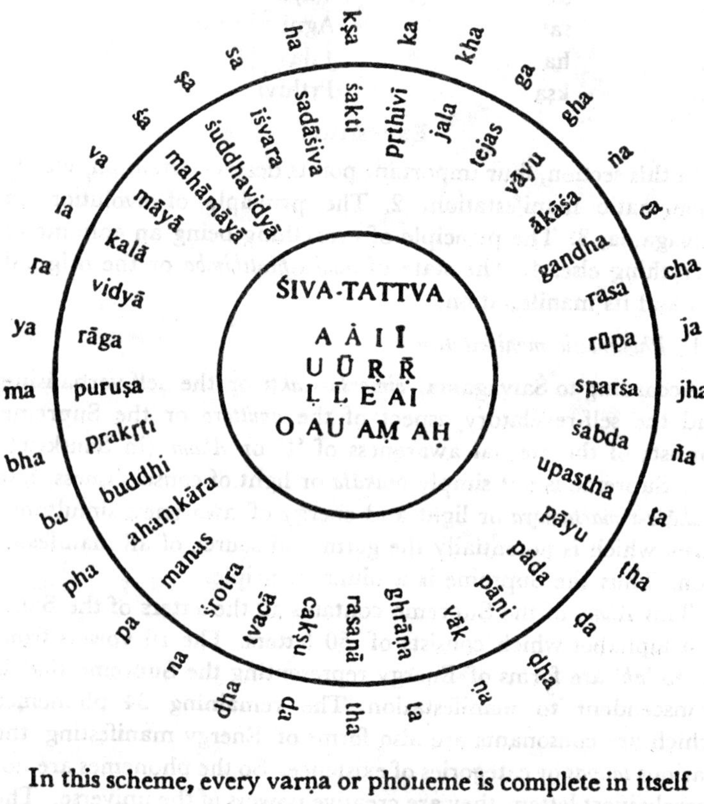

In this scheme, every varṇa or phoneme is complete in itself

a—cit	ū—ūnatā	e—asphuṭa kriyāśakti	ou—sphuṭatama kriyāśakti
ā—ānanda	ṛ—amṛta bīja	ai—spuṭa kriyāśakti	oṃ—Śivabindu
i—icchā	ṝ—amṛta bīja	o—sphuṭatara kriyāśakti	aḥ—Śivavisarga
ī—īśanā	ḷ—amṛta bīja		
u—unmeṣa	ḹ—amṛta bīja		

CHART 4

ARRANGEMENT OF LETTERS ACCORDING TO MĀTṚKĀ IN PARĀPARA-SAṂVITTI IN SARVA MADHYARŪPATĀ

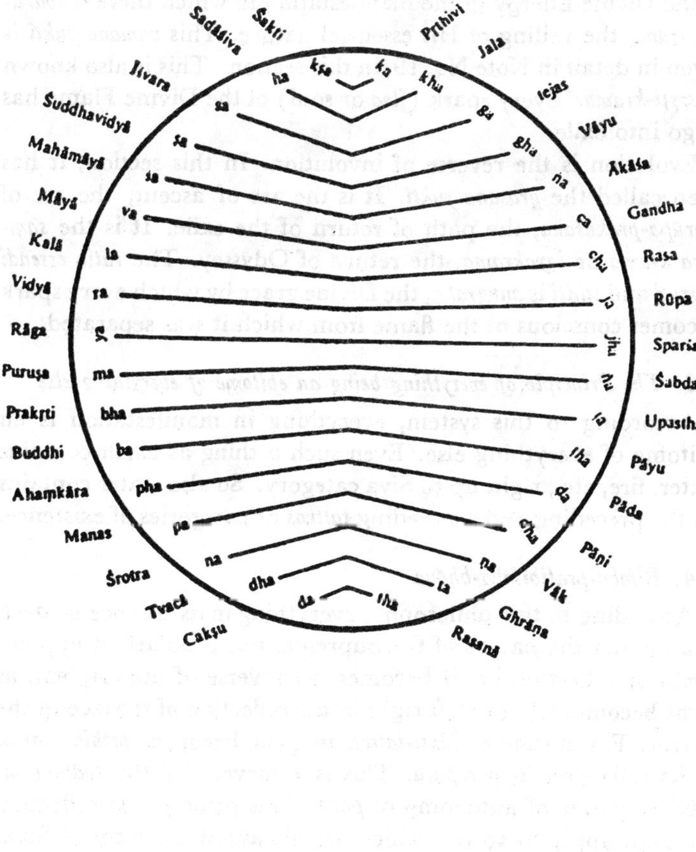

busy creating the universe and in effecting everyday activity of life. *Mātṛkā* when realized by the soul also becomes *mantra* that saves the soul and brings about its liberation.

2. *The Principle of Evolution in Śaivāgama*

This section also contains the philosophy of Evolution according to Śaivāgama. There is in manifestation first of all the arc of descent of the Divine right up to the solid earth. This is the process of involution known as *vamana yukti*, the process of projection of the Divine Energy in the manifestation in which there is *svarūpagopana*, the veiling of His essential nature. This *vamana yukti* is given in detail in Note No. 19 in this section. This is also known as *sṛṣṭi-krama*. Every spark (*jīva* or soul) of the Divine Flame has to go into exile.

Evolution is the reverse of involution. In this section, it has been called the *grasana yukti*. It is the arc of ascent, the arc of *svarūpa-prakāśana*, the path of return of the exile. It is the *saṃhāra krama* or *layakrama*, the return of Odyssey. The *ratio essendi* of *sṛṣṭi* and *sthiti* is *anugraha*, the Divine grace by which every spark becomes conscious of the flame from which it was separated.

3. *The Principle of everything being an epitome of everything else*

According to this system, everything in manifestation is an epitome of everything else. Even such a thing as earth contains water, fire, etc., right up to Śiva category. So also water contains all the preceding and succeeding *tattvas* or categories of existence.

4. *Bimba-pratibimba-bhāva*

According to this philosophy, everything in its essence is *anuttara* i.e. has the nature of the Supreme, but is polarised in *pratibimba* or reflection i.e. it becomes the reverse of the original, as right becomes left and left right in the reflection of the face in the mirror. For instance *Śakti-tattva* in *parā* becomes *pṛthivī tattva* in its reflection in *parāparā*. This is achieved by the *svātantrya-śakti* or power of autonomy of *parā*. This principle of reflection does not apply to vowels which are always of the form of Śiva. The diagram *Pratibimba* or reflection in *bimba* shows that *pṛthivī* or earth category represented by the letter '*ka*' is reflected as *śakti* represented by the letter '*kṣa*' and vice-versa.

For further details, see the diagrams (Charts No. 1, 2, 3, 4).

Mālinī and *Mātṛkā* in relation to Śiva *tattva* in the aspect of *parā*.

Text

From *evaṃ ca sthite* on p. 51, l. 22 to *samāviṣṭaṃ* on p. 52, l. 8.

Translation

Such being the case, since everything is in everything else, let us, first of all, see how the first sixteen letters of *Mālinī* (*Ihatya*), viz. '*na, ṛ, ṝ, ḷ, tha, ca, dha, i, ṇa, u, ū, ba, ka, kha, ga*' give an idea of Śiva seriatim in relation to the supreme or transcendental consciousness.

(*parasaṃvidam apekṣya*) [The pervasion of Śiva in the first sixteen letters of *Mālinī* in the *parā* or Supreme Consciousness on the basis of *sarvāgrarūpatā*]

1. '*Na*' which symbolizes *śrotra* (hearing) in *Mātṛkā cakra* and is a consonant appears in the supreme consciousness in *Mālinī* as *nāda* which, in other words, is *ahaṃ-parāmarśa* or the divine I-consciousness in this context.

2. It enters the group of four phonemes (*i.e. ṛ, ṝ ḷ, ḹ*) which are the ambrosial seeds inasmuch as they are the womb of immortality being the essential nature of Śiva. The I-consciousness in the form of *nāda* thrives here and attains maturity (*vṛṃhitattvam avāpya*).

3. *Tha* in *Mālinī* symbolizes *rasanā* or flavour in the group of *Mātṛkā* letters. So immediately entering this stage, the I-consciousness enjoys the flavour of its own nature as 'I'.

4. The phoneme '*ca*' in *Mālinī* symbolizes *gandha* or smell in *Mātṛkā cakra*. *Gandha* (as is well known) is the attribute of earth. In the *para* or transcendental consciousness, *gandha* is symbolic of *pratyabhijñā* or recognition in the form 'I have always been like this'.

5. The phoneme '*dha*' in *Mālinī* symbolizes '*tvak*' or touch in *Mātṛkā cakra*. In its very state of self-recognition (*tatraiva*) the I enjoys the consciousness of contact with Śakti, or Spiritual Energy and recognizes its identity with it.

6. The above state is known as *śāktam yaunaṃ dhāma*' or the

state of procreative Energy. Now it is established in the procreative Energy through *iśāna bija* or Śiva *bija* represented by the phoneme '*i*' in *Mālinī*.

7. '*Na*' in *Mālinī* symbolizes that sense-power in *Mātṛkā cakra* which is known as *vāk*. This is the *karaṇa-śakti* or in other words *māyāśakti* which is non-different from *anuttara*. Being reflected in this.

8. Further than the *karaṇa-śakti*, there is the state of efflorescence (*unmeṣa*) indicated by the phoneme '*u*' in *Mālinī*. This is the introvertive state.

This is followed by the tendency towards *prasāra* or extension (*ūrdhvāśrayaṇa*) i.e. a state of extroversion indicated by the phoneme *ū* in *Mālinī*.

The phoneme '*ba*' in *Mālinī* symbolizes '*buddhi*' in *Mātṛkā cakra*. The function of *buddhi* is ascertainment. So it resorts to perfect ascertainment of its self-existence in Śakti represented by *buddhi* (*buddhirūpam śākta yonim adhiśayya*) (hinting that it is not only transcendent to manifestation but also immanent in it).

9. The phoneme '*ka*' in *Mālinī* symbolizes '*pṛthivī*' or solidity in *Mātṛkā cakra*. *Pṛthivī* or solidity indicates '*sthairya*' or firmness. This means that the I-consciousness attains firmness in its own nature as Śiva.

The phoneme '*kha*' in *Mālinī* symbolizes *jala* or liquidity in *Mātṛkā cakra*. The characteristic of *jala* (water) is *rasa* which symbolizes savour or delight. This means that the I-consciousness is immersed in its own bliss as Śiva.

The phoneme '*ga*' in *Mālinī* symbolizes *agni* or fire in *Mātṛkā cakra* which indicates *prakāśa* or light. This means that the I-consciousness knows itself as *prakāśa* or Light in its own nature as Śiva.

(This is known as Śiva-*tattva* in *parasaṃvitti* or Supreme State)

Exposition

In this relationship of *Mālinī* to the *para* or transcendental state, Abhinavagupta brings out the following points:

1. '*Sarvaṃ sarvātmakaṃ*'—'Everything consists of everything else'. This is the basic principle. Śiva is immanent in manifestation. Since Śiva is not confined to any particular element, but is the all-of-Reality, therefore, there is nothing in the universe

which does not contain the all-of-Reality. When it is said for instance, that *pṛthivī* is solidity and has the attribute of *gandha* or smell, it does not mean that solidity is the only thing that is represented by *pṛthivī*. It only means that solidity is predominant in *pṛthivi*, but it contains the other elements also in miniature.

Trika philosophy maintains that the entire manifestation is an expression of *parā śakti* or *parā vāk* or transcendental logos. This *parā vāk* is creative energy. Every letter of the alphabet represents energy in some form. The letters of the alphabet are arranged in two schemes in Trika, viz., *Mātṛkā* and *Mālinī*. *Mātṛkā* means the little mother or phonematic creative energy. *Mālinī* literally means the Devī who wears a *mālā* or garland of fifty letters of the Sanskrit alphabet. *Mātṛkā* also wears a garland of fifty letters. That is why sometimes *Mātṛkā* is called as *pūrvamālinī* and *Mālinī* is called as *uttara-mālinī*. But the word *Mālinī* is rarely used for *Mātṛkā*. Another etymology of *Mālinī* is '*malate viśvam iti Mālinī*', i.e. the *śakti* of letters which holds the entire universe within itself (the root '*mal*' meaning 'to hold').

The main difference between *Mātṛkā* and *Mālinī* consists in the arrangement of letters. In *Mātṛkā*, they are arranged in a regular order, i.e. the vowels come first, and the consonants come next in a serial order. In *Mālinī*, they are arranged in an irregular way i.e. the vowels and consonants are mixed and no serial order is observed.

On the principle of '*sarvaṃ sarvātmakaṃ*', Abhinavagupta has tried to show that the first sixteen letters of the *Mālinī* order represent Śiva *tattva* just as the first sixteen vowels of the *Mātṛkā* order do. Out of the sixteen letters of the *Mālinī* order seven, viz., *ṛ*, *ṝ*, *ḷ*, *ḹ*, *i*, *u* and *ū* are vowels and as such, they are the constituents of Śiva *tattva* itself. Therefore, they do not represent any outgoing movement. They have only an intrinsic significance. *Ṛ*, *ṝ*, *ḷ*, *ḹ*, are called *amṛta bīja*, immortal germs or vowels, because they are the resting place of I-consciousness; they do not produce anything; they do not change. I connotes *iśānā bīja* or the power of mastery. *U* connotes '*unmeṣa*' or introvertive effloresence of knowledge, and *ū* connotes *ūrdhvāśrayaṇa* or the tendency to extroversion. All these vowels are concerned only with the inner life of Śiva.

So far as the other nine letters of *Mālinī* are concerned viz., *na, tha, ca, dha, ṇa, ba, ka, kha, ga,* Abhinavagupta shows, as given in the translation above, that they denote, on the principle of '*sarvaṃ sarvātmakaṃ*', certain aspects of *Mātṛkā* order as well.

The whole role of these sixteen letters (of *Mālini*) vis-à-vis *Mātṛkā* with reference to *parā saṃvid* or supreme consciousness can be seen in Chart 5.

Chart 5

Letters of Mālinī together with their representation with reference to Supreme Consciousness or *parasaṃvitti*:

Śivatattva

Letters of Mālinī	Symbolic of aspects in Mātṛkā scheme	Symbolic of aspects in Śiva
Ṅa	Śrotra-Hearing	Nāda as I-consciousness
[*ṛ, ṝ, ḷ, ḹ*-Amṛtabīja as a mass of Cidānanda of Śiva]		
Tha	Rasanā—Flavour	The joy of Śiva's realization as I
Ca	Gandha—Smell	Pratyabhijñā or Recognition of I-consciousness
Dha	Sparśa—Touch	Identity of I-consciousness with Śakti
Ī [Īśāna bīja indicating Śiva's autonomous staying in His nature]		
Na	Vāk-Speech	Siva's reflection as I in vāk
U [Unmeṣa indicating introvertive state of knowledge and bliss in Śiva]		
Ū [ūrdhvāśrayaṇa or tendency to extroversion in Śiva]		
Ba	Buddhi	Confirmation of I-consciousness
Ka	Pṛthivī—solidity	Firmness in I-consciousness
Kha	Āp—Liquidity	Taste of the bliss of I-consciousness
Ga	Agni—Light	Primordial Light of Consciousness as Śiva

Mâlinī and Mâtrkâ in Relation to Parâpara i.e., Supreme-Cum-Non-Supreme Consciousness:

Text

From *paśyantīrūpānusṛtyā* to *bhavati* on p. 52, l. 10 to l. 20

Translation and Exposition

In accordance with *paśyanti*, that is to say, in *parāpara* or supreme-cum-non-supreme state,

1. *Na* of *Mālinī* which represented *śrotra* or hearing in *Mātṛkā* in the *para* or supreme state and *nāda* in Śiva *tattva* in the same state is reflected as *ṇa* in *Mātṛkā* in the *parāpara* or supreme-cum-non-supreme state. *Ṇa* in the *Mātṛkā* scheme represents *vāk* (speech or sound), the faculty of intuitive comprehension (*grahaṇātmaka-rūpaṃ*), symbol of I-feeling in Śiva *tattva*.

Now this I-feeling expands, i.e. gets strengthened in the *amṛta-bīja* or the ambrosial vowels *ṛ, ṝ, ḷ, ḹ* (*tattraiva bījeṣu prasṛtya*). Of this, there is no reflection or transformation.

2 *Tha* of *Mālinī* which represented *rasanā* or taste in *Mātṛkā* in the supreme state and *ānanda rasa* or the rapture of bliss in Śiva *tattva* in the same state is reflected as *da* in *Mātṛkā* in the *parāpara* state. *Da* in the *Mātṛkā* scheme in this state represents the faculty of seeing (*cākṣuṣyāṃ bhuvi*) and *sākṣātkāra* or self-awareness in Śiva *tattva*.

3. *Ca* of *Mālinī* which represented *gandha* in *Mātṛkā* in the supreme state and self-recollection in Śiva *tattva* in the same state is reflected as '*va*' in *Mātṛkā* in the *parāpara* state. *Va* in the *Mātṛkā* scheme in this state represents *māyā* which here means pure *māyā-śakti* united with Śiva (*tatsāmānyāśuddhavidyā karaṇe*). In Śiva *tattva*, it represents *svātantrya śakti*, the autonomous power of Śiva. (It should be borne in mind that *śuddhavidyā* in this context does not mean *śuddha-vidyā-tattva* but *māyā*, not *māyā* in the ordinary sense of *māyā-tattva*, but as the *māyā-śakti* or *svātantrya* of Śiva. It is in this sense that the word *māyā* has been used in the following verse by Utpaladeva in Īśvara-Pratyabhijñā-Kārika:

"*Svāṅgrūpeṣu bhāveṣu patyurjñānaṃ kriyā ca yā māyātṛtīye te eva paśoḥ sattvaṃ rajas-tamaḥ*" (IV. I.4).

"What are admitted to be knowledge and action of the Lord in relation to objects which are identical with Him, the same together with the third, the *māyā* are the three *guṇas* of the limited subject, viz. *sattva*, *rajas*, and *tamas*.")

4. The letter '*dha*' in *Mālinī* which represented *tvak* or touch in *Mātṛkā* in the supreme state and *svarūpasparśa* or self-contact in Śiva-*tattva* in the same state is reflected as '*ta*' in *Mātṛkā* in the *parāpara* state. '*Ta*' in *Mātṛkā* scheme in this state represents the last in order of the external senses viz., *ghrāṇa* or the faculty of smelling. In Śiva *tattva*, it represents *pratyabhijñā* or self-recognition.

5. *Ī* in *Mālinī* symbolizes *Īśāna bīja* or the *svara* (vowel) representing autonomy of Śiva (here also, there is no reflection or transformation). The *ahaṃ-vimarśa* or I-feeling holding the previous state fast with the power of autonomy (*īśānabījam ākramya*) proceeds to the next step.

6. The letter '*ṇa*' in *Mālinī* which represented '*vāk*' in *Mātṛkā* in the *para* or supreme state and *svarūpa nāda daśā* in Śiva *tattva* is reflected as '*na*' or *śrotra śakti*, the faculty of hearing in *Mātṛkā* in the *parāpara* state (*śrotraśaktim ālambya*) and represents *aṅgīkṛta nāda-daśā* or acceptance of *nāda* state in Śiva *tattva*.

7. '*U*' in *Mālinī* only represents *unmeṣa* or inner efflorescence as in *para* state (of this, there is no reflection or transformation).

Similarly *ū* in *Mālinī* only indicates *ūrdhvāśrayaṇa* or the tendency to exteriorization. (Of this also, there is no reflection.) (*unmeṣordhvabīja-yogena*). With the aid of '*u*' and '*ū*', *ahaṃ-vimarśa* proceeds to the next step.

The letter '*ba*' in *Mālinī* which represented '*buddhi*' in *Mātṛkā* in the *para* state, and *svarūpa-niścaya* i.e. Self-certainty or self-assurance in Śiva *tattva* is reflected as '*tha*' in *Mātṛkā* in *parāpara* state. '*Tha*' in the *Mātṛkā* scheme in *parāpara* state represents *pāyu* or rectum (*ānandendriya-yoni*), the seat of sexual pleasure, the symbol of *saṅkoca-vikāsa*, contraction and expansion or ingress and egress (*ānandendriyayonigaṃ*).

8. The letter '*ka*' in *Mālinī* which represented *pṛthivī* or solidity in *Mātṛkā* in the *parā* state and firmness in Śiva *tattva* is reflected

as *kṣa* in *Mātṛkā* in the *parāpara* state. '*Kṣa*' here represents *śakti-cum-sadāśiva* (*Sadāśiva-maya-śakti*), according to *sarvāntyarūpatā.*

The letter '*kha*' in *Mālinī* which represented water in *Mātṛkā* in the *para* state and delight in Śiva *tattva* is reflected as '*ha*' in *Mātṛkā* in the *parāpara* state. '*Ha*' here represents Sadāśiva cum Īśvara (*Īśvara-maya-Sadāśiva*) (according to *sarvāntyarūpatā*).

The letter '*ga*' in *Mālinī* which represented fire in *Mātṛkā* in *para* state and *prakāśa* or light in Śiva *tattva* is reflected as '*sa*' in *Mātṛkā* in the *parāpara* state. '*Sa*' here represents *śuddhavidyā-cum-Īśvara* (*Śuddhavidyā-maya Īśvara*) (according to *sarvāntya-rūpatā*).

The last three steps denote what is meant by "*sadāśiveśveśvara-śuddhavidyāmayam bhavati*" in the text.

Thus it has been said here that Śiva *tattva* is of infinite power (*ananta-śakti*) inasmuch as it is unlimited, appearing as it does in *sarvāgra, sarvamadhya,* and *sarvānta-gāmī* phases.

Exposition

In the previous description, Abhinavagupta has shown how the various phases of *nādātmaka* I-consciousness represented by the first sixteen letters of *Mālinī* are represented in the *Mātṛkā* order with reference to *para* or supreme state of Śiva *tattva.*

In this, he has shown how the various phases of *ahaṃ-vimarśa* of Śiva *tattva* represented by the first sixteen letters of *Mālinī* are represented in the *Mātṛkā* order with reference to *parāpara-saṃvitti* or supreme-cum-non supreme state of Śiva *tattva.*

Of the sixteen letters, seven viz. *ṛ, ṝ, ḷ, ḹ, i, u* and *ū* are *bīja* letters or vowels. As such, they are aspects of Śiva both in *Mālinī* and *Mātṛkā* and therefore undergo no change. They have the same function in *parāpara* as in *para.*

The phonemes, according to Trika philosophy, have three aspects: *sarvāgrarūpatā, sarvamadhyarūpatā* and *sarvāntagāmitā. Sarvāgrarūpatā* refers to a phoneme as it is in itself. *Sarvamadhyatā* refers to phonemes undergoing transformation, and *sarvāntagāmitā* refers to phonemes reaching finally the state of *Śuddhavidyā, Īśvara, Sadāśiva* and Śakti.

Six consonants of *Mālinī,* viz. *na, tha, ca, dha, ṇa* and *ba* are reflected in *Mātṛkā* in different phonemes in *parāpara* state under the law of *sarvamadhya-rūpatā* as shown in the chart.

Three consonants of *Mālinī*, viz. *ka, kha* and *ga* after undergoing the changes into *kṣa, ha,* and *sa* respectively under the law of *sarva-madhya-rūpatā* point to the final destiny, viz., of passing into *śuddhavidyā, Īśvara,* Sadāśiva, and Śakti. They, therefore, refer to *sarvāntagamitā* state. *Ka* which represents *pṛthivī* in *Mātṛkā* is reflected into *kṣa* which symbolizes Śakti, but in the *parāpara* state, it is not simply Śakti but *sadāśivamaya-Śakti*. The *parāmarśa* or comprehension of Sadāśiva is *ahaṃ idam* (I am this, the unity of subject and object); the *parāmarśa* of Śakti is only *ahaṃ* or I, for in *para* state, there is no *idam* or objectivity separately; everything is only I or *ahaṃ*. Since this is a description of *parāpara* state, therefore, *kṣa* or Śakti is described as *Sadāśivamaya-Śakti*. Similarly, '*ha*' which represents Sadāśiva is in *parāpara* state *Īśvara-maya-sadāśiva*. Similarly '*sa*' which represents Īśvara is in *parāpara* state *Śuddhavidyāmaya-Īśvara*.

Thus the pervasion of Śiva full of invariable and infinite Śakti is described through the first sixteen letters in the order of the letters of the *Mālinī* group from the point of view of *sarvāgrarūpatā* (*parāsaṃvitti*) and *sarvamadhyarūpatā* and *sarvāntyarūpata* (*parāparasaṃvitti*).

The mixture of the remaining tattvas of Mālinī in aparā saṃvitti

TEXT

From *mālinyāmihatya* on p. 52, l. 22 up to *pṛthivī ca pha* on p. 53, l. 10.

TRANSLATION

Now the phonemes are described with reference to *apara* (non-supreme) state in *Mālinī* and their reflections with reference to *paśyantī* i.e. *parāpara* (supreme-cum-non-supreme) state. '*Gha*' which represents Sādākhya or Sadāśiva in *Mālinī* in the *apara* state appears as *vāyu* (the element of air) in *Mātṛkā* in the *parāpara* state. (The same process should be understood successively in the case of all the letters. The description of each letter is given in *Mālinī* in *apara saṃvitti* and of the corresponding letter in *Mātṛkā* in *parāpara saṃvitti* or *paśyantī*). *Na* which represents Īśvara in the *apara* state in *Mālinī* is reflected as *nabha* i.e., *ākāśa* or ether in *Mātṛkā* in the *parāpara* state. 'I' which represents *śuddhavidyā* of the *aparā*

(*Continued on page* 144)

CHART 6

PARASAMVITTI (SUPREME CONSCIOUSNESS)-SARVĀGRARŪPATĀ

In this every tattva or category of Existence is complete in itself. Letters in order of mātṛkā

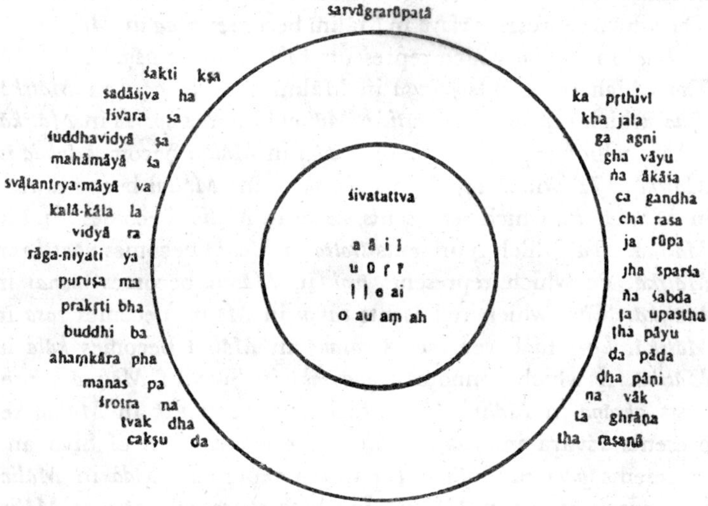

Explanation of the vowels which are of the nature of Śiva:

a denotes cit or consciousness

ā denotes ānanda or bliss

i denotes icchā or will to manifest, but still unaffected by objectivity

ī denotes īśanā or mastery. This is the state in icchā or will which is coloured by objectivity

u denotes unmeṣa or jñānaśakti (power of knowledge)

ū denotes ūnatā or deficiency of knowledge, the cause of objective appearance

ṛ ṝ ḷ ḹ } denotes amṛtabīja, imperishable letter, not subject to any change

e denotes asphuṭa kriyāśakti or indistinct power of activity

ai sphuṭa kriyāśakti or distinct power of activity

o sphuṭatara kriyāśakti or more distinct power of activity

au sphuṭatama kriyāśakti or most distinct power of activity

aṃ denotes Śiva-bindu or undivided knowledge of the universe

aḥ denotes visarga represented by two perpendicular dots. The lower dot, symbolizing Śakti, means that there is an expansion of an objective world. The upper dot, symbolizing Śiva, means that the entire universe rests in the I-consciousness of Śiva

state in *Mālinī* appears as *icchā śakti* in *parāpara* state. '*A*' which represents *māyā* in the *aparā* state in *Mālinī* represents *anuttara* (the unsurpassable Absolute) in *Mātṛkā*. '*Va*' which is *niyati* in *Mālinī* becomes *māyā* in *Mātṛkā*. '*Bha*' which is *kāla* in *Mālinī* becomes *prakṛti* in *Mātṛkā*. '*Ya*' which is *rāga* in *Mālinī* becomes *niyati* in *Mātṛkā*. '*Ḍa*' which represents *vidyā* in Mālinī becomes *pāda* in *Mātṛkā*.

'*Ḍha*' in *Mālinī* which represents *kalā* becomes *pāṇi* in *Mātṛkā*. *Ṭha* which represents *puruṣa* in Mālinī become *pāyu* in *Mātṛkā*. '*Jha*' which represents *prakṛti* in *Mālinī* becomes *sparśa* in *Mātṛkā*.

'*Ña*' which represents *dhī* or *buddhi* in *Mālinī* becomes *śabda* in *Mātṛkā*. '*Ja*' which represents *ahaṃkāra* in *Mālinī* becomes *rūpa* in *Mātṛkā*. *Ra* which represents *manas* in *Mālinī* becomes *vidyā* in *Mātṛkā*. '*Ṭa*' which represents *śrotra* in *Mālinī* becomes *upastha* in *Mātṛkā*. *Pa* which represents *tvak* in *Mālinī* becomes *manas* in *Mātṛkā*. '*Cha*' which represents *cakṣu* in *Mālinī* becomes *rasa* in *Mātṛkā*. *La* which represents *rasanā* in *Mālinī* becomes *kāla* in *Mātṛkā*. *Ā* which connotes *ānandaśakti* in Śiva in *Mātṛkā* represents *ghrāṇa* in *Mālinī*. '*Sa*' which represents *vāk* in *Mālinī* represents Īśvara in *Mātṛkā*. *Aḥ* is the *visarga śakti* of Śiva and represents *pāṇi* in *Mālinī*. *Ha* which represents *pāda* in *Mālinī* becomes Sadāśiva in *Mātṛkā*. *Ṣa* which represents *pāyu* in *Mālinī* becomes *śuddhavidyā* in *Mātṛkā*. '*Kṣa*' which represents *upastha* in *Mālinī* becomes Śakti in *Mātṛkā*. '*Ma*' which represents *śabda* in *Mālinī* becomes *puruṣa* in *Mātṛkā*. *Śa* which represents *sparśa* in *Mālinī* becomes *mahāmāyā* in *Mātṛkā*. *Aṃ* is Śiva's *bindu śakti* and represents *rūpa* in *Mālinī*. *Ta* represents *rasa* in *Mālinī* and appears as *ghrāṇa* (*nāsikā*) in *Mātṛkā*. *E* which is the *sātvika kriyāśakti* of Śiva represents *gandha* in *Mālinī*. The same in its long form i.e., as *Ai* represents *nabha* or ether in *Mālinī*. Similarly, *O* represents *vāyu* and *Au* represents *tejas* or *agni* in *Mālinī*. (In *Mātṛkā* *e*, *ai*, *o* and *au* being of the very nature of Śiva cannot undergo any modification). '*Da*' in *Mālinī* represents *āp* or water and becomes *cakṣu* in *Mātṛkā*. *Pha* represents *pṛthivī* in *Mālinī* and becomes *ahaṃkāra* in *Mātṛkā*.

Exposition

In the first two descriptions of *Mālinī* with reference to *para* and *parāpara* state of Śiva *tattva*, Abhinavagupta has selected only

(*Continued on page* 147)

CHART 7

IN PARĀPARA SAṂVITTI—SUPREME-CUM-NON-SUPREME CONSCIOUSNESS SARVAMADHYA-RŪPATĀ IN THE ORDER OF MĀTṚKĀ-LETTERS.

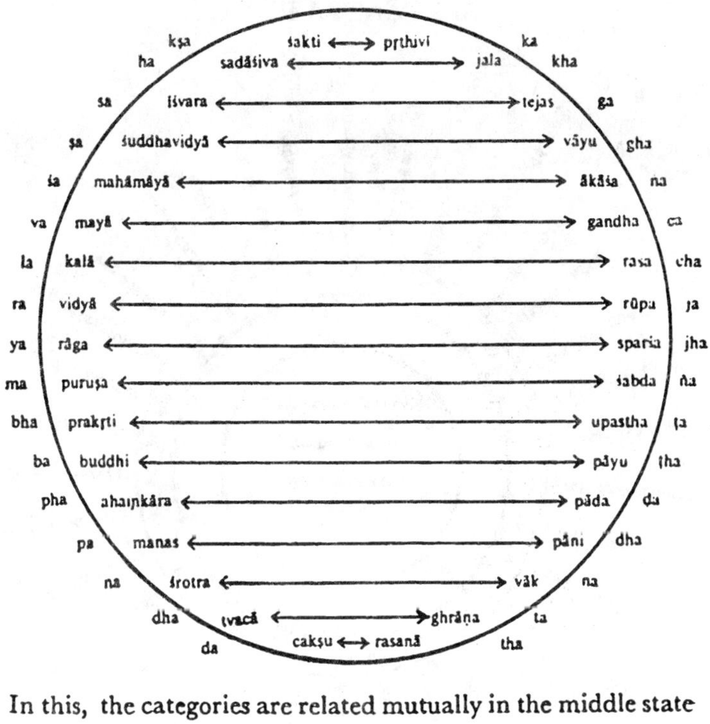

In this, the categories are related mutually in the middle state

CHART 8

ARRANGEMENT OF LETTERS ACCORDING TO MĀTṚKĀ IN PARĀPARA SAṂVITTI IN SARVĀNTYA-RŪPATĀ

In this every succeeding category absorbs within itself the preceding one.

the first sixteen letters which in the *Mālinī* phase are concerned with Śiva.

In the *para* state, the seven vowels, viz. *ṛ, ṝ, ḷ, ḹ, i, u* and *ū* undergo no change. The first four vowels are the resting place of I-consciousness. I connotes Śiva's power of autonomy, and *u* and *ū* indicate His introvertive and extrovertive states. The other nine letters which are consonants show the relationship of *Mālinī* and *Mātṛkā* and the expansion of I-consciousness in various phases.

In *parāpara* state, Abhinavagupta shows how the nine consonants of *Mālinī* are reflected in different letters of *Mātṛkā* which point to different aspects of I-consciousness. Both have to do with the I-consciousness of Śiva. Only they show the expansion of I-consciousness in different ways. So both are concerned with Śiva *tattva*. In the *aparadaśā* of *Mālinī*, it is the modification of the remaining thirty-four letters of *Mālinī* which has been depicted. In the *para-daśā*, it is only the expansion of Śiva's I-consciousness that has been described. There the phonemes are concerned only with Śiva's inner life, not with manifestation. That is where it is known as *para-daśā*. In the *apara-daśā* of *Mālinī*, the phonemes are concerned with the *tattvas* and their modification. In other words, they are concerned with manifestation. That is why this state is known as *apara* or non-supreme. Their corresponding modification is shown in the *parāpara* state in *Mātṛkā*. In the *apara* state in *Mālinī*, the seven vowels i.e. *a, aḥ. aṃ, e, ai, o, au* represent *tattvas* or elements of manifestation but they represent only different *śaktis* of Śiva in *Mātṛkā*; they do not represent elements of objectivity there. So there is no question of their corresponding modification in *Mātṛkā*. (See chart 9 for details.)

CHART 9

Mālinī in *apara saṃvitti*	*Mātṛkā* in *paśyantī* or *parāpara saṃvitti*
1. Gha—Sadāśiva	1. Gha—Vāyu
2. Ṅa—Īśvara	2. Ṅa—Nabha or Ākāśa (ether)
3. I—Śuddhavidyā	3. I—Icchā of Śiva
4. A—Māyā	4. A—Anuttara

5. Va—Niyati
6. Bha—Kāla
7. Ya—Rāga
8. Ḍa—Vidyā
9. Ḍha—Kalā
10. Ṭha—Puruṣa
11. Jha—Prakṛti
12. Ña—Dhī or Buddhi
13. Ja—Ahaṃkṛta
14. Ra—Manas
15. Ṭa—Śrotra
16. Pa—Tvak
17. Cha—Cakṣu
18. La—Rasanā
19. Ā—Ghrāṇa
20. Sa—Vāk
21. Aḥ—Pāṇi
22. Ha—Pāda
23. Ṣa—Pāyu
24. Kṣa—Upastha
25. Ma—Śabda
26. Śa—Sparśa
27. Aṃ—Rūpa
28. Ta—Rasa
29. E—Gandha
30. Ai—Nabha or ether
31. O—Vāyu
32. Au—Tejas or fire
33. Da—Jala
34. Pha—Pṛthivī

5. Va—Māyā
6. Bha—Prakṛti
7. Ya—Niyati
8. Ḍa—Pāda
9. Ḍha—Pāṇi
10. Ṭha—Pāyu
11. Jha—Sparśa
12. Ña—Śabda
13. Ja—Rūpa
14. Ra—Vidyā
15. Ṭa—Upastha
16. Pa—Manas
17. Cha—Rasa
18. La—Kalā or Kāla
19. Ā—Ānandaśakti of Śiva
20. Sa—Īśvara
21. Aḥ—Visarga Śakti of Śiva
22. Ha—Sadāśiva
23. Ṣa—Śuddhavidyā
24. Kṣa—Śakti
25. Ma—Puruṣa
26. Śa—Mahāmāyā
27. Aṃ—Śiva's Binduśakti
28. Ta—Ghrāṇa
29. E—Asphuṭa-kriyāśakti of Śiva
30. Ai—Sphuṭa-kriyāśakti of Śiva
31. O—Sphuṭatara-kriyāśakti of Śiva
32. Au—Sphuṭatama-kriyāśakti of Śiva
33. Da—Cakṣu
34. Pha—Ahaṃkāra

Text

From *atraiva ca yathoktaṃ* on p. 53, l. 11 upto *iti* after *śeṣā varṇā-stukevalāḥ* on p. 54, l. 11.

Translation

In these very letters of *Mālinī*, the structure of the *śākta-śarīra* has been described (in Mālinī-vijaya) for the purpose of *nyāsa* (mental assignment of the various parts of the body to tutelary deities by placing one's fingers on them). Thus the principle that 'everything else is in everything' has been completely demonstrated. It is the venerable supreme verbum (*parā vāk*) which, according to the principle enunciated, casting its reflection in *paśyantī*, simultaneously attains in *madhyamā* established as identical with itself a form of letters in which consonants are intermingled with vowels in an irregular order, and thus becomes *Mālinī* itself which is characterized by difference in the reckoning of the various vowels (*kula-puruṣa*) and the various consonants (i.e. *kulaśakti* indicated by the word *ādi*) in innumerable ways owing to the endless diversity of intermixture of consonants (*yoni*) and vowels (*bīja*). As has been said:

"One should worship *Mālinī* whose corpus is constituted by a group of many vowels (*kuladeha*)[1] and consonants (*kulaśakti*)."

By adopting this practice, the *yogī* who is engrossed in the practice of repeated meditation acquires supernormal power in respect of various *bhuvanas*, *tattvas*, centres of energy in the body (*śārīreṣu cakreṣu*)[2] everywhere in respect of body and *prāṇa*.

As certain medicines produced by the mixture of certain ingredients bring about certain result, even so *bhāvanā* (religious discipline) by intermingling certain religious practices, e.g. *mantra* (repetition of a sacred word of power), *nyāsa* (mental assignment of various parts of the body), *homa* (oblation) etc., brings about the attainment of certain spiritual power. Even here the success comes about by the non-transgression of the working of *niyati-śakti*.[3]

In every sacred literature, the assemblage of letters (in a *mantra*) has been brought about differently by placing the letters in different arrangements. This has been done in accordance with certain fixed succession (*niyataparipāṭi*) determined by the predominance of certain letters considered as appropriate according to the *vijñāna*[4] of each Śāstra (*nijanija vijñāna-samucita-tattad-varṇa-bhaṭṭāraka prādhānyena*). It is in this way that a *mantra* is selected and presented, to show how *parā*[5] (inclusive of *Mātṛkā* and

Mālinī) imparts radiance to a *mantra* invigorated by its creative energy (*tāmeva mātṛkā-rūpāṃ tathāvidhavīryadā-anopabṛṃhita mantra-sphurattādāyinīṃ darśayituṃ*).

As has been said in Nityātantra, the arrangement of letters in *Mālinī* beginning with '*na*' and ending with '*pha*' has been determined principally in accordance with their state in *para nāda*, i.e. *parāpaśyanti*.[6] In *Mālinī*, the aim of placing the vowels (*kulapuruṣa*) and consonants (*kulaśakti*) in this intermixed form is this very penetration into *paranāda* or *parā-paśyanti*. It is not simply the mystery-mongering of the letters and *mantras* that constitutes their advantage. As in Vājasaneyatantra, after placing the letters in their proper order, it is said:

"This is the divine order of letters of *Mātṛkā*, which has reached the abode of Viṣṇu i.e. this is the *Mātṛkā-cakra* which has reached the infinite space of *Mālinī*. When it is fully understood from the teaching of the *guru* (the spiritual director), it cuts asunder the noose of the limited, empirical man."

Similarly, it is said in Trikahṛdaya: "It is the power of the weapons or of anything else, that matters. So also, it is not only the position of the letters of a *mantra*, but the power of creative energy that is inherent in it that matters. It is by being preserved with that creative energy, that the *mantras* are really preserved, otherwise (i.e. without the creative energy) what remains constitutes merely a number of letters."

Notes

1. The difference of *kulabheda* or *kulapuruṣa* i.e., vowels and *kulaśakti* i.e. consonants appears in three ways:—(a) *Varṇabheda* i.e. difference in letters i.e., vowels and consonants, (b) *Mantrabheda*, i.e. difference of *mantras* having no vowels and *mantras* having vowels, (c) *Avasthābheda* i.e. difference of *kulapuruṣa* as *siddhas* and *kulaśakti* as *yoginīs*.

2. *Siddhi* in *bhuvanas* or spheres means that once a *yogī* has acquired power over a particular *bhuvana*, he is no longer born in that particular *bhuvana*. So also *siddhi* over a particular *tattva* or category of existence means that he has arisen above that category of existence. *Siddhi* over the *cakras* means that if a *yogī* has acquired control over a particular *cakra*, he will no longer be governed by the forces of the *cakras* below it.

3. *Niyati-śakti.* It is a technical term which means that the success in a certain supernormal power depends on the controlling power of the Divine.

4. *Vijñāna* is a technical term here meaning the name of the *mantras* and their structure.

5. According to tradition, *Mātṛkārūpāṃ* means *mātṛkā-mālinīrūpāṃ parā,* i.e. *parā* inclusive of *Mātṛkā* and *Mālinī.*

6. According to tradition, *paranāda* means *parā-paśyanti* in its aspect of *bimba* or matrix, *parāparanāda* denotes *parāmadhyamā* in its aspect of matrix, and *aparanāda* denotes *parā vaikharī* in its aspect of matrix.

Text

From *tathā hi mantrāṇām* on p. 54, l. 11 upto *vidhirānantya-vedane* on p. 54. l. 25.

Translation

1. Even when the letters of the *mantras* are considered by themselves, and not in any other aspect, those very *mantras* have differences (*anyathātvaṃ*) in the Śāstras in accordance with the division of *āṇava, śākta* and *śāmbhava upāya.*[1]

2. There is a difference in the seminal *mantra* of *māyā,* viz.: *hrīṃ* delineated in Śaiva Śāstra, of *praṇava* or '*oṃ*' delineated in Vaiṣṇava Śāstra, of the immortal germ of the heart (*amṛtabīja*) which includes all the *tattvas,* viz. '*sauḥ*' delineated in the Śāstras of the left-hand path,[2] or there is a difference in the *praṇava mantra* (lit. the four aspected *mantra*) in the Vedic scripture (where it is OṂ), and in Kaulottara etc. i.e., the Śākta Tantras (where it is *hrīṃ*), and in the Ucchuṣma or Bhairava Śāstra (where it is *hūṃ*).[3]

Here is recorded the rule of the use of the *mantras* for the worthy practitioners of *yoga* in respect of the manifold differences of vowels (*kulapuruṣa*) and consonants (*kulaśakti*). "All the vowels (*pūrve*) should be placed before (*apare*) the consonants (*pareṣāṃ*) and the consonants (*pare*) should be placed after (*pṛṣtha*) the vowels, and the vowels (*pūrve'pica*) should be placed in regular succession. This is considered to be the rule of the use of *Mātṛkā mantra.*"

Thus also should be made the form (of the other i.e., *Mālinī*) with an inter-mixture (*bhinna-yoni*) of vowels and consonants. This goddess *Mālinī* with the combination of various consonants *etc.* (*śāktādi*) becomes innumerable (*asaṃkhyā*). It is still known as *Parā* or *Anuttara Mālinī.*

Further, "In the *mantras* (*dhāmasu*) consisting of *halanta* letters i.e. consonants without any vowel (*bhedasaṃkhyeṣu*), placed one below the other (*adho'dho viniviṣṭeṣu*), there is only one dot (*bindu*) on the final letter. In the others i.e., the *mantras* which consist of letters with vowels, there is a dot on each previous letter (*anyeṣu prāk*). In such kind of *mantras*, each *mantra* (*ekataḥ*) should be cast by placing a dot (*saṃkhyā*) on the top of each letter (*svapṛṣṭha-gāṃ*) both on the previous letters and the final one (*prāktanāntya-gāṃ*). Thus the dot will differ in the case of *mantras* the letters of which are without a vowel (*iṣṭaihi*) and those which are with a vowel (*aspṛṣṭaihi*). This is the order of such *mantras*. This is the rule (*vidhi*) of the combination of vowels (*kulapuruṣa*) and consonants (*kulaśakti*) as has been described above (*yathoktaḥ*) in order to point out the infinity of such *mantras* (*ānantyavedane*)."[4]

EXPOSITION

In this, Abhinavagupta mentions the following important points about the *mantras*:

1. In spite of the similarity of letters, they become different when used for different *upāyas.* When a *mantra* is used as *āṇava upāya*, it is *prāṇa-apāna* or *kriyāśakti* that is predominant. When it is used as *śāktopāya*, it is *jñānaśakti* that is predominant. When it used as *śāṃbhavopāya*, it is *icchā śakti* that becomes predominant.

2. There is a difference in the seminal *mantras*. In the Vaiṣṇava Śastras, it is OṂ; in Śaivaśāstras, it is *hrīṃ*; in the left-hand Śāstras, it is *sauḥ.*

3. There is a difference in *praṇava* itself in the different Śāstras. In the Vedic scriptures, it is 'OṂ'; in the Śākta Tantras it is *hrīṃ*; in the Bhairavaśāstra, it is *hūṃ*.

4. Again, there are differences in the formation and the arrangement of the letters in a particular order. The first verse cited, beginning with *pūrvepareṣām* etc. shows the difference of arrangement of letters in *Mātṛkā* and *Mālinī.* In this verse, the word '*pūrva*' has been used for vowel, and the word '*para*' has been used for consonant. The verse says that in *Mātṛkā,* all the

vowels should be placed in regular succession. In *Mālinī* there is an inter-mixture of vowels and consonants.

The second verse cited, beginning with '*adho'dho*' contains very archaic Sanskrit words in a technical sense. *Bhedasaṃkhyā* has been used for *halant* letters, *dhāma* has been used for *mantra*, *saṃkhyā* for *bindu* or a dot etc. For details, see the translation. In this quotation, Abhinavagupta gives an example of two kinds of *mantras*. The first is that in which (i) *halanta* letters i.e. consonants without any vowel are placed one below the other, and (ii) in which there is a *bindu* or dot only on the final letter which has a vowel. The following *navātma mantra* is an instance of this kind of *mantra*. Such *mantras* are known as *saṃyuktākṣari mantras*.

For instance: *h* or: *h*, *s*, *r*, *kṣ*, *m*, *l*, *v*, *y*, *ṇūṃ*

s
r
kṣ
m
l
v
y
ṇūṃ

The other is that kind of *mantra* in which each consonant has a vowel and there is a dot (*bindu*) on each letter, e.g. *yaṃ*, *raṃ*, *laṃ*, *vaṃ*. Such *mantras* are known as *asaṃyuktākṣari mantras*.

Text

From *tadetena* on p. 55, l. 1 upto *padamanāmayam*, on p. 55, l. 6.

Translation

Thus, in accordance with this precept, those spiritual practitioners who are devoted to the right rules of vowels (*kulapuruṣa*) and consonants (*kulaśakti*) of the *mantras*, e.g. Mantramaheśvaras (beings always steeped in the essential nature of Śiva) become unqualified (to impart *mantra* to others); they cannot impart *mantra* for deliverance, for a *mantra* from them cannot bear fruit. This does not apply to *Mantras*, for even when they are completely absorbed in meditation, they do not reach the extreme state of *anāmaya* in which one loses one's personality in Śiva.[1]

It has been rightly said:

"In this world in which beings come into existence right from Brahmā upto a tuft of grass, three and a half crores of *mantras* appointed by Śiva (for helping creatures) are quite enough. After conferring grace on the entire lot of creatures, they have reached the *anāmaya* state i.e. the state of being completely immersed in Śiva. In other words, they have become Mantramaheśvaras." (M.V.T. I, 40-41)

Notes

1. Mantramaheśvaras are the divinities who abide in Sadāśiva *tattva*, Mantreśvaras abide in Īśvara *tattva*, and Mantras are the divinities who abide in Śuddhavidyā. Mantra in this context means a divinity, not a sacred word of power.

Text

From *tadevaṃ bhagavati* on p. 55, l. 7 upto *evaṃ yo vetti tattvena ityādi* on p. 57, l. 22.

Translation

The goddess *parā vak* who assumes different states (i.e. the state of *paśyanti*, *madhyamā* etc.) becomes in her chief mode i.e. *madhyamā* (i.e. *parāparā* state) goddess Mālinī herself. At this stage, She becomes so infinite, that considering the varied forms which She assumes she appears omnifarious, and thus being of all forms, She assumes the state of letter (*varṇa*), a word (*mantra*) and sentence (*pada*) through the predominance of three aspects viz. *para* (supreme), *parāpara* (i.e. subtle or *sūkṣma*) and *apara* (gross or *sthūla*) i.e. even in *parāpara* state, She appears as *para*, *parāpara* (*sūkṣma*) and *apara* (gross).[1] This threefold aspect should be regarded from the standpoint of effecting purification. The sources of bondage appearing in *paśyanti* are indeed subtle. They have to be purified in their subtle aspect, for the sources of bondage are lying within. The sources of bondage at the *paśyanti* level are subtle; therefore their purification has to be effected at the subtle level, for a bondage is bondage when it lies within the subtle aspect. At the level of *madhyamā* in which the external expansion of Śakti becomes more and more perceptible, *paśyanti* appears as an instrument of purification (*śodhana-karaṇa-tayaiva bhavati*).

Just as by washing the dirt or impurity lying in the inner fold of a cloth, the dirt lying on the upper portion gets automatically washed, even so by the removal of dirt lying at the subtle level, the dirt lying at the *madhyamā* level gets automatically removed.[2]

So, the stage of *vaikharī* as lying within the *parā-saṃvid* is being considered. The state of *vaikharī* in the *parā* (supreme) state is not impossible.[3]

Though the development of speech-organs (*sthāna*) and articulation (*karaṇa*) becomes manifest in children in two or three years, yet it is an established fact that their proficiency of the language increases day after day and month after month. If in *madhyamā* (which is inherent in *parāvāk*) there were no appearance of the lineaments of the letters in accordance with the speech organs and articulation that become distinct with the expansion of *vaikharī*, then there would be no difference in the development of language between a child a day old, a month old, or a year old. The proficiency (*vyutpatti*) in the development of language in a child increases as the impressions of words heard and objects seen are associated in his mind. *Parāmarśa* or mental association is not possible without word (gross or subtle). Word whether expressed externally in a manifest or gross form or implied internally in an unmanifest subtle form is an aspect of *vaikharī*.

In a new-born child even when the vocal organs are not yet developed, the subtle form of *vaikharī* inheres in *madhyamā* by which he is able to associate heard word and seen object by means of an inner, subtle, unmanifest implicit proto-language.

It has also to be admitted that the constituent elements of *vaikharī* are present in his mind in an implicit form for without these, he could not have been able to have even an implicit form of language and without this he could not have been able to associate the seen object and the heard word.

If it be said that it is *madhyamā* itself that becomes distinguished by the difference resulting from such development, we may ask how? Let us discuss this point carefully.

The child hears the words and sees the objects and thus develops his acquisition of language. He mentally lays hold on the words heard. The words heard are of the level of *vaikharī* (articulate speech). In regard to these words, he is like one born blind in regard to forms. (He hears the sounds but does not know what they refer to). Therefore, *vaikhari* constituted by speech organs and articulation certainly inheres in *madhyamā*.

Similar is the condition even in the dumb. It has already been said that the consciousness of the goddess *parā* is all-containing (*sarvātmaka*).

Thus *vaikhari* herself, who has acquired development through *madhyamā*, so long as she remains in herself with words and their referents perfectly manifest, expressing mutual diversity and having the net-work of the categories of existence within herself, so long she is *aparā*. The development of the *madhyamā* stage which inheres in *parā* is known as *parāparā*, and also the growth of *paśyanti* (is known as *parāparā*). In her own self, *parā* is the divine goddess.

Śodhaka, Śodhana and Śodhya

Thus in the state of purified and purifier, there is a threefold position. The purifier (*śodhaka*) is the Universal Divine whose expansion is universal. It has already been said that the expansion occurs in this very way (i.e. in the way of triad).[4] In the matter of the means of purification (*śodhana*) the action is that of the Divine Being Himself who assumes self-imposed limitation through His own autonomy and reposes in the state of the glory of His *śakti*. (*śāktamahimaviśrāntasya*). That which is to be purified (*śodhya*) is the network of bondage of the limited empirical being (*narātmanaḥ*) who is full of a sense of difference which is first incipient in the *paśyanti vāk* stage, which is a *śakti* of limited beings expanded by the *parāparā* goddess who is the pulsating *paśyanti* of the form of *pati-śakti*, who is also *paśu-śakti*[5] developed by the *jñānaśakti* of Sadāśiva, who is similar in rank to venerable *parā* that is nondifferent from venerable Bhairava who is the unified form of the triad (sun, fire and moon)[6] and who transcends the thirty-seven categories.[7] This is a settled fact.

As has been said by revered Somānanda in Śivadṛṣṭi: "May Śiva who has entered into us as the Subject (as *śodhaka*) make obeisance by Himself (in the form of *mantra* as *śodhana*), to Śiva who is extended as the universe, by means of *parā* who is His own Śakti in order to remove all obstacles which are but Himself." (Ś.D. I, 1)

The entire group of activities (whether *śodhaka*, *śodhana* or *śodhya*) indicates this form of Śiva in Śiva-Dṛṣṭi.

In the matter of purification, the succeeding state has to be dissolved in the preceding.[8]

"Leave both (*śodhya*) *dharma* and *adharma*, both truth and falsehood (i.e. dissolve them in the true Self). Having left both truth and falsehood (i.e. the *śodhya*), leave also that by which you leave everything (i.e. give up also the *mantra* in the form of *śodhana* by which you give up the *śodhya*).

This is the eminence of Trika Śāstra, this is the glory that even the purifier,[9] and the means of purification has to be purified. All the three (i.e. *śodhaka*, *śodhana*, and *śodhya*, in other words, *paśyanti*, *madhyamā* and *vaikharī*) exist simultaneously in *parā* (the supreme *vāk*).

Man speaks something through *vaikhari*, ideates through *madhyamā*, experiences some indeterminate state through *paśyantī* and experiences inwardly some truth through *parā*.

It is Lord Bhairava only who abides completely full in all the three states (*tāvati*). By closely investigating the traditional teaching of the primordial experience, it will be established that it is the met-empirical consciousness of oneself. This is a fact that cannot be controverted.

This is not simultaneous in a temporal sense. Owing to its being subtle, it is not marked. So there is only a presumption of simultaneity. Just as the piercing of a hundred flowers and buds together appears to be simultaneous, so is that. If it be said that simultaneous means occuring at the same time, what does it really mean? According to the principle enunciated by me earlier, viz. that time is only a thought-construct, what is time in the introverted consciousness? The essence of time consists in the experience of successive appearance and disappearance of objects. Its essence consists in the non-presence of the awareness of introverted consciousness which is time-less.

The objection that though time is experienced in juxtaposition with successive objects (as *prāṇa-apāna*, change of season etc.), it can overpower the non-temporal consciousness, is not valid, for the successive object is in itself known through the underlying consciousness which is not successive. Otherwise how could time itself be known as a distinct object? The rise of the fallacy of mutual dependence is due to the separation of a thing from the light of consciousness which is found in one's own self. Every thing that can be uttered has to fall back upon indeterminate consciousness (*nirvikalpa jñāna*). The same fallacy of mutual dependence lies in saying that the piercing of many flowers and twigs together means piercing the many. A whole atom does not come about by the addition of the last one with the others, for this phenomenon is not a *karma* (operation).[10]

A congruous connexion cannot be established in the absence of indeterminate knowledge (*jñānābhāvena*). Investigation of congruous connexion is not possible if there is a break in memory (*smṛtibhede*), and memory depends on indeterminate knowledge (*jñāna*). So investigation of congruous connexion cannot be carried out without indeterminate knowledge. I have examined this problem in detail in my commentary on 'Padārthapraveśa-nirṇaya'.[11] So what is the use of this fruitless tangle of words which only ends in creating an obstacle in the teaching of the subject under discussion?

Thus the goddess *parā* abides as purifier; *parāparā* also acts as purifier where abide the powers '*aghorā*'[12] etc. with whose aid, the spiritual practitioners Vijñānākalas have become Mantramaheśa etc. Through the grace of Brāhmī and other goddesses, the minor spiritual practitioners have become Brahmā, Viṣṇu and others. Indeed, it is the Lord, venerable Bhairava who being, through the multitude of His powers, perfect and whole in Himself, infuses by His autonomy, His own power into Brahmā and others and thus makes them autonomous (in their own spheres). What else can there be other than this?

Thus this is another excellence of Trika, viz., that even the purifier has to be purified.[13] It has been rightly said, "Trika is higher even than Kula". So, owing to the triadic nature of purifier, agency of purification and the one to be purified Trika is invariable.

As has been said by myself in one of my hymns: "When there are three aspects of the group of three (*trika*)" there is no *regressus ad infinitum* in this, for every thing of this teaching is of a piece with the highest consciousness of the Lord. "Leave that *śodhana* also through which you do away with the *śodhya* (the one to be purified)"——one should consider it in this way. Finally, the purifier has also to be purified, inasmuch as the idea of difference that arises in him is also a bondage. Purification is also in its highest sense that fire which is non-different from the consciousness of Bhairava which is proficient in burning away all impurities. When every thing viz., that which is to be purified (*śodhya*), the means of purification (*śodhana*), and the purifier (*śodhaka*) enters into Bhairava, then it is perfection itself. As will be said, "Thus who truly knows etc." (Verse 25 of this book).

Notes

1. In the *para* or supreme state, she is the repository of *varṇa* or letters, in the *parāpara* or supreme-cum-non-supreme state (i.e. *sūkṣma* state) she is the repository of *mantra* or words; in the *apara* state (*sthūla* state) she is the repository of *pada* or sentences. *Mālinī* is symbolic of *parāpara* state, but even in *parāpara* state, she appears as *para*, *parāpara* (*sūkṣma*), and *apara* (*sthūla*).

2. The sense is that the gross form is *śodhya* (to be purified), and the subtle form is the *śodhaka* or purifier; the subtle form is *śodhya* (to be purified) and the *para* (Supreme) form is its *śodhaka* (purifier). This chain goes on until *anuttara* or the Highest.

3. In the womb of *parāśakti* lies *parāvāk*, in *parāvāk* lies *paśyantī*, in *paśyantī* lies *madhyamā* and in *madhyamā* lies *vaikharī*. Consequently *vaikharī* is inherent in *parāsaṃvit*.

4. The triad refers to Śiva-Śakti-*nara*, *varṇa-mantra-pada*, *para-parāpara-apara*, *śodhaka-śodhana-śodhya*.

5. In this context, *parāpara* goddess signifies the original *bimba paśyantī* (or *pati-śakti*) and *paśu-śakti* signifies the *pratibimba* or reflected *paśyantī-vāk*. The first is without *kṣobha*, the second is with *kṣobha*.

6. The triad consists of the sun, fire and moon. The sun or *sūrya* symbolizes *pramāṇa* or knowledge, the fire or *agni* symbolizes *pramātā* or the experient or subject; the moon or *soma* symbolizes *prameya* or object. Again *sūrya* or the sun is the symbol of *jñāna* or knowledge; *agni* or fire is the symbol of *icchā* or will, and *soma* or the moon is the symbol of *kriyā* or activity. Bhairava is the unified form of all these triads.

7. *Anuttara* has three eyes, *agni* (fire), *soma* (moon), and *sūrya* (sun). These three have 10+16+12, i.e. 38 *kalās* or phases. 37 *kalās* being *vedya* or objects are not *svabhāva* or essential nature

of *Anuttara*. The 38th *kalā* is the Bhairava-*svabhāva* or the essential nature of *anuttara*.

8. *Śodhya* or that which has to be purified has to be dissolved in *śodhana* or the means of purification and *śodhana* has to be dissolved in *śodhaka* or the purifier.

9. This means that finally both *śodhya* and *śodhana* have to be given up. Be established in your real Self, and then nothing else would be required.

10. What Abhinavagupta is trying to express means that what is a 'whole', an integral fact is above time. It is not constituted by the sum of the parts what becomes a 'whole' by the addition of parts, it is the result of *karma* or operation which is temporal, but a real whole or *paripūrṇa* is not the result of *karma* or operation. It is an expression of *kriyā śakti* which is beyond time.

11. This book is untraced.

12. 'Aghorā' are those Śaktis who help the spiritual practitioners in the realization of Śiva-nature.

13. This *śodhaka* or purifier refers to such *śodhakas* as Mantramaheśvara etc. The idea in the purifier, viz. 'I am purifier' is also a stain. This has also to be given up.

Text

From *tat parasaṃvidekamaya* etc. on p. 57, l. 22 up to *hṛdayaṃgamikṛtam* on p. 63, l. 6.

Translation

Thus *Parāparā* divinities being identical with the highest consciousness are omnifarious (*sarvātmaka*) and therefore include infinite variety of secular and sacred words and their referents, as has been said in Mālinīvijaya III, verses 59-60.

The very powerful *yoginis* which are like limbs of *parāpara mantra*[1] are eight.[2] They include successively five, six, five, four, and two, three letters twice.[3] They are constituted by the nominatives of address amounting to seven, eleven, one and one-and-half letter twice, i.e. twenty-two letters.[4]

Thus this relation of the purifier and the one to be purified is constituted by the inclusion of endless pre-concerted signs (*saṃketa*) pertaining to *mantras* already composed or to be composed in future. This does not amount to *regressus ad infinitum* (*anavas-*

thā), nor to irrelevance (*ati prasaṅga*) nor to too wide pervasion (*ativyāpti*). Nor can it be said that a conventional sign cannot indicate spiritual knowledge. This is accepted. This being the position, we are now pursuing the topic under discussion.

The syntactical connexion of the words in the fifth verse indicates that at first there are '*a*' and other vowels (upto *au*). At their end, through the connexion of *kriyāśakti* (*kālayogena*) occur what are known as *soma* (moon) and *sūrya* (sun).[5] By the word '*tat*' in the phrase '*tadantaḥ*' is to be understood '*akula*' i.e. *anuttara* or Bhairava referred to in a previous verse. Therefore '*akula*' is that which includes within itself the effectuating power (*kalanā*), for the *kulaśakti* (the cosmic creative power) inheres in it.[6] It is the *vimarśaśakti* (the energy of the creative I-consciousness) that is the effectuating power (*kalanātmikā*). Without this *vimarśaśakti* even *akula* which transcends the fourth state, is mere nothing, for it is only inherent in the deep sleep state. The states that come immediately after *turya* (i.e. *suṣupti*, *svapna* and *jāgrat*) are also similar to *turya* (i.e. they are also mere nothing without *vimarśa śakti*). *Vimarśaśakti* abides as the supreme, divine, unsurpassed (*niratiśaya*), autonomous *śakti* of venerable Bhairava, full (*pūrṇa*), emaciated (*kṛśa*), both full and emaciated, neither full nor emaciated.[7]

In the *vimarśaśakti* of Bhairava, this is no stain either of the appearance of succession or simultaneity. According to the precept referred to previously, viz., that time is only a thought construct, succession should be deliberated upon (*kramo vicāraṇīyaḥ*) in accordance with the fact that the very nature of the massive creative Self-consciousness (*vimarśaikaghana*) of the supreme (*parābhaṭṭarikā*) gives rise to infinite, future absorption and emanation and that there is an appearance of succession and non-succession (*kramākramāvabhāsaḥ*) in that nature of the Divine which is above both succession and simultaneity (*kramayaugapadyāsahiṣṇu*). As has been said: "Lord Bhairava is autonomous, perfect, whole and omnipresent. That which does not appear in the mirror of His Self does not exist." Non-succession can have its existence only in consciousness in which there is an appearance of both succession and non-succession (*akramasya tatpūrvakeṇa saṃvidyeva bhāvāt*) so succession has to be accepted for the sake of exposition. Since succession has its *ratio essendi* in consciousness only, all this mental grip in the form of speech is only succession (*sarva evāyaṃ vāgrūpaḥ parāmarśaḥ kramika eva*). That grip which is of the inner consciousness is non-successive only. Thus the divine supreme Śakti (*parābhaṭṭārikā*) is always of this kind, i.e. multifarious and variegated (*vicitrā*). Therefore it is in accordance with succession i.e. in order to indicate succession in non-succession, the grammarians have formed '*at*' by placing '*t*' after '*a*'.*

Thus the autonomy (*svātantryaśakti*) of the Lord in the form of Will in which the manifestation of existents has not yet started (*anumilita-bhāva-vikāsā*) and the essence of which consists in an inner massive I-consciousness is designated '*a*'. That *svātantrya-śakti* (power of autonomy) abiding in the Transcendent (*anuttara*) is designated Will[8] in which that which is to be willed has not yet become prominent. This will is only a state of consciousness of the transcendental being (*anuttara-sattā*). The highest Lord is always conscious of His own nature. He is *akulaśakti*. Though in being aware of His form, He makes use of *kulaśakti*, yet there is a distinction in the concept of *akulaśakti* from that of *kulaśakti*. *Akula* is the creative I-consciousness (*vimarśasattā*) of Bhairava.[9] That *svātantryaśakti* expanding further is known as '*ā*' which denotes *ānandaśakti*. Perfect *icchā* or Will is '*i*'. *Icchā* itself wishing to perceive (lit. to seize) the future *jñāna* or knowledge through its autonomy becomes '*ī*' which denotes *īśanā* or sovereignty. *U* is the *unmeṣa* or appearance of *jñānaśakti* which is the source of all objective existents desired to be known.

When *unmeṣa* or the arising of knowledge (*unmiṣattā*) has, in consciousness, the desire for further objectivity (*unmimiṣatāyām*), the transcendental consciousness becomes diminished (*ūnībhūta anuttarasaṃvit*) owing to contraction (*saṅkocavaśena*) which is due to all forms lying within or tending to assume subsequent objectivity (*antaḥprāṇa sarvasvarūpa-unmeṣottaraika-rūpairapi*) and to the multitude of existents which lie within as nearly objective, in which the aspect of difference is almost indistinct and which are tending to appear objectively (*antaḥkaraṇa-vedyadeśīya-asphuṭa-prāyabhedāṃśa-bhāsanānabhāvarāśibhiḥ*). This reduced consciousness, because of its retention within itself of all objectivity (*sarvabhā-*

*According to Pāṇini's Sūtra '*taparastatkālasya*'.

vagarbhīkāreṇa), is like the udder of the wish-fulfilling celestial cow, viz. the *parāśakti* (*anaṅga-dhainavīrūpā-paradevatāyāḥ-ūdhorūpā*), and upholding the multitude of entire objectivity, becomes manifest (*sphuṭa*), wide-spreading *jñāna śakti*, i.e. '*ū*'.

These viz., *i*, *ī*, and *u*, *ū* are the two powers (viz., *icchāśakti* and *jñānaśakti*) of Lord Bhairava. The first (viz. *i*, *ī*) being the completely full nature of Bhairava is perfect and being non-different from the Somaśakti abides as *soma* in accordance with the etymological interpretation 'one who abides with *Umā*, (*umā saha*) i.e. transcendental *icchā* or Will is *soma*. Thus *svātantrya śakti* (the power of autonomy) in the form of *icchā* (will) resting in its own *ānanda* (bliss) is designated *mahāsṛṣṭi* (transcendental emanation).[10] As will be said (in verse 29 in this book): "The heroic *sādhaka* (*vīraḥ*) should thereafter worship *sṛṣṭi* (emanation)." The second one (viz., *u*, *ū* or *unmeṣa*, *ūnatāmayī jñānaśakti*) becomes prominent by being engaged in the separation (*recana*) i.e. external expansion of the multitude of objects which abide identically with the *icchāśakti* of Bhairava and by being engaged in the *anupraveśa* i.e. in withdrawing them and effecting their entrance in *anāśrita* Śiva.

By the separation of the multitude of objects, she becomes emaciated, as she is engaged in the manifestation and expansion of objects. Thus she is like the sun.[11] Being identical with the essential nature of Bhairava, by the desire to withdraw the creative consciousness into *anāśrita* Śiva (*kulasaṃvitsaṃjihiṣātmikā*), she is known as *jñānaśakti* who has the tremendous power of withdrawal. Again, reviewing her former expanding form, she, within herself,/ looks for the previous state of her own transcendental consciousness, symbolized by moon (*soma*) with the disposition of the retention of the successive form of the sun and the moon.[12] In an inverse state she looks for the aspect of the moon, the symbol of manifestation (*sṛṣṭi*) and the sun, the symbol of withdrawal (*saṃhāra*).

In this changing state, now wishing *saṃhāra* and now wishing *sṛṣṭi*, *jñāna* and *icchā* sometimes tending towards expansion and sometimes not, one should not attribute the fallacy of non-finality (*na ca atrānavasthā iti vācyam*), for the expansion (*prasara*) and non-expansion (*aprasara*) go on changing their position. Sometimes there may be expansion (*prasara*) of *icchā* (will), and non-expansion (*aprasara*) of *jñāna*, and sometimes there may be expansion (*prasara*) of *jñāna* (knowledge) and non-expansion of *icchā*. Desist from wandering in the error of external appearance. Set out on the path of subtle reflection.

When there is the knowledge of the round shape, colour etc. of a jar, at that very time, the self-shining indeterminate knowledge (*svayamprathaṃ jñānam*) i.e. *nirvikalpaka* knowledge mingled with the knowledge of the object, viz., the jar or *savikalpaka jñāna* (determinate knowledge) also displays itself. In the knowledge of the jar, that is also communicated (*saṃvedya*) which displays the initial, subtle appearance of the variegated form of the jar (*tadrūpakarburībhāve ghaṭādi*) the origin of the appearance is the same (*ekabhāvodgamasya prathamānatvāt*) viz., the *nirvikalpa* or indeterminate consciousness, there being the complete absence of any other *agency* (*anyataḥ kutaścit abhāvasya*).

It is the autonomy of this indeterminate consciousness only which desirous of projecting objects is known as *īśanā* or sovereignty. This is known by the testimony of one's own experience.

Eternal Pervasion of Anuttara and Ānanda in Icchā and Jñāna

That indeterminate consciousness (*nirvikalpa*) which is not yet limited by the cluster of objects, which is massive consciousness, perfect and whole, whose very being is autonomy is perfectly autonomous only because of its having within itself a mass of beatitude. Therefore the presence of *ānanda* (beatitude) in it cannot be gainsaid. *Anuttara* (*a*), the unsurpassable, the possessor of Śakti or creative energy, who is beyond all appellation or description, whose essence is supreme amazement of beatitude, who is venerable Bhairava, of course, shines everywhere (i.e. both as Śiva from '*a*' to '*aḥ*' and as *jagat* (world from *ka* to *kṣa*) as the autonomous active agent.

If one reflects on the essential nature of *anuttara* (*a*) *ānanda* (*ā*), (*akṣubdha* or calm) *icchā* (*i*), (*kṣubdha* or perturbed *icchā*) i.e. *īśana* (*ī*), (*akṣubdha* or calm *jñāna*), *unmeṣa* (*u*) (*kṣubdha* or perturbed *jñāna*), *ūnatā* (*ū*)—one will find that the above six phonemes rest in the indivisible plane of consciousness i.e. *anuttara* or '*a*' phase as their base and that these divinities, the (six) energies of consciousness (though appearing separately) are not separate from their basic essential nature (*ananyā eva sva-saṃvidaḥ*), for being perfect, there is no difference in their nature.[14]

These *śaktis* appear to be different because of the objects of experience with which they are associated (*saṃvedyopadeśca*). This difference lasts only so long as the objects of experience are due to the physical limitation (*tasyā-upādhiḥ dehasaṃvedya mātra-tayaiva bhāvāt*). Therefore in Tantrasāra, it has been said that reality has to be understood through the example of the shadow of the best part of the body i.e. the head. "Just as (when) one tries to jump over the shadow of one's head with one's foot, the head will never be at the place of one's foot, so (also) is it with *baindavi kalā*."[15] Thus this group of six *śaktis* (from '*a*' to '*ū*') which has been determined covers the powers upto *jñāna*.

Now we are going to deliberate on *kriyāśakti*, the power of activity that has begun to move forward. *Icchā* (will) and *jñāna* themselves by heterogenous intermixture[16], by admitting the succession of the preceding and following which are full of marvellous strangeness are termed *kriyā*. Impetuous eagerness is the essence of *kriyā*. Whatever intermixture occurs owing to the expansion of *kriyāśakti* with something else, is due to the fact that *anuttara* (the Absolute) enters suddenly in a sphere of reality which is beyond mental grasp (*anāmarśanīya*), and void (i.e. the state of *anāśrita* Śiva) just as a frog by a simple leap reaches another place from one place. The consciousness that is *anuttara* (*a*) and *ānanda* (*ā*) does not expand in the first four spheres (i.e. *ṛ*, *ṝ*, *ḷ*, *ḹ*) (*na prasarati*), of *kriyāśakti*, for that is an unnamable (*anākhyā*) state, not being the object of name and form (*nāma-rūpa*).

Anuttara and *ānanda* being the final support of everything (*paryantabhittirūpatvāt*) and after having been the foundation of the entire activity in every kind of knowledge cease (from expansion), *akṣubdha icchā* ends in *kṣubdha īśanā*. So far as its relation to impetuous eagerness is concerned, it is capable of expanding both in its own field and also in *anuttara* and *ānanda* because of its capacity for succession.

Then that *kriyāśakti* full of impetuous eagerness, penetrating into its own form (denoted by *ṛ*, *ṝ*, *ḷ*, *ḹ*) which is void (i.e. devoid of all manifestation), immerges at first into a luminous form which is *tejas* or fire (denoted by the experience of *ṛ*). Thus arise *ṛ* and ṝ. How can it be denied that in these letters, the energy of *icchāśakti* (*i*) and that of *īśanāśakti* (*ī*) are associated with the sound of '*R*' whose essential nature is luminosity.[17] This is what the glorious Puṣpadanta says: "The *tejas* and mobility found in ṛ, ṝ are established with the general sound of '*r*'."

When *icchā-īśanā* desires to enter the void, i.e. the state of *anāśrita* Śiva who is free of any manifestation, they have first to pass through the stages of luminosity (*bhāsvararūpa*) i.e. the stages ṛ and ṝ united with the *r* sound. After this, *icchā-īśanā* following the sound '*l*' assumes the form of ḷ and ḹ which indicates immobility, the essential nature of the earth (*pārthivarūpa-salattva*).[18] Finally, it is the energy of *īśanā*, which passing over all the states of objectivity, jumping over the longer state (*dīrghataraṃ plutvā*), after reaching the immobile state of vacuity i.e. *l*, attains to the prolated state (*plutatvameti*) i.e. ḹ in accordance with the principle of Sanskrit grammar that phoneme 'ḷ' does not have the long form (*dīrgha*) of the phonemes '*a*' etc., the prolated state is only a longer form of the long one. In accordance with the rule stated already,[19] one should not search for the long form of ḷ separately. Enough of this. This group of four letters on account of its penetration into vacuity is like burnt seed and is said to be eunuch.[20] There is in them no total absence of germ i.e. the state of a vowel. Nothing can exist which is neither germ nor womb which symbolize Śiva and Śakti, for the existence of any other thing has not been mentioned either in Pūrva Śāstra (Mālinīvijaya) or any other Śāstra. Even in worldly pleasures, there is felicity in repose of this kind. That is why this group of four letters is said to be the germ of immortality.

When *icchā* (*i*) and *īśanā* (*ī*) penetrate the aspect of *ānanda* and the sphere of *anuttara* which are anterior to all and never lapse from their essential nature, we have '*a*' (*anuttara*) or *ā* (*ānanda*) plus *i* or *ī* as *e* as is said, the letter '*a*' combined with the letter '*i*' becomes *e*.

In the inverse state (i.e., if '*a*' and '*ā*' come after '*i*' and '*ī*') with the penetration of '*a*' and '*ā*' there will arise a different letter. If '*i*' or '*ī*' penetrates *ānanda* i.e. '*ā*', there will be a long state (*sphuṭatā*) of the vowel '*e*'. If '*i*' or '*ī*' penetrates *anuttara* i.e. '*a*', there will be a short state (*sūkṣmatā*) of '*e*'.[21] Similarly, glorious Patañjali says:

"Among those who recite the Vedas (*chandogānāṃ*) the followers of the sub-branch *satyamugri* of the branch Rāṇāyanīya enunciate also as half i.e. short *e* and short *o*" [Here *satya* is symbolic of 'short' and *ugri* is symbolic of long].

Among the common folk also, this practice is quite manifest. In the Śaivaśāstras also (*pārameśvareṣu api*) the short aspect of '*e*' and '*o*' in comparison to '*ai*' and '*au*' which is noticed in the application of *aṅgavaktra* i.e. in connexion with limbs or mouth, should be considered in this light viz., '*e*' becomes '*aya*' in place of long *ai* and '*o*' becomes '*ava*' in place of long *au*. Thus the position with regard to the vowels '*e*' and '*o*' is settled.

Now when '*e*' combines with '*a*' and '*ā*' (*tathā śabalibhūtaṃ*), it becomes '*ai*'. Similarly in the case of *unmeṣa* i.e., '*u*', when it coalesces with '*a*' or '*ā*' we have '*o*'. So also when *ū* coalesces with '*a*' or '*ā*' we have '*o*'. When '*o*' combines with *a* or '*ā*' we have '*au*' [*e* is the fifth stage of *kriyāśakti*, *ai* is the sixth, *o* is the seventh, and *au* is the eighth and final stage of *kriyāśakti*].

Though *unmeṣa* i.e., *jñānaśakti* expanding can penetrate into the void, yet it can do so only when it enters at first *icchā* and *īśanā* (*asya īśanecchātmakobhayarūpa praveśa eva śūnyatā*). It is only thus that there can be an entry in the void. In the case of *icchā* and *īśanā*, there is no question of change of their essential nature.[22] So, their position remains as before. Thus *icchā* and *jñāna* (i.e. *i*, *ī*, *u*, *ū*) by entering the essential nature of *anuttara* (i.e. *a*) become developed, i.e. reach *au* which is symbolic of full development of *kriyāśakti*. After this, they abandon the variation of those *śaktis*, and mounting to the state of non-difference, get immersed in the remaining form of a *bindu* i.e. *aṃ*, a dot which represents awareness (*vedanā*) of the very nature of the Reality that is pure consciousness (*cinmayapuruṣatattvasatattva*), and get immersed in the *anuttara* state. So they get dissolved in the state of *anuttara*. The vibration of *kriyāśakti* ends in *au*. The vibration of *icchā* and *jñāna* comes to a stop here, for *icchā* and *jñāna* are included in *kriyāśakti*.[23] In the Trika Śāstra, the nature of *au* is determined as a trident[24] in the enunciation of topics, in the following verse:

"The venerable *parā vāk* pervades the three spheres (*aṇḍa*) viz. *pṛthivī*, *prakṛti* and *māyā* with the letter '*sa*', with the trident i.e., '*au*', she pervades the fourth (i.e. the Śakti *aṇḍa*). With '*aḥ*' she pervades that which transcends all."[25]*

The dot (*bindu*) represents the remainder, viz., pure awareness only. [The twofold nature of expansion and the beginning of *śāktaprasara* or *śākta* expansion]. When the highest Lord emanates within Himself the entire cosmos as only pure awareness in order to express unity (*ekagamanāya*) at first as predominantly the possessor of Śakti, i.e., as Śiva (*śaktimat-rūpapradhānatayā*), and next as predominantly Śakti (*śākta-visargapradhānatayā*) with the creative means of that (*tannirmāṇena* i.e. *icchā*, *jñāna* and *kriyā*). The *visarga* '*aḥ*' is symbolic[26] of *śākta visarga*.

In respect of fully developed *kriyāśakti* of such an extent (*etāvati*) upto the end of *au*, it is the aspects of the pulsation of *icchā*, the initial, *jñāna*, the middle, and *kriyā*, the final appearing first as the desire to manifest (*icchā*), then the comprehension of manifestation (*jñāna*) and finally the actual manifestation (*kriyā*) that constitute the very nature of venerable Bhairava or the unsurpassable (*anuttara*) who has penetrated into all these. These are clearly experienced by *yogis* who are engaged in subtlest meditation and are described by Svacchanda and other practical Śāstras as *prabuddha* connoting *icchā*, *prasaraṇa*, connoting *jñāna*, and *āvaraṇa*, connoting *kriyā*.[27] Therefore, it has been said in the seventh chapter in Śivadṛṣṭi: "By meditating on the supreme Self (*parātmani*) who is *cit* (*sunirbharatarā*), *ānanda* (*ahlāda*), fullfledged '*a*' i.e. *anuttara* (*bharitākāra-rūpiṇi*) and in whom all the three *śaktis* (viz. *icchā*, *jñāna* and *kriyā*) are fused (one acquires the nature of Śiva)." Again, "It is His Śakti that has acquired the form of the cosmos, just as a mass of clay acquires the form of a jar." (ŚD, VII, 28). And finally having described that 'There is only one principle (viz. Śiva), there is no difference in Him on account of the number of phases (like the four spheres of *pṛthivī*, *prakṛti*, *māyā* and Śakti or, three Śaktis, five states etc.), it declares

---

*Two points in this verse are noteworthy:

1. The earlier aspect of *kriyā* with *icchā* refers to transcendent state (*viśvottīrṇamayatā*): the latter aspect refers to immanence of Śiva (*viśvamayatā*).

2. *Sa* + *au* + : make the mantra *sauḥ* of which '*sa*' represents the three spheres of *pṛthivī*, *prakṛti* and *māyā* i.e. the 31 *tattvas*, *au* represents *śuddhavidyā*, *īśvara* and *sadāśiva* and the *visarga* represents Śiva and Śakti. Thus *sauḥ* represents the entire divine manifestation.

that it is Śiva only who having assumed plentitude (*bharitatā*) of wondrous delight the effect of pulsating energy which is only an expression of the expansion of autonomy that is infinite and wonderful, has acquired the aspect of Bhairava.

In Śiva-Dṛṣṭi, this is the position which has been described in the first chapter which lays down the tradition of Trika: "When *anuttara* abides only in the experience of its consciousness and bliss (*cidānanda*), at that time its *icchā-śakti* (as known of the form of *abhyupagama*), *jñānaśakti* (of the form of *prakāśa* or light) also abide in the same consciousness and bliss (*cidānanda*). Thus Śiva abides with perfect fusion of the three subtle Śaktis (viz. *icchā*, *jñāna* and *kriyā*) in Himself. That supreme Reality is then the highest *cit* (consciousness) and *ānanda* (beatitude) without any differentiation (*nirvibhāgaḥ*)." (ŚD I, 3-4)

Referring to the knowledge of an object, such as a jar, the same text says:

"Even at the time of the knowledge of an object, such as a jar etc. (these five aspects viz. *icchā*, *jñāna*, *kriyā*, *ānanda* and *cit* are present); 'one knows the jar'—this indicates *kriyāśakti*, 'knows' this fact indicates *jñāna-śakti* and if one does not have *icchā*, knowledge would not be possible (lit., there would be destruction of knowledge). When a thing has been known (i.e. after *pramiti*) the absence of inclination towards that thing (*aunmukhyābhāva*) indicates his abstention (*nivṛtti*) from that thing, but this is not possible without the experience of *ānanda* (*nirvṛtti*); that is why one does not advance towards that which one dislikes; and knowledge is not possible without *cit*." (ŚD I, 24-25).

Similarly:

"Because one desires, therefore one proceeds to know or do. Activity takes place only with desire. Of this (i.e., of activity with desire), two aspects have to be assumed, viz. the earlier and the later (ŚD I, 19). The earlier consists of the acquisition of *ānanda* (beatitude) accruing from accomplishing a deed; the later consists of its inclination towards manifestation which is its expansion. Śiva does not at all become gross by this inclination towards manifestation" (ŚD I, 17).

This treasure of Āgama has been accepted on account of its reasonableness as one's very life.

Notes

1. The *parāpara mantra* consists of 19 *padas*. They are the following:
1. *Oṃ* 2. *aghore* 3. *hṛīḥ* 4. *paramaghore* 5. *huṃ* 6. *ghorarūpe* 7. *haḥ* 8. *ghoramukhi* 9. *bhime* 10. *bhīṣaṇe* 11. *vama* 12. *piba* 13. *he* 14. *ru ru* 15. *ra ra* 16. *phaṭ* 17. *huṃ* 18. *haḥ* 19. *phaṭ*

In this *mantra, ru ru ra ra phaṭ huṃ haḥ phaṭ* pertain to Śiva, so we are not concerned with these in this context. The remaining *padas* pertain to Śakti with which we are concerned here.

2. The eight *yoginis* like limbs of *parāpara mantra* are the following:

1. Brāhmī 2. Māheśvarī 3. Kaumārī 4. Vaiṣṇavī 5. Vārāhī 6. Indrāṇī 7. Cāmuṇḍā 8. Yogeśvarī.

3. They include 30 letters as shown below:

	Divinities	*Mantras*	*No. of letters*
1.	Brāhmī	*Oṃ aghore hṛīḥ*	5
2.	Māheśvarī	*Parama ghore huṃ*	6
3.	Kaumārī	*Ghora rūpe haḥ*	5
4.	Vaiṣṇavī	*Ghoramukhe*	4
5.	Vārāhī	*Bhime*	2
6.	Indrāṇī	*Bhīṣaṇe*	3
7.	Cāmuṇḍā	*Vama*	2
8.	Yogeśvarī	*piba he*	3
		Total:	30

4. The nominatives of address amounting to 22 letters are the following:

1. Aghore	3
2. Paramaghore	5
3. Ghorarūpe	4
4. Ghoramukhi	4
5. Bhīme	2
6. Bhīṣaṇe	3
7. He	1
	22

5. See the note on Soma and Śiva on the verse 5 earlier.

6. *Akula-kula*: *Akula* is Bhairava, the transcendental energy; *kula* is the Śakti that brings about manifestation. *Akula* contains *kula* as '*a*' contains all the other phonemes.

7. *Pūrṇa-kṛśa-vimarśa-śakti*: the Divine Creative Energy is said to be full or *pūrṇā* because it is she who goes on projecting things out of herself which indicates that she is perfectly full and rich. She is said to be *pūrṇā* from the point of view of *sṛṣṭi* or emanation.

She is said to be *kṛśā* or emaciated, because she reabsorbs all that she has emanated which indicates that she is depleted and must take back the manifested objects to make up her loss. She is said to be *kṛśā* from the point of view of *saṃhāra* or withdrawal. She is said to be both, *tadubhayatā*, because she both emanates and withdraws.

She is said to be none of these—*tadubhaya-rahita*—because in herself, she transcends all these conditions. All the adjectives which are applied to her only point to the limitations of human speech. In reality, she is inexpressible in any human language.

8. *Icchā* is different from *icchāśakti*.

9. *A* is the state of *sāmarasya* (identity) of *akula*, *anuttara* and *kulaśakti*. This is known as '*bhairavaśaktimadvimarśasattā*.'

10. There is triple *sṛṣṭi*: (i) that which is only transcendental emanation at the level of *parā vāk* or Supreme Verbum is *mahā-sṛṣṭi*. This is undifferentiated. (ii) When it is reflected in *parā-parā śakti* i.e., at the level of *paśyanti* and *madhyamā* it is known as *parāparā sṛṣṭi*. (iii) When it is fully differentiated in *aparā śakti* at the level of *vaikharī*, it is known as *aparā sṛṣṭi*.

11. *Sūryarūpā*: She is compared to the Sun, because the sun projects his energy outwards.

12. *Soma* here represents the *viśvottīrṇa* or the transcendental state and *sūrya* or the sun represents the *viśvamaya* or the immanent state. In an inverse state, *soma* or moon is the symbol of manifestation and *sūrya* or sun is the symbol of withdrawal.

13. Just as '*a*' pervades all the phonemes from '*a*' to '*ū*', even so these also rest in the *anuttara* '*a*'. So is the base both from the point of view of expansion from *ā* to *ū* and contraction from *ū* to *ā*.

14. On the basis of *sarvātmaka-bhāva* (each is the epitome of all), the other five are inherent in each.

15. *Baindavī kalā*: *Baindavī* means pertaining to *bindu*. *Bindu* or *vindu* which ordinarily means a dot represents the *paraḥ pramātā*, the Highest Self. Just as it is impossible for one to catch the shadow of one's head with one's feet, for the shadow of the head always eludes them, even so it is impossible to know the knower by the various means of knowing, for these owe their own existence to the knower. In this particular context what is meant to be said is that *icchā śakti* cannot be grasped by means of the objects of *icchā* (desire) with which it is associated, for objects owe their very existence to *icchā* or desire.

16. Heterogenous intermixture is such as *ṛ=r+i, ṝ=r+ī, l=ḷ+i, ḹ=ḷ+ī, e=a+i, ai=a+e, o=a+u, au=a+o*. There is no intermixture from *ā* to *ū* as they are homogenous. Eight vowels from *ṛ* upto *au* are the field of *kriyāśakti*.

17. In that void is experienced a faint sound of '*r*' which together with '*i*' of *icchāśakti* becomes '*ṛ*' and with *ī* of *īśanāśakti* becomes *ṝ*. Thus '*r*' is the seed letter (*bīja svara*) of *tejas* or fire.

18. *R* which is *agnibīja* (the seed letter of fire) is symbolic of heat and mobility and *l* which is *pṛthivībīja* (the seed letter of earth) is symbolic of solidity and compactness.

19. The reference to the rule implies that the transcendental *anuttara-tattva* prone to spreading externally at first being averse to external appearance suddenly enters a state of vacuity known as the state of *anāśrita-śiva*. In terms of the phoneme *ḷ*, it may be said that transcending the long aspect of *ḷ*, it comes to cessation in the *pluta* or prolated aspect of *ḹ*.

20. This group of four letters i.e. *Ṛ*, *Ṝ*, *Ḷ*, *Ḹ* is said to be eunuch, because these letters are neither purely vowels nor purely consonants. They have a semblance of both, just as a eunuch has a semblance of both male and female. They are called eunuch also because they are unable to produce any other letter, just as a eunuch cannot produce a child. They are called germless only because having entered into the state of void, they are like burnt seed unable to proceed into further expansion. Being vowels, they are not totally germless.

21. In the inverse state i.e. if '*a*' and '*ā*' come after '*i*' and '*ī*', and not before, there will be '*ya*' instead of '*e*' according to Pāṇini's rule of *sandhi*—"*iko yaṇaci*".

22. Though according to the grammar of classical Sanskrit,

both *e*, *ai* and *o* are long, yet in the aspect of *mantra* in Śaiva-śāstra and the Vedas '*e*' and '*o*' are short also. So *a*+*i* or *i*=*e* (short) and *ā*=*i* or *ī*=*e* (long). In the Trika, the short vowel symbolizes Śiva and the long one symbolizes the union of Śiva-Śakti.

23. *Icchā* and *īśanā* do not have any other element in them. *Unmeṣa* or *jñāna* has the elements of both *icchā* and *jñāna* in it.

24. *Au* is called *triśūla* or *śūlabīja* i.e. trident because all the *śaktis*, *icchā*, *jñāna*, and *kriyā* are present in it in the clearest form.

25. The internal expansion of manifestation within *anuttara* itself comes to a stop at *au*, for this letter indicates the termination of *kriyāśakti* within *anuttara* itself. After this, the expansion of manifestation is withdrawn into the *unity* of *anuttara*. The dot (*bindu*) in '*aṃ*' is symbolic of the dissolution of the inner manifestation in *anuttara*.

This inner manifestation is the *bimba* or origin of its *pratibimba* or reflection in the external manifestation in the world. The inward manifestation is accomplished inwardly in *anuttara* itself and is known as *svarūpa-sṛṣṭi* or the manifestation within the inward nature itself.

The vowels from '*a*' to '*au*' represent the inner manifestation within *anuttara*, and the vowel *aṃ* represents the dissolution (*saṃhāra*) of the inner manifestation within *anuttara* itself and identification with '*cinmaya-puruṣa-tattva*' i.e., with *Śāmbhava-tattva*.

The developed form of *icchā-śakti* is *jñāna-śakti*, and the developed form of *jñāna-śakti* is *kriyā-śakti*. So *kriyā-śakti* includes both *icchā* and *jñāna*.

Abhinavagupta says in Tantrāloka III, Verse 111:

> uditāyāṃ kriyāśaktau somasūryāgni dhāmani /
> avibhāgaḥ prakāśo yaḥ sa binduḥ paramo hi naḥ //

"When *kriyāśakti* is accomplished in the phases represented by *soma* or *icchā-śakti*, *sūrya* or *jñānaśakti* and *agni* or *kriyāśakti* i.e. in the entire *svarūpa-sṛṣṭi* or inner manifestation of *anuttara*, the experience at the bottom of all this that flashes forth is the dot known as Śiva-*bindu* (or *vindu*) i.e. that which is undivided light, that which, in spite of all differentiation, does not change, remains unaffected and does not deviate from its inherent oneness is *vindu* (the dot expressed by *aṃ*=.)"

26. The two dots of *visarga* (:) indicate the truth that though from the point of view of Śakti symbolized by the lower dot, there is an expansion of an outer world, yet from the point of view of Śiva or *śaktimat* symbolized by the upper dot, the entire universe rests in the I-consciousness of Śiva.

27. In manifesting the world, there is no *vikāra* or change in Śiva. All manifestation is the outcome of his Śakti, but he is not changed in the gross physical world. Trika does not believe in *pariṇāmavāda*. Its doctrine is that of *svātantryavāda*. Śiva brings about the manifestation of the world by means of his *svātantrya* or absolute autonomy by which he effects all changes without undergoing any change in himself. This is represented by the dot in *aṃ* (.).

TEXT

From *sa eṣa parameśvaro visṛjati* on p. 63, l. 6 upto *prāgeva uktametat* on p. 69, l. 3.

[The nature of Śakti-*visarga* and activity]

TRANSLATION

The Lord (always coupled with His emanatory Energy) emanates the universe. That energy of emanation (*visargaśakti*) extends from the earth to '*śakti*' (from the point of view of *tattva*) or from '*ka*' to '*kṣa*' (from the point of view of letter). This is declared as the 'sixteenth *kalā*'[1] (also as *amā kalā*) in the following verse: "In the *cinmaya puruṣa*, i.e. Śiva who is of 16 *kalās*, the 16th *kalā* is known as *amṛtakalā* (the immortal or 'changeless *kalā*')." This is the standpoint neither of Sāṃkhya nor of Vedānta, but only of Śaiva Śāstra. The *visargaśakti* of the supreme Lord is the seed of the highest beatitude.

Thus '*a*' and other letters (i.e. *ā*, *i*, *u*, *ṛ* and *ḷ*) having acquired compactness (*ghanatā*) and assuming the form of *śāktayoni* or consonant do not deviate from their essential nature. All these, by their transmission in consonants (*yoni rūpa*) which are however, their own essential nature, are known as having acquired the position of *visarga* i.e. expansion. As has been said, "O great goddess, that, where the vowels finally reach their state of repose i.e., the consonants, is said to be the face of the *guru* (*guru-*

vaktra) or *visarga pada*, and the collective whole of the *śaktis* (*śakti-cakra*)."[2]

The condensation of '*a*' itself makes the class '*ka*', all of them being guttural; the condensation of '*i*' makes the '*ca*' class, all of them being palatal. The condensation of '*u*' gives rise to '*pa*' class, all of them being labial. The condensation of *ṛ* brings about the '*ṭa*' class, all of them being cerebral. The condensation of '*ḷ*' bring about the '*ta*' class, all of them being dental, '*ya*' and '*śa*' go along with '*ca*' class; '*ra*' and '*ṣa*' go along with '*ṭa*' class being cerebral. '*La*' and '*sa*' go along with '*ta*' class, being dental. '*Va*' issues from '*ta*' and '*pa*' class i.e., it is labio-dental. Even in Vijñānākala who has either *svātantrya* or *śakti*, but lacks *bodha* or awareness, or has merely *bodha* (*cinmātrasyāpi*) but not *svātantrya*, there is the *kriyāśakti* (i.e., even his *cinmātratā* or *bodha* is a subtle form of *kriyāśakti*). That compactness (*ghanatā*) accruing at *visarga-pada*, according to the mode as described earlier (*uktanītyā*) is produced by the group of six *śaktis*, viz., *a*, *ā*, *i*, *ī*, *u*, *ū*; or *anuttara*, *ānanda*, *icchā*, *īśanā*, *unmeṣa*, and *ūnatā*. Thus the five classes of *cit*, *ānanda*, *icchā*, *jñāna*, and *kriyā* multiplied by six *śaktis* (*anuttara* etc.) referred to above become thirty. With the addition of the six referred to above,the total becomes thirty-six *tattvas*.

Thus Śiva-*bīja* i.e. *svara* (vowel) becoming condensed through its autonomy and abiding in the *śākta-rūpa* in a *śakti* form as *kusuma* (blood) is called *yoni* i.e. a consonant.[3] (By the combination of Śiva-*bīja* and *Śākta-yoni*, there is universal manifestation).

That red sperm of Śakti or female principle according to the principle referred to before, consisting of three angles viz., *grāhya* (object), *grahaṇa* (knowledge), *grāhaka* (subject) when mingled with the semen of Śiva or male principle becomes the place of procreation (*visargapada*) or external expansion. It is only by the meeting of both Śiva and Śakti that there is the activity of *puṣpa* or the female creative red sperm, i.e. in the female aspect, it is known as *yoni* or female organ of generation because of its fitness for mating by the Śiva aspect or male. Therefore, that red sperm (*kusumam eva*) itself being three-angled represents the *yoni* or female organ of generation. At this stage, the triad of *grāhya* or *prameya* (object), *grahaṇa* or *pramāṇa* (knowledge), *grāhaka* or *pramātā* (subject) symbolizes clearly the three forms of *soma* (moon), *sūrya* (sun), *agni* (fire), *sṛṣṭi*, *sthiti*, *saṃhāra*, *iḍā*, *piṅgalā*, *suṣumnā*, *dharma*, *adharma*, and mixed form of the two i.e. *dharmādharma*. The triadic Śakti of the Supreme is known as Bhairavī. The meeting point or union of Śiva and Śakti now appears in the form of a hexagonal (*ṣaṭkoṇa*) *mudrā* and being the spot and basis of the generation of manifestation is designated as *yoni* or the female organ of generation. (While both Śiva and Śakti are separately triadic, their union is hexagonal).[5]

In the chapter on *khaṇḍacakravicāra* in Kubjikāmata, it is with reference to this matter that it has been declared: "There is *mahāmāyā* above *māyā* who is the very embodiment of bliss because of her being of a triangular aspect." Therefore, the union of Śiva and Śakti which is represented by semen (*bīja*) and ovum (*kusuma*) being fused into one compactness should be worshipped by oneself in the form of his Self. This is what has been advised in Trikatantrasāra:

"The spiritual aspirant who experiences his identity with the incipient unity of Śiva-Śakti found in *icchā-śakti* and with their compact unity found in *jñāna-śakti* should worship the highest triad of the union of the triangular aspect of Śiva and the triangular aspect of Śakti."

Therefore, though the condensation of the phonemes becomes distinct only in the *vaikharī* or gross aspect, yet it abides primarily in the supreme verbum (*parāvāk*) which is all inclusive (*sarvasarvātmaka*).

In that (i.e. in *parā*), even the organs of speech (*sthāna*) such as throat, lips and manner of articulation (*karaṇa*) are all-inclusive. This is the special point to be noted. Even inwardly one mutters and envisions. This is a matter of distinct experience. Their difference is due to the various organs of utterance, for audition is the very life of the letters. Moreover, even a child, when he is being taught the use of words, learns the names of various objects by muttering the words within. Even while he thinks in the opposite way or in an uncertain way, so long as he uses his mind, he does know something. All understanding is due to use of words. So letters which are produced by contraction of the throat (*saṃvāra*), expansion of the throat (*vivāra*), which are unaspirated (*alpaprāṇa*) and which are aspirated (*mahāprāṇa*) with the aid of breath and sound are present, according to their appropriate nature, inwardly (in *madhyamā* and *paśyantī,*) as they are in *vaikharī*). Otherwise (i.e., if it were not so) then on account of there being no difference in the letters produced by the same organ of articulation, the powers of the senses uttering the letters separately would disappear even in *vaikharī*. Besides diversity of ideas like 'I hear' (in *vaikharī*) and 'I heard' (in *madhyamā* and *paśyantī*); 'I see' (in *vaikharī*) and 'I saw' (in *madhyamā* and *paśyantī*); 'I ideate' (in *vaikharī*) and 'I ideated' (in *madhyamā* and *paśyantī*) would otherwise be impossible (i.e., if these diversities were not present in the inner states).

So by this repeatedly thought-out reasoning, entering more and more in the interior, cherish that consciousness which is a mass of awareness and is all-inclusive,[6] and therefore the abode of guttural and labial energies (also), and in which inheres that creative I-consciousness, viz. *ahaṃ* which is the very quintessence of autonomy, which is the venerable phoneme, the highest *mantra*, and is (always) inherent within. If one were to object, "in that undifferentiated mass of consciousness, how can there be a division like: this is the organ of utterance, this the articulation, this the letter etc.?" my reply would be: "that unbounded, absolute freedom brings about in the supreme Self of every one different apprehensions like 'this is a jar' (external object); 'this is happiness' (internal object); 'this is knowledge' (*pramāṇa*); 'I am the knower' (*pramātā* or subject)." In this diversity of experiences what and how much is the exertion?[7]

Therefore one and the same venerable supreme verbum (*ekaiva parābhaṭṭārikā*), being all inclusive, abides as the highest Lord in all, whether stone, tree, animal, man, god, Rudra, *pralayākala* or *vijñānākala* (*kevalī*), Mantra, Mantreśvara, Mantramaheśvara and others. Therefore, *Mātṛkā* whose body consists of letters (and sounds) which reside in various stations as their very soul either in indistinct (*asphuṭa*) or imperceptible (*avyakta*) way as in *madhyamā* or in distinct (*sphuṭa*) or perceptible (*vyakta*) way as in *vaikharī* is declared as the efficacious potency of *mantra* (*mantravīrya*).

Similarly it is said that the same note produced at different places in different instruments like the *vīṇā*, *vipañcī* (a *vīṇā* with nine strings), *kacchapī* (another *vīṇā* with a tortoise-shaped soundboard), *muraja* (a kind of drum) is said to be belonging to the same register (*ekasthāna*).[8]

Similarly, the basic or the starting note (*sthāyi svara*) in different registers, such as bass (*mandra*), middle (*madhya*) and upper (*tāra*) is said to be the same. Similarly the same phoneme is produced in some creatures from different organs. For instance, it is found that in crows, the sounds '*ka*', '*ṭa*' and '*ra*' are produced jointly by so many organs, such as stomach, anus, throat, palate. Though they (*ka, ṭa, ra* etc. of crows) are indistinct, they are all right in themselves, being phoneme, and a phoneme apart from *Mātṛkā* is impossible. If it is said that certain phonemes are separate from *Mātṛkā*, and being indistinct and meaningless, they are useless, therefore, they should not be accepted, we say that this is not correct. There is usefulness even of an indistinct phoneme, such as the sound of a *muraja* (a kind of drum) or of an ocean in as much as it is helpful in bringing about joy or sorrow. What other utility is desired? In Śaiva Śāstra also, mostly those have been chosen as *mantra* whose phonemes are indistinct, for instance (indistinct sound of *praṇava* in) *ardhacandra* etc. are said to be the very essence of a *mantra*. It is also said that the *mantra* at the stage of *nirodhinī* makes only a hissing sound. The (indistinct) sound of bell, cymbal etc. which strikes the ear has also been (agreeably) indicated in the teaching about *nāda-yoga*. It has been said in Guhyayoginī Tantra: "As the horse neighs, as the tame ox bellows, as the lion roars, as the camel produces a guttural sound, even so the powerful *yoginīs* (*balādhikāḥ*) by muttering a *mantra* (of indistinct sound) draw down the very life of *paśus* (empirical beings). This is the application of *mahāmantra* which is used in drawing towards oneself even that which cannot be overpowered". This is only an expedient.

In fact, "It is the inner sound that is *mantra*". *Mahāmantras* which have distinct and meaningful phonemes can be easily used both by you and us.

Therefore, the indistinct sound also is definitely of the form of phoneme, just as a jar placed even at a distance is jar all the same. This is settled. That a phoneme, though produced in different places, through the difference of *prāṇa*, like that of a bird or kettle-drum etc., is the same phoneme--this is also settled. Therefore what the sage Patañjali says, viz. "There can be a knowledge of the sound of all beings to the yogī," is fully realized by me now. Otherwise how can that which is a commingling of word, object and idea (*śabdārthapratyayānām*) by mutual imposition (*itaretarādhyāso*), and that acquisition of Supreme Genius which can distinguish them in their minutest detail by means of a combined operation (*saṃyama*) of *dhāraṇā* (concentration), *dhyāna* (meditation) and *samādhi* (entranced attention) on each of them separately and in the knowledge of the cooing of birds etc. without their distinct phoneme (*asphuṭa varṇa*)? When those indistinct phonemes also (i.e. the *asphuṭa* or indistinct phonemes like those of birds etc.) acquire the status of words which have perfectly clear meaning (lit., whose meanings are really identical with those words) like distinct phonemes (*varṇānāmiva*), then according to the principle mentioned, the cooing of birds and even the sounds of kettle drum etc. become full of meaning. Then as the cooing of birds has some meaning, even so the sound of drum may be indicative of either conquest or defeat (in battle). It is from that point of view only that the different *Sūtras* of Śikṣā (the science of proper articulation and pronunciation of words) etc., according to some '*ha*' and *visarga* are to be pronounced 'from the chest', according to others, they are to be pronounced 'from the root of the teeth', can have some sense, not at all otherwise. This is the reason why on the basis of slight difference, grammarians being in doubt about the different forms of phonemes have increased the list of phonemes to sixty-four by considering the following as different phonemes:

1. *Jihvāmūlīya* and *upadhmānīya* from *visarjanīya*.[10]
2. The five *yama akṣaras*: *ṅuṃ*, *ñuṃ*, *ṇuṃ*, *nuṃ*, *muṃ* as different from the five nasal phonemes *ṅa*, *ña*, *ṇa*, *na*, *ma* though they are only varied forms of the latter.[11]
3. By taking the varied form of *ḍa*, *ḍha*, *ya*, *ra*, *la*, *va*, *kṣa* by means of a short form of articulation as different from those letters.

In this division of phonemes, there is the same difference between *ṛ* and *r* as between vowel and consonant. It has been said in Trikaratnakula also: "The *Mātṛkā* whose variety has been determined by multiplying eight by eight (8×8=64) alone should be considered as *kulacakra* (i.e. *śakti cakra*).[12] That *kulacakra* pervades the entire universe. The difference of these 64 phonemes has been determined in detail in the work 'Mātṛkājñānabheda'.

Here (i.e. in Trika), there is no fondness for that procedure for integral wholeness or perfection is the essence of this system. So, there is such method of the entrance into the supreme consciousness everywhere. Whether in *jñānaśakti* (*saṅkalpyamānaḥ*) or in *kriyāśakti* (*kriyamāṇaḥ*), every object rests on the superb splendour of the *mantra* of supreme verbum, viz. the pure, creative I-consciousness (*vimarśātma*) which is one's essential nature (*svarūpabhūta*) and which is non-*māyiya* (non-empirical) and unconventional (*asāṅketika*). It is that state which is lauded by all the schools of philosophy as indeterminate (*nirvikalpa*). That splendour of the supreme *mantra* (*paramantramahaḥ*) is present in earth category etc. both in unmixed or mixed state in the form of vowels (*bīja*) and consonants (*piṇḍa*) in phonemes like '*ka*' etc. Otherwise there would have been no difference between the determinate different pairs of knowledge, such as Meru-mountain and Jujube fruit, water and fire, jar (an external experience) and pleasure (an inner experience) and their indeterminate knowledge. Even determinate knowledge (*vikalpa*) which arises only from the heedlessness (of the indeterminate state) would have followed the same path (i.e. in that also there would not have been mutual distinction). On the contrary, it could not have been able to make the distinction-less indeterminate state as the basis of all distinctions. The fact is that the *mantra* (of I-consciousness or *parāvāk*) which transcends all conventionality is taught as the object of worship by the all-knowing teachers even when they know that that *mantra* is the source of all the mutually distinctive conventions. It is, indeed, in that non-conventional splendour of the supreme verbum (*vāṅmahasi*) i.e. into *aham* (I) that all empirical (*māyiya*) conventional symbols so terminate that they i.e., the *māyiya* (empirical) symbols attain identity with that transcendental, non-conventional *mantra*, viz., *aham*. The only signification of those empirical (*māyiya*) conventional symbols consists in the attainment of the experience of the essential nature of the non-conventional, there is no other signification of these symbols. By constant repetition when one enters the sphere of the non-conventional, one recollects clearly that the consciousness of the word '*go*' (cow) attained in a remote past (or in a previous life) and later, on the occasion of conventional use, the consciousness attainable of a visible cow—both merge ultimately in a higher sphere of another kind of consciousness transcending conventionality and beyond the pale of *māyā*. Even in a child, there is at first, the predominance of only *cit* (pure, unconditioned consciousness). Therefore, even in the present life after a previous one, there exists in him a consciousness which transcends conventionality. Otherwise there would be no support for his conventionality to stay. So it is on the basis of the non-conventional that there can be the possibility of the comprehension of the conventional, not otherwise. This is what was ascertained by venerable Utpaladeva in his commentary on Īśvara-pratyabhijñā.[13]

The means for entrance into the non-conventional state is described in the following words by revered Kaṇṭhapāda: "Where one sees something else, hears something else, does something else, talks something else, thinks something else, eats something else--in all such conditions, there is the stance of the non-conventional reality (i.e. it is the non-conventional that controls all these functions). The attention is cast elsewhere, the eye is directed elsewhere. That is how *prāṇa* always proceeds effortlessly." (Sv. T. VII, 58).

So, the conventional sign i.e., the determinate knowledge (*savikalpaka jñāna*) pursuing its source terminates in the *anuttara* or the transcendental state. That transcendental state whose very nature is an eagerness always to exhibit that kind of multitudinous variety, always goes on expanding from the point of view of manifestation (*visarga*).

It is that impulsion to manifest that brings about expansion upto '*ha*' aspect. Of that, viz., of that impulsion to manifest (*visargasya*) there is the aspect of *śakti-kuṇḍalinī* designated as half of '*ha*' (in Trika) which assuming the shape of a dot (*bindu*) that is a means of identity with the essential nature of Śiva, passes back again into the *anuttara* (transcendental) state, and thus rests in the essential nature.

The consciousness symbolized by one phoneme, viz. '*a*' i.e., the *anuttara* or transcendental consciousness indeed by its very nature transcends all concept of space, time and causality and which, according to the previously stated principle, is wholly perfect, resorts instantly to the stage of *para visarga*, i.e., the supreme stage of manifestation.

It is only after connexion with the stage of *para-visarga* i.e.

the supreme creative elan, that there is the stance of *ānanda*, *icchā*, *iśanā*, *unmeṣa*, its expansion, i.e. *ūnatā* or *ū*, its diversity i.e., *ṛ*, *ṝ*, *ḷ*, *ḹ* and the product of *kriyāśakti* viz. *e*, *ai*, *o*, *au*.

That supreme, energy of manifestation (*para* or *śāmbhava visarga*) becomes supreme-cum-non-supreme energy (*parāpara*) which expands because of its excessive plentitude and because of its being inseparably connected with that supreme energy (*svasattā-nāntarikatayā*) and instantly becomes the aspect of '*ha*' i.e., *apara visarga* or external manifestation. It is the acquisition of the state of '*ha*', i.e. external manifestation that actually brings about the existence of a network of innumerable categories symbolized by '*ka*' etc. It is again this very '*ha kalā*' or external manifestation which entering the *bindu* i.e., *aṃ* of '*ahaṃ*' terminates into the *anuttara* state.

Thus it is that supreme venerable Goddess, the supreme verbum who is only one, non-dual, wholly integral and perfect and who is present as *saṃvedanasattā*, i.e. as *vimarśamayi-kriyāśakti* or conscious Creative Energy. There is no question of succession (of space, time and form) in this act of manifestation. In the aspect of manifestation, this is known as '*ahaṃ*' (*a-ha-m*) or Śiva-Śakti-*nara*; inversely in the aspect of withdrawal this is known as '*ma-ha-a*' or *nara*-Śakti-Śiva. Though appearing as two, this is really one consciousness.

Thus, everywhere, even in the consciousness of jar (external), or pleasure (internal) etc., it is the I-consciousness whose whole treasure consists in calm repose within itself. As has been said by Utpaladeva: "The resting of all objective and subjective experience within oneself is what is meant by I-feeling" (Ajaḍa-pramātṛ-siddhi, verse 22). In reality, that I-consciousness is all-inclusive according to the principle already enunciated (viz., *sarvaṃ sarvātmakaṃ*—everything is in everything). That I-consciousness is Bhairava Himself pervaded by the Supreme Energy. As has been said by myself in the following hymn of praise:

"I make an obeisance, through my own joy, to that highest reality which is wondrous delight (*paramārtha-camatkṛti*) which blossoms forth everywhere in the multitude of objects without cessation (*bhāva-paṭale parijñābhamāna viccheda-śūnya*), which is the I in the perfect mode of existence (*pūrṇavṛtti aham iti*), which is full of lustre (*devīm*), whose nature it is to shed light all round (*prathanasvabhāvāṃ*) and who abides in one's own self (*svātmasthitiṃ*)". One should understand that this is the doctrine that has been taught in the Advayasampattivārtika composed by Vāmana. So it is settled that the phoneme '*a*' only is endowed with fullest richness i.e., is perfect in every way. In words like '*harṣa*', '*ghaṭa*', '*nīla*', the letters '*ha*' etc. have to be combined together with the preceding and the following letters (in order to make a complete word). Otherwise (i.e., if the letters are not combined in a synthetic whole), if only the last letter is added to the group of letters such as '*ha*', etc., it would not form a complete whole, the word would be concealed within and would be unable to give rise to a concept.[14]

Thus in all kinds of knowledge, all the divinities of letters (*devatāḥ* i.e., *varṇa-devatāḥ*) arising together simultaneously, would bring about concepts of strange kinds. It is with this idea in view that in the chapter on *kāla* (time) in Svacchanda Tantra it has been described that in the duration of one breath, even in the sixteenth part or one *tuṭi* or space covered by 2¼ fingers of one breath (of a yogī), there are, along with an explanation of the passage of sixty or its double number of years, the rise and dissolution of eight Mātṛkās, eleven Rudras, ten guardians of quarters (*lokapālas*), twenty-seven constellations, eight Nāgas and other divinities. Thus, timelessness is the highest truth of reality. If the highest Reality is what is to be decidedly the empirical (*māyīya*) measure of truth, it would only lead to atheism (in as much as it is beyond the empirical understanding). But in the supreme or transcendental consciousness, it appears immediately in that state (of timelessness). Therefore, what has been said, by way of teaching viz., 'he sees something else, thinks something else', etc., refers to one *anuttara* consciousness (*ekasyāmeva jñānakalanāyāṃ*) that *anuttara* or transcendental consciousness being the substratum (simultaneously) of the three divinities, viz. *parā* (*parā vāk*), *parāparā* (*paśyantī* and *madhyamā*), and *aparā* (*vaikharī*) is certainly invariable truth. Really speaking, the highest truth of all kinds of knowledge is I-consciousness.

So this is established, viz., the supreme divine impulse to manifestation (*visarga* in its aspect of *prasāra* or expansion) in its plenitude of beatitude (*ānanda-śaktibharitaḥ*) goes on ejecting the entire cosmos which is lying within it first as *para visarga* and then in its progressive congealment, it becomes external manifestation ('*ha*' i.e., *apara visarga*) (*hakārātmatām pratipadya*) and the *visarga* simultaneously goes on reabsorbing its manifestation in its aspect of *saṃhāra* or withdrawal and after diverse combinations finally it becomes '*kṣa*'.[15] This very emanation (*sa eva eṣa visargo*) whose nature it is to give rise to a multitude of innumerable objects which spring up from the middle *suṣumṇā* stage (*madhyamasauṣumṇa padocchalat-tattadanantabhāvapaṭalātmā*), now making a combination of two consonants[16] (*dūtyātmakaśāktayoni-saṃghaṭṭa*), viz. of the appropriate consonants (*ka* and *sa*) which in active state resorts to a state in which there is no actual impact (*anāhatanāda-daśāśrayaṇena*) (and thus) putting an end to all combination (*viśliṣyan*) enters the transcendental stage which is constant (*dhruvadhāmni anuttarapade*). This has been said even before.[18]

Notes

1. From '*a*' to '*aṃ*', there are 15 *kalās* (energies of letter) and '*aḥ*' is the sixteenth *kalā*. This is the essential nature of the Lord. This sixteenth *kalā* of *aḥ* is known as *visarga-kalā*. From '*ka*' to '*kṣa*' which represents external manifestation, there is always *prasāra-saṅkoca* (expansion-contraction), but the *visarga-kalā* remains changeless in its nature. In *prāṇāyama* also, fifteen *tuṭis* go on increasing or decreasing but the 16th *tuṭi* remains unchanged. In the moon also, 15 digits go on increasing or decreasing, but the 16th digit, the background of all and hidden from view, remains unchanged.

The *visarga śakti* or the emanative Energy of Śiva is called *amṛta kalā*, because in spite of all the changes brought about by the energy of Śiva, Śiva or His energy does not undergo any change whatsoever.

(a) *Parā visarga śakti*: There are three phases of *visargaśakti-parā, parāparā* and *aparā*. *Parā* is also known as *śāṃbhava* or *Śaiva visarga*. It is transcendental emanation, an interior emanation within the divine consciousness. It is the source and primary principle of *ānanda* or the highest divine beatitude. It is represented by the phoneme '*ā*'. That is why it has been said to be *paramānanda-bhūmi*.

(b) *Parāparā visarga-śakti* or *parāparā visarga*:

This is known also as *śakti visarga*. This is intermediate between the *parā* or supreme *visarga* and the *aparā* or non-supreme *visarga*. It is, at the same time, in unity with the non-dual supreme consciousness, and contains in a subtle way the potentiality of the empirical diversity. It is represented by the phoneme '*aḥ*'. It is known as *śākta visarga*.

(c) *Aparā visarga-śakti* or *apara visarga*:

This brings about the diversity of empirical manifestation, the manifestation of limited beings. This is why it is also known as *āṇava visarga*. It is represented by the phoneme '*ha*'.

2. Śakti is said to be mouth (*vaktra*) of Śiva because it is through Śakti that one can get entry in Śiva. The guru is also like Śiva. *Visarga-śakti* is also like *guru-mukha*. Therefore in this context *visarga-śakti* is also called '*guru vaktra*.'

3. It is difficult to bring out the *double entendre* used in this passage. Śiva represents the male-principle and Śakti the female principle. Śiva-*bija* is the white semen of the male, and *kusuma* the red menstruation of the female. In the present context the *bīja* is the *svara* or vowel and *yoni*, the female organ, is the consonant. Just as the combination of the male semen and the female sperm gives rise to fetus, so the *bija* of Śiva and *yoni* of Śakti brings about the full consonant.

4. *Kusuma* and *puṣpa* (lit. flower) are symbols of procreative energy.

5. The union of Śiva-*trikoṇa* which is *bija* and Śakti-*trikoṇa* which is *yoni* is known as *Ṣaṭkoṇa mudrā*. This is illustrated in the following diagram:

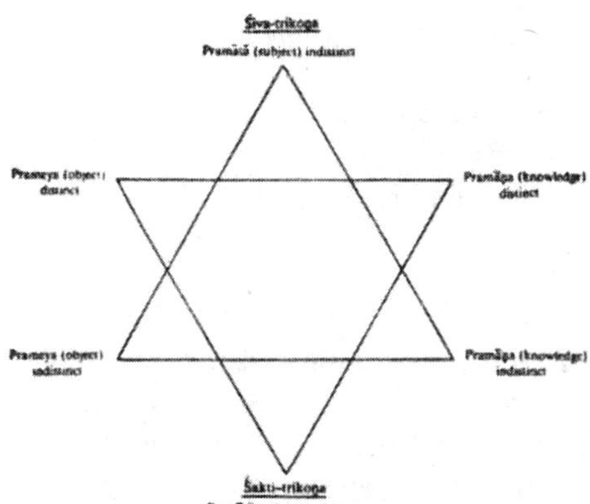

The three angles expressive of *pramātā*, *pramāṇa* and *prameya* in Śiva are indistinct, while the three angles expressive of the same in Śakti are distinct.

6. This refers to *parā vāk* or supreme Verbum which is only the product of '*ahaṃ vimarśa*' or the creative I-consciousness of Śiva.

7. A.G.'s reply means that the diversity of experience is not due to the effort of any individual but to the autonomous will of the Lord who has brought about manifestation in this fashion.

8. *Sthāna* in this context is a technical word of music which in Western music is known as register. There are three *sthānas* in music, viz. *mandra* (low and deep sound), *madhya* (middle) and *tāra* (high), known as bass (low), middle and upper register. A.G. means to say that a note struck in a particular register in different instruments, though differing in the position of production in the different instruments, is always the same.

9. The *mantras* pertaining to *ardhacandra*, *nirodhi*, *nāda*, *nādānta*, *śakti*, *vyāpinī*, *samanā*, and *unmanā* are *avyakta* (indistinct).

10. *Jihvāmūlīya*: uttered from the root of the tongue, especially the *visarga* before '*k*' and *kh*, written as ᳵ क, ख, *upadhmānīya*: the *visarga* as pronounced before '*p*' and '*ph*', written as ᳵ प, फ.

11. The five *yamas* are *ṅuṃ*, *ñuṃ*, *nuṃ*, *ṇuṃ*, *muṃ*.

12. This is how sixty-four phonemes are arrived at:

a, *i*, *u*, *ṛ*--pronounced short, long and prolated—(4 x 3)	=12
ḷ-short and prolated	2
e, *ai*, *o*, *au*--long and prolated	8
Sparśa varṇas from *ka* to *ma*	25
Antaḥstha varṇas i.e. *ya*, *ra*, *la*, *va*	4
Ūṣma varṇas or spirants *śa*, *ṣa*, *sa*, *ha*	4
Anusvāra and *visarga*	2
Jihvāmūlīya and *upadhmānīya*	2
Yamas	5
	64

13. The Īśvara-pratyabhijña-ṭīkā of Utpaladeva is now lost. It is said to have contained six or eight thousand verses.

14. Each word is a 'gestalt', an organized whole, in which the letters are synthetically combined in a unitary configuration.

15. The phoneme '*kṣa*' being a combination of *k*, *ṣ* and '*a*', denotes the union of Śiva and Śakti. It is known as *kūṭa-bīja*. *Kūṭa* is a technical name for a letter which results from the combination of two *halanta* letters. The two *halanta* letters are *k* and *ṣ*. The combination of '*a*' makes it *kṣa*.

The phoneme '*a*' itself descending at the level of '*ha*' becomes '*ka*'. The phonemes '*a*', '*ka*', '*ha*' and the *visarga* belong to the same organ of articulation (*akuhavisarjanīyānāṃ kaṇṭhaḥ*). '*Sa*' is only another form of *visarga*. *Kṣa* is the external symbol of Śiva and Śakti.

16. *Dūtyātmaka-śākta yoni* is a technical term for consonant.

Text

From *amīcākārādyāḥ* on p. 69, l. 3 upto *svato rasāt* on p. 74, l. 27.

Translation

In accordance with the principle that there are sixteen *tuṭis*[1] in one movement of *prāṇa*, the '*a*' etc., viz. the 16 vowels while inhering within as phonemes divide the *tuṭis* into half and half and including the cessation in the first half and the rise of *prāṇa* into the second half, represent the fortnight of time (15 *tithis*) in the external world.[2] These *tithis* are also said to be *kalās* or digits of the moon. When the sixteenth digit, which has the *śakti* or power to expand (*visargakalā* or *amā kalā*) remains apart i.e., does not expand, it is designated the seventeenth digit in Śrī Vādya and other scriptures in the following words:[3]

"That 16th or *visargātmikā kalā* by itself becomes half of '*ha*' i.e. *visarga* (:) and further half of *visarga*, i.e. *bindu* (.) Then it is known as the seventeenth goddess or *kalā*." Because of *visarga* being half of '*ha*' and further half of this being *bindu*, which is *viśleṣa*, i.e. apart, not taking part in expansion is known as the 17th *kalā*.[4]

If it is objected, "How can there be division of one phoneme '*a*' (into 16th and 17th *kalās*), for '*a*' which is *anuttara* is partless?" We reply, "In our system, every thing is partless, being non-different from the light of consciousness." Just as, through the unimpeded autonomy of Śiva, even when parts appear, partlessness of Reality is invariable, even so is the case with '*a*'. Where is the inconsistency? Thus the propriety of the development of phonemes is maintained, because of the appearance of partlessness in parts. Otherwise (on the occasion of utterance), how can the air whose nature it is to produce impact successively through the dental, labial, guttural, palatal phonemes strike the palate after having struck the throat? If it were to spread simultaneously in all the organs of articulation, then there would ensue simultaneity in the utterance of all the sounds. Consequently, the sound that is produced by impact of the air in the throat would become similar to the sound that is produced by impact in the palate. That which is experienced after breath and resonance is called '*anupradānam*'.[5] In letters having two or three *mātrās*, i.e. in *dirgha* or *pluta* letters the inclusion of one or two *mātrās* is implied. Similarly, in one *mātrā* also, the inclusion of half a *mātrā* is to be understood. As has been said by Bhaṭṭanārāyaṇa: "I bow to Śiva (*sthānu*) who is *citprakāśa* above the three genetic constituents of *prakṛti*, who is subtler than even half the *mātrā* indicated on the top of '*oṃ*' and greater than even a cosmic egg". (St. C. verse 7)

Here the fifty phonemes or even the universe is one without succession. At some places in the Mata Śāstra, etc., there is assumed to be 18th *kalā* or phase in the state resting on *anuttara* or the transcendental by means of the *viśleṣa* or separation of *visarga*, i.e. by means of the second dot, viz. the half of *visarga* (:). So the phenomena of fifty phonemes or in other words the entire universe is 'one' without succession.

So these *kalās*, i.e., the phonemes '*a*' etc. of *anuttara* are called *svara* on account of their revealing the delightful mental state. The etymological explanation of *svara* is as follows. The root '*svṛ*' means (i) those which utter a sound (*śabdayanti*) i.e. indicate a delightful mental mode (*sūcayanti cittaṃ*) and (ii) which (in the state of withdrawal) yield their essential nature to Śiva, the highest subject (*svaṃ ca svarūpam ātmānaṃ rānti*)," i.e. which dissolve completely in *anuttara*.[6] Thus the word '*svaraḥ*' means "those which transmitting their essential nature to the highest experient (i.e. *anuttara*) offer themselves i.e. get dissolved in *anuttara* (as vowels) (in the aspect of *saṃhāra* or withdrawal) and offer their form as consonants like '*ka*' etc. i.e., display (existents) externally (in the aspect of *prasāra* or expansion). These *svaras* as mere sound (*nādātmakāḥ*) are indicative of mental mode like pathos (*karuṇa*), the amatory sentiment (*sṛṅgāra*), contentment (*śānta*) by means of lamentation, pleasing words, laudatory expressions respectively either merely by themselves or by penetrating consonants. They display mental modes even of animals, a day-old creatures by appearing suddenly, without the slightest trace of any hindrance of conventional sign etc., and by acquiring the form of exclamatory enunciation (*svarakākvādirūpatām aśnuvānāḥ*), since they are so close to direct feeling. Thus *udātta* etc., have been taught as having the characteristic of expressiveness. They are indicative of mental mode by means of musical notes, such as *ṣaḍjā* etc. Thus everywhere in all kinds of knowledge, these phonemes from '*a*' to '*kṣa*', ingenious in bringing about varied acts, coming together in their several, distinctive forms (*samāpatantyo'haṃ ahamikayā*), (fundamentally) appearing without succession (*akramam eva bhāsamānaḥ*) displaying the transition of forms one after the other by their effectuating powers (*kalanāmayatayaiva mūrtikramasaṃkramaṇam eva diśyamānaṃ*) bring about spatial distinctions.

Otherwise (i.e. in the absence of spatial distinction of forms), there would have been no difference between the Meru mountain and an atom.

Thus these phonematic divinities enclose within themselves the varied activity of forms (*kriyāvaicitryātmakaṃ*) expressive of spatial distinctions and (also) time expressive of succession, bring into prominence (*ullāsayantyaḥ*) within (*antar* i.e. in *prāṇacāra*) and externally (in manifestation) devour i.e. absorb within the essential nature (the entire universe of objects). (From *prollāsasamaye* upto *bhagavatī sṛṣṭiḥ*, several ideas are telescoped into one another. Therefore, it is better to translate the sentence into parts.)

In the process of interiorization:

It enters the *anuttara* stage when *udyoga*, *avabhāsa*, *carvaṇa* and *vilāpana* are seized by *pramiti kalā* (state of awareness) and by residing in the awareness state and developing and gradually being impregnated with 16 forms[8] of manifestation reach the perfect state. '*Tadamṛtānanda*' refers to *ṛ*, *ṝ*, *ḷ*, *ḹ*. They are known as *amṛta varṇa* inasmuch as they are not productive of any external manifestation. So '*tadamṛtānanda viśrāntirūpaṃ*' means the immortal, essential, restful nature indicated by *ṛ, ṝ, ḷ, ḹ*.

Having the state of this restful nature, and being of the essence of *camatkāra*, i.e. the Divine I-consciousness, projecting the external manifestation of the four *kalās* (aspects) of *udyoga* etc. (with reference to the limited empirical subjects, means of knowledge, and objects), enjoying the swing of *pūrṇa* and *kṛśa*, i.e. introvertive and extrovertive emanation, expert in *grāsa* or devouring i.e. in *saṃhāra* or withdrawal of external manifestation and *vamana* (emitting) i.e. *prasāra* or projection of external manifestation and weaving the network of *soma* (the moon), symbolic of *pramāṇa* or means of knowledge of 16 *kalās* and *sūrya* (the sun), symbolic of *prameya* or the universe of objects of 12 *kalās*, upholding in the beginning '*a*', in the middle the group of consonants from '*ka*' to *kṣa* i.e. the '*ha*' *kalā* and the dot (i.e. *anusvāra*) at the end, i.e. in the form of '*ahaṃ*', the divine *Mātṛkā* (from '*a*' to '*kṣa*') is the creative goddess.[9]

So it has been said by Somānanda in his commentary:

"*Aḥ* and *aṃ* are the modified and unmodified forms of *Mātṛkā*."[10]

He maintains that the vowel '*a*' denotes '*anuttara*' (the Absolute), and the 15 vowels from *ā* to '*aḥ*' denote 15 *tithis* or lunar days. Alternatively he has given another interpretation of the verse "*athādyāḥ...tadantaḥ*", viz. '*aṃ*' is symbolic of *bindu* separately, the remaining fifteen vowels from '*a*' to '*aḥ*' are denotative of fifteen lunar days (*tithis*), but the final '*aḥ*' should be taken as denotative of *visarga*. At the same time, he has taught that the *visarga* is '*spanda*', i.e. the essential nature of Consciousness. '*Spanda*' is defined as slight movement. If there is a going forth from oneself to another object (i.e. other than the self) it won't be 'slight movement', it would connote full movement. Otherwise (i.e., if there is no 'going forth' or movement from oneself), the very idea of 'movement' would become meaningless. Therefore, it is only because of a slight pulsation within the essential nature (of the Self) consisting of succession-less wondrous delight (not because of moving from oneself to another object) that it has been indicated in the Āgamas by words, such as '*ucchalattā*' (jerking up), '*ūrmi*' (billow), '*matsyodarī*' (throbbing in the stomach of a fish). This is what is said to be '*spanda*' (because of slight pulsation within the essential nature of the Divine). This '*spanda*' is of the nature of the union of Śiva-Śakti. It is of two kinds--*sāmānya* (general) and *viśeṣa* (particular).[11] This has been explained already.

The fifteen '*a*' etc. are all the vowels ending in a dot, i.e. *anusvāra* (or *aṃ*, the nasal '*a*'). They are the fifteen *tithis* or lunar days. At their end, through the connexion of *kriyāśakti* (*kāla-yogena*) occur what are known as *soma* (moon) and *sūrya* (sun) which constitute the terminal point of *akula* or *anuttara* (verse 5) i.e. the last vowel is *aḥ* of which the upper dot is symbolized by the moon and the lower is symbolized by the sun.

The earth and other categories of existence right upto quintuple *brahma* (*brahmapañcaka*) i.e., *śa, ṣa, sa, ha,* and *kṣa* (the symbol of Śakti) repose in the vowels. How? The answer is '*kramāt*' (verse 6).

The etymological meaning of *kramāt* is the following: "*Krama*+*at* which is derived from the root '*ad*' 'to devour' means devouring of succession (*kramasya adanam-bhakṣaṇam*) i.e., swallowing up of time (*kāla-grāsaḥ*)". *Kramāt* is used here in an adverbial sense i.e. 'by swallowing up time'.

'*Suvrate*' in verse 6 means the following: *su* = *śobhana* or magnificent. *Vrata* = holy practice. *Suvratā,* therefore, means one who has two holy practices, viz. (1) *bhoga* i.e., enjoyment which consists in emptying her energy in manifestation (*riktatve*), and (2) *bhoga-nivṛtti* i.e., abstention from manifestation or withdrawal of manifestation in herself, thus making up the loss and becoming full (*pūrṇatve*). '*Suvrate*' which is the vocative case of *suvratā* should be explained as above.

Amūlā in verse 8 means 'who is rooted in '*a*', and one who has no beginning or origin' (*avidyamānamūlā*), for she has no beginning (i.e. she is timeless, eternal).[12] (Now A.G. explains *amūlā tatkramā*.)

She is *kaulikī śakti* whose course (*krama*) is this i.e., whose course consists of identity (*praśleṣaṇa*), distinction (*atadrūpo*), identity cum-distinction (*anyathārūpo*). In spite of all these activities, she remains *amūlā*--one whose origin has no beginning, one whose origin is unknown.

(Now A.G. explains *amūlā*+*ātat*+*kramāḥ*)

'*Ātat*' means extension or expansion of the one who is rooted in '*a*' (*amūlasya yadātananamātat*). She is the one whose course or method is this extension (*tadeva ca kramo yasyāḥ*).[13]

She is unknown (*ajñeyā*) for she is the knower of all (and, therefore, cannot be reduced to the status of the known), (from another point of view), she is the only one to be known, i.e. worth knowing (*eṣaiva ca jñeyā*), for anything other than she does not exist (*anyasya abhāvāt*).

(Now A.G. gives the meaning of '*akṣāntā*' in the following words:) '*Akṣāntā*' means '*a*' i.e., *avidyamānaṃ kṣāntaṃ* i.e., *tūṣṇim āsanaṃ yasyaḥ* i.e. one who has no quiet seat or one who does not stay quiet; in other words 'in whom there is no cessation of activity by way of manifestation etc.' (*aviratam sṛṣṭyadi-rūpatvena*).

(Now A.G., interprets the word *ākṣāntā* in the following way:).

'*Ākṣāntā*: '*ākṣa*' means pertaining to '*akṣa*' or the senses. So '*ākṣāntā*' would mean 'one who does not end with the sensuous perception from before' (*aindriyakāṇāmante samīpe prāgaparyavasānā yā*). This *ākṣāntā* is the adjective of *sṛṣṭi*. Figuratively, this means that this is manifestation in which there is an unparalleled taking away or seizure (*apūrvam āharaṇaṃ*), that is to say, in which there is the withdrawal of manifestation by way of entrance within the Self (*svātmānupraveśātma-svarūpam saṃhāra-rūpaṃ yasyāṃ*).

This creative goddess, viz., *Mātṛkā* is the source of all *vidyā* or knowledge assuming the form of *vedanā* or inward feeling, indicative of the throb of Śakti, and as a product of germinal energy in the form of Śiva-*bīja* or vowels and *prasara* or consonants, of the attribute of protection or reflection of the *mantras* in the form of *vācya* i.e. the *devatās* or inherent goddesses and their *vācakas* or wordings. This creative goddess is the same everywhere i.e. by nature she is neither less nor more (anywhere). She is said to be the bestower of success in all the Tantras, in all the spiritual disciplines, in all activities and at all times. '*Ākhyātā*' (is said to be) has to be interpreted in another form also, i.e. *ā*+*akhyātā* i.e. in the external state, she is evident (*prakaṭa*) in her state of *akhyāti* i.e. in the state of self-forgetfulness, for in the stage of *vaikharī* or empirical utterance, the difference in the phonemes is due to *māyā*. Thus, those very phonemes existing in the mind as pure *mantra*[14] at first (i.e. under the influence of *māyā*), having reached the state of intellectual creation (*bhāvasṛṣṭi*) of the form of *pratyayas* i.e., thought-constructs like the fivefold *viparyaya*,[15] *aśakti*[16] etc., cast a pall over the essential nature (of the soul).

"There are five varieties of *viparyaya* i.e., wrong knowledge. *Aśakti* or inefficacy due to the impairment of the senses has twenty-eight varieties. There are nine kinds of *tuṣṭi*[17] or contentment. *Siddhi*[18] or fulfilment is of eight kinds." These creations of the intellect (*pratyayāḥ*) (Sp. K. Verse 47) are primarily bonds (*pāśaḥ*) which pertain to the class of bound souls. As has been said in Spanda Kārikā:

"The powers are ever in readiness to conceal his real nature, for without the association of words, ideas cannot arise." Similarly, "The rise, in the bound soul, of all sorts of ideas marks the disappearance of the bliss of supreme immortality. On account of this, he loses his independence. The appearance of the ideas has its sphere in sense-objects". (Sp. K. III, 14) etc. Therefore by setting aside the sphere which is the creation of the intellect, non-*māyīya* sphere of phonemes has been designated which is distinctly audible, which is appreciable by means of the ear, which is the embodiment of the primal, highest purity of Śiva, and which bestows the reward of various spiritual practices. In Pūrvaśāstra or Mālinīvijayottara Śāstra also, it has been said: "The Lord, of His own accord thus illuminated Aghora with this method teeming with the sense of all the Śāstras." "Thus being awakened with the Lord's teaching, exciting the *vimarśa yoni* with the Lord's powers, created innumerable *mantras* (i.e. inner phonemes) with suitable sounds for being employed by creatures of various categories" (M.V.T. III, 27).

"These *mantras* (inner phonemes) only being embraced by Aghora etc., the various *mantra* experients bestow on the main users of them the fruits of all desires, not otherwise". (M. V. III, 28).

Thus described, the *mantras*, though manifest from the point of view of phonematic creativity are unmanifest to those who are blinded by *māyā*.

(Now A.G. takes the word *khyātāḥ* as noun and explains it in the following manner:).

'*Sarvadaiva khyātāḥ*'—"They are always shining or manifest in the form of pure knowledge" or it may mean: "whose expansion is unimpeded according to the power of the nature of each".

The following is the sense of the whole teaching in a concise form:

"The Supreme Power, who is Bhairavī, whose characteristic is wondrous delight issuing from her unique autonomy, shines externally by herself. He (i.e. Śiva) who is in union with Her nature, who is unimpeded in His activity and is always present, always shines as consciousness, whose essence is self-consciousness. He shines in the form of Sadāśiva, earth, animals, blue, yellow, and pleasure that are an expression of His own nature (i.e. He shines without any external aid). Knowing every thing in its own form[19] (*svasvasaṃvedanaṃ*) is called means of proof. This appears as common to all experients whether a child or an animal.

The following are the *pramāṇas* or means of knowledge: (1) sensuous knowledge or perception by means of the senses; (2) three kinds of inference (*trirūpaṃ ca liṅgaṃ*),[20] (3) the word of a great, credible person[21] (*paravacaḥkramaḥ*), proof by analogy[22] (*svārūpya*), inference from circumstance (*anyathāyoga*)[23], cessation of a further desire to know (*pratītyanudaya*),[24] proof on the basis of non-existence (*yama*)[25]— all these are described simply as means to that self-consciousness whose light is never interrupted, which shines equally even in lower creatures like birds etc., which do not know perceptual or inferential proof even by name.

So the light of consciousness (*bhāsā*) is by nature reflective of Self (*svarūpamarśanātmikā*). That which is Self-consciousness is itself the supreme Verbum (*paravāg-vapuḥ*). It is its very nature to appear in diverse forms of existence. Therefore, it shines as the cosmos of variegated existence. It never undergoes the state of dependence on others. As it is not dependent on anything (outside itself), how can any impediment possibly exist in it? Therefore, self-consciousness which is void of convention transcends all space, time, *kalā*, *māyā*, limitation of place or activity. It is perfect in itself, it is the all and yet different from all forms and figures. It is the natural, supreme consciousness characterized by excellent refinement, of the pure form of *śuddhavidyā*[26], it is the *ahaṃ* or I in both ways, i.e. both as Śiva and Śakti, both as consciousness and its expression as Energy.. That '*aham*' (I) itself as *Mātṛkā*, is the very essential nature of earth etc. In the highest sense, its fluid form is said to be the vowel (*bīja*) and the solid form the consonant (*yoni*), the very nature of Śiva and Śakti.

By the union of Śiva and Śakti (i.e. vowel and consonant), by their mutual union crops up the delight of the visible universe. The virile energy (of *anuttara* or I-consciousness) which is the highest reality (*pāramārthika-sadvapuḥ*) and which is present in the universe inherent within up to its extreme limit is designated as *visarga* both in its aspect of '*viśleṣa*' i.e. external expansion or *prasāra* and its aspect of '*yojanā*' i.e. inward withdrawal or *saṃhāra*. This *visarga* is the invariable domain (of the aspirants), this the easy means of attaining to *anuttara*. In Śrī-Pūrva (i.e. Mālinī-vijayottara), a phonematic creation from *na* to *pha* has been described which is different from this non-*māyīya* multitude of phonemes i.e. the *Mātṛkā* group from '*a*' to '*kṣa*'. That is known as *Mālinī* which is *bhinna*, i.e. mingled with vowels and consonants and is formed with reference to *māyā*.

Khecarī-vaiṣamya or the State of Paśu

The *Mālinī* being divided into fifty phonemes at the stage of *māyā* gives rise to *vikalpas* or thought-constructs. In this form, it is by nature such that it casts a pall over the essential nature of the Self and leads to bondage of the empirical selves. Involved in this phonematic creation, the various *khecarī śaktis* lead to *vaiṣamya* or dis-similarity of the essential nature, and carry out the recurrence of the variegated cycle of temporal existence full of the *kārmika*, *māyīya*, and *āṇava* limitations.

Khecarī-sāmya or the State of Pati

Khecarī, by nature, has the sameness or identity with pure Bhairava. This has already been said. In *khecarī sāmya*, it is the highest state i.e. the state of Śiva[26] or *pati* both in life and liberation. The highest aspect of non-differentiation in the phonematic creation of difference is the virility of the *mantra* by the preservation of which the *mantra* is preserved. This *sāmya* is '*aham*' (I) itself or which is the *visarga* status of *anuttara*. When the awakened one realizes it as his supreme nature, he is forthwith liberated in life itself. The *yogis* who desire supernormal power etc., by means of this I-consciousness meditate on *ahaṃ* in a limited way in the navel or the heart-centre. I have briefly concluded it according to (the teaching of) my *guru* and the Āgamas. As to what happens by resorting to this I-consciousness, ask your personal experience. I have only shown a little bit of the path. One should not rest contented with this much.

Who can say with certainty 'this much is all' regarding the divine consciousness? The divine grace has been vouchsafed to me only to this extent. By that (grace), I have been privileged to disclose this much (as means) (viz., *khecarī sāmya* or identity with the divine consciousness). Subtler *tarka* then this (i.e. *sat-tarka*) may occur to other experients either today (in the present) or at some other time (past or future) i.e., the *tarka*[27] either may occur in the present (*bhavati*), or occurred in the past (*abhūt*), or will occur in the future (*bhavitā*). Among all the lights of the component parts[28] of *yoga*, this (i.e., *tarka*) has been determined in Śrī Pūrva Śāstra (i.e. Mālinī-vijaya) as the brilliant sun (*gabhastimān*) by which one gets liberated and liberates others. This (i.e., *tarka*) should be clearly understood in every way and reflected on by the clear-sighted ones (*vicakṣaṇaiḥ*) desirous of the supreme state (*parepsubhiḥ*) by abandoning for a moment jealousy common to mortal beings. The aspirant is established in the essential nature of the Self immediately after *sat-tarka* (*ālocana*) and, therefore, the specks of cloud[29] that cover the sun of consciousness are dissolved automatically by the savour of delight that the aspirant experiences at this moment.

Notes

1. *Tuṭi* is a division of breath. It covers an extension of 2¼ fingers. Normally, there are 16 *tuṭis* in one round of breath (including inspiration and expiration). One round of breath thus covers an extension of 36 fingers.

2. Breath rising within and going out is known as *prāṇacāra*, and rising outside and entering within is known as *apānacāra*. In *prāṇacāra*, the point within from which *prāṇa* arises is known as *antaḥ-dvādaśānta*, and the point where it ceases externally is known as *bāhyadvādaśānta*. On the other hand, in *apānacāra*, the external point where *prāṇa* arises is known as *bāhyadvādaśānta* and the point where it ceases internally is known as *antaḥdvādaśānta*. The space between these two *dvādaśāntas* is 36 fingers or 16 *tuṭis*. These 16 *tuṭis* cover the 16 vowels from '*a*' to '*aḥ*'. The vowels from '*a*' to *aṃ* represent the fifteen *tithis* or lunar days in the external world. The *prāṇacāra* represents the 15 *tithis* of the dark fortnight, and

apānacāra represents the bright fortnight. The vowel *aḥ* is changeless. It represents the 16th digit of the moon which is changeless and is known as *amā kalā*.

3. The *visargātmikā kalā* is said to be divided into two by itself of which the successive *kalā* is known as the 17th.

4. When *visarga kalā* is involved in manifestation or expansion, it is known as *visarga* (:); when it ceases from manifestation, it is known as *vindu* or *bindu* (.). In Trika philosophy, ordinarily both *visarga* and *vindu* are known as *visarga,* for in the aspect of *saṃhāra, visarga* becomes *vindu* and in the aspect of *sṛṣṭi, vindu* is *visarga. Visarga-vindu* is in all conditions eternal and immutable.

5. '*Anupradānaṃ*': This is a technical word of Sanskrit Grammar. It is an effort outside the mouth in the production of sound at the different vocal organs which is looked upon as external effort or *bāhyaprayatna.*

There are three main factors in the production of sound, viz. (1) *sthāna,* (2) *karaṇa* or *ābhyantara prayatna,* (3) *anupradāna* or *bāhyaprayatna.* There are two main varieties of *anupradāna,* known as (i) (*śvāsānupradāna* (emission of breath) and (ii) *nādānupradāna* (resonance), [vide, 'A Dictionary of Sanskrit Grammar' by K.U. Abhyankar, p. 23].

6. So long as '*a*' etc. are only an inner apprehension, they are known as *kalā* and when they assume an external sound, they are known as vowels or *svara.*

7. The *anuttara* principle accepting the limited condition of *pramātā* (knower), *pramāṇa* (knowledge) and *prameya,* (the known), manifests the universe as something external. There are four aspects of this manifestation, viz. *udyoga, avabhāsa, carvaṇa,* and *vilāpana.*

(1) *Udyoga* is the initial preparation in the form of Will.
(2) *Avabhāsa* is the appearance of a mental experience, e.g., blue as something external.
(3) *Carvaṇa* i.e. relishing the above experience for some time as a form of the I-consciousness.
(4) *Vilāpana* i.e. withdrawal or re-absorption of the expanse in the essential nature of the Self.

Even in the work-a-day pragmatic experience, these aspects are at play, for instance at first there is will to perceive a jar (*udyoga*), then there is the actual perception of the jar (*avabhāsa*), relishing of the perceptive experience (*carvaṇa*), and finally assimilating the perceptive experience of the jar to the essential nature of the Self.

When the above (*udyoga, avabhāsa*, etc.) without bringing about the limited experience of the knower, known, etc., reside in the pure state of awareness, it is the perfect *parā-śakti* of 17 *kalās*. It is a state of pure awareness in which inhere 16 forms of experience.

The four forms of *pramātā, pramāṇa, prameya* and *māyā* multiplied by the four forms of *udyoga, avabhāsa, carvaṇa* and *vilāpana* make up 16 forms.

The perfect form of *pramiti*, therefore, is 1 *kalā* of the pure *pramiti* itself plus the above 16 *kalās* inherent in it, i.e. of 17 *kalās*. This perfect *pramiti* (awareness) is *svātantrya* or autonomy, the third eye of Śiva, symbolic of *saṃhāra-mudrā*.

8. This is the form of 16 *kalās* of the goddess. This does not include the perfect *pramiti kalā*. This is called the *somanetra* or the lunar eye of Śiva. This is expressive of *prasāra-mudrā*, the state of external expansion.

9. Thus there are three states, viz.:

(1) *Pramiti* which is signified by Agni, which is known as the *bhāla netra* or the central eye of Śiva. It is a state of pure awareness, perfect or *pūrṇa*, which including the 16 vowels from '*a*' to '*aḥ*' is of 17 *kalās*. This is only an inner state without any external manifestation.

(2) The Right Eye (*dakṣiṇa netra* of Śiva). This is also known as *soma kalā* or *pramāṇa-kalā*. This indicates the external manifestation of the inner 16 vowels. The *pramātā, pramāṇa, prameya* and *māyā* multiplied by *udyoga, avabhāsa, carvaṇa* and *vilāpana* (4 x 4) work out to sixteen.

(3) The Left Eye (*vāmanetra*) of Śiva—also known as Sūrya *kalā* or *prameya kalā* is the external manifestation of 12 *kalās* without the play of *ṛ, ṝ, ḷ, ḹ* i.e. when these phonemes are in a state of *viśrānti* or rest in *pramiti*. *Pramātā, pramāṇa*, and *prameya* multiplied by *udyoga, avabhāsa*, etc. (3 x 4) work out to 12.

10. Somānanda has designated '*aḥ*' as *vikṛta* or modified form of *Mātṛkā*, because it denotes external manifestation, and '*aṃ*' as

avikṛta, because it denotes introversion. '*Aḥ*' is centrifugal, therefore, *vikṛta* or modified; '*aṃ*' is centripetal and therefore, *avikṛta* or unmodified. There is *saṅkoca* (contraction) and *vistāra* (diffusion) simultaneously in the heart of Śiva. Both are denoted by the common word '*visarga*'. There is no such common word in English.

11. Movement (*calanam*) in this context is not to be taken in the sense of physical movement. It is an inward pulsation or throb in Consciousness denoting the ever-present activity of the delight of Self-consciousness of the Divine. It is the dynamic activity of Consciousness. It is motionless movement so to speak. Just as a wave in the ocean rises up only in the ocean itself but does not move out, even so '*spanda*' is a throb in the divine consciousness of Śiva-Śakti.

Spanda is of two kinds, *sāmānya* (general) and *viśeṣa* (particular). *Sāmānya spanda* is the foundational *spanda* of Śiva-Śakti, on which is based the working of the *guṇas* of *prakṛti* which are the *viśeṣa spanda*, leading to particular experiences of psychic and physical phenomena. The particular experiences are popularly known as the *spanda* of Śakti.

12. '*Amūlā*' has also been used in two senses, viz. (1) '*a mūlaṃ yasyāḥ*' which means that '*a*' is the origin of the entire phonematic manifestation and (2) '*avidyamānaṃ mūlaṃ yasyāḥ*' which means that 'being beginningless (*anādi*), it has no origin other than the essential nature of *anuttara*'.

13. The sense of this is that the entire phonematic manifestation is only *ātat* or expansion of '*a*'.

14. So long as *varṇas* or phonemes exist only in the mind, they are known as *mantra*. Usually, it is only when they are uttered by the vocal organs that they are known as *varṇa*.

15. '*Sva-sva-saṃvedana*' is of two kinds—(i) *śivātmaka-saṃvedana* born out of *prātibha-jñāna* i.e., knowledge born of spontaneous divine influx which ensures a knowledge of Śiva in every object, (2) perceptive knowledge through the senses, as that of a jar.

16. The five kinds of *viparyaya* are (1) *Tamas* or darkness, (2) *Moha* (delusion), (3) *Mahāmoha* (great delusion), (4) *Tāmisra* (gloom), (5) *Andhatāmisra* (blinding gloom).

17. *Aśakti* or inefficacy due to the impairment of the senses is

of 28 kinds—11 due to defect in the senses and 17 due to imperfection in *buddhi.*

18. The nine kinds of *tuṣṭi* are (i) *Prakṛti,* (ii) *Upādāna,* (iii) *Kāla,* (iv) *Bhāgya,* (v) *Arjana,* (vi) *Rakṣaṇa,* (vii) *Kṣaya,* (viii) *Saṅga,* (ix) *Hiṃsā.*

The eight kinds of *siddhi* are (1) *Ūha,* (2) *Śabda,* (3) *Adhyayana*; prevention of three kinds of *duḥkha,* viz. (4) *Ādhyātmika duḥkha,* (5) *Ādhibhautika duḥkha,* (6) *Ādhidaivika duḥkha* (7) *Suhṛtprāpti,* (8) *Dāna.* For details see Sāṃkhya Kārikā, Verses 47-51.

19. '*Aghora*' is Anantabhaṭṭārakanātha.

20. The three kinds of inference are (1) *Pūrvavat,* (2) *Śeṣavat* and (3) *Sāmānyato-dṛṣṭam.*

(1) *Pūrvavat* literally means 'as before'. It has been noticed before that whenever there is cloud, there is rain. So, now when cloud is noticed in the sky, the inference is that it will rain. It is an inference from cause to effect.

(2) *Śeṣavat* is an inference from the part to the whole. If a little water of the ocean when tasted appears to be saltish, the obvious conclusion is that the remaining water must also be saltish.

(3) *Sāmānyato-dṛṣṭam*: As Caitra who is now seen in Prayāga is later seen in Kāśī leads one to infer that he moves about, even so planets when seen in different positions lead one to infer that they move about.

21. This is known as inference based on *āptavacana* i.e., on the word of a reliable and credible person. It is also known as *śabda-pramāṇa.*

22. This is known as *upamāna pramāṇa* or inference by analogy, such as a *gavaya* is like a cow.

23. *Anyathāyogā*: This is also known as *arthāpatti,* or an inference from circumstance. Devadatta does not eat during the day and yet he is stout. The obvious inference is that he must be eating at night.

24. *Pratītyanudaya*: This is also known as *uparama pramāṇa.* When one has known a thing, his curiosity ceases. There is no further desire to know about it.

25. This inference is based on *abhāva* or non-existence of a thing. Since there are no mice here, there must be cats in this place.

26. Śuddhavidyā refers to Śiva-vidyā or Sahaja-vidyā, not to Śuddhavidyā *tattva.* This is *khecarī* in the primal form, not the consciousness of the empirical individual, but the consciousness of Śiva. It is the universal activity of the supreme energy of Śiva. It is the identity with this *khecarī* (*khecarī-samatā* or *khecarī-sāmya*) which is the object of Devī's enquiry and the aim of every aspirant.

27. *Tarka* means reasoning. This is known as *sat-tarka* or the true reasoning. It is reasoning in conformity to the teaching of the Āgama. It does not mean logic-chopping.

28. The component parts of *yoga* are, according to Śaivāgama, six, known as *ṣaḍaṅga.* These six limbs or component parts are: (1) *Prāṇāyāma,* (2) *Dhyāna,* (3) *Pratyāhāra,* (4) *Dhāraṇā,* (5) (*Śat*)-*Tarka,* and 6. *Samādhi.*

29. The specks of cloud refer to the *āṇava mala* of the soul that is automatically dissolved now.

Text

From *evamuttarasyāpyanuttaramiti* on p. 75, l. 14 upto *kriyāśakti-samarpaṇamuktaṃ* on p. 79, l. 9.

Translation

Introduction to the succeeding Sūtras:

Thus it has been said earlier (in verse 3) viz. "that is *anuttara* even of *uttara*". From the portion 'it is *anuttara* even of *uttara*' it has been described in detail that the expansion of manifestation (consisting of 36 *tattvas*) is due to *kula* or Śakti. It has been determined that even the subsequent one i.e. expansion of the universe has the *anuttara* or the transcendental as its precedent. Now it is the nature of the transcendental which requires a detailed consideration. So while considering both prescriptive rule (*vidhi*) and explanatory reiteration (*anuvāda*), the nature of both *vidhi* and *anuvāda* has to be characterized. In the mental recitation of the name of Śiva (which is *vidhi*), and the appearance of all happiness (which is *anuvāda*) both are discernible. Though in this system, *anuttara* or the transcendental is nothing different from the *uttara* or the posterior—for if it were something other, that would also fall within the category of the *uttara,* even then there is this difference brought about by the autonomy of the Lord from the point of view of the disciple and the teacher. Therefore, a quotation of further verses is given in order to determine the nature of the transcendental in detail. This is what it describes:

CATURDAŚAYUTAṂ BHADRE
TITHĪŚĀNTASAMANVITAM// 9/
TṚTĪYAṂ BRAHMA SUŚROṆI
HṚDAYAṂ BHAIRAVĀTMANAḤ/
ETANNĀYOGINĪJĀTO
NĀRUDRO LABHATE SPHUṬAM// 10/
HṚDAYAṂ DEVADEVASYA
SADYO YOGAVIMUKTIDAM/
ASYOCCĀRE KṚTE SAṂYAṄ
MANTRAMUDRĀGAṆO MAHĀN// 11/
SADYASTANMUKHATĀMETI
SVADEHĀVEŚALAKṢAṆAM/
MUHŪRTAṂ SMARATE YASTU
CUMBAKENA ABHIMUDRITAḤ// 12/
SA BADHNĀTI TADĀ SARVAṂ
MANTRAMUDRĀGAṆAṂ NARAḤ/
ATĪTĀNĀGATĀNARTHĀN
PṚṢṬO'SAU KATHAYATYAPI// 13/
PRAHARĀDYADABHIPRETAṂ
DEVATĀRŪPAM UCCARAN/
SĀKṢĀT PAŚYATYASANDIGDHAM
ĀKṚṢṬAM RUDRAŚAKTIBHIḤ// 14/
PRAHARADVAYAMĀTREṆA
VYOMASTHO JĀYATE SMARAN/
TRAYEṆA MĀTARAḤ SARVĀ
YOGĪŚVARYO MAHĀBALĀḤ// 15/
VĪRA VĪREŚVARĀḤ SIDDHĀ
BALAVĀÑ CHĀKINĪGAṆAH/
ĀGATYA SAMAYAṂ DATVĀ
BHAIRAVEṆA PRACODITĀḤ// 16/

YACCHANTI PARAMĀṂ SIDDHIṂ
PHALAṂ YADVĀ SAMĪHITAM /
ANENA SIDDHĀḤ SETSYANTI
SĀDHAYANTI CA MANTRIṆAḤ// 17 /
YATKIÑCID BHAIRAVE TANTRE
SARVAMASMĀT PRASIDDHYATI /
ADṚṢṬAMAṆḌALO' PYEVAM..../ / 18 /

Translation

The Description of Amṛtabīja or Sauḥ mantra

"O thou gracious one, thou with beautiful thighs, it is the third *brahma*[1] (i.e. *sat* or rather '*sa*') united with the fourteenth vowel (i.e. *au*) and well-joined with that which comes at the end of the lord of the vowels[2] (i.e. *visarga*). (*Sa*+*au*+*visarga* = *sauḥ*). This is the heart[3] of Bhairava. Or this *sauḥ* or *amṛtabīja* is the *bhairavīya hṛdaya* of the *narabhāva* or phenomenal aspect which is only of the essence of Śakti (*tṛtīyaṃ brahmabhairavātmānaḥ naḥ bhairavātma hṛdayaṃ*: *naḥ* in this syntax means *asmākam* i.e. of our system). 9-10.

He who is not born of *yoginī*[4] or is not united with Rudra[5] cannot clearly obtain this (i.e., *sauḥ*). This is the (very) heart (i.e. *hṛdaya-bīja*, the *mantra sauḥ*) of the God of gods i.e., *parama* Śiva, and bestows immediately (both) *yoga*[6] and liberation. 10-11.

When this *mantra* (i.e. *sauḥ*) is perfectly well recited*[7] the grand multitude of *mantras* and *mudrās* immediately appears before him (i.e. they become favourable to him) being characterized by their absorption in his body (*svadehaveśalakṣaṇam*). 11-12.

The man i.e. the *yogī* (i.e., in this context) who has a mindfulness[8] of this *mantra* even for a *muhūrta*[9] or forty-eight minutes is sealed with *cumbaka*[10] and binds i.e., brings under his control the entire multitude of *mantras* and *mudrās*. He also narrates past and future events, when interrogated. 12-13.

---

*The word *uccāra* which literally means 'to recite or to sound' is used here in a technical sense, viz. (1) full realization of *sauḥ* in the form of *vimarśa* or (2) joining *sauḥ* with the current of *prāṇa* and *apāna* according to the instruction of the *guru*.

If he calls up the form of any divinity that he desires, for a *prahara* i.e., 3 hours, he sees it with his eyes, without doubt, drawn near to himself by the powers of Rudra. 14.

If he has the mindfulness of a divinity for two *praharas*, i.e. six hours, he becomes established in the expanse (lit. sky) of pure consciousness. 15a.

If he continues the above practice for three *praharas* i.e. nine hours, then all the mothers,[11] all the greatly powerful *yogiśvaris*,[12] the *viras*,[13] *vireśvaras*,[14] the *siddhas*[15], the multitudes of powerful *śakinis*,[16] impelled by Bhairava, come to him after making an appointment[17] and offer to him the supreme felicity viz. *mokṣa* supernormal power or the fruit desired by him. By this *bijamantra*, i.e. *sauḥ*, the practisers of the *mantra* are practising *yoga* in the present (*sādhayanti*), by its practice they became perfect in the past (*siddhati*) and by this they will gain perfection in future (*setsyanti*). 15-17.

All the perfections described in Bhairava Tantra are accomplished by this *bijamantra* (i.e. *sauḥ*). This *amṛtabija* removes entirely the sense of difference prevalent in the *māyiya aṇḍa* (the sphere of *māyā*). On the other hand, being the heart of every object and state, it also abides, having accepted the limitation prevalent in all the four *aṇḍas*. 18.

Commentary

The Explanation of Bhairavātmanaḥ hṛdayaṃ etc.

The essential nature of the universe which is simply a form of Bhairava, which by demonstrated experience (*pradarśita*), reasoning (*yukti*) (in accordance with the teaching of the *guru*), and Āgama (the traditional teaching) is ascertained to be venerable *aparā* or non-supreme manifestation is *śākta* i.e., pertaining to Śakti. The heart or the essence of that *śākta* nature is Śiva who is held in firm embrace by the divine Śakti, viz. the venerable supreme power (*parā*).

By the word 'Bhairava' is to be understood Śakti, the Divine Energy, of the universe according to the principle that everything is the form of everything else (*sarvasarvātmakatā vapuḥ*).

The heart or the essential nature of the phenomenal reality (*nara rūpasya*) permeated by that Śakti is Śiva who is identified with the supreme non-differentiation (*pareṇa abhedena*) by the above principle, for without this even differentiation would not be possible i.e. if Śiva and Śakti were not prevalent in phenomenal reality, its state of difference would not have been possible. This has been stated before. *Suśroṇi* (O with beautiful hip and thighs), is the vocative case. (A.G. by splitting *bhairavātmanaḥ* into two i.e. *bhairavātma* and '*naḥ*' and by adding *hṛdayaṃ* with *suśroṇi* and turning it into a compound word, viz. *suśroṇi-hṛdayaṃ* gives the following explanation:)

That which is irremovably involved even in repugnant *māyā* and consists of pure consciousness is the core between the two thighs, viz., the female organ (*yonirūpam*). The Śakti in the form of *yoni* (female organ) is the state of Bhairava that indicates the wholeness (*pūrṇatā*) of the *nara-bhāva* or phenomenal reality which includes within itself the entire host of experients from *sakalas* (i.e. limited experients), (divinities like) Mantra, Mantra-maheśvara down to immobile beings (like plants etc.) whose very life consists of empirical I-feeling and which is rightly designated as 'ours' (*naḥ*).

The Explanation of tṛtiyam brahma

Brahman (accepted in Trika) is that in whom the virility of the universe is inherent and who is full of the mass of bliss (*ānanda-śaktighanaṃ*) that is surging forward for *visarga-viśleṣaṇa* i.e. *visarga* or separation from Śiva and *viśleṣaṇa* or union with Śakti. Such Brahman is vast (*bṛhat*), all-pervading (*vyāpaka*) and fully nurtured with the union of Śakti. This Brahman is certainly not like that which is accepted by the readers of Vedānta and which is not far removed from absolute nihilism. This is called the third Brahman, because it is more identical with Śiva than *nara* or Śakti. Therefore, in Tantras and particularly in Parātrīśikā (*atra*), this i.e. the union of the male principle and the female principle is the very core which has been taught as the object of worship. Even in the case of ordinary people whose mind has not penetrated into the core of that sort of virility, by the mere pursuit of external ritual, the bonds that govern the state of *paśu*[18] (limited empirical being) become at first gradually slack and finally completely loosened, at first slowly splitting and then finally completely split asunder and then they automatically attain to the state of penetrating into that core (which is the union of Śiva and Śakti). This penetration into the core is not like a literal statement as in "I have entered the heart, it is the supreme goddess", rather it is the search inside the heart. This has been already said in detail. "Neither the restrictions of Śāstras (religious texts) can confine the heart within narrow limits, nor can popular views contaminate consciousness. That alone is the state of plenitude which is infused with the joyful condition of absorption or *khecarī sāmya* which is completely replete with the attribute of the essential nature of the Divine". As has been said by myself in one of my hymns: "In those whose mind has been made purer by being fully dominated by devotion unto you, this state is clearly established in the heart in a moment." Therefore on the angles (i.e. *parā*, *parāparā* and *aparā*) of the triangular Śakti, the three goddesses and in the centre the transcendental goddess who is the churning Śakti of Bhairava, the embodiment of supreme beatitude[19] have to be worshipped. In the tradition of the deities, there is bliss through *kṣobhātmaka visarga* which is due to the incessant flow of bliss of the eternal beatitude.[20] In *yāmala* or *vīra-yoginī* or *vīra-dūtī* tradition, there is physical union (*saṃghaṭṭa*) between the *vīra* and *yoginī*. The purpose is only to stimulate the *nityānanda* or eternal beatitude by means of the contact of sex-organs. By this contact, there is *kṣobhātmaka visarga*. It gives intense delight.[21] In a single person (*ekavīratāyāmapi*) occurs also by concentration of the mind on the essential delight of the Self the same (sexual) delight. In the case of the ordinary run of mankind, on the occasion of intercourse, on account of the close compactness of the union of the sexual organs of the man and the woman right from the deepest part upto the foremost part, the mind of both is dissolved (in the supreme Śakti), and the delight that resides in the ejaculatory part of the sexual organ of man and the nether aspect of the triangular region i.e. the *yoni* or the female sexual organ is consequently exceedingly generated.[22] In this connexion, the mystic sense of the intercourse has been expressed in the following verse:

"One should throw (i.e. concentrate) the delightful mind in the middle of *vahni* (the region of contraction) and *viṣa* (the region of expansion) both ways, whether by itself or permeated by *vāyu* (prāṇic breath). One would then be joined to the bliss of sexual union"[23] (V. Bh. verse 68). Thus it is the association of beatitude which is the worship of the 'heart' i.e., the essential nature of *parādevī*.

As has been said in Trikatantrasāra:[24]

"The expansion of beatitude is 'worship'. One should perform this worship on the Trikoṇa (triangle)[25] with sweet smell like that of flowers, incense etc., which give satisfaction to the heart." Everything is pervaded with two *mudrās* which are essentially *jñāna* and *kriyā śakti*. Only among deities, the display of *jñāna-mudrā* or Śiva-*trikoṇa* is prominent internally and that of the display of *kriyā-mudrā* or Śakti-*trikoṇa* is external, whereas among the *vīras*, it is just the reverse. So far as the entrance in the region of delight or *madhya-dhāma* i.e. *suṣumṇā* is concerned, there is both similarity and difference. It is from this point of view that it has been mentioned that the *kriyāśakti* or the symbol of the female organ should be offered to *jñānaśakti* or the symbol of the male sexual organ.

Notes

1. *Tṛtīyam brahma*: The usual nomenclature of *brahma* is '*auṃ tat sat*; *Sat* is the third *brahma*. '*Sa*' with which begins the third *brahma*, viz. '*sat*' is symbolically designated as the third *brahma*.

2. *Tithīśa* or the lord of the vowels is '*aṃ*'. At the end of this comes *aḥ* or *visarga*. So *sauḥ* is the *mantra* that indicates *anuttara* or the transcendental.

3. Heart or *hṛdayaṃ* is the centre of Bhairava. It is the *pratiṣṭhāsthānaṃ*—the place of repose of the Lord. In his commentary on verse 2 in P.T.V., A.G. says "*paraṃ pratiṣṭhāsthānaṃ saṃvidātmāhṛt*"--the heart is the very consciousness of *anuttara*; it is its most interior place of repose, the very centre of consciousness. In his commentary, L.V., A.G. explains it as "*Bhairavātmano bhagavataḥ śabdarāśeḥ viśvaśarīrasya hṛdayaṃ sārabhūtaṃ*". If we take the universe as a body, it would be its very heart, i.e., the very essence of the universe which in other words, is a mass of sound (congealed). Commenting on the word '*hṛdayaṃ*' occurring in verse 9, A.G. says in P.T.V. that it is *yonirūpam*, the source of all creative energy.

4. Ordinarily, *yoginīs* are those initiated ones who have acquired

supernatural powers. Here the word seems to be used for those deities who are liberated and identified with Śiva.

5. Rudra in this context, also appears to be a liberated soul, identified with Rudra Śiva.

6. The word '*yoga*' stands here for supernatural powers and union with Śiva.

7. *Saṃyak uccāra* in this context does not mean mere vocal recitation, but silent, spontaneous, subtle movement of the *mantra* within. It is its union with the breath that leads to realization. Commenting on this in his L.V., A.G. says: "*Asya bījasyoccāre prāṇarūpatāyāṃ samāveśena tavāt hṛtamātra eva jñānakriyāśakti-śarīrā mantramudrāḥ sadya eva sammukhatām uccārayitur ābhimukhyaṃ prati-padyante*".

"When by the *uccāra* of this *mantra*, the *yogī* becomes totally absorbed in *prāṇa*, then by that alone, the *mantras* and *mudrās* which are the embodiment of knowledge (*jñāna*) and activity (*kriyā*) turn towards the *yogī* who is reciting the *mantra* and offer him all that he desires."

8. *Smarate* does not simply mean memorizing but constant attention on the *mantra*. That is why it has been translated as 'has a mindfulness'.

9. *Muhūrta* = two *ghaṭikās*. One *ghaṭikā* = 24 minutes. So *muhūrta* = 48 minutes.

10. *Cumbaka* is *śākta sparśa*, the embrace of *śakti cakra* occurring in *suṣumṇā* or *madhya nāḍī*. *Cumbaka* means magnet. Just as a magnet draws iron-fillings towards itself, even so the *śākta-sparśa* draws the aspirants toward itself.

11. The 'mothers' refers to the eight deities Yogīśvarī, Brāhmī, Maheśvarī, Kaumārī, Vaiṣṇavī, Vārāhī, Aindrī and Cāmuṇḍā presiding over the various groups of phonemes.

12. They are chiefs of the *yoginīs*.

13. A.G. says in his L.V. that the *vīras* are Aghora etc. In P.T.V. he says that the *vīras* are the *buddhi* (intellect), and organs of action (*kriyendriyākhyāḥ* etc.) when they are introverted towards Śiva.

14. *Vīreśvaras*: In L.V., A.G. says that these are the deities associated with *navātmā mantra*.

15. *Siddhas*: A.G. says in L.V. "*taccakrabhyāsjāta-vibhūtyaśca siddha jayante*"--those become *siddhas* who acquire supernatural

powers by their mastery of *śakti-cakra* i.e., the wheel or group of energies.

16. Śākinī: A.G., in his L.V. says "*Śākinīnām śaktīnām khecaryādibhedabhinnānām*", i.e. they are *śaktis* different from *khecarī* etc. Lakṣmīrāma, in his Vivṛti says that they are a group of *yoginis*. Svāmī Lakshmanjee thinks that they are a group of *yoginis*. They seem to be female *yoginis* who have acquired supernatural powers.

17. '*Samayaṃ datvā*'-- Monier Williams in his Sanskrit-English Dictionary says that '*samayaṃ dā*' means "to propose an agreement", and "*samayaṃ kṛ*" means "to make an agreement or engagement". The expression has been used here in the sense of "having made an engagement or appointment."

18. These bonds are *āṇava, māyīya* and *kārma malas*.

19. The three recommended to be worshipped are the *parā* (supreme), *parāparā* (supreme-cum-non-supreme) and *aparā* (non-supreme) *śaktis*. The transcendental or *parātītā devī* is in the centre.

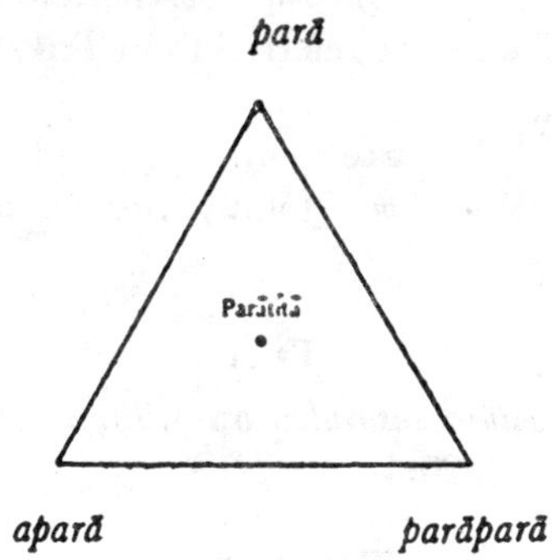

20. In the tradition of the deities, there is no physical contact with any female. Those aspirants who have attained to this level feel the influx of an internal delight owing to the awakening of the *kuṇḍalinī*. *Kṣobhātmaka visarga* refers to the process of the flow of *śabda* (sound), *sparśa* (contact), *rūpa* (form and colour), *rasa* (flavour), and *gandha* (smell) that well up out of sheer delight.

This union is *jñānamudrā*, an internal spiritual union, not *kriyāmudrā*, not an actual intercourse.

21. Only those men and women were entitled to be designated *vīra* and *yoginī* who had attained *khecarī sāmya*. They could have the union of *kriyāmudrā* (actual intercourse). They develop such capacity as enables them to enter *śākta* stage suddenly without

ejaculation on the occasion of orgasm. They have intercourse not for momentary sexual pleasure but for the transformation of consciousness by an inward *śākta* delight.

22. In the four kinds of intercourse described, there is the pervasion of *parā* aspect of Śakti in the first, of *parāparā* in the second and third and of *aparā* in the fourth.

In the first three, there is the contact of *kuṇḍa-golaka* and in the fourth, there is the contact of '*śukra-śoṇita*' in the intercourse.

The intercourse of the '*vīras*' and '*yoginīs*' is called technically the '*ādi-yāga*' which literally means the 'primal sacrifice'.

23. *Smarānanda*--the bliss of sexual union by recollection. There is no actual intercourse here. It is only 'inverted *kāma*' or sexual delight.

24. This book is not available now.

25. *Trikoṇa* is a technical word. It symbolizes both Śiva-*trikoṇa* in which *jñānaśakti* or the male sexual organ is predominant and Śakti-*trikoṇa* in which *kriyā-śakti* or the female sexual organ is predominant. The *trikoṇa* referred to in Trikatantrasāra is Śakti-*trikoṇa*.

26. Separately, they are known as simply *trikoṇa-mudrā* or as Śiva-*trikoṇa* or Śakti-*trikoṇa*. Jointly, the two triangles are known as *ṣaṭ-koṇa-mudrā*.

TEXT

From *evametat caturdaśasuyutam* on p. 79, l. 9 upto *etadbhairavātma hṛdayaṃ* on p. 82, l. 20.

TRANSLATION

Explanation of the terms caturdaśayutam, tithīśāntasamanvitaṃ, tṛtīya-brahma, and hṛdayaṃ

(Now A.G. is giving an explanation of the text from verse 9 onwards).

1st interpretation :

This i.e., the third *brahma*, viz. '*hṛdaya*-'*sa*' (or *amṛta-bīja*) joined with the fourteenth vowel i.e., '*au*', is linked with the sixteenth i.e., *visarga*, '*aḥ*', which occurs at the end of *tithīśa*, the soul of fifteen *kalās*. (Thus it becomes '*sa+au+aḥ*' = *sauḥ*.)

'*Yutaṃ*' may be interpreted as '*yugmam*' or a pair. With the fourteenth, the pair makes sixteenth which is the '*iśa*' or the presiding deity of the fifteen vowels, viz. *visarga* (*aḥ*).

Its (i.e. of the *visarga*) end is the seventeenth, viz., the *anuttara* or the transcendental aspect (of Reality). *Hṛdaya* or heart is that which is linked with it (i.e. with *anuttara*). It has already been stated in detail that all things whether external such as a jar, or internal, such as pleasure, take hold of that germ (the source of all existence) as the highest Reality. Therefore that (*anuttara*) is the heart or core (of Reality).

2nd interpretation

(A.G. gives this interpretation by splitting *caturdaśa* into '*catur*' (four) and *daśā* (states).) This is an interpretation with reference to the phoneme '*a*'. That which is *brahma*, i.e., *sāmarasya* or equipoise, in other words, which is the conjunction of the four states (*caturdaśa*) i.e., '*udyoga*', '*avabhāsa*', '*carvaṇa*' and '*vilāpana*' of the subject and the object is the primal undifferentiated state. Being linked with that means 'inseparable from that'.

The vowels which are up to the end of '*ū*' are known as *tithiśa*, because out of them, the other remaining phonemes are born. The last ones of the vowels coming at the end of the above *tithiśa* vowels are the four immortal phonemes viz., *ṛ*, *ṝ*, *ḷ*, *ḹ*. *Brahma* is well connected with these vowels. From the point of view of ascent, Śiva who is higher than *nara* and Śakti is the third. Therefore, the third *brahma* is identical with supreme Śiva.

The subject (*vedaka*), moving forward by means of the four states of *udyoga*, *avabhāsana*, *carvaṇa* and *vilāpana*, with his eagerness increased by those states, dissolving the *amṛtakalās* (i.e. *ṛ*, *ṝ*, *ḷ*, *ḹ*) within his Self, unifies the entire objectivity with his Self. Thus, by accomplishing the fusion of the stir of the state of the subject and object within the Self, he enters the state of *anuttara*, the very heart of the universe which can be accessible only to *jñāna* (gnosis) characterized by identity, or *yoga* characterized by activity. As has been said in Bhagavadgītā: "One who is established in *yoga* regards everything as the same (divine) in all cases. He sees the Self (in all beings[5]) and all beings in the Self"[6] (VI, 30).

3rd interpretation: (from the point of view of *ānanda* i.e., with reference to the phoneme '*ā*'.)

It is *ānandaśakti* (the power of beatitude) which is the base of the rise of pure[7] *icchāśakti* (will), i.e. pure *icchāśakti* is implicit in *ānanda*. In a reverse order, *icchā* is the third with reference to *kriyā śakti* (e.g. 1. *kriyā*, 2. *jñāna*, 3. *icchā*). This *icchā* (will) in its initial aspect, being untainted with desired objects is *brahman* (*tadeva prāk-koṭau-iṣyamānādi-akaluṣam brahma*).

Caturdaśa may be interpreted as forty by analyzing the word into '*Catur ye daśa*' i.e., four times ten. Bhairava together with his three *śaktis* (viz. *parā* or supreme, *parāparā* or supreme-cum-non-supreme and *aparā* or non-supreme) plus the thirty-six categories (*tattvāni*) would make forty. As has been (rightly) said, "The thirty-six *tattvas* are to be purifed. The purifier is the supreme Bhairava. The means (of purification) is the supreme triad (viz. *parā*, *parāparā*, *aparā*). This initiation is the highest one".

'*Caturdaśa yutam*' means 'connected with these forty.' *Ānanda śakti* is already supreme and being perfect, united with all the vowels and their subsequent phonemes i.e., the consonants which indicate earth etc. (*tadantaiḥ-yonirūpadharādibhiḥ samanvitaṃ*). '*Samanvitam*' is to be taken as an adverb in the sense of 'having been unified'.

This *brahma* is the *hṛdaya* or heart i.e., the centre. This is apprehended immediately (*sakṛd-vibhātaṃ*) everywhere (in the form of vowels and consonants and subjects and objects) and is realized mainly by intuition (*prasaṃkhyāna-gamyam mukhyataḥ*).

It should be borne in mind that for those who, purified by the supreme grace, are competent for this realization, the practice of *yoga* is useless like sham illusion (*vṛthaindrajālika-kalanā-sadṛśo*)

4th interpretation: (from the point of view of *icchā*[8] i.e. with reference to the phoneme '*i*'.)

Now interpretation is being given from the point of view of *icchā* (aspect of Śiva.). The third is *icchā*. That is *brahma*; '*brahma*' is one who is '*bṛṃhita*' (grown, swollen, evolved). In this context, it is *brahman*, because being identified with the objects of desire, it is fully grown and is thus full *brahma* (*bṛṃhitaṃ iṣyamāṇena abhinnena pūrṇam brahma*).

'*Caturdaśayuta*' may be interpreted as that with which forty are united. The word '*yuta*' coming after *caturdaśa* can also be taken in the sense of 'unseparated', i.e. the forty inhere only in *brahma* as *icchā*; they are not separate from *brahma*. *Tithiśānta-samanvitam* may be interpreted as follows. '*Tithiśa*' means of the lord of vowels, i.e. *anuttara* or '*a*'. *Tithīśānta* means 'at the end of '*a*' or '*ā*' of *ānanda śakti*'. '*Samanvitam*' may be analysed into *sam*+*anu*+*itam*. '*Anu*' means 'after' (*paścāt*). '*Sam*' means well (*saṃyak*), '*itam*' means 'known'. So '*samanvitaṃ*' means well known after *ānanda*. (Śiva is well known after *ānanda* as *icchā*. That is the *hṛdaya* or core of Bhairava). This *icchātmaka brahma* is *bodhamaya* i.e. pure consciousness.

5th interpretation: (from the point of view of *īśāna*, i.e. with reference to the phoneme '*ī*'.)

Now the interpretation is being given with reference to *īśāna*, i.e. the phoneme '*ī*' (*īśānāpekṣayā*). '*Tṛtiyam brahma*' may be interpreted thus: The third i.e., *icchā* is *brahma*. This means that owing to expansion (*prasāra-vaśāt*), it has become great (*bṛhatbhūtām* which is the etymological meaning of *brahma*) i.e., it has acquired *īśānatā* or rulership (*īśānatām āpannaṃ*). *Caturdaśayutaṃ*' means 'in which the forty *tattvas* or categories have mingled with one another'.

Tithīśa may be interpreted as follows: Of *akula* or *anuttara* who is the lord of the vowels (*tithīśvarasya akulamaya anuttarātmanaḥ*). *Antaḥ* means *saṃkṛtiḥ* i.e., absorption i.e., absorption in *anuttara*, i.e. the initial pulsation of *kulaśakti* that is absorbed in *akula* or *anuttara*. So *tithīśāntasamanvitam* means 'joined with the primal pulsation of *kulaśakti* that is absorbed in *akula* the lord of the vowels.' (That is the *hṛdaya* or core of Bhairava).

6th interpretation: (from the point of view of *unmeṣa* or the phoneme '*u*'.)

Now the interpretation is given from the point of view of *unmeṣa* or *jñāna-śakti* (the energy of knowledge).

The third *brahma* is *īśāna* or ruler.

When the forty categories are just separating from *unmeṣa*, i.e., when there is the first pulsation for an external manifestation, then that state is known as *caturdaśayutaṃ* (*yutaṃ* meaning separation in this context). *Tithīśāntena* means with the initial pulsation. The whole thing means with the desire to shoot forth (*praruruksutayā*); it is well linked with the initial pulsation of *kulaśakti* that is absorbed in *akula*, 'the lord of the vowels'. The word '*sam*' in '*samanvitam*' connotes '*bharaṇa*' or maintenance, i.e. nourishing the state of objectivity.

7th interpretation: (from the point of view of *ūnatā* i.e., from the point of view of the phoneme '*ū*'.)

Ūnatā i.e., *ū* is the intermediate point between *jñānaśakti* and *kriyāśakti*. This has been indicated before. Its nature is *ūḍhatā*, i.e. to hold the division of the categories of existence prior to manifestation in *jñānaśakti* itself. In accordance with this established practice (*rūḍhyā*), the third *brahma* at this stage is that which holds the entire mobile and immobile manifestation within. In contrast to the *aśuddha sṛṣṭi* (the entirely differentiated order of manifestation), and *śuddhāśuddha sṛṣṭi* (the differentiated-cum-undifferentiated order of existence), it is a purely undifferentiated order of manifestation (*śuddha-sṛṣṭyātmakaṃ*). Hence it is the third *brahma*. Phonematically, it is joined with the *tithīśas* which are the very heart of Reality, i.e. the vowels and with the consonants, beginning with '*ka*' and ending with '*kṣa*' coming after the vowels (*tadantaiḥ*).

8th interpretation:

The interpretations are given with reference to the four void vowels (*śūnya-catuṣka*), viz. *ṛ*, *ṝ*, *ḷ*, *ḹ*. First of all the interpretation is being given with reference to *ṛ*. That is the void or empty *ākāśa* (ether) symbolized by *ṛ* in which the condition (*daśā*) of the four (*catur*), viz. the earth, water, fire and air either disappears in the gross form in *saṃhāra* or withdrawal of the world-process or in the subtle form remains as void ether. The *icchā* (*i*) inhering in *ṛ* (*r*+*i*=*ṛ*), considered in a reverse order with reference to *kriyā* (*ānanda, icchā, jñāna, kriyā*) is the third *brahma*. Linked (*yutam*) with that void ether, the third *brahma* may be termed *icchā*. This *brahma* is full of the external glow of *tithīśvara*, i.e. the sun.[6] *Arka* or the sun is the symbol of *pramāṇa* or knowledge. So *tithīśānta-samanvitaṃ* means joined with the *tejas* or glow of *pramāṇa* or knowledge.

9th interpretation: (with reference to the phoneme *ṝ*.)

This also is to be interpreted in accordance with the explanation given above. *Tṛtīyam brahma* is now to be taken in connection with *īśāna*, the symbol of long '*ī*' which appears in *ṝ* (*r*+*ī*.). This also is to be interpreted as the previous one i.e., as joined with the glow of *pramāṇa* or knowledge.

10th interpretation: (with reference to the phoneme *ḷ*.)

The third *brahma* is known as *icchā* inasmuch as *i* inheres in *ḷ* (*l*+*i*=*ḷ*). It is *vyoma* or *śūnya* (ether) which is the inner state (*antaradaśā*) of four viz., earth, water, fire and air, is its base (*ādhāra*). Therefore, it is linked with that. This *brahma* being connected with some reality which follows the *tithiśānta* i.e. the glow of fire (*vahni*), known as *pramātṛ-tejas* is of the nature of the void (*vyomātma*).

11th interpretation: (the interpretation with reference to the phoneme *ḹ*)

As in *ṝ* phoneme, the third *brahma* inherent in the phoneme *ḹ* is *īśāna* (*ḷ*+*ī*=*ḹ*) itself. This also is connected, on the one hand, with the ether, the inner void, the base of the four categories of earth, water, fire and air (*caturdaśa-yutam*) and on the other, with something indefinable that follows the *pramātṛ-tejas* (*tithiśānta*).

Only this one plunges with tremendous momentum into the fullest form of the void (*paripūrṇa śūnya*) which is Bhairava itself.

What this means is the following: When *icchā* together with *īśāna* which is its own nature, reaches the *vyoma* plane (i.e., the plane of the void) of objective experience (*vedya*), then it rests in slight luminosity for a while, suddenly enters the plane of the void (*vyomebhūmim*) which is unbounded (*aparyantatām*), invariably steady (*niścalām*) almost like wood or stone. About such *yogis* as have entered the state of the void which is like deep sleep without the awareness of any object whatsoever (*apavedya-suṣupta*), it has been said: "Even the sound of a kettle drum or bronze cymbal cannot awaken him from his state of absorption".

12th interpretation: (with reference to *e*.)

Now in accordance with the process explained before, when the six vowels (*a*, *ā*, *i*, *ī*, *u*, *ū*) enter another, there occurs diversity of forms. Keeping this in view, the nature of the third *brahma* is as follows: When *icchā* (will) together with *īśāna* (*i*, *ī*) is oriented towards entering *anuttara* (*a*, *ā*), then it experiences the joy of the emotional excitement generated by the union of *śakti-kṣobha* or *icchā-śakti* and *anuttara*, and this is what is said with regard to that state.

Sāmānya spanda[7] is the fourth state of the particular (*viśeṣa*) *spandas* of the qualities of consciousness flowing externally in the form of a vowel of slow tempo, predominantly of the nature of *sattva*, or a vowel of middle tempo, predominantly of the nature of *rājas*, or a vowel of fast tempo, predominantly of the nature of *tamas*. This is indicated by the word *catuḥ* (four). That is *akula* when the state of *sāmānya spanda* is present. *Icchā* with *iśāna* (*i*) joined with that *akula* or in other words *anuttara* is the third *brahma* in this context. This *brahma* is also joined with *ā* occurring after the termination of the phoneme '*a*' i.e., *tithiśa* (*tithiśasya akārasya antyena ānandaśaktyātmanā anvitam*).

13th interpretation: (with reference to *ai*)

(In this connexion, A.G. splits *bhairavātmanaḥ* into two, viz., *bhairavātma* and *naḥ*.)

Similarly when that phoneme *e* enters the highest state, i.e. *anuttara* with *ānanda-śakti* (*a*, *ā*), then acquiring the long state i.e. *ai* (*dirghībhūtaṃ*), it abides in the perfect form of Bhairava, and is our (Śaivas') *brahma*.

Thus this pair of vowels, viz. *e* and *ai* (*bijayugmam*) by entering the vowels, viz., *a* and *ā* in various ways[8], become '*ācchāda*[9]/*samartha*' and '*prasava-samartha*'[10] which are stated to be of the nature of '*kāmatattva*' and '*vāk-tattva*.'[11] This is supported by such lines as: "All desired objects (*kāmān*) should be accomplished with *kāma* (power of desire). This *śakti* should be willingly (*kāmam*) applied to all objects of desire".

"The *bija* or vowel inhering in *e* and *o* i.e. *anuttara* state is meant to give utterance to *kāma-tattva* (inhering in *ai* and *au*)."

14th interpretation: (with reference to *o* and *au*)

With reference to the fifth and sixth phonemes i.e. *u* (*unmeṣa*) and *ū* (*ūnatā*), the explanation that has been given earlier, viz., that is the third *brahma* which is joined with the distributed form of forty categories and the group of vowels and consonants will be helpful here. When this enters the *anuttara* state, it becomes *a*, *ā*—*u*, *ū*, equal to *o*; *a*, *ā*—*o* equal to *au*. So in the context *o* and *au*, this is the third *brahma*, identical with Bhairava.

15th interpretation: (With reference to the phoneme '*aṃ*' or *bindu kalā*.)

In accordance with what has been said earlier, *brahma* joined with the distributed form of the forty categories and the group of vowel-consonants, i.e. *brahma* appearing in the innumerable form of the external world is the *bindu* or dot (*anusvāra*). It is the *hṛdaya* or the very core of Reality, viz., Bhairava in his aspect of knowledge. Consequently, this core or *bindu* is the nature of the third *brahma*.

16th interpretation: (with reference to the phoneme *aḥ*)

(i) *From the point of view of external visarga*

All this multitude of categories darts forth as Bhairava and being emitted outside and expanding, it is known as *brahma* inasmuch as it is of the nature of expansion and abides externally.

(ii) *From the point of view of internal visarga*

It is the stage of *visarga* which is identified with Bhairava, which by setting aside all exclusion indicative of difference and having acquired 'the state of everything being all things' has grown and is thus present also as an internal *visarga*. (Consequently there are with reference to *visarga* two aspects of the third *brahma*—external and internal). This has been determined with attentiveness.

Thus the pervasion of the third *brahma* of sixteen kinds has been described with reference to vowels. Its pervasion with reference to each consonant has already been described.

Now the expressions '*caturdaśayutam, tithīśānta-samanvitam, tṛtīyam brahma*, and *hṛdayam Bhairavātma*' have to be explained with reference to the various stages of life.

Third brahma with reference to the classification of bodily states

Caturdaśayutam: taking the word *daśa* as *daśā*, *caturdaśayutam* means joined with the four states. The four states are (i) childhood, (2) youth, (3) old age, and (4) taking on another body (after death). Being an aggregation of these four states (*catuṣṭayasamāhāramayam*), having a gross body composed of the five gross elements (*pañcabhautikam*) and inwardly united with *tithīśānta*, i.e. *prāṇa* and *apāna* which are breaths going out (expiration) and coming in (inspiration) respectively (*antaḥ tithīśāntan praveśanirgamātmanā prāṇāpāna-rūpeṇa yutam*), the *puryaṣṭaka*[13] is also the third *brahma*. Being pervasive (*bṛhattvāt*), it is void, and the heart abiding in it is that of Śakti (*atra ca hṛdayaṃ śaktyātma*).[14] In fact, it is Śiva-*bīja* (*bīja* i.e. source of all existence) who is all awareness (*bodhātmaka*) and who in progressive compactness or solidification having adopted (1) physical body, (2) *prāṇa*, (3) *puryaṣṭaka*, (4) *śūnya* or consciousness devoid of any object, and (5) *turya* or the fourth state of consciousness or the metaphysical Self has expanded into five kinds of experients with particular kinds of vehicles. These are called respectively (1) external self (*bāhyātmā*), (2) *prāṇa* as the self (*bhūtātmā*), (3) the subtle body as the self which carries the soul from one state of existence to another (*ātivāhikātmā*), (4) the inner self (*antarātmā*), and (5) the supreme self (*paramātmā*). This is the *hṛdaya* (centre) i.e., Bhairava Himself.

Notes

1. The five main powers of Śiva are *anuttara* (*a*) or *cit*, *ānanda* (represented by the phoneme *ā*), *icchā* (represented by the phoneme '*ī*'), *jñāna* or *unmeṣa* (represented by the phoneme '*u*'), and *kriyā* (represented by the phonemes, *e*, *ai*, *o*, *au*). *Icchā* comes after *ānanda*.

2. This experience is known as *vedaka-tādātmya*--the identity of the subject with all.

3. This experience is known as *vedya-tādātmya*--the identity of all manifestation with the Self.

4. *Icchā* is implicit in *ānanda*. But in this aspect, it is not tainted by any desired object. Hence it is called pure.

5. '*Yu miśraṇe amiśraṇe vā*': The root '*yu*' connotes both mingling and separation. In this context it connotes mingling.

6. The difference between *icchā* mentioned earlier and *icchā* mentioned now is that the earlier is of *pūrva koṭi* i.e. of the first aspect where there is not even a trace of the desired object; whereas the *icchā* mentioned now is of the second aspect where there is a subtle incipience of the desired object.

7. As soon as *anuttara* oriented towards external expansion begins to throb as *vimarśa*, there is a lapse of its essential nature. But it has not yet emerged from the state of *jñāna* and reached the state of *kriyā* by which it manifests itself as the external world. This is an intermediate state of *śūnyātiśūnya*. This state is called

vyomasamādhi by the mystics. *Ṛ* symbolizes the initial stage of this *samādhi* (ecstasy) and *ḷ* the final.

The following indicates the four stages of this *samādhi*:

ṛ— Unsteady *vyomasamādhi* followed by *pramāṇa-tejas* or glow of knowledge.

ṝ slightly steady *vyomasamādhi* followed by *pramāṇa-tejas*.

ḷ— Semi-steady *vyomasamādhi* followed by *pramātṛ-tejas* or glow of the subject.

ḹ— Fully steady *vyomasamādhi* followed by *pramātṛ-tejas*.

8. *Sāmānya spanda*: This is the universal *vimarśa-śakti* of the Divine, the universal creative pulsation. When it is exteriorized and flows in the form of different objects, when it becomes the manifestation of the *guṇas* of *prakṛti*, it is known as *viśeṣa spanda*.

9. "Various ways" (*vaicitryānupraveśāt*) is to be understood thus:

1. *e* = *a*+*i*, *ī*, i.e. mingling of *anuttara*, *icchā* and *īśāna*
2. *e* = *ā*+*i*, *ī*, i.e. mingling of *ānanda*, *icchā* and *īśāna*
3. *ai* = *a*+*e*, i.e. mingling of *anuttara* or *trikoṇabīja* i.e. *e*
4. *ai* = *ā*+*e*, i.e. mingling of *ānanda* and *trikoṇabīja*, i.e. *e*

In Śārada script *e* is written as IV. Hence it is called *trikoṇabīja*, i.e. a vowel having three angles.

10. *Ācchāda-samartha* literally means 'with the virility covered' i.e. in-operative. It is also called '*akṣubhdha-samartha*', i.e. with inoperative vitality. In the state in which the male principle and the female principle or in other words the vowel and the consonant are not in actual union or in the case in which vowel and consonant do not mingle with each other, in that there is no external manifestation or expression. This state is known as '*ācchāda-samartha*'. *Kāmatattva* so long as it is not manifest, so long as it is not operative in *kāma-vāk*, it is not of practical use.

The mystery of *kāma-vāk* lies in the actual union of the male and the female principle or vowel and consonant. The *kāma* aspect of Śiva-Śakti lies in their *saṃghaṭṭa* or union.

The vowel '*e*' is short (*hrasva*) which symbolizes only Śiva without the union of Śakti. Hence it is only '*ācchāda-samartha*.'

11. *Prasava-samartha*: Literally, it means capable of begetting or procreation. *Ai* is always long (*dīrgha*), hence it is symbolic

of the eternal union of Śiva-Śakti, and therefore, it is *prasava-samartha*. This means that both *kāma-tattva* and *kāma-vāk* or *kāma-vāṇi* are present in it. The phoneme *ai* is thus symbolic of complete or entire (*paripūrṇa*) Bhairava, for the union of Śiva-Śakti is whole Bhairava according to Trika.

12. *Kāma-tattva* and (*kāma*)-*vāk-tattva*:

Kāma-tattva refers only to the potency of procreation. Hence it is indicative only of *ācchāda-samartha*. (*Kāma*)-*vāk-tattva* refers to the actual manifestation of the potency in creativity. It is *prasava-samartha*.

Phonetically, a pure vowel uncombined with consonant is representative only of Śiva who is *ācchāda-samartha*, or *kāma-tattva*, but a vowel combined with consonant is representative of the union of Śiva-Śakti. Hence it symbolizes *prasava-samartha* or *vāk-tattva*.

In the present context, *e* symbolizes the former and *ai* symbolizes the latter.

13. *Puryaṣṭaka* is the subtle body composed of the five *tanmātras* (*śabda*—sound, *rūpa*—form and colour, *rasa*—flavour, *sparśa*—touch, and *gandha*—smell) and *manas*, *buddhi* and *ahaṃkāra*. This is also *ātivāhika deha*. It is called *ātivāhika*, because it carries the Self from one birth to another. Till death the Self resides in *puryaṣṭaka* or *ātivāhika deha*. According to Abhinavagupta, this is also *brahma*.

14. *Śaktyātma and the five kinds of experients*:

The liquid Śiva-*bīja* itself in its progressive solidification becomes *spanda-śarīra*, *śākta-śarīra*, *puryaṣṭaka-śarīra*, *prāṇa-śarīra*, *sthūla-śarīra* (the external gross body). Since they are all expressions of Śiva's energy, they are, according to Abhinavagupta, a kind of self. Thus there are five different kinds of self, viz., (1) the external self—*bāhyātmā*, (2) the prāṇika self—*bhūtātmā*, (3) the subtle body that carries the Self from one form of existence to another—*ātivāhikātmā*, (4) the inner Self—*antarātmā*, (5) the supreme Self--*paramātmā*. All this is *brahma*.

Text

From *praveśopāyo'tra* on p. 82, l.20 upto *bhāvanā saṃvedana yuktyā niyama eva* on p. 89, l. 23.

The means for entry into this brahma

Translation

The means of entering this (which is the heart of Bhairava) is the following: One should constantly contemplate the various stages of the experients as integrally Bhairava. What this means is the following:

'*Caturdaśa-catvāriṃśat-yutaṃ-dviguṇam-aśītiḥ*' means ten (*daśa*) multiplied by four = *catvāriṃśat* i.e. forty. *Catvāriṃśat-yuta* forty twice i.e. 80

Tithayaḥ pañcadaśa means the lunar fortnight i.e. 15

Īśāḥ i.e. Rudrāḥ 11

Antaḥ samanvita yuktā dviguṇitā kālāstrayaḥ means double the three times (present, past, future)... 6

112

The word '*marma*' in this context means 'measure of fingers'. Therefore, '*dvādaśottaraśatamarmagata*' means 'stretching up to the dimension of 112 fingers.'

The whole sentence means: 'One should (constantly) contemplate on the very corporeal existence (*śarīrasattām eva*) integrally (*anavacchedena*) of all the stages of experients stretching upto the dimension of 112 fingers,[1] viz., *sthūla śarīra*, the gross body, *sūkṣma śarīra*, the subtle body, *para śarīra*, the causal body, *śākta śarīra*, and *spanda śarīra*, throbbing with the expansion of the energy of I-sense (*mantra-vīrya-vikāsa-sphurīkṛta*), full of the excitement brought about by *visarga-viśleṣa* i.e. the emission of the semen of the male state and *visarga-saṃghaṭṭa* i.e. the spot of the union of the emission or the female state as Bhairava himself.

In accordance with the tradition of simultaneous entrance or *caryākrama*, *caturdaśayutam* is to be explained as follows:

Catasro daśā yasya (*tat caturdaśayutam*) i.e., that which has four aspects, viz. sweet, astringent, bitter and sour i.e., various kinds of wine such as *madya*, *surā*, *āsava* etc.

Tithiśānta in this context means the substance that issues forth from both, viz. *vīra*, and *yoginī* or *kuṇḍa-golaka*.

Samanvitaṃ means the secretion existing within their generative organs and denoted by the word '*kusuma*'. '*Tṛtīyam brahma*' means the ashes that remain after the fuel in the form of the world is completely burnt out (i.e. *pramiti* or awareness). *Bhairavātma* means full and satiating liquid. '*Hṛdayam*' or heart signifies the seminal fluid of *vīra* and the thick secretion of *yoginī* existing within the generative organs of the two. These substances (wine etc.) in as much measure as is obtainable destroy all taint of difference. The following process is generally observed. Doubt which brings about narrowness of mind is generative of the first sprout of the mundane tree, and then it expands, becomes mature, and finally brings about the very fruit (i.e., complete involvement) of mundane existence. It has been fabricated by the awakened ones in such a way that it may become stationary in the case of the unawakened ones. In the case of fools, once a doubt is entertained, it gets rooted in their mind, it fructifies in diverse ways for them, according to their peculiar nature.

Therefore, on account of diverse imagination doubts assume different forms and are described as *adharma* (unrighteous) etc. They vary according to each scripture, and each country. As has been said, "Just as a plunderer carries away the valuables of the house, even so depression saps away the vitality of the body." (Sp. K. III, 8).

When that doubt is instantly dissolved, then the stain of the trouble of the psycho-physical limitations of the aspirant is cast out (*nirasta-pāśava-yantraṇā kalaṅko*) and he enters the heart of Bhairava. Therefore, one should in every way, practise the discipline that leads to the heart of Bhairava. This is the sense of the teaching of Tilaka-Śāstra. It has also been said in Bharga-śikhā: "One should welcome the mode of life of the *vīras*[3] and should practise it in due order." In Sarvācāra also, it has been said:

"It is the fool who is subject to doubt owing to ignorance, and thence arise birth and death. All the *mantras* are of the nature of phonemes, and all the phonemes are of the nature of Śiva. All that is considered as drinkable or non-drinkable is (after all) simply water; all that is considered to be eatable or not eatable is (after all) simply what comes from the element earth. Whether beautiful or ugly, everything is (after all) the product of the element fire. Touchable and untouchable are considered to be only a matter of the element air. The hole (whether of the male organ or the female organ) is only a matter of space.

Sweets offered (to the deity), the person who offers, and one who accepts the offer they are all, O goddess, a mass of the five elements. There is nothing which is not a product of the five elements. For what is one to entertain a desire (as desirable)? And regarding what one is to hesitate as undesirable?"

In Vīrāvali Śāstra also, this is the opinion.

In Kramastotra also, it has been said:

"I bow to Kālī who, for regulating the affairs of the world (*jagato yamāya*) portrays the form of those who carry out the option of doing this or that (*yamasya yantuḥ*), the option characterized by intentness in accepting one object by keeping off other ones (*sarvārthasaṃkarṣaṇa saṃyamasya*), and to Kālī who simultaneously assimilates (lit. swallows up) in her inner being the advanced souls above *vikalpas* and enjoys the grand play of involving limited experients in *vikalpas* (*mahāgrāsavilāsa-rāgāt*) i.e., who carries out *saṅkoca* and *vikāsa* at the same time."

This has been explained by me in detail in the gloss on it, viz. Kramakeli. Therefore, in Trika Śāstra, this very activity almost without any curb is worship. All things are available for the fulfilment of this worship. The course of knowledge has been described in detail. Of the castes—Brāhmaṇas, etc., there is no fixed principle, for the caste distinction is artificial. The specification that Brāhmaṇas alone are entitled for instruction can convince only the silly herd. This has been conclusively clarified in detail by the Lord in 'Mukuṭasaṃhitā'. In Trika, it is established without any effort at proving.

(Now another interpretation of the text is taken up)

The treatment of amṛtabīja

The fourteenth vowel, i.e. the middle one between *o* and *aṃ* is *au*. *Tithīśānta* i.e., the final of the vowels is *visarga* i.e. *aḥ*. *Tṛtīyam brahma* is that which comes in between '*ṣa*' and '*ha*' i.e. '*sa*'. This is really the *mantra* (i.e. *sauḥ*) which is the generating seed of the universe. Whatever existent (*sat*) represented by that '*sa*' appears whether in the sphere of earth, *prakṛti* or *māyā* that falling within *icchā*, *jñāna* or *kriyā* is a triad (represented by *au*) and being an epitome of all, is delivered in and by Śiva (represented by the *visarga, aḥ*).[3] Thus this indeterminate (*nirvikalpaka*) continuum of manifestation goes on ceaselessly.

A determinate thought-construct is used when it is meant to express predominantly a sense of difference, connected as it may be with the three series of time, as for instance, 'this was done in such a manner by women, friend, etc., this is being done in such a manner (by them), this will be done in such a manner (by them). On the contrary, even the stage of Śiva which is plain liberation (and *amṛtabīja*) is for the unfortunate ones always (i.e., in both *nirvikalpa* and *savikalpa* states) a desert or a vast forest owing to the fear of transmigratory state. "(For the unfortunate ones) there appears to be a heap of tangled flames in the form of submarine fire bursting forth from water. From the full moon, the very abode of nectar-like light, there appears to be splitting of thunderbolt from fear. Through thought-construct, there is fear of transmigratory existence even from the expansion of sovereignty (of *anuttara*). What strange things extend in different ways through the development of evil fate !"

In Īśvarapratyabhijñā also, it has been said: "He who knows that all this glory (of manifestation) is mine (i.e. belongs to the Self), who realizes that the entire cosmos is his Self possesses *maheśatā* (lordship) even when dichotomising thought-constructs have their play" (Āgamādhikāra IIA, 12). As among figures, the four-armed Viṣṇu, the three-eyed Śiva etc., among spirituous liquors, *surā, āsava*, etc. lead one forcibly as it were to the state of Bhairava, even so, among all the phonemes, '*sa*' leads to the state of Bhairava.

'*Sa*', the nature of which is the ambrosia of the highest beatitude, casting the host of all other phonemes within itself, shines forth in manifestation. That which is the highest nature of *satya* (truth), *sukha* (happiness), *sampat* (acquisition), *sattā* (existence), all beginning with '*sa*', is experienced at the time of the appearance of the sound '*si*' to express pleasurable sensation when there is the quivering of the male organ and contraction-cum-expansion of the female organ. That is really the non-māyīya nature of *satya* etc.

Those who by means of the grasp of the supreme core i.e., *amṛtabīja*, have become versed in knowing a thing by a mere hint or gesture can, by penetration into truth through '*sa*' (*tāvati satyapade anupraveśāt*), know the desired object of others only by means of the phoneme '*ga*' etc., out of the innumerable words such as '*gagana*', '*gavaya*' and '*gava*', occurring initially, in the middle or at the end. Thus even one phoneme can express the real sense. As has been said "There is an intermixture of word, the object denoted and the knowledge (indicated by the word) by mutual imposition. If one practises *saṃyama*[4] on each of them separately, he can acquire the knowledge of the sound of all creatures." (Yogasūtra III, 17).

Therefore, for the most part even phonemes '*a*', '*ca*' which are mere 'particles' and affixes etc., even in the state of *māyā* (i.e. even in the work-a-day world), as in the highest state express such a sense of negation and totality (*niṣedhasamuccayādikamartham abhidadhati*) as are absorbed in the state of the subject and have not yet acquired objectivity and being destitute of external gender and number have not yet acquired the status of '*sattva*' or a definite word of declension and are non-different from things that are yet to become the objects of negation and totality. This is the sense also of what respected Bhartṛhari says in the following lines in Vākyavicāra i.e. Vākyapadīya:

"Every word is initially complete in itself separately but (in a reciprocal relation of word, sense and knowledge) that same word becomes a correlative".

In Vedic grammar and divine Śāstras like Śiva-Sūtras, an etymological explanation of words occurring as *mantra* (sacred formula) or in initiation, in accordance with the intent of each letter of the word is considered to be perfectly appropriate. That is not conventional; the etymological explanation of every word, owing to unforeseen destiny has not reached the common people. So the nature of the phoneme '*sa*' is also like this. The explanation of *au* and the *visarga* (of the mantra *sauḥ*) has already been given. It has been said in Pūrva-Śāstra (Mālinīvijaya):

"Three spheres (viz. *pṛthivi*, *prakṛti* and *māyā*) are pervaded by the phoneme '*sa*', the fourth one (viz. the Śakti sphere) is pervaded by the trident i.e. '*au*' and the one that transcends all, viz. Śiva is indicated by *visarga* i.e. *aḥ*. This is how the pervasion of *parā* is described." (M.V. IV, v. 25).

"The mystery of this can be understood only when the spiritual director (*guru*) is satisfied with the physique, monetary position, knowledge of the Śāstras, good caste, good morals and good qualities of the pupil. O goddess, venerated by the *vīras* it is only when the mystery (of this *mantra*) is unravelled (*bheditā*) by the *guru*, pleased in heart, it is only then that it should be considered as bringing about fulfilment (*siddhi* i.e. liberation), not otherwise." (M.V. III, 57-58.) Elsewhere also it has been said:

"There is only one *sṛṣṭi-bīja* (i.e. *amṛtabīja* or *sauḥ*), one *mudrā* viz. *khecarī*. One in whom both of these are engendered is situated in a stage of surpassing peace."

Therefore, the rule is that mystic knowledge or this *mantra* is not to be recorded (clearly) in a book. In Pūrva-Śāstra (i.e. Mālinīvijaya) also '*sauḥ*' has been described in a disguised way in the following form: "United with the left thigh, the creature has come according to tradition" in which 'united with the left thigh' (*vāmajāṅghānvitaḥ*) really means 'united with *au*', the creature (*jīva*) really means '*sa*', 'has come according to tradition' (*pāramparyakramāgatāḥ*) really means *visarga*, i.e. (so the whole thing really means *sa*+*au*+: i.e. *sauḥ*). In this book also, it will be said "As lying in the seed of a banyan tree".

Explanation of etannaḥ...yogavimuktidam

[*Naḥ* = *na*+*a*+*aḥ* i.e. *na*, the first letter of *Mālinī*, *a*, the first letter of *Mātṛkā*, symbol of *vīra*, and *aḥ*, symbol of *visarga-śakti yoginī*. The person born from the union of these is known as *yoginī-jāta*]. Only such a person can have realization of the heart of Bhairava i.e. *amṛtabīja* or the *mantra sauḥ* in whom:

1. The state of an experiencer has arisen (*jātaḥ prādurbhūta-pramātṛbhāvaḥ*) from the union of Śiva-*vīra* who is to be cognized by means of '*na*' (the first letter of *Mālinī*) and '*a*' (the first letter of *Mātṛkā*) and *visargaśakti* (i.e. *yoginī*).*

2. Or in him who is Rudra. Rudra is one who can successfully keep off or destroy the bonds of *māyā*. He is the veritable man. He alone can clearly realize it. He who is not Rudra, nor born of *yoginī* cannot realize it. The realization of *amṛtabīja* can bestow *sadyoga* or identity with Bhairava, which is ascertained as libera-

*Such a person was known as *yoginībhūḥ*. Abhinavagupta himself was a *yoginībhūḥ*.

tion (in Trika). The word '*sadyaḥ*' denotes immediately. This suggests that he who realizes it is of this kind i.e., Rudra or born of *yoginī*; no one else can obtain it. He who is of the above kind realizes it clearly. Thus he realizes the heart i.e., '*sauḥ*' which offers liberation immediately.

Explanation of 'asya uccāra kṛte...svadehāveśalakṣaṇam'

Mantras are the sacred phonemes both worldly and divine. They save by reflection (*mananatrāṇarūpāḥ*). For worldly purposes, they are of the form of thought-construct i.e., *vikalpa*; as divine or transcendental, they are full of *saṃvit-śakti* (the power of higher consciousness). The *mudrās* are the particular dispositions of the hands and feet of the nature of *kriyāśakti*. *Mantramudrāgaṇa*, therefore, means a host of great powers brought into being by *mantra* and *mudrā*, which in the collective form is identical with *parāśakti* (the supreme Śakti).*

[A.G. explains *svadehāveśalakṣaṇam* in the following ways:]

(1) '*Sva*' means 'of one's own' (*svasya-ātmanaḥ*) *dehasya*—of the body means 'of *prāṇa, puryaṣṭaka, śūnya* etc.' *Āveśaḥ* means immediately by the entrance (in oneself) of the highest nature, there is the disappearance of the stupefaction which connotes dependence on others and the emergence of the stage of the conscious subject permeated by autonomy. (2) *svadehāveśaḥ* may be analysed into *svadā*+*ihā*+*āveśaḥ*. '*Svadā*' means 'that which imparts its own nature (of *prakāśa* and *vimarśa*) to all objects'. *Īhā* means expansion of intial *icchā* up to *kriyā*. *Tayā āveśaḥ* means penetration by such *īhā*. So the whole phrase (*svadehāveśalakṣaṇam*) means in a manner characterized by the penetration in him of the expansion of *īhā* which has the divine nature of *prakāśa* and *vimarśa*. The supreme state of the Experient characterized by such *īhā* is *svadehāveśaḥ*. That is the (real) enunciation of this *mantra* i.e. *sauḥ* which arises in the above manner, being established in the highest aspect i.e., the aspect of the supreme conscious Self (*ūrdhvācaraṇe sthitau satyām*).

*In the ordinary life, a sense is meant for a specific purpose. The eye for instance can only see, not hear. There is, however, a general state of the sense-activities in which the functions of all the senses can be performed simultaneously without the use of the gross senses. This is the collective state of the senses.

The way by which this state can be brought about has been determined very often. (Now A.G. interprets *sadyas tanmukhatām* etc.). By the word '*sadyaḥ*' (immediately) is suggested absorption in the *anuttara* stage. '*Tanmukhatām eti*' means that after *samāveśa*, one acquires supreme consciousness (*para-rūpa*). This penetration is not the like that of the animals whose real nature of Bhairava on the contrary is concealed. (Now A.G. takes up '*muhūrtam smarate*' for explanation). '*Muhūrtam*' in this context means 'fortyeight minutes'. Though *amṛtabīja* is undetermined by time (*akālakalitatve'pi*) yet the word '*muhūrta*' is used here with reference to the experience of other experients which is temporal (*para-kalanāpekṣayā*). '*Yaḥ smarati*' means he who establishes congruous connexion with *amṛtabīja* (*anusandhatte*). He alone holds captive (*saṃbadhnati*) i.e. makes identical with himself (*svātmani ekīkaroti*) the multitude of *mantra* and *mudrā* already explained because of his unity consciousness (*advayataḥ*). How does he do so? He alone can do it who by means of *cumbaka* i.e. by means of *śākta-śarīra* which contacts the universal aspect, having impressed with *mudrās* on all fronts, establishes congruous connexion with *amṛtabīja*.

The particle '*tu*' is used in the sense of certainty. He who being stamped with the pulsation of Śakti, has joined his consciousness in congruous unity with Śiva who is the embodiment of this kind of true state i.e., *sauḥ*; he alone accomplishes this, not stone etc., which come under the category of *nara*. (The explanation of *atītānāgata...kathayati eva* is as follows):

He tells by mere will (*saṅkalpanāt*) all the events which have no obvious meaning (*anartharūpam*), goes on telling all about them till the very end (*kathāparyantatām nayati*), events of the past (*atīta*), or likely to occur in the future (*anāgata*) or which may be not existing (*prāgabhāva*), or non-existent in any other form (*anyābhāvāt*), i.e. in the form of *pradhvaṃsābhāva* (non-existence caused by utter destruction), *atyantābhāva* (absolute non-existence), or *anyonyābhāva* (mutual non-existence) or of any other kind of non-existence (*itaradapi*). Under what circumstances does he do so? The answer is when he is interrogated about a certain matter (*pṛṣṭam tad yasyāsti sa tathā*)—he is all-knowing. Only when a question is put (*praśne*), then what he desires to know (*yadeva kila jñīpsyati*) that which is already lying within him, he expresses outwardly in *vaikhari* or gross speech (*tadeva antargataṃ bahiṣkurute*). As has been said:

"As the sustainer of this universe (i.e. Śiva) when eagerly entreated with desire accomplishes all the desires abiding in the heart of the embodied *yogi* who is awake after causing the rise of the moon (*soma*) and the sun (*sūrya*)."[5] (Sp. K. III, 1) (i.e. by means of *jñāna* and *kriyāśakti*). One and the same *yogi* even in memory (which refers to the past) and imagination (which refers to the future) remains equally in the present. Past and future do not exist for him. As has been said:

"It is better to remain in the present which is not limited by the past and the future."[5a] When the state of the experient has been existing from before (from endless time) and there cannot be any increase or decrease in it, how can it tolerate such limitations of the present? "So and so knows *this*, does *this*". Therefore, it has '*sakṛdvibhātatva*', i.e. it is shining eternally. Therefore has it been said. It is because of this i.e. limitation that the present time requires a reference to the past etc. i.e., to the past and the future. In the absence of limitation, because of non-applicability of expectancy, reality is undetermined by time. This has been repeatedly stated. It is the Lord alone who makes the variegated power of time manifest. "Moreover in any waking condition, that which is considered to be a *ghaṭikā* i.e. twenty four minutes, in that very time those experients, who are undergoing varied experiences in a dream, experience the diversity of a day, three hours (*prahara*), a year etc.".

(Now A.G. is giving an interpretation of the fourteenth verse, viz. *praharādyadabhipretam...rudraśaktibhiḥ*. The vision of the Deity by means of *rodhana* and *drāvaṇa*.)

Rodhana-praharaḥ = prakṛṣṭoharaḥ; *sāksāt = sākṣa + ad.*

Praharaḥ has been explained by A.G. as the state of complete dissolution. The sense is: the aspirants after having realized the *amṛta-bija* or *sauḥ*, and having assimilated the objective world grasped through the senses into the Self (*sākṣāt*), or in other words achieved its dissolution in *akula* or *anuttara*.

Drāvaṇa-sakṣa + at

Making the same sense-grasped (*sākṣa*) objective world which is now internalized, externalize (*at*), bringing it face to face with *jñānaśakti* residing in Sadāśiva, the so-called *preta* (*preta-śabda-*

vācya-sadāśiva-niviṣṭa-jñānaśakti-ābhimukhyena), undoubtedly (*asaṃdigdhaṃ kṛtvā*), realizes the goddess *icchā-śakti*—the source of effecting all external forms (*rūpāṇām kalanam*) and attracted by the simultaneous process of *rodhana-drāvaṇa-śakti*, i.e. the simultaneous Śakti of assimilating inwards the sense-grasped objective world (*sākṣasya-sendriyasya rūpasya adanaṃ bhakṣaṇam kṛtvā*) and effecting externalization of the assimilated objective world (*atanam ca sātatyagamanaṃ kṛtvā*), (realizes the goddess *icchā-śakti*).

'*Ru*' denotes *rodhana* and '*dra*' denotes *drāvaṇa*. *Rodhana* in this context is a technical term. It means *saṃhāra*, i.e. withdrawal or dissolution. *Drāvaṇa* is also a technical term in this context. It means *sṛṣṭi* i.e. manifestation. Being drawn i.e. going in a state of absorption through the *saṃhāra* and *sṛṣṭi śaktis*, he (the *yogī*) fully perceives i.e. experiences. This is what is meant to be said. (First of all, there is *rodhana*—the state of inward dissolution and then there is *drāvaṇa*, the state of external expansion).

1. *Rodhana—the state of inward dissolution*

What is said to be perception or experience (*yadidaṃ darśanaṃ nāma*) that comes to the *yogī* who, having reached the state of *akula* in which the waves of all the external *vikalpas* (thought-constructs) have dissolved (*tat-sarva-taraṅga-pratyastamayārdhya-akula-sattādhirūḍhasya*) and full of *icchā-śakti* which has reached its highest capacity by coming in contact with *svātantrya* (divine autonomy) full of endless glory (*ananta-mahima-svātantrya-yogāt*), realizes the dissolution of *icchā* in *anuttara*.

2. *Drāvaṇa—the state of external expansion.*

Then the same *icchā* becoming externally oriented assumes the aspect of *jñānaśakti*, having slightly indistinct appearances of difference as its object.

Rodhana even in external orientation and Drāvaṇa even in internal orientation

The *jñānaśakti* of the nature of *sāmānya spanda* (general pulsation) expanding towards the outside, assumes the form of the senses of the nature of specific *spanda* and the *yogī* at this state achieves the *rodhana* or arresting of the senses in the same condition outside. This is indeed *atana* in *rodhana* i.e. *sātatyāgamana* or continuous movement in *rodhana* or arresting. Therefore, *rodhana* is both *drāvaṇa* or expansion and *bhakṣaṇa* (swallowing) or dissolution. This process is known as *vamana-bhakṣaṇa*, i.e. both ejecting outside and swallowing within. *Darśana* or experience is of the nature of *prathā* i.e. it involves both *sāmānya* or general *jñāna* and *viśeṣa* or specific *jñāna* and what is *prathā* involves diversity of expansion (*prathāyāśca tathavidha-vaicitrya-yogāt*). A state of indecision or doubt depends on two alternatives, e.g., whether this is the trunk of a tree or a human being. Even this uncertainty has an element of certainty about it (for certainly it is one of these and cannot be anything else). Thus the divine power achieves what is hard to accomplish.

Explanation of prahara...smaraṇa

Such a *yogi* is verily Bhairava who has the power of memory which is *parāpara* i.e. which assimilates a past experience to a present one. That is why it has been said only in 'two *praharas*' i.e. by placing two cognitions (*para* and *apara*) together. The *para* or the previous or the past *prahara* is that of actual experience and the *apara* or the second *prahara* is the cognition of the sameness in the present. Remembering the *amṛtabija* in this way (i.e. in *parāpara** way) he becomes settled in *vyoma* or empty space (*vyomastho jāyate*) i.e. he acquires the status of an experient in *puryaṣṭaka* (at the time of perception or first experience) and *śūnya* or void (at the time of *apohana*). When his perceptual experience is characterized by *prahara* i.e. by complete absorption, he deliberates upon it by calling it up in memory again and again. "*Sākṣāt paśyati asaṃdigdhaṃ...rudra śaktibhiḥ*" is connected with this as with the previous one. It has been said that till that time even the memory is like the original experience itself. It is said that he is united with the *vikalpa śakti* of the nature of *apara* i.e., *apohana* i.e., he experiences even the gap occurring between the first experience and its recall.

(Now A.G. is explaining the 15th and 16th verses). When perceiving, then remembering, then settled in *vyoma* i.e., in *apohana* (the experience of the gap between the first experience and its recall), he experiences again by means of these processes unitedly (*trayeṇa*) then with three kinds of cognition characterized

**Parāpara* means that together with *darśana* or *anubhavajñāna*, the *yogī* has *smṛtijñāna*, *vikalpajñāna* and *apohanajñāna*.

by the expression *praharatraya*, the *mātaraḥ sarvā* i.e., all the inner *pramātaras*, in other words the inner supreme energies of the senses,[6] being experients become *siddha* or perfect in experiencing the objects regardless of the other experients being successful in experiencing them.[7]

Yogeśvaryaḥ means those who have gained *aiśvarya* i.e., *svātantrya* or autonomy by means of *yoga* characterized by identity with the inner genuine experient. *Mahābalāḥ* means '*mahat balaṃ yāsāṃ tāḥ*' i.e., they whose prowess is great. The *bala* or prowess here means the power of expanding in all directions without any check in contrast to the external senses. 'They' refers to the inner *śaktis* (*antaḥ-karaṇa-didhatayaḥ*) viz., *manas*, *buddhi* and *ahaṃkāra*. These are also perfect because regardless of the restraints advocated by all the ordinary empirical texts, they are full of activity prompted by the ardour or autonomy.

Virāḥ—*Vircs* in this context are what are called the organs of sense and the organs of action (of such *yogis*). They also become perfect. *Vīreśvarāḥ* i.e., the lords of the *viras* or in other words, the energies of *ka* and other phonemes also become perfect.

'*Śākiniganaḥ*' means Brāhmī and other divinities who appear with the manifestation of '*ka*' and other phonemes and who are a host of powers denoting different mental modes such as attraction, aversion etc. This host of powers also becomes perfect. Since it is perfect, therefore it is powerful (*balavān*).

Paramāṃ siddhiṃ yacchanti means (they) offer the *paramā*-perfection; *paramā* means *parasyamā* i.e., *pramiti* or correct notion of the supreme experient (*parasya*). This *siddhi* or perfection is *vikalpātmikā*, i.e., even with external means of proof, the *yogi* is able to pinpoint the nature of the supreme, e.g., such is the supreme (*asau paraḥ*) or they offer the (most) desired object of the *yogi*, viz. the realization of the (real) 'I'. Two alternative courses would be applicable (*vikalpayoga*) successively (*kramaśaḥ*) both to the *yogi* who carries on the yogic practice as a matter of course without knowing its full value (*ajñātārthakriye*) and also to the *yogi* who carries on the yogic practice with full knowledge of its purport (*jñātārthakriye*).

Explanation of 'anena...prasidhyati'

In short (*kim bahunā*), those adepts (*mantriṇaḥ*) who practise the discipline of spiritual perfection (*sādhayanti*) in accordance with the *mantra* of other scriptures, they also will become perfect by this creative *mantra* (*hṛdayam* i.e., *sauḥ bija*) and will become liberated while alive. Without this (*mantra*) the highest perfection will not be achieved. This is the sense.

The interpretation of the last lin , viz. '*yat kiñcit bhairava* etc' is the following: '*Siddhāḥ* or they who have become perfect (through *jñāna*), *sādhayanti* or they who are carrying on the discipline of spiritual life (through *yoga*), *setsyanti* or they who will become perfect gradually by means of powers like *aṇimā* etc., all these have achieved or will achieve perfection only through this *mantra* (i.e., *sauḥ*). Without penetration in this central creative *mantra*, even success in the pragmatic life will not be achieved, or in *tantra* i.e., in the practical discipline of *yoga*, all that is due to this (*mantra*) only.

Thus the highest Lord himself is this *hṛdaya bija* i.e., *sauḥ mantra.* In this way strengthened by the three *śaktis* (of *parā*, *parāparā* and *aparā*,), he is full of *udaya-saṃhāra-maya** and identical with infinite Consciousness.[8]

(A.G. is now explaining *adṛṣṭamaṇḍalo'pi*)

(1) *From the standpoint of pati*

Thus, '*adṛṣṭa*' is that which is unseen i.e., unknown, the sphere of ignorance, the limitation of *māyā* (*akhyāti-rūpam aṇḍaṃ māyā-malam*). This *hṛdaya-bija* (*sauḥ*) realized in this way removes (*lumpati*) the limitation of *māyā* which brings about a sense of differentiation and also the primal ignorance (*akhyāti rūpaṃ*) of the true nature of the Self.

(2) *From the standpoint of paśu* (*adṛṣṭaṃ, aṇḍāni eva lopaḥ, tadyogi*)

At the same time, this *amṛta-bija* having accepted the limitation (*lopa* or *saṅkoca*) pervading the four spheres of Śakti, *māyā* etc. is present in the form of limitation also.

Thus the highest Lord who is a mass of consciousness has *vidyā* (i.e. *anubhava* or the *parā* state), *māyā* (i.e., *apohana* or the *aparā*

---

* *Udaya-saṃhāra-maya* is a technical term. It means that at the time of experience, it is *udīyamāna* (rising), at the time of memory (*smṛti*), it is *udaya-saṃhāra-maya*, at the time of *apohana*, it is only *saṃhāra-maya. Udaya-saṃhāra* includes all the three.

state) and both (i.e., *smṛti* or *parāparā* state). As has been rightly said:

"*Darśana* i.e., experience is the supreme Śakti (*parā*), *smaraṇa* or memory is the supreme-cum-non-supreme Śakti (*parāparā*); *vikalpa* or alternation or *apohana* is the non-supreme Śakti (*aparā*). The Lord has all the three Śaktis. He has both the powers of *māyā* (the power of differentiation) and *vidyā* (the power of non-difference or identity). *Māyā* has four spheres (viz., *pṛthivī*, *prakṛti*, *māyā* and *śakti*). *Vidyā* is the consciousness of Self, full of grace, the beneficent Energy of Śiva."

If the above verses have to be interpreted primarily in accordance with *yoga* then as prescribed in Śri-pūrvaśāstra (Mālinīvijaya) etc., one should first follow holy observance (of fasting etc.) and then enunciate this *mantra* (i.e. *sauḥ*). The verses should be interpreted evidently in this way, for in the fixed practices of *yoga* (*dṛṣṭakāryeṣu*) the numerous practices depending on a fixed order refer only to certain fixed rules. The *yogis* also have to observe a fixed discipline in connexion with nerves, vortices of energy (*cakra*), *karaṇas*[9], creative contemplation (*bhāvanā*), etc.

NOTES

1. The throb of the corporeal I-sense will be clear from the following chart:

Dimension	The state of the Experient	Name of the body	Dimension of the fingers	Folds of the Body
From the toe of the foot up to the head	Bāhyātma pramātā	Sthūla-śarīra	84	The external fold of the body
From the toe of the foot up to Brahma-randhra	Bhūtātma-pramātā	Sūkṣma-śarīra	12 (84+12) = 96	The inner second fold
From the toe of the foot upward upto	Ātivāhika-ātma-pramātā or	Para-śarīra	12 (96+12) = 108	Third fold measured up-to 12 fingers

108 fingers	puryaṣṭaka			above Brahma-randhra
From the toe of the foot downward in the earth upto two fingers	Antarātma-pramātā	Śākta-śarīra	2 (108+2) = 110	Fourth fold
Two fingers above the Ātivāhika	Paramātma-pramātā	Spanda-śarīra	2 (110+2) = 112	Fifth fold

2. '*Vīra*': This means literally a 'hero'. The term designates a special category of Tāntrika initiates characterized by courage and an inclination towards orgiastic practices.

3. This means that the *mantra* '*sauḥ*' covers the entire manifestation.

4. *Saṃyama* is a technical word of the Yoga-Sūtras of Patañjali. It includes the three practices of *dhāraṇā* or fixing the attention, *dhyāna* or meditation and *samādhi* or complete absorption of the mind.

5. Here *soma* or the moon symbolizes *jñāna-śakti* (the power of knowledge) and *sūrya* or sun symbolizes *kriyāśakti* (the power of action).

5.a cf. Mālinīvijaya Vārttika I, 156, with the *sukhī bhavet*.

6. *Parameśa-śakti* means the inner supreme energy of the senses. The word *mātaraḥ* connotes these inner *śaktis* or energies of the senses. There is a difference between *indriya-śakti* and *indriyavṛtti*. *Indriyaśakti* means the inner energy of the senses, *indriyavṛtti* means the mode in which senses perceive objects. *Indriyavṛtti* is extroverted; *indriyaśakti* is introverted. *Indriyaśakti* has *abhedajñāna* or identity-consciousness; *indriyavṛtti* is concerned with *bhedajñāna*, the difference and variety of objects.

7. When all perceivers perceive the same object as it is, e.g., when all perceive a jar as jar, then the perception is confirmed and it is considered to be the right perception. The *yogī*'s perception is perfect whether other people perceive a particular object in the same way or not. Moreover, the perception of other

people is of the kind of *indriyavṛtti*, whereas the perception of the *yogī* is of the kind of *indriyaśakti* which is of a different order.

8. *Ananta-saṃvidaikyaśāli*: This includes the ideas of '*prasāra-hṛdaya*' and *saṃhāra-hṛdaya. Prasāra-hṛdaya* is *a-ha-m*'. This is known as '*hṛdaya-bīja*'. *Saṃhāra-hṛdaya* is *m-ha-a*. This is technically known as *piṇḍa-nātha*. Both refer to the identity of the infinite I-consciousness.

9. *Karaṇa* is one of the *āṇava upāyas* by which the aspirant contemplates over the body and the nervous system as an epitome of the cosmos.

INTRODUCTION TO VERSE 19

It has been said that 'Trika is higher than Kula'. Now of this Trika, *anuttara* is that which transcends all. It is this which the Tantra is going to describe.

ADṚṢṬAMAṆḌALO'PI EVAṂ
YAḤ KAŚCID VETTI TATTVATAḤ
SA SIDDHIBHĀGBHAVEN NITYAṂ
SA YOGĪ SA CA DĪKṢITAḤ //19/

TRANSLATION

Whosoever thus knows truly (the *bījamantra sauḥ*) even if he has not seen the *maṇḍala*, he enjoys the success of perfection eternally. He is (perfect) *yogī*, he is (really) initiated.

TEXT

From *maṇḍalam* on p. 90, l. 7 upto *nityamiti* on p. 90, l. 19.

TRANSLATION

Maṇḍala[1] means a mystic circle (diagram) in which the deity is installed. *Adṛṣṭa* means one who has not seen or one who has not joined the association of *yoginis* (*aprāptamelako'pi*) by means of *caryā* or observance of certain religious rites through *śakti* process (*śāktopāya*) or *niśāṭana* i.e., a religious rite practised at night through *āṇava* process or *haṭhapāka* i.e. a persistent process of assimilating experience to the consciousness of the experient classed under *śāmbhava* process.

Another explanation of *maṇḍala* may be the system of nerves as medium of prāṇic currents and a smaller group of nerves.

So '*adṛṣṭamaṇḍalaḥ*' according to this interpretation of *maṇḍala* would mean 'one who has not perceived the group of nerves etc.

(*Continued on page* 238)

CHART No. 10

The outline of the Maṇḍala of the Trident and Lotuses (*triśūlābjamaṇḍalam*) prescribed by MVUT 9.6-31 (TĀ 31.62-85b).
Diagram Courtesy: A. Sanderson

by means of yogic practice', it may be interpreted as not even having seen the diagram of the trident with lotuses.[2] In the matter of realization, *maṇḍala* or the ceremony of initiation is of no use.

'*Evam* means '*evameva*' i.e. all of a sudden.

'*Yaḥ kaścit*' means: he who has been favoured with the highest grace (*parāśaktipātānugṛhīto*), '*vetti*' means he alone knows. 'This realization alone is *dīkṣā*, what else is *dīkṣā* (initiation)?'

Therefore thus knowing, he has (really) been initiated by omnipresent revered Bhairava. The statement that "The man with little intelligence who adopts a *mantra* by himself (without the help of a *guru*) gets into trouble"[3] applies only to *mantras* other than this central seminal *mantra*, not to this *mantra*, viz., *sauḥ bīja*, for it is the very heart of Bhairava. This *mantra* transcends even such deities as Mantra, Mantreśvara and Mantramaheśvara.

This cannot be expressed in a book. It is the very core of the Divine. It has (already) been clearly laid down that this is truly acquired only by the favour of the highest grace. So 'any one' suggests that any one can acquire it irrespective of caste, religious vow, *caryā* etc.; insight into it is the main point.

That *yogi* enjoys full perfection. Since a *yogī* is one who yearns after communion with the Divine, initiation characterized by the gift of spiritual insight (*jñāna-dāna*) and the destruction of *māyā* (*māyākṣapaṇa*)[4] is imparted to him alone. The particle '*ca*' has been used in the sense of certainty. Therefore he should be wholly considered a *yogi*. That is why it is said, "He alone is the *yogī* who has attained full perfection. He alone is ever initiated."

Notes

1. *Maṇḍala*: A.G. interprets it in three ways:

(1) *devatācakram*, a circle in which a deity is installed. This is the usual meaning of the word, (2) the group of nerves for the passage of *prāṇic* currents, and (3) the diagram of the trident with lotuses.

2. *triśūlābjādimaṇḍalaṃ*: This is the diagram of a triangle representing the divine Śakti or Devī in all her aspects. A white lotus (*abja*) is placed on each prong of the *triśūla* for worship. The diagram is given on the previons page.

On the occasion of initiation, a diagram like this was drawn with lines of lime and shown to the disciple before initiation.

3. The full verse referred to is as follows:

> Svayaṃgṛhīta mantrāśca kliśyante cālpabuddhayaḥ
> Lipisthitastu yo mantro nirvīryaḥ so'trakalpitaḥ //

"People with little intelligence who adopt a *mantra* by themselves (without its being imparted by a *guru*) get into trouble. That *mantra* which is simply recorded in a book is without any power. This is what is declared here."

4. This is hermeneutic interpretation of *dīkṣā*. The letter '*dī*' means '*dīyate jñānam*' i.e. insight is imparted; the letter '*kṣa*' means '*kṣiyate pāpam*' i.e., sin is destroyed.

Text of the Verse

ANENA JÑĀTAMĀTREṆA JÑĀYATE SARVAŚAKTIBHIḤ

Translation

By mere knowledge of this *mantra* he (being perfect) is known by all the *śaktis*.

Translation of the Commentary (p. 90, l. 22 to l. 24)

He is known by all the *śaktis* means 'by all the omniscient deities'. By mere knowledge of this *mantra*, he knows whatever is known by those *śaktis*. This should be interpreted as before; '*Sarvābhiḥ śaktibhiḥ*' is used in an instrumental sense.

Text of the Verse

ŚĀKINĪKULASĀMĀNYO
BHAVED YOGAṂ VINĀPI HI //20//

Translation

Even without *yoga*, he becomes equal to the family of Śākinīs.

Translation of the Commentary (p. 91, l. 4 to l. 6)

Merely by having an insight in this *mantra*,[1] without the practice of *yoga* which brings about identity with the Divine after the end of this body formed by *māyā*, the aspirant not only becomes equal to the family of Śākinīs—but becomes even superior to them, for the group of Śākinī has only *viśeṣa spanda* (particular *spanda*) (which only leads to behaviour and intercourse characterised by differentiation), whereas he (the aspirant) becomes identified with *sāmānya spanda* or universal pulsation of the Divine, with the energy of the unsurpassed *akula* (*sāmānya spandarūpo akularūpaḥ*) and becomes the master of the group of *śaktis*.

Notes

1. *Anena jñātamātreṇa* (by merely having an insight in this *mantra*): In L.V. A.G. explains it thus: *Etatsamāveśābhyāsāt* i.e., by the practice of absorption in this (i.e. *sauḥ*).

2. *Śākinikulasāmānyo*: In L.V., A.G. explains it thus: *Śākinikulena devatācakreṇa sāmānyastulyo bhavati, anenajñātamātreṇa sarvasyavastunaḥ pūraṇāt*, i.e. He becomes equal to the group of divinities, for merely by the knowledge of this (*mantra*), there is the plenitude of all things.

In his Vivaraṇa commentary on Parātrīśikā, A.G. says that the aspirant who has acquired a knowledge of the *mantra sauḥ* not only becomes equal to the Śākinīs but even rises superior to them, for the Śākinīs are confined only to *viśesa spanda*, whereas this aspirant acquires the energy of *sāmānya* or universal *spanda*.

Text of the Verse

AVIDHIJÑO VIDHĀNAJÑO
JĀYATE YAJANAṂ PRATI //21//

Translation

Even if he is ignorant of the injunctions pertaining to rituals, he acquires the knowledge of the injunctions concerning sacrifice (by himself).

Translation of the Commentary (p. 91, l. 10 to l. 15)

Vidhi means both knowledge (*jñānam*) (of the injunctions pertaining to religious ceremonies) and its practical application (*kriyā*). He who has not got these two is a mere animal. As has been said in Kiraṇāgama: "He who is engaged only in thinking of the means of (sensuous) enjoyment (*bhogopāyavicintakaḥ*) is always a mere formless animal, ignorant, incapable of doing anything, having no qualities, wanting in power, diffusive (*vyāpi*), confined only within *māyā*, and steeped in her interior."

Even such an animal by mere insight into this *mantra* becomes a *vidhānajña* of sacrifice. '*Vidhānajña*' is one who has both knowledge of the injunctions and their practical application (*vidhānaṃ jñaca yasya saḥ*) i.e., he is both a knower and performer of the ceremony appropriate to a certain religious obligation (*viṣaya-saṃgata karaṇam prati kartā jñātā ca*).

Though the sacrifice that he performs may not be formally perfect, yet it brings about the full fruit for him, for this central seminal *mantra* is all-inclusive.

Text of the Verse

KĀLĀGNIM ĀDITAḤ KṚTVĀ
MĀYĀNTAṂ BRAHMADEHAGAM
ŚIVO VIŚVĀDYANANTĀNTAḤ
PARAṂ ŚAKTITRAYAṂ MATAM // 22 //

Translation

Beginning from *kālāgni* i.e., the earth right up to *māyā*, thirtyone *tattvas* rest in *brahma*-body. Śiva i.e. *anāśrita* Śiva with Śakti rests in *an*[2]+*anta*+*antaḥ* i.e., in *visarga* (coming) at the end of '*a*', i.e. *aḥ*. In the remaining (*para*)[3] i.e., *au* beginning from *Śuddhavidyā* (*viśvādi*), rests Śakti, *śakti-traya* i.e., *śakti-triśūla*—Sadāśiva, Īśvara and Śuddhavidyā of the nature of *icchā*, *jñāna* and *kriyā*. This Śakti-*triśūla* is acknowledged as the Supreme (*tacca paraṃ matam*) or Creative force (*visargamaya*).

Translation of the Commentary (p. 91, l. 21 to p. 92, l. 2)

Kālāgni is the initial *bhuvana* of the earth category. So '*Kālāgnim āditaḥ kṛtvā māyāntaṃ*' means from the earth category upto *māyā*. All these rest in the body i.e., the essential nature of *brahma*, i.e. in '*sa*'.

Viśvādi means from *śuddhavidyā* up to *anāśrita* Śiva with Śakti. *Anantaḥ* = *an*+*anta*+*antaḥ*. *An* means the vowel '*a*', *antaḥ* means the end of vowels i.e. *visarga*. *Param* that which expands (*visargātmakam*) i.e., expands in Śuddhavidyā, Īśvara and Sadāśiva.

Śakti-trayam[4] means that which consists of three *śaktis* viz. *icchā*, *jñāna* and *kriyā*. That which is constituted by these, i.e. *sa*+*au*+*aḥ*: is considered to be the supreme. The same thing has been declared by the verse, beginning with the phoneme '*sa*'. (The phoneme '*sa*' is symbolic of 31 *tattvas* from the earth up to *māyā*, '*au*' is symbolic of Śuddhavidyā, Īśvara, and Sadāśiva and '*aḥ*' is symbolic of Śiva and Śakti. Thus '*sauḥ*' includes all the 36 *tattvas*.)

Notes

1. *Brahmadehagam*: Brahma in this context means '*sa*'. This interpretation is based on Bhagavadgītā which says that Brahma is *om*, *tat*, *sat*. The '*t*' of '*sat*' is dropped, and '*sa*' is considered to be Brahma. It is generally called *tṛtīyam brahma*, the third name of Brahma, the first two names being *om* and *tat*.
2. '*a*' with: becomes *aḥ* i.e. *visarga*. The phoneme '*a*' is generally called *ananta* in Trika inasmuch as it is the basis of all expansion.
3. The word '*para*' being repeated twice yields two meanings. The first *para* means 'in the remaining' and the second *para* means the supreme.
4. *Śakti-trayam* means that which is constituted by three *śaktis*, viz. *icchā*, symbolic of Sadāśiva, *jñāna*, symbolic of Īśvara, and *kriyā*, symbolic of Śuddhavidyā.

Text of the Verse

TADANTARVARTI YATKIÑCIT
ŚUDDHAMĀRGE VYAVASTHITAM /
AṆURVIŚUDDHAM ACIRĀT
AIŚVARAṂ JÑĀNAM AŚNUTE // 23 //

Translation

Whatever is established (in the universe), all that reposing in that i.e., *sauḥ*, is in the pure way i.e. it is implicit in *sauḥ* in a pure way i.e., without any *mala* or limitation. The limited individual soon enough obtains the pure knowledge of the Divine (after the realization of *sauḥ*).

Translation of the Commentary (p. 92, l. 7 to l. 10)

Whatever is established in a variegated way i.e. in *bhedābheda* and *bheda* in the universe, all that reposes in the central seminal *mantra sauḥ* in a pure state i.e. in a state of undifferentiated unity. *Aṇu* is (1) one who breathes or (2) one who experiences and utters in a limited way. Even he (after the realization of *sauḥ*) becomes topmost of living beings (*mūrdhanyo bhavan*) and obtains by the influence of this *mantra* (*tatprabhāvāt*) the Divine knowledge very soon. How?

Text of the Verse

TACCODAKAḤ ŚIVOJÑEYAḤ
SARVAJÑAḤ PARAMEŚVARAḤ /
SARVAGO NIRMALAḤ SVACCHAS
TṚPTAḤ SVĀYATANAḤ ŚUCIḤ // 24 //

Translation

(The first line has two senses:) (1) The *guru* who inspires to know the secret of that *amṛta-bija* should be considered as Śiva.

(2) It should be known that He who inspires to know this *mantra* is Śiva. He is unknown to others but He is Himself omniscient, Supreme Lord. He is omnipresent, spotless, pure, fully satisfied, abiding in His own essential nature, unsullied.

Translation of the Commentary (p. 92, l. 16 to l. 19)

The *guru* or spiritual director who inspires this *mantra* to realize should be understood to be Śiva Himself. It is Śiva alone who inspires it. He is beyond comprehension, for he is the (eternal) subject (and cannot be reduced to an object). *Svāyatana* is one who (while abiding in his essential nature) emanates his own (*sva*) *ayas* i.e., the exiṣtence or objects in the form of consciousness. All this has been delineated in detail (earlier).

Thus having described it in detail, the scripture emphasizes the purport in conclusion.

Text of Verses 25 and 26

YATHĀ NYAGRODHABĪJASTHAḤ
ŚAKTIRŪPO MAHĀDRUMAḤ /

TATHĀ HṚDAYABĪJASTHAṂ
JAGADETACCARĀCARAM // 25 //
EVAṂ YO VETTI TATTVENA
TASYA NIRVĀṆAGĀMINĪ /
DĪKṢĀ BHAVATYASAṂDIGDHĀ
TILĀJYĀHUTIVARJITĀ // 26 //

Translation

As the great banyan tree lies in the form of potency in its seed, even so this universe with all the mobile and immobile beings lies in the seminal *mantra* (*sauḥ*), the very heart of the Supreme. 25.

He who knows this *mantra* in its essence, becomes competent for initiation leading to *nirvāṇa* (liberation) undoubtedly, without any formal ceremony consisting of oblation (*āhuti*) with sesamum indicum (*tila*) and *ghee* (melted butter). 26.

Translation of the Commentary (p. 93, l. 7 to p. 94, l. 5)

It has already been said that there is nothing in this world which is simply non-existent. Everything (in its place) is all-inclusive. Just as in the seed of the banyan tree lie all the relevant parts, viz. sprout, branches, leaves, and fruits, even so this universe lies in the heart of the Supreme. The certain conviction of this is (in itself) undoubted initiation for liberation (*nirvāṇa*). As has been said:

"This is the acquisition of ambrosia leading to immortality; this alone is the realization of Self (lit. grip of Self). This alone is the initiation of liberation (*nirvāṇa-dīkṣā*) leading to identity with Śiva". (Sp. K. II, 7)

There are other kinds of initiation also which may offer worldly enjoyments, but the insight into this (*mantra*) is the essential initiation. That is why it (Trika-Śāstra) is superior to every other Śāstra; it is even superior to Kulaśāstra.

As in the weights of a balance, though there may be only a limited removal of the weight there arises a good deal of difference in the measure of a thing only by slightly raising or lowering the balance, even so there occurs a good deal of difference in respect of the knowledge of space, time, and enjoyment of the higher and higher *tattvas* (categories of existence).

It is even possible that the sphere of experience (*saṃvedana*) rising higher and higher may exceed the thirty-six categories. Since insight (*saṃvedana*) into the *hṛdaya-bīja* or *sauḥ* is initiation (*dīkṣā*), therefore is it said that *vīra* and *yoginī* who have penetrated this insight (*etat saṃvit anupraviṣṭo*) stand initiated (*kṛta-dīkṣan*) by the grace of the I-consciousness described as revered, supreme Bhairava who is the ruler of the collective whole (*cakreśvara*) of the twelve* external and internal sense-divinities (*raśmi-devatā-dvādaśaka*) that are constantly present (*satatodita*) in the supreme reality (*para-sattā*) and are transcendent to *māyā* (*amāyīya*). 25-26.

Thus the way in which the transcendental (*anuttara*) state occurs without abandoning the external extension has been determined many a time both separately and in a composite way.

Now this is what is to be said. In every Śāstra it is said: "Those who are devoted to *hṛdaya-bīja* or *sauḥ*, the very import of Trika, even when they do not realize its full virility, are the very lord, in a veiled form, having entered the human body."

How is this worship to be performed? Even though this external worship is without its full virility, there must be in it the impact of *anuttara*-reality (*anuttara sattā*), for *anuttara* is after all *anuttara*. What is the operational method of this worship? In order to give a definite answer to this query, the author lays down the following verses:

Text of the Verse

MŪRDHNI VAKTRE CA HṚDAYE
GUHYE MŪRTAU TATHAIVA CA /
NYĀSAṂ KṚTVĀ ŚIKHĀM BADDHVĀ
SAPTAVIṂŚATIMANTRITĀM // 27 //

Translation

External Worship

After making *nyāsa*[1] on skull (*mūrdhā*), mouth, heart, private part,[2] and the whole body[3] and tying the tuft of the hair (*śikhā*) with twenty-seven *mantras*.

*The twelve sense-divinities are 5 organs of sense plus 5 organs of action plus *manas* and *buddhi*.

Notes

This external worship is to be performed by *vīra* and *yoginī*, together.

1. *Nyāsa*: mental assignment of various parts of the body to deities (by placing the fingers on them).

2. The private part of both *vīra* and *yoginī*.

3. The *mantra* has to be repeated five times on each part for each of the five deities, viz. Īśāna, Tatpuruṣa, Aghora, Vāmadeva and Sadyojāta with the *mantras* of *Mātṛkā* and *Mālinī*. The *Mātṛkā mantra* is *akṣa hrīṃ* and the *Mālinī mantra* is *napha hrīṃ*. The *āvartana* or repetition is made in the following way:

25 *mantras*

First *āvartana* or repetition:

1. akṣa hrīṃ īśānamūrdhne namaḥ
2. napha hrīṃ tatpuruṣa vaktrāya namaḥ
3. akṣa hrīṃ aghorahṛdayāya namaḥ
4. napha hrīṃ vāmadevaguhyāya namaḥ
5. akṣa hrīṃ sadyojātamūrtaye namaḥ

Second *āvartana*:

1. akṣa hrīṃ tatpuruṣamūrdhne namaḥ
2. napha hrīṃ aghoravaktrāya namaḥ
3. akṣa hrīṃ vāmadevahṛdayāya namaḥ
4. napha hrīṃ sadyojātaguhyāya namaḥ
5. akṣa hrīṃ īśānamūrtaye namaḥ

Third *āvartana*:

1. akṣa hrīṃ aghoramūrdhne namaḥ
2. napha hrīṃ vāmadevavaktrāya namaḥ
3. akṣa hrīṃ sadyojātahṛdayāya namaḥ
4. napha hrīṃ īśānaguhyāya namaḥ
5. akṣa hrīṃ tatpuruṣamūrtaye namaḥ

Fourth *āvartana*:

1. akṣa hrīṃ vāmadevamūrdhne namaḥ
2. napha hrīṃ sadyojātavaktrāya namaḥ
3. akṣa hrīṃ īśānahṛdayāya namaḥ
4. napha hrīṃ tatpuruṣaguhyāya namaḥ
5. akṣa hrīṃ aghoramūrtaye namaḥ

Fifth *āvartana*:

1. akṣa hrīṃ sadyojātamurdhne namaḥ
2. napha hrīṃ īśānavaktrāya namaḥ
3. akṣa hrīṃ tatpuruṣahṛdayāya namaḥ
4. napha hrīṃ aghoraguhyāya namaḥ
5. akṣa hrīṃ vāmadevamūrtaye namaḥ

27 mantras for tying the tuft of hair (Śikhā)

1.	Sṛṣṭirūpecchātmikayā	parārūpayā	Śikhāyā	bandh-anaṃ	karomi	namaḥ
2.	„	parāparārūpayā	„	„	„	„
3.	„	aparārūpayā	„	„	„	„
4.	Sṛṣṭirūpajñānātmikayā	parārūpayā	„	„	„	„
5.	„	parāparārūpayā	„	„	„	„
6.	„	aparārūpayā	„	„	„	„
7.	Sṛṣṭirūpakriyātmikayā	parārūpayā	„	„	„	„
8.	„	parāparārūpayā	„	„	„	„
9.	„	aparārūpayā	„	„	„	„
10.	Sthiti rūpecchātmikayā	parārūpayā	„	„	„	„
11.	„	parāparārūpayā	„	„	„	„
12.	„	aparārūpayā	„	„	„	„
13.	Sthiti rūpajñānātmikayā	parārūpayā	„	„	„	„
14.	„	parāparārūpayā	„	„	„	„
15.	„	aparārūpayā	„	„	„	„
16.	Sthiti rūpakriyātmikayā	parārūpayā	„	„	„	„
17.	„	parāparārūpayā	„	„	„	„
18.	„	aparārūpayā	„	„	„	„
19.	Saṃhārarūpecchātmikayā	parārūpayā	„	„	„	„
20.	„	parāparārūpayā	„	„	„	„
21.	„	aparārūpayā	„	„	„	„
22.	Saṃhārarūpajñānātmikayā	parārūpayā	„	„	„	„

23. „ parâparârūpayâ „ „ „ „
24. „ aparârūpayâ „ „ „ „
25. Saṃhârarūpakriyâtmikayâ
parârūpayâ „ „ „ „
26. „ parâparârūpayâ „ „ „ „
27. „ aparârūpayâ „ „ „ „

Text

EKAIKAṂ TU DIŚĀM BANDHAṂ
DAŚĀNĀM API YOJAYET /
TĀLATRAYAM PURĀ DATTVĀ
SAŚABDAṂ VIGHNAŚĀNTAYE // 28 //

Translation

Then one should fetter the ten directions with only one *mantra* (viz. *sauḥ*), but before doing so, in order to remove all obstacles, one should clap three times by muttering inwardly (through *madhyamā vāṇī*) *s* (the first time), *au* (the second time), *aḥ* (the third time).

Notes

The directions have to be fettered thus:

1. Sauḥ indradiśâ bandhanaṃ karomi namaḥ
2. Sauḥ agnidiśâ bandhanaṃ karomi namaḥ
3. Sauḥ yamadiśâ bandhanaṃ karomi namaḥ
4. Sauḥ nairṛtyadiśâ bandhanaṃ karomi namaḥ
5. Sauḥ varuṇadiśâ bandhanaṃ karomi namaḥ
6. Sauḥ vâyudiśâ bandhanaṃ karomi namaḥ
7. Sauḥ kuberadiśâ bandhanaṃ karomi namaḥ
8. Sauḥ īśânadiśâ bandhanaṃ karomi namaḥ
9. Sauḥ ūrdhvadiśâ bandhanaṃ karomi namaḥ
10. Sauḥ adhodiśâ bandhanaṃ karomi namaḥ

Text

ŚIKHĀSAṂKHYĀBHIJAPTENA
TOYENĀBHYUKṢAYET TATAḤ /
PUṢPĀDIKAṂ KRAMĀT SARVAṂ
LIṄGE VĀ STHAṆḌILE'THAVĀ // 29 //

Translation

Then after consecrating water with the same number of *japas* as are meant for tying the tuft of hair, i.e. the same twenty-seven *mantras* as are meant for *śikhā-bandhana*, one should sprinkle with the consecrated water over flowers and all other objects of worship successively. All this should be done by the *vira* on the female organ (*sthaṇḍila*) of the *yogini* and by the *yogini* on the male organ (*liṅga*) of the *vira*.

Text

CATURDAŚĀBHIJAPTENA
PUṢPEṆĀSANAKALPANĀ /
TATRA SṚṢṬIṂ YAJED
VĪRAḤ PUNAREVĀSANAṂ TATAḤ // 30 //

Translation

One has to form a seat with flowers consecrated with fourteen *mantras* by putting a dot on each of the vowels from '*a*' to '*au*'[1]. The *vira* should worship the *sṛṣṭi-bija* (*hṛdaya-bija*), on this seat and then should fashion another seat by means of the same process.[2]

Notes

1. The flowers have to be consecrated with fourteen *mantras* in the following way:

1. aṃ	āsanapakṣaṃ		śodhayāmi	namaḥ
2. āṃ	"	"	"	"
3. iṃ	"	"	"	"
4. īṃ	"	"	"	"
5. uṃ	"	"	"	"
6. ūṃ	"	"	"	"
7. ṛṃ	"	"	"	"
8. ṝṃ	"	"	"	"
9. ḷṃ	"	"	"	"
10. ḹṃ	"	"	"	"
11. eṃ	"	"	"	"
12. aiṃ	"	"	"	"
13. oṃ	"	"	"	"
14. auṃ	"	"	"	"

2. This whole practice is shrouded in mystery.

The Internal Supreme Worship

TEXT

SṚṢṬIṂ TU SAṂPUṬĪKṚTYA
PAŚCĀD YAJANAM ĀRABHET /
SARVATATTVA-SUSAMPŪRṆAṂ
SARVĀBHARAṆA-BHŪṢITĀM //31//
YAJED DEVĪṂ MAHEŚĀNĪṂ
SAPTAVIṂŚATI-MANTRITĀM
TATAḤ SUGANDHIPUṢPAISTU
YATHĀŚAKTYĀ SAMARCAYET //32//
PŪJAYET PARAYĀ BHAKTYĀ
ĀTMĀNAṂ CA NIVEDAYET /
EVAṂ YAJANAM ĀKHYĀTAM
AGNIKĀRYE'PYAYAṂ VIDHIḤ //33//

TRANSLATION

After the *sampuṭīkaraṇa* of *sṛṣṭi*,[1] one should start the *yajana* i.e. the internal supreme worship. One should worship the goddess Maheśānī who is fully equipped with all the *tattvas* or categories of existence, is decorated with all the ornaments and who is consecrated with (the previously described) twentyseven *mantras*. Then with fragrant flowers one should pay the goddess due honour according to his capability together with *yoginī* (*yathāśakti*).[2] 31-32.

In this way, both (*vīra* and *yoginī*) should worship with supreme devotion and surrender themselves completely to her. The internal worship has been described in this way. The same procedure should be followed in the matter of *agnihotra* or sacrificial libation to fire associated with this worship. 33.

NOTES

1. The *sampuṭīkaraṇa* of *sṛṣṭi* has two meanings, viz. 1. The group of letters from '*a*' to '*kṣa*'. It is known as *varṇa-sṛṣṭi*. *Sṛṣṭi* in this context is symbolic of *hṛdaya-bīja* in which all the letters from '*a*' to '*kṣa*' are present. 2. It also means the coitus of *vīra* and *yoginī*

2. There is double meaning in *yathāśakti* also. Literally, it

means, not transgressing one's capacity or capability. It also suggests that the worship has to be performed along with *śakti* i.e., with *yoginī* in this context.

Text of the Commentary

From *mūrdhādini* on p. 95, l. 13 upto *mālinyādimantrāṇāmanupraveśa* on p. 95, l. 19.

Translation of the Commentary

The esoteric aspect of the limbs pertaining to nyāsa

The *nyāsa* on the head etc., is all right from the exoteric point of view. Really speaking, however, they being symbolic of *mantra* are

(1) indications of the five quintuple gross elements, viz. from ether down to earth which are said to be the external forms of the Supreme *brahma*,
(2) essence of Īśāna, Tatpuruṣa, Aghora, Vāmadeva, and Sadyojāta, the five mouths of Bhairava,
(3) forms of *cit* (consciousness), *unmeṣa* in the sense of *ānanda* or bliss, *icchā* or will, *jñāna* or knowledge, *kriyā* or activity

Their *mantras* are the following:

1. *īśānamūrdhne*, 2. *tatpuruṣa-vaktrāya*, 3. *aghorahṛdayāya*, 4. *vāmadeva-guhyāya*, 5. *sadyojāta-mūrtaye*.

Really speaking there is no difference among the five (*etat pañcaka-avibhāgātmakatve*). Each of these is quintuple. Therefore, the number of the *mantras* is twentyfive. The *Mālinī mantra* (*napha hrīṃ*) and *Mātṛkā mantra* (*akṣa hrīṃ*) are both included within these twentyfive.

Notes

The esoteric aspect of *nyāsa* would be the following:

Number	Limb (*aṅga*)	*Tattva*	*Mukha* of *Śiva*	*Śakti*
1.	Mūrdhā (head)	Ākāśa (ether)	Īśāna	Cit
2.	Vaktra (mouth)	Vāyu (air)	Tatpuruṣa	Ānanda
3.	Hṛdaya (heart)	Agni (fire)	Aghora	Icchā

4.	Guhya (private part)	Jala (water)	Vāmadeva	Jñāna
5.	Sarvāṅga (mūrti, the whole body)	Pṛthivī (earth)	Sadyojāta	Kriyā

Text

From *tisraśca devyaḥ* on p. 95, l. 19 upto *sarvasarvātmakatva nirṇayenaiva* on p. 96, l. 3.

Translation

Śikhā-bandhana (tying the tuft of hair):

There have become nine forms of the three goddesses, viz. *parā*, *parāparā*, and *aparā* because of each of them being connected with *icchā*, *jñāna* and *kriyā*. Each of them being associated with *sṛṣṭi*, *sthiti* and *saṃhāra* again becomes threefold. Thus their number becomes twenty-seven. All of them derive their nurture from *hṛdaya-bīja*.

Śikhā symbolizes the autonomy of the Divine diffused from Śiva upto the earth; its tying indicates identity, the quintessence of the non-differentiation of all.

Though the limbs, head, mouth etc., have been indicated separately, yet each one of them is specifying the other. This fact has already been established by the principle: 'Everything is the epitome of all' (*sarvaṃ sarvātmakaṃ*).

Text

From *diśyamānā ghaṭādyāḥ* on p. 96, l. 3 upto *ityetadapi nirṇītameva* on p. 96, l. 18.

Translation

Diśābandhana:

Jars etc. related to space indicate directions. These are ten with reference to oneself, i.e. to one's body. In this case also, tying or fettering is symbolic of Self-realization.

Three clappings:

This should be done with three clappings. Clapping is symbolic of stability (*pratiṣṭhā*) i.e., being stable in Self. In clapping, the *hṛdayabīja* starting with '*s*' is the *mantra* i.e. the first clapping should be done with the muttering of '*s*', the second with the muttering of *au*, the third with the muttering of *aḥ*.

The *mantra* should be a mere mumble i.e. it should be uttered only indistinctly in *madhyamā vāṇi*. Inner *vimarśa* is the essence of sounding. That is accomplished in *madhyamā vāṇi*. It has been stated frequently that *vaikharī* or gross speech is only an appendage of *madhyamā vāṇi* i.e. gross speech is only external manifestation of what is inwardly mumbled in *madhyamā*.

Pacification of obstacles:

(In the esoteric sense), obstacles are the stain of waves of difference of which the essence is limitation and division in the Supreme Self (*paramātmani*) which is free of all difference and division. Their pacification connotes identification with the Bhairava-ocean in which there is no wave of difference or division.

As has been said by venerable Somānanda:

"May Śiva who has entered into us as (the empirical) subject make obeisance by Himself to Śiva who is extended as the universe by means of *parā* who is His own Śakti in order to remove all obstacles which are but Himself." (Ś.D. I, 1)

Arghya-pātra:

Arghya-pātra-vidhi is the ceremony for purifying the water and the small vessel containing the water to be offered to the deity. Both the vessel and the water to be sprinkled should be consecrated first with the twenty-seven *mantras* mentioned before. Water in this context means everything that melts the heart (*hṛdaya-dravātmā*, i.e. wine) because of non-restraint and non-hesitation.

So far as flower is concerned, it has already been explained.

Liṅga-Emblem:

With regard to the worship of the emblem (*liṅga*), the view expressed in the following verse should be borne in mind:

"Do not worship the emblem of Śiva made of clay or stone or mineral or gem. Worship that spiritual emblem in which is absorbed the entire universe consisting of the mobile and immobile beings" (M.V. XVIII, 2-3).

This has also been conclusively explained.

TEXT

From *viśvātmanitattve* on p. 96, l. 18 upto *śabdapratītipaurvāparyamātre* on p. 97, l. 4.

Translation

Āsana (Seat):

That is *āsana* (seat) which is determined by the agent through his autonomy, for when the aspect of universality is the main principle, then in the act of sitting, the location and seat are determined through autonomy only.

Fourteenth Mantra:

By fourteenth is meant '*au*', for it has already been said that that is the *triśūla* or trident (which symbolizes *icchā*, *jñāna* and *kriyā*).

Sṛṣṭi in this context means (*varṇa-sṛṣṭi* i.e.) the series of phonemes from '*a*' to '*kṣa*'. It is the *hṛdaya* (*-bīja* or the *mantra sauḥ*) which is identified with the phonemes '*a*' to '*kṣa*'.

That is the reason why the entire *āsana* is also covered with the same *mantra*, for the place of location (*ādhāra*) and that which is to be located are indissolubly connected.

(What this means is that there is no difference between Śiva-*trikoṇa* and Śakti-*trikoṇa*. Śakti-*trikoṇa* is the *ādhāra* and Śiva-*trikoṇa* is the *ādheya*.)

As has been said in Bhagavadgītā:

"One who being united to *yoga* views the Self as seated in all beings (as the subject) and all beings residing in one's Self regards all things as the same". (VI, 29).

The sampuṭīkaraṇa of sṛṣṭi:

1. *From the point of view of esoteric worship of the Supreme*:

Sṛṣṭi here means the arising and subsiding of all the phonemes from '*a*' to '*kṣa*' severally and cumulatively in the Supreme principle through *hṛdaya-bīja*. *Sampuṭīkaraṇa* of *sṛṣṭi* implies that *sampuṭa* should be made by means of the *mantra sauḥ* at first of all the letters severally from '*a*' to '*kṣa*' and then cumulatively of all the letters. It has already been said that there cannot be *regressus ad infinitum* (*anavasthā*) in this matter.

2. *From the point of view of the tradition of vīra-yoginī*:

In the case of Śakti and Śaktimān i.e. the female and male partner, *sampuṭīkaraṇa* of *sṛṣṭi* implies the exciting enjoyment of coitus between the *vīra* and *yoginī* and the substance produced by their union is also used.

In '*saṃpuṭikṛtya*' occurring in the verse 31, there is the use of the suffix '*ktvā*' merely to show the precedence and succession of words.

Notes

The words *sṛṣṭi* and *saṃpuṭikaraṇa* have two meanings. In the first case, *sṛṣṭi* denotes *varṇa-sṛṣṭi*, the series of phonemes from '*a*' to '*kṣa*'. *Sampuṭikaraṇa* in this context is a technical word which means the utterance of an additional *mantra* before and after the principal *mantra*. For instance, there is *saṃpuṭa* of *auṃ* both before and after the principal *gāyatrī mantra*. In the present case, there would be the *saṃpuṭa* of '*ahaṃ*' *mantra* both before and after the '*sauḥ*' *mantra*.

Saṃpuṭa is a hemispherical bowl with two movable covers which encloses something. Here the *mantra ahaṃ* is the *saṃpuṭa* which encloses the *mantra sauḥ*.

In the second case, *sṛṣṭi* denotes conjugal relation and *saṃpuṭikaraṇa* denotes the actual coitus of the two. The 'substance' refers to *kuṇḍagolaka*, cf. TĀ XXIX, 22-24.

Note of the Editor: Cf. Tantrasāra 22: One should meditate upon the *āsana* as the location and the located object, as identified with pure consciousness. The *saṃpuṭikaraṇa* is to be done between the universe (*viśva*) and pure consciousness (*saṃvit*).

Text

From *sarvatattvaiḥ suṣṭhu abhedena* on p. 97, l. 4 to *tṛtiyā ca tatraivoktā* on p. 97, l. 12.

Translation

Sarvatattvaiḥ...pūrṇatvaṃ—means that the supreme Devī is fully (*saṃyak*) and invariably (*anapāyitayā*) equipped with all the *tattvas*.

She is decorated with all the *ābharaṇas* (ornaments). This means—

1. (*Sarvābharaṇa* = *sarvatra ā-bharaṇam*)

The Supreme goddess is making every-thing in all directions (*sarvatra*), even in the atoms wholly (*samantāt*) her own (*ātmīkaraṇam*).

2. (*Sarvābharaṇa = sarvair-ā-bharaṇam*)

It has already been explained that all external objects, such as jar etc., all inner experiences, such as pleasure etc., all experients such as animal, man, Brahmā, Viṣṇu, Rudra, Mantra, Sadāśiva are like congruous limbs (*avayava*) of the Supreme goddess so that her being a uniform (*ekarasa*) organism (*avayavī*) is fully justified. That is why meditation on any definite form or weapon of hers has not been prescribed, for all this is (only) artificial.

(If it is not necessary to meditate on any definite form or weapon of the goddess), how can one desirous of mounting to the highest stage in spirituality, and desirous of following the path recommended by Trika achieve his object?

If this is the question, the reply is: 'Who is constrained to mount? If there is any such being, let him not mount. Let him follow the process advocated by Siddhā-tantra etc., let him resort to the narrow method of meditation etc. prescribed according to their mode of thinking (*tadāśayenaiva nirūpita*). Such a person is not privileged to enter the stage of *anuttara* which is without any limitation or restriction."

(Explanation of *yajed...vidhiḥ*, verses 32 and 33)

This is the eternal form of homage to the deity. So far as scent and flower are concerned, they have been conclusively described. The word '*yathā*' in *yathāśaktyā* has been used in the sense of 'with', i.e. 'with *śakti* or the female partner' and the instrumental suffix has also been used in that sense.

Text

From *parayaiva hṛdayarūpayā pūjayet* on p. 97, l. 12 upto *nirmitaprāyameva* on p. 98, l. 18.

Translation

The word '*parayā*' implies that the worship has to be done with heart's devotion. How?

(Three kinds of *bhakti*):

1. (*Bhakti* from the root '*bhaj*' meaning 'to serve')

By identifying ourself with *hṛdaya-bīja* or *sauḥ* (*tādātmya*) by entering into it (*anupraveśa*), and with a spirit of service or submissiveness (*prahvatātmatā*).

2. (*Bhakti* from the root '*bhaj*' meaning 'to divide')

Bhaktyā—with the self-contrived division of the worshipped and the worshipper. The one to be worshipped is (imaginatively) fashioned by oneself. The self-created object of worship has to be supreme, full of autonomy and consciousness for such is the power of the autonomy of *anuttara* (the Absolute). It cannot be insentient like a jar. That is the distinction of this system (*iti viśeṣatra*). It has been rightly said in Īśvara-pratyabhijñā:

> "The Lord, by His non-dualistic autonomy, having fashioned His own free self into Īśvara (Brahmā, Viṣṇu etc.) causes the world to worship Himself through them". (I. 5, 16)

3. (*Bhakti* as *samāveśa* or compenetration)

By *samāveśa* which is formally known as worship, one realizes the Supreme Reality (*paraṃ tattvam lakṣyate*). The recognition of *samāveśa* in all forms of ritual observance (*sarva-kriyāsu*) is the best means (to the realization of Supreme Reality), just as written letters are a means for the production and understanding of all empirical phonemes, and the empirical phonemes are a means of penetration into their energy.

Offering of One's Self

Ātmānaṃ nivedayet means one should offer one's self, for there is nothing else worth offering than this. The purport is that (according to the etymology of '*nivedayet*': *niḥ*—completely, *vedayet*—one should experience or understand oneself). One should, in conformity to the Absolute Reality, consider one's Self to be the Absolute Reality itself. Here the potential mood (*liṇ*) in *nivedayet* has been used in the sense of possibility, for it has already been said that any stance connected with Self is always one of possibility.

Yajana—homage

The meaning of the expression '*ākhyātaṃ*' occurring in verse 33 is *ā-samantāt, sarvatra, sadā* i.e., wholly, everywhere, always. *Khyātam* connotes the *khyāti* or realization of the supreme, pure nature of Śiva. This is the true *yajana* or homage of the goddess *Parāsaṃvit* (Supreme Consciousness). The root *yaja* 'in *yajam*' connotes three meanings:

(1) *Yaja* in the sense of worship means: 'This is her true worship'.

(2) *Yaja* in the sense of *saṃgati* means: 'This kind of worship offers the opportunity of appropriate meeting (*saṃyag-gamana*) of the worshipper and the worshipped, in other words the identity with the Supreme.'

(3) *Yaj* in the sense 'to make an offer, to donate' means the following: 'This worship by removing the narrow, limited sense of I-consciousness of the empirical individual, denotes the sense of unification of the self with the perfect mass of Consciousness which is Śiva-Śakti.'

Agnikārya or oblation in the sacrificial fire

This is the real oblation in the sacrificial fire, viz. the oblation, i.e. inner burning of the residual traces of all desires in the mighty flame of Supreme Bhairava which is always ablaze with the *araṇi*[1] of Supreme Śakti excited by union with Śiva, which is burning brightly with the eager consumption of all objects as its fuel, which is aglow with the abundant light of lubricous melted butter of worldly attachments. This alone is the real injunction regarding oblation right up to initiation. There is none other different from this. This is the real purport of it.

> "Recognition of One's essential nature—this is the highest *mantra*. This is the real initiation. This is the real sacrifice. Among all the ceremonies, this is the highest rite."

It has been said earlier that just as in other scriptures, in the earlier part, ceremonies of worship with *mantra* are described, in the latter part the conclusion is made with *jñāna*, in the present Śāstra, it is not so. What has been indicated in the *sūtra* '*uttarasyāpi anuttaraṃ*' has been carried out to the end in this work. Sacrifice, initiation, ceremonies etc. are only aspects of *hṛdayabīja* and that is really *anuttara* (transcendent).

Revered Somānanda after having said that *hṛdayabīja* endures everything, has in order to prove its undivided character, enjoined the purification or cleansing of *sruk*, *sruva*.[2] In the beginning, the description of *nyāsa* on limbs, heart, powder (*dhūli*), etc. is perfectly in order. There is no inconsistency in this, nor is discrepancy perceivable. Nor is the Trika system dependent on the inferior Śāstras that advocate otherwise. There has been a clarification of all these points. (27-33)

Notes

1. *Araṇi*: A piece of wood, taken generally from Śamī tree, used for kindling the sacred fire by attrition.

2. *Sruk, sruva-(sruc)*: A sort of wooden ladle for pouring clarified melted butter on sacrificial fire.

Sruva or *Sruvā* is a small wooden ladle for pouring clarified melted butter into the large ladle or *sruk*.

Text

From *kim evam upāsāyām* on p. 98, l. 19 upto *taṃ yogamārgaṃ nirūpayituṃ granthaśeṣo'vatarati* on p. 100, l. 20.

Translation

What is the result of the worship of *hṛdaya-bīja* in this way? (In reply to this query), the book lays down the following:

"Mentally dwelling on the *hṛdaya-bīja* (*sauḥ*), the adept who performs the worship in the proper manner attains to his goal i.e. liberation while alive (*jivan-mukti*)." (34)

Translation of the Commentary

1. Thus ceaselessly even in worldly affairs, the aspirant who carries on worship, while remembering the *hṛdaya-bīja*, leaving aside other disciplines like Kaulaśāstra, Śaiva and Vaiṣṇava Śāstra, having entered into the essence i.e. *hṛdaya-bīja* of revered Bhairava, making an outward display of object just for pastime, created by the blissfil force of one's own *parāsaṃvit* (Supreme Consciousness), is verily liberated while alive. The use of the word '*smaraṇa*' (remembering) connotes the repetition of one's own experience, nothing else. In Śrīmata-Śāstra also the same idea has been expressed.

2. The worshipper who has not penetrated into the very heart of the energy of the great *mantra*, by rightly remembering the *hṛdaya-bīja* through the efficacy of *krama-pūjā*, having gradually attained to the power of the *mantra* as *hṛdaya-bīja*, also achieves the realization of the highest perfection or the power of the *mantra* of *hṛdaya-bīja*, either through the gradual superiority of the efficacy of the *kramapūjā* or by himself, or through the exhortation from the mouth of a pleased *guru* (spiritual director) and becomes liberated while alive.

In this process, there is neither any advantage nor any disadvantage (*khaṇḍanā*) in the (traditional) worship of '*dvārapūjā*'[2] or *guru*. That is why revered Somānanda has laid down the following:

"In this matter an auspicious period (*parva*) prescribed according to Kula-Śāstra and a *pavitram*[3] are meant only to enhance the propriety of the process of worship."

NOTES

1. *Krama-pūjā*—a regular course of graded worship as detailed in verses 27 to 33.

2. *Dvārapūjā* means the worship of Gaṇeśa or Baṭuka.

3. *Pavitraṃ* as a noun means 'a ring of *kuśa* grass worn on the fourth finger on certain religious occasions.' The rite of offering *pavitraka* to the Lord: cf. Tantra-sāra, 20, where it is described that after performing the worship of the Lord one should offer 4 *pavitrakas* to Him: one goes down to the knee, one going down to navel, one to the throat and one on the head. They may be made of gold, pearl, jewels, *kuśa* grass or cotton threads with knots numbering 36 representing *tattvas*, or *bhuvanas*, *varṇas* etc. They are generally offered to the deity or to the *guru*.

(A SUMMARY OF THE CHAPTER)

"O aspirants that have reached the *prabuddha* stage, that in which the entire universe shines, that which (by itself) shines everywhere, that sparkling Light (which is both *prakāśa* and *vimarśa*) alone is the highest core of Reality."

Just as a she-ass or a mare expanding and contracting her female organ (*jagajjanmadhāma*) simultaneously experiences delight in her heart, on the occasion of the coitus of both (*vira* and *yogini*), in the heart of *suṣumṇā* full of supreme delight, there is the heart, throbbing in the form of simultaneous expansion and contraction characterized by *sṛṣṭi* (i.e. *sṛṣṭibija* or *sauḥ*). Meditate on that.

That in which, whether meditating, remembering, reflecting, or acting, everything comes to rest, and from which everything comes forth in manifestation—that is the heart.

That heart is only one i.e. shines primarily as *nirvikalpa* (indeterminate), in which abide other determinate knowledge (*paraṃ vaikalpikaṃ jñānam*), the thirtysix categories of existence, expanse of (hundred and eight) *bhuvanas* (worlds), and all the experients from Śiva to the limited souls—all these assuming diverse forms, though non-different from the highest Reality, making even the wonderful Supreme Consciousness (*parāsaṃvid*) variegated, appear as shining in it.

The worship of this central reality is ever present in the heart of the aspirant. Whether he may be associated with any country, matter, activity, place, thought-construct, in every case, his mind is ever set upon the *hṛdaya-bija* without the least hesitation.

So far as *krama-pūjā* is concerned, Trika discipline is of the opinion that with the observance of auspicious period prescribed by Kula-Śāstra and by means of offering *pavitraka* the appropriateness of this worship is increased.

As has been said (with regard to *krama-pūjā*):

As among fluid substances is semen, among phonemes is *sṛṣṭi-bīja*, i.e. *sauḥ*, among scriptures is Trika, in states of liberation is the attainment of the state of Bhairava, in meditation is the state of absorption, in vows is the pious observance of the *vīras* (most excellent), even so, among auspicious occasions are those of Kula (most excellent), according to Trika-Śāstra.

The use of *pavitraka* is essential for the full accomplishment of the rites connected with *krama-pūjā*. Those worshippers who do not carry out the injunction regarding the use of *pavitraka* four times, thrice, twice or at least once during the auspicious period do not know the significance of the auspicious period according to Kula-Śāstra. In the case of such people, the potency of the *mantra* does not function at its maximum.

Thus the nature of *anuttara* (transcendental reality) has been described in detail. In it, there is no room for contemplation. In it only gnosis (*prasaṃkhyānam*) functions as the bearer of mountains fit for the burden of means (*upāya-dhaureya-dharādharāṇi dhatte*) upto the end of firm realization of Self identified with *hṛdaya-bija* which is characterized by steadfast spiritual delight.

Now the *yoga* for those who are desirous of attaining supernormal powers (for show) has to be described. Though the supernormal powers pertaining to *dṛṣṭayoga*[1] are possible only by means of the autonomy of the Absolute and they are beyond the sphere of popularly known and determinate laws, yet they cannot (wholly) transgress the divinely fixed order, 'yet the means for the supernormal powers pertaining to strange matters has to be described with respect', as said by Somānanda in Śiva-Dṛṣṭi.

Even in the matter of *yoga* for the display of supernormal powers (*dṛṣṭa-yoga*), there is no violation of the transcendental nature, for like the effort to attain the supernormal powers for display, their actual attainment, and the cessation of all effort in their maturity—everything is due to the grace of the Supreme. But in comparison to liberation in life, such an attainment would be said to be due to faint grace of the divine, for *it does not lead to perfection.*[2]

It is, however, the *yoga* which is due to faint grace that is described in the remaining part of the book.

Notes

1. *Dṛṣṭayoga-siddhi*: The supernormal powers which are meant for display to the people, and which arouse in them a weird sense of mystery are said to be '*dṛṣṭa-yoga-siddhi*'.

2. That alone is said to be the highest *yoga* which leads the aspirant to the recognition of his self as identical with the divine I-consciousness, and the world as the glow of Śiva's Light in various forms.

Text of the verse

ĀDYANTARAHITAṂ BĪJAM
VIKASAT TITHIMADHYAGAM /
HṚTPADMĀNTARGATAṂ DHYĀYET
SOMĀṂŚAṂ NITYAM ABHYASET //35//

Translation

The *yogi* must meditate on this *bīja* which has neither beginning nor end, which has expanded into fifteen vowels (*vikasat-tithimadhyagam*) and which resides in the heart-lotus of Śiva. He should also practise the lunar part (*somāṃśam*, i.e. view all objects of the world as nothing but the manifestation of *sauḥ*).

Commentary

From *etadeva* on p. 101, l. 1 upto *bhaṭṭa-dhaneśvaraśarmā*, l. 10.

Translation of the Commentary

Explanation from the point of view of Śāktopāya

Anādya-antam bījam

This central seminal mantra (*hṛdayabīja* or *sauḥ*) is without beginning or end (1) for it does not require any extraneous light, i.e. it shines by its own light (*dīpakābhāvāt*), (2) for it is without variation, without coming in and going out (*gamāgama-śūnyatvāt*), (3) for it is ever actively present (*satatoditatvāt*).

Vikasat and tithimadhyagam:

This, on the one hand, has expanded in the form of the external objective world and thus reached its complete manifestation. On the other hand, it inheres in the sixteen *tithis*,[1] being their innermost essence.

Hṛtpadmāntargataṃ dhyāyet:

The *yogī* should meditate on *kanda* and *guhya* (i.e. the male *yogī* or *vīra* on the female organ (*guhya*) and the female *yogī* or *yoginī* on the male organ (*kanda*), as if it were the heart-lotus. These two organs have been called 'lotus' only in a figurative sense, for like lotus they are endowed with the characteristic of contraction and expansion (*saṅkoca-vikāsa-dharma-upacarita-padmabhāve*).

Kiñcāsya dhyānam āha:

What sort of meditation is this? The following is its description (*āha*):

Somāṃśaṃ nityam abhyaset—abhyaset to be taken in the sense of *abhi*+*asyet*.

The aspirant should cast the *somāṃśa* i.e. *apāna* current (the current of inhalation) full of sixteen *tuṭis* from all sides (*abhitaḥ*) towards the male organ or the female organ. This means that the aspirant should project the *apāna* current of breath which is synonymous with full moon into *hṛtkarṇikā*[2] upto *puṣpa* i.e. the point of origin of the creative energy existing in each one at an inner distance of twelve fingers.

Then after coming in contact with *amṛta* i.e. *kuṇḍalinī-śakti*, in accordance with the inner vibration that is surging up, he acquires *kākacañcupuṭa-mudrā*[3] characterized by the electro-magnetism of *śakti-sparśa*.

Then the *apāna* current being withdrawn and expanding with the relish of the nectar of Śakti, excites the vibration within. The aspirant should make the *apāna* current fully developed by drinking in the nectar which is churned out by the vibratory force.

After this, at the moment of the rise of the *prāṇa* (*sūrya kalā*), the exhalatory breath-current, resting in vowel-less '*s*' (vowel-less '*s*' of *sauḥ mantra*), he should continue his practice, supported by the experience of thrill, stoppage (of breath), an inner sensation of springing up, tears, tremor etc. This is *śāktopāya* according to Bhaṭṭa Dhaneśvara Śarmā.

Notes

1. The *tuṭis* of *prāṇacāra* are $\frac{1}{2}+15+\frac{1}{2}=16$. The *tuṭis* of *apāna-cāra* are $\frac{1}{2}+15+\frac{1}{2}=16$.

2. *Hṛt-karṇikā* is a centre in *suṣumnā*.

3. *Kākacañcupuṭa-mudrā*: When the *apāna* current pierces the *hṛt-karṇikā*, there is contact with Śakti. At this moment, the *kākacañcupuṭa mudrā* is formed and as a result the vowel-less *s-s-s* sensation arises.

Translation of the 35th verse according to Śāmbhava-upāya

The *hṛdaya-bīja* is without beginning or end. Of the *mantra* '*sauḥ*' '*s*-part which betokens *prāṇa*, and '*au*'-part which betokens *apāna* being devoured, what remains is only the *visarga* (:)-part. The actual nature (*svarūpa*) of this *visarga* is the seventeenth *bindu-kalā* which transcends the sixteenth *kalā* inherent in the fifteen *tithis* each of the passage of *prāṇa* and *apāna*. This has to be realized only in the heart-lotus. One should always practise the repetition of *somāṃśa* i.e. all the external objects like blue etc. and internal mental contents like pleasure etc. as *prameya* or objectivity.

Note

There is no essential difference between *bindu-kalā* and *visarga-kalā*. The sixteenth *visarga-kalā* itself assumes the form of the seventeenth *bindu-kalā*. In the inner aspect *visarga* becomes *bindu* and in the external aspect, *bindu* becomes *visarga*.

Commentary on the above

From *ādyantarahitaṃ sakāramātram*, p. 101, l. 11 upto *sambhāva-nāyaṃ liṇ*, p. 101, l. 24.

2. Explanation according to *śāmbhava upāya*:

The aspirant should make the *hṛdaya-bija*, (i.e. *sauḥ*) without beginning or end i.e. without '*au*' and '*aḥ*' so that only '*s*' remains. Then together with the sixteen *tithis* i.e. '*a*' to '*aḥ*', i.e. together with the sixteen-phased *apāna* current, he should project it by the contrivance of *grāsana* (dissolution) into *hṛdaya* (i.e. *kanda* or *guhya*, male or female organ). Just as in pouring water in a pipe, there is at first movement with slow tempo (*calana*), then medium tempo (*kampana*), and finally fast tempo (*spandana*), so by the practice of slow, medium and fast tempo, the aspirant should penetrate *mūlādhāra*, *trikoṇa*, *bhadrakāli*, *kanda*, *hṛdaya* and *mukha*, i.e. *hṛt-karṇikā*. After this, simultaneously using slow, medium, and fast movement he reaches the culminating point at which there is a tremendous current owing to which both *prāṇa* (*sūrya*) and *apāna* (*soma*) become dissolved.

From the point of view of succession of the phonemes, without the beginning and the next i.e. without '*s*' and *au* of *hṛdaya bija* (*ādyantābhyām etat-bijaṃ-mātṛkāpekṣayā aukāra-sakārābhyāṃ rahitaṃ*) is meant the sixteenth *kalā*, viz. the *visarga*.

(1) which is without '*au*' denoting *apāna* and '*s*' denoting *prāṇa*,

(2) the acquaintance of whose virility can be obtained only by *viśleṣaṇa*,

(3) which is *dhruva* i.e. invariable *anuttara*,

(4) which is very Śiva (*visargātmakam*),

(5) which is the very centre of the expanding fifteen *tithis* and in which there is no *tithi* whatsoever, that is to say in which there is neither *prāṇa* nor *apāna*, and in which are swallowed up all the sixteen digits.

The aspirant rises even higher than this which is the seventeenth *kalā*, the commencement of *ūrdhvakuṇḍalini*. He or she should always meditate on the *amṛta-aṃśa*, which is the sixteenth aspect i.e. the *visarga-kalā* in the *hṛtkamala* or in other words the generative organ of *vira* or *yogini*. This is what my *guru* (Śambhunātha) says.

The mystic explanation of *somāṃśa* is the following:

According to the etymological analysis—*saha umayā* (*vartate*) i.e. he who abides with Umā or Śakti, *soma* means Śiva, for Śiva is constantly in union with goddess *parāśakti*, and is in a state of *spanda* (*kṣobhena*) due to union which is indicative of the state of churning together of the two *tattvas*. *Aṃśa* in *somāṃśa* means that all objects, internal like pleasure and external like blue, are like organs of the organic whole who is Śiva, and who is perfect I-consciousness.

So the aspirant should practise the meditation over and over again with the *japa* of his senses both in an extroverted way in which he regards objective manifestation (*sṛṣṭi*) as Śiva and in an introverted way in which he regards the withdrawal of manifestation (*saṃhāra*) also as Śiva.* This is the ever-present *hṛdaya-japa*. The potential mood has been used in the sense of possibility, competence.

Notes

Mūlādhāra-trikoṇa-bhadra-kanda-hṛt-mukha-mudrāsu:

This mentions the mystic physiology of *suṣumṇā*. In *suṣumṇā*, there is *mūlādhāra cakra*. In *mūlādhāra*, there is a triangular form known as Śiva-*trikoṇa*. Joined with this, there is another one known as *bhadra-kālī* (Śakti-*trikoṇa*). Then there is *kanda* which is a *saṃpuṭa* of Śiva and Śakti. Then, there is the *hṛt* or centre. Finally, there is the *mukha-mudrā* or *hṛt-karṇikā*. All these together form one *hṛt-padma*. Its centre is the *hṛt-karṇikā*. This is the *hṛdaya* known as *amṛta-bīja*.

Commentary

From *anye tu* on p. 101, l. 25 upto *evaṃ pūrveṣvapi ślokasūtreṣu*, p. 102, l. 9.

Translation of the Commentary

3. Explanation according to *āṇava upāya*:

Others i.e. those who follow the *āṇava upāya* explain this *Sūtra* in the following way:

The starting point of breath is the heart, and the movement of

*Svamiji says that this is *krama mudrā* described by Kṣemarāja in Pratyabhijñā-Hṛdayam in Sūtra No. 19.

prāṇa from that point upto *bāhya* (external) *dvādaśānta* measures upto thirty-six fingers. From that point, beginning with *prāṇavāyu* (*sūryatayā ullāsya*), the aspirant should restrain it at the point of *bāhya-dvādaśānta* for half a *tuṭi*[1] (before beginning the movement of *apāna-vāyu*). Then after the rise of the movement of *apāna vāyu* which is known as the '*somakalā*', the imperishable, *amṛta*-like *visarga*, the aspirant should increase the *candrakalā* or in other words the *apāna kalā* at every *tuṭi* which measures two and a quarter fingers. Thus when fifteen *tuṭis* are completed, the *apāna vāyu* becomes '*soma*' or moon of sixteen digits at the point of *hṛtpadma*, i.e. the *antaḥ* (inner) *dvādaśānta*, for there has to be a pause of half a *tuṭi* there also. In this way, all told the passage of *apāna* current is completed at thirty-six fingers. (Pause of ½ *tuṭi* at *bāhya-dvādaśānta*+15 *apāna-cāra*+pause of ½ *tuṭi* at *antaḥ-dvādaśānta* totals to 16 *tuṭis*. Each *tuṭi* being of 2¼ fingers, the 16 *tuṭis* make 36 fingers).

In such a state, without beginning or end only means that since the *parābija* or *amṛtabija* (*sauḥ*) is ever present at the first half *tuṭi* (on the occasion of pause at the *bāhya dvādaśānta*) and the last half *tuṭi* (on the occasion of pause at *antaḥ dvādaśānta*), it cannot be limited by time. Therefore, it is without beginning or end.

Leaving aside these two half *tuṭis*, the aspirant should practise the dissolution of the *kalās*, by meditating on the *somāṃśa* i.e. on *visarga kalā* (*aḥ*) without '*s*' and '*au*' within the remaining *tuṭis*, separating it within himself in the form of the seventeenth *bindu-kalā*.[2]

All these three explanations should be considered to be appropriate. This verse is a Sūtra. Therefore, by turning its words this way or that way, many kinds of explanations would become quite fit, as has been said that 'a Sūtra is that which gives scope for manifold senses.' The respected teachers have averred that Parātrīśikā is an unsurpassable Sūtra. In this way, there can be many interpretations of the earlier verses also which are indeed like Sūtras.

Notes

1. *Tuṭi*: *tuṭi* is that time in which the breath covers 2¼ fingers.
2. The seventeenth *bindukalā* is that where the movement of both *prāṇa* and *apāna* ceases.

3. The *bāhya-dvādaśānta* is called the '*ādi-koṭi*', and the *antaḥ-dvādaśānta* is called the '*anta-koṭi*'. Practice of meditation on these two spots is called '*ādyanta-koṭi-nibhālana*'.

Commentary

kim itthamabhyāse sati bhavati? ityāha

What happens by means of the practice of this *yoga*? Inan swer to this query, the author says:

Text of the Verse

YĀN YĀN KĀMAYATE KĀMĀṂS
TĀNSTĀÑ CHHĪGHRAM AVĀPNUYĀT /
ASMĀT PRATYAKṢATĀM ETI
SARVAJÑATVAṂ NA SAṂŚAYAḤ //36//

Translation of the text

The *yogī* obtains immediately whatever objects he desires. Therefore, omniscience becomes as direct to him as perception. There is no doubt about this.

Text of the Commentary

From *evam abhyāsāt* upto *dehena iti* on p. 102, l. 15 to 18.

Translation of the Commentary

Thus he becomes full of endeavour, perseverance, eagerness, and zeal through firmness of will brought about by the potency of the omnifarious *sauḥ mantra* (*sarvamaya hṛdaya-virya-samuccha-lita-icchā prasara*) and so by repetition of the continuous state of the *yoga* (*tat sthiti-rūḍhi-rūpa-abhyāsāt*), he acquires so much power that he obtains immediately whatever he desires. In short, in this very physical body, he acquires omniscience that is characteristic of the Supreme Bhairava. 36.

Concluding portion

From *sarvamuktvā upasaṃhriyate* on p. 102, l. 18 upto *so yamu-pasaṃhāra* on the same page, l. 19.

Translation of the Commentary

After examining from all points of view, the book is now being concluded. In the end, the progress of the *yogi* terminates in the attainment of this transcendental state (*akula-sattā-asādane*) which means resting in one's essential Self; this alone is the state of Bhairava. This has been mentioned repeatedly. Now this is the concluding verse.

Text of the Verse

EVAṂ MANTRA-PHALĀVĀPTIR-
ITY ETAD RUDRAYĀMALAM /
ETAD ABHYĀSATAḤ SIDDHIḤ
SARVAJÑATVAM AVĀPYATE // 37 //

Translation

Such is the gain from the practice of this *mantra* (viz. *hṛdayabīja orsauḥ*). This betokens the union (*yāmala*) of Rudra and Rudrā or Śiva and Śakti. By the continuous practice of this is acquired the supernormal power of omniscience.

Commentary

From *mantrāṇām* upto *iti śivam* on p. 103, l. 1 to 6.

Translation of the Commentary

In this way, the fruit of all *mantras*, even of the *mantras* with the phonemes of the other Śāstras also, is obtained, not otherwise. The word '*iti*' connotes conclusion.

In conclusion, it is said that this connotes the union of Rudra and Rudrā (Rudrayāmala) i.e. of Śiva and Śakti where there is no division of question and answer, which is the state of awareness of the essential Self (*svarūpa-amarśana*).

Beginning from a consideration of this up to the external state in which there are infinite, innumerable cases of manifestation and absorption—all this is indeed summarized in *akula* or *anuttara*, the transcendental Reality. This is the conclusion (of the dialogue between Bhairava and Devī) from the point of view of intuitive gnosis (*prasaṃkhyāna*).

"From the practice of this accrues the power of omniscience"—this is the conclusion from the point of view of *yoga*.

This (i.e. Rudrayāmala state) is ever-present in everybody. May there be good to all!

Notes

The whole book may be regarded as a complete five-membered syllogism according to Nyāya-Śāstra. The first verse, viz. "*anuttaraṃ kathaṃ deva...vrajet*" is the *pratijña* or introduction of the topic. The intervening verses constitute the *hetu* (logical reason), *udāharaṇa* (example) and *upanaya* (application). The 35th and 36th verses constitute the *nigamana* (conclusion).

AUTOBIOGRAPHICAL VERSES OF ABHINAVAGUPTA

Thus being born of Cukhulaka, resident of Kashmir, I, a black bee at the lotus-feet of Maheśvara, intent on lifting up mankind looking upto me (for spiritual succour), have written this commentary pregnant with the deliberation of the mystery of Trika. (1)

Who can estimate emphatically that so much only is the doctrine pertaining to Śiva? There is no bar to words in this matter. All that which is within my comprehension appears here regarding the Universal Spirit (*akhilātmani*). Therefore, the wise should not be averse to it. (2)

This is a work of such nature that it makes firm the knowledge of the ignorant, of one who is full of doubts or of one who has contrary views. In the case of those in whom conviction has already started, in whom it is fully grown (*rūḍhasya*), it makes the settled conviction of their heart harmonize with its teaching. (3)

In Kashmir, there was the chief minister of the king, Yaśaskara. He was named Vallabhācārya. He was a Brahmin of the most excellent lineage. His son, Śauri is worthy of renown on account of all his good qualities and is like the ocean in dedication to the feet of the crescent-crested Śiva, is the abode of virtue, one who fully deserves the great fame that has spread about him, is a pleasant object of affection and who has an inborn tendency towards compassion on all people.

His life-companion (wife) is named Vatsalikā. Because of the abounding devotion to her husband, her mind is filled with an inner disposition towards spiritual matters and expands with delight by the worship of Śiva. (4-5)

He has a son, named Karṇa who is a Brahmin who very well understands the mystery of the manifestation and maintenance of the world, who delights in the meditation and reflection on and worship of Śiva, who even in boyhood and youth, abandoning attachment to objects of sense, has resorted to unwavering reflection which eradicates transmigratory existence. (6)

My own brother by name Manoratha Gupta, having a longing for the Supreme Self, is engrossed in the Śaiva Śāstras, who, in order to destroy transmigratory existence, is eager to examine the entire range of Śāstras and Tantras in order to attain the supreme status of Śiva. (7)

There is also another person, Rāmadeva by name, who is devoted to Śaiva Śāstras, who is well-versed in grammar (*pada*), Mīmāṃsā (*vākya*) and Nyāya (*pramāṇa*), · nd who brings about veritable adornment to his birth in the highest caste (i.e. Brāhmaṇa). (8)

May that which I have written with heart full for the good and delight of all these serve as a guide for all for the attainment of (the nature of) Śiva. (9)

Atrigupta who was born in an excellent family in Antarvedi (the land between Gaṅgā and Yamunā) came (to settle down in) Kashmir the borders of which were hallowed by innumerable sages who were the incarnations of moon-crested Śiva. (10)

In his great lineage was born Varāhagupta whose son was Cukhula by name who was averse to worldly affairs and whose heart was set on Śiva alone. (11)

From him who had examined and understood the entire lot of categories and principles did obtain Abhinavagupta the human body sanctified by the Supreme Lord. (Even in this embodied condition), having obtained full freedom from care and doubt, he has instilled into the hearts of his pupils the secret lore of Trika. (12)

To those who are devoid of right judgement, I can only make a bow. There are others who deliberate but are unable to reach a successful conclusion. One can but pity these senseless people. There may be someone else, though only one among a lakh (a hundred thousand) who has become steady in mind after having attained the quintessence of deep deliberation. The above may bring my effort to a successful issue. (13)

Any earnest request to those who are lazy in discerning their Self will not bear any fruit other than harrying oneself. There are those of unsteady mind who only make a fuss regarding the discernment of the universe. I only bow my head in respect to appease them. (14)

There are dull-witted people who are confused themselves and throw the senseless multitude of creatures into confusion. Having bound them fast with fetters, they bring them under their subjection by influencing them with tall talk of their qualities. Having thus seen creatures who are simply carriers of the burden of *gurus* and their (blind) followers, I have prepared a trident of wisdom in order to cut asunder their bondage. (15)

I was also thrown into confusion by many who presumed to be teachers of truth by declaring 'that (Brahma of Śiva) am I' but whose tongue had not even contacted the two words 'that' and 'thou' (*tat tvam varṇayugamapi*). (16)

The Lord has set in motion the heart of the *guru* with compassion for lifting up those who have taken refuge (at his feet). That glorious *guru* has set me on the path of truth. (17)

I have written this work after (fully) reflecting on the doctrine of Somānanda which has spontaneously entered my heart which shares that pure state of truth taught by my *guru*. (18)

O goddesses full of streams of ardent delight rushing forth lavishly from you as you move about freely in the domain of *hṛdaya-bīja* and acting as the upper sharp edge of the wisdom-spike that is proficient in cutting asunder crores of my fetters, my mind, speech and body free of the reawakening of the fear of migratory existence are already surrendered at your feet. May you, therefore, confer your favour on me exceedingly and quickly, and dwell in my heart as Grace abounding. (19)

O goddesses, having your beautiful and ingenious continued existence in that *hṛdayabīja* (*tatcakra*), assigning the position of a *guru*, it is you who have employed me in the act of exposition etc. Therefore forgive this capriciousness of my speech and mind. (20)

In nineteen hundred (ways or verses) this Parātrīśikā has been explained. This will cut asunder the knots of doubts in all the Trika Śāstra. This has been written by Abhinavagupta.

The commentary on Parātrīśikā is completed.

GENERAL INDEX

अथ

श्रीपरात्रीशिकाग्रन्थः

श्रीमदभिनवगुप्ताचार्यकृततत्त्वविवेकाख्यव्याख्योपेतः

विमलकलाश्रयाभिनवसृष्टिमहा जननी
भरिततनुश्च पञ्चमुखगुप्तरुचिर्जनकः ।
तदुभययामलस्फुरितभावविसर्गमयं
हृदयमनुत्तरामृतकुलं मम संस्फुरतात् ॥ १ ॥

यस्यामन्तर्विश्वमेतद्विभाति
बाह्याभासं भासमानं विसृष्टौ ।
क्षोभे क्षीणेऽनुत्तरायां स्थितौ तां
वन्दे देवीं स्वात्मसंवित्तिमेकाम् ॥ २ ॥

नरशक्तिशिवात्मकं त्रिकं
हृदये या विनिधाय भासयेत् ।
प्रणमामि परामनुत्तरां
निजभासां प्रतिभाचमत्कृतिम् ॥ ३ ॥

जयत्यनर्घमहिमा विपाशितपशुव्रजः ।
श्रीमानाद्यगुरुः शंभुः श्रीकण्ठः परमेश्वरः ॥ ४ ॥

निजशिष्यविबोधाय प्रबुद्धस्मरणाय च ।
मयाभिनवगुप्तेन श्रमोऽयं क्रियते मनाक् ॥ ५ ॥

श्रीदेवी उवाच

अनुत्तरं कथं देव

सद्यः कौलिकसिद्धिदम् ।

येन विज्ञातमात्रेण

खेचरीसमतां व्रजेत् ॥ १ ॥

परमेश्वरः पञ्चविधकृत्यमयः, सततम् अनुग्रहमय्या परारूपया शक्त्या आक्रान्तो वस्तुतोऽनुग्रहैकात्मैव, नहि शक्तिः शिवात् भेदमामर्शयेत् । सा च शक्तिः लोकानुग्रहविमर्शमयी प्रथमतः परामर्शमय्या पश्यन्त्या आसूत्रयिष्यमाणानन्तशक्तिशताविभिन्ना प्रथमतरं परमहामन्त्रमय्याम् अदेशकालकलितायां संविदि निरूढा, तावत् पश्यन्त्युद्भविष्यदुक्तिप्रत्युक्त्यविभागेनैव वर्तते । सैव च सकलप्रमातृसंविदद्वयमयी सततमेव वर्तमानरूपा, ततस्तु पश्यन्ती यद्यत् अभीप्सितं तत्तदेव समुचितकारणनियमप्रबोधितं बोधसूत्रणमात्रेण विमृशति, यथा अनेकभावाभावज्ञानसंस्कारसंस्कृताया मेचकधियः स्मृतिबीजप्रबोधकौचित्यात् किंचिदेव स्मृतिर्विमृशति; नहि प्रथमज्ञानकाले भेदोऽत्र आस्फुरत्, यत्र वाच्यवाचकविशेषयोः अभेदः, मध्यमा पुनः तयोरेव वाच्यवाचकयोः भेदमामर्श्य सामानाधिकरण्येन विमर्शव्यापारा, वैखरी तु तदुभयभेदस्फुटतामय्येव,—इति तावत् व्यवस्थायां स्वसंवित्तिसिद्धायां यैव परावाग्भूमिः, सैवामायीयशब्दशक्तिपरमार्थस्वभावासांकेतिकाकृतकपारमार्थिकसंस्कारसारा वक्ष्यमाणनयेन मन्त्रवीर्यभूतांशचोदिता, तदुत्तरं पश्यन्त्यादिदशास्वपि वस्तुतो व्यवस्थिता, तया विना पश्यन्त्यादिषु अप्रकाशतापत्त्या जडताप्रसङ्गात् । तत्र च इदम्, एवम्, अत्र, इदानीम्—इत्यादिभेदकलना न काचित् । तत एव च परमहामन्त्रवीर्यविसृष्टिरूपाया आरभ्य वैखरीप्रसृतभावभेदप्रकाशपर्यन्तं यत् इयं स्वचमत्कृतिमयी स्वात्मन्येव प्रकाशनमये विश्रम्य स्फुरति, तदेवं स्फुरितमविच्छिन्नतापरमार्थम् 'अहम्' इति । तदेतत् अग्रे स्फुटीभविष्यति ।

तन्मध्य एव तु पश्यन्त्यां यत्र भेदांशस्यासूत्रणं, यत्र च मध्यमायां भेदावभासः, तत्र उभयत्र ज्ञानक्रियाशक्तिमये रूपे सदाशिवेश्वरसारे सैव 'अहम्' इति चमत्कृतिः अन्तःकृतानन्तविश्वेदन्ताचमत्कृतिपूर्णवृत्तिः तत् पश्यन्तीमध्यमात्मिका स्वात्मानमेव वस्तुतः परसंविदात्मकं विमृशति । परैव च संवित् 'देवी' इत्युच्यते । इयता पश्यन्त्यादिसृष्टिक्रमेण बाह्यनीलादि-पर्यन्तेन स्वविमर्शानन्दात्मना क्रीडनेन, सर्वोत्तीर्णत्वेन सर्वोत्कर्षावस्थितेः भगवतो भैरवस्य तथा स्थातुमिच्छया विजिगीषात्मना, इयदनन्तज्ञान-स्मृतिसंशयनिश्चयादिव्यवहारकरणेन, सर्वत्र च भासमाने नीलादौ तन्नीला-द्यात्मभासनरूपेण द्योतनेन, सर्वैरेव तदीयप्रकाशावेशैः तत्प्रवणैः स्तूयमानतया, यथेच्छं च देशकालावच्छेदेन सर्वात्मतावगमनेन; अत एव मुख्यतो भैरवनाथस्यैव देवत्वमिष्यते, तच्छक्तेरेव च भगवत्या देवीरूपता । यदुक्तम्—'दिवु क्रीडाविजिगीषाव्यवहारद्युतिस्तुतिगतिषु ।' तथा च एवं-विधमुख्यपारमेश्वर्यमयदेवत्वांशांशिकानुग्रहात् विष्णुविरिञ्च्यादिषु देवता-व्यवहारः । एवं भगवती पश्यन्ती मध्यमा च स्वात्मानमेव यदा विमृशति 'अहमेव परावाग्देवतामयी एवमवोचम्' इति, तदा तेन रूपेण उल्ल-सन्मायारम्भतया स्वात्मापेक्षतया तन्मायीयभेदानुसारात् तामेव पराभुवं स्वात्ममयीं भूतत्वेन अभिमन्वाना भेदावभासप्राणनान्तर्बहिष्करणपथ-व्यतिवर्तिनीयत्वात् परोक्षतया सूर्यादिसंचारायत्तदिनविभागकृताद्यतना-नवच्छेदात् ब्रह्मणोऽनेककल्पसंमितमहः, ततोऽपि विष्णुप्रभृतेः अन्तश्च प्राणचारादौ प्राणीयशतसहस्रांशेऽपि अहर्व्यवहारः,—इति अनवस्थितं, काल्पनिकं च अद्यतनत्वम् अकाल्पनिके संविद्वपुषि कथम् ? इति न्यायात् भूतानद्यतनपरोक्षार्थपरिपूरणात् परोक्षोत्तमपुरुषक्रमेण विमृशेत्, 'अहमेव सा परावाग्देवीरूपैव सर्ववाच्यवाचकाविभक्ततया एवमुवाच' इति तात्पर्यम् । 'सुप्तोऽहं किल विललाप' इति हि एवमेव उपपत्तिः । तथाहि—ताम् अतीतामवस्थां न स्मरति प्रागवेद्यत्वात्, इदानीं पुरुषान्तरकथित-माहात्म्यात् अतिविलापगानादिक्रियाजनितगद्गदिकादिदेहविक्रियावशेन

वा तदवस्थां चमत्कारात् प्रतिपद्यते; नहि अप्रतिपत्तिमात्रमेव एतत् 'मत्तः सुप्तो वा अहं किल विललाप' इति मदस्वप्नमूर्छादिषु हि वेद्यविशेषानवगमात् परोक्षत्वं, परावस्थायां तु वेद्यविशेषस्य अभाव एव,—इति केवलमत्र वेदकवेद्यतादात्म्यप्रतिपत्त्या तुर्यरूपत्वात्, मदादिषु तु मोहावेशप्राधान्यात्—इति इयान् विशेषः, परोक्षता तु समानेव। एवं सर्व एव प्रमाता गुरुशिष्यादिपदे अन्यत्र वा व्यवहारे स्थितः, सर्वकालमेव यत्किंचित् कुर्वाणः एनामेव संविदमनुप्रविश्य सर्वव्यवहारभाजनं भवति, अतः तामेव वस्तुतो विमृशति 'देवी उवाच' इति यावदुक्तं स्यात्, अहमेव सततं सर्वमभेदेन विमृशामि पराभूमौ, अन्यथा पश्यन्तीमध्यमाभूमिगं स्फुटमिदं प्रथनं न स्यात्, तावदेव उक्तं भवति 'देवी उवाच' इति। एवमेव पुरस्ताद् 'भैरव उवाच' इति मन्तव्यम्। तत्रापि हि स्वपरशक्त्यविभागमयो भैरवात्मैव अहमुवाच—इत्यर्थः। केवलं शक्तिप्रधानतया सृष्टिस्वभावाख्यामर्शे 'अहम्' इति उचितो देवीपरामर्शः, शक्तिमत्प्रधानतया संहारावेशविमर्शे 'महअ' इति भैरवरूपचमत्कारः। स्फुटयिष्यते च एतत्। एतच्च पश्यन्तीमध्यमाभुवि ज्ञानशक्तिमय्यामेव परस्या इच्छाशक्तिमय्याः संविदो विमर्शनम्। तदेव च सर्वारम्भपर्यन्तशास्त्रप्रयोजनम्; अत एव ज्ञानशक्तावेव सदाशिवमय्यां पूर्वोत्तरपदवाक्यक्रमोल्लासात् वास्तवपरमहामन्त्रवीर्यविमर्श एव दकार-एकार-वकार-यकार-उकार-वकार-आकार-चकार,-भकार-ऐकार-रेफ-अकार-वकार-अकारादिपदवाक्ययोजना। उक्तं च स्वच्छन्दतन्त्रे (भाग ४, पृष्ठ २०)

'गुरुशिष्यपदे स्थित्वा स्वयं देवः सदाशिवः।
पूर्वोत्तरपदैर्वाक्यैस्तन्त्रं समवतारयत्'॥

इति। एवं च अनुग्रहशक्तिः सततं सर्वप्रमातृषु अनस्तमितैव इति। सैष षडर्धसारशास्त्रैकप्राणः पर एव संबन्धः। अत्र अनुत्तरे संबन्धान्तराणां महदन्तराल-दिव्यादिव्यादीनामुक्तोपदेशेन परैकमयत्वात्। तदुक्तं त्रिकहृदये

'नित्यं विसर्गपरमः स्वशक्तौ परमेश्वरः ।
अनुग्रहात्मा स्रष्टा च संहर्ता चानियन्त्रितः ॥'

इति । एवम् अमुना क्रमेण सदोदितता, एवं परमार्थमयत्वात् परमेश्वरस्य चित्तत्त्वस्य यदेव अविभागेन अन्तर्वस्तु स्फुरितं, तदेव पश्यन्तीभुवि वर्ण-पद-वाक्यविबिभाजयिषया परामृष्टं, मध्यमापदे च भेदेन स्थितं वस्तुपूर्वकं संपन्नं यावत् वैखर्यन्तम् 'अनुत्तरं कथम्' इत्यादि भिन्नमायीय-वर्ण-पद-वाक्यरचनान्तम् । एतदेव तदनुपलक्ष्यं भैरववक्त्रं सृष्टिपरामर्शात्मकम्, अनुत्तराहंभावसाराकाराकाररूपशिव-शक्तिसंघट्ट-समापत्तिक्षोभात्मकं त्रिकशास्त्रप्रसरबीजं ध्रुवपदं मौलिकं सर्वजीवतां जीव-नैकरूपम् । अत एव व्यवच्छेदाभावात् स्थाननिर्देशाद्ययोगात् स्थानादि-पूर्वकत्वं नोपपन्नम् । वस्तु च प्रश्नतदुत्तररूपं सर्वतोदितमेव प्रथममवि-भागमयम्, तेन एतावदेव अत्र तात्पर्यम्—स्वात्मा सर्वभावस्वभावः स्वयं प्रकाशमानः स्वात्मानमेव स्वात्माविभिन्नेन प्रश्नप्रतिवचनेन प्रष्टृप्रतिवक्तृ-स्वात्ममयेन अहन्तया चमत्कुर्वन् विमृशति,—अहमेव एवं-विचित्रचमत्का-रेच्छुः तथा जानन्नेव तथैव भवामि—इति यावत् तावदेव 'देवी उवाच, अनुत्तरं कथम्' इत्यारभ्य 'भैरव उवाच, शृणु देवि' इति मध्यतो यावत् 'इत्येतद् रुद्रयामलम्' इति । यद्वा सर्वाणि पञ्चस्रोतःप्रभृतीनि शास्त्राणि यावत् लौकिकोऽयं व्यवहारः, स एष उक्तः परः संबन्धः ।

गोप्यमुपदेशसारं सद्यो भैरवपदावहं सततम् ।
अभिनवगुप्तेन मया व्याख्यातं प्रश्नसर्वस्वम् ॥

शिष्यहितपरतया तु इदमेव संगृह्य अभिदध्मः

सर्वेषु व्यवहारेषु ज्ञेयं कार्यं च यद्भवेत् ।
तत्परस्यां तुर्यभुवि गतभेदं विजृम्भते ॥
भेदासूत्रणरूपायां पश्यन्त्यां क्रमभूजुषि ।
अन्तःस्फुटक्रमायोगो मध्यायां तद्विभेदभाक् ॥

मध्या पश्यन्त्यथ परामध्यास्याभेदतो भृशम्
परोक्षमिव तत्कालं विमृशेन्मत्तसुप्तवत् ॥
'जाहणकुणहजहिं गिहपहिलउउशिअसब्वो
विअलिअरोओविअम्वइजाणिब्व उका
अब्वईणजोअन्तिहि मज्जिअभेदस्फुरन्तु
कामेण आसरिसेइणओअव
इसोच्चिअरेच्चभेरेणमतुउजिमणि
अवत्थबहिभणुसंधेइखनेन ॥'

एवमेव एतदनुत्तरत्वं निर्वक्ष्यति—इति । तदुक्तं श्रीसोमानन्दपादैः
'पञ्चविधकृत्यतत्परभगवद्भैरवभट्टारकस्य प्रथमशाक्तस्पन्दसमनन्तरम् ।'
इत्यादि निजविवृतौ । तद्ग्रन्थिनिर्दलनार्थं एव अयमस्माकं तच्छासन-पवित्रितानां यत्नः । उक्तः संबन्धः । अभिधेयं 'त्रीशिका' इति, तिसृणां शक्तीनाम् इच्छा-ज्ञान-क्रियाणां सृष्ट्याद्युद्योगादिनामान्तरनिर्वाच्यानाम् ईशिका ईश्वरी, ईशना च ईशितव्याव्यतिरेकेणैव भाविनी,—इति एत-च्छक्तिभेदत्रयोत्तीर्णा तच्छक्त्यविभागमयी संविद्भगवती भट्टारिका परा अभिधेयम्, तद्योगादेव च इदमभिधानं त्रीशिकाख्यम् । 'त्रिशका' इत्यपि गुरवः पठन्ति, अक्षरवादसाम्यात् च निरुक्तमाहुः—तिस्रः शक्तीः कायति—इति त्रिशका, न तु त्रिंशत्श्लोकयोगात् त्रिंशिका; एतावतोऽपि त्रिशका-र्थत्वात् । तथाहि श्रीतन्त्रसारे

'त्रिशकार्थस्त्वया प्रोक्तः सार्धकोटिप्रविस्तरः ।'

इति । अभिधानाभिधेययोश्च पर एव संबन्धः तादात्म्यात्—इति उक्त-प्रायम् । प्रयोजनं च सर्वप्रमातृणां विभोः परशक्तिपातानुग्रहवशोत्पन्नैता-वदनुत्तरज्ञानभाजनभावानाम् इत्थं निजस्वरूपहृदयङ्गमीभावेन निजामो-दभरक्रीडाभासितभेदस्य निखिलबन्धाभिमततत्त्वव्रातस्य स्वात्मचमत्कार-पूर्णाहन्तातादात्म्यभैरवस्वरूपाभेदसमावेशात्मिका जीवत एव मुक्तिः । प्राणदेहादिभूमावेव हि अन्तर्बहिष्करणविषयायां प्रेरणाख्यायाम् उद्योग-

बलजीवनादिरूपायां रूढस्य बन्धाभिमतेभ्यो मुक्तिः,—इति गीयते। त्रुटितेऽपि हि मायोये संस्कारमात्रे केयं मुक्तिवाचोयुक्तिः, किमपेक्षया वा ?, इति। तदुक्तं श्रीस्पन्दे

'इति वा यस्य संवित्तिः क्रीडात्वेनाखिलं जगत्।
स पश्यन् सततं युक्तो जीवन्मुक्तो न संशयः ॥'

(स्प. का. २।५)

इति। स्फुटीभविष्यति च एतत् अविदूर एव।

'जहि जहि धावइ जंकुण तहि तहि बिअविअकाउ।
अच्छन्त उपरिउणबिअपाय इहलइफलसिवणाओ ॥'

तदनेन स्वसंवेदनेन प्रयोजनमेव अत्र सकलपुमर्थपर्यवसानम्—इति प्रयोजनप्रयोजनानवकाशः। उक्तान्येव संबन्धाभिधेयप्रयोजनानि।

अथ ग्रन्थार्थो व्याख्यायते। 'अनुत्तरम्' इति, न विद्यते उत्तरमधिकं यतः, यथा हि तत्त्वान्तराणि षट्त्रिंशत् अनाश्रितशिवपर्यन्तानि परभैरव-बोधानुप्रवेशासादिततथाभावसिद्धीनि संविदमधिकयन्ति, नैवं परा परिपूर्णा परभैरवसंवित्, तस्याः सदा स्वयमनर्गलानपेक्षप्रथाचमत्कारत्वात्। तथा न विद्यते उत्तरं प्रश्नप्रतिवचोरूपं यत्र, यत एव हि महासंवित्सिन्धोः उल्लसदनन्तप्रतिभापर्यन्तधाम्न उल्लास्यप्रश्नप्रतिभानादिपात्रं भवति शिष्यः, तदेव वस्तुतः तत्त्वं सततोदितम्,—इति किमिव आचार्योयमुत्तर-मन्यत् स्यात्। उत्तरणम् उत्तरो भेदवादाभिमतोऽपवर्गः, स हि वस्तुतो नियतिप्राणतां नातिक्रामति। तथाहि प्रथमं शरीरात् प्राणभूमावनुप्रविश्य, ततोऽपि बुद्धिभुवमधिशय्य, ततोऽपि स्पन्दनाख्यां जीवनरूपतामध्यास्य, ततोऽपि सर्ववेद्यप्रक्षयात्मशून्यपदमधिष्ठाय, ततोऽपि सकलमलतानवतार-तम्यातिशयधाराप्राप्तौ शिवत्वव्यक्त्या अणुरपवृज्यते आरोपव्यर्थत्वात्—इति। ईदृश एव नाभिहृत्कण्ठतालुब्रह्मभैरवबिलाद्यधिष्ठानक्रमप्राप्त ऊर्ध्व-तरणक्रम उत्तरः, तथा उत्तरन्ति अत इति उत्तरो बन्धः, उत्तरणमुत्तरो मोक्षः, तत् एवं-विधा उत्तरा यत्र न सन्ति; उत्तरं च शब्दनं तत् सर्वथा

'ईदृशं तादृशम्' इति व्यवच्छेदं कुर्यात्, तत् यत्र न भवति अव्यवच्छिन्नम् इदम् अनुत्तरम्। इदम् इत्यपि हि व्यवच्छिन्नोत्तरव्यवच्छेदप्राणमेव,—इति व्यवच्छेदकत्वात् विकल्पात्मैव, अत एव यावदनुत्तरे रूपे प्रविविक्षुः मायीयः प्रमाता तावत् कल्पित एव विशेषात्मनि, तत्र तु अविकल्पितं यत् अविनाभावि तद्विना कल्पितरूपास्फुरणात्, तदेव वस्तुतोऽनुत्तरम्। तत्र हि भावनादेः अनुपपत्तिरेव वस्तुतः,—इति भावनाकरणोज्झितत्वमुक्तं, न तु अनुपयुक्तित एव, तत् ईदृशमनुत्तरं व्यवहारवृत्तिष्वपि एवमेव—इति। तदुक्तं मयैव स्तोत्रे

'वितत इव नभस्यविच्छिदेव
प्रतनु पतन्न विभाव्यते जलौघः।
उपवनतरुवेश्मनीध्रभागा-
द्युपधिवशेन तु लक्ष्यते स्फुटं सः॥ इति।
....तद्वत् परभैरवोऽतिसौक्ष्म्याद्
अनुभवगोचरमेति नैव जातु॥
अथ देशाकृतिकालसन्निवेश-
स्थितिसंस्पन्दितकारकत्वयोगाः।
जनयन्त्यनुभाविनीं चितिं ते
झटिति न्यक्कृतभैरवीयबोधाः॥'

इत्यादि। तथा च वक्ष्यते 'उत्तरस्याप्यनुत्तरम्' इति। व्याख्यायते च एतत्। एवमेव नरात्मनः शाक्तमुत्तरं ततोऽपि शाम्भवं, तथा तेष्वपि भूततत्त्वात्ममन्त्रेश्वरशक्त्यादिभेदेन स्वात्मन्येव उत्तरोत्तरत्वं, भूतादिष्वपि पृथिव्यादिरूपतया, जाग्रत उत्तरं स्वप्नः, ततः सुप्तं ततस्तुर्यं ततोऽपि तदतीतं, जाग्रदादिष्वपि स्वात्मन्येव चतुरादिभेदतया उत्तरोत्तरत्वम्। तदेतत् श्रीपूर्वपञ्चिकायां मयैव विस्तरतो निर्णीतम् इह अनुपयोगात् ग्रन्थगौरवात् च न वितत्य उक्तम्। तत् ईदृशमौत्तराधर्यंद्वैतसंमोहापायि

उत्तरत्वं, तथा विप्रराजन्यवैश्यशूद्रान्त्यजातिविभागमयम् ऊनाधिकत्वं यत्र न स्यात्, भावप्राधान्यमुत्तरशब्दस्य। उत्तराः पश्यन्त्याद्याः शक्तयः, पराद्याः ता यत्र न स्युः, 'नुद प्रेरणे' इत्यस्य नोदनं नुत्, तथा तरणं दीक्षाक्रमेण तरः शिष्यचैतन्ये गुरुचैतन्यं प्रेर्यते तेन हंसप्राणादिशून्यविषुवत्प्रभृतिस्थानभेदपरिपाट्या सकले निष्कलेऽपि वा पूर्णाहुतियोजनिकादिस्थित्या मोक्षदां दीक्षां विधत्ते; तत् अत्र चैतन्यस्य स्वप्रकाशस्य व्यापिनो देशकालाकारविशेषितस्य कथङ्कारम् इमा विडम्बनाः ?। तत् एवंविधो 'नुदा' प्रेरणेन 'तरः' तरणं यत्र न भवति तत् अनुत्तरम्। यत् वक्ष्यते

'एवं यो वेत्ति तत्त्वेन तस्य निर्वाणगामिनी।
दीक्षा भवति······(प. श्री. २५) ॥

इति। अनिति श्वसिति इति क्विपि अन्—अणुः आत्मा देहपुर्यष्टकादिः, तथा अननं जीवनम् अन् देहाद्यन्तर्गतैव भिन्नभिन्नशक्त्याद्यहन्ताशून्यप्राया जीवनाख्या वृत्तिः, यः शून्यप्रमाता इति अभिहितः, तस्यैव उत्तरत्वं सर्वतः परमार्थतया आधिक्यं यत्र—भैरवैकमयत्वात्। जडाजडभरिते जगति जडैः जीवदेकमग्नैः स्थीयते, जीवतां च जीवनं नाम प्रागुक्तं ज्ञानक्रियारूपमेकं पारमेश्वर्यं सर्वेषां, परत्रापि हि स्ववत्। देहादिरेव पृथक्कया भाति। यत् पुनः प्राणनं तत् अभेदेनैव स्वप्रकाशम्, एतदेव च परमार्थः। यदुक्तं श्रीमदुत्पलदेवपादैः

'ज्ञानं क्रिया च भूतानां जीवतां जीवनं मतम्।' (प्र. का. १।१४)

इति। तथा च जीवनं ज्ञानक्रिये एव इति। 'अ' इति च या इयम् अमायीयाश्रौतनैसर्गिकमहाप्रकाशविश्रान्तनिस्तरङ्गचिदुदधिस्वात्मचमत्काररूपा शाक्तोल्लासमयविश्वामर्शनरूपपरिपूर्णाहंभावप्रथमपर्यवसानोभयभूमिगा कला तस्या एव वक्ष्यमाणनयेन या इयं 'नुत्' विसर्गान्तता तस्या एव 'तरः' प्लवनं—सर्वोपरिवृत्तित्वं यत्र। अविद्यमाना देशकालगमनागमनादिद्वैतसापेक्षा 'नुत्' प्रेरणा क्रमात्मकक्रियामयी यत्र तत्

'अनुत्' आकाशादि लोकप्रसिद्धया, ततोऽपि सातिशयमनुत्तरम्, तस्यापि हि आकाशादेः संयोगिघटादिचित्रोपाधिवशात् समवायिशब्दादियोगात् च स्यादपि ईदृशी सक्रमा क्रिया। संवित्तत्त्वे तु सर्वतोऽनवच्छिन्नपूर्णस्वातन्त्र्यैश्वर्यसारे विच्छिन्नचमत्कारमयविश्रान्त्या स्वीकृतशङ्क्यमानोपाधिभावसकलेदन्तास्पदभावपूगपरिपूरिताहमात्मनि निराभासे सदाभासमाने स्वीकाराभासीकृतानाभासे इदन्ताभासतदनाभाससारदेशकालापेक्षक्रमाभावात् अक्रमैव स्वात्मविमर्शसंरम्भमयी मत्स्योदरीमतादिप्रसिद्धा विमर्शाभिधा क्रिया इति तदेव अनुत्तरम्। अतिशयमात्रे तमपो विधिः, द्विवचनविभज्योपपदे अत्र तरप्। तत्र अयं शुक्लोऽयं शुक्लः, अयमनयोः अतिशयेन शुक्लः इति वाक्येऽयमर्थः—अनयोः शुक्लयोः मध्यात् अतिशयेन अयं शुक्लः शुक्लतरः, एषां तु शुक्लानामयमतिशयेन शुक्लः इति कोऽयमधिकोऽर्थः, तथाहि—अयं प्रासादः शुक्लः, अयं पटश्च शुक्लः, अयं हंसश्च शुक्लः, एषां सातिशयः शुक्लतमः इति, तत्र प्रासादोऽपि शुक्लः पटोऽपि शुक्लः इति किमिव अधिकमुक्तं स्यात्। तस्मात् तमपि प्रत्यये एवंविधवाक्यकरणमयुक्तमेव। न च तरपः तमप् अधिकमतिशयमभिदध्यात्। एवं तावत् तु स्यात्—अविवक्षिते प्रतियोगिविशेषे तमप्प्रयोगः, प्रतियोगिविशेषापेक्षायां तु तरप्, प्रतियोग्यपेक्षैव द्विवचनविभज्योपपदार्थः, एक एव हि प्रतियोगी भवेत्, अनयोः अयं शुक्लोऽतिशयेन इति न तृतीयः प्रतीयते, निर्धारणार्थेन प्रथमस्यैव प्रतियोगित्वावगतेः। न च द्विप्रभृत्यपेक्षा भवति एकस्य, युगपत् एकैकापेक्षा मता—इति तस्य क्रमेण नाधिकोऽर्थः कश्चित्। 'तारतम्यम्' इति तु प्रयोगः क्रमातिशयेऽव्युत्पन्न एव रूढः, न तु तरप्तमप्प्रत्ययार्थानुगमात् 'तार्यं ताम्यम्' इत्याद्यपि हि स्यात्। तदलम् अकाण्डे श्रुतलवकौशलप्रथनेन। इह तु उत्तरक्रमिकप्रतियोग्यपेक्षायां 'तरप्'। प्रतियोग्यनपेक्षायाम् 'अनुत्तमम्' इत्यपि प्रयोगे अयमेव अर्थः। तथाहि आगमान्तरे

'अद्यापि यन्न विदितं सिद्धानां बोधशालिनाम्।

न चाप्यविदितं कस्य किमप्येकमनुत्तमम् ॥'

इति। एवं स्वातन्त्र्यसाराकलितक्रियाशक्तिशरीरमनुत्तरम्। तदुक्तमुत्पलदेवपादैः

'सक्रमत्वं च लौकिक्याः क्रियायाः कालशक्तितः।
घटते न तु शाश्वत्याः प्राभव्याः स्यात्प्रभोरिव ॥' (प्र. का. २।१,२)

इति। तत् व्याख्यातमिदमनुत्तरं षोडशधा। यदुक्तं त्रिकसारशास्त्रे

'अनुत्तरं तद्धृदयं हृदये ग्रन्थिरूपता।
ग्रन्थि षोडशधा ज्ञात्वा कुर्यात्कर्म यथासुखम् ॥'

इति। तथा

'हृदये यः स्थितो ग्रन्थिः……'……।'

इत्यादि। तत् ईदृक् अनुत्तरं केन प्रकारेण किमुत्तररूपपरित्यागेन उत स्वित् अन्यथा ?—इति। कश्च अयं प्रकारः—यदनुत्तरं सर्वमिदं हि ज्ञानज्ञेयजातं सर्वत एव अन्योन्यं भेदमयं विरोधमुपलभते, ततश्च इदम् औत्तराधर्यं भवेदेव—इति कस्मिश्च प्रकारे मोक्षे एव किं वा बन्धाभिमतेऽपि ?—इति थमुप्रत्ययस्य विभक्तिविशेषार्थानियमेन प्रकारमात्रे विधानात् प्रकारमात्रविषय एव अयं प्रश्नः। 'देव' इति व्याख्यातम्। कुलं स्थूलसूक्ष्मपरप्राणेन्द्रियभूतादि-समूहात्मतया, कार्यकारणभावात् च। यथोक्तम्

'संहत्यकारित्वात्'

इति। तथा कुलं बोधस्यैव आश्यानरूपतया यथावस्थानात् बोधस्वातन्त्र्यादेव च अस्य बन्धाभिमानात्। उक्तं हि 'कुल संस्त्याने बन्धुषु च' इति। नहि प्रकाशैकात्मकबोधैकरूपात् ऋते किमपि एषामप्रकाशमानं वपुरुपपद्यते, तत्र कुले भवा कौलिकी सिद्धिः—तथात्वदार्ढ्यं परिवृत्त्य आनन्दरूपं हृदयस्वभावपरसंविदात्मकशिवविमर्शतादात्म्यं, तां सिद्धिं ददाति अनुत्तरस्वरूपतादात्म्ये हि कुलं तथा भवति। यथोक्तम्

'व्यतिरेकेतराभ्यां हि निश्चयोऽन्यनिजात्मनोः ।
व्यवस्थितिः प्रतिष्ठाथ सिद्धिर्निर्वृत्तिरुच्यते ॥' (स्प. ५।१०)

इति। सद्य इति शब्दः समाने अह्नि इत्यर्थवृत्तिः, उक्तनयेन अह्नोऽनवस्थितत्वात् 'समाने क्षणे' इत्यत्र अर्थे वर्तते। समानत्वं च क्षणस्य न सादृश्यम्, अपितु तत्त्वपर्यवसाय्येव, एवमेव सद्यःशब्दात् प्रतीतेः। अतस्तस्मिन्नेव क्षणे इति वर्तमानक्षणस्य सावधारणत्वेन भूतभविष्यत्क्षणान्तरनिरासे तदुभयापेक्षकलनाप्राणां वर्तमानस्यापि कालतां निरस्येत, यतो यद् इदं परमेश्वरस्य भैरवभानोः रश्मिचक्रात्मकं निजभासास्फारमयं कुलमुक्तम्, तत् च यदा अन्तर्मुखपरभैरवसंवित्तादात्म्यलक्षणं निरोधमेति, तदा एव परमानन्दामृतास्वादमयम् अदेशकालकलितम्, अनुत्तरं ध्रुवं विसर्गरूपं सततोदितम्। तदुक्तं श्रीवाद्यतन्त्रे

'संरुध्य रश्मिचक्रं स्वं पीत्वामृतमनुत्तमम् ।
कालोभयापरिच्छिन्नं वर्तमाने सुखी भवेत् ॥'

इति। विस्तारितश्च विस्तरतोऽन्यत्र मयैव कालोभयापरिच्छेदः। तथा कुलात् प्राणदेहादेः आगता सिद्धिः भेदप्राणानां नीलसुखादीनां निश्चयरूपा तां ददाति इति—शरीरादयो हि झगिति अनुत्तरध्रुवविसर्गवीर्यवेशेन अकालकलितेन प्राणादिमध्यमसोपानारोहेणेव भावानां तथात्वनिश्चयरूपां सिद्धिं विदधते। यथोक्तम्

'अपि त्वात्मबलस्पर्शात् पुरुषस्तत्समो भवेत्। (स्प० १।८)

इति। तथा

....करणानीव देहिनाम्। (स्प० २।१०)

इति। तथा कुले शिवशक्त्यात्मनि संनिहितेऽपि सिद्धिरुक्तनयेन जीवन्मुक्तामयी समभिलषिताणिमादिप्रसवपदा, तां सद्यः अनाकलितमेव भावनाकरणादिरहितत्वेनैव ददाति। यदुक्तं श्रीसोमानन्दपादैः

'भावनाकरणाभ्यां किं शिवस्य सततोदितेः। (शि. दृ. ७।१०१)

इति । तथा

'एकवारं प्रमाणेन शास्त्राद्वा गुरुवाक्यतः ।
ज्ञाते शिवत्वे सर्वस्थे प्रतिपत्त्या दृढात्मना ॥
करणेन नास्ति कृत्यं क्वापि भावनयापि वा ॥ (शि. दृ. ७।६)

इति । कुले जाता सिद्धिः शाक्त-हृदिरूपप्रसरणात् आरभ्य बहिर्भावपटल-विकासपर्यन्तं भेदावभासमानता तां ददाति । तदेव हि अनुत्तरं महा-प्रकाशात्म अन्तःकृतबोधमयविश्वभावप्रसरम् अनुत्तरादेव निरतिशय-स्वातन्त्र्यैश्वर्यचमत्कारभरात् भेदं विकासयति । नहि अप्रकाशरूपं भाव-विकासप्रकाशे कारणं भवेत्, प्रकाशात्मकं चेत्, नूनं तत् परमेश्वरभैरव-भट्टारकरूपमेव—इति किमपरेण वाग्जालेन । तथा येन अनुत्तरेण विशेषेण ज्ञाता मात्रा मानेन प्रमात्मना त्राणं पालनं पतित्वं यासां प्रमातृप्रमाणप्रमेय-प्रमितिरूपाणां ता मात्रा विज्ञाता येन तत् विज्ञातमात्रम् । तथा विशेषेण प्रतिपत्तिदार्ढ्यबन्धेन यत् ज्ञातं तत् विभातमेव, न पुनः भावनीयं सकृद्वि-भातात्मत्वात् । तथा ज्ञातमात्रं ज्ञावमेव ज्ञेयैकरूपत्वात्, न तु कदाचित् ज्ञातृरूपं घटादि, तथा ज्ञाता ज्ञेयरूपा भेदमयी इयं माया, तदुभयं विगतं यत्र तत् विज्ञातमात्रं, घटादयो यत्र ज्ञात्रेकरूपत्वेन स्वप्रकाशात्मानः, यत्र च माया न प्रभवति, तेन विज्ञातमात्रेण । खे ब्रह्मणि अभेदरूपे स्थित्वा चरति—विषयमवगमयति, तथा हानादानादिचेष्टां विधत्ते स्वरूपे च आस्ते इति खेचरी, अन्तर्बहिष्करणतदर्थसुखादिनीलादिरूपा । तथाहि वेद्यवेदकभावानुल्लासिपदे शून्ये संविन्मात्रदृगुल्लासे संवेद्यगतान्तरैक्यरूप-दिश्यमानभेदोल्लासे स्फुटभेदोद्रेके च क्रमेण व्योमचरी-गोचरी-दिक्चरी-भूचरीभूता याः शक्तयः ता वस्तुत उक्तनयेन स्वभावचरखेचरीरूप-शक्त्यविभक्ता एव—इत्येकैव सा पारमेश्वरी शक्तिः । यदुक्तम्

'शक्तयोऽस्य जगत् कृत्स्नं शक्तिमांस्तु महेश्वरः ।'

इति । ततः स्त्रीलिङ्गेन निर्देशः । नहि आत्मनो मनसः इन्द्रियाणां बाह्यानां च भेदविषयस्य व्यवस्थापनं युज्यते—अभिसंधानाद्ययोगात्

अप्रकाशत्वात् च। सैव खेचरी कामक्रोधादिरूपतया वैषम्येन लक्ष्यते, तस्याः समता सर्वत्रैव परिपूर्णभैरवस्वभावात्। अणुमात्रमपि अविकलानुत्तरस्वरूपापरिज्ञानमेव चित्तवृत्तीनां वैषम्यम्। स एव च संसारः, अपूर्णाभिमानेन स्वात्मनि अणुत्वापादनात् आणवमलस्य, तदपूर्णरूपपरिपूरणाकाङ्क्षायां भेददर्शनात् मायाख्यस्य मलस्य, तच्छुभाशुभवासनाग्रहेण कार्ममलस्य च उल्लासात् स्वरूपापरिज्ञानमयतद्वैषम्यनिवृत्तौ मलाभावात् क्रोधमोहादिवृत्तयो हि परिपूर्णभगवद्भैरवभट्टारकसंविदात्मिका एव। यदुक्तं श्रीसोमानन्दपादैः

'……………………तत्सरत्प्रकृतिः शिवः।' (शि. दृ. ३।९४)

इति। तथा

'सुखदुःखे विमोहे च स्थितोऽहं परमः शिवः।' (शि. दृ. ७।१०५)

इति।

'दुःखेऽपि प्रविकासेन स्थैर्यार्थे धृतिसंगमात्।' (शि. दृ. ५।९)

इत्यादि। क्रोधादिवृत्तयो हि चिच्चमत्कारतादात्म्यात् अन्यथा तत्स्वरूपलाभस्यैव अयोगाच्च। पारमेश्वर्यः करणदेवता एव भगवत्यस्तास्ताः क्रीडा वितन्वन्त्यः शिवार्कस्य दीधितिरूपाः, तथा ता एव तत्तत्परस्परसांकर्यलब्धासंख्येयरूपाः तत्तदुच्चाटन-मारण-शान्त्यादिरूपेषु कर्मसु परिकल्पिततत्तत्समुचितसौम्यरौद्रप्रकाराः कृत्यादिभेदात् देवतात्वेन उपास्या उक्ताः, मतादिशास्त्रेषु भगवद्भैरवभट्टारकपरिवारभूताश्च। यथोक्तम्

'उच्चाटने काकवक्त्रा …………… ।'

इत्यादि उपक्रम्य

'ता एव देवदेवस्य रश्मयः कादिधारिकाः॥'

इत्यादि। तथात्वेन तु अपरिज्ञातस्वरूपाः चिच्चमत्कारं विकल्पेऽपि निर्विकल्पैकसारं तेन तेन विचित्रवर्णाक्षरपुञ्जात्मना घोरतरात्मना विकल्परूपेण देवतात्मना शङ्कातङ्कानुप्रवेशेन तिरोदधत्यः सांसारिकपाश्यपशुभावदायिन्यः। यथोक्तम्

'पीठेश्वर्यो महाघोरा मोहयन्ति मुहुर्मुहुः ।'

इति । तथा

'विषयेष्वेव संलीनानधोऽधः पातयन्त्यणून् ।'

इत्यादि । तथा

'शब्दराशिसमुत्थस्य शक्तिवर्गस्य योग्यताम् ।
कलाविलुप्तविभवो गतः सन् स पशुः स्मृतः ॥' (स्प.का. ३।१३)

इति । ज्ञातस्वरूपाः ता एव उक्तयुक्त्या जीवन्मुक्ताप्रदायिन्यः । तथा उक्तम्

'यदा त्वेकत्र संरूढस्तदा तस्य लयोद्भवौ ।
नियच्छन् भोक्तृतामेति ततश्चक्रेश्वरो भवेत् ॥' (स्प.का. ३।१९)

इति । स्वरूपपरिज्ञानं च एतावदेव—यत् एतासु क्रोधादिषु वृत्तिषु उदयसमयनिर्विकल्पैकरूपासु विकल्पोऽपि उदयमानो वर्णराशिसमारब्धतत्तद्विचित्रशब्दारूषितत्वेऽपि न तादृशेन वर्णपुञ्जात्मना शक्तिचक्रेण युज्यते, यत् तस्य प्राक्तननिर्विकल्पैकव्यवहारमयस्य विकल्पात्मनो मातुः स्वरूपं खण्डयेत् । न च विकल्पा अनुभवात् विकल्पान्तराद्वा भिन्नाः, अपि तु स एव एकः स्वातन्त्र्यभेदितभावोपरागलब्धभेदभूताद्यभिधविज्ञानचक्रप्रभुः, तदेवं खेचरीसाम्यमेव मोक्षः, तत् च अनुत्तरस्वरूपपरिज्ञानमेव सततोदितं परमेश्वर्याः शिवात्मनि संघट्टसमापत्त्या उभयविमर्शानन्दरूढि । शिवो हि परवाङ्मयमहामन्त्रवीर्यविसृष्टिमयः परमेश्वरीविसृष्ट्या तद्वीर्यघनतात्मकप्रसूननिर्भरया सृष्ट्या युज्यते तथा हि सर्वेषामन्तर्बहिष्करणानां यत् यत् अनुप्रविशति तत्तत् मध्यनाडीभुवि सर्वाङ्गानुप्राणनसारायां प्राणात्मना चेतनरूपेण आस्ते यत् ओज इति कथ्यते । तदेव सर्वाङ्गेषु अनुप्राणकतया तदविभक्तवीर्यरूपत्वेन ततोऽपि पुनरपि नयनश्रवणादीन्द्रियद्वारेण बृंहकरूपं रूपशब्दादि अनुप्रविशत् बृंहकत्वादेव तत् वीर्यक्षोभरूपकामानलप्रबोधकं भवति । यथोक्तम्

'आलापाद् गात्रसंस्पर्शात्………………॥'

इत्यादि। एकेनैव च रूपाद्यन्यतमेन उद्रिक्तप्राक्तनबलोपबृंहितस्य सर्वविषयकरणीयोक्तक्षोभकरणसमर्थत्वं सर्वस्य सर्वस्य सर्वसर्वात्मकत्वात्। स्मरणविकल्पादिनापि सर्वमयमनोगतानन्तशब्दादिबृंहणवशात् जायत एव क्षोभः, परिपुष्टसर्वमयमहावीर्यमेव पुष्टिसृष्टिकारि न तु अपूर्णं नापि क्षीणं समुचितशैशववार्द्धकयोरिव। वीर्यविक्षोभे च वीर्यस्य स्वमयत्वेन अभिन्नस्यापि अदेशकालकलितस्पन्दमयमहाविमर्शरूपमेव परिपूर्णभैरवसंविदात्मकं स्वातन्त्र्यमानन्दशक्तिमयं सुखप्रसवभूः। नयनयोरपि हि रूपं तद्वीर्यक्षोभात्मकमहाविसर्गविश्लेषणयुक्त्या एव सुखदायि भवति। श्रवणयोश्च मधुरगीतादि। अन्यत्रापि इन्द्रिये अन्यत् केवलं परिपूर्णसृष्टितां न अश्नुते, स्वात्मन्येव उच्छलनात्। तथा च तद्वीर्यानुपबृंहितानाम् अविद्यमानतथाविधवीर्यविक्षोभात्मकमदनानन्दानां पाषाणानामिव रमणीयतरतरुणीरूपमपि नितम्बिनीवदनघूर्णमानकाकलीकलगीतमपि न पूर्णानन्दपर्यवसायि यथा यथा च न बृंहकं भवति तथा तथा परिमितचमत्कारपर्यवसानम्। सर्वतो हि अचमत्कारे जडतैव; अधिकचमत्कारावेश एव वीर्यक्षोभात्मा सहृदयता उच्यते। यस्यैव एतद्भोगासङ्गाभ्यासनिवेशितानन्तबृंहकवीर्यबृंहितं हृदयं, तस्यैव सातिशयचमत्क्रिया। दुःखेऽपि एष एव चमत्कारः, अन्तर्व्यवस्थितं हि यत्तत् दयितासुतसुखादि वीर्यात्मकं तदेव भावनासदृशदृगाक्रन्दादिबोधेन क्षोभात्मकं विकासमापन्नं पुनर्न भविष्यति इति नैरपेक्ष्यवशसविशेषचमत्क्रियात्म दुःखसतत्त्वम्। तदुक्तम्

'दुःखेऽपि प्रविकासेन.............................।' (शि. दृ. ५।९)

इति। यदा सकलेन्द्रियनाडीभूतमरुदादिपरिपूरणे तु महामध्यमसौषुम्नपदानुप्रवेशे निजशक्तिक्षोभतादात्म्यं प्रतिपद्यते तदा सर्वतो द्वैतगलने परिपूर्णस्वशक्तिभरविमर्शाहन्तामयचमत्कारानुप्रवेशे — परिपूर्णसृष्ट्यानन्दरूपरुद्रयामलयोगानुप्रवेशेन तन्महामन्त्रवीर्यविसर्गविश्लेषणात्मना ध्रुवपदात्मकनिस्तरङ्गाकुलभैरवभावाभिव्यक्तिः। तथाहि तन्मध्यनाडीरूपस्य उभयलिङ्गात्मनोऽपि तद्वीर्योत्साहबललब्धावष्टम्भस्य कम्पकाले सकल-

वीर्यक्षोभोद्विगमिषात्मकम् अन्तःस्पर्शसुखं स्वसंवित्साक्षिकमेव। न च एतत्कल्पितशरीरनिष्ठतयेव केवलं तदभिज्ञानोपदेशद्वारेण इयति महामन्त्र-वीर्यविसर्गविश्लेषणावाप्तध्रुवपदे परब्रह्ममयशिवशक्तिसंघट्टानन्दस्वातन्त्र्य-सृष्टिपराभट्टारिकारूपेऽनुप्रवेशः। तद्वक्ष्यते .

'ततः सृष्टिं यजेत् .... ।' (प. त्री. २९)

इत्यादि। तथा

'यथा न्यग्रोधबीजस्थः .... ।' (प. त्री. २४)

इत्यादि। तथा

'...............................इत्येतद्द्वयामलम् ॥' (प. त्री. ३५)

इत्यादि। अन्यत्रापि उक्तम्

'लेहनामन्थनाकोटैः स्त्रीमुखस्य भरात्स्मृतेः।
शक्त्यभावेऽपि देवेशि भवेदानन्दसंप्लवः ॥' (वि. भै. ७०)

इति। भरात् स्मर्यमाणो हि संस्पर्शः तत्स्पर्शक्षेत्रे च मध्यमाकृतिमपरात्मकशक्तिनालिकाप्रतिबिम्बितः तन्मुख्यशाक्तस्पर्शाभावेऽपि तदन्तर्वृत्ति-शाक्तस्पर्शात्मकवीर्यक्षोभकारी भवति इत्यभिप्रायेण। तथा

'शक्तिसंगमसंक्षोभशक्त्यावेशावसानिकम् ।
यत्सुखं ब्रह्मतत्त्वस्य तत्सुखं स्वाक्यमुच्यते ॥' (वि. भै. ६९)

इति।

'...............................स्नेहात् कौलिकमादिशेत् ।'

इति च। महावीरेण भगवता व्यासेनापि

'मम योनिर्महद्ब्रह्म तस्मिन् गर्भं दधाम्यहम्।
संभवः सर्वभूतानां ततो भवति भारत ॥' (भ. गी. १४।३)

इति गीतम्। सोमानन्दपादैरपि निजविवृतौ

'भगवत्या रतस्थायाः प्रश्न इति परैकमयत्वेऽपि
तन्मयमहदन्तरालाभिप्रायेण'

इति ।

तदलम् अमुना त्रिकशास्त्ररहस्योपदेशकथातिप्रस्तावेन । तदिदम् 'अनुत्तरं कौलिकसिद्धिदं येन ज्ञातमात्रेण खेचरीसाम्यम्' उक्तनयेन ॥ १ ॥

एतद्गुह्यं महागुह्यं कथयस्व मम प्रभो ।

गुह्यम् अप्रकटत्वात् यतो गुहायां मायायां स्वरूपापरिज्ञानमय्यां सत्यां स्थितमपि अप्रकटम् । अथ च महत् अगुह्यं सर्वस्य एवंविधचमत्कारमयत्वात् । मातृमानमेयमयभेदाविभागशालिनी भगवती शुद्धविद्यैव त्रिकोणा मायायामतिशयप्रतिफलितभेदावग्रहा भवति इति, मायापि जगज्जननभूः विद्यैव वस्तुतः, तत् उक्तेन नयेन सा एवंभूतत्वेन अपरिज्ञायमानत्वात् अभेदमाहात्म्यतिरोहिततत्प्रमात्रादिकोणत्रयत्वात् महागुहा इति उच्यते, सैव च वस्तुतः पूजाधाम त्रिशूलं त्रिकार्थे । तदुक्तम्

'सा त्रिकोणा महाविद्या त्रिका सर्वरसास्पदम् ।
विसर्गपदमेवैष तस्मात् संपूजयेत्त्रिकम् ॥'

इति । तथा

'उदेत्येकः समालोकः प्रमाणार्थप्रमातृगः ।'

इति । ततश्च ईदृश्यां महागुहायां शुद्धविद्याहृदयमय्यां महासृष्टिरूपायां जगज्जन्मभूमौ स्वचमत्काररूपेण भवति यत् 'मह-अ' इति तद् एतत् गुह्यम् । एतेन हि यत् इदमविच्छिन्नभैरवभासा विमर्शरूपं स्वातन्त्र्यं, भावेभ्यः स्वरूपप्रत्युपसंहारक्रमेण आत्मविमर्शविश्रान्तिरूपत्वं, प्रकाशस्य हि स्वाभाविकाकृत्रिमपरवाङ्मन्त्रवीर्यचमत्कारात्म अहमिति । यथोक्तम्

'प्रकाशस्यात्मविश्रान्तिरहंभावो हि कीर्तितः ।' (अ. प्र. सि. २२)

इति । तदेव गुह्यम् अतिरहस्यम् । तथाहि—सृष्टिक्रमेण यथा अविकृतानुत्तरध्रुवरूपविश्रान्तो भैरवभट्टारकः सकलकलाजालजीवनभूतः सर्वस्य आदिसिद्धोऽकलात्मकः, स एव प्रसरात्मना रूपेण विसर्गरूपतामश्नुवानो

विसर्गस्यैव कुण्डलिन्यात्मक-ह्-शक्तिमयत्वात् पुनरपि तच्छाक्तप्रसराभेद-तदेकरूपबिन्द्वात्मना नररूपेण प्रसरति। तथा पुनरपि तन्मूलत्रिशूलप्राण-परशक्तित्रयोपसंहारे तद्विसर्गविश्लेषणया मूलध्रुवपदानुत्तरप्रवेशः सर्वदा, स्फुटयिष्यते च एतत् अविदूर एव। महे—परमानन्दरूपे पूर्वोक्ते, यदिदम् उक्तनयेन अ इति रूपं तदेव गुह्यम् एतदेव च महागुह्यं—जगज्जननधाम। तथा उभयसमापत्त्या आनन्देन अगुह्यं, सर्वचमत्कारमयम्। स्व !आत्मन्नेव, हे प्रभो एवंविधवैचित्र्यकारितया प्रभवनशील, आमन्त्रणमेतत्। तच्च आमन्त्र्यस्य आमन्त्रकं प्रति तादात्म्यमाभिमुख्यं प्रातिपदिकार्थात् अधिकार्थदायि। यथोक्तम्

'संबोधनाधिकः प्रातिपदिकार्थः।'

इति। निर्णीतं च एतत् मयैव श्रीपूर्वपञ्चिकायाम्। एतत् कथय—परावाग्रूपतया अविभक्तं स्थितमपि पश्यन्त्यादिभुवि वाक्यप्रबन्धक्रमासूत्रणेन योजय। यथोक्तं प्राक्

'गुरुशिष्यपदे स्थित्वा स्वयं देवः सदाशिवः।'

इत्यादि। पराभट्टारिकायाश्च पश्यन्त्यादितादात्म्यं निर्णीतं प्रागेव। तथा मम इत्यस्य प्रत्यगात्मसंबन्धित्वस्य इदंभावस्य यत् गुह्यं मह अ इत्युक्तम् अहमिति। तथा हि मम इदं भासते इति यत् भासनं, तस्य विमर्शः पुनरपि अहंभावैकसारः, स पुनः अहंभावो भावप्रत्युपसंहरणमुखेन इति मह अ इत्येतद्रूप एव यथोक्तं प्राक्। यदुक्तम्

'इदमित्यस्य विच्छिन्नविमर्शस्य कृतार्थता।
या स्वस्वरूपे विश्रान्तिर्विमर्शः सोऽहमित्ययम्॥' (अ. प्र. सि. १५)

इति। अन्यत्रापि

'घटोऽयमित्यध्यवसा नामरूपातिरेकिणी।
परेशशक्तिरात्मेव भासते न त्विदन्तया॥'

(ई० प्र० १।५।२०)

इति । तदुक्तं श्रीसोमानन्दपादैः निजविवृतौ

'अ'बीजं शुद्धशिवरूपम्'

इत्यादि । तदेव अस्माभिः विपश्चितमिति । तथा स्वमम—सुष्ठु अविद्यमानं मम इति, यस्य अहन्ताभरैकरूपत्वात् विश्वं न किंचित्, यस्य व्यतिरिक्त-निर्देशप्राणषष्ठ्यर्थयोगि विश्वं न भवति । शास्त्रान्तरदीक्षितानां विज्ञाना-कलानां प्रलयकेवलिनां च यद्यपि ममेति व्यतिरिक्तं नास्ति, तथापि भेद-योग्यतावसाना स्यादेव प्रबोधसमये तद्विकासात् अहंभावरूढिः तदपाकृत्यै सुष्ठुशब्दार्थे सुः । यदुक्तं मयैव स्तोत्रे

'यत्र किंचन ममेति दीनतां
प्राप्नुवन्ति जडजन्तवोऽनिशम् ।
तत्र किंचन ममास्मि सर्वमि-
त्युद्धुरां धुरमुपेयिवानहम् ॥'

इति । शोभनेन द्वैतकलङ्काङ्कनाकालुष्यलेशशून्येन अनेन परमार्थोपदेशा-द्वयात्मना ज्ञानेन, मानम् अवबोधो यस्य स्वप्रकाशैकरूपत्वात् । अमतीति अमा । अ मा इति यत्र अविद्यमानं मा मानं निषेधश्च नित्योदितत्वात् संहारश्च यत्र नास्ति, सा भगवती अमा इति उच्यते । सा शोभना सततोदिता अत्र । मायां प्रमाणप्रमेयव्यवहृतौ सा तादृशी अमा यस्य इति बहुव्रीह्यन्तरो बहुव्रीहिः । परमेश्वरो हि प्रमाणादिव्यवहारेऽपि पर-शक्तिमय एव सर्वथा अद्वैतरूपत्वात् । तस्य आमन्त्रणमात्मन एव ॥ १३ ॥

इदमेवं सार्धश्लोकनिरूपितानन्तप्रश्नतात्पर्यसंग्रहेण एतदुक्तं भवति, इति निर्णेतुं निरूप्यते

हृदयस्था तु या शक्तिः
कौलिकी कुलनायिका ।
तां मे कथय देवेश
येन तृप्ति लभाम्यहम् ॥ २ ॥

सर्वस्य नीलसुखादेः देहप्राणबुद्ध्यादेश्च परं प्रतिष्ठास्थानं संविदात्म हृत्, तस्यैव निजस्वातन्त्र्यकल्पितभेदा अया—विचित्राणि घटादिज्ञानानि, तत्स्था या इयं स्फुरणमयी शक्तिः, कुलस्य नायिका शरीरप्राणसुखादेः स्फुरत्तादायिनी, ब्राह्म्यादिदेवताचक्रस्य वीर्यभूता, निखिलाक्षनाडीचक्रस्य मध्य-मध्यमरूपा जननस्थानकर्णिकालिङ्गात्मा अस्ति। तत्रैव च कुले भवा-कुलरूपा (भवा अकुलरूपा) कौलिकी। यद्वा कुले भवमकुलात्म कौलं तत् यस्यामन्तः तादात्म्येन अस्ति सा कौलिकी, कुलं हि अकुलप्रकाश-रूढमेव तथा भवति। यदुक्तम्

'अपि त्वात्मबलस्पर्शात्।' (स्प. का. १।८)

इति। तथा

'तदाक्रम्य बलं मन्त्राः सर्वज्ञबलशालिनः।
प्रवर्तन्तेऽधिकाराय करणानीव देहिनाम्॥'

(स्प. का, २।१०)

इति। देवानां ब्रह्मविष्णुरुद्रादीनाम् ईशस्य आमन्त्रणम्। तन्मे कथय इत्यपि पठन्ति श्रीसोमानन्दपादाः, व्याचक्षते च तत् तस्मात् इति। यद्वा तत् कथय येन तृप्तिं परमानन्दमयीं लभे परमाद्वयनिर्वृतिस्वातन्त्र्यरसा भवामि इति समन्वयः। व्रजामि इत्यपि पाठः। अहमित्यनेन सर्वप्रमातृजीवन-रूपमेव सततं परामृश्यते, तत् च एवमभिहितस्वरूपोपदेशेन प्रत्यभिज्ञाय निजमीश्वररूपं परिपूर्णभावात्मिकां तृप्तिं विन्दति इति प्राक् प्रकटितमेव। तदुक्तं सोमानन्दपादैः स्वविवृतौ

'हृदि भयो गमनं ज्ञानम्'

इत्यादि।

इति शिवरसं पातुं येषां पिपासति मानसं
सततमशिवध्वंसे सक्तं शिवेन निवेशितम्।
हृदयगगनग्रन्थिं तेषां विदारयितुं हठाद्
अभिनव इमां प्रश्नव्याख्यां व्यधात्त्रिकतत्त्वगाम्॥

तदत्र प्रश्नसर्वस्वे

श्रीभैरव उवाच

व्याख्यातं प्रागेव एतत् किं पुनरुक्ततापादनेन, भैरवो भरणात्मको महामन्त्ररवात्मकश्च, केवलमत्र शक्तिमत्प्राधान्यं संहाररूपेण मह्म इत्येवं रूपम् इत्युक्तं प्राक्, स्फुटीभविष्यति च अग्रत एव। तत् इयान् अत्र तात्पर्यार्थः

परा भगवती संवित्प्रसरन्ती स्वरूपतः।
परेच्छाशक्तिरित्युक्ता भैरवस्याविभेदिनी ॥
तस्याः प्रसरधर्मित्वं ज्ञानशक्त्यादिरूपता।
परापरापरारूपपश्यन्त्यादिवपुर्भृतिः ॥
तदेवं प्रसराकारस्वरूपपरिमर्शनम्।
प्रश्न इत्युच्यते देवी यन्मयप्रश्नकारिणी ॥
तस्य प्रसररूपस्य परामर्शनमेव यत्।
तदेव परमं वक्तुं तत्प्रश्नोत्तररूपकम् ॥
तदेवापरसंवित्तेरारभ्यान्तस्तरां पुनः।
परसंविद्घनानन्दसंहारकरणं मुहुः ॥
अन्तर्भावितनिःशेषप्रसरं भैरवं वपुः।
प्रतिवक्तृस्वरूपेण सर्वदेव विजृम्भते ॥
एतौ प्रसरसंहारावकालकलितौ यतः।
तदेकरूपमेवेदं तत्त्वं प्रश्नोत्तरात्मकम् ॥
तदेवं परसंबन्धमनुत्तरतयान्वितम्।
षडर्धसारसर्वस्वं गुरवः प्राङ्न्यरूपयन् ॥

पफिलउ फुरइ फुरण
अवि आरिणा होइपरावर
अवरविहइण
देवि विसरिम इऊ उ।

सासच्चिअ परिसरि
सेइसऊअउदेउ
विलोमइ भेरव ऊअउ
उत्तरु एहु अणुतुल ॥

शृणु देवि महाभागे
उत्तरस्याप्यनुत्तरम् ॥ ३ ॥
कौलिकोऽयं विधिर्देवि
मम हृद्व्योम्न्यवस्थितः ।
कथयामि सुरेशानि
सद्यः कौलिकसिद्धिदम् ॥ ४ ॥

देवि इति प्राग्वत् । महान् भागो यस्याः, या भज्यमाना उक्तवक्ष्यमाणोपदेशानुशीलनेन सेव्यमाना पारमेश्वर्याख्यमहाबलदा भवति इति । महत्—परममहद्रूपतया प्रसिद्धोऽनाश्रितशिवरूपः स यस्याः भागः अंशः, पारमेश्वरी हि शक्तिः अनन्तषट्त्रिंशदादितत्त्वगर्भिणी । महान्—बुद्ध्यादिस्तत्त्वविशेषो भागो विभागकलापेक्षि रूपं यस्याः, पारमेश्वरी हि संविदेकघनशक्तिः स्वस्वातन्त्र्योपकल्पितभिन्नज्ञेयकार्यप्रतिष्ठापदत्वे बुद्धिरित्युच्यते । यदुक्तं श्रीसोमानन्दपादैः

..............................अपरस्थितौ,
सा बुद्धिर्यत्पुनः सूक्ष्मं सर्वदिक्कमवस्थितम् ।

ज्ञानं बोधमयं तस्य शिवस्य सहजं सदा ॥ (शि. दृ. १।२०, २७)

इति । भागो भेदः स यत्र अस्ति इति मत्वर्थीयाकारप्रत्ययान्तेन भागशब्देन विभक्तं रूपमुच्यते । विभक्ते च वपुषि परिच्छेदोऽन्योन्यव्यवच्छेदेनैव भवति इति प्रसादात्मकविषयनिश्चयो बुद्धावुपजायमानोऽपररम्यारम्यादिविश्ववर्तिनो भावान् अस्पृशन्नेव, प्रत्युत तान् व्यवच्छिन्दन् उपजायते

इति। सुखवृत्तिबुद्धेः धर्मैश्वर्यादिरूपत्वात् सत्त्वात्मको गुणनिःष्यन्दः इति गीयते। यदि तु तत्रापि अन्तस्तमाम् अनुप्रविश्यते तत् तद्द्वारेणैव तन्मूलवर्तिनि परमानन्दधाम्नि भवेदेव सततमुदयः। 'महस्य' सर्वतोऽखण्डितपरिपूर्णनिरर्गलनिरपेक्षस्वातन्त्र्यजगदानन्दमयस्य आ—ईषत् भागाः सुखलक्षणा अंशा यतः। यत् यत् किल सुखं तत् महानन्दनिर्वृतिपरमधाम्नि विसर्गशक्तौ अनुप्रवेशात् तथाऽचेत्यमानतया कियद्रूपतां प्राप्तम्। तदुक्तं भट्टनारायणेन

'त्रैलोक्येऽप्यत्र यो यावानानन्दः कश्चिदीक्ष्यते।
स बिन्दुर्यस्य तं वन्दे देवमानन्दसागरम्॥

इति। प्राङ्नयेन यदुक्तं 'महअ' इति रूपं तदेव भजनीयं यस्याः। परमेश्वरस्य हि स्वचमत्कारबृंहितं यत् 'अहम्' इति तदेव शाक्तं वपुः, तदेव च पराभट्टारिकारूपमिति उच्यते। अत एव सैव च परमेश्वरी सर्वं शृणोति—श्रवणाख्यया सत्तया तिष्ठन्ती तस्याः श्रवणसंपुटस्फुटक्रमिकस्वस्पन्दमयवर्णराशिनिष्ठमैकात्म्यापादनरूपसंकलनानुसंधानाख्यं स्वातन्त्र्यम्। तेन हि विना कलकललीनशब्दविशेषं शृण्वन्नपि—न शृणोमि इति व्यवहरति प्रमाता। कलकलमात्रविषयमेव तु संकलनमिति तत्रैव श्रुतमिति व्यवहारः। वस्तुतस्तु स कलकलध्वनिः श्रोत्राकाशे अनुप्रविशन् न वर्णान् अनुप्रवेशयन् तथा भवेत् तद्वर्णातिरिक्तस्य कलकलस्यैव भावात्। तद्वर्णविशेषविवक्षायां च कलकलस्य च कारणाभावादेव अनुत्पत्तिः स्यात्—तद्विवक्षोत्पन्नस्फुटवर्णमयशब्दकार्यत्वे सजातीयशब्दोत्पत्त्या अनुपपत्तेः कलकलस्य। सर्वथा त एव वर्णाः तेन स्फुटरूपेण संकलनामगच्छन्तः कलकलशब्दवाच्याः। तत्संकलनावधानोद्युक्तस्य भवेदेव कियन्मात्रस्फुटोपलम्भ इति संकलनमेव अत्र उपयोगि। संकलनं च भगवती सैव परा परमेश्वरी करोति। यदुक्तम्

तदाक्रम्य बलं मन्त्राः (स्प. का. २।१०)

इत्यादि । वस्तुतो हि शृणोति पश्यति वक्ति गृह्णाति इत्यादि भगवत्या एव रूपम् । यथोक्तम्

'येन रूपं रसं गन्धं स्पर्शशब्दौ च मैथुनम् ।

एतेनैव विजानाति किमत्र परिशिष्यते ॥' (क.ठ० २।१।३)

इति वेदान्ते परमेश्वरेण । न तु श्रवणं नाम स्फुटकलकलात्मकतारगद्गदादिरूपवर्णाकर्णनमेव । तथाहि—श्रीपरमेश्वर एव श्रीस्वच्छन्दशास्त्रे जपविभागनिर्णयावसर एवमेव निरूपितवान्

'आत्मना श्रूयते यस्तु स उपांशुरिति स्मृतः ।' (स्व. तं. २।१४६)

अत्र हि मध्यमापदे आत्मैव संशृणुते नापरः इत्युक्तम्, स्थानादिप्रयत्नस्फुटतायां दन्तोष्ठपुटादिसंयोगविभागेन अतिनिभृतमपि शब्दोच्चारे निकटतरवर्तिपरश्रवणमपि स्यादिति सशब्दतापत्तिरेव ।

'परैः संश्रूयते यस्तु सशब्दोऽसौ प्रकीर्तितः ।' (स्व. तं. २।१४७)

इत्युक्तम्, यतः न चात्र निकटादिविशेषः कश्चित् इति । परप्रमातृदर्शनमात्रगोचरजिह्वोष्ठपुटादिसंयोगेऽपि आत्मन एव श्रवणं स्यात् न परस्य, यतः मध्यमापदमेव एतत् संपद्यते—वर्णस्य बहिरात्मलाभाभावात् । वाय्वभिघातात् हि स्फुटवर्णो निष्पन्न एव, न च तत्र वाय्वभिघातो बाह्यतापत्तिपर्यन्तः स्यात् । ओष्ठादिचलनमपि न तत्र वर्णांशेऽनुप्रविशेत्, अपि तु स्वात्मनिष्ठमेव तात्कालिकं तत्स्यात्, तात्कालिकेङ्गितनिमिषितकरव्यापारादिस्थानीये स्फुटस्थानकरणप्रयत्नयोगे तु वर्णनिष्पत्तावपि यदि नाम ध्वनीनां तारतम्येन तारमन्द्रादिविभागे दूरादूरादिश्रवणं स्यात्, सर्वथा परैः श्रूयते—इति वैखरीपदमेव एतत्, इत्यलं प्रसक्तानुप्रसक्त्या । सैव परमेश्वरी आमन्त्रणयोगेन स्फुटं शक्तिरूपतयोक्ता । नर-शक्ति-शिवात्मकं हि इदं सर्वं त्रिकरूपमेव । तत्र यत् केवलं स्वात्मनि अवस्थितं तत् केवलं जडरूपयोगि मुख्यतया नरात्मकं घटः तिष्ठति इतिवत्, एष एव प्रथमपुरुषविषयः शेषः । यत् पुनरिदमित्यपि भासमानं, यदामन्त्र्यमाणतया

आमन्त्रकाहंभावसमाच्छादिततद्भिन्नेदंभावं युष्मच्छब्दव्यपदेश्यं तच्छाक्तं रूपं, त्वं तिष्ठसि इत्यत्र हि एष एव युष्मच्छब्दार्थः, आमन्त्रणतत्त्वं च। तथाहि यथा अहं तिष्ठामि तथैव अयमपि इति। तस्यापि अस्मद्रूपावच्छिन्नाहंभावचमत्कारस्वातन्त्र्यमविच्छिन्नाहंचमत्कारेणैव अभिमन्वान आमन्त्रयते, यथार्थेन मध्यमपुरुषेण व्यपदिशति, सेयं हि भगवती परापरा। सर्वथा पुनरविच्छिन्नचमत्कारनिरपेक्षस्वातन्त्र्याहंविमर्शे अहं तिष्ठामि इति पराभट्टारिकोदयः, यत्र उत्तमत्वं पुरुषस्य, यदुक्तम्

'यस्मात्क्षरमतीतोऽहमक्षरादपि चोत्तमः।
अतोऽस्मि लोके वेदे च प्रथितः पुरुषोत्तमः॥' (भ. गी. १५।१८)

इति। अत्र क्षराक्षररूपात् उभयतोऽपि हि उत्तमत्वम् अस्मि इत्यस्मदर्थेन उक्तम्। नहि अत्र सर्वत्र अहमिति परिमितं शरीरादि अपदिश्यते तस्य प्रत्यक्षेणैव तादूप्यविरोधात्। तदेवमीदृशं स्वयंप्रथात्मकं शिवात्मकं रूपम्। अत एव बोधस्यास्य स्वसंवित्प्रथात्मकस्य किंचिन्न ऊनं नाप्यधिकं—तस्याप्रकाशरूपस्य चिन्मये अननुप्रवेशात्। तदपेक्षया च माध्यस्थ्यमपि न किंचित्—इत्युपचयापचयमध्यस्थानीयेदन्तानिर्देश्याभावलब्धप्रतिष्ठाने न प्रभवन्ति तद्बोधाविच्छेदरूपास्मदर्थाः, विच्छेदितोऽपि युष्मदर्थ एवमेवेति, अत एव 'अलिङ्गे युष्मदस्मदी' गीते। देहगतसंख्याद्युपचारेण परापरादिशक्तिगर्भीकारात् संख्यायोगस्तु उपपद्यते। तथाहि—स्वस्वातन्त्र्योपकल्पितभेदावभासस्य अनन्तशरीराद्येकतयैव विमृशेत् 'आवां युवां वयं यूयं' इति च। उपचयाद्यास्तु देहगता उपचरितुमपि न शक्याः—चिद्रूपस्य ऊनाधिकतानुपपत्तेः। सर्वं हि सर्वात्मकमिति नरात्मानो जडा अपि त्यक्ततत्पूर्वरूपाः शाक्त-शैवरूपभाजो भवन्ति—शृणुत ग्रावाणः, मेरुः शिखरिणामहं भवामि, अहं चैत्रो ब्रवीमि इत्यपि प्रतीतेः। शाक्तमपि युष्मदर्थरूपमपि नरात्मकतां भजत एव शाक्तरूपमुज्झित्वा, त्वं गतभयधैर्यशक्तिरिति अनामन्त्रणयोगेनापि प्रतिपत्तेः। भवानित्यनेन 'पादा, गुरव' इत्यादिप्रत्ययविशेषैश्चापरावस्योचितनरात्मकप्रथमपुरुषविषयतयापि प्रती-

तिसद्भावात्। त्यक्तशाक्तरूपस्यापि च अहंरूपशिवात्मकत्वमपि स्यात् वयस्ये दयिते त्वमेव अहं भवामि इति प्रत्ययात्। शिवस्वरूपमपि च उज्झितचिद्रूपमिव नरशक्त्यात्मकं वपुराविशत्येव। कोऽहम्, एषोऽहम्, अहो अहं, धिक् माम्, अहो मह्यम् इत्यादौ हि अहमिति गुणीकृत्या-विच्छिन्नं स्वातन्त्र्यं, मुख्यतया तु विच्छिन्नैव इदन्ता प्रतीयते यत्र भगवत्या अपराया उदयः। हे अहम् इत्यादौ परापरशाक्तस्पन्दस्पर्श एव शिवस्य, किं तु पूर्वं पूर्वमव्यभिचरितमुत्तरत्र। तेन नररूपं स्फुटयैव प्रति-पत्त्या शाक्त-शांभवधुरमारोढुं शक्नुयादेव, न पुनर्वैपरीत्येन आरोहणं स्फुटप्रतीतिमयम्। अत्यक्तनिजनिजरूपतया त्र्यात्मकत्वात् एक-द्वि-बहुरूप-भागित्वमेति प्रत्येकमेतत् त्रिकम्। उक्तं हि

'एकं वस्तु द्विधा भूतं द्विधा भूतमनेकधा।'

इति। एकात्मकत्वे हि अप्रतियोगित्वात् शिवता, प्रतियोगिसंभवे शाक्तत्वम्, अनेकतायां भेद एव नरात्मभाव एकस्यैव घटः घटौ घटाः घटपटपाषाणा इत्यपि हि तिष्ठति तिष्ठतः तिष्ठन्ति इति च एकेनैव क्रियाशक्तिस्फुरितमेव एतत्, यथोक्तं

'अनेकमेकधा कृत्वा को न मुच्येत बन्धनात्।'

इति। अत एव नर-शक्ति-शिवात्मनां युगपदेकत्र परामर्शे उत्तरोत्तरस्वरू-पानुप्रवेश एव—तस्यैव वस्तुतः तत्परमार्थरूपत्वात्, स च त्वं च तिष्ठथः, स च त्वं च अहं च तिष्ठामः इति प्रतीतिक्रम एव अकृतकसंस्कारसारः शाब्दिकैर्लक्षणैरनुगम्यते, तथा च निजभाषापदेष्वपि संस्कारस्य यत्र नामापि न अवशिष्यते बौद्धान्ध्रद्रविडादिषु तत्रापि अयमेव वाचनिकः क्रमः, वचनक्रमश्च हार्दीमेव प्रतीतिं मूलतोऽनुसरन् तत्प्रतीतिरसरूपतया प्रतीतेरपि एवंरूपत्वमवगमयेत्, यथोक्तं मयैव

'न सा गीर्या न हृदयंगमगामिनी'

इति। तत् सर्वथा अकृतका एवंप्रतीतिः, यथोक्तम्

'न तैर्विना भवेच्छब्दो नार्थो नापि चितेर्गतिः ।'

इति । श्रीमालिनीतन्त्रेऽपि

'एवं सर्वाणुसंघातमधिष्ठाय यथा स्थिता ।
तथा ते कथिता शंभोः शक्तिरेकैव शांकरी ॥' (मा. वि. ३।३४)

इति । श्रीतन्त्रसमुच्चयेऽपि

नर-शक्ति-शिवावेशि विश्वमेतत्सदा स्थितम् ।
व्यवहारे क्रमीणां च सर्वज्ञानां च सर्वशः ॥'

इति । तदेव नरशक्तिशिवात्मकं स्फुटप्रतिपत्तिसंप्रदायोपदेशेन दर्शितम् । नरः शक्तिः शिव इति तु सर्वसहः प्रतिपत्तिक्रमः परमेश्वरेच्छास्वातन्त्र्यसृष्टः । इत्यलं परशक्तिपातपवित्रितबहुश्रुतसहृदयसोपदेशकतिपयजनहृदयहारिण्या प्रसक्तानुप्रसक्त्या । तत् व्याख्यातं 'शृणु देवि' इति । 'उत्तरस्यापि' इति, यदुक्तं—कथमनुत्तरमिति, तत्र प्रतिवचनम्—उत्तरस्यापि संनिहितस्य यत् अनुत्तरं, प्रागुक्तक्रमेण हि उत्तरमपि अनुत्तरतादात्म्येनैव भवेत् नान्यथा, अत एव उत्तरमपि अनादृत्य 'अनादरे षष्ठी' (पा. २।३।३८) । उत्तरं रूपं हि अनादृततद्भावमनुत्तररूपमेव । भेदो हि अयमुत्तररूपो नितरामेव अभेदभुवमधिशय्य तथा भवेत् । यथोक्तं

'परव्यवस्थापि परे यावन्नात्मीकृतः परः ।
तावन्न शक्यते कर्तुं यतो बुद्धः परः परे' ॥

इति । तथा उत्तरस्यापि ग्रन्थभागस्य अनुत्तरं तेनापि उत्तरीतुं न शक्यते । पश्यन्त्या अपि पराभट्टारिकायाः प्रथमप्रसरत्वात्, उत्तरस्यापि च मदीयस्य एतदेवानुत्तरं परमार्थः । उत्तरस्य त्रिशूलप्रेरणादिमयस्य यत् अनुत्तरं विश्रान्तिस्थानम् । किं तत् ? इत्याह—अयं कौलिको विधिः—कुलाकुलात्मा प्राक् व्याख्यातो विधीयमानत्वात् विधिः महासृष्टिरूपो गर्भीकृतानन्तसृष्ट्यादिकोटिशतो यस्मात्प्रसृत एतदेव तदनुत्तरं, यदुक्तम्
'............यतः सर्वं......................'

इति। तथाहि इदं विश्वं चिच्चित्तप्राणदेहसुखदुःखेन्द्रियभूतघटादिमयमेकस्यां परस्यां परमेश्वर्यां भैरवसंविदि अविभागेनैव बोधात्मकेन रूपेण आस्ते। यद्यपि बोधात्मकं रूपं नास्तमेति जातुचिदपि तदस्तमये अप्रकाशमानतापत्तेः, तथापि परस्पराभावात्मकोऽवच्छेदः तत्र नास्ति, विश्वात्मान एव भावाः। तत्र च यदि एषामवस्थितिः न स्यात् तत् प्रथमानुसंधानादिकमेव अक्षप्रेरणोपयोग्यपि न भवेत् इति समुचितानुदितेदन्ताकमहंपरामर्शमात्राभिन्नमेव भावजातं विगतभेदकलनं तिष्ठति। न तत्र कश्चित् अवच्छेदः। तथा यद् यत्र स्पष्टः सन्नयं विधिः कौलिकः स्थितो विश्रान्ति प्राप्तः। सर्वमिदं हि षट्त्रिंशदात्म, ततः सामान्यस्पन्दसंविदात्मनः शक्तिमतः परशक्तिप्रधानात् शिवात् स्वशक्त्या सृष्टमपि सत् तत्रैव भैरवविशेषस्पन्दात्मनि शक्तिप्रधाने स्वस्वरूपे विश्राम्येत्, तदेव स्वस्वभावनिष्ठितत्वं भावानाम्। यदुक्तं

'यस्मिन्सर्वं.........................'

इति। तदेतत् शिवशक्त्यात्मैव सामान्यविशेषरूपमेकात्मकमपि परमेश्वरेणैव उपदेशोपायप्रवेशाय पृथक्कृत्य निरूप्यमाणं वस्तुतः पुनरेकमेव स्वतन्त्रचिन्मयमहमित्यैश्वर्यशक्तिसारमनुत्तरम्। कीदृशे स्वस्वरूपेऽवस्थितः 'मम हृद्व्योम्नि'—ममेति यत् एतत् हृदयं सर्वभावानां स्थानं प्रतिष्ठाधाम, नीलादीनां हि अन्ततः क्रिमिपर्यन्तं चिदंशानिविष्टानां न किंचित्। नीलादि रूपमिति प्रमातुरेव। यत् 'ममेति' अविच्छिन्नचमत्कारांशोपारोहित्वं 'मम नीलं भातम्' इति तदेव नीलादिरूपत्वमिति, तस्य ममेत्यस्य नीलाद्यनन्तसर्वभावहृदयस्य यत् व्योम—यत्र तत् ममकारात्मकं विश्वं वीतं—सम्यक् धृतम्, अत एव त्यक्तभिन्ननिजरूपतया शून्यरूपं व्योम यत्र। तथा ममेत्यस्य भिन्नाभिन्नरूपपरापरसंविदात्मनो यत् हृदयं पर्यन्तप्रतिष्ठाधाम 'अहमिति' तस्यापि व्योम संहाररूपकलनेन 'म ह अ' इति नरात्मकं लीनं बिन्द्वात्मशक्तौ म-इति, कुण्डलिनी-ह-कलारूपायां प्रविश्य, परिपूर्णनिरर्गल-

चमत्कारे सर्वाविच्छिन्ने अ-इत्यनुप्रविष्टं तथा भवति, एतदेव मम हृद्व्योम। एवं यत्र इदं प्रसृतं यत्र च विश्रान्तं तदेव नित्यमनावृतस्वभावं स्वयं प्रथमानम् अनपह्नवनीयमनुत्तरम्। यथोक्तम्

'यत्र स्थितमिदं सर्वं कार्यं यस्माच्च निर्गतम्।
तस्यानावृतरूपत्वान्न निरोधोऽस्ति कुत्रचित् ॥' (स्प. का. १।२)

इति। आवरकत्वेन निरोधकाभिमतोऽपि हि तदावरणादिस्वातन्त्र्येण प्रकाशमानो दृक्क्रियात्मक एव परमेश्वरः। यदित्ययं निपातः सर्वविभक्त्यर्थवृत्तिः अपरवाक्यीयसंबन्धौचित्यात् विशेषे स्थास्नुरत्र पञ्चम्यर्थे च वर्तते। अयं हि आञ्जस्येन अर्थः—यदयं कौलिकः सृष्टिप्रसरः, यच्च मम हृद्व्योम्नि अवस्थितः तदेवानुत्तरम्। एवं तस्यैव प्रसरविश्रान्त्युभयस्थानत्वं निरूप्य प्रसरक्रमस्वरूपं क्रियाशक्तिस्पन्दविसर्गं निरूपयति 'कथयामि' इत्यादि। तदेव हि रूपम् अहं परानुत्तरात्मपरापरादिमयपश्यन्त्यादिप्रसरपरिपाट्याऽविच्छिन्नैकतापरमार्थः। कथयामीति समुचितव्यपदेशं पराभट्टारिकोदयभागि वैखर्यन्तं वाक्यप्रबन्धं शास्त्रीयलौकिकादिबहुभेदं व्यक्तयामीति, तदुक्तम्

'..........सर्वतश्च यः'

इति। प्रथमपर्यन्तभुवि परभट्टारिकात्मनि तत्प्रसरात्मनि च परापरादेवतावपुषि अनुत्तरध्रुवपदविजृम्भैव, तदाहुर्निजविवृतौ श्रीसोमानन्दपादाः—कथयामि इति उच्चारयामि उत्कलिकात इति, तथाहमेव सर्वस्य अन्तश्चिद्रूपेण कथयामीति, तदेवास्माभिः युक्त्युपदेशसंस्कारैः निर्मलय्य हृदयङ्गमीकृतम्। स्वरूपं चास्य परमेश्वरस्य 'सद्य' इति—'य एव च परमेश्वरो भैरवात्माकुलानुत्तरध्रुवधामतया'—उक्तः, तदेवेदं सर्वं 'सत्'—कौलिकविधिरूपं, नहि प्रकाशविमर्शशुद्धभैरवस्वरूपातिरेकि किंचित् भावानां सत्त्वम्। सत्तासंबन्धार्थक्रियाकारित्वादीनामपि सत्ताहेतुता पराभिमतानामपि, सत्तायोगे तथात्वानुपपत्तेः, सत्त्वान्तरार्थक्रियान्तरयोगे चानवस्था-

पत्तेः, प्रथमत एव तथा विमर्शजीवितप्रकाशमयत्वमेव सत्त्वं, तत् च स्वातन्त्र्यविमर्शसाराहंभावभरितमिति भैरवरूपमेव। यद्वा सति सद्रूपे यस्यति यत्नं करोति क्रियाशक्तिप्राणत्वात् तत् सद्य इति क्विपि नपुंसकनिर्देशः। सद्यदिति केचित् गुरवः पठन्ति। तदुक्तं श्रीसिद्धसन्ताने

'प्रकाशमानाभासैव यद्भूतिस्तत्सदेव हि।'

इति। श्रीस्पन्देऽपि

'............तदस्ति परमार्थतः।' (स्प. का. १।५)

इति। श्रीसोमानन्दपादैरपि

'यत्सत्तत्परमार्थो हि परमार्थस्ततः शिवः।'

इति स्वरूपमुक्तम्। तदुक्तं

'यः सर्वं................'

इति। अस्यैव क्रियाशक्तिप्रसरं निरूपयति 'कौलिकसिद्धिदम्' इति, कौलिकं यत् व्याख्यातं तस्य सिद्धिः तथात्वदार्ढ्यं तत् यतो भवति, तत्र हि परमार्थप्रमातरि सकलं कुलाकुलादि तथा भवति यत्र प्रतीयमानं सर्वं तथात्वदार्ढ्यं भजते। तदुक्तं

'........परात्परतरं त्रिकम्।'

इति। अन्यत्रापि

'वेदाच्छैवं ततो वामं ततो दक्षं ततः कुलम्।
ततो मतं ततश्चापि त्रिकं सर्वोत्तमं परम्॥'

इति। श्रीनिशाचारेऽपि

'वाममार्गाभिषिक्तोऽपि दैशिकः परतत्त्ववित्।
संस्कार्यो भैरवे सोऽपि कुले कौले त्रिकेऽपि सः॥'

इति। श्रीसर्वाचारेऽपि

'वाममार्गाभिषिक्तोऽपि देशिकः परतत्त्ववित्।
क्रमाद्भैरवतन्त्रेषु पुनः संस्कारमर्हति॥'

इति। क्रमश्च अस्य एष एव, यत् सर्वलोकवेदसिद्धान्तवामदक्षिणकुलमत-भूमिषु परमार्थप्रमातृभाव इति। यथोक्तम्

'यश्च सर्वमयो नित्यं तस्मै सर्वात्मने नमः।'

इति। तदेवानुत्तरमेतत्सर्वं गर्भीकृत्योक्तं निजविवृतौ सोमानन्दपादैः, किंबहुना सर्वमेवानुत्तरमनुत्तरत्वात् इति। अयं तात्पर्यार्थः—

'सअल बहुसंवेअणफुरितमत्त
उजहित हिंचि अजत्तो हित्तउपफुर।
इज कुट्टि उस अलभाव
संवेअणरअणणिहाणुइउ॥
परिआणहुएत्तिअणुतुरुछत्तुहजसठुउसम्मूढतुणिअ-
च्छहतुहअत्तासिअऊउऊउसुबाहिरबितुरहुंबन्धुण-
मोक्खतउइरिअवहुविकुणसिबिसग्गुणिमसिद्वउपुण-
संहरसिज्जितिपविण्णुविरिश्चरुद्रमअलक्खहिमसर-
णिरोहचिन्तइमलक्खएक्कवाअपरिआणहुअत्ताणउप-
रमतथअण्णुणकोइबिआसुबहुइउसअलउसत्थत्थ।'

इतीदृक् व्याख्यानं त्यक्त्वा यत् अन्यैः व्याख्यातं तत्प्रदर्शनं दूषणम्। यद्यपि पदवाक्यसंस्कारविहीनैः सह व्रीडावहा गोष्ठी कृता भवति, तथापि सचेतसोऽनुत्तरमवबोधयितुं तत् एकवारं तावत् लिख्यते—'अनुत्तरम्' इत्यादिना सार्धेन श्लोकेन शिवविषयः प्रश्नः। 'हृदयस्था' इत्यादिना श्लोकेन शक्तिविषयः। तथा 'शृणु देवि' इत्यत्र प्रतिवचनग्रन्थे 'उत्तरस्याप्यनुत्तरम्' इति, तत्रार्थः उत्तरं च शृणु अनुत्तरं च इति। अत्र यदि एषा त्रिकार्थाभिप्रायेण व्याख्या तत् नरविषयप्रश्नप्रसङ्गः। अथ तु यामलाभिप्रायेण तत्रापि न द्वे वस्तुनी शिवशक्त्यात्मके यामलमुच्यते, येन पृथक् प्रश्नविषयतोपपत्तिः, अथशब्दार्थश्च न संगच्छते—स हि सजातीयक्रियानन्तर्यवृत्तिः, उत्तरस्वरूपावधारणमन्तरेण च अनुत्तरविषयस्यैकप्रश्नस्य

अनुपपत्तिः। तथाहि केषुचित् वृद्धपुस्तकेषु ईदृक् श्लोकान्तरं दृश्यते

'श्रुतं देव महाज्ञानं त्रिकाख्यं परमेश्वर।
उत्तरं च तथा ज्ञानं त्वत्प्रसादादवधारितम् ॥'

इति। तस्मात् श्रीसोमानन्दपादनिरूपितव्याख्यानुसारेणैव यत् गुरवः समादिक्षन् तदेव सर्वस्य करोति शिवम्।

इत्यसंस्कृतदुर्व्याख्यातामसोन्मूलनव्रतः।
षडर्धशासनापूतहृदम्बुजविकासकः ॥
संस्त्यानानन्तपाशौघविलापनलसद्रुचिः।
दीप्तोऽभिनवगुप्तेन व्याख्याभानुः प्रकाशितः ॥

एवं यतोऽयं कौलिको विधिः प्रभवति, यत्र च प्रतिष्ठापदवीं भजते, यन्मयं च इदं कौलिकं, तदेवानुत्तरमित्युक्तम्। तत्र कस्तावत् कौलिको विधिः? कथं च अस्य प्रसरोऽनुत्तरात्? कथं चात्रैव अस्य प्रतिष्ठा? कथं च अनुत्तरैकरूपत्वम्? यच्चोक्तम्—उत्तरस्याप्यनुत्तरमिति, तत् सर्वं युक्त्यागमस्वसंवेदननिष्कर्षणतत्त्वावबोधावाप्तविमर्शनिपुणान् शिष्यान् प्रति वितत्य निर्णिनीषुः भगवान् प्रस्तौति ग्रन्थान्तरम्, एतावददृढोपदेशनिर्दलितभेदाभिमानविकल्पानल्पसंस्काराणां तु सर्वमेतावतैव 'अनुत्तरं कथम्' इत्यादिसार्धश्लोकयुगलनिगमितेन प्रश्नेन, 'शृणु देवि' इत्यादिना सार्धश्लोकनिर्णीतेन चोत्तरेण अनुत्तरपदप्राप्तिवशाविष्टजीवन्मुक्तभावानां कृतकृत्यता। अतस्तावन्मात्र एव दृढप्रतिपत्तिपवित्रीकृतैर्विश्रमणीयम्—इत्युद्गुजाः फूत्कुर्मः। तदनुत्तरपरभैरवपदविमलदर्पणान्तर्निविष्टकौलिकपदप्रविविक्तये ग्रन्थान्तरमवतरति, इत्युक्तम् ॥ ४ ॥

तद्यथा

अथाद्यास्तिथयः सर्वे
स्वरा बिन्द्ववसानगाः।

तदन्तः कालयोगेन

सोमसूर्यौ प्रकीर्तितौ ॥ ५ ॥

पृथिव्यादीनि तत्त्वानि

पुरुषान्तानि पञ्चसु ।

क्रमात् कादिषु वर्गेषु

मकारान्तेषु सुव्रते ॥ ६ ॥

वाय्वग्निसलिलेन्द्राणां

धारणानां चतुष्टयम् ।

तदूर्ध्वं शादि विख्यातं

पुरस्ताद् ब्रह्मपञ्चकम् ॥ ७ ॥

अमूला तत्क्रमाज्ज्ञेया

क्षान्ता सृष्टिरुदाहृता ।

सर्वेषामेव मन्त्राणां

विद्यानां च यशस्विनि ॥ ८ ॥

इयं योनिः समाख्याता

सर्वतन्त्रेषु सर्वदा ।

तत्राकुलमनुत्तरमेव कौलिक सृष्टिरूपमिति निर्णीयते। अथ तत्सृष्टिरिति संबन्धः, तदे'वानुत्तर-पदं'—सृष्टिरित्यर्थः। यद्यपि च सृष्टावपि प्राक्तननयेन कालापेक्षि पौर्वापर्यं न स्यात् तथापि उपदेश्योपदेशभावलक्षणो भेदो यावत् स्वात्मनि स्वातन्त्र्यात् परमेश्वरेण भास्यते ताव-त्पौर्वापर्यमपि-इति तदपेक्षया अथ-शब्देनानन्तर्यम्—अनन्तरमकुलमेव सृष्टिरूपमिति यावत्। न तु प्रश्नप्रतिज्ञाभ्यामानन्तर्यमथ-शब्देनोक्तम्—एकप्रघट्टकगत-

सजातीयप्रमेयापेक्षक्रमतात्पर्यंप्रतीतिप्रवणत्वादस्य। अन्यथा तूष्णींभावादे-रनन्तरमिदम्, इत्यपि सर्वत्र तत्प्रयोगावकाशः। अस्तु—क इव अत्र भवतः क्लेशः? इति चेत्—न कश्चित्—ऋते प्रतीत्यभावात्। यत्तु श्रीसोमानन्दपादाः

'अकारः शिव इत्युक्तस्थकारः शक्तिरुच्यते।'

इत्यागमप्रदर्शनेन अथ इत्येतावदेवानुत्तरम् इति व्याचचक्षिरे, थकार-हकारसमव्याप्तिकताभिप्रायेण सर्वत्र प्रथमोल्लासे प्रसरदनन्तानन्तवस्तुसृष्टि-शक्त्यभेदरूपत्वात् सर्वभूतस्थजीवनरूपपरनादावलम्बनरूपत्वाच्च अथ-शब्दार्थस्य। तत् नास्माभिः वितत्य विवेचितम्,—तादृशस्य आगमस्य यतो न साक्षाद्वयमभिज्ञाः। तैस्तु तथा-विधागमसाक्षात्कारिभिरनेकयुक्ति-शतसहिष्णुता सूत्रग्रन्थस्य सूत्रितैवम्। धूलिभेदप्रदर्शनमपि तेनैवाभिप्रायेण तैरितश्च अमुतश्च विततम्। वयं तु तच्छासनपवित्रितास्तद्ग्रन्थग्रन्थिनिर्द-लनाभिलषितस्वात्मपवित्रभावाः तैः निर्णीतेषु एवमादिषु अर्थेषु उदासीता एव। धूलिभेदादिना च कल्पितसामयिकलिप्यपेक्षणमपि भवेदपि कस्यचित् उपायाय, न तु तत्सकलदेशकालगतशिष्यविषयम्—इति नास्माभिः वितत्य विपश्चितम्। एतदनुभवयुक्त्यनुप्रविष्टानां च तदकार्यंकरं, स्वकल्प-नाभिश्च सुकरम्। अन्येषां च एतदुपदेशानभिज्ञानां तदुपदेशनमपि अकिं-चित्करम्, इत्यलमनेन प्रकृतविघ्नविधायिना। प्रस्तुतमनुसरामः—'अ' आद्यो येषां स्वराणाम्। यदि वा थकारेण सुखोच्चारणार्थेन सह अथ् आद्यो येषामिति। आद्य-शब्दश्च अत्र न व्यवस्थामात्रे नापि सामीप्यादौ, अपि तु आदौ भव आद्यः, तथाहि अमीषां वर्णानां परावाग्भूमिरियमिह निर्णीयते, यत्रैव एषामसामयिकं नित्यमकृत्रिमं संविन्मयमेव रूपम्। संविन्मये च वपुषि सर्वसर्वात्मकता सततोदितैव। सा च परमेश्वरी पराभट्टारिका तथाविधनिरतिशयाभेदभागिन्यपि पश्यन्त्यादिकाः परापराभट्टारिकादि स्फाररूपा अन्तःकृत्य तत्तदनन्तवैचित्र्यगर्भमयी, नहि 'तत्र यन्नास्ति तत् क्वाप्यस्ति' इति न्याय्यम्, परामृशति च प्रथमां प्रतिभाभिधां संकोच-

कलङ्ककालुष्यलेशशून्यां भगवतीं संविदम् । तथाहि—यत्किंचित् चरमचरं च तत् पारमार्थिकेन अनपायिना रूपेण वीर्यमात्रसारात्मना तदुद्भविष्य-दीषदस्फुटतमेषदस्फुटतरेषदस्फुटादिवस्तुशतसृष्टिकालोपलक्ष्यमाणतत्तदनन्त-वैचित्र्यप्रथोन्नीयमानतथाभावेन संविदि भगवद्भैरवभट्टारकात्मनि तिष्ठत्येव । तथावधानातिशयरूढैः सहसैव सर्वज्ञताभूमिरसंकुचितपरमार्था अकृत्रिम-तद्रूपा अधिशय्यते एव, परानुग्रहपवित्रितैरभ्यासक्रमशाणनिघर्षनिष्पेषित-तदप्रत्ययरूपकम्पाद्यनन्तापरपर्यायविचिकित्सामलैः सविचिकित्सैरपि प्रति-भात-कियन्मात्रवस्तुसत्यतावलोकनेन कियन्मात्रदत्तसंकोचा—न त्वकृत्रिमा । यदाहुः श्रीकल्लटपादाः

'तुटिपाते सर्वज्ञत्वसर्वकर्तृत्वलाभः ।'

इति । एवमेष स्वप्रकाशैकरूपोऽपि अर्थो युक्त्या प्रदर्श्यते—यत् यत् स्वसामर्थ्योद्भूतोत्तरकालिकार्थक्रियायोग्यतादिवशनिःशेष्यमाणसत्यतावशा-वाप्ताविचलसंवादं विरोधावभासिसंमतक्रमिकविकल्प्यमाननीलादिनिष्ठ-विकल्पपूर्वभावि निर्विकल्पसंविद्रूपं तत्तद्विकल्पनीयविरुद्धाभिमतनीलपीता-द्याभासाविभागि भवति, यथा चित्रज्ञानशिखरस्थसंविन्मेचकबोधादि, यत्तु तद्विरुद्धरूपनीलपीताद्याभासाविभक्तं न भवति तत्तदनन्तस्वसामर्थ्योद्भूत-नीलपीताद्याभासविकल्पपूर्वभाग्यपि न भवति, यथा नीलैकसाक्षात्कारि ज्ञानम् । भवति च इदमस्तमितोदेष्यदुभयविकल्पज्ञानान्तरालवर्ति उन्मेष-प्रतिभादि शब्दागमगीतं निर्विकल्पकं ससंवादविरुद्धाभिमतनीलादिविकल्प-पूर्वभावि । तस्मात्तदनन्तावभासाविभागमयमेवेति उभयोश्च ज्ञानयोरन्त-रालमनपह्नवनीयं—ज्ञानयोर्भेदादेव, तच्च संविदात्मकमेव, अन्यथा तेनैव संवित्संस्कारोच्छेदे स्मरणाद्यनुसंधानाद्ययोग इति प्रतिभास्यस्य धर्मिणः सर्ववादिनः प्रति अविवाद एव इति न असिद्धिः, संकेतव्युत्पत्तिकालानव-लम्बनात् च अस्य अविकल्पत्वमेव सहजासामयिकतयापरामर्शयोगे हि जडविलक्षणसंविद्रूपनान्तरीयकस्य न विकल्पतुल्यत्वं—भेदानुल्लासात्, भेदसारतालब्धतया तु अर्थभावं कुर्यात्, विकल्पानां च अविकल्पं विना

नोदयः, अस्वातन्त्र्यात् । स्वातन्त्र्यं च संकेतादिस्मरणोपायत्वात्, संकेतादिस्मरणं च तथा अनुभवं विना कुतः, संविदश्च प्राङ्न्यायेन कालादिपरिच्छेदाभावः, इति एकैव सा पारमेश्वरी प्रतिभा अस्मदुक्तिमाहात्म्यकल्पिता एवंविधा अपरिच्छिन्नस्वभावा सर्वात्मैव । मध्येऽपि वर्तमानभूतभविष्यद्रूपविकल्पान्तरप्रसवभूरेव, तथा च विवेककुशलैरालयविज्ञानमेवमेवोपगतम् । ससंवादत्वं च तदनन्तरभाविनां विकल्पानां दर्शितमेव इति नासिद्धो हेतुः साध्यधर्मिणि, न च एकावभासिविकल्पसंविभागकारिणि अविकल्पकेऽविपक्षे सदा वा कदाचिदपि वा वर्तते, न च ततोऽस्य व्यावृत्तिः संदिग्धा—इति न विरुद्धो नानैकान्तिको न संदिग्धविपक्षव्यावृत्तिः । दृष्टान्तधर्मिणि अपि चित्रज्ञानादौ हेतोरेवमेवासिद्धतादिदोषाः परिहृता भवन्त्येव । हेतुदोषेषु तु परिहृतेषु दृष्टान्तादिदोषा निरवकाशा एव । इत्यादि बहु निर्णीतकल्पमपरैरेव, इति किं तदनुभाषणक्लेशेन । सिद्धं तावद् ह्येतत्

यत्प्रातिभं निखिलवैषयिकावबोध-
पूर्वापरान्तरचरं निखिलात्मकं तत् ।
तस्यां प्रलीनवपुषः परशक्तिभासि
ग्लानिर्घटेत किमभाववशोपक्लृप्ता ॥
शरीरप्राणादौ परघनसुखास्वादपटल-
मनालोक्य स्वस्मिन्स्पृशति हृदये ग्लानिमसमाम् ।
प्रविष्टा चेदन्तर्निखिलजगतीसूतिसरसा
परा देवी हन्त प्रविलसति पूर्णाहुतिरिव ॥

तदुक्तं स्पन्दे

'ग्लानिर्विलुण्ठिका देहे तस्याश्चाज्ञानतः सृतिः ।
तदुन्मेषविलुप्तं चेत्कुतः सा स्यादहेतुका ॥' (स्प. का. ३।८)

इति ।

'एकचिन्ताप्रसक्तस्य यतः स्यादपरोदयः ।
उन्मेषः स तु विज्ञेयः स्वयं तमुपलक्षयेत् ॥' (स्प. का. ३।९)

इति च।

मायीयकार्ममलमूलमुशन्ति तावद्
अज्ञाननाममलमाणवमेव भद्राः।
बीजं तदेव भवजीर्णतरोः परस्मिन्
संविन्निशातदहने दहते क्षणेन॥

यथाहुः

'मलमज्ञानमिच्छन्ति संसाराङ्कुरकारणम्।' (मा. वि. १।२३)

इति।

'तदुन्मेषविलुप्तं चेत्...'

इति। एवमेव च व्याख्यातम्, अतोऽन्यथा, ग्लानेः विलोपकत्वमस्याश्च अज्ञानात् सरणम्, अज्ञानस्य च उन्मेषेण विलोपः—इति किं केन संश्लिष्टम्, इति नृपनिरूपणप्रायमेव भवेत्

सइवरिउण्णपमरुउत्ताण
उतहुगहिअबुणभज्जिअणिज्जइ।
अजाणिअविहडइअक्षाण
उजम्पुसुअच्छइपूरिअकज्ज॥

तदेवं भगवती परावाग्भूमिः गर्भीकृतस्वस्वातन्त्र्यसत्तोद्भविष्यत्पश्यन्त्यादि-विनिविष्टपरापराभट्टारिकादिप्रसरा तद्गर्भीकारवशाविवादघटितसकल-भूतभुवनभावादिप्रपञ्चप्रबोधैक्यचमत्कारसारा परमेश्वरभैरवभट्टारकाबि-र्भावप्रथिततथाविधाद्भुतभूतपरमार्थस्वरूपा स्वात्मविमलदर्पणनिर्भागिता-नन्तसृष्टिस्थितिसंहारैक्यमयमहासृष्टिशक्तिरादि-क्षान्तरूपा 'अथाद्या' इत्या-दिना ग्रन्थेन निःशेषं भगवता निर्णीयते, इति स्थितम्। तदेवं स्थिते ग्रन्थार्थो निर्णीयते—अकारादि-विसर्गान्तं शिवतत्त्वं, कादि-ङान्तं धरादि-नभोऽन्तं भूतपञ्चकं, चादि-ञान्तं गन्धादि-शब्दान्तं तन्मात्रपञ्चकं, टादि-णान्तं पादादि-वागन्तं कर्माक्षपञ्चकं, तादि-नान्तं घ्राणादि-श्रोत्रान्तं बुद्धि-

करणपञ्चकं, पादि-मान्तं मनोऽहंकार-बुद्धि प्रकृति-पुरुषाख्यं पञ्चकं, वाय्वादि-शब्दवाच्या यादयो वकारान्ता राग-विद्या-कला-मायाख्यानि तत्त्वानि, धारयन्ति—पृथग्भूततया अभिमानयन्ति इति धारणानि, द्वौ अत्र णिचौ प्रयोज्यप्रयोजकभावद्वैरूप्यात्, तथा हि—ध्रियन्ते स्वात्मनि एव सर्वे भावाः प्रकाशात्मनि परमपरिपूर्णे पदे भैरवात्मनि सर्वात्मनि, यथोक्तं शिवदृष्टौ

'आत्मैव सर्वभावेषु स्फुरन्निर्वृतचिद्वपुः ।

अनिरुद्धेच्छाप्रसरः प्रसरद्दृक्क्रियः शिवः ॥' (शि. दृ. १।२)

इति । यथोक्तं स्पन्दे

'यत्र स्थितमिदं सर्वं............ ।'

इति । एवं स्वात्मन्येव प्रभास्वरे प्रकाशनेन ध्रियमाणान् भावान् धारयति स्वयमप्रकाशीभावेन—जडतास्वभावेदंभावास्पदताप्रापणेन प्रकाशयति परमेश्वर एव, पुनरपि अहंभावेनैव आच्छादयति । तदियं भगवत्सदाशिवेश-दशा शुद्धविद्यामयी एकेन णिचा ध्वनिता, तत्रापि च यत् इदन्ताया अहन्तया आच्छादनं तदाच्छादनीयेदन्तोपपत्तौ उपपद्यते, न च शुद्धपरमे-श्वरचिन्मयरूपापेक्षं भिन्नप्रथात्मकमिदन्ताख्यं रूपमुपपद्यते—इति आच्छा-दनीयानुपपत्तौ तद्वशेन तदाच्छादकतापि अहंभावस्य नोपपन्ना, इति तथाविधेश्वरबोधानुपपत्तिः, तदनुपपत्तौ च न किंचित् भासेत—कारणा-भावात्, इत्युक्तमसकृत् । भासते च इदम् । तद्भासाव्यतिरेकरहितमपि परमेश्वरशक्तित एव बहिः प्रथते—कारणान्तरासंभवात् । स्वसंविदि च संविद एव सर्वमयत्वप्रथनात् । तदेवं स्वात्मरूपं जगत् भेदेन भासमानं प्रकाशात्मन्येव अहमात्मनि भासते सामानाधिकरण्येन । इति इयता एता-वत् अवश्यमेवाक्षिप्तं—यद् ईश्वर एव कस्यापि वेदितुर्भिन्नान् वेद्यान् अहन्तया पश्यति । यश्चासौ कोऽपि भासनात् स्वात्ममय एव—इति स्वात्मनि तथाविधाः शक्तीरधिशेते याभिरसौ तदेव भिन्नवेद्यवेदकीभावमुपाश्नुवीत । रागादिभिरेव च तथाविधत्वमस्येति रागादय एव आध्रियमाणान् भावान्

उक्तन्यायेन धारयन्तमीश्वरं प्रति प्रयोजकतां गच्छन्ति, अतस्तस्यैव पुंस्त्वव्यपदेशकारणैकभूता द्वितीये णिचि उत्पन्ने, धारणशब्दवाच्याः, णिजुत्पत्तावपि सर्वत्रैव प्रकृत्यर्थान्वियानपायो—ध्रियमाणतया प्रकाशमानस्यैव हि धार्यमाणता—प्रकाशनासंज्ञा उपपद्यते। यथोक्तं मयैव शिवदृष्ट्यालोचने

'प्रेर्योऽपि स भवेद्यस्य शक्तता नाम विद्यते।'

इति। भर्तृहरिरपि

'अप्रवृत्तस्य हि प्रैषे प्रच्छादेर्लोड्विधीयते।
प्रवृत्तस्य यदा प्रैषस्तदा स विषयो णिचः॥

इति। तदेवं धारणशब्देनापरशास्त्रेषु कञ्चुकनामधेयप्रसिद्धान्येव तत्त्वानि इह निरूपितानि, यदुक्तं श्रीतन्त्रसारे

'धारयन्ति पशोः पाशान्भावान्स्वात्ममयांस्तथा।
विद्यामायानियत्याद्याः शोध्यास्तेन प्रयत्नतः॥'

इति। यत्तु श्रीसोमानन्दपादैः धारणशब्देन अङ्गानि निरूपितानि पक्षान्तराश्रयणेन, तत्र परपक्षसर्वंदृश्यत्वप्रथनमात्मनि अभिप्रायः, तेषां हि ईदृशी शैली

'स्वपक्षान्परपक्षांश्च निःशेषेण न वेद यः।
स्वयं स संशयाम्भोधौ निमज्जंस्तारयेत्कथम्॥'

इति। शादि-क्षान्तं महामायाविद्येश्वरसदाशिवशक्त्याख्यं तत्त्वपञ्चकम्। तथाहि- मायातत्त्वस्य उपरि विद्यातत्त्वाधश्च अवश्यं तत्त्वान्तरेण भवितव्यम्—यत्र विज्ञानाकलानां स्थितिः। यथोक्तम्

'मायोर्ध्वे शुद्धविद्याधः सन्ति विज्ञानकेवलाः।'

इति। तथाहि महामायाभावे मायापदे प्रलयकेवलानामवस्थितिः, विद्यापदे च विद्येश्वरादीनाम्—इति किमिव तत् विज्ञानकेवलास्पदं स्यात्, अत एव विद्यापदप्रच्युतानामपि एषां भेदमयभावराशिगतभिन्नवेद्यप्रथानुदयात्

मायीयाभिधानमलानुल्लासे, "तत्र विज्ञानकेवलो मलैकयुक्तः" (मा. वि. १।२२,२३) इति अज्ञानात्मकाणवमलावलम्बित्वं श्रीपूर्वशास्त्रे कथितम्। त एव शुद्धविद्यापदानुग्रहात् बोधिता मन्त्रतदीशादिभावभागिनो भवन्ति इति। तत्रैवोक्तं

'विज्ञानकेवलानष्टौ बोधयामास पुद्गलान्।'

इत्यादिना,

'मन्त्रमहेश्वरेशत्वे संनियोज्य ततः पुनः।

मन्त्राणामसृजत्तद्वत्सप्तकोटीः समण्डलाः॥' (मा. वि. १।२१)

इत्यादिना च। केषुचित्तु शास्त्रेषु सा महामाया भेदमलाभावोपचारात् विद्यातत्त्वशेषतयैव निर्णीयते, क्वचित् पुनरज्ञानमलसद्भावोपरोधात् मायातत्त्वपुच्छतया। यथा केषुचित् शास्त्रेषु 'रागतत्त्वं पुंस्येव लग्नम्' इति न पृथक् परामृष्टम्। यथा वा इहैव श्रीत्रिकागमेषु नियतिकालौ न पृथक् निरूपितौ। अत्र मते विद्याद्यनाश्रितशिवान्तं ब्रह्मपञ्चकम्। निर्णेष्यते च एतत्। एषां च तत्त्वानां बृंहकत्वं च प्रायो भेदसमुत्तीर्णत्वात् संसारसूतिकर्तृत्वात् च। एवमेतानि चतुस्त्रिंशत्तत्त्वानि प्रक्रियात्मना स्थितानि अकारमेव आदिरूपतया भजन्ते। तत्र इदं विचार्यते—प्रथमतः शिवतत्त्वम् 'अ' वर्गे, ततो भूतानि इत्यादि यावदन्ते शक्तितत्त्वम्—इति कोऽयं सृष्टिसंहारस्थित्यवतारक्रमाणां मध्यात् क्रमः, सर्वत्र च श्रीमालिनीविजयोत्तर-सिद्धातन्त्र-स्वच्छन्दादिशास्त्रेषु क्षकारात् प्रभृति अवर्गान्तं पार्थिवादीनां शिवान्तानां तत्त्वानां निवेश उक्तः

'आद्यधारिक । ऽधास्तं तत्रैकं तत्त्वमिष्यते।

एकमेकं पृथक् क्षार्णं पदार्णमनुषु स्मरेत्॥' (मा. वि. २।५०)

इत्यादिना, तत्रैव च पुनर्भिन्नयोनिमालिनीभट्टारिकानुसारेण फकारादीनां मभिन्नयोनिमातृकानिवेशावाप्ततत्त्वान्तरस्थितीनामपि

'फे धरातत्त्वमुद्दिष्टं दादिझान्तेऽनुपूर्वशः।

त्रयोविंशत्यबादीनि प्रधानान्तानि लक्षयेत्'॥ (मा. वि. ४।१५)

इत्यादिना पार्थिवादितत्त्वयोजना निरूपिता। पुनरपि च तत्रैव श्रीविद्यात्रयानुसारेण

'निष्कले पदमेकार्णं त्र्यर्णेकार्णद्वयं द्वये।' (मा. वि. ४।१९)

इति परापराभट्टारिकानुसारेण, ओंकारं शिवतत्त्वम् अघोरे इत्यत्र शक्तितत्त्वम् इत्यादिक्रमेण तत्त्वयोजना। श्रीमदपराभट्टारिकाभिप्रायेण च

'सार्धेनाण्डद्वयं व्याप्तमेकैकेन पृथग्द्वयम्।
अपरायाः समाख्याता व्याप्तिरेषा विलोमतः॥' (मा.वि. ४।२४)

इत्यादिना फट्कारे पार्थिवप्राकृताण्डद्वयम्, हुंकारे मायीयं, ह्रींकारे शाक्तमण्डं च इति तत्त्वनिवेशः। श्रीपराभट्टारिकाव्याप्तिनिरूपणे च

'सार्णेन त्रितयं व्याप्तं त्रिशूलेन चतुर्थकम्।
सर्वातीतं विसर्गेण परा व्याप्तिरुदाहृता॥' (मा.वि. ४।२५)

इति अन्यथैव प्रक्रियायोजनं निरूपितम्। पुनरपि मातृकासद्भावरतिशेखरकुलेश्वरादिमन्त्रभट्टारकाद्यभिप्रायेण अन्यथा अन्यथा च, अपरतन्त्रेष्वपि एवमेव विपर्यस्तप्रायं बहु बहुशो निरूपितम्, तत् पुनरिह सर्वमेवान्यथा इति परिदृश्यते—इति महानयम् आगमविदः स्वकटकक्षोभ इव सर्वविनाशकः समुद्भूतः। न च सांकेतिकमिदं येन पुरुषेच्छावशोपकल्पितेन रूपेण च अन्यथा अन्यथा निरूप्यमाणमिह संगतं भवेत्, यथा—दाक्षिणात्याः चोरशब्देन ओदनं व्यपदिशन्ति, सैन्धवास्तु तेनैव दस्युम्, ओदनं तु क्रूरश्रुत्या, तया तु काश्मीरिका वितुषितयवगोधूमतण्डुलान्, इति—सांकेतिकत्वे हि अनवस्थितत्वात् अपारमार्थिकत्वात् च शोध्यशोधकभावाद्यनुपयोगात् अनिरूपणीयत्वमेव स्यात्। संकेतस्यापि परमार्थसत्त्वेव, नहि संकेतो नाम अन्यः कश्चित्—ऋते परमेश्वरेच्छातः, प्रसिद्धो हि संकेतो भगवदिच्छाप्रकल्पितः, तन्नामाक्षरलिप्यादिगताप्यायनादिकर्मविधिजनितच्छान्तिकादिफलसंपत्तेः, इति चेत्—तर्हि एकेनैव संकेतेन सर्ववस्तुसंपत्तौ किं संकेतान्तराश्रयेण। तदाश्रयणे वा स्वशास्त्रितशास्त्रा-

न्तरीयलौकिकपार्षददैशिकगणकृतप्रतिपुरुषनियताद्यनन्तसंकेतनिवेशनपूर्वकं, तदपि निरूप्यमेव। न तावद्भिरुपयोगः, एतावतैव कार्यसिद्धिः—इत्यपि निरक्षरकुक्षिकुहरैः उच्यमानं श्रूयमाणं च शोभत एव। अविकला भगवदिच्छा न विचारपदवीमधिशेते ? इति चेत्—अलं ग्रन्थधारणवाचनव्याख्यानविचारणादिमिथ्यायासेन। परित्याज्य एवायं गुरुभारः। तूष्णींभावशरणैरेव स्थेयम्, भगवदिच्छैवोत्तारणीयमुत्तारयेत्, तदिच्छैव अनुग्रहात्मा एवं विचारणायां पर्यवसाययति। न खलु पादप्रसारिकयैव सुखं शयानैः भुञ्जानैश्च स्वयम् अविमृशद्भिः स्वापेक्षतीव्रतरादिपरमेश्वरानुग्रहोत्पन्नाधिकाधिकसूक्ष्मतमविमर्शकुशलधिषणापरिशीलनपराङ्मुखैः वा स्थातव्यमिति। तत् सर्वथा विमृश्यमिदं वर्तते—इति एतावत् न जहीमः। तत् अत्र अवधार्यं स्थीयतां यावत् परिहरामः। सर्वमिदं-किंचित् न-वस्तुतः चोद्यजातं परमेश्वर्यां परावाग्भुवि अनुत्तरदुर्घटकारितात्मकनिरपेक्षस्वातन्त्र्यसारायां पारतन्त्र्यांशलेशमात्रपरमाणुनापि अनुपरक्तायाम्—इति प्रायः प्रागेव प्रतिसमाहितमदः, तथापि विस्तरतः परिह्रियते—यत् तावदुक्तं शिवतत्त्वं, ततः पृथिवी इत्यादि कोऽयं क्रम इति, तन्न कश्चित् क्रमः—इति ब्रूमः, अक्रमं यत् एतत् परं पारमेश्वरं विचित्रं गर्भीकृतानन्तवैचित्र्यं स्वातन्त्र्यं त्रिकार्थरूपं तदेव एतत्, तथाहि—येयमपरा परापरा पराभट्टारिका पारमेश्वरी भैरवीया सत्ता, सा सदाशिवतत्त्वानाश्रितशिवतत्त्वस्यापि उपरिवृत्तिः—तदन्तस्यापि आसनपक्षीकृतत्वात्। तथाहि

'ईश्वरं च महाप्रेतं प्रहसन्तं सचेतनम्।' (मा. वि ८।६८)

इत्यनेन सदाशिवान्तमासनं नादान्तपक्षनिविष्टं श्रीपूर्वशास्त्रोपसंहृतम्,

'इत्येवं सर्वमासनम्'। (मा. वि. ८।६८)

इत्युक्त्वा।

'तस्य नाभ्युत्थितं शक्तिशूलशृङ्गत्रयं स्मरेत्' (मा. वि. ८।६९)

इति शक्तिव्यापिनीसमनात्मकशृङ्गत्रयमुक्तम्। तत्रापि उन्मनसोर्ध्वकुण्डलिकापदपरमधामसितकमलत्रयरूपतया निरूपितम्, इत्येतत् परमासनं—

परापर्यन्तत्वात् इति, तदुपरि च देवीनां स्थितिः इति। तदेतत्परं पश्यन्त्याख्यं ज्ञानशक्तेरेव पर्यन्तधाम नादाख्यरूपमतिक्रमणीयत्वेनैव स्थितम्। यथोक्तं शिवदृष्टौ

'अथास्माकं ज्ञानशक्तिर्या सदाशिवरूपता।

वैयाकरणसाधूनां सा पश्यन्ती परा स्थितिः॥' (शि. दृ. २।१)

इति।

प्रत्यगात्मनि हि बुद्धिः पश्यन्ती रुद्रदेवता। परं सदाशिवज्ञानशक्तावेव अनाश्रितशिवशक्त्यात्मनि विश्राम्यति। मनोऽहंकारयोः ब्रह्मविष्णुदेवतयोः वैखरीमध्यमापदे पत्योरीशसदाशिवक्रियाशक्तिपदमेव परा प्रतिष्ठाभूः। इति तावत् आगमसिद्धं स्वसंवेदनबृंहितं च। तत् पश्यन्त्युपरि पराभूमिः भगवती—यत्र सर्वमभेदेनैव भाति च विमृश्यते च। यद्यपि हि विद्यापदे मायापदेऽपि अभेदेन भासना स्थितापि तत्र विमर्शोऽन्यथा, विद्यापदे हि इदमिति प्रमातृप्रमेयजातमेकतोऽहमात्मनि संक्रामेत्, तदाच्छादितं विमृश्यते—'अहमिदम्' इति, तत् एतत् समाने चिदात्मनि अधिकरणे उभयं प्रतिबिम्बितमभेदेनैव अवभासमानं सामानाधिकरण्यमुक्तम्। अत एव ईश्वरावस्थायां परापरात्मिकां दशां भावा भजन्ते, तथैव मायाध्वनि अपराम्। न तु सैव परापराशक्तिः अपरा वेति। अत एव यत् ईश्वरतत्त्वं प्रति अभिहितं श्रीमदुत्पलदेवपादैः, तत् प्रदर्शितागमविपर्यासशङ्कायुक्तम्— इति न मन्तव्यम्, मन्त्रमहेशादिषु तु रूपं बोधैकपरमार्थमपि अपरबोधैक-परमार्थात् 'अन्यदहम्'। 'इदं पुनरिदमेव' इति संवित्, विज्ञानाकलानां तु बोधैकपरमार्थेनापि रूपेण 'अहं' नेदम् इति संवित्। अप्रबोधात् 'अह-मित्येव' तत्र अप्रबुद्धम्, प्रलयकेवलिनाम् 'इदमहम्' इत्यप्रबुद्धमेव, अत्र मायापदे च तन्निर्विकल्पकताभासेन यद्यपि अस्ति तथाविध एव प्राणभूतो विमर्शः, तथापि तद्रूपव्यवहारकस्य तत्प्रसादासादितसत्ताकस्यापि तदव्यति-रिक्तस्यापि वा पश्चात्तनस्य विमर्शस्य 'इदं शरीरादि, अहमहं, योऽसौ ज्ञाता, इदं घटादिकम्, इदं यत्तत् ज्ञेयम्' इति भेदेनैव विमर्शरूपतया

व्यवहारो विकल्पात्मैव, तत्र तु तथाविधत्वे कारणान्तरासंवेदनात्कल्प्यमानेऽपि च कारणे पुनरपि तथाविधबोधाविनिर्भागमात्रपर्यवसानात् तस्यैव अविकल्पसंविदात्मनः तथा सामर्थ्यम्। तथा सामर्थ्ययोगादेव च तदनन्तवैचित्र्यात्मकम् ऐश्वर्यमनपायि सिद्ध्येत्। अस्यां च सत्तायामैश्वर्यमनपेतं—यतो वैखर्यात्मनि एवं मायीये वेद्येऽपि वा मध्यमामये धाम्नि भासनातिरेकी न संभाव्य एवं विमर्शः। अत्र तु परसंविदि यथैव भासः तथैव व्यवहारमयोऽपि विमर्शः। तेन—जल इव जलं ज्वालायामिव ज्वाला सर्वथा अभेदमया एव भावा भासन्ते, न तु प्रतिबिम्बकल्पेनापि केवलम्। यावत् एषापि परमेश्वरी उपदेशाय निरूप्यते तावत् अधरसत्ताक्लृप्त्या तथा भवति। एवं च भासात्मकं भैरवरूपं स्वतः सिद्धम् अनादि प्रथमं सर्वतः चरमं च सर्वतश्च वर्तमानमिति किमपरं तत्र उच्यताम्। तत्त्वभावविकासात्ममयमात्मैक्येनैव स्वप्रकाशं प्रकाशयति, तथैव च विमृशति अनपेततथाचमत्कारत्वेऽपि। यच्च तत् तथा विमर्शनं तत् भाविमायीयानन्तसृष्टिसंहारलक्षकोट्यर्बुदपरार्धसाक्षात्कारिणि भासने भवन् तथारूपमेव भवति। तथा भवच्च तत् यदि सृष्टौ प्राथमिकं माध्यमिकं वा पदं भासनात् न विमृशेत् तत् पूर्वस्य तदुत्तरव्यभिचारणाशंकासंभावनानपगमात् अपरिपूर्णप्रथितेतरभावराशिखण्डिताभेदकथम् अनिर्व्यूढपरभैरवमहाधामसमाश्रिताधरस्तनपश्यन्त्यादिनिष्ठभेदासूत्रणात्मकं तथाविधवस्तुपोषणवशनाममात्रीभूतपराभट्टारिकारूपं भवेत्। एतावृशधारारोहणाभावे च न किंचित् इदं विजृम्भमाणं भासेत विजृम्भेत इति। व्रजतु अपूर्णता, प्रतिष्ठितभावराशिरभेदकथा खण्ड्यताम्, मा निर्वाक्षीद्भैरवाश्रयता, भेदकलङ्कमुद्वहतु नामधेयमात्रेण परत्वम्—इति न वक्तुं युक्तम्। तत् एतदेव भवति संगच्छते च, यदि प्रथमतरं सर्वचरमे एवमाभासा पतन्ती तत्रैव विमर्शेनापि पदं बन्धयेत्, स हि चरमो भागः तथा तावत् स्वात्मरूपं बिभ्रत् तत्स्वात्मरूपनान्तरीयकतास्वीकृततदनन्तनिजपूर्वपूर्वतरादिभागान्तरो भासमानो विमृश्यमानश्च पूर्ण एव, तत्पूर्वोऽपि भागः तदुत्तरभागपृष्ठपातिवृत्तपूर्वपरिपूर्णभासासारविमर्श-

तादात्म्यात् तदुत्तररूपपरिपूर्णतामजहत् स्वयं च स्वरूपनान्तरीयकताहठकृष्टस्वपूर्वपूर्वतरादिभागान्तराभोगो भासमानो विमृश्यमानश्च तथैवाखण्डितः—इत्येवं तत्पूर्वपूर्वगतभासा तत्तद्द्वित्रादिनिजनिजोत्तरभागभासाविभागे लब्धभैरवभावस्वभावाव्यभिचारानुरोधबलस्वीकृतस्वस्वपूर्वभागचमत्कार एकैकमपि परं पूर्णं भवति। यावत् स्वप्रकाशनिजभैरवाभिमतनिकटतरवर्ति रूपं, तदेव स्वेच्छाविश्रान्तिधाम वा भैरवाख्यं वपुः, स्वयमेव तद्विमर्शकुशला भवत प्रसंख्यानपराः। ह्रद-गिरि-तरुप्रभृत्युपाधिसंकोचेन रहिते तद्वत्यपि वा अरण्यानीप्रदेशे दूरादखण्डिता दृष्टिरेवमेव अखण्डिततामुपाश्नुवाना भैरवबोधानुप्रवेशं प्रति संप्रदायतामासादयेत्

'निर्वृक्षगिरिभित्त्यादौ देशे दृष्टिं विनिक्षिपेत्।' (वि. भै. ६०)

इत्यादि, अन्यथा भागशः पाते प्रथमभागात् आरभ्य यदि वा सावयवमेव एतत् तर्क इव अपरसंवेदनेभ्योऽपूर्णाभिमतेभ्यो विशेषः। विशेषस्तु गर्भीकृतानन्तवैचित्र्यचमत्कारकृत एव अपूर्णसंविदन्तरेभ्यः पूर्णाभिमतसंवेदनस्य—इति स्वयमेव जानन्तु सोपदेशाः पारमेश्वराः। परमेशशक्तिपातकिरणाविकसिते तु पशुजनहृदयकुशेशये न अस्मदीयैर्वचनशतैरपि अतितीक्ष्णाभिधेयसूचिभिरपि संभेदोऽथ विकासोऽथ वितरीतुं शक्यः, घटेऽपि एवमेव परिपूर्णो दृष्टिपातः, तत्रापि हि अविकल्पा संवित् झगिति चरमभागे एव निपतति, ततस्तु क्रमात् विकल्पसंविद आ चरमनिकटभागात् अन्तरान्तरामन्तस्तमां च अनुप्रविशन्ति, इति किमन्येन। तदेवमेव इहापि शिवतत्त्वं सदा अविकल्पमेव विकल्पसूति स्वातन्त्र्यसरसमनादि सर्वादिभूतं सिद्धम्। अत्र तावत् न विमतिः। तत्तु परिपूर्णं तथा भवति यदि सर्वचरमां पार्थिवीमेव भुवमधिशेते। धरासंवित् हि तथा धरां विषयतयापि अभेदेनाभासयेत् विमृशेत् च यदि तत्स्वरूपं सर्वस्वावभासविमर्शयोः व्याप्रियेत। स्वरूपसतत्त्वं च अस्याः परिपूर्णप्रसरतत्स्वातन्त्र्यक्लृप्तप्ररूढाभेदतत्पूर्वकैकरसभेदावभासतद्वशोदितसंकुचच्चित्स्वातन्त्र्यसत्तामयमायाग्राहकतद्ग्राह्यचक्राविभेदात्मकप्रधानतद्विकारधीतत्त्वतत्परिणामात्मकाहंकार-

तन्मूलकरणपूर्वकतन्मात्रवर्गप्रसूतखादिजलान्तभूतवर्गाधरवृत्तितया अवस्थानं धरायाः। सा हि यावदाक्षेपेणैव वर्तमाना तावत् स्वरूपसतत्त्वैव, यावदेव पञ्चगुणत्वात् तन्मात्राणि आक्षिपेत् तावत् तानि आक्षिप्यमाणानि निजस्वरूपोपक्लृप्तये समाक्षिप्तप्राक्तनप्रातिष्ठिकमूलान्तरपरम्परानुबन्धिस्वकपूर्वकमूलान्येव। नहि 'उपादानाभिमतकारणस्वरूपान्वयः कार्यसत्तायां स्यात्' इति न्याय्यम्, निमित्तकारणादीनि कथंचित् न अन्वीयुरिति उच्येतापि कदाचित्। एतच्च प्रकृतविघातकमन्यत्र तदभिधानप्रवणे शास्त्रे निष्कुष्य निष्कुषितमस्माभिरेव—इति न इह विततम्। तदेवं प्रथमं तावत् धरा। ततोऽपि जलं तथैव स्वरूपसाकल्येन भासमानं विमृश्यमानं च तद्भासा-विमर्शचमत्कारमन्तःकृत्य तथाविधधरणितत्त्वसंस्कारसत्ताकं पूरयेदेव इति यावत्, अन्ते सैव पूर्णसंविद्भगवती शिवात्मैव, तत् अनेनैव उपदेशयुक्तिनयेन 'प्रदेशमात्रमपि ब्रह्मणः सर्वरूपम्। एकैकत्रापि च तत्त्वे षट्त्रिंशत्तत्त्वमयत्वं' शास्त्रेषु निरूपितम्। एवं च श्रीस्पन्दशास्त्रोपदेशो

'दिदृक्षयेव सर्वार्थान्यदा व्याप्यावतिष्ठते।
तदा किं बहुनोक्तेन स्वयमेवावभोत्स्यते॥' (स्प. का. ३।११)

इत्ययं हृदयंगमीकर्तव्यः। चरमेण पादेन तदेवात्र सूचितमिति किमन्यत्। यच्च येन विना न भवति तत् तावत् स्वरूपं यथा शिंशपात्वं वृक्षत्वरूपम्। पारमेशस्वातन्त्र्यतिरोहितनियतिविजृम्भायां यत्तु यस्य स्वरूपं न भवति तत् तेन विना भवत्येव। यथा वृक्षत्वमृते शिंशपात्वापवादो, न भवन्ति च धरादीनि उत्तरोत्तरतत्त्वानि जलादिपूर्वंपूर्वं विना—इति तावत्स्वरूपाण्येव। धरा हि न जलं विना भवेत्—धृतेरेव काठिन्यदर्शनात् इत्येवं क्रमेण भूतानि तन्मात्रैर्विना कथम्। तान्यपि इन्द्रियजृम्भया विना कथम्। इन्द्रियाण्यपि तत्तथाविधाध्यवसायेन विना कथम्। सर्वाणि चैतदाद्याविभक्तान्वितसूक्ष्मरूपमूलकारणविनाकृतानि न भवन्ति। मूलप्रकृतिरपि

भोग्या भोक्तारं विना। तद्भोग्यविभागभागित्वादेव संकुचितं, संकोचवशादेव च स्वात्मारोहितकालकलादि-पाशजालं संविदात्मकं चान्तरेण कथम्। संविदश्चाखण्डरूपायाः कथं संकोचकारणस्वातन्त्र्यं मायापरपर्यायं विना संकुचितत्वं स्वातन्त्र्यं च संकोचकाले असंकुचिततासारतत्संकोचिततारतम्याक्षेपि भवदीषदसंकुचितासंकुचितेषद्विकासिविकस्वररूपं विरहय्य नैव भवेत्। सर्वमेव चेदं प्रथमानं स्वतन्त्रपरिपूर्णप्रथासारभैरवं विना किंचिदेव न—इति स्वसंवित्तिसिद्धोऽयं तत्त्वक्रमः। श्रुतिरपि जलात्मिका काठिन्यं विना क्व इति धरापि सलिल-पूर्विका अस्तु इति कथ्यमानम् अपि किं नश्छेदयेत्। प्रत्युत परिपूर्णसर्वात्मकभैरवभट्टारकात्मकपरासंवित्परिपोषणायैव स्यात्। सर्वश्चायं परापराभट्टारिकादिरूपपश्यन्त्यादिसत्तासमयोद्भविष्यदीषत्स्फुटस्फुटतरादितत्त्वभेदानुसारेण पराभट्टारिकामहसि तदुचितेनैव वपुषा विराजते। भविष्यदपि वस्तु चरममपि प्रथमप्रकाशे भासेतैव केवलमेकरसतद्भेदसारस्फुटरूपापेक्षया भविष्यत्ता। तथाहि—भविष्यति कर्की हनिष्यत्यधर्मपरान्—इत्यादि यदि न प्रकाशितं तत् कथं पुराणेषु निबद्धम्, क्वचन सर्गे बभूव कर्की तथैव व्यधित—इति चेत् किं स एवासावन्य एव वा, अन्यश्चेदप्रकाशोऽसौ, स एव चेत् कथं कालभेदः, अकालकलितश्चेत् कथमिव? चित्त्वाद्विश्वरूपत्वात्—इति चेत् तर्हि अकालकलिते संविदात्मनि सततविश्वशक्त्यवियुक्ते स्वातन्त्र्यवशसंकोचविकासावभासितसंहृतिसृष्टिशताविरुद्धैकरूपतदात्मकवपुषि परमेश्वरेऽस्मज्जिह्वाग्रहृदयानपायिनि भैरवभट्टारके सर्वमस्ति—इत्यस्माभिरुपन्यस्यमानमेव मुक्तमन्दाक्षं कथं नाद्रियते विवृततरकण्ठमेव वा स्वयमेव न निर्णीय निरूप्यते। तस्मात् शिवतत्त्वमिदमनाद्यन्तं स्वयं प्रथमानं पूर्णतात्मकनिरपेक्षतामात्रसतत्त्वस्वातन्त्र्यसारमन्तःक्रोडीकृत्यात्मतैकपरमार्थं तत्त्वजातं अवस्थाशब्दव्यपदेशासहिष्णोत् सर्वाविरोधित्वात् निखिलानुग्राहकत्वाच्च अवस्थाशब्दव्यपदेशासहिष्णो यावदकालकलितमासीनं भैरवरूपमवतिष्ठते, तावदेतच्छास्त्रसमुचितेनैव महासृष्ट्यादिरूपेण न तु मितसृष्ट्यादिक्रमेण—

इति सिद्धम् । स एष एव संपुटयोगे, अस्मद्गुरूणां संप्रदायः—शुद्धपरसत्तया सर्वस्यैव एकैकतत्त्वस्य निखिलस्य च तत्त्वौघस्य संपुटीकरणात् अवतिष्ठते । वक्ष्यते चाप्येतत् 'पश्यन्तीदशायाश्चारभ्य भेदासूत्रणात् पाशांशोल्लासः' इति । ततः प्रभृत्येव शोध्यशोधकभाव इति तावद्व्यवस्थाऽनपह्नवनीया, यथोक्तम्

'यत्सदाशिवपर्यन्तं पार्थिवाद्यं च सुव्रते ।
तत्सर्वं प्राकृतं ज्ञेयं विनाशोत्पत्तिसंयुतम् ॥' (स्व. ५।५४८)

इत्यादि । पश्यन्ती च परापराभट्टारिकासतत्त्वा परशक्तेरेव स्वात्मशक्तिदर्पणकल्पा, यत्र तत्पराभट्टारिकास्वरूपमेव चकास्ति—प्रतिबिम्बवत् । यच्च रूपं सदा बिम्बे प्रतिबिम्बे चैकतापरमार्थं मुखपरामर्शमात्रमिव न तत्प्रतिबिम्बितमुच्यते—तन्मात्रसतत्त्वादेव । यत्तु तत्रान्यथा तथा च भाति मुखाकार इव पूर्वापरवामदक्षिणतादिविपर्ययात् एतदेवापि तदेवापि, तदेव प्रतिबिम्बितमुच्यते । तच्च तत्समानधर्मैव भवति, न तु विजातीयम्, एवं च पश्यन्तीसतत्त्वपरापराविमलमुकुरिकायां तत्तत्तथाविधोक्तक्रमम् अपूर्णपृथिव्यादितत्त्वसामग्रीनिर्भरम्, अन्तस्तथाविधसहजाकृत्रिमपारमार्थिकानपायिकादिपरामर्शक्रोडीकारेणैव वर्तमानमपि श्रीपराभट्टारिकावपुः प्रतिबिम्बमर्पयत् स्वरूपान्यथात्वसहिष्णुकादिपरामर्शानन्यथाभावेनैव प्रकटयति । तत्परैकरूपं परामृश्यं धरण्यम्भःप्रभृति तथोल्लसद्भेदसूत्रणया सजातीयायां विमलायां च यावत्प्रतिबिम्बयति तावद्धरादितत्त्वानां विपर्यास एवोपजायते । यत् परसंविदि शक्तितत्त्वं तदेव परापरात्मनि पृथिवीतत्त्वं, यत्तु धरातत्त्वं तच्छक्तितत्त्वम्, इति क्षकारात् प्रभृति धरादीनां स्थितिः । भगवद्भैरवभट्टारकस्तु सदापूर्णोऽनन्तस्वतन्त्र एव न विपर्यस्यते जातुचिदपि—चिद्रूपातिरेकाद्यभावात् इति उक्तं बहुशः । परात्मनि परामर्शे परामर्शैकतत्त्वान्येव तत्त्वानि, परामर्शश्च कादि-क्षान्तशाक्तरूपपरमार्थ इति । तत्र अभेद एव । परापरायां तु भेदस्य

अभेदात्मकता प्रतिबिम्बन्यायेन। सा च परापरामर्शमयी कादि-क्षान्तवर्ण-मालाशरीरा यावत्स्वोर्ध्वव्यवस्थितपराभट्टारिकानिविष्टतत्त्वप्रतिबिम्बानि धारयति तावत् तेष्वेवामायीयाश्रौतकादि-क्षान्तपरमार्थपरामर्शेषु ऊर्ध्वाधर-विपर्यासेन तत्त्वानि संपद्यन्ते। ऊर्ध्वबिम्बाधरप्रतिबिम्बधामस्वभाव-महिम्ना—इति तात्पर्यम्, ततः पृथिवी 'क्षकार' इत्यादिशोध्यरूपापेक्षया न किंचिद्विरुद्धम्। तत्रापि परदशानपायात् एष एव कादिवर्णसंतानः। तत्रैव च स्वांशोद्रेकात् स्वांशान्तर्वर्तिमध्यमापदोल्लासात् स्वरूपवर्तमान-वैखरीरूपप्रावण्याच्च वर्ण-मन्त्रपदरूपता शोध्यांशवृत्तिः—इत्यास्ताम् अप्र-कृतमेतत्। निर्णीतं च मयैव श्रीपूर्वप्रभृतिपञ्चिकासु। यदप्युक्तं श्रीमालिनी-भट्टारिकानुसारेण 'अन्यथा चान्यथा स्थितिः' इति, तदपि निर्णीय निरूप्यमाणं विमृशन्तु त्रिकोपदेशविशीर्णाज्ञानग्रन्थयः पारमेश्वराः। अनाश्रितशक्त्यात्मकपश्यन्तीपरमकोटिमतिक्रम्य 'पारमेश्वर्यां परसंविदि देवतास्तिस्र' इति यदुक्तं तत् तावन्न विस्मर्तुमर्हन्ति तत्रभवन्तः। एवं च परसंविदन्तर्वर्तिनि मध्यमापदे परापराभट्टारिकाविजृम्भास्पदे स्थिति-र्विमृश्यते, मध्यमा तावत्स्वाधिकारपदे क्रियाशक्त्यात्मनि ऐश्वरे पदे स्फुटवेद्यप्रच्छादकवेदनरूपा वाच्ये वाचकं तत्रापि वाच्यमध्यस्यते। विश्वत्र वाच्ये विश्वात्मनि वाचकमपि यदि विश्वात्मैव तदेवं परम्परा-च्छादनलोलीभावात्मा निर्वहेत् अध्यासः, न त्वन्यथा। न हि त्रिचतुरङ्गुल-न्यूनतामात्रेऽपि पटः पटान्तराच्छादकः स्यात्। विश्वात्मकत्वं च परस्परस्वरूपव्यामिश्रतया स्यात्, बीजात्मनां स्वराणां वाचकत्वं योनि-रूपाणां च व्यञ्जनानां वाच्यत्वं—क्रमेण शिवशक्त्यात्मकत्वात्

'बीजमत्र शिवः शक्तिर्योनिरित्यभिधीयते।' (मा. वि. ३।१२)

इति। तथा

'बीजयोन्यात्मकाद्भेदाद् द्विधा बीजं स्वरा मताः।
कादिभिश्च स्मृता योनिः ·················· ॥' (मा.वि. ३।१०-११,

इति श्रीपूर्वशास्त्रनिरूपणात् शिव एव हि प्रमातृभावमत्यजन् वाचकः स्यात्, प्रमेयांशावगाहिनी शक्तिरेव वाच्या। भेदेऽपि हि वाचकः प्रतिपाद्य-प्रतिपादकोभयरूपप्रमातृस्वरूपाविच्छिन्न एव प्रथते। शिवात्मकस्वर-बीजरूपा श्यानतेव शाक्तव्यञ्जनयोनिभावो—बीजादेव योनेः प्रसरणात्, इति—समनन्तरमेव निर्णेष्यामः, अत एव स्वरात्मकबीजव्यामिश्रीभावश्चे-द्योनेः तत्समस्तफलप्रसवो हन्त निर्यत्नः—इत्यपवर्गभोगावकृष्टपच्यावेव भवतः। बीजवर्णोऽपि स्वात्मनि योनिवर्णोऽपि तथैव—इति किं कस्य भेदकम्—इति कथ्यमानं नास्मानाकुलयेत्, ये वयमेकां तावदनन्तचित्रता-गर्भिणीं तां संविदात्मिकां गिरं संगिरामहे। मायीयेऽपि व्यवहारपदे लौकिकक्रमिकवर्णपदस्फुटतामयी एकपरामर्शस्वभावैव प्रत्यवमर्शकारिणी प्रकाशरूपा वाक्। अन्यैश्च एतत्प्रयत्नसाधितम्। इह च एतावदुपदेश-धाराधिशयनशालिनामप्रयत्नत एव सिद्ध्यति इति नास्माभिरत्र वृथा वैयाकरणगुरुगृहगमनपूतशरीरताविष्क्रियामात्रफले निर्बन्धो विहितः, एव-मेव नवात्मपिण्डप्रभृतिष्वपि मालामन्त्रेष्वपि च क्रमाक्रमपूर्वापरादिभेद-चोद्यप्रतिवादनं सिद्धमेव। एवं भगवती मालिन्येव मुख्यपारमार्थिकमध्यम-धामशक्तिसतत्त्वम्, अत एवोक्तं श्रीपूर्वशास्त्रे

> यथेष्टफलसंसिद्ध्यै मन्त्रतन्त्रानुवर्तिनाम्।
> न्यसेच्छाक्तशरीरार्थं भिन्नयोनिं तु मालिनीम्॥ (मा. वि. ३।३५-३६)

इति। भिन्नयोनित्वं च निर्णीतम्, अन्यत्रापि

> 'न पुंसि न परे तत्त्वे शक्तौ मन्त्रं निवेशयेत्।
> जडत्वान्निष्क्रियत्वाच्च न ते भोगापवर्गदाः॥'

इति। एवं च स्थिते सर्वसर्वात्मकत्वात् यदेव 'न ऋ ॠ ऌ ॡ थ च ध ई ण उ ऊ ब क ख ग' इत्यभिहितम् इहत्यपरसंविदमपेक्ष्य क्रमेण—

(अ)

(१) श्रोत्रं नादात्मकभावरूपं योन्यात्म

(२) अमृताप्यायकारि-बीजचतुष्काप्यायभूमौ पतितं बृंहितत्वमवाप्य

(३) झटिति ग्रहणात्मकरसतत्त्व-रसनामयत्वं प्रतिपद्य

(४) धरण्याकार-गन्धविशेषीभूय

(५) तत्रैव स्पर्शकरणतां श्रित्वा

(६) एतावच्च शाक्तं यौनं धाम ईशानबीजेन अधिष्ठाय

(७) वागात्मनि करणशक्तौ प्रतिफलितम्

(८) ततोऽपि करणशक्तेर् उन्मेष-ऊर्ध्वाश्रयण-बीजरूपतया बुद्धिरूपां शाक्त-योनिम् अधिशय्य

(९) पृथिवी-अप्-तेजोयोनिसमाविष्टं (शिवतत्त्वम् अत्रोक्तं भवति) ।

(आ)

पश्यन्तीरूपानुसृत्या तु—

(१) (श्रोत्रं) ग्रहणात्मक-वाग्-रूपं तत्रैव बीजेषु प्रसृत्य,

(२) चाक्षुष्यां भुवि;

(३) तत्सामान्या शुद्धविद्याकरणे;

(४) तत्सर्वान्त्यकरणे घ्राणे च स्थित्वा,

(५) ईशानबीजेनाक्रम्य,

(६) श्रोत्रशक्तिम् अवलम्ब्य,

(७) उन्मेष-ऊर्ध्वबीजयोगेन आनन्देन्द्रिययोनिगं;

(८) सदाशिव-ईश्वर-शुद्धविद्यामयं भवति,

इति सर्वाग्र-मध्य-अन्तगामित्वेन अपरिच्छिन्नम् अनन्तशक्तिशिवतत्त्वम् अत्रोक्तं भवति ।

(इ)

मालिन्याम् इहत्य-अपरसंविद्-अनुसृत्या पश्यन्त्यात्मकसत्तानुसृत्या च क्रमेण—

"वायुः सादाख्यं च 'घः', नभ ईश्वरश्च 'ङः', इच्छैव शिवमयी शुद्धविद्या 'इ', अनुत्तर एव स्वतन्त्रोऽहंभावः 'अ' शिवाख्यो माया, माया

नियतिश्च 'वः', प्रकृतिः कालश्च 'भः', रागः नियतिश्च 'यः', पादः विद्या च 'ड':, पाणिः कला च, 'ढकारः' पुमान् पायुश्च 'ठ':, स्पर्शः प्रकृतिश्च 'झः', शब्दश्च 'ञः' धीरूपञ्च, रूपम् अहंकृत् च 'जः', 'रः' विद्या मनश्च, आनन्देन्द्रियं 'टः' श्रोत्रं च, मनस्त्वक् च 'पः', रसः चक्षुश्च 'छः', 'लः' कला रसना च, आनन्दशक्तिः शैवी 'आ' घ्राणं च, ईश्वरो वाक् च 'सः', विसर्गशक्तिः 'अः' पाणिश्च, सदाशिवः पादश्च 'हः', शुद्धविद्या पायुश्च 'ष':, शक्ति-पृथिवी उपस्थश्च 'क्षः', पुमान् शब्दश्च 'मः', महामाया 'शः' स्पर्शश्च, बैन्दवी शिवशक्तिः 'अं' रूपं च, नासिका रसश्च 'तः', शिवशक्तिः सात्त्विकी 'ए' गन्धश्च, सैव दीर्घा 'ऐ' नभश्च, तथैव वायुतेजसी 'ओ, औ', चक्षुर् आपश्च 'दः', अहंकृत् पृथिवी च 'फः'।

अत्रैव च यथोक्तं शरीरनिवेशः—इत्येवं सर्वसर्वात्मकत्वं निर्व्यूढं भवेत्। पराभट्टारिकैव हि प्रोक्तनयेन पश्यन्त्यां प्रतिबिम्बं स्वकमर्पयमाणा तत्सम-कालमेव स्वात्मतादात्म्यव्यवस्थितमध्यमाधाम्नि भिन्नयोनितामश्नुवाना तत्तद्योनिबीजपरस्परसंभेदवैचित्र्यस्य आनन्त्यादसंख्येनैव प्रकारेण तत्तत्कुल-पुरुषादिपरिगणनभेदेन भेद-भागिनी मालिन्येव। यथोक्तम्

'अनन्तैः कुलदेहैस्तु कुलशक्तिभिरेव च।
मालिनीं तु यजेद्देवीं परिवारितविग्रहाम्॥' इति।

अनेनैव च क्रमेण बहिर्भुवनेषु तत्त्वेषु शारीरेषु च चक्रेषु अभ्यासपरो योगी तत्तत्सिद्धिभाक् सर्वत्रैव देहे प्राणे च भवति। यथा काश्चिदेवौषध्यः समुद्भूय किंचिदेव कार्यं विदधते तथा काचिदेव समुद्भूय भावना मन्त्रन्यास-होमादिरूपा कांचिदेव सिद्धिं वितरेत्, अत्रापि यावन्नियतिव्यापारानति-क्रमात्। तथाहि प्रतिशास्त्रमन्यथा चान्यथा च वर्णनिवेशपुरःसरं निज-निजविज्ञानसमुचिततत्तद्वर्णभट्टारकप्राधान्येन तत्तद्वर्णानुसारायातनियतपरि-पाटीपिण्डितवर्णसमूहरूपः प्रस्तारो निरूपितः। तत एव च मन्त्रोद्धारो निरूपितः, तामेव मातृकारूपां तथाविधवीर्यदानोपबृंहितमन्त्रस्फुरत्ता-

दायिनीं दर्शयितुम्। यथा श्रीनित्यातन्त्रेषु परनादात्मनिवेशप्राधान्यात् तदनुसारापतितश्रीमन्त्रादिफान्तक्रमेणैव निवेशः। अत्र कुलपुरुषाणां कुलशक्तीनां च एष एव निवेशोऽभिप्रायः, न च वर्णमन्त्रादिगुप्तिमात्रमेव फलं, तथा श्रीवाजसनेयतन्त्रे वर्णान् यथोचितं निवेश्योक्तम्

'इत्येतन्मातृकाचक्रं दिव्यं विष्णुपदास्पदम्।
ज्ञातं गुरुमुखात्सम्यक् पशोः पाशान्निकृन्तति॥'

इति। तथा श्रीत्रिकहृदयेऽपि

आयुधानां च शक्तीनामन्यस्यापि च कस्यचित्॥
यो निवेशस्तु वर्णानां यद्वीर्यं तत्र मन्त्रगम्।
तेन गुप्तेन ते गुप्ताः शेषा वर्णास्तु केवलाः॥

इति। तथाहि—मन्त्राणामक्षरमात्रान्यथाभावेऽपि तेषामेव शास्त्रेष्वाणवशाक्तशाम्भवादिविभागेनान्यथात्वम्। यथा मायाबीजस्य प्रणवस्य सर्वस्यामृतबीजस्य च वैष्णव शैव-वामादिशास्त्रेषु, यथा वा चतुष्कलभट्टारकस्य कौलोत्तरादौ श्रीमदुच्छुष्मशास्त्रे च अन्यथात्वम्। अत्र च कुलपुरुषकुलशक्तिबहुभेदप्रकटनायामभियुक्तानामुपायो लिख्यते

'पूर्वे परेषामपरे परे पृष्ठवदेव च।
पूर्वेऽपि च यथापूर्वं मातृकाया विधिर्मतः॥
एतेनैवानुसारेण भिन्नयोनिस्वरूपतः॥
शाक्ताद्यसंख्या देवीयं परैवोत्तरमालिनी॥'

इति।

'अधोऽधो विनिविष्टेषु भेदसंख्येषु धामसु।
एकं बिन्दुरथापि प्रागन्येषु प्राक्तनान्त्यगाम्॥
स्वपृष्ठगां च तां संख्यां विनिवेश्यैकतः क्षिपेत्।
अस्मादन्यैर्भवेत्सख्या-स्पृष्टैरिष्टैः पुनः क्रमः॥
यथोक्तः कुलशक्तीनां विधिरानन्त्यवेदने।'

तदेतेन विधिना ये कुलपुरुषशक्तियोगिनो निरधिकारीभूता मन्त्रमहेश्वराः, तेभ्यो नैव मन्त्रोद्धारः, तस्य निष्फलत्वात्। न तु मन्त्राः, तेषां स्वलयावसरेऽनामयपदपर्यन्तताभावः। यथोक्तम्

'ब्रह्मादिस्तम्बपर्यन्ते जातमात्रे जगत्यलम् ॥

मन्त्राणां कोटयस्तिस्रः सार्धाः शिवनियोजिताः।

अनुगृह्याणुसंघातं याताः पदमनामयम् ॥ (मा. वि. १।४० ४१)

इति। तदेवं भगवती पराभट्टारिका पदभेदशालिनी मध्यमया मुख्यया वृत्त्या भगवन्मालिनीरूपेव अनन्ता परिगणनप्रदर्शितवैश्वरूप्यस्वस्वरूपा, तत्रापि च तथैव स्वात्मनि सर्वात्मकत्वेनांशत्रयोद्रेकात् वर्ण-पद-मन्त्रात्मकत्वमेति। एतच्च शोधनकरणभावेन इति मन्तव्यम्। पश्यन्त्यंशोल्लसन्तो हि पाशाः सूक्ष्मा एव शोध्या भवन्ति—अन्तर्लीनत्व एव पाशत्वात्। उदितोदितविजृम्भामयशाक्तप्रसरे तु मध्यमापदे शोधनकरणतैव अन्तर्लीनपटमलापसरणे बाह्यस्थूलमलस्येव तत्। पराभट्टारिकासंविदन्तर्गतं तु वैखरीपदं विमृश्यते। न हि तत्र वैखर्या असंभवः। तथाहि—बाला द्वित्रैर्वर्षैः यद्यपि स्फुटीभूतस्थानकरणा भवन्ति, तथापि एषां मासानुमासदिनानुदिनमेव वा हि व्युत्पत्तिरधिकाधिकरूपतामेति—इति तावत् स्थितम्। तत्र यदि मध्यमापदे तथाविधवैखरीप्रसरस्फुटीभविष्यत्स्थानकरणविभागवर्णांशस्फुरणं न स्यात्, तदहर्जातस्य बालकस्य मासजातस्य संवत्सरजातस्य वा व्युत्पत्तौ न विशेषः स्यात्, मध्यमैव सा व्युत्पत्त्या विशिष्यते ? इति चेत्, कथमिति चर्च्यतां तावत्—शृण्वन्नेव तान् शब्दान् पश्यंश्चार्थान् व्युत्पद्यते, वर्णांश्च श्रूयमाणानेव परामृशेत्, श्रूयन्ते च वैखरीमयाः, तेषु च असौ रूप इव जात्यन्धवत्। तस्मात् अन्तर्मध्यमानिविष्टस्थानकरणादिमयी अस्त्येव वैखरी। मूकेऽपि एवमेव। सर्वात्मकत्वं च संविदो भगवत्या एव इति उक्तम्। एवं च वैखरीपदमेव मध्यमाधामलब्धविजृम्भं स्वांशे परस्परवैचित्र्यप्रथात्मनि स्फुटवाच्यवाचकभावोल्लासे तत्त्वजालमन्तःकृत्य यावदास्ते तावदपराभट्टारिका। तदन्तर्वर्तिमध्यमापदोल्लासे

परापरा, पश्यन्त्युल्लासे च। स्वरूपतो भगवती देवी च। इति शोधकभावेन स्थितिः त्रैधमेवावतिष्ठते। शोधको हि विश्वात्मा विततरूपो, वैतत्यं चैवमेव भवतीत्युक्तम्। शोधनं प्रति तु कर्तृत्वं कर्तुरेव स्वस्वातन्त्र्यगृहीतसंकोचस्य शाक्तमहिमविश्रान्तस्य भगवतः। शोध्यता तु संकोचैकरूपस्य सप्तत्रिंशातिक्रान्तत्रिकैकरूपभैरवभट्टारकाविनिर्भक्तपराभट्टारिकातुल्यकक्ष्यपरापरादेवताक्षोभात्मकसदाशिवज्ञानशक्तिविस्फारितपशुशक्तिरूपपश्यन्तीधामप्रथमासूत्रितभेदात्मनो नरात्मनः पाशजालस्य, इति निर्णयः। यथोक्तं श्रीसोमानन्दपादैः शिवदृष्टौ

'अस्मद्रूपसमाविष्टः स्वात्मनात्मनिवारणे।
शिवः करोतु परया नमः शक्त्या ततात्मने॥' (शि. दृ. १।१)

इति सर्वक्रियाकलाप एवंरूपतासूचकः शिवदृष्टौ। तत्रापि च उत्तरोत्तरं शोध्यशोधकानामपि विगलनम्

'त्यज धर्ममधर्मं च उभे सत्यानृते त्यज।
उभे सत्यानृते त्यक्त्वा येन त्यजसि तत्त्यज॥'(म.भा. १२।३१६।४०)

इति। तदियमेतावती धारा यच्छोधकमपि शोधनमपि शोध्यमेव—इति श्रीषडर्धशास्त्रे स्वोत्कर्षः। तिसृणामपि चासां युगपत् स्थितिर्भवत्येव। वक्ति ह्यन्यत्, विकल्पयंश्च अन्यत् जल्पत्यविकल्पमेव अन्यत्पश्यति। अत्र तु परिपूर्ण एव तावति भगवान् भैरव एव—इत्याद्यनुभवसंप्रदायोपदेशपरिशीलनेन—अस्यार्थस्य स्वसंविन्मयस्यानपलापनीयत्वात्। न तत् युगपत्, अपि तु 'तथा-सौक्ष्म्यादलक्ष्यम्' इति यौगपद्याभिमानः शिरीषकुसुमपल्लवशतव्यतिभेद इव—युगपत् इति, समानकालम्—इति चेत्। केयं खलु भाषा। अन्तर्मुखे संविदात्मनि प्रोक्तनयेन कः कालः। तस्य ज्ञेयरूपप्राणगमागमादिमयाभासतदभावप्राणत्वात् ज्ञेयोपाधिगतोऽपि ज्ञानमवस्कन्देत् सः, इति चेत्—ज्ञेयस्य स्वात्मनि भासामयेऽन्यथा वा कोऽस्य विशेषो ज्ञानमुखेनोक्त इतरेतराश्रयसंप्लवः स्वतो भेदात्। सर्वमुच्यमानं ज्ञान-

मुखमेवापतेत्। तथा च स एव दोषो बहुतरत्रुसुमपल्लवशतव्यतिभेदोऽपि चानेक इत्युच्यमाने—परमाण्वन्तावयवयोगात् नास्ति कर्म—इत्यापतेत्। न च अनुसंधानं ज्ञानाभावेन सह स्यात्—अनुसंधायाः स्मृतिभेदे तस्याश्च अनुभवोपजीवित्वेनुभवाभावात्। वितत्य च विचारितं मयैतत् पदार्थ-प्रवेशनिर्णयटीकायाम्,—इति किमिह वृथावाग्जालेन प्रकृतोपदेशविघ्न-पर्यवसायिना। एवं भगवती परा शोधकभावेन स्थिता। परापरापि च यत्र भगवतीनामघोरादीनां शक्तीनां स्थितिः—यद्योगात् विज्ञानाकल-साधकयोगिनो मन्त्रमहेशादिरूपाः संपन्नाः। ब्राह्म्याद्यादिशक्त्यनुग्रहेणैव साधकाणवो ब्रह्मविष्ण्वादयः सम्पन्नाः। परमेश्वरो हि भैरवभट्टारकः समग्रशक्तिपुञ्जपरिपूर्णनिर्भरवपुर्निजशक्तिनिवेशनया ब्रह्मादीन् स्वतन्त्रान् करोति इति किमन्यत्। एवं शोधकस्यापि शोध्यत्वमित्यन्य उत्कर्षः

'......................कुलात्परतरं त्रिकम्।'

इति स्थित्या ततश्च शोध्यशोधनशोधकानां सर्वत्रैव त्र्यात्मकत्वात् त्रिक-मनपायि। यथोक्तं मयैव स्तोत्रे

'.........—यत्र त्रिकाणां त्रितयं समस्ति।'

इति। न चैवमनवस्था—सर्वस्यास्य भगवत्परसंविदेकमयत्वात्

'..................येन त्यजसि तत्त्यज।'

इत्येवमेव मन्तव्यम्। अन्ततः शोधकोऽपि वा भेदांशोच्छलत्तायां पाशात्म-कत्वात् शोध्य एव। शोधनं च परमार्थतः सर्वमलप्लोषचतुरभैरवसंविदभेदि हुतवह एव सर्वस्यानुप्रवेशे परिपूर्णतैव, यद्वक्ष्यति

'एवं यो वेत्ति तत्त्वेन' (प. श्री. २५)

इत्यादि। तत् परसंविदेकमयपरापरादिदेवतानां सर्वात्मकत्वात्

'परापराङ्गसंभूता योगिन्योऽष्टौ महाबलाः।
पञ्चषट्पञ्चचत्वारि द्वित्रिवर्णाः क्रमेण तु॥
ज्ञेयाः सप्तैकादशार्णा एकार्धार्णद्वयान्विताः।' (मा.वि. ३।५९-६०)

इत्यादिवचनात् लौकिकशास्त्रान्तरीयादिवाच्यवाचकानन्त्यमपि संगृहीतम्। तत् एवं कृतकरिष्यमाणाद्यनन्तसंकेतगर्भीकारेणैव अयं शोध्यशोधकभावः। न चानवस्था नातिप्रसङ्गो नातिव्याप्तिर्न संकेतितस्यापारमार्थिकता—इति स्थितम्। एवं स्थिते प्रकृतमनुसरामः—अकाराद्या एव कालयोगेन सोमसूर्यौ यौ तदन्तः प्रकीर्तिताविति संबन्धः। तच्छब्देन प्राक्तनश्लोकोक्तमकुलं भैरवात्म परामृश्यते। तेनाकुलमेवान्तर्गृहीतकलनाकं—कुलशक्तेरत्रैव निवेशात्, कलनात्मिका हि विमर्शशक्तिः। तामन्तरेणाकुलमपि तुर्यातीतं नाम न किंचित्—सौषुप्तपदाविष्टत्वात्, तुर्यानन्तरताया अपि समानत्वात्। विमर्शशक्तिश्च परा परमेश्वरी भैरवभट्टारकस्य निरतिशयस्वातन्त्र्यात्मिका पूर्णकृशतदुभयात्मतदुभयरहितत्वेनावतिष्ठते। तत्र न कश्चित् क्रमयौगपद्योदयकलङ्कः—प्रोक्तोपदेशनयेन एतावत्याः पराभट्टारिकासंविदोऽनन्तागामिप्रलयोदयात्मकस्वस्वभावविमर्शैकघनत्वादिति।

'स्वतन्त्रः परिपूर्णोऽयं भगवान्भैरवो विभुः।
तन्नास्ति यन्न विमले भासयेत्स्वात्मदर्पणे॥'

इति नीत्या क्रमयौगपद्यासहिष्णुस्वात्मरूपमध्य एव यावत् क्रमाक्रमावभासः, तावत् तदनुसारेणायं क्रमो विचारणीयः, अक्रमस्य तु तत्पूर्वकेण संविद्येव भावात्। तत्प्रतिपादनाय अस्तु क्रमः। तथा च सर्व एवायं वाग्रूपः परामर्शः क्रमिक एव अन्तःसंविन्मयस्त्वक्रम एव—इति सदैवेयमेवंविधैव विचित्रा पारमेश्वरी पराभट्टारिका। ततस्तत्क्रमानुसारेण अत् इत्यादिव्यपदेशः कार्यः। एवं परमेश्वरस्य स्वात्मनि इच्छात्मिका स्वातन्त्र्यशक्तिरनुन्मीलितभावविभासा अन्तर्घनसंवित्स्वभावविमर्शसारा 'अ' इत्युच्यते। सा चावस्थानेन इच्छेति व्यपदेश्या इष्यमाणानुद्रेका। तत एवानुत्तरसत्तापरामर्शात्मिकैव एषा। परमेश्वरः सततं स्वस्वरूपामर्शकोऽकुलशक्तिपदात्मकमपि रूपमामृशन् यद्यपि कुलशक्तीरनुयातु, तथापि कुलपरामर्शांतोऽस्य स्यादेव विशेषः—इति भैरवशक्तिमद्विमर्शसत्तेयम्। तादृश्येव पुनः प्रसरन्ती आनन्दशक्तिः 'आ' इति प्रसृता। परिपूर्णेच्छा 'इ' इति।

इच्छेव भाविज्ञानशक्त्यात्मकस्वातन्त्र्येण जिघृक्षन्ती ईशानरूपा 'ई' इति। उन्मिषन्ती तु ज्ञानशक्तिरीक्ष्यमाणसकलभावोन्मेषमयी 'उ' इति। उन्मिषत्तैव उन्मिमिषतायामपि अन्तःप्राणसर्वस्वरूपोन्मेषोत्तरैकरूपैरपि अन्तःकरणवेद्यदेशीयास्फुटप्रायभेदांशभासमानभावराशिभिः संकोचवशेन ऊनीभूतानुत्तरसंवित्सर्वभावगर्भीकारेण अनङ्गधेनवीरूपपरदेवताया ऊधोरूपा ऊढसकलभावराशिः सुस्फुटा प्रसृता ज्ञानशक्तिः 'ऊ' इति। तदेवमेते परमेश्वरस्य भैरवस्य द्वे शक्ती। प्रथमा स्वरूपपरिपूरणारूपत्वात् पूर्णा चान्द्रमसी शक्त्यव्यतिरेकाच्च सहोमया वर्तत इति सोमरूपा स्वानन्दविश्रान्तिभावा इच्छाख्या कलना महासृष्टिव्यपदेश्या। यद्वक्ष्यते 'ततः सृष्टिं यजेदिति' (प. श्री. २९)। द्वितीया तु तत्स्वरूपभावराशिरेचनानुप्रवेशोद्रिक्ता तद्रेचनादेव कृशा भावमण्डलप्रकाशनप्रसारणव्यापारा सूर्यरूपा स्वरूपभूता कुलसंवित्संजिहीर्षात्मिका महासंहारशक्तिर्ज्ञानाख्या। तत्रापि च प्रसरत्प्राक्तनरूपपर्यालोचनावशात् स्वात्मनि यथाक्रमं सोमसूर्यरूपतायुगलकभावेन स्वसंविदात्मकं भावाख्यं च रूपमपेक्षते। विपर्ययेऽपि सोमसूर्यात्मकसृष्टिसंहृतिकलनयोः रूपमपेक्षते। न च अत्रानवस्था, ज्ञानेच्छयोरपि प्रसराप्रसरान्तरादिरूपत्वं, तयोरपि प्रसराप्रसरयोरिच्छाज्ञानप्रसराप्रसरान्तरादिपरिकल्पनाप्रसङ्गात् इति वाच्यम्, उपसंहरत बाह्यविभ्रमभ्रमणं तावत्। अनुप्रविशत सूक्ष्मां विमर्शपदवीम्। यावद्धि घटादावपि विज्ञानं जायते तावदेव ज्ञेयघटाद्यंशकर्बुरीकृतस्वयंप्रथं ज्ञानं प्रथत एव। तत्रापि च तद्रूपकर्बुरीभावघटादिप्रथमसूक्ष्मोल्लासोऽपि संवेद्यः—एकभावोद्गमस्य, अन्यतः कुतश्चिदभावस्य प्रथमानत्वात्। संविदः स्वातन्त्र्यम् एव भावोज्जिगमिषात्मकमीशनं स्वसंवित्प्रमाणलब्धमेव। तद्भावानुपचयरूपा संविद्घना परिपूर्णा स्वातन्त्र्यमत्तापि स्वात्मन्यानन्दघना भवन्ती स्वतन्त्रा स्यात्—इत्यानन्दोऽपि नापह्नवनीयः। अनुत्तरश्च शक्तिमानव्यपदेश्यपरचमत्कारसारो भैरवभट्टारकः सर्वत्र कर्तृत्वेन भासत एव। तत्रापि त्वनुत्तरानन्देच्छेशनोन्मेषणोनतायां स्वरूपविमर्शे, तेषामविच्छेदविचारणेन ज्ञानभूमि-

मधिशयानानां ता एव भगवत्यः संविच्छक्तयः समापतन्त्यनन्या एव स्वसंविदः—परिपूर्णत्वेनाभेदात्। संवेद्योपाधेश्च भेदकत्वात्—तस्य देह-संवेद्यमात्रतयैव भावात्। अत एव श्रीतन्त्रसारे 'निजोत्तमाङ्गच्छाया-तत्त्वम्' इत्युक्तम्

'स्वपदा स्वशिरश्छायां यद्वल्लङ्घितुमीहते।
पादोद्देशे शिरो न स्यात्तथेयं बैन्दवी कला॥

इति। तदेवं षट्कं प्रवृत्तं ज्ञानशक्त्यन्तम्। क्रियाशक्तिस्तु प्रसरन्ती विचार्यते—इच्छाज्ञाने एव परस्परस्वरूपसांकर्यवैचित्र्यचमत्कारमयपूर्वा-परीभूतस्वरूपपरिग्रहे संरम्भसारा क्रिया, तत्र यद्यदन्यव्यामिश्रितसांकर्य-मन्यसंबन्धादेति तत्तदनामशंनीयशून्यप्रायस्वरूपाक्रमणपुरःसरीकारेण तथा भवति—प्लवनमिव भेकादेः। तत्रानुत्तरानन्दात्मकं वपुर्न प्रसरति, अव्यप-देश्यरूपत्वात्। तत्सर्वज्ञानेषु सर्वाधारवृत्तित्वेन पर्यवस्यति, पर्यन्तभित्ति-रूपत्वात्। किन्तु क्रमसहिष्णुत्वात् संरम्भेच्छैवेशनान्ता स्वात्मनि अनुत्तरा-नन्दपदे च प्रसरणक्षमा। ततः सैव शून्यात्मकं स्वं वपुरवगाहमाना भास्वरं रूपं तेजोमयमिव प्रथमं गाहते 'ऋ-ॠ' इति। अत्र हि 'इ-ई' इत्यनुगमो भास्वररूप-रेफश्रुत्यनुगमश्च कथमपह्नूयताम्, यथाह भगवान्पुष्पदन्तः

'रश्रुतिसामान्याद्वा सिद्धम्'

इति। शून्ये हि निश्चले रूपे अनुप्रविविक्षायां भास्वररूपसंवित्तिसोपा-नाक्रमणं स्थितमेव, ततो निश्चलरूपानुप्रवेशात् पार्थिवरूपसतत्त्वनिश्चल-तात्मक-लकार-श्रुत्यनुगमे 'ऌ-ॡ' इति। तथा च पर्यन्ते ईशनरूपतैव समग्रभावात्मस्वरूपोल्लङ्घनेन दीर्घतरं प्लुत्वा निश्चलां शून्यां सत्तामेत्य प्लुतत्वमेति। 'लृवर्णस्य दीर्घा न सन्ति' इति न्यायात्, अवर्णादीनां तु दीर्घस्यैव दीर्घतरता प्लुतत्वम्। तच्च प्राङ्नीत्या दीर्घत्वमेव पृथगपर्येषणीयम्। इत्यास्तां तावत्। एतच्चतुष्कं शून्यरूपतानुप्रवेशात् दग्धबीजमिव षण्ढरूपं भण्यते। न तु सर्वथा बीजरूपत्वाभावात्, बीजयोन्यात्मकशिवशक्त्यु-भयातिरेकिणः कस्यचिदप्यभावात्, श्रीपूर्वादिशास्त्रेषु चानभिधानात्।

लौकिकसुखादिषु चैवंविधैव विश्रान्तिरानन्दरूपतेति। तदेवामृतबीजचतुष्कमित्युक्तम्। तदेवमिच्छेशनं चानन्दवपुषि अनुत्तरपरधामनि च प्राग्भाविनि स्वरूपादप्रच्याविनि अनुप्रविश्य 'अ आ इ ई' इति च। यथोक्तम् 'अवर्णे इवर्णे ए' इति। विपर्यये चानुत्तरपदानुप्रवेशे स्यादपि कश्चिद्विशेषः। आनन्दपदानुप्रवेशे हि स्फुटता, अनुत्तरधामसंभेदे तु सूक्ष्मता तदपेक्षया, तथाहि भगवान् भुजगविभुरादिशत्

'छन्दोगानां सात्यमुग्रिराणायनीया
अर्धमेकारमर्धमोकारं चाधीयते।' (म. भाष्य १. १. ४७)

इति। लोकेऽपि प्राकृतदेशभाषादौ स्फुट एव एष सन्निवेशः। पारमेश्वरेष्वपि एकारौकारयोरैकारौकारापेक्षया यत् ह्रस्वत्वमङ्गवक्त्रादिविनियोगे दृश्यते, तदेवमेव मन्तव्यम्—अय एकार, अव ओकाराभिप्रायेण। एवम्—'ए ओ' इति बीजं स्थितम्। एतदपि तथाशबलीभूतं संविद्वपुः तथैव च तदेव रूपमनवसत् 'अ, आ, ए, 'ऐ' इति। एवमुन्मेषेऽपि वाच्यम्—'अ, आ, उ, ऊ' ओ इति। 'अ, आ, ओ, 'औ' इति। केवलमुन्मेषो ज्ञानशक्त्यात्मा प्रसरन् यद्यपि शून्यतावगाहनं कुर्यात्, तथापि अस्येशनेच्छात्मकोभयरूपप्रवेश एव शून्यता। इच्छेशनयोस्तु स्वपरिवृत्तिरूपं नास्ति—इत्युक्तनयेनैव स्थितिः। एवमिच्छाज्ञाने अनुत्तरस्वरूपानुप्रवेशेन प्राप्तोपचये पश्चात् परित्यज्य तथाविधोपाधिपरिस्पन्दसत्तामभेदसत्तारोहणचिन्मयपुरुषतत्त्वसतत्त्ववेदनारूपबिन्दुमात्रावशेषेण वपुषा तथानुत्तरपदलीनें 'अमिति'। तथाहि ओकारे एव क्रियाशक्तिपरिस्पन्दः परिसमाप्यते इति—इच्छाज्ञानयोरत्रैवान्तर्भावात्। त्रिशूलरूपत्वमस्य षडर्धशास्त्रे निरूपितम्

'सार्णेनाण्डत्रयं व्याप्तं त्रिशूलेन चतुर्थकम्।'
सर्वातीतं विसर्गेण पराया व्याप्तिरिष्यते॥ (मा. वि. ४।२५)

इत्याद्युद्देशेषु। बिन्दुः पुनर्वेदनामात्रशेषतैव। सर्वस्य वेदनामात्राविशेषमपि विश्वं यदा स्वात्मन्येकगमनाय विसृजति स्वात्मनश्च सकाशात् तन्निर्माणेन

विसृजति स एव परमेश्वरः प्रथमं शक्तिमद्रूपप्रधानतया, इदानीं तु शाक्तविसर्गप्रधानतया 'अः' इति। औकारपर्यन्ते हि निर्भरीभूते क्रियाशक्तिप्रसरे एतावति अनुप्रविष्टानुत्तरपदस्य भैरवभट्टारकस्य स्वरूपसतत्त्वस्य इच्छा-ज्ञान-क्रियात्मकशक्तिपरिस्पन्दादिमध्यान्तभागा उल्लिलसिषा-उल्लसत्ता-उल्लसिततास्वभावाः सूक्ष्मतमप्रसंख्यानगृहीततावद्भूमिकाधिरूढयोगिजनस्फुटलक्षणीयाः श्रीस्वच्छन्दादिप्रक्रियाशास्त्रेषु प्रबुद्धप्रसरणावरणादिरूपत्वेनोक्ताः। अत एव शिवदृष्टिशास्त्रे सप्तमाह्निके

'सुनिर्भरतराह्लादभरिताकाररूपिणि।
निलीनशक्तित्रितये परात्मन्यनुभावनात् ॥'

इत्यादि

'तस्यापि शक्तिर्मृत्पिण्डघटवद्विश्वतां गता।' (शि. दृ. ७.२८)

इत्यन्तं निरूप्य

'एकमेव हि तत्तत्त्वं न संख्यातोऽतिरिक्तता।'

इति यच्छिवतत्त्वमेव अनन्तविचित्रस्वातन्त्र्यस्फारस्फुरणशक्तिचमत्कारभरिततोपात्तभैरवभावं निर्णीतम्। तत्रायमेवोक्तक्रमः। संप्रदायप्रथमाह्निकेऽपि

'स यदास्ते चिदाह्लादमात्रानुभवतल्लयः।
तदिच्छा तावती तावज्ज्ञानं तावत्क्रिया हि सा ॥
सुसूक्ष्मशक्तित्रितयसामरस्येन वर्तते।
चिद्रूपाह्लादपरमो निर्विभागः परस्तदा ॥ (शि. दृ. १।३-४)

इति। तथा घटज्ञानमुद्दिश्य

'घटादिग्रहकालेऽपि घटं जानाति सा क्रिया।
जानाति ज्ञानमत्रैव निरिच्छोर्वेदनक्षतिः ॥
औन्मुख्याभाववतस्तस्य निवृत्तिर्निर्वृतिं विना।
द्वेष्ये प्रवर्तते नैव न च वेत्ति विना चितिम् ॥'
(शि. दृ. १।२४-२५)

इति। तथा

यत इच्छति तज्ज्ञातुं कर्तुं वा सेच्छया क्रिया।

तस्याः पूर्वापरो भागो कल्पनीयो पुरा हि या॥ (शि. दृ. १।१९)

तत्कर्मनिर्वृतिप्राप्तिरौन्मुख्यं तद्विकासिता।

न चौन्मुख्यप्रसङ्गेन शिवः स्थूलत्वभाक् क्वचित्॥' (शि.दृ. १।१७)

इत्यादि एतदागमसर्वस्वप्राणतयेव युक्तियुक्ततया हृदयंगमीकृतम्। स एष परमेश्वरो विसृजति विश्वम्। तच्च धरादिशक्त्यन्तं कादि-क्षान्तरूपम्—इति एतावती विसर्गशक्तिः 'षोडशी कला' इति गीयते

'पुरुषे षोडशकले तामाहुरमृतां कलाम्।'

इति। एषा हि न सांख्येया नापि वैदान्तिकी दृक्, अपि तु शैव्येव, विसर्गशक्तिरेव च पारमेश्वरी परमानन्दभूमिबीजम्। एवं हि अकारादिरूपं घनतापत्त्या योनिरूपतां गृहीत्वा स्वरूपाप्रच्युतम्। तदेव स्वस्वरूप एव योनिरूपे संक्रामद्विसर्गपदमित्युच्यते, यथोक्तम्

'स विसर्गो महादेवि यत्र विश्रान्तिमृच्छति।

गुरुवक्त्रं तदेवोक्तं शक्तिचक्रं तदुच्यते॥'

इत्यादि। अकारस्यैव घनता 'कवर्गः'—कण्ठ्यत्वात्, इकारस्य 'चवर्गः'—तालव्यत्वात्, उकारस्य 'पवर्गः'—ओष्ठ्यत्वात्, ऋकारस्य 'टवर्गो'—मूर्धन्यत्वात्, 'ऌकारस्य तवर्गो'—दन्त्यत्वात्, 'यशौ' चवर्गस्यान्तः, 'रषौ' टवर्गस्य, 'लसौ' तवर्गस्य, वकारोऽपि 'तपवर्गयोः' घनता। अबोधस्यामूर्तस्यापि चिन्मात्रस्यापि क्रियाशक्तिरूपतैव। सा चोक्तनीत्या शक्तिषट्कक्रमेणैवोपजायते—तेन पञ्च प्रसृताः षड्गुणिताः त्रिंशत्। षड्भिः सह षट्त्रिंशत् भवन्तीति। तदेवं शिवबीजमेव स्वातन्त्र्यात् घनीभूततया क्वचिद्वपुषि शाक्तरूपे कुसुमतया तिष्ठत् योनिरित्यभिधीयते। तदेव हि पुष्पं पूर्वोक्तनयेन ग्राह्यग्रहणग्राहककोणत्रयमयं वस्तुतः प्रसूतिपदं बीजसंमिश्रतयेव भवति, तदेव पुष्परूपत्वात्। अन्यदा तु योग्यतयेव तथाव्य-

पदेशः, ततश्च तत् कुसुममेव त्रिकोणतया योनिरूपं तत्स्फुटीभूतविभक्त-ग्राह्यादिरूपसोमसूर्याग्नि-सृष्टिस्थितिसंहृति-इडापिङ्गलासुषुम्णा-धर्माधर्म-शबलादिकोणत्रितया पारमेश्वरी भैरवी भट्टारिका मुद्रा तद्रूपयोन्याधारतया योनिरिति निर्दिष्टा। तथा च श्रीकुब्जिकामते खण्डचक्रविचारे अमुमेवार्थं प्रधानतयाधिकृत्यादिष्टम्

'मायोपरि महामाया त्रिकोणानन्दरूपिणी।'

इत्यादि। अत एव तथाविधबीजकुसुमैकघनभावशिवशक्तिसंघट्टः स्वयं स्वात्मनैव पूज्य इत्युपदिष्टं श्रीत्रिकतन्त्रसारे

'शिवशक्तिसमापत्त्या शिवशक्तिघनात्मकः।
शिवशक्तिसमापत्तित्रिकं संपूजयेत्परम् ॥'

इति। एवं च घनीभावोऽपि वैखरीरूपे यद्यपि स्फुटीभवति, तथापि सर्वसर्वात्मनि परावाग्वपुषि मुख्यतयावतिष्ठते। तत्र परं कण्ठोष्ठस्थानकरणान्यपि सर्वसर्वात्मकान्येव इति विशेषः। तथाहि—अन्तरपि संजल्पेत् पश्येदिति स्फुट एवानुभवः। भेदश्च स्थानादिकृत एव—श्रुत्येकप्राणत्वात् वर्णानाम्। किं बहुना बालोऽपि व्युत्पाद्यमानोऽन्तः तथारूपतया विमृशति भावजातम्। विपर्ययेण संशयेनापि वा यावत् विमृशति तावत्संवेदयत एव। स च वाग्विमर्शकृत एव। अत एव संवारविवाराल्पप्राणमहाप्राणताश्वासनादानुप्रदानादियोगोऽपि च अन्तस्तथासमुचितस्वभावः स्यादेव। अन्यथा सस्थानेषु भेदायोगात् अन्तर्हितकरणशक्तयो वैखर्यामपि भवेयुः। श्रृणोम्यश्रौषं पश्याम्यद्राक्षं संकल्पयामि समकल्पयमित्यादेरपि संकल्पस्यान्यथा-वैचित्र्यायोगात्। तदनया युक्त्या निभालितयान्तरधिकमधिकमनुप्रविश्य परिशीलयतां संविदम्। यत्र सर्वसर्वात्मकबोधैकघनकण्ठोष्ठादिधाम्नि तथाविधबोधैकघनविमर्शात्मकस्वातन्त्र्यसारमहामन्त्ररूपवर्णभट्टारकनिवेशः। बोधैकघनतानिर्विशेषतायाम् इदं स्थानम्, इदं करणम्, अयं वर्ण इति कथंकारं विभाग इति चेत्? तदेव स्वातन्त्र्यं तथाविधे स्वात्मनि घटोऽयं, सुखमिदं, ज्ञानमिदं, ज्ञाताहम् इत्यवभासयति। तस्यैवंविधचित्र-

तररूपावभासने को वा कियान् वा प्रयासः ? अत एव सर्वे पाषाणतरु-तिर्यङ्मनुष्यदेवरुद्रकेवलिमन्त्रतदीशतन्महेशादिका एकैव पराभट्टारिका-भूमिः सर्वसर्वात्मनैव परमेश्वररूपेणास्ते इति। तद्विचित्रस्थानादिसार्वा-त्म्यविनिविष्टस्फुटास्फुटव्यक्ताव्यक्तादिरूपशब्दशरीरा 'मन्त्रवीर्यम्' इति गीयते। तथाहि वीणाविपञ्चीकच्छपिकामुरजादिषु स एव स्वनोऽन्यतो-ऽन्यतो देशादप्युद्भवन्नेकस्थान इति कथ्यते। एवं तारमध्यमन्द्रेष्वपि तत्स्थायिस्वरैकात्म्येऽपि वाच्यम्। अत एव च स एव वर्णः क्वचित्प्रा-णिनि स्थानान्तरसमुल्लास्यपि भवति। यथा ध्वांक्षेषु ककारटकाररेफा उच्चरन्तः सर्व एवोदरपायुकण्ठतालुनिर्वर्त्या उपलभ्यन्ते अव्यक्तत्वेऽपि त एव तावन्तः शब्दत्वात्। शब्दस्य च मातृकातिरेकिणोऽभावात्। मातृकातिरेक्यपि अव्यक्तः शब्दोऽनुपयोगान्न संगृहीतव्यः इत्यप्ययुक्तम्। अव्यक्तवर्णरूपस्यापि मौरुजसामुद्रादिध्वनितस्य ह्लादपरितापकारित्वमपि अस्त्येव—इति कोऽन्योऽभिमत उपयोगः। पारमेश्वरेऽपि अव्यक्तध्वनेर्मुख्य-तयैव प्रायशो मन्त्रत्वं निरूपितम्—अर्धचन्द्रादीनामेव मन्त्रव्याप्ति-सारत्वेनाभिधानात्। तत्र च

'निरोधिनीमनुप्राप्तः शब्दः शुमशुमायते।'

इत्याद्युक्तम्—घण्टाकांस्यादिध्वनीनां श्रोत्रघट्टनादीनां च नादोपदेशे निरूपणात्।

'हयो हेषति यद्वच्च दान्त उद्रवतीव च।
सिंहो गर्जति यद्वच्च उष्ट्रः सीत्कुरुते यथा॥
तथोदीर्य पशोः प्राणानाकर्षन्ति बलाधिकाः।
महामन्त्रप्रयोगोऽयमसाध्याकृष्टिकर्मणि ॥'

इत्युक्तं गुह्ययोगिनीतन्त्रे। तत्रोपायमात्रमेतत्। वस्तुतस्तु 'आन्तर एवासौ नादात्मा मन्त्र' इति तु कथ्यमानं भवद्भिरपि अस्माभिरपि व्यक्त-वर्णमालादिमन्त्रेष्वपि न न संचारयितुं शक्यते। तस्मात् अव्यक्तोऽपि

वर्णात्मैव शब्दः। यथा विदूरगतोऽपि घटो घट एव इति स्थितम्। स च प्राणभेर्यादिभेदेन स्थानान्तरमपि अनुसरन् स एवेत्यपि स्थितम्। अत एवेदानीं सर्वभूतरुतज्ञानं यच्छेषमुनिना भगवतोपदिष्टं तद्धृदयंगमीभूतम्। अन्यथा शब्दार्थप्रत्ययानां य इतरेतराध्यासो यच्च ध्यानधारणासमाधिसंयमेन तत्प्रविभागपर्यन्तपरलाभः स कथमस्फुटवर्णरूपत्वातिरेकिविहगादिकूजितज्ञानाय पर्यवस्येत्। यदा तु त एव वर्णा वर्णानामेव परमार्थतोऽर्थतादात्म्यलक्षणं वाचकत्वं यान्ति तदा युक्त्या त एव विहगादिरुतज्ञानं भेर्यादिशब्दा अपि हि अर्थवन्त एव—जयाजयसूचकतयोपदेशात् विहगादिरुतवत्। तदभिप्रायेणैव शिक्षासूत्रकारसूत्राणि "हविसर्जनीयावुरस्यावेकेषाम्", "रदनमूलमेकेषाम्" इत्यादीनि वाचकीभवन्ति न तु अपरथा कथंचिदपि। अत एव किंचिद्वैचित्र्यमालम्ब्यान्यत्वम् अन्यत्वं चाशङ्कमानैः विसर्जनीयाजिह्वामूलीयोपध्मानीयौ, अनुनासिकेभ्यः पञ्च च यमान्, डकारढकारयरलवक्षकारेभ्यः तानेव लघुप्रयत्नतरान् भेदेनाभिमन्य चतुःषष्टिर्वर्णा उक्ताः, अन्यत्वं चात्र स्वरव्यञ्जनयोरिव ऋवर्ण-रशब्दयोः श्रीत्रिकरत्नकुलेऽपि उक्तम्

'अष्टाष्टकविभेदेन मातृका या निरूपिता।
तदेव कुलचक्रं तु तेन व्याप्तमिदं जगत्॥'

इति। मातृकाज्ञानभेदे विस्तरतो निरूपितमेतत्। इह तु तत्प्रक्रियानभिनिवेशः—पूर्णतैकसारत्वात्। तदेवं सर्वत्रायमीदृशः संविदनुप्रवेशक्रमः। पदार्थः संकल्प्यमानः साक्षात् क्रियमाणो वा अमायीयासांकेतिकस्वरूपभूतशुद्धविमर्शात्मपरवाङ्मन्त्रमहामहसि तावत् प्रतिष्ठां भजते। यत्र या सर्ववादिभिरविकल्पा दशा गीयते। तच्च परमन्त्रमहः पृथिव्यादौ शुद्धव्यामिश्रादिपारमार्थिकबीजपिण्डरूपकादिवर्णात्मकमेव। अन्यथा मेरुबदरजलज्वलनभावाभावघटसुखनिर्विकल्पज्ञानानि—इत्येकमेव सर्वं स्यात्। विकल्पोऽपि तत्प्रमादोत्थः तामेव सरणिमनुसरेत्। न तु प्रत्युत तत्स्वरूपं भिन्द्यात्। तथा च यदेव तदसांकेतिकं मन्त्रवपुः, तदेव अन्योन्यविचित्ररूपं पश्यद्भिः सर्वज्ञैः संकेतोपायमुपास्यतया उपदिश्यते। तत्रैव चासां-

केतिके वाङ्महसि तथा खलु मायीयाः संकेताः पतन्ति। यथा त एवा-मायीयासंकेतितमन्त्रतादात्म्यं प्रतिपद्यन्ते। तथा स्वरूपप्रतिपत्तिरेव हि तेषां वाचकताभावो नान्यः कश्चित्। अत्र स्फुटमभिज्ञानमभ्यासवशात् असांकेतिकतामापन्ने चिरतरपूर्ववृत्तगोशब्दपरामर्शः। तथैव संकेतकाले गोपरामर्शोऽपि अन्यामायीयासांकेतिकपरामर्शधामन्येव निपतति। यावत् बालस्यापि जन्मान्तरानुसरणेऽपि चित्स्वभावस्यादौ स्थितैवासांकेतिकी सत्ता—अन्यथानवस्थानात्। एवमेव संकेतग्रहणोपपत्तिः नान्यथा। इतीश्वरप्रत्यभिज्ञाटीकायामपि श्रीमदुत्पलदेवपादैर्निर्णीतम्। अत्र चानुप्रवेशयुक्तिः

'पश्यत्यन्यच्छृणोत्यन्यत्करोत्यन्यच्च जल्पति।
चिन्तयत्यन्यदा भुङ्क्ते तत्रासांकेतिकी स्थितिः॥'

इति। भट्टारकश्रीश्रीकण्ठपादाः

'मनोऽप्यन्यत्र निक्षिप्तं चक्षुरन्यत्र पातितम्' (स्व. तं. ८।५८)

इत्याद्यप्यवोचन्। तदपि सांकेतिकमन्त्रवपुः स्वबीजमनुधावदनुत्तरपदपर्यवसायि भवति। तदप्यनुत्तरपदं सततं तथाविधानन्तसमुदायवैचित्र्यसंरम्भसारं विसर्गदृष्ट्या प्रसरत्येव, विसर्गस्यैव हकलापर्यन्ततया प्रसरात्। तस्यापि हकारार्धाख्यशक्तिकुण्डलिन्याः स्वरूपाभेदात्मकबिन्दुस्वरूपद्वारेण अनुत्तरपद एव संक्रमात् स्वरूप एव विश्रान्तिः। एकाक्षरसंवित् किल स्वरूपत एव देशकालकलनोपादानादिनैरपेक्ष्येणैव प्रागुक्ततत्त्वपूर्णतानयेन झगिति पर-विसर्गभूमौ धावति। परविसर्गभूमिश्लेष एव आनन्देच्छेशनोन्मेषतत्प्रसृतितद्वैचित्र्यक्रियाशक्तिमयानाम् आकारादीनां स्थितिः। स एव विसर्गः स्वसत्तानान्तरीयकतयैव तथैवातिभरितया सत्तया प्रसरन् द्रागित्येव हकलामयः संपद्यते। हकलामयतासंपत्तिरेव वस्तुतः कादिसत्तानन्ततत्त्वजालस्थितिः। हकलैव च पुनरपि बिन्दावनुप्रविशन्त्यनुत्तरपद एव पर्यवस्यति। इत्येकैवाद्वयपरिपूर्णरूपा संवेदनसत्ताभट्टारिकेयं परा भगवती परमेश्वरी। न तत्र क्रमादियोगः कश्चित्। तदेतदुच्यते 'अहमिति' विपर्यये तु संहृतौ 'महअ' इति। द्वैधमपि च इयमेकैव वस्तुतः संवित्।

एवमेष स सर्वत्र घटसुखादिप्रकाशेऽपि स्वात्मविश्रान्तिसर्वस्वभूतोऽहंभावः। यथोक्तं

'प्रकाशस्यात्मविश्रान्तिरहंभावो हि कीर्तितः।' (अ. प्र. सि. २२)

इति। स च वस्तुतः सर्वात्मकः—समनन्तरनिर्णीतनीत्या इति पराभट्टारिकानुविद्धो भैरवात्मक एव, यथोक्तं मयैव स्तोत्रे

'विश्वत्र भावपटले परिजृम्भमाणा
विच्छेदशून्यपरमार्थचमत्कृतिर्या।
तां पूर्णवृत्त्यहमिति प्रथनस्वभावां
स्वात्मस्थितिं स्वरसतः प्रणमामि देवीम्॥'

इति। एष एव श्रीवामनविरचिते अद्वयसंपत्तिवार्त्तिके उपदेशनयो बोद्धव्यः। तेन स्थितमेतत्—अकार एव सर्वाद्यः। यत्रापि हर्षघटनीलादौ हकाराद्या अपि वर्णाः, तत्रापि तथाविधानन्तनिजपूर्वापरवर्णसमाक्षेप एव। अन्यथा तस्यैव हादेः समुदाययोगान्ते परमाक्षिप्यमाणत्वादेवान्तर्निलीना विकल्पगोचरत्वमप्राप्ताः स्युः। अत एव सर्वत्र विज्ञाने सर्वा एव देवताः सममेव समुदयं दधत्यश्चित्रां संवित्तिवृत्तिं वर्तयन्ति। तदनेनैवाशयेन कालाधिकारादावेकस्मिन्नेव प्राणे प्राणषोडशांशेऽपि वा षष्टितद्द्विगुणाद्यब्दोदयपूर्वकं मातृरुद्रलोकपालग्रहनागादीनामुदयप्रलयाश्चित्रा निरूपिता एकस्मिन्नेव प्राणचारे। इत्यकालकलितत्वमेव तत्त्वं—वस्तुतः परमार्थः। यदि परमेतावन्मात्रं मायीय–अध्यवसाय–अनध्यवसेयम् इति नास्तिकताअभिमानकारि, परसंविदि तु तत्कालं भासते एव। अत एवैकस्यामेव ज्ञानकलनायां 'पश्यत्यन्यद्विकल्पयत्यन्यत्' इत्याद्युपदेशेन यदुक्तं देवतात्रयाधिष्ठानं तत्सर्वत्रैवानपायि। सर्वाण्येव च संवेदनानि वस्तुतोऽहमितिपरमार्थानि विमर्शमयान्येव। तदेवं स्थितम्—एतद्विश्वमन्तःस्थितमानन्दशक्तिभरितो वमन् प्रसमानश्च विसर्ग एव परमेश्वरो घनीभूय हकारात्मतां प्रतिपद्यानन्तसंयोगवैचित्र्येण क्षरूपतामप्येति। स एवैष द्व्यात्मकशाक्त-

योनिसंघट्टसमुचितवर्णात्मकक्षोभरूपानाहतनाददशाश्रयणेन मध्यमसौषुम्न-पदोच्छलत्तत्तदनन्तभावपटलात्मा विसर्गो विश्लिष्यन् ध्रुवधाम्नि अनुत्तर-पद एव प्रविशति, इति प्रागपि उक्तमेतत्। अमी चाकाराद्याः स्थितिमन्तः प्राणे तुटिषोडशकादिस्थित्या एकां तुटिं संधीकृत्यार्धार्धभागेन प्रलयो-दययोर्बहिरपि पञ्चदशदिनात्मककालरूपतां तन्वते, इति—तिथयः कलाश्चोक्ताः, षोडश्येव च कला विसर्गात्मा विश्लिष्यन्ती, सप्तदशी कला श्रीवाद्यादिशास्त्रेषु निरूपिता

'सा तु सप्तदशी देवी हकारार्धार्धरूपिणी।'

इति। विसर्गस्य हकारार्धत्वात् ततोऽपि विश्लेषस्यार्धत्वादिति निरव-यवस्यैकवर्णस्य कथमेषा विकल्पना? इति चेत्—अस्मत्पक्षे सर्वमेवानव-यवं चिन्मयैकावभासनानतिरेकात्। तथापि च स्वातन्त्र्यादेव अवयवा-वभासेऽपि अनवयवतैवानपायिनी, तथा इहापि अस्तु को विरोधः। एवमेव वर्णोपपत्तिः। अपरथा दन्त्योष्ठ्यकण्ठ्यतालव्यादिवर्णेषु क्रमप्रसारी पवन आघातकः कथं कण्ठं हत्वा तात्वाहन्ति इति। युगपदापूरकत्वेऽपि समान-कालता स्यात्। यत्तु कण्ठघातोत्थं रूपं तत् तु ताल्वाहतिजं सर्वत्र संभवति। श्वासनादयोश्च पश्चात्प्रतीयमानतया 'अनुप्रदानत्वम्' उच्यते। द्विमात्रत्रिमात्रेषु च द्विकादियोगो गर्भीकृतः। तथैव मात्रकेऽपि अर्ध-मात्रादियोगः संवेद्यः। यथोक्तं भट्टनारायणेन

'प्रणवोर्ध्वार्धमात्रातोऽप्यणवे महते पुनः।
ब्रह्माण्डादपि नैर्गुण्यगुणाय स्थाणवे नमः॥' (स्त. चि. ७)

इति। इह तु पञ्चाशद्वर्णा विश्वमपि वा अक्रममेकमेव। क्वचित्तु मतादि-शास्त्रेषु विसर्गविश्लेषस्यैव अनुत्तरपदसत्तालम्बनेनाष्टादशी कला इत्यभ्युप-गमः। तदेवमेताः कला एव ह्लादनामात्रचित्तवृत्त्यनुभावकाः 'स्वराः' इत्युक्ताः। स्वरयन्ति शब्दयन्ति सूचयन्ति चित्तं स्वं च स्वरूपात्मानं रान्ति। एवं परप्रमातरि संक्रामयन्तो ददति, स्वं च आत्मीयं

कादियोनिरूपं रान्ति—बहिः प्रकाशयन्तो ददति इति स्वराः। एत एव हि चित्तवृत्तिसूचका नादात्मकाः करुणशृङ्गारशान्तादिकां चित्तवृत्ति-माक्रन्दनचाटुकस्तुत्यादौ केवला वा योनिवर्णनिविष्टा वा तिर्यक्तदहर्जाता-दिष्वपि प्रथमत एवापतन्तः संकेतविघ्नादिनैरपेक्ष्येणैव संविदासन्नवर्ति-त्वात् स्वरकाक्वादिरूपतामश्नुवानाः प्रकाशयन्ति—इत्यर्थधर्मा उदात्तादय उपदिष्टाः, तेषामेव चित्तवृत्त्यनुभावकषड्जादिस्वरूपत्वात्। एवं सर्वत्र संवेदने सर्वा एवैता वैचित्र्यचर्याचारचतुराः शक्तय आदिक्षान्ताः समा-पतन्त्योऽहमहमिकया अक्रममेव भासमानाः कलनामयतयैव ज्ञानक्रम-संक्रमणमेव दिश्यमानं देशमुत्थापयन्ति, अन्यथा मेरुपरमाण्वोरविशेषात्। इति गर्भीकृतदेशात्मकवैचित्र्यं क्रियावैचित्र्यात्मकं क्रमरूपं च कालम् अन्तर्बहिर्योजनयोल्लासयन्त्यः स्वात्मनि युञ्जानत्वेन ग्रसमानाः प्रोल्लास-समये रिक्तरूपतया उद्योगावभासचर्वणविलापनरूपेण द्वादशात्मिकां कृशरूपतामाश्रयन्त्यः, तद्गृहीतप्रमितिगतोद्योगादिकलाचतुष्टयपरिपूर्ण-तयापि सालसं षोडशात्मकभरितपूर्णरूपतया प्रविशन्त्योऽन्तर्बहिश्च तद-मृतानन्दविश्रान्तिरूपं चमत्कारसत्तासारकलाचतुष्कं विसृजन्त्य एवं-विधामेव पूर्णकृशात्मकदोलालीलां निर्विशमानाः सोमसूर्यकलाजालग्रसन-वमनचतुरा अकारमेवादितया मध्ये च कादियोनिजातमवसाने च बिन्दुं दधती 'अहम्' इत्येषैव भगवती सृष्टिः। तदुक्तं श्रीसोमानन्दपादैर्निजविवृतौ 'अः अं इत्येषैव विकृताविकृतरूपा मातृका' इत्यादि। ते तु 'अ' इत्येतदनुत्तरमाकाराद्याश्च तिथयः। यद्वा बिन्दुरंकारः अकाराद्यास्तिथय-स्तदन्तो विसर्ग इत्यपि व्याचक्षते। तदेव संवित्सतत्त्वं 'स्पन्द' इत्युपदिशन्ति। स्पन्दनं च किंचिच्चलनम्। स्वरूपाच्च यदि वस्त्वन्तराक्रमणं तच्चलनमेव न किंचित्त्वम्। नो चेत् चलनमेव न किंचित्। तस्मात् स्वरूप एव क्रमादिपरिहारेण चमत्कारात्मिका—उच्छलत्ता ऊर्मिरिति मत्स्योदरीति-प्रभृतिशब्दैरागमेषु निदर्शितः 'स्पन्द' इत्युच्यते—किंचिच्चलनात्मकत्वात्। स च शिवशक्तिरूपः सामान्यविशेषात्मा तद्व्याख्या-

तम् । 'आद्यास्तिथयः बिन्द्ववसानगाः कालयोगेन सोमसूर्यौ' तस्यैवाकुलस्यान्तः पृथिव्यादीनि च यावत् ब्रह्मपञ्चकं तावत्तेषां स्वराणामन्तः । कथम् । क्रमात् क्रमस्यादनं भक्षणं कालग्रासः तथा कृत्वेति क्रियाविशेणम् । शोभने व्रते भोगे रिक्तत्वे भोगनिवृत्तौ च पूर्णत्वे सुव्रते, आमन्त्रणमपि एतत् एवं व्याख्येयम्, एवममूला—अकारमूला अविद्यमानमूला च अनादित्वात् । स क्रमो यस्याः प्रश्लेषेणातद्रूपोऽन्यथारूपोऽपि क्रमो यस्याः तथाप्यमूला । अमूलस्य यदाततनमाततं ततस्तदेव च क्रमो यस्याः । एषा चाज्ञेया ज्ञातृरूपा । एषैव च ज्ञेया—अन्यस्याभावात्, अविद्यमानं क्षान्तं तूष्णीमासनमविरतं सृष्ट्यादिरूपत्वेन अस्याम् । आक्षाणामैन्द्रियिकाणामन्ते समीपे प्रागपर्यवसाना या भवेदित्युपचारादाक्षान्वा सृष्टिरपूर्वमाहरणं स्वात्मानुप्रवेशात्मस्वरूपं संहाररूपं यस्याम् । एषैव च शिवात्मकबीजप्रसररूपाणां मननत्राणधर्माणां सर्वेषामेव वाच्यवाचकादिरूपवर्णभट्टारकात्मनां मन्त्राणां, शक्त्यात्मकयोनिस्पन्दानां, सर्वासां तद्बीजोद्भूतानां वेदनारूपाणां विद्यानाम् (योनिः) । इयं समा सर्वत्रानूनाधिका सर्वेषु तन्त्रेषु तन्त्रणासु च सर्वासु क्रियासु सर्वकालं च सर्वं ददती सिद्धिसंघम् आख्याता-प्रकटा । अख्यातिरूपां मायामुद्दिश्य भेदो वर्णानाम् । तथाहि—त एव शुद्धमन्त्ररूपा वर्णाः प्रथमं पञ्चविधविपर्ययाशक्त्यादिरूपप्रत्ययात्मकभावसृष्टितामेत्य स्वरूपमावृण्वते,

'पञ्च विपर्ययभेदा भवन्त्यशक्तिश्च करणवैकल्यात् ।
अष्टाविंशतिभेदा तुष्टिर्नवधाष्टधा सिद्धिः ॥' (सा. का. ४७)

इति हि एत एव प्रत्ययाः पाशवसृष्टिरूपाः पाशा मुख्यतया, यथोक्तम्

'स्वरूपावरणे चास्य शक्तयः सततोत्थिताः ।
यतः शब्दानुवेधेन न विना प्रत्ययोद्भवः ॥' (स्प. का. ३।१५)

इति । तथा

'परामृतरसापायस्तस्य यः प्रत्ययोद्भवः ॥' (स्प. का. ३।१४)

इत्यादि, एवं प्रत्ययसृष्टित्वान्तरालीकरणेन स्फुटश्रूयमाणश्रुत्यात्मकक्रमाभासमानमायीयवर्णसृष्टिराद्यपारमार्थिकशुद्धरूपालिङ्गिता तत्तत्कार्यफलप्रसवदायिनी निरूपिता श्रीपूर्वशास्त्रे

'सर्वशास्त्रार्थगर्भिण्या इत्येवं विषयानया ।
अघोरं बोधयामास स्वेच्छया परमेश्वरः ॥' (मा. वि. ३।२६)

इत्येवं-विषया

'स तया संप्रबुद्धः सन् योनिं विक्षोभ्य शक्तिभिः ।
तत्समानश्रुतीन्वर्णांस्तत्संख्यानसृजत्प्रभुः ॥' (मा. वि. ३।२७)

इत्यादि,

'तैस्तैरालिङ्गिताः सन्तः सर्वकामफलप्रदाः ।
भवन्ति साधकेन्द्राणां नान्यथा वीरवन्दिते ॥' (मा. वि. ३।२८)

इत्यादि च । एवमाख्याता प्रकटापि अप्रकटा मायान्धानाम् । सर्वदैव ख्याता प्रकाशा शुद्धवेदनात्मिका यस्याः, सर्वत्र स्वस्वभावात्मकप्रभावप्रख्यप्रसरानिरोधो यस्या वा । तदयमत्र संक्षेपार्थः

'स्वातन्त्र्यैकरसावेशचमत्कारैकलक्षणा ।
परा भगवती नित्यं भासते भैरवी स्वयम् ॥
तस्याः स्वभावयोगो यः सोऽनिरुद्धः सदोदितः ।
सदाशिवधरातिर्यङ्नीलपीतसुखादिभिः ॥
भासमानैः स्वस्वभावैः स्वयंप्रथनशालिभिः ।
प्रथते संविदाकारः स्वसंवेदनसारकः ॥
स्वस्वसंवेदनं नाम प्रमाणमिति वर्ण्यते ।
बालतिर्यक्सर्वविदां यत्साम्येनैव भासते ॥
इन्द्रियाणि त्रिरूपं च लिङ्गं परवचःक्रमः ।
सारूप्यमन्यथायोगः प्रतीत्यनुदयो यमः ॥
इत्यादिको यस्य सर्वं द्वारमात्रं निरूप्यते ।
तत्स्वसंवेदनं प्रोक्तमविच्छेदप्रथामयम् ॥

येषां नाक्षत्रिरूपादिनाममात्रेऽप्यभिज्ञता ।
तेषामपि तिरश्चां हि समा संवित्प्रकाशते ॥

एवं भासा स्वभावेन स्वरूपामर्शनात्मिका ।
स्वरूपामर्शनं यच्च तदेव परवाग्वपुः ॥

तद्विचित्रस्वभावत्वाद्विचित्रप्रथनामयम् ।
प्रथते पारतन्त्र्यं हि न जातु भजते क्वचित् ॥

अपारतन्त्र्यात्संकेतप्रत्यूहादेः कथं स्थितिः ।
अतः संकेतरहितं स्वस्वरूपविमर्शनम् ॥

देशकालकलामायास्थानाघातक्रियोत्तरम् ।
परिपूर्णं स्वतः सर्वं सर्वाकारविलक्षणम् ॥

स्वाभाविकमहासंवित्सत्संस्कारैकलक्षणम् ।
शुद्धविद्यात्मकं रूपमहमित्युभयात्मकम् ॥

तदेव मातृकारूपं खरादीनां निजं वपुः ।
तत्पारमार्थिकाकारं द्रुत्याश्यानस्वरूपतः ॥

बीजयोन्यात्मकं प्रोक्तं शिवशक्तिस्वरूपकम् ।
शिवशक्त्योस्तु संघट्टादन्योन्योच्छलितत्वतः ॥

परस्परसमापत्तिर्जगदानन्ददायिनी ।
अन्तःस्थविश्वपर्यन्तपारमार्थिकसद्वपुः ॥

यद्वीर्यमिति निर्णीतं तद्विश्लेषणयोजना ।
विसर्ग इति तत्प्रोक्तं ध्रुवधाम तदुच्यते ॥

अनुत्तरपदावाप्तौ स एष सुघटो विधिः ।
अस्मादेव तु मायीयाद्वर्णपुञ्जान्निरूपिता ॥

मायामालम्ब्य भिन्नैव श्रीपूर्वे सृष्टिराक्षरी ।
पञ्चाशद्भेदसंभिन्नप्रत्ययप्रसवात्मिका ॥

बन्धरूपा स्वभावेन स्वरूपावरणात्मिका ।
अत्रैवान्तर्गतास्तास्ताः खेचर्यो विषमात्मिकाः ॥

तन्वते संसृतिं चित्रां कर्ममायाणुतामयीम् ।
अस्याः साम्यं स्वभावेन शुद्धभैरवतामयम् ॥

प्रोक्तं प्रागेव जीवत्वं मुक्तत्वं पारमार्थिकम् ।
भिन्नाया वर्णसृष्टेश्च तदभिन्नं वपुः परम् ॥

वीर्यमित्युक्तमत्रैव यद्गुप्त्या मन्त्रगुप्तता ।
तदेतदहमित्येव विसर्गानुत्तरात्मकम् ॥

स्वस्वभावं परं जानञ्जीवन्मुक्तः सकृद्बुधः ।
सिद्ध्यादिप्रेप्सवस्तेन क्लृप्तसंकोचसूत्रितम् ॥

नाभिमण्डलहृद्व्योम्नि योगिनोऽहमुपासते ।
तदेतत्किल निर्णीतं यथागुर्वागमं मनाक् ॥

एनां संविदमालम्ब्य यत्स्यात्तत्पृच्छ्यतां स्ववित् ।
नैतावतैव तुलितं मार्गीशस्तु प्रदर्शितः ॥

इयतीं तु व्यवच्छिन्द्याद्भैरवीं संविदं हि कः ।
एतावाञ्छक्तिपातोऽयमस्मासु प्रविजृम्भितः ॥

येनाधिकारितैरेतदस्माभिः प्रकटीकृतम् ।
अस्माकमन्यमातॄणामद्य कालान्तरेऽपि वा ॥

भवत्यभूच्च भविता तर्कः सूक्ष्मतमोऽव्ययम् ।
यः सर्वयोगावयवप्रकाशेषु गभस्तिमान् ॥

श्रीपूर्वशास्त्रे निर्णीतो येन मुक्तश्च मोचकः ।
एतत्तु सर्वथा ग्राह्यं विमृश्यं च परेप्सुभिः ॥

क्षणं मर्त्यत्वसुलभां हित्वासूयां विचक्षणैः ।
आलोचनक्षणादूर्ध्वं यद्भवेदात्मनि स्थितिः ॥

चिदर्काभ्रलवास्तेन संशाम्यन्ते स्वतो रसात् ।'

परसंवेअणाभासमऊइणाऊरअरमहसोआइमऊइणसइभा-
सइम अलाहि शरणिअपसरहु परिसरिसन जतुहसो पश्चअप
हिलुअवर्णं परिगाहरु इर वसत्तिपलमहस्म ओहुभितुर कदसुख
विसरिपि असिद्धि धराइम उस अल विपरिसि अभासइ वाहिर-
विहरिणो एहि विसर्गभूमि अनार्दहुक्तइ लर्थ ईण पवि मिणं
दहुअमलाहं विहरिणी कुइलित्यत अणुत्तर परपइ जश्चि अभवि
अतत तचमप्पइ भस्मइवि बिन्दुविसरि सुताए हुप आसत्त तअह
सत्तमल हिपुविसि विभेत विहंसः तमालि निमाइ अअह सुत-
तस्मह भोअममण अइलं मरु निभुंऊ अपारहमरल पदुद्यो प्रन्तीप
सारइमात द्वय भासि विगमइ विलाअनु सोश्नि अं असि तमर्थं
अहिसा अइपविमन्ती अलसइरसा मच्छेअरि परिदेवितरंगणि
प्रफऊ असुह सारंगिणि रितत्तस्म कीलालसा तुहि मत्तिदिविरह
एणि हानुण पिब्भति जतस्माइ लालणमहो संमअलालसा ।

एवमुत्तरस्याप्यनुत्तरमिति यदुक्तम् 'तन्मयोऽसावुत्तरस्य' इत्यंशेनोपात्तः कुलात्मा शाक्तः सृष्टिप्रसरः स विस्तरतो निर्णीतः। तच्चोत्तरमपि यथानुत्तरं तथा निरूपितम्। इदानीं त्वनुत्तरमेव स्वरूपेण विस्तरतो विचारपदवी-मपेक्षते। एवं विध्यनुवादो निर्वहतो अनूद्यमानो विधीयमानश्चांशः स्वरूपतो लक्षितौ स्याताम्। यथा यदेव शिवनामस्मरणमेतदेव समस्तसौख्यो-च्छलनमिति द्वावप्यंशौ लक्ष्यौ, इह तु यद्यपि अनुत्तरं नाम अन्यद्वस्तु किंचिन्नास्ति—अन्यत्वे तस्याप्युत्तरत्वे एवाभिपातात्, तथापि स्वातन्त्र्य-कल्पितोपदेश्योपदेशकभावाभिप्रायेणेयं व्यवस्था इत्युक्तं प्राक्। ततश्च विस्तरतोऽनुत्तरस्वरूपनिरूपणाय ग्रन्थान्तरावतारः—

तन्निरूपयति

चतुर्दशयुतं भद्रे
तिथीशान्तसमन्वितम् ॥ ९ ॥

तृतीयं ब्रह्म सुश्रोणि
हृदयं भैरवात्मनः ।
एतन्नायोगिनीजातो
नारुद्रो लभते स्फुटम् ॥ १० ॥

हृदयं देवदेवस्य
सद्यो योगविमुक्तिदम् ।
अस्योच्चारे कृते सम्यङ्-
मन्त्रमुद्रागणो महान् ॥ ११ ॥

सद्यस्तन्मुखतामेति
स्वदेहावेशलक्षणम् ।
मुहूर्तं स्मरते यस्तु
चुम्बकेनाभिमुद्रितः ॥ १२ ॥

स बध्नाति तदा सर्वं
मन्त्रमुद्रागणं नरः ।
अतीतानागतानर्थान्
पृष्टोऽसौ कथयत्यपि ॥ १३ ॥

प्रहराद्यदभिप्रेतं
देवतारूपमुच्चरन् ।
साक्षात्पश्यत्यसंदिग्ध-
माकृष्टं रुद्रशक्तिभिः ॥ १४ ॥

प्रहरद्वयमात्रेण
व्योमस्थो जायते स्मरन् ।
त्रयेण मातरः सर्वा
योगीश्वर्यो महाबलाः ॥ १५ ॥

वीरा वीरेश्वराः सिद्धा
बलवाञ्छाकिनीगणः ।
आगत्य समयं दत्त्वा
भैरवेण प्रचोदिताः ॥ १६ ॥

यच्छन्ति परमां सिद्धिं
फलं यद्वा समीहितम् ।
अनेन सिद्धाः सेत्स्यन्ति
साधयन्ति च मन्त्रिणः ॥ १७ ॥

यत्किञ्चिद्भैरवे तन्त्रे
सर्वमस्मात्प्रसिद्ध्यति
अदृष्टमण्डलोऽप्येवं
.... ॥ १८ ॥

भैरवरूपस्य विश्वस्य प्रदर्शितयुक्त्यागमनिरूपितनररूपापराभट्टारिका-स्वभावः शाक्तः, तस्य हृदयं सारं शिवरूपं परमेश्वर्या श्रीमत्पराभट्टारिकया समालिङ्गितम् । भैरवशब्देन विश्वस्य सर्वसर्वात्मकतावपुः शक्तिरूपं तत्सहितस्यात्मनो नररूपस्य एतावच्छिवात्मकं हृदयं परेणाभेदेन सर्वात्मकतया एव । तेन, तया च विनास्य भेदस्यैवायोगात् इत्युक्तं प्राक् ।

'सुश्रोणि' इत्यामन्त्रणम्। अशोभनमायात्मकतायामपि अनपेतं शुद्धचिन्मयं यदेतत् श्रोण्यां हृदयं योनिरूपमुक्तं तत्रः—अन्तःकृतसकलमन्त्रमहेशादिभिः स्थावरान्तप्रमातृजालस्याहमात्मनोऽस्माकमिति समुचितापतितव्यपदेशस्य भैरवात्मपूर्णतामयम्। अन्तर्गतविश्ववीर्यसमुच्छलत्तात्मकविसर्गविश्लेषानन्दशक्त्यैकघनं ब्रह्म बृहत् व्यापकं बृंहितं च। न तु वेदान्तपाठकाङ्गीकृतकेवलशून्यवादाविदूरवर्तिब्रह्मदर्शने इव। एतच्च तृतीयं नराद्यपेक्षया शिवपरैकरूपम्। अत एवामीषु शास्त्रेषु अत्र च मुख्यतया तदेव हृदयं पूज्यतयोपदिष्टम्। अननुप्रविष्टतथावीर्यव्याप्तिसारहृदया अपि तावन्मात्रबाह्याचारपरिशीलनेनैव क्रमवशशिथिलीभवच्छिथिलितविदलद्विदलितपाशवनियमबन्धना एतद्धृदयव्याप्तिं स्वयमेव समधिशेरते। नहि एतद्धृदयानुप्रवेश एव 'एतद्धृदयेऽनुप्रविष्टोऽस्मि इयं देवी परा' इत्येतच्छाब्दविकल्पकल्प्यः, हृदयान्तरमार्गणादित्युक्तं विस्तरतः।

संकोचयन्ति हृदयं नहि शास्त्रपाशा
नो संविदं कलुषयेद्यदयं च लोकः।
सम्यक्स्वभावपदवीपरिपूर्णरूपा
सैवोल्लसल्लयभरा भरिता स्थितिः स्यात्॥

यदुक्तं मयैव स्तोत्रे

'भवद्भक्त्यावेशाद्विशदतरसंजातमनसां
क्षणेनैषावस्था स्फुटमधिवसत्येव हृदयम्।'

इति। अत एव कोणेषु पूज्यास्तिस्रो, मध्ये देवी परानन्दभैरवनिर्मथनरूपा नित्यानन्दरसप्रसरेणैव क्षोभात्मकविसर्गेण—इति देवतानां संप्रदायो, यामलयोगे वीराणामपि आनन्देन्द्रियनित्यानन्दक्षोभात्मकदूतीसंघट्टजेन इति। एकवीरतायामपि स्वरूपानन्दविश्रान्तियोगेन, पुंसोऽपि आनन्देन्द्रियनिःसरणधामत्रिकोणकन्दाधोविनिविष्टचित्तनिवेशात् आनन्दक्षोभप्रसवं करोति तदिन्द्रियमूलतत्पर्यन्तसंघट्टघनतायाम्, अत्रोक्तम्

'वह्नेर्विषस्य मध्ये तु चित्तं सुखमयं क्षिपेत् ।'
केवलं वायुपूर्णं वा स्मरानन्देन युज्यते ॥ (वि. भै. ६८)

इति । एवमानन्दयोग एव हृदयपूजा । यथोक्तं त्रिकतन्त्रसारे

'आनन्दप्रसरः पूजा तां त्रिकोणे प्रकल्पयेत् ।
पुष्पधूपादिगन्धैस्तु स्वहृत्संतोषकारिणीम् ॥'

इति । सर्वं हि मुद्राद्वयानुविद्धं—ज्ञानक्रियाशक्तिसारत्वात् । केवलं देवतासु ज्ञानमुद्रा अन्तरुद्रिक्ता, क्रियामुद्रा बहिः । वीरेषु विपर्ययः । अनुप्रवेशस्तु समतया विपर्ययाच्च । अनेनैवाभिप्रायेण ज्ञानशक्त्यात्मके लिङ्गे क्रियाशक्तिसमर्पणमुक्तम् । एवमेतत् चतुर्दशसु युतं संश्लिष्टं पञ्चदशात्मकं तिथीशान्तेन विसर्गेण षोडशेनान्वितम् । यद्वा चतुर्दशसहितं युतं युग्मं षोडशं तिथीनां पञ्चदशानामीशो विसर्गः, तस्यान्तः सप्तदश्यनुत्तरकला तदन्वितं हृदयं—सर्वाणि घटसुखादीनि वस्तूनि तामेव बीजसत्तां परमार्थरूपेणाक्रामन्तीत्युक्तं विस्तरतः, अत एव तत् हृदयम् । तथानुत्तरानुसारेण यदेतत् ब्रह्मसामरस्यं वेद्यवेदकयोश्चतसृणां दशानामुद्योगादीनां समाहारोऽविभागभूः प्राथमिकी, तया युतमविभागि, य एते तिथीनामीशा ऊकारान्ताः तत्प्रभवत्वादन्यस्येति हि उक्तम् । तेषां तिथीशानामन्ता—अमृतवर्णाः चत्वारः तैः सम्यगन्वितम् । तच्च तृतीयं—नराद्यपेक्षया शिवरूपं परम् । वेदकश्चतसृभिर्दशाभिरुल्लसन् वेद्यमेव ताभिराप्यायकौतुकात्मना ता एवामृतकलाः स्वात्मनि एकीकुर्वन् वेद्यवेदकक्षोभसमापत्त्या ऐकात्म्यलक्षणप्रसंख्यानेनाभ्यासेन वा गम्यं भैरवात्मना विश्वहृदयमनुत्तरं प्रविशेत् । यथोक्तम्

'सर्वभूतस्थमात्मानं सर्वभूतानि चात्मनि ।
ईक्षते योगयुक्तात्मा सर्वत्र समदर्शनः ॥' (भ. गी. ६।३०)

इति । इच्छोल्लसत्तात्मनि आनन्दशक्तौ यदेतत् संहृत्य अनुसृत्या क्रियाशक्तिमपेक्ष्य तृतीयं रूपमिच्छात्म, तदेव प्राक्कोटाविष्यमाणाद्यकलुषं ब्रह्म, चतुर्थे दश चत्वारिंशत् भैरवभेदापेक्षया परभैरवपरशक्तित्रयसहितानि

तत्त्वानि, यथोक्तम्

'षट्त्रिंशच्छोधनीयानि शोधको भैरवः परः।
परं त्रिकं तु करणं दीक्षेयं पारमार्थिकी।।'

इत्यादि, तेयुंतम्। आनन्दशक्तिर्हि प्राक्पररूपा पूर्णा, कथं तिथीशैर्बीजैः तदन्तैश्च योनिरूपधरादिभिः समन्वितम्—इति क्रियाविशेषणम्। तदेव हृदयं, सर्वत्रात्र सकृद्विभातं प्रसंख्यानगम्यं रूपं मुख्यतः। तत्र योग्यानां तु परशक्तिपातपवित्रितानां वृथेन्द्रजालिककलनासदृशो योगाभ्यास इति मन्तव्यम्।

इच्छाभिप्रायेण तृतीयमिच्छा, तच्च बृंहितमिष्यमाणेनाभिन्नेन पूर्णं ब्रह्म, चतुर्दश चत्वारिंशद्युतानि निर्विभागभाञ्जि। यतोऽनन्तरं युतशब्दो विभक्तवाचि तिथीश्वरस्य अनुत्तरकलात्मनोऽन्तः आनन्दः तस्यानु—पश्चात् सम्यगितं बोधमयम्।

ईशानापेक्षया तृतीयमिच्छारूपं प्रसरवशादबृहद्भूतमीशानताम् आपन्नं चतुर्दशानां चत्वारिंशत्तत्त्वानां उक्तायाः, युतं परस्परव्यामिश्रता यत्र तिथीश्वरस्याकुलमयानुत्तरात्मना अन्तःसंहृतिः—कुलशक्तिप्रथमस्पन्द-स्तेनान्वितम्।

उन्मेषात्मकज्ञानशक्तियोगेन तृतीयं ब्रह्मेशनमेव। यदा चतुर्दशानां तस्या एव तत्त्वचत्वारिंशतो युतं प्रथमविभागो यत्र, तथाविधं भवति, तथा तिथीशान्तेन –कुलशक्तिप्रथमस्पन्देन सम्यक् प्ररुरुक्षुतया अन्वितम्। संशब्दोऽत्र भरणापेक्षः।

तज्ज्ञानशक्तिक्रियाशक्तिमध्यकोटिरूपप्राङ्निर्णीत-ऊकारकलालम्बितो-द्वतारूक्षया यदेतत् ब्रह्म। यत्किंचिच्चराचरं, तदशुद्धशुद्धाशुद्धसृष्ट्यपेक्षया तृतीयं शुद्धसृष्ट्यात्मकं यत्, अत एव तिथीश्वरैः हृदयभूततया तदन्तैश्च कादिक्षान्तैः समन्वितम्।

अथ शून्यचतुष्कानुसृत्या चतुर्णां धरादीनां दशा विनाशात्मिका विद्यते यत्र तद्व्योम तेन युतं तृतीयं ब्रह्मेच्छाख्यं तिथीश्वरस्यार्कस्य अन्तेन बाह्येन तेजसान्वितम् ।

व्याख्यातक्रमेण तृतीयं ब्रह्मेशनम् एतदपि एवमेव ।

तृतीयं ब्रह्मेच्छाख्यं चतुर्णां धराप्रभृतीनाम्, अन्तर्दशा यत्र आधारतया, तया युतम् । तिथीशान्तस्य वह्नेः तेजसो यदनुसरद्रूपं तेन सहितं व्योमात्म ।

तथैव तृतीयं ब्रह्म, चतुर्दशयुतं तिथीशान्तसमन्वितं परिपूर्णशून्यरूपप्लुत्या भैरवात्म ।

इच्छा खलु निजस्वभावभूतेशानसहिता वेद्यभूमेर्व्योमसत्तां यदाक्रामति तदा किंचित्प्रकाशभुवि विश्रम्य झटिति अपर्यन्तां काष्ठपाषाणप्रायां निश्चलां व्योमभूमिमनुप्रविशति, यत्रापवेद्यसुषुप्तमहाव्योमानुप्रविष्टान् योगिनः प्रत्युच्यते

'भेरीकांस्यनिनादोऽपि व्युत्थानाय न कल्पते ।'

इत्यादि ।

अधुनोक्तव्याप्त्या यदेतत्परस्पररूपसांकर्यवैचित्र्यं शक्तीनां तदुद्देशेन एवम्—"इच्छा यदानुत्तरपदप्रवेशशालिनी भवति तदा शक्तिक्षोभस्य रसनानन्तरम्, तत्रोच्यते—विलम्बितमध्यद्रुतानां चिद्विशेषस्पन्दानां सत्त्वादियोगजुषां चतुःशब्दोपलक्षिता चतुर्थी दशा यत्रास्ति सामान्यस्पन्दरूपा तदकुलम् । तेनाकुलेन अनुत्तरेण युतं तृतीयं ब्रह्मेच्छात्म ईशानसहितं तिथीशस्याकारस्यान्तेनानन्दशक्त्यात्मना अन्वितम्" ।

तदपि तथैव पुनरपि परां सत्तामनुप्रविशति यदा, तदा भैरवात्म परिपूर्णं दीर्घीभूतं नः—अस्माकमिति पूर्ववत् । अत एवैतदेव बीजयुग्मम् एवंविधबीजवैचित्र्यानुप्रवेशात् आच्छादप्रसवसमर्थम्—इति कामवाक्स्वोपयोगेनोच्यते ।

'कामेन कामयेत्कामान् कामं कामेषु योजयेत् ।'

(वामकेश्वरीमत ४।४६)

इत्यादि

'ए-ओकारगतं बीजं वाग्विधानाय केवलम् ।' (वा. म. १।८३)

इत्यादि, पञ्चमषष्ठवर्णद्वयेन यदुक्तं 'चतुर्दशयुतं तृतीयं ब्रह्म तिथीशान्तसमन्वितं' तदेव भैरवात्मानुत्तरपदानुप्रविष्टम् ।

एतत् ब्रह्म चत्वारिंशद्युतमुक्तनीत्या तिथीशान्तसमन्वितं भैरवात्मवेदनरूपतया बिन्द्वात्मकं हृदयम् ।

सकलमिदं तत्त्वजालं भैरवात्मतयोच्छलत्, अत एव बहिर्विसृज्यमानं बृंहितं ब्रह्म विसर्गात्मकं बहिःस्थितं च, भैरवात्मतयैकीभूतं भेदात्मकव्यवच्छेददारिद्र्यापसारणेन सर्वसर्वात्मकपदप्राप्त्या बृंहितम्—इति विसर्गपदम्, निर्णीतं चैतदवधानेन ।

एवं षोडशात्मिका बीजव्याप्तिरुक्ता । योनिव्याप्तिस्तु प्रतिवर्णं प्रागेवोक्ता, वर्गीकरणाभिप्रायेण तु निरूपणीया, बाल्ययौवनस्थाविरदेहान्तरग्रहणरूपदशाचतुष्टयसमाहारमयं पाञ्चभौतिकम्, अन्तः तिथीशान्तेन प्रवेशनिर्गमनात्मना प्राणापानरूपेण युतं तृतीयं पुर्यष्टकात्म ब्रह्म वृहत्त्वाच्च शून्यम् । अत्र च हृदयं शक्त्यात्म । त एते सर्व एव शरीरप्राणपुर्यष्टकशून्यतुर्यशक्तिरूपा बोधात्मकशिवबीजसातिशयघनताक्रमप्राप्तकायिकतयाभावा बाह्यात्मभूतात्मातिवाहिकात्मान्तरात्मपरमात्मव्यपदेश्याः प्रमातारः, एतद्भैरवात्म हृदयम् । प्रवेशोपायोऽत्र—"सर्वाः प्रमातृभूमीरनवच्छेदेनाक्रामेत् अन्तर्बहिष्करणत्रयोदशकं प्रकृत्या सह च । चतुर्दश चत्वारिंशद्युतं द्विगुणितमशीतिः । तिथयः पञ्चदश, ईशा रुद्रा एकादश, अन्तसमन्वितं—समन्विता युक्ता द्विगुणिताः कालाग्नयः, एवं—द्वादशोत्तरशतममंगतस्थूलसूक्ष्मपरशाक्तस्पन्दरूपमन्त्रवीर्यविकासस्फुरीकृतविसर्गविश्लेषणसंघट्टक्षोभात्मिकां शरीरसत्तामेव भैरवरूपां परिशीलयेत्" । ... युगपन्निवेशसंप्रदाय-

युक्त्या चतस्रो मधुरकषायतिक्ताम्लदशा यस्य मद्यसुरासवादेस्तत् तिथी-शान्तम्—उभयविसर्गात्मद्रव्यम्, समन्वितं—तदिन्द्रियद्वयान्तर्वर्ति कुसुम-शब्दवाच्यं मलम्। तृतीयं ब्रह्म जगदिन्धनदाहशेषं भस्म, भैरवात्म भरिता-कारमाप्यायकमम्बु हृदयं च उभयेन्द्रियान्तर्वर्तिरसाश्यानोभयरूपम्। तदे-तानि द्रव्याणि यथालाभं भेदमलविलापकानि। तथाहि दृश्यते एवायं क्रमः—यदियं संकोचात्मिका शङ्केव समुल्लसन्ती रूढा, फलपर्यन्ता, संसार-बीजतरोः प्रथमाङ्कुरसूतिः। सा चाप्रबुद्धान् प्रति स्थितिर्भवेत्—इति प्रबुद्धैः कल्पिता। बालान् प्रति कल्प्यमानापि च तेषां रूढा वैचित्र्येणैव फलति। अत एव वैचित्र्यकल्पनादेव सा बहुविध-अधर्मादिशब्दनिर्देश्या प्रतिशास्त्रं प्रतिदेशं चान्यान्यरूपा। यथोक्तम्

'ग्लानिर्विलुण्ठिका देहे तस्याश्चाज्ञानतः सृतिः।' (स्प. का. ३।८)

इति। सेयं यदा झटिति विगलिता भवति तदा निरस्तपाशवयन्त्रणाकलङ्को भैरवहृदयानुप्रविष्टो भवति। इति सर्वथा एतदभ्यासे यतितव्यम्। इति श्रीतिलकशास्त्रेऽयं भावः। श्रीभर्गशिखायामपि उक्तम्

'वीरव्रतं चाभिनन्देद्यथायोगं समभ्यसेत्।'

इत्यादि। श्रीसर्वाचारेऽपि

'अज्ञानाच्छङ्कते मूढस्ततः सृष्टिश्च संहृतिः।
मन्त्रा वर्णात्मकाः सर्वे वर्णाः सर्वे शिवात्मकाः॥
पेयापेयं स्मृता आपो भक्ष्याभक्ष्यं तु पार्थिवम्।
सुरूपं च विरूपं च तत्सर्वं तेज उच्यते॥
स्पृश्यास्पृश्यौ स्मृतो वायुश्छिद्रमाकाश उच्यते।
नैवेद्यं च निवेदी च नैवेद्यं गृह्णते च यः॥
सर्वं पञ्चात्मकं देवि न तेन रहितं क्वचित्।
इच्छामुत्पादयेत् कुत्र कथं शङ्का विधीयते॥'

इति । श्रीवीरावलिशास्त्रेऽपि अयमेवाभिप्रायः, उक्तं च क्रमस्तोत्रे

'सर्वार्थसंकर्षणसंयमस्य
यमस्य यन्तुर्, जगतो यमाय ।
वपुर्महाग्रासविलासरागात्
संकर्षयन्तीं प्रणमामि कालीम् ॥'

इति । व्याख्यातं चैतन्मया तट्टीकायामेव क्रमकेलौ विस्तरतः । अत एव षडर्धशास्त्रेष्वेषैव क्रिया प्रायो नियन्त्रणारहितत्वेन पूजा, तत्परिपूरणायैव सर्वद्रव्यलाभात् । इति विज्ञानक्रमो विस्तरत उक्तः । जातीनां च ब्राह्मणादीनां नास्ति स्थितिः—कल्पितत्वात्, उपदेशव्यङ्ग्तेति तु दुर्बुद्धीन् पशून् प्रत्याययेत्—इति च भगवता मुकुटसंहितायां विस्तरतो निर्णीतम्, इह तु अयत्नसिद्धमेव ।

चतुर्दशः ओकार-अंकारमध्यगः । तिथीशान्तो विसर्गः, तृतीयं ब्रह्म ष-हमध्यगम् । एतद्बीजं वस्तुतो विश्वस्य । तथाहि—यत्किंचित् सत् पार्थिवप्राकृतमायीयरूपं भासते तत् इच्छायां ज्ञाने वा क्रियायां वा पतितमपि सर्वात्मकत्वात् त्रिकरूपं परत्र शिवपदे विसृज्यते सर्वं च शिवपदात् विसृज्यते—इत्यविरतमेष एव प्रबन्धो निर्विकल्पकः । विकल्पो हि प्रमदारातिप्रभृतिरेवंकार्यभूत्, एवंकारी भवति, एवंकारी भविष्यतीति वर्तमानकालत्रयानुसंधितो भेदपरमार्थतयैव विसर्ग इति । प्रत्युत मोक्षमयशिवभूमिरपि सदैव देवदग्धानां संसारभयमरुमहाटवी संपन्ना ।

जलात्स्फूर्जज्ज्वालाजटिलवडवावह्निनिवहः
सुधाधाम्नः पूर्णाद्द्वयसदनदम्भोलिदलना ।
विकल्पादैश्वर्यप्रसरसरणेः संसृतिदरः
कियच्चित्रं चित्रं हतविधिविकासात्प्रसरति ॥

ईश्वरप्रत्यभिज्ञायामप्युक्तम्

'सर्वो ममायं विभव इत्येवं परिजानतः ।
विश्वात्मनो विकल्पानां प्रसरेऽपि महेशता ॥'
(आगमाधिकार २।१२)

इति । यथा चाकृतिमध्य एव चतुर्भुजत्रिनयनाद्या आकृतयो द्रव्यमध्ये च सुरासवाद्या बलादेव तां सत्तां समधिशाययन्ति । एवं सर्ववर्णमध्येऽपि अयं वर्णः, तथाहि—सकारस्तावत् परमानन्दामृतस्वभाव उल्लसन् एव समस्तं वर्णजालमाक्षिप्य उल्लसति । यद्यत्सत्यसुखसंपत्सत्तादीनां पारमार्थिकं वपुः सीत्कारसमुल्लासशेपकम्पवराङ्गसंकोचविकासोपलक्ष्यम्, तदेव हि सत्यादीनाममायीयं वस्तुतो रूपम् । तथाहि परहृदयग्रहणेङ्गितनिपुणा गगनगवयगवाद्यनन्तपदप्राङ्मध्यान्तभाविनोऽपि गकारादिमात्रादेवाभीष्टं चिन्वते—तावति सत्यपदेऽनुप्रवेशात्, एवमेकैकस्यैव वर्णस्य वास्तवं वाचकत्वम् । यथोक्तम्

'शब्दार्थप्रत्ययानामितरेतराध्यासात्संकरः
तत्प्रविभागसंयमात्सर्वभूतरुतज्ञानम् ।' (यो. सू. ३।१७)

इति । अत एव प्रायशोऽमी अकार-चकाराद्या वर्णा एकवर्णात्मानो निपातविभक्त्यादयो मायापदेऽपि पारमार्थिकमिव प्रमातृपदलीनमिदन्तापराङ्मुखमसत्त्वभूतं तत्तन्निषिध्यमानसमुच्चीयमानाभिन्नरूपनिषेधसमुच्चयादिकमर्थमभिदधति । एष एव भावस्तत्रभवतो भर्तृहरेः, यदाह

'पदमाद्यं पृथक्सर्वं पदं साकाङ्क्षमित्यपि ।' (वा. प. २।२)

इति वाक्यविचारे । तथा च वेदव्याकरणे पारमेश्वरेषु शास्त्रेषु मन्त्रदीक्षादिशब्देषु अक्षरवर्णसाम्यात् निर्वचनमुपपन्नम् । तत्तु न रूढं नियतिवशाद्विति न लोकपर्यन्तम् । तदेवं सकार ईदृशः । औकारविसर्गावपि व्याख्यातो । तदुक्तं श्रीपूर्वशास्त्रे

'सार्णेन त्रितयं व्याप्तं त्रिशूलेन चतुर्थकम् ।
सर्वातीतं विसर्गेण परा व्याप्तिरुदाहृता ॥' (मा. वि. ४।२५)

इति । तथा

'शिष्येणापि तदा ग्राह्या यदा संतोषितो गुरुः ।
शरीरद्रव्यविज्ञानजातिकर्मगुणादिभिः ॥
भेदिता तु यदा तेन गुरुणा हृष्टचेतसा ।
तदा सिद्धिप्रदा ज्ञेया नान्यथा वीरवन्दिते ॥'

(मा. वि. ३।५७-५८)

इति । अन्यत्रापि

एकं सृष्टिमयं बीजम् एका मुद्रा च खेचरी ।
द्वावेतौ यस्य जायेते सोऽतिशान्तपदे स्थितः ॥

इति । अत एवालेख्यं पुस्तके इति नियमः, श्रीपूर्वशास्त्रेऽपि

'वामजङ्घान्वितो जीवः पारम्पर्यक्रमागतः । (मा. वि. ३।५४)

इति । इहापि वक्ष्यते

'यथा न्यग्रोधबीजस्थः··· ·········· ।'

इति । तदेतत् भैरवात्मनो हृदयं—मालिन्यपेक्षया नकारात्, वस्तुतस्तु अकाराद्योगिन्याश्च विसर्गशक्तेः जातः प्रादुर्भूतप्रमातृभावो, रुद्रो रोधको द्रावकश्च पाशानां, स एव ना—पुरुषः एतत् स्फुटं लभते । न तु अरुद्रो नापि अयोगिनीगर्भसंभवः । सद्योयोगो भैरवैकात्म्यम् । स एव मोक्षो निर्णीतः । तं ददाति इति । (सद्यः) यो लभते स एवंविधो नान्यः । यश्चैवंविधः स स्फुटं लभत एव हृदयं, लभते—सद्योयोगविमोक्षदमेवेति । मन्त्रा वर्णभट्टारका लौकिकपारमेश्वरादिरूपा मननत्राणरूपा विकल्पसंविन्मयाः, मुद्राश्च सकलकरचरणादिकरणव्यापारमय्यः क्रियाशक्तिरूपाः । तत्कृतो गणः समूहात्मपरशक्त्येकरूपः । स्वस्यात्मनः प्राणपुर्यष्टकशून्यादेः देहस्य य आवेशः—झटिति परस्वरूपानुप्रवेशेन पारतन्त्र्यात्मकजडतातिरोधानेन स्वतन्त्रकर्तृत्वानुविद्धप्रमातृतोदयः । तथा स्वं स्वभावं पदार्थस्य ददातीति स्वदा, ईहा इच्छाद्या क्रियान्ता प्रसृतिः, तया आवेशः, तदेव लक्षणं यत्र तथा कृत्वा य उदेति सोऽस्य बीजस्योच्चारे ऊर्ध्वचरणे स्थितो

सत्याम्। यथैतत् तथा निर्णीतं बहुशः। सद्य इत्यनेन अनुप्रवेशः सूच्यते। तन्मुखतां तत्पररूपप्राधान्यमेति। न तु पशूनामिव तद्रूपं प्रत्युत तिरोधत्ते। अत एव मुहूर्तम्—अकालकलितत्वेऽपि परकलनापेक्षया उन्मेषमात्रं यः स्मरति—अनुसंधत्ते स एव व्याख्यातं मन्त्रमुद्रागणं संबध्नाति—स्वात्मन्येकीकरोति अद्वयतः। कथं?—चुम्बकेन विश्वस्पर्शकेन शाक्तेन रूपेणाभितः सर्वतो मुद्रितं मुद्रणं कृत्वा, तुरवधारणे। य एवं शाक्तस्पन्दमुद्रित एवंविधतत्त्वमयविरूपानुसंधायकः स एवैवं करोति। न तु नरैकरूपः पाषाणादि। यदतीतं यच्चानागतं यदनर्थरूपं प्रागन्याभावात् इतरदपि स कथयति एव—कथापर्यन्ततां नयति। संकल्पनात्। कथं? पृष्टः—पृष्टं तद् यस्यास्ति स तथा। प्रश्न ञीप्सा—यदेव किल ञीप्स्यति तदेव अन्तर्गतं बहिष्कुरुते।

यथोक्तम्

'यथेच्छाभ्यर्थितो धाता जाग्रतोऽर्थान्हृदि स्थितान्।
सोमसूर्योदयं कृत्वा संपादयति देहिनः॥' (स्प. का. ३।१)

इत्यादि। एको हि असौ स्मरणोत्प्रेक्षणादावपि तावानेव वर्तमानः। न स्तो भूतभविष्यती, यथोक्तम्

'कालोभयापरिच्छिन्ने वर्तमाने स्थितिर्भवेत्।'

इत्यादि। प्राग्भवत एवानधिकरूपस्य पुनरिदं जानाति करोति इत्यादिसंकोचासहिष्णोः सकृद्विभातत्वम्। अत एवोक्तं 'भूताद्यपेक्षा वर्तमानकालस्य तदभावे वस्तुतः अप्रसक्तेः अकालकलितत्वमेव वस्तुतत्त्वम्'। इति हि उक्तमसकृत्। स एव तु कालशक्तिमवभासयति चित्राम्।

'किं च जाग्रति कस्मिंश्चिद्घटिकाभिमतापि या।
तस्यामेव प्रमातारः स्वप्नगाश्चित्रताजुषः।
दिनप्रहरवर्षादिवैचित्र्यमपि चिन्वते॥'

इति नीत्या प्रकृष्टो हरः संहारोऽकुलाख्यः, तथोऽनन्तरमभिप्रेतं प्रेतशब्द-वाच्यसदाशिवतत्त्वनिविष्टज्ञानशक्त्याभिमुख्येन देवताया इच्छाया रूपं रूपाणां कलनम्। साक्षस्य सेन्द्रियस्य रूपस्यादनं भक्षणमतनं च सातत्य-गमनं कृत्वा। रोधनद्रावणशक्तिभिराकृष्टं पश्यति असंदिग्धं कृत्वा, एतदुक्तं भवति—यदिदं दर्शनं नाम तत्सर्वंतरङ्गप्रत्यस्तमयास्याकुलसत्ताधिरूढस्य अनन्तमहिमस्वातन्त्र्ययोगाद् भवति। इच्छाशक्तिमतः सेवेच्छा स्वान्तर्गता। इष्यमाणवस्तुन ईषदस्फुटभेदावभासनरूपज्ञानशक्त्यात्मकतामेति। तज्ज्ञान-शक्तिविशेषस्पन्दरूपसमस्तेन्द्रियाणां बहीरोधनम्। एतदेव सातत्यगमनम्, तच्च द्रावणं तदेव भक्षणम्। एते एव वमनभक्षणे। दर्शनस्य सर्वप्रथैक-मपत्वात् प्रथायाश्च तथाविधवैचित्र्ययोगात्। अनिश्चितोभयालम्बनत्वमपि स्थाणुपुरुषादावपि असंदिग्धमेव। एवं दुष्करमयी परमेशशक्तिः। एवं तु असौ परापररूपस्मृतिशक्तिमान् भैरव इत्याह 'प्रहरद्वयेत्यादि'। एवं तु स्मरन् (व्योमरूपः) जायते व्योम विद्यते यत्र पुर्यष्टके शून्ये च, तत्प्रमातृ-रूपतामादधानः प्रहरोपलक्षितं दर्शनाख्यं रूपं यदा पुनः पुनः परामृशति स्मरन्नपि च। प्राग्वत् 'साक्षात्पश्यत्यसंदिग्धमाकृष्टो रुद्रशक्तिभिः' इति संबन्धः। तावद्धि तदपि दर्शनमेव, इत्युक्तम्। एवं तु 'अपरात्मकविकल्प-शक्तियुक्त' इत्युच्यते। त्रयेणेति—पश्यन् स्मरंश्च व्योमस्थो यदा पुनरपि पश्यति तदनेन प्रहरोपलक्षितदर्शनत्रयेण मातरोऽन्तःप्रमातृमय्यः परमेश-शक्तयः ताश्च प्रमातृत्वादेव सिद्धाः प्रमात्रन्तरविषयसिद्ध्यनपेक्षाः तद्रूपै-कात्म्यलक्षणेन योगेनैश्वर्यं तथा गृहीतस्वातन्त्र्यांशाः, महत्—बाह्येन्द्रिय-वृत्त्यपेक्षया सर्वत्राप्रतिहतप्रसरत्वं बलं यासां ता अन्तःकरणदीधितयः ता अपि सिद्धा एव—विश्वत्र पाशवशासनयन्त्रणानिरपेक्षतयैव सरभसप्रवृत्ति-रूपत्वात्। वीरा बुद्धिक्रियेन्द्रियाख्याः तेऽपि सिद्धा एव। तेषामपि चेश्वराः कादिवर्णात्मानः तेऽपि सिद्धाः। तत्कादिवर्णोद्धारोदितश्च ब्राह्म्यादिदेवतात्मा तत्तद्द्वेषरागादिचित्तवृत्तिरसमयः शक्तिसमूहः, सोऽपि सिद्ध एव। अत एव बलवान्। एते सर्वे संभूय पराज्ञया—

परस्य मां मानमयीम् इति विकल्पात्मिकां सिद्धिम्, यद्वा समीहितं फलमेव 'अहं' ददति प्रयच्छन्ति। अज्ञातार्थक्रिये ज्ञातार्थक्रिये च एष क्रमेण विकल्पयोगः। किं बहुना ये मन्त्रिणोऽपरशास्त्रमन्त्रसिद्धाः साधयन्ति च तेऽपि अनेन हृदयेन सेत्स्यन्ति जीवन्मुक्ता भवन्ति। एतेन विना पारमार्थिकी सिद्धिर्न भवतीति भावः। 'यत्किंचिद्भैरवेत्यादि' तथा ये सिद्धाः साधयन्ति च ये च सेत्स्यन्ति अणिमादियोगात् तेऽपि अनेनैव। नहि एतद्धृदयानुप्रवेशं विना व्यावहारिक्यपि सिद्धिः। यतो—भैरवे विश्वात्मनि तन्त्रे क्रियाकलापे यत् किंचित् सिद्धिजातं तदत एव। एवमेष परमेश्वर एव हृदयात्मा। एवंरूपतया शक्तित्रितयबृंहितसततोदयमानसंह्रियमाणानन्तसंविदैक्यशाली।

१. एवम्—अदृष्टम्—अख्यातिरूपम्, अण्डं मायामलं,
अण्डं च भावानां भेदाख्यं सारं, लुम्पति एतत् हृदयम्।

२. एतत् हृदयमण्डलोऽपि—चत्वारि अण्डान्येव
लोपः संकोचः तद्योगि।

एवमेष विद्यामायोभयात्मा परमेश्वर एक एव चिद्घनः, यथोक्तम्

'दर्शनं तु परा देवी स्मरणं च परापरा।
विकल्पस्त्वपरा देवी त्रिकशक्तिमयः प्रभुः॥

मायाविद्ये उभे तस्य माया तु चतुरण्डिका।
विद्या स्वरूपसंवित्तिरनुग्रहमयी शिवा॥'

इति। यदि तु योगप्राधान्यं तदा श्रीपूर्वादिशास्त्रनिरूपितं पूर्वमेव व्रतादि कृत्वा 'अस्योच्चारे कृते' इत्यादि स्पष्टमेव व्याख्येयम्। यतो दृष्टकार्येषु नियतिपरतन्त्र-क्रियाकलापं नियतमेवाक्षिपति। योगिनामपि हि नाडीचक्रकरणभावनासंवेदनयुक्त्या नियम एव॥ १८॥

अस्येदानीं त्रिकार्थस्य यदुक्तं 'कुलात्परतरं त्रिकम्' इति सर्वोत्तर-मनुत्तरत्वं, तन्निरूपयति

अदृष्टमण्डलोऽप्येवं
यः कश्चिद्वेत्ति तत्त्वतः ।
स सिद्धिभाग्भवेन्नित्यं
स योगी स च दीक्षितः ॥ १९ ॥

मण्डलं—देवताचक्रम्, अपश्यन्नपि—अप्राप्तमेलकोऽपि चर्यानिशाटन-हठादिना । मण्डलानि शरीरनाडीचक्रानुचक्ररूपाणि योगाभ्यासेनासा-क्षात्कुर्वन्नपि, त्रिशूलाब्जादिमण्डलमदृष्ट्वापि, नात्र मण्डलादिदीक्षोपयोगः । एवमेव कश्चित्—परशक्तिपातानुगृहीतो वेत्ति यः 'एतज्ज्ञानमेव हि दीक्षा कान्यात्र दीक्षा' । अत एव एवं जानन् विभुना भैरवभट्टारकेण दीक्षितः । अत एव 'स्वयं गृहीतमन्त्राश्च'—इत्येतद्धृदयातिरिक्तमन्त्रविषयम् । नहि अयं मन्त्रो—हृदयमयत्वात् । मन्त्रमहेशतन्महेशरूपोत्तीर्णत्वात् अस्य । पुस्तकेष्वलेख्यमेवेदं 'हृदयमिति' । परशक्तिपातानुग्रहादेव एतल्लाभस्तत्त्वत इति निर्णीतम् । तथा यः कश्चिदिति—जातिव्रतचर्यादिनैरपेक्ष्यमत्र वेदनमेव हि प्रधानम् । स सिद्धिभाक् योगी—'योगमेकत्वमिच्छन्ति' इति, यतो—ज्ञानदानमायाक्षपणलक्षणा च तस्यैव दीक्षा । चकारोऽवधारणे । सतश्च सर्वतो मन्तव्यः । तदाह—स एव सिद्धिभाग्योगी । स एव च दीक्षितः नित्यमिति ॥ १९ ॥

अनेन ज्ञातमात्रेण
ज्ञायते सर्वशक्तिभिः ।

सर्वाभिः देवताभिः सर्वशक्तिभिश्च सर्वज्ञैरसौ ज्ञायते । एतज्ज्ञानश्चेव तैरपि यत्किंचित् ज्ञायते तदनेन ज्ञातमात्रेण ज्ञायते इति प्राग्वत् । सर्वाभिः शक्तिभिरिति करणे तृतीया ।

तथा

शाकिनीकुलसामान्यो

भवेद्योगं विनापि हि ॥ २० ॥

अनेन ज्ञातमात्रेण योगमाभ्यासिकं मायीयदेहपातावाप्ततदैवयरूपं च विनापि शकिनीकुलस्य—विशेषस्पन्दात्मनः, सामान्यस्पन्दरूपोऽकुलरूपः शक्तिचक्रेश्वरो भवेदिति ॥ २० ॥

किंच

अविधिज्ञो विधानज्ञो

जायते यजनं प्रति ॥ २१ ॥

विधिः—क्रिया ज्ञानं च तद्यस्य द्वयं नास्ति स पशुः, यथोक्तं किरणायाम्

'पशुर्नित्यो ह्यमूर्तोऽज्ञो निष्क्रियो निर्गुणोऽप्रभुः ।
व्यापी मायोदरान्तःस्थो भोगोपायविचिन्तकः ॥'

इति । स पशुरपि अनेन ज्ञातमात्रेण, विधानं ज्ञा च यस्य स—कर्ता ज्ञाता च विषयसंगतकरणं प्रति जायते । यजनं च अस्यापूर्णमपि पूर्णं भवतीति—सर्वमयत्वात् हृदयस्य ॥ २१ ॥

तथाहि

कालाग्निमादितः कृत्वा

मायान्तं ब्रह्मदेहगम् ।

शिवो विश्वाद्यनन्तान्तः

परं शक्तित्रयं मतम् ॥ २२ ॥

कालाग्नेर्धरातत्त्वादिभुवनात् मायातत्त्वं यावत्, ब्रह्मणः सकारस्य देहे, विश्वभुवनात्—विद्यातत्त्वादेरारभ्य शिवोऽनाश्रितशक्तिरूपश्च,

अनन्तस्य—अकारस्य अन्तः परं विसर्गात्मकं शक्तित्रयं, तच्च परं मतम्। उक्तं च 'स्रार्णेन' इत्यादि ॥ २२ ॥

तदन्तर्वर्ति यत्किचित्
शुद्धमार्गे व्यवस्थितम्।
अणुर्विशुद्धमचिरा-
दैश्वरं ज्ञानमश्नुते ॥ २३ ॥

यत् किंचिद्वस्तु व्यवस्थितं विचित्रावस्थं तत् हृदयबीजान्तर्वर्ति शुद्धं भवेत्, तदेव चैश्वरं ज्ञानम्। अणुः—अण्यते प्राणिति अणति नदति परिमितोच्चारान् मूर्धन्यो भवन् तत्प्रभावाद् ऐश्वरं ज्ञानम् अचिरादेव प्राप्नोति ॥ २३ ॥

कथम्

तच्चोदकः शिवोऽज्ञेयः
सर्वज्ञः परमेश्वरः।
सर्वगो निर्मलः स्वच्छ-
स्तृप्तः स्वायतनः शुचिः ॥ २४ ॥

यः—तच्चोदको गुरुः स शिव एव ज्ञेयः, शिव एव तच्चोदकः। स चाज्ञेयो ज्ञातैव। स्वायतनः—स्वान् अयान् विज्ञानरूपान् भावांस्तनोतीति। सर्वं चैतद्विस्तरतो निर्णीतमेव ॥ २४ ॥

एवं विस्तरतोऽभिधाय तात्पर्येण निगमयति

यथा न्यग्रोधबीजस्थः
शक्तिरूपो महाद्रुमः।

तथा हृदयबीजस्थं
जगदेतच्चराचरम् ॥ २५ ॥
एवं यो वेत्ति तत्त्वेन
तस्य निर्वाणगामिनी ।
दीक्षा भवत्यसंदिग्धा
तिलाज्याहुतिर्वर्जिता ॥ २६ ॥

इह असत् न तावत् किंचित्—इत्युक्तम् । विश्वं च विश्वात्मकमिति । ततश्च यथा वटबीजे तत्समुचितेनैव वपुषा अङ्कुरविटपपत्रफलानि तिष्ठन्ति, एवं विश्वमिदं हृदयान्तः । एवं परिज्ञानमेव असंदिग्धा निर्वाणदीक्षा । यथोक्तम्

इयमेवामृतप्राप्तिरयमेवात्मनो ग्रहः ।
इयं निर्वाणदीक्षा च शिवसद्भावदायिनी ॥ (स्प. का. २।७)

इति । अन्या अपि दीक्षा भोगान् वितरेयुरपि, एतत्परिज्ञानमेव तु तत्त्वतो दीक्षेति । तत एवात्र सर्वोत्तरत्वं—कुलशास्त्रेभ्योऽपि आधिक्यात् । यथाहि तुलाङ्केषु ऊर्ध्वमूर्ध्वं परिमितेऽपि उन्नत्यवनतियोगेऽनन्तमन्तरं परिमाणस्य भवति, एवमूर्ध्वोर्ध्वतत्त्वेषु देशकालभोगसंवेदनानाम् अनन्तमेवान्तरमिति । एवम् एव अधिकीभवन् षट्त्रिंशतोऽपि अधिकं भवेदिति । यतश्च संवेदनमेव दीक्षा, तत एव उक्तम्—एतत् संविदनुप्रविष्टो वीरो वा योगिनी वा निजपरसत्तासततोदितामायीयबाह्यान्तःकरणरश्मिदेवताद्वादशकचक्रेश्वरपरभैरवभट्टारकात्मकनिर्णीततत्त्वाहंरूपानुग्रहेण कृतदीक्षो इति ॥ २५-२६ ॥

एवमनुत्तरपदमुत्तररूपापरित्यागेनैव यथा भवति तथा व्याससमासाभ्यां भूयसा निर्णीतम्, अधुना तु इदं वक्तव्यम् । उच्यते तावत्सर्वशास्त्रेषु

'मनुष्यदेहमास्थाय च्छन्नास्ते परमेश्वराः ।
निर्वीर्यमपि ये हार्दं त्रिकार्थं समुपासते ॥

इति । तत्कथमस्योपासा ? तथापि चानुत्तरसत्तया अत्रापि भाव्यम्—अनुत्तरत्वादेव । सा च कथम् ? इत्याकाङ्क्षां निर्णिनीषुर्ग्रन्थान्तरमवतारयति

मूर्ध्नि वक्त्रे च हृदये
गुह्ये मूर्तौ तथैव च ।
न्यासं कृत्वा शिखां बद्ध्वा
सप्तविंशतिमन्त्रिताम् ॥२७॥

एकैकं तु दिशां बन्धं
दशानामपि योजयेत् ।
तालत्रयं पुरा दत्त्वा
सशब्दं विघ्नशान्तये ॥२८॥

शिखासंख्याभिजप्तेन
तोयेनाभ्युक्षयेत् ततः ।
पुष्पादिकं क्रमात्सर्वं
लिङ्गे वा स्थण्डिलेऽथ वा ॥२९॥

चतुर्दशाभिजप्तेन
पुष्पेणासनकल्पना ।
तत्र सृष्टिं यजेद्वीरः
पुनरेवासनं ततः ॥३०॥

सृष्टिं तु संपुटीकृत्य

पश्चाद्यजनमारभेत् ।

सर्वतत्त्वसुसंपूर्णां

सर्वाभरणभूषिताम् ॥३१॥

यजेद्देवीं महेशानीं

सप्तविंशतिमन्त्रिताम् ।

ततः सुगन्धिपुष्पैस्तु

यथाशक्त्या समर्चयेत् ॥३२॥

पूजयेत्परया भक्त्या

आत्मानं च निवेदयेत् ।

एवं यजनमाख्यात-

मग्निकार्येऽप्ययं विधिः ॥३३॥

मूर्धादीनि बाह्यतयोचितरूपाणि । वस्तुतः परब्रह्मरूपाभिहित-पञ्चात्मकव्योमादिधरण्यन्तसतत्त्वेशानादिसारचिदुन्मेषेच्छाज्ञानक्रियारूपाण्येव—मन्त्रलिङ्गात्, यथा मन्त्राः

'१ ईशानमूर्ध्ने, २ तत्पुरुषवक्त्राय, ३ अघोरहृदयाय, ४ वामदेव-गुह्याय, ५ सद्योजातमूर्तये'

इति, तत्रैतत्पञ्चकाविभागात्मकत्वे पञ्चानामेकैकशः पञ्चात्मकता—इति पञ्चविंशतिः । अत्रैव मालिन्यादिमन्त्राणामनुप्रवेशः । तिस्रश्च देव्यः प्रत्येकमिच्छादित्रययोगात् नवात्मतां प्राप्ताः । पुनरपि सृष्टिस्थितिसंहृतिवशात् त्रैधमापन्ना इति सप्तविंशतिसंभृतहृद्बीजेन । शिखाया—एवंरूपधरण्यन्त-

परिकल्पनस्वातन्त्र्यरूपायाः बन्धनं—सर्वाविभागसारं तादात्म्यम् । मूर्धादिषु केवलेष्वपि प्रत्येकं सर्वाणि वक्त्रादीनि परस्परं विशेषणानि । तच्च निर्णीतमेव सर्वसर्वात्मकत्वनिर्णयेनैव, दिश्यमाना घटाद्या एव दिशः । ताश्च स्वापेक्षया दशैव भवन्ति । तत्रापि एतदेव बन्धनम्—आत्मसाक्षात्कारात्मकम् । एतच्च तालत्रयेण, ताला प्रतिष्ठाविश्रान्तिः । तत्र सकारादि हृदयमेव । तच्च सशब्दं मध्यमान्तं, शब्दनं हि शब्दः । तच्च मध्यमेव । वैखर्याः तच्छेषात्मकत्वात्—इत्युक्तं बहुशः । एषा च विघ्नानाम्—अभेदात्मनि अखण्डिते परमात्मनि खण्डनात्मकसंकोचसारभेदकल्लोलकलङ्कानां, शान्तिः—अभेदभैरवार्णवतादात्म्यमेव । यदाहुः श्रीसोमानन्दपादाः

'अस्मद्रूपसमाविष्टः स्वात्मनात्मनिवारणे ।
शिवः करोतु परया नमः शक्त्या ततात्मने ॥' (शि. दृ. १।१)

इति । एवमेव सप्तविंशतिजप्तं तोयमित्यर्घपात्रविधिः । तोयमत्र सर्वमेव हृदयद्रवात्म—अनियन्त्रितत्वात् असंकोचदानाच्च, पुष्पं व्याख्यातम्, लिङ्गं च

'मृच्छैलधातुरत्नादिभवं लिङ्गं न पूजयेत् ।
यजेदाध्यात्मिकं लिङ्गं यत्र लीनं चराचरम् ॥' (मा. वि. १८।१,३)

इत्येतदपि निर्णीतमेव । विश्वात्मनि तत्त्वे आसि-क्रियायामधिकरणस्य कर्तुश्च आसनस्य स्वातन्त्र्यात् कल्प्यमानस्य, स्वातन्त्र्येण कल्प्यमानत्वम् । चतुर्दशेन औकारेण—तस्यैव त्रिशूलरूपत्वात् इत्युक्तमेव । सृष्टिः—आदिक्षान्ततादात्म्यमयं हृदयम् । अत एव आसनमपि सर्वं तत्रैव—आधाराधेययोः परस्परैकरूपत्वात् । यथोक्तम्

'सर्वभूतस्थमात्मानं सर्वभूतानि चात्मनि ।
ईक्षते योगयुक्तात्मा सर्वत्र समदर्शनः' ॥ (भ. गी. ६।२९)

इत्यादि ।

संपुटीकरणसृष्टेरादिक्षान्तायाः प्रत्येकं सर्वशश्च हृदयबीजेन परतत्त्व एवोल्लासात् संहाराच्च। न चानवस्थेत्युक्तमेव। सृष्टेश्च संपुटीकरणमुभयसंघट्टप्रक्षोभानन्दरूपम्। तदुत्थद्रव्योपयोगोऽपि। क्त्वा अत्र शब्दप्रतीतिपौर्वापर्यमात्रे। सर्वतत्त्वैः सुष्ठु अभेदेन सम्यगनपायितया पूर्णत्वम्। सर्वत्र च परमाणावपि यदा समन्तात् भरणं—सर्वात्मीकरणम्। सर्वैर्वा घटसुखतिर्यङ्नरविरिञ्चिविष्णुरुद्रमन्त्रसदाशिवादिप्रमातृरूपैः अवयवमानैरहमेकरस—अवयवित्वं निर्णीतमेव। अत एव विशिष्टाकृत्यायुधादिध्यानमत्र नोक्तम्—तस्य निर्मेयत्वात्। आरुरुक्षुरेतावत्त्रिकार्थाभिलाषुकश्च कथमारोहतु ? इति चेत्—कस्यायमर्थिभावः। मा तर्हि आरुक्षत् सिद्धातन्त्रादिविधिमेव, तदाशयेनैव निरूपिततद्ध्यानादिसंकोचमालम्बताम्, असंकोचितानुत्तरपदे हि अनधिकृत एव। एष एव सदोदितो यागः गन्धपुष्पादि निर्णीतम्, यथाशब्दः सहार्थे, तृतीया च तत्रैवोक्ता। परयैव हृदयरूपया पूजयेत्, कथं ? १. भक्त्या—तादात्म्यानुप्रवेशप्रह्वतात्मना, २. भक्त्या—स्वयं क्लृप्तेन पूज्यपूजकविभागेन। पूज्यो हि स्वयं सृज्यते, स परं स्वतन्त्रचिन्मयतापरमार्थ एव—अनुत्तरस्वातन्त्र्यबलात्। न घटादिरिव जड इति विशेषोऽत्र, तदुक्तं श्रीप्रत्यभिज्ञायाम्

> 'स्वातन्त्र्यामुक्तमात्मानं स्वातन्त्र्यादद्वयात्मनः।
> प्रभुरीशादिसंकल्पैर्निर्माय व्यवहारयेत् ॥' (प्र. का. १।५।१६)

इति। ३. भक्त्या च लक्षणया पूजनेन परं तत्त्वं लक्ष्यते—सर्वक्रियास्वेवंरूपताप्रत्यभिज्ञानमुपायत्वात् १—लिप्यक्षरस्येव मायीयवर्णव्युत्पत्तौ, २—तस्यापि च वर्णवीर्यानुप्रवेशे। आत्मानं निवेदयेत्—अन्यस्य निवेद्यस्याभावात्। एवं च आत्मानमेव निःशेषेण निरुत्तरपदं वेदयेत्—अनुत्तरसत्तानुसारेण। अत्र संभावनायां लिङ्—सततमेवंमयत्वेनैवावस्थितेः इति हि उक्तम्।

एवम् आ—समन्तात् सर्वत्र सदा यत् ख्यातं 'पारमार्थिकशुद्धशिव-

स्वरूपप्रथात्मिका ख्यातिः', तदेव यजनं परभैरवसंविद्देवतायाः (१) पूजनात् (२) तया च तादात्म्यसम्यग्गमनरूपताकरणात् (३) सर्वत्र च परिमितात्मीयात्मरूपस्वत्वनिवृत्त्या परिपूर्णचिद्घनशिवशक्त्यात्मका—आत्मरूप—स्वत्वापादनात्मकाद् दानाच्च।

एतदेव अग्निकार्यं—सर्ववासनाबीजानां सर्वपदार्थेन्धनग्रासलाम्पट्य-जाज्वल्यमाने, शिवसंघट्टक्षोभक्षुभितपरशक्त्यरणिसततसमुदितपरभैरव-महामहसि, सर्वाभिष्वङ्गरूपमहास्नेहाज्यप्राज्यप्रतापे हवनात्—अन्तर्दाहात्। अयमेव अग्निकार्ये विधिर्दीक्षापर्यन्तोऽपि, नान्यः पृथक् कश्चित्—इति तात्पर्यम्।

'स्वस्वरूपपरिज्ञानं मन्त्रोऽयं पारमार्थिकः।
दीक्षेयमेष यागश्च क्रियायामप्यनुत्तरः॥'

अत एव प्रागेवोक्तम्—यथान्यत्र मन्त्रोपासादिक्रिया उत्तरेण ज्ञानग्रन्थेनोत्तीर्यते नैवमिहेति। यदुक्तम् 'उत्तरस्याप्यनुत्तरम्' इति सूत्रे तदेवैतदन्तेन ग्रन्थेन निर्व्यूढं—हृदयस्यैव यागदीक्षाक्रियारूपत्वात् तस्य चानुत्तरत्वात्। श्रीसोमानन्दपादैस्तु स्रुक्स्रुवसंस्कारादि सर्वंसहत्वप्रतिपादनेन, अखण्डितत्वाभिप्रायेण निरूपितम्। एवमादौ अङ्गहृद्भेदघूलिभेदाद्यपि तद्रूपं युज्यते, न किंचिदत्र; नाप्युपपद्यते, नाप्यस्ति; नाप्यधरशास्त्रपातित्वेन तदुपजीवकत्वम् इति निर्णीतप्रायमेव॥ २७-३३॥

किमेवमुपासायां भवति? इत्यवतरति

कृतपूजाविधिः सम्यक्

स्मरन् बीजं प्रसिद्ध्यति॥३४॥

एवमनवरतं व्यवहारेष्वपि बीजं स्मरन्नेव—स्मरणादेव कृतपूजाविधिः (१) प्रकर्षेणान्यकुलशास्त्रादिशैववैष्णवान्तशास्त्रातिरेकेणैव भगवद्भैरव-भट्टारकरूपसमाविष्टः निजपरसंविच्चमत्कारवशनिर्मितभावक्रीडाडम्बरो जीवन्मुक्त एव भवति, इत्यनुभव एवायमावर्तते न त्वन्यत् किंचिदिति

'स्मरणम्' उक्तम्। श्रीमतशास्त्रेष्वेवमेव—(२) उपासकस्त्वननुप्रविष्टवीर्यसत्तासारहृदयोऽपि क्रमपूजामाहात्म्यात् बीजं सम्यक् स्मरन् प्राप्तहृदयाख्यतत्त्वमन्त्रवीर्यः प्रकर्षेण सिद्ध्यति—क्रमपूजामाहात्म्यादेव तारतम्यातिशयात् स्वयं वा प्रसन्नगुरुभट्टारकवदनकमलाद्वा मन्त्रवीर्यं हृदयात्मकमासादयति जीवन्मुक्तश्च भवतीति यावत्। अत्र द्वारपरिवारगुरुपूजनं गुणं खण्डनां वा न वहति। तत एव भट्टपादैः न्यरूपि। अत्र तु कुलपर्वाणि पवित्रं चेति सम्यक्त्वं पूजाविधेः ॥३४॥

(संक्षेपार्थः)

'यत्रान्तरखिलं भाति यच्च सर्वत्र भासते।
स्फुरत्तैव हि सा ह्येका हृदयं परमं बुधाः॥

रासभी वडवा वापि स्वं जगज्जन्मधाम यत्।
समकालं विकास्यैव संकोच्य हृदि हृष्यति॥

तथोभयमहानन्दसौषुम्णहृदयान्तरे।
स्पन्दमानमुपासीत हृदयं सृष्टिलक्षणम्॥

ध्यायन्स्मरन्प्रविमृशन्कुर्वन्वा यत्र कुत्रचित्।
विश्रान्तिमेति यस्माच्च प्रोल्लसेद्धृदयं तु तत्॥

तदेकमेव, यत्रैतज्ज्ञानं, वैकल्पिकं परम्।
तत्त्वानि भुवनाभोगाः शिवादिपशुमातरः॥

स्वं स्वं विचित्रं विन्दन्तः स्वरूपं पारमार्थिकम्।
चित्रीकुर्वन्त्येव भान्ति तां चित्रां संविदं पराम्॥

देशद्रव्यक्रियास्थानज्ञानादिष्वपि सर्वशः।
अशङ्कयैव संक्रामः पूजास्य सततोदिता॥

क्रमपूजनमात्रं च कुलपर्वपवित्रकैः।
सहात्र पूजने प्रोक्तं सम्यक्त्वं त्रिकशासने॥'

यथोक्तम्

'द्रवाणामिव शारीरं वर्णानां सृष्टिबीजकम् ।
शासनानां त्रिकं शास्त्रं मोक्षाणां भैरवी स्थितिः ॥

उपासायाः समापत्तिर्व्रतानां वीरवृत्तिता ।
तथैव पर्वमध्ये तु कुलपर्वाणि शासने ॥

सर्वेषां चापि यागानां पूरणाय पवित्रकम् ।
पवित्रकं न कुर्वन्ति चतुस्त्रिद्विःसकृत्तु ये ॥

कुलपर्व न जानन्ति तेषां वीर्यं न रोहति ।'

फुरइ फुरणम अलह कामब्बह पर देउ सोहि अउस मगाहू सब्ब काल नीसंकसऊ सहजा जाणु पूजस पब्ब इ इ उ उ हू ॥

एवमनुत्तरस्वरूपं विस्तरतो निर्णीतं—यत्र भावनाद्यनवकाशः। प्रसंख्यानमात्रमेव दृढचमत्कारलक्षणहृदयङ्गमतात्मकप्रतिपत्तिदार्ढ्यपर्यन्तं यत्रोपायधौरेयधाराधराणि धत्ते। सिद्धिप्रेप्सुषु तु योगो वक्तव्यः। स्वातन्त्र्यानीयमानास्वपि दृष्टयोगसिद्धिषु लौकिकप्रसिद्धिनियत्युत्तरत्वेऽपि पारमेशव्यवस्थारूपनियत्यनतिक्रमात्, यदुक्तं शिवदृष्टौ

'तथापि चित्रकर्मार्थमुपायो वाच्य आदरात् ।'

इति। तत्रापि चानुत्तररूपस्य नास्ति खण्डना काचित्—दृष्टसिद्धीप्सा-यत्नमेव तदाप्तितत्फलविश्रान्त्यादेरपि परैकमयत्वात्। किन्तु जीवन्मुक्ता-पेक्षया मन्दशक्तिपातोऽसावुच्येत, अपूर्णप्रायत्वात् ॥

तं योगमार्गं निरूपयितुं ग्रन्थशेषोऽवतरति

आद्यन्तरहितं बीजं
विकसत्तिथिमध्यगम् ।
हृत्पद्मान्तर्गतं ध्यायेत्
सोमांशं नित्यमभ्यस्येत् ॥ ३५ ॥

१. एतदेव हृदयबीजं दीपकाभावात् गमागमशून्यत्वात् सततोदितत्वाच्च अनाद्यन्तं, तदेव विकसत् परिपूर्णत्वं यातं तिथीनां मध्यगं—हृदयत्वात्, तदेव संकोचविकासधर्मोपचरितपद्मभावे कन्दे गुह्ये हृदीव ध्यायेत्। किं च अस्य ध्यानमाह—'सोमांशं' षोडशकलात्मकं सोमरूपम् अभितः समन्तादस्येत् क्षिपेत्—परिपूर्णचन्द्रस्यास्य हृत्कर्णिकानिवेशिकलया स्वस्वद्वादशान्तगपुष्पाद्युदयस्थानात् आहृतामृतस्पर्शः, प्रोद्यन्नादानुसारचुम्बिकालक्षणकाकचञ्चुपुटमुद्रामुद्रितः, पुनस्तदपसृतशिशिरामृतरसास्वादविकस्वरहार्दसोमप्रसरन्नादनिर्मथितसुधापानपूरित-चन्द्रमाः, पुनः सूर्यकलोदयमयानच्कसकारमात्रविश्रान्तो रोमाञ्चस्तोभोत्पतनबाष्पकम्पाद्यनुगृहीतदेहोऽभ्यासं कुर्यादिति भट्टधनेश्वरशर्मा।

२. आद्यन्तरहितं सकारमात्रं षोडशाकारादितिथिसहितं कलाग्रासक्रमेण हृदयेऽन्तर्निक्षिपेत्। नालिकाजलाकर्षणवत् चलनकम्पनस्पन्दनसमाविष्टमूलाधारत्रिकोणभद्रकन्दहृन्मुखमुद्रासु युगपदेव विलम्बितमध्यद्रुततरतदतिशयादिधाराप्राप्तिवशगलितसोमसूर्यकलाजालग्रासे आद्यन्तरहितं कृत्वा आद्यन्ताभ्यामेतद्बीजमातृकापेक्षया औकारवकाराभ्यां रहितं विश्लेषणयुक्तिलब्धवीर्यपरिचयं, ध्रुवं विसर्गात्मकं, विकसतां पञ्चदशानां तिथीनां यन्मध्यं तिथिरहितमेव ग्रस्तकलं षोडशं, ततोऽपि गच्छति यत्—'सप्तदशी कला' इत्युक्तम्। सोमस्य षोडशात्मकम् आमृतमंशं हृत्कमले ध्यायेत् तदेव नित्यमभ्यस्येदित्यस्मद्गुरवः। तथाहि—सह उमया भगवत्या संघट्टात्मकसमापत्तिक्षोभेण तत्त्वनिर्मथनात्मना वर्तते इति सोमो भट्टारकः, तस्य समग्रभावावयविनः परिपूर्णाहमात्मनोंऽशो नीलसुखादिः, तदेवमभ्यस्यति स्वस्वरूपावर्तनसृष्टिसंहारावर्तचक्राक्षमालिकया पुनः पुनरावर्तयतीति यत् संभाव्यते। स एव एष सततोदितो हृदयजपः, संभावनायां लिङ्।

३. अन्ये तु हृत्स्थानात् द्वादशान्तं यश्चारः षट्त्रिंशदङ्गुलः, तत्र सूर्यरूपतयोल्लास्य, बहिरर्धतुटिमात्रं विश्रम्य अविनाश्यमृताख्यविसर्गरूप-

सोमकलोदये सपादाङ्गुलद्वितयमात्रायां तुटौ तुटौ चन्द्रकलापरिपूरणे, पञ्चदश्यां तुटौ पूर्णायां, हृत्पद्मे पूर्णश्च भवति; अर्धतुटिमात्रं च तत्रापि विश्रान्तिः। एवं षोडशतुट्यात्मा षट्त्रिंशदङ्गुलश्चारो भवति। इत्यवस्थायाम् 'आद्यन्तरहितम्'—अनस्तमितत्वात्। विकसत्सु द्वितीयादिषु अन्तर्गतं सोमांशं विसर्गरूपं विश्लिष्य सप्तदशात्मकं, परिशीलनेन ध्यायन् कलाग्रासाभ्यासं कुर्यात्—इत्यादि समादिशन्। सर्वं चैतत् युक्तमेव मन्तव्यम्। अत्र चावृत्यानन्तं व्याख्यानं सूत्रत्वादुपपन्नमेव, यत उक्तम् 'अनन्तार्थसूत्रणात् सूत्रम्' इति 'त्रीशिका चानुत्तरसूत्रम्' इति गुरवः। एवं पूर्वेष्वपि श्लोकसूत्रेषु ॥ ३५ ॥

किम् इत्थमभ्यासे सति भवति ? इत्याह

यान्यान्कामयते कामां-

स्तांस्ताञ्छीघ्रमवाप्नुयात्।

अस्मात्प्रत्यक्षतामेति

सर्वज्ञत्वं न संशयः ॥ ३६ ॥

एवमभ्यासात् यद्यत्कामयते तत्तदचिरादेव तथाविधसर्वमयहृदयवीर्यसमुच्छलितेच्छाप्रसरावष्टम्भविशेषबलोद्योगसंरम्भसोत्साहः, पुनः पुनः तत्स्थितिरूढिरूपाभ्यासात् प्राप्नोति। किं बहुना सर्वज्ञत्वं—परभैरवात्मकत्वमनेनैव देहेन—इति ॥ ३६ ॥

सर्वमुक्त्वोपसंह्रियते। पर्यन्ते हि प्रसरस्योपसंहारे विश्रान्तिरूपाकुलसत्तासादने भैरवता इत्युक्तमसकृत्। सोऽयमुपसंहारग्रन्थः

एवं मन्त्रफलावाप्ति-

रित्येतद् रुद्रयामलम्।

एतदभ्यासतः सिद्धिः

सर्वज्ञत्वमवाप्यते ॥ ३७ ॥

मन्त्राणां शास्त्रान्तरीयाणां वर्णानां च फलमेवमवाप्यते नान्यथेति समाप्तौ रुद्रस्य रुद्रायाश्च यद्यामलं—संघट्टः निर्विभागप्रश्नोत्तररूपस्वरूपामर्शनप्रसरात् आरभ्य यावद्बहिरनन्तापरिगणनीयसृष्टिसंहारभासनं यत्रान्तः, तदेतदकुलोपसंहृतमेव—इति प्रसंख्याननिगमनम्। 'एतदभ्यासात्सर्वज्ञत्वम्' इति योगफलनिगमनम्। सततोदितं हि एतत्सर्वस्य इति शिवम्॥

॥ समाप्तमिदं परात्रीशिकाविवरणम्॥

इत्थं प्रपन्नजनतोद्धरणप्रवृत्त-
श्रीमन्महेश्वरपदाम्बुजचञ्चरीकः।
वृत्तिं व्यधात्त्रिकरहस्यविमर्शगर्भां
कश्मीरिकाच्चुखुलकादधिगम्य जन्म॥ १॥

एतावदेतदिति कस्तुलयेत्प्रसह्य
श्रीशांभवं मतमनर्गलितात्र वाचः।
एतत्तु तावदखिलात्मनि भाति यन्मे
भातं ततोऽत्र सुधियो न पराङ्मुखाः स्युः॥ २॥

अज्ञस्य संशयविपर्ययभागिनो वा
ज्ञानं प्रकम्परहितं प्रकरोति सम्यक्।
रूढस्य निश्चयवतो हृदयप्रतिष्ठां
संवादिनीं प्रकुरुते कृतिरीदृशीयम्॥ ३॥

कश्मीरेषु यशस्करस्य नृपतेरासीदमात्याग्रणीः
श्रीमान्वल्लभ इत्युदाहृततनुर्यः प्राग्र्यजन्मा द्विजः।
तस्य स्वाङ्गभवः प्रसिद्धिपदवीपात्रं समग्रैर्गुणैः
श्रीशौरिः शिशुचन्द्रचूडचरणध्यानैकरत्नाकरः॥ ४॥

शीलस्यायतनं परस्य यशसो जृम्भास्पदं नर्मभू-
वात्सल्यस्य समग्रलोककरुणाधर्मस्य जन्मस्थितिः ।
श्रीमद्वत्सलिकाभिधा सहचरी तस्यैव भक्त्युल्लसत्
प्रोद्रिक्तान्तरवृत्ति शंकरनुवो यस्या मनो जृम्भते ॥ ५ ॥

तस्यैवात्मभवो विभावितजगत्सर्गस्थितिः शकर-
ध्यानार्चापरिचिन्तनैकरसिकः कर्णाभिधानो द्विजः ।
यो बाल्येऽप्यथ यौवनेऽपि विषयासक्तिं विहाय स्थिरा-
मेनामाश्रयते विमर्शपदवीं संसारनिर्मूलिनीम् ॥ ६ ॥

भ्राता ममैव शिवशासनरूढचित्तः
प्रेप्सुः परात्मनि मनोरथगुप्तनामा ।
यः शास्त्रतन्त्रमखिलं प्रविवेक्तुकामः
प्राप्तुं परं शिवपदं भवभेदनाय ॥ ७ ॥

शिवशास्त्रैकरसिकः पदवाक्यप्रमाणवित् ।
रामदेवाभिधानश्च भूषितोत्तमजन्मकः ॥ ८ ॥

एतत्प्रियहितकरणप्ररूढहृदयेन यन्मया रचितम् ।
मार्गप्रदर्शनं तत् सर्वस्य शिवाप्तये भूयात् ॥ ९ ॥

अन्तर्वेद्यामत्रिगुप्ताभिधानः
प्राप्योत्पत्तिं प्राविशत्प्राग्र्यजन्मा ।
श्रीकश्मीरांश्चन्द्रचूडावतारै-
र्निःसंख्याकैः पावितोपान्तभागान् ॥ १० ॥

तस्यान्ववाये महति प्रसूताद् वराहगुप्तात् प्रतिलब्धजन्मा ।
संसारवृत्तान्तपराङ्मुखो यः शिवैकचित्तश्चुखुलाभिधानः ॥ ११ ॥

तस्माद्विवेचितसमस्तपदार्थजाता-
लब्ध्वापि देहपदवीं परमेशपूताम् ।
प्राप्ताभयोऽभिनवगुप्तपदाभिधानः
प्रावेशयत्त्रिकसतत्त्वमिदं निगूढम् ॥ १२ ॥

ये तावत्प्रविवेकवन्ध्यहृदयास्तेभ्यः प्रणामो वरः
केऽप्यन्ये प्रविविक्षते न च गताः पारं धिगेताञ्जडान् ।
यस्त्वन्यः प्रविमर्शसारपदवीसंभावनासुस्थितो
लक्षैकोऽपि स कश्चिदेव सफलीकुर्वीत यत्नं मम ॥ १३ ॥

स्वात्मानं प्रविवेक्तुमप्यलसतां ये बिभ्रति प्रार्थना
तान्प्रत्यात्मकदर्थनान्न परतः किंचित्फलं सोष्यते ।
विश्वस्यास्य विविक्तये स्थिरधियो ये संरभन्ते पुनः
तानभ्यर्थयितुं मयैष विहितो मूर्ध्ना प्रणामादरः ॥ १४ ॥

भ्राम्यन्तो भ्रमयन्ति मन्दधिषणास्ते जन्तुचक्रं जडं
स्वात्मीकृत्य गुणाभिधानवशतो बद्ध्वा दृढं बन्धनैः ।
दृष्ट्वेत्थं गुरुभारवाहविधये यातानुयातान्पशून्
तत्पाशप्रविकर्तनाय घटितं ज्ञानत्रिशूलं मया ॥ १५ ॥

बहुभिरपि सोऽहमेव भ्रमितस्तत्त्वोपदेशकंमन्यैः ।
तत्त्वमिति वर्णयुगमपि येषां रसना न पस्पर्श ॥ १६ ॥

परमेश्वरः प्रपन्नप्रोद्धरणकृपाप्रयुक्तगुरुहृदयः ।
श्रीमान्देवः शंभुर्मामियति नियुक्तवांस्तत्त्वे ॥ १७ ॥

तत्तत्त्वनिर्मलस्थितिविभागिहृदये स्वयं प्रविष्टमिव ।
श्रीसोमानन्दमतं विमृश्य मया निबद्धमिदम् ॥ १८ ॥

हंहो हृच्चक्रचारप्रविरचनलसन्निर्भरानन्दपूर्णा
देव्योऽस्मत्पाशकोटिप्रविघटनपटुज्ञानशूलोर्ध्वधाराः ।
चेतोवाक्कायमेतद्विगतभवभयोत्पत्ति युष्मासु सम्यक्
प्रोतं यत्तेन मह्यं व्रजत किल हृदि द्राक्प्रसादं प्रसह्य ।। १९ ।।

व्याख्यादिकर्मपरिपाटिपदे नियुक्तो
युष्माभिरस्मि गुरुभावमनुप्रविश्य ।
वाक्चित्तचापलमिदं मम तेन देव्य-
स्तच्चक्रचारुचतुरस्थितयः क्षमध्वम् ।। २० ।।

शतैरेकोनविंशत्या त्रीशिकेयं विवेचिता ।
सर्वेषु त्रिकशास्त्रेषु ग्रन्थीन्निदलयिष्यति ।।

।। कृतिरभिनवगुप्तस्य समाप्ता ।।

LIST OF ADDITIONS & CORRECTIONS
(SANSKRIT TEXT)
शुद्धिपत्र

Page	line	अशुद्ध	शुद्ध
४	२२	add after quotation: स्व० ८/३२	
५	२५	अन्तःस्फुटक्रमायोगो	अन्तःस्फुटक्रमयोगे
७	१५	चमत्कारत्वात्	चमत्कारसारत्वात्
६	३	add अघोराद्याः before पराद्याः	
६	७	देशकालाकारविशेषितस्य	देशकालाकारविशेषा-विशेषितस्य
१२	२	स्प० ५/१०	अ.प्र.सि. १२
१३	२६	व्यवस्थापनं युज्यते	व्यवस्थापनं व्यवस्था च युज्यते
१४	११	सुखदुःखे	सुखे दुःखे
१५	५	योग्यताम्	भोग्यताम्
१७	२२	भ.गी.१२/१३	भ.गी. १४/३
१८	५	delete सत्यां at the end of the line	
१६	२	तदेकरूप..	वेदकरूप
१६	१४	add after quotation: स्व० ८/३१	
२०	१३	अनेन	अमेन
२०	१५	अमा इति यत्र	delete यत्र
२०	१७	अत्र	यत्र
२०	१७	मायां	मायायां
२१	२४	निवेशितम्	निवेशिताम्
२२	१२	प्रश्न	प्रश्नम्
२२	१२	यन्मयप्रश्न	तन्मयप्रश्न
२२	१४	वक्तुं	प्रोक्तं
२४	६	add after quotation: स्त० चि० ६१	
२४	१६	श्रतमिति	श्रुतमिति
२६	२२	शृणत	शृणुत
२८	८	दर्शितन्	दर्शितम्
२८	२२	after विधिः add: कौलिकः	

३०	८	पञ्चम्यर्थे च	पञ्चम्यर्थे सप्तम्यर्थे च
३२	२२	नरविषय प्रश्न...	नरविषयतृतीयप्रश्न..
३४	१७	कौलिक सृष्टिरूपमिति	कौलिकसृष्टिरूपमिति
३६	१०	सवं	सर्वं
		add after quotation: स्प० का० ११२	
३६	२४	कोऽपि भासनात्	कोऽपि वेदयिता सोऽपि भासनात्
४०	६	add after quotation: वा.प. ३।७।१२६	
४१	१४	तत्त्वानां बृंहकत्वं	तत्त्वानां बृंहत्त्व बृंहकत्वं
४७	१८	वृक्षत्वरूपम्	वृक्षत्वस्वरूपम्
४६	७	स्व० ५।५४८	स्व० ५।५।४८
५०	१७	परम्परा—	परस्परा—
५१	२	...गाहिनी शक्तिरेव	...गाहिनी च शक्तिरेव
५१	१५	...प्रतिवादनं	...प्रतिविधानं
५१	२५	नादात्पक	नादात्मक
५२	६	बीजरूपतपां	बीजरूपतयां
५६	१६	स्वोत्कर्षः	एवोत्कर्षः
५७	४	अनुभवोपजीवित्वेनुभवा..	अनुभवोपजीवित्वेऽनुभवा
५६	१	ईशानरूपा	ईशनरूपा
६०	२३	delete । after पृथगपर्येषणीयम्	
६१	१४	उ, ऊ' ओ इति	उ, ऊ' 'ओ' इति
७०	८	ज्ञानक्रम	मूर्त्तिक्रम
७०	१४	तयापि सालसं	तयापि अङ्कुरीभूय सालसं
७०	२६	add । after सामान्यविशेषात्मा	
७२	१३	यस्याः	v.l. यशः
७८	१२	कल्प्यः,	कल्प्यः, अपि तु
७६	२१	सर्वभूतस्थमात्लानं	सर्वभूतस्थमात्मानं
८१	१७ and २१	delete "...."	
८२	१६	वृहत्त्वाच्च	बृहत्त्वाच्च
८२	२० and २५	delete "..."	
८२	२१	delete । after सह च	
८७	७	...तत्त्वमयविरूपानु...	...तत्त्वमयशिवरूपानु
८८	१३	(व्योमरूपः)	(व्योमस्थः)
८८	२६	साऽपि	सोऽपि

८६	१	मानमयीम् इति	मानमयीम् असौ पर इति
६१	५	शकिनीकुलस्य	शाकिनी कुलस्य
६१	१२	after quotation add: १/१२	
६६	२४	भ. गी. ६/२६	भ. गी. ६/३०
१००	१६	after quotation add: ७/६	
१०१	१५	औकारवकाराभ्यां	औकारसकाराभ्यां
१०२	१	तुटौ तुटौ चन्द्र . . .	तुटौ तुटौ प्रत्येकं चन्द्र . .
१०२	५	विसर्गरूपं विश्लिष्य	विसर्गरूपं हृत्पद्ममध्ये विश्लिष्य

INDEX OF HALF-VERSES OF PARĀTRIŚIKĀ*

श्लोकार्द्धानुक्रमणिका

*I thank Dr. (Miss) Sushama Pandey for preparing the Indexes (Editor).

INDEX OF QUOTATIONS
उद्धरण-सूची